Social Science Quotations

Social Science Quotations

Who said What, When, and Where

David L. Sills
&
Robert K. Merton,
editors

Transaction Publishers
New Brunswick (U.S.A.) and London (U.K.)

This book is printed on acid-free paper that meets the American National Standard for Permanence of Paper for Printed Library Materials.

Library of Congress Catalog Number: 00-023402
ISBN: 0-7658-0720-3
Printed in the United States of America

Library of Congress Cataloging-in-Publication Data

Social science quotations : who said what, when, and where / David L. Sills & Robert K. Merton, editors.

p. cm.
Originally Published: The Macmillan book of social science quotations : who said what, when, and where. New York : Macmillan Publishing Company, 1991. With new codicil.
Includes bibliographical references and index.
ISBN 0-7658-0720-3 (pbk. : alk. paper)
1. Social sciences—Dictionaries. 2. Social sciences—Quotations.
I. Sills, David L. II. Merton, Robert King, 1910-

H41 .S64 2000
300' .3—dc21 00-023402

To the memory of
PAUL F. LAZARSFELD
1901–1976

Contents

List of Advisers

The editors wish to thank the following individuals who nominated quotations for inclusion in this volume or suggested other scholars who might be asked for nominations.

Andrew B. Abel
University of Pennsylvania

Robert Amdur
Columbia University

Abram Amsel
University of Texas

Solomon E. Asch
Princeton, New Jersey

Barbara Babcock
University of Arizona

Bernard Bailyn
Harvard University

John D. Baldwin
University of California, Santa Barbara

Terence W. Ball
University of Minnesota

Bernard Barber
Columbia University

Karen Barkey
Columbia University

George A. Barnard
Brightlingsea, Colchester (United Kingdom)

William J. Baumol
Princeton University and New York University

Peter J. Behrens
Bethlehem, Pennsylvania

Piers Beirne
University of Southern Maine

Daniel Bell
Harvard University

Reinhard Bendix
University of California, Berkeley

Lee Benson
University of Pennsylvania

Abram Bergson
Harvard University

Robert Bierstedt
University of Virginia

Peter M. Blau
University of North Carolina

Mark Blaug
Institute of Education (London)

Kenneth E. Bock
University of California, Berkeley

Kenneth E. Boulding
Boulder, Colorado

Jo Ann Boydston
The Center for Dewey Studies, Southern Illinois University

William Bright
University of California, Los Angeles

Adrian Brock
York University

Jerome S. Bruner
New School for Social Research

James M. Buchanan
George Mason University

Frederick Burkhardt
Bennington, Vermont

Charles Camic
University of Wisconsin

Francis Canavan
Fordham University

Albert H. Cantril
Harvard University

Theodore Caplow
University of Virginia

Robert Carneiro
American Museum of Natural History (New York)

Bliss Carnochan
Stanford University

John J. Cerullo
University of New Hampshire

Ranjit Chatterjee
University of Chicago

Harvey M. Choldin
University of Illinois

Geraldine J. Clifford
University of California, Berkeley

John L. Clive
Harvard University

Richard A. Cloward
Columbia University

Ansley J. Coale
Princeton University

I. Bernard Cohen
Harvard University

Randall Collins
University of California, Riverside

Deborah J. Coon
Harvard University

Lewis A. Coser
Boston College

Rose Laub Coser
Boston College

Lawrence A. Cremin
Teachers College, Columbia University

Joseph Cropsey
University of Chicago

Charles H. G. Crothers
University of Auckland

Jacqueline L. Cunningham
University of Texas

G. David Curry
University of Chicago

Robert A. Dahl
Yale University

Ralf Dahrendorf
St. Antony's College (Oxford)

Kurt Danziger
York University

Robert Darnton
Princeton University

Kingsley Davis
The Hoover Institution (Stanford, California)

Mary Jo Deegan
University of Nebraska

Arthur P. Dempster
Harvard University

Solomon Diamond
Los Angeles, California

Lesley A. Diehl
State University of New York, Oneonta

Wilton S. Dillon
Smithsonian Institution (Washington, D.C.)

Paul DiMaggio
Yale University

Karin Dovring
Urbana, Illinois

Dinesh D'Souza
Washington, D.C.

Otis Dudley Duncan
University of California, Santa Barbara

Abraham Edel
University of Pennsylvania

Carolyn Eisele
Hunter College, City University of New York

Jean B. Elshtain
University of Massachusetts

Mary Evans
University of Kent

Lorraine D. Eyde
Arlington, Virginia

George A. Feaver
University of British Columbia

Joseph V. Femia
University of Liverpool

Stephen E. Fienberg
Carnegie Mellon University

David J. Finney
International Statistics Institute (Voorburg)

George K. Floro
Studies of Voluntarism and Social Participation, Inc. (Alpine, Texas)

William J. Frazer, Jr.
University of Florida

Milton Friedman
The Hoover Institution (Stanford, California)

Alfred H. Fuchs
Bowdoin College

Hans G. Furth
Catholic University of America

John F. Galliher
University of Missouri

Mike Gane
Loughborough University of Technology

Howard Gardner
Harvard University

Peter Gay
Yale University

Anthony Giddens
King's College (Cambridge)

Christiane Gillieron
University of Geneva

Charles C. Gillispie
Princeton University

Sidney Goldstein
Brown University

Albert E. Gollin
Newspaper Advertising Bureau (New York)

Richard A. Gonce
Grand Valley State College

Loren R. Graham
Massachusetts Institute of Technology

Richard Grathoff
University of Bielefeld

Howard E. Gruber
University of Geneva

Joseph Gusfield
University of California, San Diego

Peter Hall
The Australian National University

Geoffrey C. Harcourt
Jesus College (Cambridge)

Benjamin Harris
University of Wisconsin

Molly R. Harrower
Gainesville, Florida

Albert H. Hastorf
Stanford University

Robert L. Heilbroner
New School for Social Research

Mary Henle
New School for Social Research

Frank Heynick
Eindhoven University of Technology

Bert G. Hickman
Stanford University

John R. Hicks
Nuffield College (Oxford)

Ernest R. Hilgard
Stanford University

Michael R. Hill
Benton Harbor, Michigan

Gertrude Himmelfarb
The Graduate Center, City University of New York

Albert O. Hirschman
Institute for Advanced Study (Princeton, New Jersey)

George C. Homans
Harvard University

Irving Louis Horowitz
Rutgers University

Michael Hovland
U.S. Bureau of the Census (Washington, D.C.)

Dell Hymes
University of Virginia

Eleanor C. Isbell
Columbia, Connecticut

Ira Jacknis
The Brooklyn Museum (New York)

Paul C. Jefferson
Haverford College

Barry C. Johnston
Indiana University

Robert Alun Jones
University of Illinois

Charles Kadushin
The Graduate Center, City University of New York

John H. Kautsky
Washington University

Christopher Kelly
University of Maryland

William S. Kern
Western Michigan University

Israel M. Kirzner
New York University

Joseph M. Kitagawa
University of Chicago

Mirra Komarovsky
Columbia University

Isaac Kramnick
Cornell University

Paul F. Kress
University of North Carolina

William H. Kruskal
University of Chicago

Adam Kuper
Brunel University

Edmund R. Leach
King's College (Cambridge)

Erich L. Lehmann
University of California, Berkeley

Charles C. Lemert
Wesleyan University

Donald N. Levine
University of Chicago

Charles E. Lindblom
Yale University

Seymour Martin Lipset
Stanford University

Colin Loader
University of Nevada

David MacGregor
King's College, University of Western Ontario

Marcello Maestro
New Rochelle, New York

Roger D. Masters
Dartmouth College

Bruce Mazlish
Massachusetts Institute of Technology

Robert C. Merton
Harvard University

Rolf Meyersohn
The Graduate Center, City University of New York

Neal E. Miller
Yale University

Henry L. Minton
University of Windsor

Judith Modell
Carnegie Mellon University

Franco Modigliani
Massachusetts Institute of Technology

Michael J. Mooney
Lewis and Clark College

David Cresap Moore
Cambridge, Massachusetts

Sally Falk Moore
Harvard University

Jill Morawski
Wesleyan University

Robert J. Morgan
University of Virginia

Denton E. Morrison
Michigan State University

K. P. Moseley
University of Port Harcourt

Frederick Mosteller
Harvard University

Stephen O. Murray
Instituto Obregón (San Francisco)

Paul Neurath
University of Vienna

Elizabeth Noelle-Neumann
Institut für Demoskopie Allensbach (Allensbach, Germany)

John O'Neill
York University

Abraham Pais
The Rockefeller University

R. R. Palmer
Princeton University

Lewis J. Paper
Keck, Mahin & Cate (Washington, D.C.)

Ann K. Pasanella
Columbia University

Don Patinkin
The Hebrew University of Jerusalem

Philip J. Pauly
Rutgers University

J. D. Y. Peel
University of Liverpool

John C. Pelzel
Harvard University

Robert G. Perrin
University of Tennessee

William Petersen
Carmel, California

R. L. Plackett
University of Newcastle-upon-Tyne

Nanneke Redclift
University of Kent

Albert Rees
Alfred P. Sloan Foundation (New York)

Shulamit Reinharz
Brandeis University

Gavin C. Reid
Darwin College (Cambridge)

Robert W. Rieber
John Jay College of Criminal Justice, City University of New York

David Riesman
Harvard University

Beate S. Riesterer
Ramapo College of New Jersey

John W. Riley, Jr.
Washington, D.C.

Paul Roazen
York University

Eugene Rochberg-Halton
Yale University

Rick Roderick
Duke University

Rosalind Rosenberg
Columbia University

Aaron Rosenblatt
State University of New York, Albany

Dorothy Ross
University of Virginia

Guenther Roth
Columbia University

Joseph R. Royce
University of Alberta

Robert A. Rutland
University of Tulsa

Murray Sabrin
Ramapo College of New Jersey

Philip Sapir
National Institutes of Health (Bethesda, Maryland)

Janet V. Sayers
University of Kent

Margaret Schabas
Harvard University

James A. Schellenberg
Terre Haute, Indiana

Arthur M. Schlesinger, Jr.
The Graduate Center, City University of New York

Morton Schoolman
State University of New York, Albany

Philip Selznick
University of California, Berkeley

Tamotsu Shibutani
University of California, Santa Barbara

Alan Sica
University of Kansas

Allan Silver
Columbia University

Michael Silverstein
University of Chicago

Herbert A. Simon
Carnegie Mellon University

Milton Singer
University of Chicago

Neil J. Smelser
University of California, Berkeley

Laurence D. Smith
University of Maine

M. Brewster Smith
University of California, Santa Cruz

C. Matthew Snipp
University of Wisconsin

Michael M. Sokal
Worcester Polytechnic Institute

David W. Southern
Westminster College

John Stanley
University of California, Riverside

Ronald Steel
University of Southern California

Nico Stehr
University of Alberta

Richard W. Sterling
Dartmouth College

Fritz Stern
Columbia University

George J. Stigler
University of Chicago

Arthur L. Stinchcombe
Northwestern University

Lawrence Stone
Princeton University

Anselm L. Strauss
University of California, San Francisco

Richard Swedberg
University of Stockholm

David L. Szanton
Social Science Research Council (New York)

Giorgio Tagliacozzo
Institute for Vico Studies (New York)

Michael S. Teitelbaum
Alfred P. Sloan Foundation (New York)

Dennis F. Thompson
Princeton University

Robert L. Thorndike
Lacey, Washington

Charles Tilly
New School for Social Research

Edward Tiryakian
Duke University

Edward R. Tufte
Yale University

Stephen P. Turner
University of Southern Florida

Carl G. Uhr
University of California, Riverside

Etienne van de Walle
University of Pennsylvania

Jaap van Ginneken
University of Groningen

Edmund H. Volkart
University of Hawaii

Immanuel Wallerstein
State University of New York, Binghamton

W. Allen Wallis
Washington, D.C.

James F. Ward
University of Massachusetts

Murray L. Wax
Washington University

E. Roy Weintraub
Duke University

Hayden V. White
University of California, Santa Cruz

John Williams
University College of Wales

Theta H. Wolf
Jupiter, Florida

Kurt H. Wolff
Brandeis University

Dennis H. Wrong
New York University

Elisabeth Young-Bruehl
Wesleyan University

Hans Zeisel
University of Chicago

Introduction

Social Science Quotations has been prepared to meet an evident unmet need in the literature of the social sciences. Writings on the lives and the theories of individual social scientists abound, but there has been no fully-documented collection of memorable quotations from the social sciences as a whole. Yet we know from the frequent use of quotations in scientific as well as literary writings that mere summaries or paraphrases typically fail to capture the full force of formulations that have made quotations memorable. After all, that is why we quote rather than paraphrase.

Most of us would hesitate to try improving upon William James's imagery of habit as "the enormous fly-wheel of society, its most precious conservative agent" or upon John Maynard Keynes's observation that "practical men, who believe themselves quite exempt from any intellectual influences, are usually the slaves of some defunct economist." Clearly, it is not their substance alone but also the words in which they are expressed that lead passages such as these to endure through repeated quotation.

We have given the book the subtitle of *Who Said What, When, and Where* in order to highlight a unique and valuable feature: the date of first publication and the source of each quotation are given in the text and the full reference is provided in the extensive Bibliography. Of obvious use to readers coming upon quotations new to them, exact references can also prove useful for swiftly locating the more familiar quotations. By leading readers back to the sources, such detailed references can help them place even extended quotations in their larger contexts. In this way, this book of quotations invites the further reading or rereading of the original texts, beyond the quotations themselves.

Social Science Quotations draws extensively upon the writings that constitute the historical core of the social sciences and social thought, those works with staying power often described as the "classical texts." Most of their authors wrote well; most of them wrote voluminously; and their ideas have had a formative impact upon much subsequent thinking. Many quotations have been drawn from these classical texts, not because the editors are Marxists or Weberians or Jamesians or Freudians or Keynesians or whatever, but because the quotations contain *memorable ideas memorably expressed*. Both consequential and memorable, these words have been quoted over the generations, entering into the collective memory of social scientists everywhere and at times diffusing into popular thought and into the vernacular as well.

There are, of course, many books of quotations available in bookstores and libraries, but none, other than this one, focused on the social sciences, broadly conceived. This broad scope has meant that the volume could not possibly include quotations from all the scholars of authority and consequence both in the long historical past of social thought and in the vastly-expanded present of the social sciences. For example, it was not possible to include quotations from all 800 or so scholars whose biographies appear in the *International*

Encyclopedia of the Social Sciences (1968; Biographical Supplement, 1979), let alone from many of the greatly-enlarged numbers of contemporary social scientists of the first rank. This is particularly true for those styles of scientific work whose undoubted importance rests on research formulations not readily captured in quotable prose.

We certainly make no claim that this volume of quotations serves as a comprehensive collection of the basic ideas and formulations of the various social sciences; it is emphatically *not* a one-volume summary of the writings of the authors included in the volume. This is typically and conspicuously the case where limitations of space and the unquotability of contributions have led to very few quotations from numerous major scholars, but it is also true for those eminently quotable figures who, much quoted from generation to generation, are cited in relative abundance. This roster includes Malinowski, Sapir, and Lévi-Strauss in anthropology; Adam Smith, Jevons, Keynes, and Schumpeter in economics; Ibn Khaldûn, Gibbon, and Macaulay in history; Hobbes, Locke, Machiavelli, and Rousseau in political thought; Freud, James, Jung, and G.H. Mead in psychology; Tocqueville, Durkheim, Simmel, and Max Weber in sociology; and Holmes, Pollock and Maitland, and Cardozo in the law. To these must be added such monumental social thinkers as Bentham, John Stuart Mill, Marx, and Pareto, who are enduringly quoted in a variety of disciplines. The notion that one, two, or for that matter, ten pages of quotations could convey the essentials of their thought is, of course, absurd, but the quotations included in the volume do serve to make some of their most memorable formulations easily accessible.

In selecting quotations, the editors have tried to cast as wide a net as possible, making relevance to the social sciences—their history, ideas, methods, and findings—the major criterion. We have included quotations from classical authors—Herodotus, Thucydides, Gibbon, and Macaulay, for example—who during the recent heyday of the behavioral sciences were identified as "literary" historians. Since this is a volume for ready reference, we have also included some quotations from the social sciences and social thought that, widely questioned as to substance, retain an enduring fame or notoriety.

In an effort to enlarge the scope of the volume, we have also included quotations on society and the social sciences drawn from the writings of poets, novelists, dramatists, philosophers, political figures, and revolutionaries, along with physicists, biologists, and mathematicians. By way of examples, there are selections from Walt Whitman and W.H. Auden; Jane Austen and Dostoyevski; Shakespeare and G.B. Shaw; Hegel, Schopenhauer, and Wittgenstein; and from the public speeches of Abraham Lincoln, Winston Churchill, Franklin D. Roosevelt, and Martin Luther King, Jr. These departures from the social sciences, narrowly defined, occupy only a small fraction of the volume but, we believe, serve an important reference function. Since this is not a book of general quotations, we have allowed ourselves only a few quotations of this kind; much more than the other quotations in the volume, their selection reflects the tastes and preferences of the editors.

Some of the quotations have had such an extensive influence for so long that they have become part of the culture. The identity of their authors is generally no longer given and, in due course, the original source becomes unknown to many making use of these anonymized quotations. This pattern in the transmission of culture has been described as "Obliteration [of source] By Incorporation [into common discourse]"—or OBI for short. Familiar instances are Francis Bacon's dictum "knowledge is power" (1597), Joseph Glanvill's "climates of opinions" (1661), John Adams's "government of laws and not of men" (1774), and Otto von Bismarck's "politics is the art of the possible" (1867). In much the same fashion, many concepts-and-phrasings—such as charisma, stereotype, opportunity costs, significant others, self-fulfilling prophecy, and double-bind—have entered the vernacular with little awareness of their sources in the social sciences.

A correlative pattern in quotation usage is misattribution. Ockham's Razor ("What can be accounted for by fewer assumptions is explained in vain by more") is generally attributed to William of Ockham, but there is no compelling evidence that it was original with him. "Bad money drives out good money" is generally and mistakenly attributed to Thomas Gresham, and "the best government is that which governs least" has been variously attributed to Thomas Jefferson, Thomas Paine, Henry David Thoreau, and the nineteenth-century editor John Louis O'Sullivan. It was Mark Twain who claimed that Benjamin Disraeli had identified three kinds of lies ("lies, damned lies, and statistics"), but there is no independent evidence for this attribution. These and other cases of misattribution are identified in bibliographical annotations to the quotations.

A number of quotations relate to each other in interesting ways that can be thought of as conversations between authors, past and present, or as echoes of earlier quotations. Some famous quotations have become so much a part of the culture of the social sciences that they are always at the ready. Consider Ranke's famous—some would now say, notorious—injunction that the historian tell what actually happened [*wie es eigentlich gewesen*]. This proves to be a nineteenth-century echo of Lucian's second-century precept that "the historian's one task is to tell the thing as it happened." This historiographic theme has been commented upon endlessly. Thus, Charles A. Beard's presidential address to the American Historical Association in 1935 was largely devoted to an attack upon it. The historian, he asserted, simply cannot find "the 'objective truth' of history, or write it, 'as it actually was'." Consider also Freud's ambiguous 1912 remark that "anatomy is destiny," which is a paraphrase of Napoleon's 1808 comment to Goethe that "politics is fate." So, too, Georg Simmel's historiographic maxim that "one need not be a Caesar truly to understand Caesar" was echoed by Max Weber in 1913 and by Alfred Schutz in the 1940s.

At times, a paraphrase takes the form of a reversal. Alphonse Karr's maxim-to-be that "the more things change, the more they remain the same" was independently inverted by Paul F. Lazarsfeld in 1962, by Gregory Bateson in 1972, and by Michael Silverstein in 1979 to read "the more things remain the same, the more they change." In like fashion, Plato's "necessity is the mother of invention" was converted by Thorstein Veblen into the consequential claim that "invention is the mother of necessity."

Many social science parables and metaphors endure in the collective memory. Montesquieu observed in 1748 that "politics are a smooth file, which cuts gradually, and attains its end by a slow progression," while Max Weber's rather more famous 1919 version has it that "politics is a strong and slow boring of hard boards." Cicero reported a parable concerning the efficacy of vows to the gods, as witness the votive pictures placed upon the beach by sailors who had survived storms at sea. But Diagoras the Atheist retorted that nowhere did he see such worshipful pictures placed by those who had drowned at sea. Francis Bacon in the seventeenth century and Laplace in the nineteenth went on to retell this story to bring out the necessity of using in research what have come to be known as control groups.

Such echoes take their most sardonic form in parodies. Thus, Herbert Spencer's 1862 definition of evolution as a process in which "matter passes from an indefinite, incoherent homogeneity to a definite, coherent heterogeneity" becomes in William James's 1880s parody "a change from a no-howish untalkaboutable all-alikeness to a somehowish and in general talkaboutable not-all-alikeness." In similar style, Ernest Gellner in 1959 transformed Wittgenstein's much-quoted 1921 injunction that "what we cannot speak about we must pass over in silence" into "that which one would insinuate, thereof one must speak."

What were our criteria in selecting quotations for inclusion in the volume? Along with the quotations with greatest staying power, others were selected by using these guidelines:

1. Frequently-quoted substantive statements that encapsulate basic contributions to the social sciences.

2. Statements marking an important event or turning point in the history of social thought and the social sciences, such as the emergence of new fields or new methodologies.

3. Ideas, words, or phrases originating in the social sciences that have diffused into popular or vernacular use.

4. Quotations that illuminate and clarify the frontiers between the social sciences and the humanities, on the one hand, and between the social sciences and the physical and biological sciences on the other.

5. Memorable observations on social science or on one of its constituent disciplines.

Assembled over a period of years, with the aid of many advisers, the quotations are drawn from a wide variety of sources: primarily books and journals, but also newspapers and magazines, collections of correspondence, diaries, epigraphs for books, and, on occasion, previously unpublished writings. In at least three cases (Thomas Jefferson, Karl Marx, and Johann Heinrich von Thünen), the quotations are engraved on their authors' tombstones.

We trust that the volume will be found useful and that readers who detect errors of any kind will call them to our attention.

June 1992

DAVID L. SILLS
ROBERT K. MERTON

Codicil to SSQ Introduction

The editors are grateful to Irving Louis Horowitz and to Mary E. Curtis for their decision to republish *Social Science Quotations* under the imprint of Transaction Books.

In the years since its first publication by the Macmillan Company in 1991, *Social Science Quotations* has served scholars and students alike in their needs for locating appropriate quotations in the social sciences and for verifying wording and identifying the sources of quotations not known with full accuracy.

The new printing—like the earlier one—is dedicated to the memory of our colleague and friend Paul F. Lazarsfeld. We also dedicate this reprinting to the memory of Charles E. Smith, an extraordinary publisher and a friend to hundreds of social scientists. His encouragement of this publication will be long remembered.

September 1999

D.L.S.
R.K.M.

Acknowledgments

This volume — like the eighteen volumes of the *Encyclopedia* that preceded it — is the product of an unusual collaboration between the academic community and the Macmillan Publishing Company. Unlike the preceding volumes, however, its preparation was greatly facilitated by several grants-in-aid. The editors gladly acknowledge financial support of the volume provided by the Eugene Garfield Foundation, the Joseph H. Hazen Foundation, the Andrew W. Mellon Foundation, the Russell Sage Foundation, the Robert Schalkenbach Foundation, and the Alfred P. Sloan Foundation.

This expression of thanks to organizations does not begin to capture our sense of indebtedness to individuals within them, particularly Eugene Garfield, Joseph H. Hazen, William G. Bowen, Neil L. Rudenstine, James Morris, Eric Wanner, Camille Yezzi, Arthur L. Singer, Jr., and Michael S. Teitelbaum.

The work of David L. Sills was greatly facilitated by a half-time sabbatical leave given him by the Social Science Research Council in 1988. Robert K. Merton was once again aided in his capacity as Foundation Scholar of the Russell Sage Foundation and, for a time, as a MacArthur Fellow.

The idea of preparing a volume of social science quotations was enthusiastically endorsed by the scholars who agreed to serve on the editorial board, and we are much obliged to them for their assistance during its preparation. We are especially grateful to Stephen M. Stigler for his almost weekly communications throughout the course of the project. The collaboration with him, begun while writing a 1984 article on "the Kelvin dictum," has allowed us to benefit from his ample stock of knowledge, wit, and wisdom.

As one means of accumulating a large store of informed quotations from which to make selections, we obtained many suggestions from other scholars specialized in the work of particular social scientists. It is a pleasure to thank them publicly for their indispensable contributions to the volume and to list their names in the accompanying roster.

In addition to receiving nominations of quotations, we benefited greatly from the advice of a number of other scholars on specific subsets of the quotations we had assembled. Daniel Bell reviewed all the quotations from Marx and Marxists, and Milton Friedman, Albert Rees, and George J. Stigler examined a large selection of quotations by economists. Charles C. Lemert was most helpful in proposing quotations from structuralists, poststructuralists, and contemporary philosophers. R. R. Palmer and David Cresap Moore reviewed the quotations from historians and Michael Silverstein reviewed those from linguists and proposed many more.

Notwithstanding all this good advice, generously given, it is the editors who made the final selection of quotations and thus are responsible for it and for remaining errors.

Documenting the quotations proved to be a substantial undertaking, with editors and editorial staff making extensive use of the New York Public Library, the Columbia University Library, the Barnard College Library, and the public libraries — all in Connecticut — of Darien, Fairfield, Greenwich, Norwalk, Rowayton, Stamford, and Westport. David Sills was given the privileges of the Frederick Lewis Allen Memorial Room at the New York Public Library, which provided him with companionable access to that magnificent collection of books and periodicals.

The small editorial staff that assisted the editors is listed on the page facing the title page. Along with these, the librarian Robin Johnson helped us in the early stages in the establishment of procedures both for documenting quotations and for the use of a computerized data base. Michael MacDonald and Thomas Smith assisted as library researchers at the beginning as did Rosa Haritos and Cheryl Kane-Piasecki in the final stages of the project.

The work of the editorial staff was carried out in the offices of a publishing consulting firm, Robert Ubell Associates, and we want to thank Robert N. Ubell, who served as executive editor, as well as his efficient and supportive staff. The Center for the Social Sciences at Columbia University and the Social Science Research Council in New York kindly served as other organizational hosts.

Charles E. Smith, then vice-president of the Macmillan Publishing Company in charge of reference books, strongly backed the idea of this new volume of the *Encyclopedia* from its inception and provided essential initial funding. His successor at Macmillan, Philip Friedman, and his associate, Elly Dickason, have provided exactly the kind of institutional aid and comfort a volume such as this requires.

A Technical Note

The quotations are presented alphabetically by author, and in that sense the volume — like a biographical dictionary — is self-indexed. The Index is alphabetically organized by subject, with most indexed entries being brief selections from a quotation. The authors are also listed in the Index, together with any references to them by other authors.

Readers seeking a quotation by a specific writer should go directly to the text, using the running heads as a guide. A brief summary of the source of each quotation is given directly below it; a complete source is given in the bibliography.

Readers seeking to learn the author of a quotation should first consult the Index, as should those seeking a quotation on a specific topic.

The editors have tried to be faithful to the original texts — to the words and intent of the authors. At the same time, we have tried to present the quotations in ways that would be understandable to the reader. The editing procedures we followed were briefly these:

(1) We have tried to quote from fairly recent, authoritative editions in English, but in all cases we have attempted to give the date of first publication as well. Quotations from sources first published in a language other than English are quoted in English translation: from a published translation, from a secondary source in English, or from an unpublished contemporary translation by the editors or others. The wording in the original language is provided at times when it is clearly necessary to convey the author's meaning.

(2) When a quoted passage begins or ends in the middle of an author's sentence, we have introduced a capital letter at the beginning and a period at the end in order to make the sentence as quoted complete.

(3) The deletion of words in the text has been signaled by ellipses. (Footnotes and references have been deleted without ellipses, since they are not taken as part of the text.)

(4) Words introduced into the quotations by the editors have been enclosed in square brackets.

(5) A number of cross-references have been placed after quotations. The Index should also be consulted for many additional interrelationships among and between quotations.

(6) Words italicized in the original have been preserved in italics in the text. However, when an entire quotation appears in italics in the source, the italics have been removed on the grounds that they no longer serve their original purpose.

(7) Citations to court cases are not included in the bibliography. In these citations, the first number is the volume of the official report on the case and the second number is the page on which the words quoted are located. The year given is the year in which the case was decided, not the year that proceedings began.

(8) Both British and archaic spellings have been preserved. British punctuation, however, has been changed to U.S. usage.

(9) Spelling and typographical errors, and some archaic punctuation marks, have been silently corrected.

Karl Abraham 1877–1925
German psychoanalyst

1 The myth is a surviving fragment of the psychic life of the infancy of the race whilst the dream is the myth of the individual.

Dreams and Myths (1909) 1955:208.

2 If when we indulge in wit we put aside strictly logical thinking, we are only reverting to the freedom we enjoyed in early childhood. The process of repression, which sets in during the fourth year of life or thereabout is, in wit, temporarily suspended.

The Cultural Significance of Psycho-Analysis (1920) 1955:129.

J. E. E. D. Acton 1834–1902
British historian

1 By liberty I mean the assurance that every man shall be protected in doing what he believes his duty against the influence of authority and majorities, custom and opinion.

The History of Freedom in Antiquity (1878) 1985:7.

2 Liberty is not a means to a higher political end. It is itself the highest political end.

The History of Freedom in Antiquity (1878) 1985:22.

3 Power tends to corrupt and absolute power corrupts absolutely.

Letter to Mandell Creighton, 5 April 1887. 1955:335.

4 There is no worse heresy than that the office sanctifies the holder of it.

Letter to Mandell Creighton, 5 April 1887. 1955:336.

5 The writer of history has to struggle as he best may with multifarious requirements, which threaten to turn him from a man of letters into the compiler of an encyclopaedia.

Introductory Note to the *Cambridge Modern History* 1902:4.

6 History must be our deliverer not only from the undue influence of other times, but from the undue influence of our own, from the tyranny of environment and the pressure of the air we breathe.

Lectures on Modern History (1906) 1952:33.

Henry Adams 1838–1918
U.S. historian

1 The difference is slight, to the influence of an author, whether he is read by five hundred readers, or by five hundred thousand; if he can select the five hundred, he reaches the five hundred thousand.

The Education of Henry Adams (1907) 1946:259.

2 Practical politics consists in ignoring facts.

The Education of Henry Adams (1907) 1946:373.

3 As he grew accustomed to the great gallery of machines, he began to feel the forty-foot dynamos as a moral force, much as the early Christians felt the Cross. The planet itself seemed less impressive, in its old-fashioned, deliberate, annual or daily revolution, than this huge wheel, revolving within arm's-length at some vertiginous speed. . . Before the end, one began to pray to it; inherited instinct taught the natural expression of man before silent and infinite force. Among the thousand symbols of ultimate energy, the dynamo was not so human as some, but it was the most expressive.

The Education of Henry Adams (1907) 1946:380. → A personal statement of a major theme in *Mont-Saint-Michel and Chartres*, published in 1904.

4 All the steam in the world could not, like the Virgin, build Chartres.

The Education of Henry Adams (1907) 1946:388.

James Truslow Adams 1878–1949
U.S. historian

1 It may be that without a vision men shall die. It is no less true that, without hard practical sense, they shall also

die. Without Jefferson the new nation might have lost its soul. Without Hamilton it would assuredly have been killed in body.

Jeffersonian Principles and Hamiltonian Principles (1928) 1932:xvi-xvii.

John Adams 1735–1826
U.S. statesman

If Aristotle, Livy, and Harrington knew what a republic was, the British constitution is much more like a republic than an empire. They define a republic to be a *government of laws and not of men.*

Novanglus (1774) 1969:106. → Novanglus is a pen name used by Adams.

In the government of this Commonwealth, the legislative department shall never exercise the executive and judicial powers, or either of them; the executive shall never exercise the legislative and judicial powers, or either of them; the judicial shall never exercise the legislative and executive powers, or either of them; to the end, it may be a government of laws, and not of men.

Constitution of the State of Massachusetts (1780) 1826:Part 1, article XXX, 11. → Although the constitution is of course unsigned, historians believe that Adams wrote it.

Alfred Adler 1870–1937
Austrian psychiatrist

Whether a person desires to be an artist, the first in his profession, or a tyrant in his home, to hold converse with God or humiliate other people; whether he regards his suffering as the most important thing in the world to which everyone must show obeisance, whether he is chasing after unattainable ideals or old deities, overstepping all limits and norms, at every part of his way he is guided and spurred on by his longing for superiority, the thought of his godlikeness, the belief in his special magical power.

Individual Psychology 1914:7.

Drama is the artistic expression of empathy.

Understanding Human Nature (1927) 1946:61.

All our institutions, our traditional attitudes, our laws, our morals, our customs, give evidence of the fact that they are determined and maintained by privileged males for the glory of male domination. These institutions reach out into the very nurseries and have a great influence upon the child's soul.

Understanding Human Nature (1927) 1946:123.

Pessimists. . . are the individuals who have acquired an "inferiority complex" as a result of the experiences and impressions of their childhood, for whom all manner of difficulties have vouchsafed the feeling that life is not easy. They always look for the dark side of life as a result of their pessimistic personal philosophy, which has been nourished by false treatment in their childhood. . . If they are children, they persistently call to their mothers, or cry for them as soon as separated. This cry for their mothers can sometimes be heard even in their old age.

Understanding Human Nature (1927) 1946:174–175.

5 I began to see clearly in every psychical phenomenon the *striving for superiority.* It runs parallel to physical growth. It is an intrinsic necessity of life itself. It lies at the root of all solutions of life's problems and is manifested in the way in which we meet these problems. All our functions follow its direction; rightly or wrongly they strive for conquest, surety, increase. The impetus from minus to plus is never-ending. The urge from "below" to "above" never ceases. Whatever premises all our philosophers and psychologists dream of — self-preservation, pleasure principle, equalization — all these are but vague representations, attempts to express the great upward drive.

Individual Psychology 1930:398.

6 Every neurotic is partly in the right.

Problems of Neurosis 1930:68.

T. W. Adorno 1903–1969
German philosopher, musicologist, and sociologist

1 In psycho-analysis nothing is true except the exaggerations.

Minimi moralia (1951) 1978:49.

2 The power of reason today is the blind reason of those who currently hold power. But as power moves towards the catastrophe it induces the mind which denies it with moderation to abdicate it. It still calls itself liberal, to be sure, but for it freedom has already become "from the sociological point of view nothing but a disproportion between the growth of the radius of effective central control on the one hand and the size of the group unit to be influenced on the other." The sociology of knowledge sets up indoctrination camps for the homeless intelligentsia where it can learn to forget itself.

The Sociology of Knowledge and Its Consciousness 1978:465. → The date of first publication of this essay is not given.

Agesilaus 444–400 B.C.
King of Sparta

1 If all the world were just, there would be no need of valour.

Quoted in Plutarch, *The Lives of the Noble Grecians and Romans*:727.

Floyd H. Allport 1890–1978
U.S. psychologist

1 *We ourselves accept and respond to the words of the leader; and therefore we believe and act upon the assumptions that others are doing so too.* The attitude and imagery involved in this reference of self-reaction to others we may call by the figurative term, *social projection.*

Social Psychology (1924) 1967:306–307.

[*See also* DANIEL KATZ AND FLOYD H. ALLPORT.]

Gordon W. Allport 1897–1967
U.S. psychologist

1 Personality is the dynamic organization within the individual of those psychophysical systems that determine his unique adjustments to his environment.

Personality 1937:48.

2 Workmanship is not an instinct, but so firm is the hold it may acquire on a man that it is little wonder Veblen mistook it for one. A business man, long since secure economically, works himself into ill-health, and sometimes even back into poverty, for the sake of carrying on his plans. What was once an instrumental technique becomes a master-motive.

Personality 1937:196.

3 The dog [in Pavlov's experiments] does not continue to salivate whenever it hears a bell unless sometimes at least an edible offering accompanies the bell. But there are innumerable instances in human life where a single association, *never* reinforced, results in the establishment of a life-long dynamic system. An experience associated only once with a bereavement, an accident, or a battle, may become the center of a permanent phobia or complex, not in the least dependent on a recurrence of the original shock.

Personality 1937:199.

4 There has been an over-emphasis upon constitutionalism, instincts, an unchanging Id, and childhood habits. Within the past few years, especially under the impact of the war, a desirable shift of emphasis to the contemporary motivational structure of the ego has occurred. One theory, in line with this modern trend of emphasis, is the doctrine of functional autonomy which holds that while the transformation of motives from infancy onward is gradual, it is none the less genuine. Just as we learn new skills, so also we learn new motives.

Geneticism versus Ego-Structure in Theories of Personality 1946:68.

5 The first experimental problem — indeed the only problem for the first three decades of experimental research — was formulated as follows: *What change in an individual's normal solitary performance occurs when other people are present?*

The Historical Background of Modern Social Psychology 1954:46.

6 Each person is an idiom unto himself, an apparent violation of the syntax of the species.

Becoming 1955:19.

Louis Althusser 1918–1990
French philosopher

1 Since Marx we know that the human subject, the political, economic or philosophical ego is not the center of history — we even know, against the Enlightenment philosophies and against Hegel, that history doesn't have a necessary "center" in our ideological misrecognitions of it. In his turn, Freud showed us that the real subject, the singular essence of the individual is not made of an ego centered on the "me" (le moi), on consciousness or on existence. . . that the human subject is decentered, constituted by a structure which also has no "center" except in the imaginary misrecognition of the "me" (moi), that is to say in the ideological formations where it finds recognition.

Freud et Lacan 1964–1965:107.

Thomas Aquinas 1225–1274
Italian theologian and philosopher

1 Practical sciences proceed by building up; theoretical sciences by resolving into components.

Commentary, *I Ethics*:Lect. 3.

2 It is natural for man, more than for any other animal, to be a social and political animal, to live in a group. . . If, then, it is natural for man to live in the society of many, it is necessary that there exist among men some means by which the group may be governed.

On Kingship:4–5.

3 When anything is done again and again it is assumed that it comes from the deliberate judgment of reason. On these grounds custom has the force of law, and abolishes a law, and is the interpreter of laws.

Summa theologiae:1a2ae 97, 151.

4 Three things are required for any war to be just. The first is the authority of the sovereign on whose command war is waged. . . Secondly, a just cause is required, namely that those who are attacked are attacked because they deserve it on account of some wrong they have done. . . Thirdly, the right intention of those waging war is required, that is, they must intend to promote the good and to avoid evil.

Summa theologiae:2a2ae 40, 81, 83.

5 To practise fraud so as to sell something for more than its just price is an outright sin in so far as one is deceiving one's neighbour to his detriment. . . The balance of justice is upset if either the price exceeds the value of the goods in question or the thing exceeds the price. To sell for more or to buy for less than a thing is worth is, therefore, unjust and illicit in itself.

Summa theologiae:2a2ae 77, 215.

Archilochos 7th century B.C.
Greek poet

1 The fox knows many tricks, the hedgehog only one; a good one.

Fragment 201:24. → In his book on Tolstoy, *The Hedgehog and the Fox* (1953), Isaiah Berlin uses this metaphor to distinguish between two types of thinkers. Foxes know many things; hedgehogs know one thing well.

Hannah Arendt 1906–1975
German-born U.S. political philosopher

1 Totalitarianism is never content to rule by external means, namely, through the state and a machinery of violence; thanks to its peculiar ideology and the role assigned to it in this apparatus of coercion, totalitarianism has discovered a means of dominating and terrorizing human beings from within.

The Origins of Totalitarianism (1951) 1979:325.

2 Wherever the relevance of speech is at stake, matters become political by definition, for speech is what makes man a political being.

The Human Condition 1958:3.

3 [Eichmann] was in complete command of himself, nay, he was more: he was completely himself. Nothing could have demonstrated this more convincingly than the grotesque silliness of his last words. He began by stating emphatically that he was a *Gottgläubiger*, to express in common Nazi fashion that he was no Christian and did not believe in life after death. He then proceeded: "After a short while, gentlemen, *we shall all meet again*. Such is the fate of all men. Long live Germany, long live Argentina, long live Austria. *I shall not forget them*." In the face of death, he had found the cliché used in funeral oratory. Under the gallows, his memory played him the last trick; he was "elated" and he forgot that this was his own funeral.

It was as though in those last minutes he was summing up the lesson that this long course in human wickedness had taught us — the lesson of the fearsome, word-and-thought-defying *banality of evil*.

Eichmann in Jerusalem (1963) 1964:252.

Aristotle 384–322 B.C.
Greek philosopher

1 All men naturally desire knowledge.

Metaphysics:Book 1, 3.

2 It is possible for all the kinds of cause to apply to the same object; *e.g.* in the case of a house the source of motion is the art and the architect; the final cause is the function; the matter is earth and stones, and the form is the definition.

Metaphysics:Book 3, 105.

3 It is equally unreasonable to accept merely probable conclusions from a mathematician and to demand strict demonstration from an orator.

Nicomachean Ethics:Book 1, 9.

4 It is. . . not of small moment whether we are trained from childhood in one set of habits or another; on the contrary it is of very great, or rather of supreme, importance.

Nicomachean Ethics:Book 2, 75.

5 All are agreed that justice in distributions must be based on desert of some sort, although they do not all mean the same sort of desert; democrats make the criterion free birth; those of oligarchical sympathies wealth, or in other cases birth; upholders of aristocracy make it virtue.

Nicomachean Ethics:Book 5, 269.

6 The difference between a historian and a poet is not that one writes in prose and the other in verse — indeed the writings of Herodotus could be put into verse and yet would still be a kind of history, whether written in metre or not. The real difference is this, that one tells what happened and the other what might happen. For this reason poetry is something more scientific and serious than history, because poetry tends to give general truths while history gives particular facts.

The Poetics:35.

7 It is evident that the state is a creation of nature, and that man is by nature a political animal.

Politics:Book 1, chap. 2, 54.

8 That man is more of a political animal than bees or any other gregarious animals is evident. Nature, as we often say, makes nothing in vain, and man is the only animal whom she has endowed with the gift of speech.

Politics:Book 1, chap. 2, 54.

9 The proof that the state is a creation of nature and prior to the individual is that the individual, when isolated, is not self-sufficing; and therefore he is like a part in relation to the whole. But he who is unable to live in society, or who has no need because he is sufficient for himself, must be either a beast or a god: he is no part of a state. A social instinct is implanted in all men by nature, and yet he who first founded the state was the greatest of benefactors. For man, when perfected, is the best of animals, but, when separated from law and justice, he is the worst of all.

Politics:Book 1, chap. 3, 55.

10 It is not the possessions but the desires of mankind which require to be equalized.

Politics:Book 2, chap. 7, 99.

11 The real difference between democracy and oligarchy is poverty and wealth. Wherever men rule by reason of their wealth, whether they be few or many, that is an oligarchy, and where the poor rule, that is a democracy. But as a fact the rich are few and the poor many; for few are well-to-do, whereas freedom is enjoyed by all, and wealth and freedom are the grounds on which the oligarchical and democratical parties respectively claim power in the state.

Politics:Book 3, chap. 9, 141.

12 A state exists for the sake of a good life, and not for the sake of a life only: if life only were the object, slaves and brute animals might form a state, but they cannot, for they have no share in happiness or in a life of free choice.

Politics:Book 3, chap. 9, 142.

13 Great then is the good fortune of a state in which the citizens have a moderate and sufficient property; for where some possess much, and the others nothing, there

may arise an extreme democracy, or a pure oligarchy; or a tyranny may grow out of either extreme — either out of the most rampant democracy, or out of an oligarchy; but it is not so likely to arise out of the middle constitutions and those akin to them.

Politics:Book 4, chap. 11, 192.

14 The universal and chief cause of . . . revolutionary feeling [is] the desire of equality, when men think that they are equal to others who have more than themselves; or, again, the desire of inequality and superiority, when conceiving themselves to be superior they think that they have not more but the same [as] or less than their inferiors; pretensions which may and may not be just. Inferiors revolt in order that they may be equal, and equals that they may be superior.

Politics:Book 5, chap. 2, 212.

Raymond Aron 1905–1983
French sociologist and journalist

1 The Left is dominated by three ideas, which are not necessarily contradictory, but usually divergent: *liberty*, against arbitrary power and for the rights of the individual; *organisation*, for the purpose of substituting a rational order in place of tradition or the anarchy of private enterprise; and *equality*, against the privileges of birth and wealth.

The Opium of the Intellectuals (1955) 1985:32.

2 Marxism now plays little part in the culture of the West. . . It is true, of course, that no modern historian or economist would think exactly as he does if Marx never existed. The economist has acquired an awareness of exploitation, or rather of the human cost of the capitalist economy, which must in fairness be credited to Marx. The historian no longer dares shut his eyes to the humble realities which rule the lives of millions of human beings. One can no longer claim to understand a society when one is ignorant of the organisation of labour, the technique of production and the relationship between the classes.

The Opium of the Intellectuals (1955) 1985:105.

3 Since men first began to reflect on politics, they have always fluctuated between two extreme positions: either that a state prospers only when the people truly desire the good of the group; or that it is impossible for the people truly to desire the good of the group, and a good government is one in which the vices of mankind conspire for the common good.

Main Currents in Sociological Thought (1965) 1968:Vol. 1, 24.

4 Sociology. . . creates a distance between the world in which one lives and the world in which one thinks. To our customs and beliefs, the very ones we hold sacred, sociology ruthlessly attaches the adjective "arbitrary." For our lived experiences, in their unique richness and indescribable depth, it substitutes indicators.

On the Historical Condition of the Sociologist (1971) 1978:76.

Kenneth J. Arrow 1921–
U.S. economist

1 The [preference] ordering, for an individual, represents his entire social ethic. . . [This] doubtless does not represent exactly the usual view of ethics; we no longer speak of "goods" but of "advantages"; in place of absolute good and evil, we speak here of a ranking of what should be *more* or *less* respected. In this view, individuals desire to act as well as possible from the moral point of view within the limits of possible actions. The conception of an ethical code and a compromise among imperfections may appear inelegant to some who prefer to devote themselves completely to the Cult of the Good.

The Principle of Rationality in Collective Decisions (1952) 1983:49.

2 To formalize the theory of choice under uncertainty, it is convenient to introduce the concept of the *state of the world*, a description of the world so complete that, if true and known, the consequences of every action would be known.

Exposition of the Theory of Choice under Uncertainty (1971) 1984:173.

3 Social good, as in the determination of a just income distribution, is an abstraction of some kind from the individual values of the members of the society. But this abstraction can only be based on interpersonally observed behavior, as in market purchases or voting, not on the full range of an individual's feelings. As is by now well known, attempts to form social judgments by aggregating individual expressed preferences always lead to the possibility of paradox. . . There cannot be a completely consistent meaning to collective rationality. We have at some point a relation of pure power; and how the distribution is going to be resolved cannot be answered unequivocally, nor can we easily say that there are objectively valid ethical criteria.

The Limits of Organization 1974:24–25.

4 The purpose of organizations is to exploit the fact that many (virtually all) decisions require the participation of many individuals for their effectiveness. In particular, . . . organizations are a means of achieving the benefits of collective action in situations in which the price system fails.

The Limits of Organization 1974:33.

5 There is one effect on organizations which has no parallel in individuals. An organization is typically composed of changing individuals. Now any individual generally has access to many communication channels, of which this particular organization is only one. In particular, education is such a channel. Thus, the organization is getting the benefit of a considerable amount of information which is free to it. Even though the code of the organization may make the internal transmission of such information costly, if there is enough of it, the behavior of the organization will change. In particular, new items will appear on the organization's agenda. If we think of edu-

cation as the primary source of new information, then it is introduced into an organization by its youngest and newest members. Thus we have the possibility of changes in organizational agenda induced by generational changes.

On the Agenda of Organizations (1974) 1984:180.

Kenneth J. Arrow 1921–
U.S. economist
and
F. H. Hahn 1925–
German-born British economist

1 The terms in which contracts are made matter. In particular, if money is the good in terms of which contracts are made, then the prices of goods in terms of money are of special significance. This is not the case if we consider an economy without a past and without a future. Keynes wrote that "the importance of money essentially flows from it being a link between the present and the future," to which we may add that it is important also because it is a link between the past and the present. If a serious monetary theory comes to be written, the fact that contracts are indeed made in terms of money will be of considerable importance.

General Competitive Analysis 1971:356–357.

[*See also* F. H. HAHN.]

Solomon E. Asch 1907–
Polish-born U.S. psychologist

1 The decisive psychological fact about society is the capacity of individuals to comprehend and to respond to each other's experiences and actions. This fact. . . alters the psychological scene for each, since to live in society is to bring into a sensible relation private and public experience. It is also an irreversible step; once in society we enter into a circle of mutuality that cannot be undone.

Social Psychology 1952:127.

2 The ego is not dedicated solely to its own enhancement. It needs and wants to be concerned with its surroundings, to bind itself to others, and to work with them. . . Accentuation of the self is often a response, not to powerful ego-centered tendencies, but to the thwarting and defeat of the need to be a part of one's group, to know that one is respected and liked, to feel that one is playing a part in the lives of others.

Social Psychology 1952:320.

John Aubrey 1626–1697
British antiquary and writer

1 When a boy, he [Aubrey] did ever love to converse with old men, as Living Histories.

Aubrey's Brief Lives: xxix. → First published in 1813; published in an expanded edition in 1898. For the origin of "oral history," see NEVINS:1.

2 One may say of him [Thomas Hobbes], as one sayes of Jos. Scaliger, that where he erres, he erres so ingeniosely, that one had rather erre with him then hitt the marke with Clavius.

Aubrey's Brief Lives:151.

3 [William Petty] hath told me that he hath read but little, that is to say, not since 25 aetat., and is of Mr. Hobbes his mind, that had he read much, as some men have, he had not known so much as he does, nor should have made such Discoveries and improvements.

Aubrey's Brief Lives:240–241.

W. H. Auden 1907–1973
British-born U.S. poet

1 *Chorus. (Singing to Mendelssohn's "Wedding March.")*
O Mr. Marx, you've gathered
All the material facts
You know the economic
Reasons for our acts.

The Dance of Death 1933:38.

2 Malinowski, Rivers,
Benedict and others
Show how common culture
Shapes the separate lives:
Matrilineal races
Kill their mothers' brothers
In their dreams and turn their
Sisters into wives.

Who when looking over
Faces in the subway,
Each with its uniqueness,
Would not, did he dare,
Ask what forms exactly
Suited to their weakness
Love and desperation
Take to govern there:

Would not like to know what
Influence occupation
Has on human vision
Of the human fate:
Do all clerks for instance
Pigeon-hole creation,
Brokers see the Ding-an-
sich as Real Estate?

When a politician
Dreams about his sweetheart,
Does he multiply her
Face into a crowd,
Are her fond responses
All-or-none reactions,
Does he try to buy her,
Is the kissing loud?

Heavy Date (1939) 1976:206.

3 If some traces of the autocratic pose,
the paternal strictness he distrusted, still
clung to his utterance and features,
it was a protective coloration

for one who'd lived among enemies so long:
if often he was wrong and, at times, absurd,
to us he is no more a person
now but a whole climate of opinion.

In Memory of Sigmund Freud (1939) 1976:217. → See GLANVILL:1.

4 Thou shalt not answer questionnaires
Or quizzes upon World-Affairs,
Nor with compliance
Take any test. Thou shalt not sit
With statisticians nor commit
A social science.

Under Which Lyre (1946) 1976:262.

Augustine 354–430
North African theologian and philosopher

1 Justice being taken away. . . what are kingdoms but great robberies? For what are robberies themselves, but little kingdoms?. . . [It] was an apt and true reply which was given to Alexander the Great by a pirate who had been seized. For when that king had asked the man what he meant by keeping hostile possession of the sea, he answered with bold pride, "What thou meanest by seizing the whole earth; but because I do it with a petty ship, I am called a robber, whilst thou who dost it with a great fleet art styled emperor."

The City of God (413–427) 1950:Book 4, 112–113.

2 The earthly city, which does not live by faith, seeks an earthly peace, and the end it proposes, in the well-ordered concord of civic obedience and rule, is the combination of men's wills to attain the things which are helpful to this life. The heavenly city, or rather the part of it which sojourns on earth and lives by faith, makes use of this peace only because it must, until this mortal condition which necessitates it shall pass away.

The City of God (413–427) 1950:Book 19, 695.

3 [If we assume that] a people is an assemblage of reasonable beings bound together by a common agreement as to the objects of their love, then, in order to discover the character of any people, we have only to observe what they love. . . And it will be a superior people in proportion as it is bound together by higher interests, inferior in proportion as it is bound together by lower.

The City of God (413–427) 1950:Book 19, 706.

Jane Austen 1775–1817
British novelist

1 [*Catherine*]: I often think it odd that it [history] should be so dull, for a great deal of it must be invention.

Northanger Abbey (1818) 1985:87.

B

Charles Babbage 1792–1871
British mathematician

1 *The cost, to the purchaser, is the price he pays for any article, added to the cost of verifying the fact of its having that degree of goodness for which he contracts.* In some cases the goodness of the article is evident on mere inspection: and in these cases there is not much difference of price at different shops. The goodness of loaf sugar, for instance, can be discerned almost at a glance; and the consequence is, that the price of it is so uniform, and the profit upon it so small, that no grocer is at all anxious to sell it whilst, on the other hand, tea, of which it is exceedingly difficult to judge, and which can be adulterated by mixture so as to deceive even the skill of a practised eye, has a great variety of different prices, and is that article which every grocer is most anxious to sell to his customers.

The Economy of Machinery and Manufactures 1832:98.

2 Political economists have been reproached with too small a use of facts, and too large an employment of theory. If facts are wanting, let it be remembered that the closet-philosopher is unfortunately too little acquainted with the admirable arrangements of the factory; and that no class of persons can supply so readily, and with so little sacrifice of time, the data on which all the reasonings of political economists are founded, as the merchant and manufacturer; and, unquestionably, to no class are the deductions to which they give rise so important. Nor let it be feared that erroneous deductions may be made from such recorded facts: the errors which arise from the absence of facts are far more numerous and more durable than those which result from unsound reasoning respecting true data.

The Economy of Machinery and Manufactures 1832:112.

3 Another kind of combination against the public. . . usually ends in a monopoly, and the public are then left to the discretion of the monopolists not to charge them above the *"growling point"* — that is, *not to make them pay so much as to induce them actually to combine against the imposition.*

The Economy of Machinery and Manufactures 1832:228–229.

4 Every moment dies a man,
Every moment $1\frac{1}{16}$ is born.

Strictly speaking, this is not correct, the actual figure is so long that I cannot get it into a line, but I believe that the figure $1\frac{1}{16}$ will be sufficiently accurate for poetry.

Letter to Alfred Tennyson. 1842? → Babbage's response to Tennyson's 1842 lines: "Every minute dies a man, Every minute one is born." As a result of Babbage's criticism, Tennyson changed "minute" to "moment" in subsequent editions.

Francis Bacon 1561–1626
British statesman and philosopher

1 Knowledge is power [*Scientia potestas est*].

De haeresibus (1597) 1892:241.

2 If a man will begin with certainties, he shall end in doubts; but if he will be content to begin with doubts, he shall end in certainties.

The Advancement of Learning (1605) 1963:41.

3 We are much beholden to Machiavel and others, that write what men do, and not what they ought to do.

The Advancement of Learning (1605) 1963:201.

4 There are four classes of Idols which beset men's minds. To these for distinction's sake I have assigned names, calling the first class *Idols of the Tribe*; the second, *Idols of the Cave*; the third, *Idols of the Market Place*; the fourth, *Idols of the Theater.*

The New Organon (1620) 1960:Book 1, aphorism 39, 47–48. → Bacon believed that these four idols hindered intellectual advance. The Idols of the Tribe are errors caused by human nature; Idols of the Cave are errors founded in idiosyncrasies; Idols of the Market Place, errors caused by misleading words; and Idols of the Theatre, errors caused by the wish to create philosophical systems.

5 The human understanding when it has once adopted an opinion (either as being the received opinion or as being agreeable to itself) draws all things else to support and agree with it. And though there be a greater number and weight of instances to be found on the other side, yet these it either neglects and despises, or else by some distinction sets aside and rejects, in order that by this great and pernicious predetermination the authority of its former conclusions may remain inviolate. And therefore it was a good answer that was made by one who, when they showed him hanging in a temple a picture of those who had paid their vows as having escaped shipwreck, and would have him say whether he did not now acknowledge the power of the gods — "Aye," asked he again, "but where are they painted that were drowned after their vows"?

The New Organon (1620) 1960:Book 1, aphorism 46, 50. → See CICERO:2 and LAPLACE:4.

6 The human understanding is no dry light, but receives an infusion from the will and affections; whence proceed sciences which may be called "sciences as one would." For what a man had rather were true he more readily believes. Therefore he rejects difficult things from impatience of research; sober things, because they narrow hope; the deeper things of nature, from superstition; the light of experience, from arrogance and pride, lest his mind should seem to be occupied with things mean and transitory; things not commonly believed, out of deference to the opinion of the vulgar. Numberless, in short, are the ways, and sometimes imperceptible, in which the affections color and infect the understanding.

The New Organon (1620) 1960:Book 1, aphorism 49, 52.

7 Men become attached to certain particular sciences and speculations, either because they fancy themselves the authors and inventors thereof, or because they have bestowed the greatest pains upon them and become most habituated to them.

The New Organon (1620) 1960:Book 1, aphorism 54, 54.

8 The understanding must not. . . be allowed to jump and fly from particulars to axioms remote and of almost the highest generality (such as the first principles, as they are called, of arts and things), and taking stand upon them as truths that cannot be shaken, proceed to prove and frame the middle axioms by reference to them; which has been the practice hitherto, the understanding being not only carried that way by a natural impulse, but also by the use of syllogistic demonstration trained and inured to it. But then, and then only, may we hope well of the sciences when in a just scale of ascent, and by successive steps not interrupted or broken, we rise from particulars to lesser axioms; and then to middle axioms, one above the other; and last of all to the most general. For the lowest axioms differ but slightly from bare experience, while the highest and most general (which we now have) are notional and abstract and without solidity. But the middle are the true and solid and living axioms, on which depend the affairs and fortunes of men; and above them again, last of all, those which are indeed the most general; such, I mean, as are not abstract, but of which those intermediate axioms are really limitations.

The New Organon (1620) 1960:Book 1, aphorism 104, 98.

9 Printing, gunpowder, and the magnet. . . these three have changed the whole face and state of things throughout the world; the first in literature, the second in warfare, the third in navigation; whence have followed innumerable changes, insomuch that no empire, no sect, no star seems to have exerted greater power and influence in human affairs than these mechanical discoveries.

The New Organon (1620) 1960:Book 1, aphorism 129, 118.

10 Above all things, good policy is to be used that the treasure and moneys in a state be not gathered into few hands. For otherwise a state may have a great stock, and yet starve. And money is like muck, not good except it be spread.

Of Seditions and Troubles (1625) 1936:48.

11 The End of Our Foundation is the knowledge of Causes and secret motions of things, and the enlarging of the bounds of Human Empire, to the effecting of all things possible.

New Atlantis (1627) 1965:447.

Walter Bagehot 1826–1877
British economic and political writer

1 I fear you will laugh when I tell you what I conceive to be about the most essential mental quality for a free people, whose liberty is to be progressive, permanent, and on a large scale; it is much *stupidity*.

Letters on the French *Coup d'État* of 1851, Letter III 20 January 1852. 1968:50–51.

2 No real English gentleman, in his secret soul, was ever sorry for the death of a political economist.

The First Edinburgh Reviewers (1855) 1965:324.

3 You may talk of the tyranny of Nero and Tiberius; but the real tyranny is the tyranny of your next-door neighbour. . . Public opinion is a permeating influence, and it exacts obedience to itself; it requires us to think other men's thoughts, to speak other men's words, to follow other men's habits.

The Character of Sir Robert Peel (1856) 1968:243.

4 A secret prerogative is an anomaly — perhaps the greatest of anomalies. That secrecy is, however, essential to the utility of English royalty as it now is. Above all things our royalty is to be reverenced, and if you begin to poke about it you cannot reverence it. When there is a select committee on the Queen, the charm of royalty will be gone. Its mystery is its life. We must not let in daylight upon magic.

The English Constitution (1867) 1974:243.

5 The sovereign has, under a constitutional monarchy such as ours, three rights — the right to be consulted, the right to encourage, the right to warn. And a king of great sense and sagacity would want no others.

The English Constitution (1867) 1974:253.

6 In this there is nothing new. . . that when a philosopher cannot account for anything in any other manner, he boldly ascribes it to an occult quality in some race.

Physics and Politics (1872) 1974:18.

7 The object of [archaic societies] is to create what may be called a *cake* of custom. All the actions of life are to be submitted to a single rule for a single object; that gradually created the "hereditary drill" which science teaches to be essential, and which the early instinct of men saw to be essential too. That [an archaic society] forbids free thought is not an evil; or rather, though an evil, it is the necessary basis for the greatest good; it is necessary for making the mould of civilisation, and hardening the soft fibre of early man.

Physics and Politics (1872) 1974:32.

8 The peculiar circumstances of his time also conducted Ricardo to the task for which his mind was most fit. He did not go to political economy — political economy, so to say, came to him.

Economic Studies (1880) 1978:344.

Bernard Bailyn 1922–

U.S. historian

1 To conceive of legislative assemblies as mirrors of society and their voices as mechanically exact expressions of the people; to assume, and act upon the assumption, that human rights exist above the law and stand as the measure of the law's validity; to understand constitutions to be ideal designs of government, and fixed, limiting definitions of its permissible sphere of action; and to consider the possibility that absolute sovereignty in government need not be the monopoly of a single all-engrossing agency but (*imperium in imperio*) the shared possession of several agencies each limited by the boundaries of the others but all-powerful within its own — to think in these ways, as Americans were doing before Independence, was to reconceive the fundamentals of government and of society's relation to government.

The Ideological Origins of the American Revolution 1967:230.

2 The real losers [in the American Revolution] — those whose lives were disrupted, who suffered violence and vilification, who were driven out of the land and forced to resettle elsewhere in middle life and died grieving for the homes they had lost — these were not the English but the Americans who clung to them, who remained loyal to England and to what had been assumed to be the principles of legitimacy and law and order which the British government embodied. They were the American loyalists, and it is their history that allows us to see the Revolutionary movement from the other side around, and to grasp the wholeness of the struggle and hence in the end to understand more fully than we have before why a revolution took place and why it succeeded.

The Ordeal of Thomas Hutchinson 1974:xi.

3 I do not know when it began — sometime in the early Middle Ages. It moved forward with varying speeds for several hundred years; was thrown back for a century or more after the first third of the fourteenth century; took a sudden lurch forward in the sixteenth century; slowed in the mid-seventeenth century; then sped precipitately ahead in the later seventeenth century to form in the eighteenth and nineteenth centuries a mighty flow that transformed at first half the globe, ultimately the whole of it, more fundamentally than any development except the Industrial Revolution. This transforming phenomenon was the movement of people outward from their original centers of habitation — the centrifugal *Völkerwanderungen* that involved an untraceable multitude of local, small-scale exoduses and colonizations, the continuous creation of new frontiers and ever-widening circumferences, the complex intermingling of peoples in the expanding border areas, and in the end the massive transfer to the Western Hemisphere of people from Africa, from the European mainland, and above all from the Anglo-Celtic offshore islands of Europe, culminating in what Bismarck called "the decisive fact in the modern world," the peopling of the North American continent.

The Peopling of British North America (1986) 1988:4–5.

Bernard Barber 1918–

U.S. sociologist

1 One essential characteristic of [the] social sciences is that they deal with the social relations between human beings, that is, with those relationships between human beings in which they interact with one another not as physical objects merely but on the basis of mutually attributed meanings.

Science and the Social Order (1952) 1962:312.

2 Knowledge is power to do good and evil alike, but we cannot throw away the power. We have faced the same dilemma in the consequences of the natural sciences, and we have chosen as we have had to choose, for the partial control that it gives us. We can give up our fear of a beehive society run by social science experts; and, having done so, we can devote ourselves to advancing social science to the point where it helps us bring our society a little more closely in accord with our social values. We have used natural science to give us relative abundance; social science can give us freedom in the same relative measure.

Science and the Social Order (1952) 1962:340.

3 Against the background of this general and comprehensive definition of trust as expectation of the persistence of the moral social order, we can proceed to two more specific meanings, each of which is important for the understanding of social relationships and social sys-

tems. . . The first. . . is the meaning of trust as the expectation of technically competent role performance. . . The second. . . concerns expectations of fiduciary obligation and responsibility, that is, the expectation that some others in our social relationships have moral obligations and responsibility to demonstrate a special concern for other's interests above their own.

The Logic and Limits of Trust 1983:14.

Chester I. Barnard 1886–1961
U.S. business executive and organizational theorist

1 A person can and will accept a communication as authoritative only when four conditions simultaneously obtain: *(a)* he can and does understand the communication; *(b) at the time of his decision* he believes that it is not inconsistent with the purpose of the organization; *(c)* at the time of his decision, he believes it to be compatible with his personal interest as a whole; and *(d)* he is able mentally and physically to comply with it.

The Functions of the Executive (1938) 1968:165.

2 The phrase "zone of indifference" may be explained as follows: If all the orders for actions reasonably practicable be arranged in the order of their acceptability to the person affected, it may be conceived that there are a number which are clearly unacceptable, that is, which certainly will not be obeyed; there is another group somewhat more or less on the neutral line, that is, either barely acceptable or barely unacceptable: and a third group unquestionably acceptable. This last group lies within the "zone of indifference." The person affected will accept orders lying within this zone and is relatively indifferent as to what the order is so far as the question of authority is concerned.

The Functions of the Executive (1938) 1968:168–169.

3 The functions of informal executive organizations are the communication of intangible facts, opinions, suggestions, suspicions, that cannot pass through formal channels without raising issues calling for decisions, without dissipating dignity and objective authority, and without overloading executive positions; also to minimize excessive cliques of political types arising from too great divergence of interests and views; to promote self-discipline of the group; and to make possible the development of important personal influences in the organization.

The Functions of the Executive (1938) 1968:225.

4 Free and unfree, controlling and controlled, choosing and being chosen, inducing and unable to resist inducement, the source of authority and unable to deny it, independent and dependent, nourishing their personalities, and yet depersonalized; forming purposes and being forced to change them, searching for limitations in order to make decisions, seeking the particular but concerned with the whole, finding leaders and denying their leadership, hoping to dominate the earth and being dominated by the unseen — this is the story of man in society told in these pages.

The Functions of the Executive (1938) 1968:296.

F. C. Bartlett 1886–1969
British psychologist

1 Remembering is not the re-excitation of innumerable fixed, lifeless and fragmentary traces. It is an imaginative reconstruction, or construction, built out of the relation of our attitude towards a whole active mass of organised past reactions or experience, and to a little outstanding detail which commonly appears in image or in language form. It is thus hardly ever really exact, even in the most rudimentary cases of rote recapitulation, and it is not at all important that it should be so.

Remembering (1932) 1967:213.

2 Propaganda is an organised and public form of the process which the psychologist calls "suggestion."

Political Propaganda (1940) 1973:51.

3 Thinking. . . is. . . not simply the description, either by perception or by recall, of something which is there, it is the use of information about something present, to get somewhere else.

Thinking 1958:74.

Bernard Baruch 1870–1965
U.S. businessman and statesman

1 As the Soviets thwarted an atomic agreement, lowered their Iron Curtain in Eastern Europe, and broke one promise after the other in those early postwar years, it became clear that they were waging war against us. It was a new kind of war, to be sure, in which the guns were silent; but our survival was at stake nonetheless. It was a situation that soon came to be known as the "cold war," a phrase I introduced in a speech before the South Carolina legislature in April, 1947.

Baruch 1960:388. → See CHURCHILL:3.

Jacques Barzun 1907–
French-born U.S. historian and cultural critic

The philosophical implication of race-thinking is that by offering us the mystery of heredity as an explanation, it diverts our attention from the social and intellectual factors that make up personality.

Race 1937:282.

2 All the steps in political progress that we most venerate were in actuality riotous, fanatical, marred by atrocities. But the political mind cannot give in to this spectator's view of history. It would be yielding to tragedy instead of acting to avert it. The statesman (and likewise the theorist of political comedy like Bagehot) must defend an interest greater than progress itself: present life. He must perpetuate order, which he does by keeping the multitudinous aggressions of men in balance against one an-

other. His task looks paradoxical because, through order, he intends that moral force, which always does have the last word, shall not speak it from beyond the grave.

Bagehot, or the Human Comedy (1946) 1962:208.

3 The use of history is for the person. History is formative. Its spectacle of continuity in chaos, of attainment in the heart of disorder, of purpose in the world is what nothing else provides: science denies it, art only invents it.

Clio and the Doctors 1974:123–124.

Frédéric Bastiat 1801–1850
French economist

1 Government *is the great fiction, through which everybody endeavors to live at the expense of everybody else.*

Government (1846) 1877:160.

2 What makes the great division between the two schools is the difference in their methods. Socialism, like astrology and alchemy, proceeds by way of the imagination; political economy, like astronomy and chemistry, proceeds by way of observation.

Economic Harmonies (1850) 1964:xxv.

3 Exchange *is* political economy. It is society itself, for it is impossible to conceive of a society without exchange, or exchange without society.

Economic Harmonies (1850) 1964:59.

Gregory Bateson 1904–1980
British anthropologist

1 Whenever we pride ourselves upon finding a newer, stricter way of thought or exposition; whenever we start insisting too hard upon "operationalism" or symbolic logic or any other of these very essential systems of tramlines, we lose something of the ability to think new thoughts. And equally, of course, whenever we rebel against the sterile rigidity of formal thought and exposition and let our ideas run wild, we likewise lose. As I see it, the advances in scientific thought come from a *combination of loose and strict thinking,* and this combination is the most precious tool of science.

Culture Contact and Schismogenesis (1935) 1972:75.

2 If it were possible adequately to present the whole of a culture, stressing every aspect exactly as it is stressed in the culture itself, no single detail would appear bizarre or strange or arbitrary to the reader, but rather the details would all appear natural and reasonable as they do to the natives who have lived all their lives within the culture.

Naven (1936) 1967:1.

3 Schizophrenia — its nature, etiology, and the kind of therapy to use for it — remains one of the most puzzling of the mental illnesses. The theory of schizophrenia presented here is based on communications analysis. . . From this theory and from observations of schizophrenic patients is derived a description, and the necessary conditions for, a situation called the "double bind" — a situation in which no matter what a person does, he "can't win." It is hypothesized that a person caught in the double bind may develop schizophrenic symptoms.

Toward a Theory of Schizophrenia (1956) 1972:201.

4 *"Plus c'est la même chose, plus ça change."* This converse of the French aphorism seems to be the more exact description of biological and ecological systems. A constancy of some variable is maintained by changing other variables. This is characteristic of the engine with a governor: the constancy of rate of rotation is maintained by altering the fuel supply. *Mutatis mutandis,* the same logic underlies evolutionary progress: those mutational changes will be perpetuated which contribute to the constancy of that complex variable which we call "survival." The same logic also applies to learning, social change, etc. The ongoing truth of certain descriptive propositions is maintained by altering other propositions.

Effects of Conscious Purpose on Human Adaptation 1972:447. → For the original aphorism, see KARR:1.

Charles A. Beard 1874–1948
U.S. historian

1 It will be admitted without controversy that the Constitution was the creation of a certain number of men, and it was opposed by a certain number of men. Now, if it were possible to have an economic biography of all those connected with its framing and adoption, — perhaps about 160,000 men altogether, — the materials for scientific analysis and classification would be available. Such an economic biography would include a list of the real and personal property owned by all of these men and their families: lands and houses, with incumbrances, money at interest, slaves, capital invested in shipping and manufacturing, and in state and continental securities.

An Economic Interpretation of the Constitution of the United States (1913) 1935:16. → Beard here advocates what is now known by the eighteenth-century term "prosopography" — the systematic study of collections of biographies.

2 The grand conclusion. . . seems to be exactly that advanced by our own James Madison in the Tenth Number of the Federalist. To express his thought in modern terms: a landed interest, a transport interest, a railway interest, a shipping interest, an engineering interest, a manufacturing interest, a public-official interest, with many lesser interests, grow up of necessity in all great societies and divide them into different classes actuated by different sentiments and views. The regulation of these various and interfering interests, whatever may be the formula for the ownership of property, constitutes the principal task of modern statesmen and involves the spirit of party in the necessary and ordinary operations of government. In other words, there is no rest for mankind, no final solution of eternal contradictions. Such is the design of the universe. The recognition of this fact is the beginning of wisdom — and of statesmanship.

The Economic Basis of Politics (1922) 1924:99.

3 The world is largely ruled by ideas, true and false.

Introduction to J.B. Bury, *The Idea of Progress* (1920) 1955:ix. → From the 1932 edition.

4 It is for us. . . to inquire constantly and persistently, when theories of national power or states' rights are propounded: "What interests are behind them and to whose advantage will changes or the maintenance of old forms accrue?" By refusing to do this we become victims of history — clay in the hands of its makers.

An Economic Interpretation of the Constitution of the United States (1913) 1935:xvii. → From the introduction to the 1935 edition. See CICERO:4.

5 The historian's powers are limited. He may search for, but he cannot find, the "objective truth" of history, or write it, "as it actually was."

That Noble Dream 1935:84. → Beard's presidential address to the American Historical Association, in which he attacked Ranke and set forth the case for historical relativism. See RANKE:1.

Charles A. Beard 1874–1948
and
Mary R. Beard 1876–1958
U.S. historians

1 At no time, at no place, in solemn convention assembled, through no chosen agents, had the American people officially proclaimed the United States to be a democracy. The Constitution did not contain the word or any word lending countenance to it, except possibly the mention of "we, the people," in the preamble. . . When the Constitution was framed no respectable person called himself or herself a democrat.

America in Midpassage 1939:Vol. 2, 922–923.

[*See also* JAMES HARVEY ROBINSON AND CHARLES A. BEARD.]

Gustave Auguste de Beaumont 1802–1866
French statesman and publicist

1 [Tocqueville and I] have ambitious plans. . . We will see America as we survey its prisons. We will survey its inhabitants, its cities, its institutions, its mores. We will learn how the republican government works. This government is not at all well known in Europe. . . Wouldn't it be good to have a book that gives an accurate notion of the American people, that paints a broad portrait of their history, boldly outlines their character, analyzes their social state, and corrects the many mistaken opinions on this subject?

Letter to his father, 25 April 1831. → The "book" described is Tocqueville's *Democracy in America* (1835–1840). See TOCQUEVILLE:2.

Simone de Beauvoir 1908–1986
French writer and critic

1 One is not born, but rather becomes, a woman. No biological, psychological, or economic fate determines the figure that the human female presents in society; it is civilization as a whole that produces this creature, intermediate between male and eunuch, which is described as feminine. Only the intervention of someone else can establish an individual as an *Other*.

The Second Sex (1949) 1968:267.

2 When we abolish the slavery of half of humanity, together with the whole system of hypocrisy that it implies, then the "division" of humanity will reveal its genuine significance and the human couple will find its true form.

The Second Sex (1949) 1968:731.

Beccaria 1738–1794
[Cesare Bonesana, marchese di Beccaria]
Italian economic and penal theorist

1 If we glance at the pages of history, we will find that laws, which surely are, or ought to be, compacts of free men, have been, for the most part, a mere tool of the passions of some, or have arisen from an accidental and temporary need. Never have they been dictated by a dispassionate student of human nature who might, by bringing the actions of a multitude of men into focus, consider them from this single point of view: the greatest happiness shared by the greatest number.

On Crimes and Punishments (1764) 1963:8. → See BENTHAM:1, 3.

2 From what has thus far been demonstrated, one may deduce a general theorem of considerable utility, though hardly conformable with custom, the usual legislator of nations; it is this: In order for punishment not to be, in every instance, an act of violence of one or of many against a private citizen, it must be essentially public, prompt, necessary, the least possible in the given circumstances, proportionate to the crimes, dictated by the laws.

On Crimes and Punishments (1764) 1963:99.

Carl L. Becker 1873–1945
U.S. historian

1 To establish the facts is always in order, and is indeed the first duty of the historian; but to suppose that the facts, once established in all their fullness, will "speak for themselves" is an illusion. It was perhaps peculiarly the illusion of those historians of the last century who found some special magic in the word "scientific." The scientific historian, it seems, was one who set forth the facts without injecting any extraneous meaning into them.

Everyman His Own Historian 1932:232. → See ALFRED MARSHALL:2.

2 [Progress] is so heavily loaded with moral and teleological overtones that no scientist with any sense of decency will use it. It implies that there are values in the world. It implies, not only that the world moves forward, but that it moves forward to some good purpose, to some more felicitous state. In short, the word Progress, like the Cross or the Crescent, is a symbol that stands for a social doctrine, a philosophy of human destiny.

Progress and Power (1936) 1949:3–4.

3 The significance of man is that he is that part of the universe that asks the question, What is the significance of man? He alone can stand apart imaginatively and, regarding himself and the universe in their eternal aspects, pronounce a judgment: The significance of man is that he is insignificant and is aware of it.

Progress and Power (1936) 1949:115.

Gary S. Becker 1930–
U.S. economist

1 The traditional theory of the household is essentially a theory of a one-person household, and it is almost, but not quite, sterile. . . In contrast, the new theory of the household is a theory of the multiperson family with interdependent utility functions, and focuses on the coordination and interaction among members with regard to decisions about children, marriage, the division of labor concerning hours worked and investments in market-augmenting and nonmarket-augmenting skills, the protection of members against hazards, intergenerational transfers among members, and so on. Economists are, therefore, only beginning to attribute to the family the same dominant role in society traditionally attributed to it by sociologists, anthropologists, and psychologists.

Marriage, Fertility, and the Family 1976:169.

2 Rotten Kid Theorem. Each beneficiary, no matter how selfish, maximizes the family income of his benefactor and thereby internalizes all effects of his actions on other beneficiaries.

A Treatise on the Family 1981:183.

3 In the 1920s, the Russian economist Nicholas D. Kondratieff claimed that capitalist economies exhibit long-term fluctuations of about fifty years' duration in output and prices. Simon Kuznets later argued that long-term fluctuations only last about twenty years. If long cycles of the Kondratieff or Kuznets type exist — we will need another 200 years of data to determine whether they do exist or are just a statistical figment of an overactive imagination — they almost certainly will depend on fertility and other family decisions that biologically require a long time to implement.

Family Economics and Macro Behavior 1988:7. → See KONDRATIEFF:1.

4 Family behavior is active, not passive, and endogenous, not exogenous. Families have large effects on the economy, and evolution of the economy greatly changes the structure and decisions of families.

Family Economics and Macro Behavior 1988:11.

Daniel Bell 1919–
U.S. sociologist

1 The analysis of ideology belongs properly in the discussion of the intelligentsia. One can say that what the priest is to religion, the intellectual is to ideology.

The End of Ideology in the West (1960) 1965:394.

2 A social movement can rouse people when it can do three things: simplify ideas, establish a claim to truth, and, in the union of the two, demand a commitment to action. Thus, not only does ideology transform ideas, it transforms people as well.

The End of Ideology in the West (1960) 1965:401.

3 The concept "post-industrial" is counterposed to that of "pre-industrial" and "industrial." A pre-industrial sector is primarily *extractive,* its economy based on agriculture, mining, fishing, timber, and other resources such as natural gas or oil. An industrial sector is primarily *fabricating,* using energy and machine technology, for the manufacture of goods. A post-industrial sector is one of *processing* in which telecommunications and computers are strategic for the exchange of information and knowledge.

The Coming of Post-Industrial Society (1973) 1976:xii. → From the foreword to the 1976 edition.

Julien Benda 1867–1956
French philosopher

1 Our age is indeed the age of the *intellectual organization of political hatreds.* It will be one of its chief claims to notice in the moral history of humanity.

The Treason of the Intellectuals [*La trahison des clercs*] (1927) 1969:27.

2 [By clerks (*les clercs*) I mean all those whose activity] is *not* the pursuit of practical aims, all those who seek their joy in the practice of an art or a science or metaphysical speculation, in short in the possession of non-material advantages, and hence in a certain manner say: "My kingdom is not of this world." Indeed, throughout history, for more than two thousand years until modern times, I see an uninterrupted series of philosophers, men of religion, men of literature, artists, men of learning (one might say almost all during this period), whose influence, whose life, were in direct opposition to the realism of the multitudes.

The Treason of the Intellectuals [*La trahison des clercs*] (1927) 1969:43–44.

3 Let me recapitulate the causes for this change in the "clerks" [*les clercs*]: The imposition of political interests on all men without any exception; the growth of consistency in matters apt to feed realist passions; the desire and the possibility for men of letters to play a political part; the need in the interests of their own fame for them to play the game of a class which is daily becoming more anxious; the increasing tendency of the "clerks" to become bourgeois and to take on the vanities of that class; the perfecting of their Romanticism; the decline of their knowledge of antiquity and of their intellectual discipline. It will be seen that these causes arise from certain phenomena which are most profoundly and generally characteristic of the present age. The political realism of the "clerks," far from being a superficial fact due to the

caprice of an order of men, seems to me bound up with the very essence of the modern world.

The Treason of the Intellectuals [*La trahison des clercs*] (1927) 1969:176–177.

Ruth Benedict 1887–1948
U.S. anthropologist

1 Normality. . . within a very wide range, is culturally defined. It is primarily a term for the socially elaborated segment of human behavior in any culture; and abnormality, a term for the segment that that particular civilization does not use. The very eyes with which we see the problem are conditioned by the long traditional habits of our own society.

Anthropology and the Abnormal (1934) 1959:276.

2 The life-history of the individual is first and foremost an accommodation to the patterns and standards traditionally handed down in his community. From the moment of his birth the customs into which he is born shape his experience and behaviour. By the time he can talk, he is the little creature of his culture, and by the time he is grown and able to take part in its activities, its habits are his habits, its beliefs his beliefs, its impossibilities his impossibilities.

Patterns of Culture (1934) 1959:2–3.

3 Custom did not challenge the attention of social theorists because it was the very stuff of their own thinking: it was the lens without which they could not see at all.

Patterns of Culture (1934) 1959:9.

4 Every human society everywhere has made [a] selection in its cultural institutions. Each from the point of view of another ignores fundamentals and exploits irrelevancies. One culture hardly recognizes monetary values; another has made them fundamental in every field of behaviour. In one society technology is unbelievably slighted even in those aspects of life which seem necessary to ensure survival; in another, equally simple, technological achievements are complex and fitted with admirable nicety to the situation. One builds an enormous cultural superstructure upon adolescence, one upon death, one upon after-life.

Patterns of Culture (1934) 1959:24.

5 Even given the freest scope by their institutions, men are never inventive enough to make more than minute changes. From the point of view of an outsider the most radical innovations in any culture amount to no more than a minor revision, and it is a commonplace that prophets have been put to death for the difference between Tweedledum and Tweedledee.

Patterns of Culture (1934) 1959:84.

6 [Boas] found anthropology a collection of wild guesses and a happy hunting ground for the romantic lover of primitive things; he left it a discipline in which theories could be tested and in which he had delimited possibilities from impossibilities.

Obituary: Franz Boas 1943:61.

7 The lenses through which any nation looks at life are not the ones another nation uses. It is hard to be conscious of the eyes through which one looks. Any country takes them for granted, and the tricks of focusing and of perspective which give to any people its national view of life seem to that people the god-given arrangement of the landscape. In any matter of spectacles, we do not expect the man who wears them to know the formula for the lenses, and neither can we expect nations to analyze their own outlook upon the world.

The Chrysanthemum and the Sword 1946:14. → This pioneering study of Japanese national character, written during World War II, is based on research reports and on interviews with Japanese-Americans in the United States.

Walter Benjamin 1892–1940
German literary and social critic

1 The products of art and science owe their existence not merely to the effort of the great geniuses that created them, but also to the unnamed drudgery of their contemporaries. There is no document of culture which is not at the same time a document of barbarism.

Eduard Fuchs (1937) 1978:233.

Jeremy Bentham 1748–1832
British political philosopher

1 It is the greatest happiness of the greatest number that is the measure of right and wrong.

A Fragment on Government (1776) 1948:3.

2 Nature has placed mankind under the governance of two sovereign masters, *pain* and *pleasure*. It is for them alone to point out what we ought to do, as well as to determine what we shall do. On the one hand the standard of right and wrong, on the other the chain of causes and effects, are fastened to their throne. They govern us in all we do, in all we say, in all we think: every effort we can make to throw off our subjection, will serve but to demonstrate and confirm it. In words a man may pretend to abjure their empire: but in reality he will remain subject to it all the while. The *principle of utility* recognises this subjection, and assumes it for the foundation of that system, the object of which is to rear the fabric of felicity by the hands of reason and of law. Systems which attempt to question it, deal in sounds instead of sense, in caprice instead of reason, in darkness instead of light.

An Introduction to the Principles of Morals and Legislation (1789) 1948:1–2.

3 By utility is meant that property in any object, whereby it tends to produce benefit, advantage, pleasure, good, or happiness, (all this in the present case comes to the same thing) or (what comes again to the same thing) to prevent the happening of mischief, pain, evil, or unhappiness to the party whose interest is considered.

An Introduction to the Principles of Morals and Legislation (1789) 1948:2.

4 *Intense, long, certain, speedy, fruitful, pure* —
Such marks in *pleasures* and in *pains* endure.
Such pleasures seek if *private* be thy end:
If it be *public*, wide let them *extend*.
Such *pains* avoid, whichever be thy view:
If pains *must* come, let them *extend* to few.

An Introduction to the Principles of Morals and Legislation (1789) 1948:29. → Bentham added these verses to a revised edition to fix in the reader's mind those points "on which the whole fabric of morals and legislation may be seen to rest."

5 To take an exact account. . . of the general tendency of any act, by which the interests of a community are affected, proceed as follows. Begin with any one person of those whose interests seem most immediately to be affected by it: and take an account,

1. Of the value of each distinguishable *pleasure* which appears to be produced by it in the *first* instance.

2. Of the value of each *pain* which appears to be produced by it in the *first* instance.

3. Of the value of each pleasure which appears to be produced by it *after* the first. This constitutes the *fecundity* of the first *pleasure* and the *impurity* of the first *pain*.

4. Of the value of each *pain* which appears to be produced by it after the first. This constitutes the *fecundity* of the first *pain*, and the impurity of the first pleasure.

5. Sum up all the values of all the *pleasures* on the one side, and those of all the pains on the other. . .

6. Take an account of the *number* of persons whose interests appear to be concerned; and repeat the above process with respect to each. *Sum up* the numbers expressive of the degrees of *good* tendency, which the act has, with respect to each individual, in regard to whom the tendency of it is *good* upon the whole: do this again with respect to each individual, in regard to whom the tendency of it is *bad* upon the whole. Take the *balance*; which, if on the side of *pleasure*, will give the general *good tendency* of the act, with respect to the total number or community of individuals concerned; if on the side of pain, the general *evil tendency*, with respect to the same community.

An Introduction to the Principles of Morals and Legislation (1789) 1948:30–31.

6 The great object, the great *desideratum*, is to know what ought and what ought not to be done by government. It is in this view, and in this view only, that the knowledge of what is done and takes place without the interference of government can be of any practical use.

Manual of Political Economy (1793–1795) 1952:224.

7 All value is founded on utility, on the use which can be made of the object. Where there is no use, there cannot be any value.

The True Alarm (1801) 1954:83.

8 Property is nothing but a basis of expectation; the expectation of deriving certain advantages from a thing which we are said to possess, in consequence of the relation in which we stand towards it.

There is no image, no painting, no visible trait, which can express the relation that constitutes property. It is not material, it is metaphysical; it is a mere conception of the mind.

The Theory of Legislation (1802) 1931:111–112.

9 *Natural rights* is simple nonsense: natural and imprescriptible rights, rhetorical nonsense, — nonsense upon stilts.

Anarchical Fallacies (1816) 1987:53. → Written in 1796; published in French in 1816; and first published in English in 1843 in Bentham's *Collected Works*.

10 As it is with *money*, so is it with all other sources or causes of pleasure: *factitious dignity* for example. Give a man a ribbon, you will produce in his mind a certain quantity of pleasure. To this ribbon add another, you may add more or less to the former quantity of his pleasure. You may *add* to it: but you will not *double* it.

The Psychology of Economic Man (1822) 1954:442. → Bentham's formulation of a principle of diminishing marginal utility.

11 The utility of all these arts and sciences, — I speak both of those of amusement and curiosity, — the value which they possess, is exactly in proportion to the pleasure they yield. Every other species of pre-eminence which may be attempted to be established among them is altogether fanciful. Prejudice apart, the game of push-pin is of equal value with the arts and sciences of music and poetry. If the game of push-pin furnish more pleasure, it is more valuable than either. Everybody can play at push-pin: poetry and music are relished only by a few.

The Rationale of Reward (1825) 1843:253. → The *Oxford English Dictionary* describes pushpin as "a child's game, in which each player pushes or flips his pin with the object of crossing that of another player."

12 To language, then — to language alone — it is, that fictitious entities owe their existence; their impossible, yet indispensable, existence.

The Theory of Fictions 1932:15. → *The Theory of Fictions* was compiled by C. K. Ogden in 1932 from a number of Bentham's writings. The date of this quotation is not identified.

Arthur F. Bentley 1870–1957

U.S. political scientist

1 Society itself is rather a nexus of actions; and it is a nexus so complex that were the investigator himself of other nature than human, its interpretation would be utterly impossible.

The Units of Investigation in the Social Sciences 1895:89.

2 If we are going to infer a soul quality from the social fact and then use the quality to explain the fact, we put ourselves on a level with animists in the most savage tribes. A branch falls. It was the life in it or behind it that threw it down. Thunder peals. It is a spirit speaking. The grain grows. It is the spirit of the corn pushing it up. This man

is a slave. It is because such is his nature. The pigeons are left unharmed. It is because we are growing more humane. We pass child-labor laws. It is because we will not tolerate abuses our fathers tolerated. That man is a boss at the head of a corrupt machine. It is because he is dishonest by nature. This man wrote a great book. It is because he had a giant intellect.

The Process of Government 1908:19.

3 Government is the process of the adjustment of a set of interest groups in a particular distinguishable group or system.

The Process of Government 1908:260.

Bernard Berelson 1912–1979
U.S. behavioral scientist

1 The political process which finds its climax in the [U.S. presidential election] campaign is a system by which disagreements are reduced, simplified, and generalized into one big residual difference of opinion. It is a system for *organizing* disagreements.

Voting 1954:183. → Written with Paul F. Lazarsfeld and William N. McPhee.

2 Happily for the [U.S. presidential electoral] system, voters distribute themselves along a continuum:

Sociable Man	Political Man	Ideological Man
(Indifferent to public affairs, nonpartisan, flexible. . .)		(Absorbed in public affairs, highly partisan, rigid. . .)

And it turns out that this distribution itself, with its internal checks and balances, can perform the functions and incorporate the same values ascribed by some theorists to each individual in the system as well as to the constitutive political institutions!

Voting 1954:323.

3 The behavioral sciences are here to stay. They have already made important contributions to our understanding of man and they will make many more. They are an indispensable approach to that understanding. They have already affected man's image of himself and permanently so. They are one of the major intellectual and cultural inventions of the twentieth century.

Introduction to the Behavioral Sciences 1963:11.

Peter L. Berger 1929–
Austrian-born U.S. sociologist

1 Alienation is the process whereby the dialectical relationship between the individual and his world is lost to consciousness. The individual "forgets" that this world was and continues to be co-produced by him. Alienated consciousness is undialectical consciousness. The essential difference between the socio-cultural world and the world of nature is obscured — namely, the difference that men have made the first, but not the second.

The Sacred Canopy (1967) 1969:85.

Peter L. Berger 1929–
Austrian-born U.S. sociologist
and
Hansfried Kellner 1927–
German sociologist

1 Sociology gives one a constant awareness of the force of consequences, including the force of (probable) unintended consequences. The moral absolutist, by contrast, dismisses or at least de-emphasizes consequences. . . With impressive regularity, moral absolutists produce consequences that are diametrically opposed to their own intentions. . . The pacifist produces war, the rebel tyranny, the puritan license.

Sociology Reinterpreted 1981:75.

2 Paradoxically, science itself has produced institutions, systems of thought and eventually social-political programs that bind people even more than the "superstitions" they replaced.

Sociology Reinterpreted 1981:102.

Peter L. Berger 1929–
Austrian-born U.S. sociologist
and
Thomas Luckmann 1927–
Yugoslavian-born U.S. sociologist

1 The sociology of knowledge understands human reality as socially constructed reality.

The Social Construction of Reality 1966:172.

2 Our conception of the sociology of knowledge implies a specific conception of sociology in general. It does *not* imply that sociology is not a science, that its methods should be other than empirical, or that it cannot be "value-free." It *does* imply that sociology takes its place in the company of the sciences that deal with man *as* man; that it is, in that specific sense, a humanistic discipline. An important consequence of this conception is that sociology must be carried on in a continuous conversation with both history and philosophy or lose its proper object of inquiry. This object is society as part of a human world, made by men, inhabited by men, and, in turn, making men, in an ongoing historical process. It is not the least fruit of a humanistic sociology that it reawakens our wonder at this astonishing phenomenon.

The Social Construction of Reality 1966:173.

Henri Bergson 1859–1941
French philosopher

1 It is of man's essence to create materially and morally, to fabricate things and to fabricate himself. *Homo faber* is the definition I propose. . . *Homo faber, Homo sapiens,* I pay my respects to both, for they tend to merge.

The Creative Mind 1946:84–85.

Adolf A. Berle 1895–1971
U.S. lawyer and diplomat
and
Gardiner C. Means 1896–1988
U.S. economist

1 A society in which production is governed by blind economic forces is being replaced by one in which production is carried on under the ultimate control of a handful of individuals. The economic power in the hands of the few persons who control a giant corporation is a tremendous force which can harm or benefit a multitude of individuals, affect whole districts, shift the currents of trade, bring ruin to one community and prosperity to another. The organizations which they control have passed far beyond the realm of private enterprise — they have become more nearly social institutions.

The Modern Corporation and Private Property (1932) 1968:46. → This book virtually created the field of research into the corporation as a social institution.

2 It is conceivable, — indeed it seems almost essential if the corporate system is to survive, — that the "control" of the great corporations should develop into a purely neutral technocracy, balancing a variety of claims by various groups in the community and assigning to each a portion of the income stream on the basis of public policy rather than private cupidity.

The Modern Corporation and Private Property (1932) 1968:312–313.

Isaiah Berlin 1909–
Latvian-born British philosopher

1 [Marxism] set out to refute the proposition that ideas decisively determine the course of history, but the very extent of its own influence on human affairs has weakened the force of its thesis. For in altering the hitherto prevailing view of the relation of the individual to his environment and to his fellows, it has palpably altered that relation itself; and in consequence remains the most powerful among the intellectual forces which are to-day permanently transforming the ways in which men think and act.

Karl Marx (1939) 1973:284.

2 Injustice, poverty, slavery, ignorance — these may be cured by reform or revolution. But men do not live only by fighting evils. They live by positive goals, individual and collective, a vast variety of them, seldom predictable, at times incompatible.

Political Ideas in the Twentieth Century (1950) 1969:40.

3 History is not identical with imaginative literature, but it is certainly no more free from what, in a natural science, would be rightly condemned as unwarrantably subjective or personal. Except on the assumption that history must deal with human beings purely as material objects in space — must, in short, be behaviourist — its method can scarcely be assimilated to the standards of an exact natural science. The invocation to historians to suppress even that minimal degree of moral or psychological evaluation which is necessarily involved in viewing human beings as creatures with purposes and motives (and not merely as causal factors in the procession of events), seems to me to rest upon a confusion of the aims and methods of the humane studies with those of natural science. It is one of the greatest and most destructive fallacies of the last hundred years.

Historical Inevitability 1954:52–53.

4 When everything has been said in favour of attributing responsibility for character and action to natural and institutional causes; when everything possible has been done to correct blind or over-simple interpretations of conduct which fix too much blame on individuals and their free acts; when in fact there is strong evidence to show that it was difficult or impossible for men to do otherwise than they did, given their material environment or education or the influence upon them of various "social pressures"; when every relevant psychological and sociological consideration has been taken into account, every impersonal factor given due weight; after "hegemonist," nationalist, and other historical heresies have been exposed and refuted; after every effort has been made to induce history to aspire, so far as it can without open absurdity, after the pure condition of a science; after all these severities, we continue to praise and to blame. We blame others as we blame ourselves; and the more we know, the more, it may be, we are disposed to blame.

Historical Inevitability 1954:58.

5 Two powerful doctrines are at large in contemporary thought, relativism and determinism. The first of these, for all that it is represented as being an antidote to overweening self-confidence, or arrogant dogmatism, or moral self-satisfaction, is nevertheless founded on a conspicuously fallacious interpretation of experience; the second, for all that its chains are decked with flowers, and despite its parade of noble stoicism and the splendour and vastness of its cosmic design, nevertheless represents the universe as a prison. Relativism opposes to individual protest and belief in moral principles the resignation or the irony of those who have seen many worlds crumble, many ideals turned tawdry or ridiculous by time. Determinism claims to bring us to our senses by showing where the true, the impersonal and unalterable machinery of life and thought is to be found.

Historical Inevitability 1954:68.

6 A great man need not be morally good, or upright, or kind, or sensitive, or delightful, or possess artistic or scientific talent. To call someone a great man is to claim that he has intentionally taken (or perhaps could have taken) a large step, one far beyond the normal capacities of men, in satisfying, or materially affecting, central human interests.

Chaim Weizmann (1958) 1981:32.

7 It is only a very vulgar historical materialism that denies the power of ideas, and says that ideals are mere material interests in disguise. It may be that, without the pressure of social forces, political ideas are stillborn: what is certain is that these forces, unless they clothe themselves in ideas, remain blind and undirected.

Two Concepts of Liberty (1958) 1969:119–120.

8 One belief, more than any other, is responsible for the slaughter of individuals on the altars of the great historical ideals — justice or progress or the happiness of future generations, or the sacred mission or emancipation of a nation or race or class, or even liberty itself, which demands the sacrifice of individuals for the freedom of society. This is the belief that somewhere, in the past or in the future, in divine revelation or in the mind of an individual thinker, in the pronouncements of history or science, or in the simple heart of an uncorrupted good man, there is a final solution.

Two Concepts of Liberty (1958) 1969:167.

9 Scepticism, driven to extremes, defeats itself by becoming self-refuting.

Introduction to *Four Essays on Liberty* 1969:liii.

Claude Bernard 1813–1878
French physiologist

1 In every enterprise. . . the mind is always reasoning, and, even when we seem to act without a motive, an instinctive logic still directs the mind. Only we are not aware of it, because we begin by reasoning before we know or say that we are reasoning, just as we begin by speaking before we observe that we are speaking, and just as we begin by seeing and hearing before we know what we see or what we hear.

An Introduction to the Study of Experimental Medicine (1865) 1957:158–159.

Bernard of Chartres d. 1126
French philosopher

1 Bernard of Chartres used to compare us to [puny] dwarfs perched on the shoulders of giants. He pointed out that we see more and farther than our predecessors, not because we have keener vision or greater height, but because we are lifted up and borne aloft on their gigantic stature.

Quoted in John of Salisbury, *The Metalogicon* (1169) 1955:167. → The original formulation of the shoulders-of-giants aphorism, as recorded by a disciple of Bernard's. See NEWTON:1.

Daniel Bernoulli 1700–1782
Dutch-born Swiss mathematician

1 The determination of the *value* of an item must not be based on its *price*, but rather on the *utility* it yields. The price of the item is dependent only on the thing itself and is equal for everyone; the utility, however, is dependent on the particular circumstances of the person making the estimate. Thus there is no doubt that a gain of one thousand ducats is more significant to a pauper than to a rich man though both gain the same amount.

Exposition of a New Theory on the Measurement of Risk (1738) 1954:24.

Jakob Bernoulli 1654–1705
Swiss mathematician

1 We define the art of conjecture, or stochastic art, as the art of evaluating as exactly as possible the probabilities of things, so that in our judgments and actions we can always base ourselves on what has been found to be the best, the most appropriate, the most certain, the best advised; this is the only object of the wisdom of the philosopher and the prudence of the statesman.

Ars conjectandi 1713.

Basil Bernstein 1924–
British sociologist and linguist

1 A number of fashions of speaking, frames of consistency, are possible in any given language and. . . these fashions of speaking, linguistic forms, or codes, are themselves a function of the form social relations take. According to this view, the form of the social relation or, more generally, the social structure generates distinct linguistic forms or codes and *these codes essentially transmit the culture and so constrain behaviour.*

A Socio-linguistic Approach to Social Learning (1965) 1974:122.

2 As the child learns his speech. . . he learns the requirements of his social structure. The experience of the child is transformed by the learning generated by his own, apparently, voluntary acts of speech. . . Every time the child speaks or listens, the social structure is reinforced in him and his social identity shaped. The social structure becomes the child's psychological reality through the shaping of his acts of speech.

A Socio-linguistic Approach to Socialization (1971) 1974:144.

Eduard Bernstein 1850–1932
German socialist

1 There can be more socialism in a good factory law than in the nationalisation of a whole group of factories. I admit it openly: I have for what is commonly called "the final goal of socialism" extraordinarily little feeling and interest. This goal, whatever it may be, is nothing to me, the movement is everything.

Die Zusammenbruchstheorie und die Kolonialpolitik 1898:555.

2 The theory which the *Communist Manifesto* sets forth of the evolution of modern society was correct as far as it characterised the general tendencies of that evolution. But it was mistaken in. . . the estimate of the *time* the evolution would take. . . It is evident that if social evolution takes a much greater period of time than was as-

sumed, it must also take upon itself *forms* and lead to forms that were not foreseen and could not be foreseen then.

Preface to English Edition of *Evolutionary Socialism* (1899) 1961:xxiv.

3 If the activity and the prospects of social democracy were dependent on the decrease of the "wealthy," then it might indeed lie down to sleep. But the contrary is the case. The prospects of socialism depend not on the decrease but on the increase of social wealth.

Evolutionary Socialism (1899) 1961:48.

Ludwig von Bertalanffy 1901–1972
Austrian-born U.S. biologist and philosopher of science

1 The fundamental problem today is that of organized complexity. Concepts like those of organization, wholeness, directiveness, teleology, and differentiation are alien to conventional physics. However, they pop up everywhere in the biological, behavioral and social sciences, and are, in fact, indispensable for dealing with living organisms or social groups. Thus a basic problem posed to modern science is a general theory of organization. General system theory is, in principle, capable of giving exact definitions for such concepts and, in suitable cases, of putting them to quantitative analysis.

General System Theory 1968:34.

Henry Digby Beste 1768–1836
British travel writer and social critic

1 The Duke of Gloucester [William Henry], brother of King George III, permitted Mr. Gibbon to present to him the first volume of The History of the Decline and Fall of the Roman Empire. When the second volume of that work appeared, it was quite in order that it should be presented to His Royal Highness in like manner. The prince received the author with much good nature and affability, saying to him, as he laid the quarto on the table, "Another d — mn'd thick, square book! Always scribble, scribble, scribble! Eh! Mr. Gibbon?"

Late Duke of Gloucester and Gibbon 1829:68. → For Gibbon's reaction to the publication of his *Decline and Fall*, see GIBBON:10.

Bruno Bettelheim 1903–1990
Austrian-born U.S. psychologist

1 *Changes in the prisoners which would make them more useful subjects* of the Nazi state. . . were produced by exposing the prisoners to extreme situations particularly created for this purpose. These circumstances forced the prisoners to adapt themselves entirely and with the greatest speed. This adaptation produced interesting types of private, individual, and mass behavior.

Individual and Mass Behavior in Extreme Situations (1943) 1979:50. → This is a report based upon the author's incarceration in Dachau and Buchenwald concentration camps in 1938–1939.

William Henry Beveridge 1879–1963
British economist

1 I profess to learn and to teach economics, politics, sociology, not from books but from observations, not from the positions of philosophers but from the conduct of mankind.

Epigraph to Lancelot Hogben (editor), *Political Arithmetic* 1938. → Beveridge is paraphrasing William Harvey's famous remark about anatomy. See HARVEY:1.

2 What is meant by "full employment," and what is not meant by it? Full employment does not mean literally no unemployment; that is to say, it does not mean that every man and woman in the country who is fit and free for work is employed productively on every day of his or her working life. In every country with a variable climate there will be seasons when particular forms of work are impossible or difficult. In every progressive society there will be changes in the demand for labour, qualitatively if not quantitatively; that is to say, there will be periods during which particular individuals can no longer be advantageously employed in their former occupations and may be unemployed till they find and fit themselves for fresh occupations. Some frictional unemployment there will be in a progressive society however high the demand for labour. Full employment means that unemployment is reduced to short intervals of standing by, with the certainty that very soon one will be wanted in one's old job again or will be wanted in a new job that is within one's powers.

Full Employment in a Free Society (1944) 1945:18. → Known as "The Beveridge Report." See BRONTË:1.

W.I.B. Beveridge 1908–
Australian-born British biologist

1 No one believes an hypothesis except its originator but everyone believes an experiment except the experimenter. Most people are ready to believe something based on experiment but the experimenter knows the many little things that could have gone wrong in the experiment. For this reason the discoverer of a new fact seldom feels quite so confident of it as others do. On the other hand other people are usually critical of an hypothesis, whereas the originator identifies himself with it and is liable to become devoted to it.

The Art of Scientific Investigation (1950) 1961:65.

Alexander M. Bickel 1924–1974
Romanian-born U.S. legal theorist

1 No society, certainly not a large and heterogeneous one, can fail in time to explode if it is deprived of the arts of compromise, if it knows no ways of muddling through. No good society can be unprincipled; and no viable society can be principle-ridden.

The Least Dangerous Branch 1962:64. → See LINDBLOM:1.

Alfred Binet 1857–1911
French psychologist

1 Heredity, to our understanding, is not capable of giving to this illness (paraphilia) its characteristic form. . . Heredity invents nothing, creates nothing anew; it has no imagination.

Études de psychologie expérimentale: Le fétichisme dans l'amour 1888:42.

2 My friend, we are going to do an experiment together, to see if you have a good memory, a better memory than that of your friends; I am going to show you a poster.

La suggestibilité 1900:248. → Unpublished translation by Jacqueline L. Cunningham. This excerpt from a research protocol illustrates how Binet treated even child research subjects as collaborators.

3 Almost all the phenomena that occupy psychology are phenomena of intelligence. . . There is in intelligence, it seems to us, a fundamental agent the lack or alteration of which has the greatest import for practical life, and that is judgment. . . To judge well, to understand well, to reason well, these are the essential springs of intelligence.

Méthodes nouvelles pour le diagnostic du niveau intellectuel des anormaux 1905:196–197. → Written with Théodore Simon.

4 At one moment [intelligence] apprehends an object, and it is a perception or an idea; at another time it perceives a connection, and it is a judgment; at yet another, it perceives connections between connections, and it is an act of reason.

The Mind and the Brain (1905) 1907:117.

5 Comprehension, inventiveness, direction, and criticism: intelligence is contained in these four words.

Les idées modernes sur les enfants 1909:118.

Alfred Binet 1857–1911
and
Théodore Simon 1873–1961
French psychologists

1 We have studied these questions with real children *(d'après nature)*, normal and abnormal. . . These examinations have permitted us to organize a *method of differential diagnosis*. . . This method is composed of three parts: psychological, pedagogical, medical. We enumerate them here in order of their decreasing importance [for] it is psychology, we insist, that ought before all to furnish the characteristic and differential signs of the idiot, the imbecile, and the moron.

Méthodes nouvelles pour diagnostiquer l'idiotie, l'imbécillité et la débilité mentale 1906:507–508.

2 Masters of science are, like princes, surrounded by clever courtesans who shade the truth to their need, attributing to the "master" the merit of a discovery, ending up by convincing him of it.

Hystérie: Historique 1910:70. → Unpublished translation by Theta H. Wolf.

Otto von Bismarck 1815–1898
German statesman

1 *Die Politik ist die Lehre vom Möglichen* [Politics is the art of the possible].

Gespräch mit dem Journalisten Friedrich Meyer von Waldeck am 11 August 1867 in Berlin. 1924:222.

William Blackstone 1723–1780
British jurist

1 In all tyrannical governments the supreme magistracy, or the right both of *making* and of *enforcing* the laws, is vested in one and the same man, or one and the same body of men; and wherever these two powers are united together there can be no public liberty.

Commentaries on the Laws of England (1765–1769) 1858:Vol. 1, 146.

2 However the crown may be limited or transferred, it still retains its descendible quality, and becomes hereditary in the wearer of it. And hence, in our law, the king is said never to die, in his political capacity, though, in common with other men, he is subject to mortality in his natural, because immediately upon the natural death of Henry, William, or Edward, the king survives in his successor.

Commentaries on the Laws of England (1765–1769) 1858:Vol. 1, 195.

3 That the king can do no wrong, is a necessary and fundamental principle of the English Constitution: meaning only, as has formerly been observed, that, in the first place, whatever may be amiss in the conduct of public affairs is not chargeable personally on the king; nor is he, but his ministers, accountable for it to the people; and, secondly, that the prerogative of the crown extends not to do any injury; for, being created for the benefit of the people, it can not be exerted to their prejudice. . . The distance between the sovereign and his subjects is such that it rarely can happen that any *personal* injury can immediately and directly proceed from the prince to any private man; and, as it can so seldom happen, the law in decency supposes that it never will or can happen at all.

Commentaries on the Laws of England (1765–1769) 1858:Vol. 3, 254–255.

4 All presumptive evidence of felony should be admitted cautiously; for the law holds that it is better that ten guilty persons escape than that one innocent suffer.

Commentaries on the Laws of England (1765–1769) 1858:Vol. 4, 358.

Peter M. Blau 1918–
Austrian-born U.S. sociologist

1 The conception of social interaction as an exchange process follows logically from the assumption that men seek to obtain rewards in their social associations. . . The individual who fails to discharge his obligations and recipro-

cate in some form for benefits received robs others of incentives to continue to befriend him. Besides, such an individual is likely to be accused of ingratitude. This very accusation indicates that reciprocation for favors freely given is expected and it serves as a social sanction to discourage men from forgetting their obligations.

Social Exchange 1968:452–453.

2 To speak of social structure is to speak of differentiation among people, since social structure is defined by the distinctions people make, explicitly or implicitly, in their role relations. An undifferentiated social structure is a contradiction in terms.

Parameters of Social Structure 1974:616.

3 A Gothic structure can support a larger and more complex edifice than a Norman one. The integration of large societies depends on the weak social ties of individuals which extend beyond particular ingroups and thereby integrate the various groups into a coherent social structure.

Inequality and Heterogeneity 1977:85. → See GRANOVETTER:1.

Marc Bloch 1886–1944
French historian

1 The clearest legacy of feudalism to modern societies is the emphasis placed upon the notion of the political contract. The reciprocity of obligations which united lord and vassal and caused with every grave dereliction by the superior the release of the inferior in the eyes of the law was transferred in the thirteenth century to the state. Practically everywhere, but with peculiar clearness in England and Aragon, the idea was expressed that the subject is bound to the king only so long as the latter remains a loyal protector. This sentiment counterbalanced the tradition of royal sanctity and finally triumphed over it.

European Feudalism 1931:210.

2 I have many times read, and I have often narrated, accounts of wars and battles. Did I truly know, in the full sense of that word, did I know from within, before I myself had suffered the terrible, sickening reality, what it meant for an army to be encircled, what it meant for a people to meet defeat? Before I myself had breathed the joy of victory in the summer and autumn of 1918 (and, although, alas! its perfume will not again be quite the same, I yearn to fill my lungs with it a second time) did I truly know all that was inherent in that beautiful word? In the last analysis, whether consciously or no, it is always by borrowing from our daily experiences and by shading them, where necessary, with new tints that we derive the elements which help us to restore the past.

The Historian's Craft (1949) 1953:44.

3 How much easier it is to write for or against Luther than to fathom his soul; to believe Pope Gregory VII about Emperor Henry IV, or Henry IV about Gregory VII, than to unravel the underlying causes of one of the greatest dramas of Western civilization.

The Historian's Craft (1949) 1953:141.

4 The reactionaries of 1815 hid their faces in horror at the very name of revolution. Those of 1940 used it to camouflage their *coup d'état*.

The Historian's Craft (1949) 1953:172. → Bloch was a leader of the French Resistance; he was killed by the Gestapo in June 1944.

5 Scarcity of watering-places would bring about the clustering of rural population, and abundance of water would disperse it, only if it were true that people made proximity to springs, wells, and ponds their supreme consideration. In reality they sometimes prefer, for the sake of security or co-operation, or even through mere gregariousness, to live in close groups even where every field has its spring; or inversely, as in certain regions of Sardinia, where everyone builds his dwelling in the middle of his little estate, they resign themselves to long walks for the scarce water as the price of isolation on which they have set their hearts. Is not man himself the greatest variable in nature?

The Historian's Craft (1949) 1953:196–197.

Leonard Bloomfield 1887–1949
U.S. linguist

1 All speaking, good or bad, is careless; only for a few minutes at a time can one speak "carefully," and when one does so, the result is by no means pleasing. In fatiguing effect and in ungracefulness, "careful" speaking is like walking a chalk-line or a tight-rope.

Literate and Illiterate Speech 1927:432.

2 Writing, like telegraphy or shorthand, is an activity that deals with language, but it is quite different, far less practised and ingrained, far more superficial in our make-up, than speech. Until quite recently only very few people knew how to read and write; even today many peoples do not write their language. Writing is based on speech, not speech on writing.

Literate and Illiterate Speech 1927:433.

3 The logical demand that a science speak in quantitative terms is met by linguistics because it speaks in terms of phonemes; for the phonemes of a language we could substitute an equal number of units of any kind.

On Recent Work in General Linguistics 1927:217.

4 If it were possible to transfer the methods of physical or of biological science directly to the study of man, the transfer would long ago have been made. . . We have failed not for lack of hypotheses which equate man with the rest of the universe, but for lack of a hypothesis (short of animism) which provides for the peculiar divergence of man. . . Let me now state my belief that the peculiar factor in man which forbids our explaining his actions upon the ordinary plane of biology is a highly specialized

and unstable biological complex, and that this factor is none other than language.

Linguistics as a Science 1930:555.

5 We have defined the *meaning* of a linguistic form as the situation in which the speaker utters it and the response which it calls forth in the hearer.

Language 1933:139. → See GEORGE HERBERT MEAD:4.

6 The categories of a language, especially those which affect morphology (*book:book*; *he:she*), are so pervasive that anyone who reflects upon his language at all, is sure to notice them. In the ordinary case, this person, knowing only his native language, or perhaps some others closely akin to it, may mistake his categories for universal forms of speech, or of "human thought," or of the universe itself. This is why a good deal of what passes for "logic" or "metaphysics" is merely an incompetent restating of the chief categories of the philosopher's language. A task for linguists of the future will be to compare the categories of different languages and see what features are universal or at least widespread.

Language 1933:270.

7 The picturesque saying that "language is a book of faded metaphors" is the reverse of the truth, for poetry is rather a blazoned book of language.

Language 1933:443.

Herbert Blumer 1900–1987
U.S. sociologist

1 Symbolic interactionism rests. . . on three simple premises. The first premise is that human beings act toward things on the basis of the meanings that the things have for them. . . The second premise is that the meaning of such things is derived from, or arises out of, the social interaction that one has with one's fellows. The third premise is that these meanings are handled in, and modified through, an interpretative process used by the person in dealing with the things he encounters.

Symbolic Interactionism 1969:2.

2 The human individual confronts a world that he must interpret in order to act instead of an environment to which he responds because of his organization. He has to cope with the situations in which he is called on to act, ascertaining the meaning of the actions of others and mapping out his own line of action in the light of such interpretation. He has to construct and guide his action instead of merely releasing it in response to factors playing on him or operating through him.

Symbolic Interactionism 1969:15.

Franz Boas 1858–1942
German-born U.S. anthropologist

1 The object of study is the individual, not abstractions from the individual under observation. . . By regarding a single implement outside of its surroundings, outside of other inventions of the people to whom it belongs, and outside of other phenomena affecting that people and its productions, we cannot understand its meaning.

The Principles of Ethnological Classification (1887) 1982:62. → From Boas's debate with Otis T. Mason over the principles of museum classification.

2 The data of ethnology prove that not only our knowledge, but also our emotions are the result of the form of our social life and of the history of the people to whom we belong. If we desire to understand the development of human culture we must try to free ourselves of these shackles. This is possible only to those who are willing to adapt themselves to the strange ways of thinking and feeling of primitive people.

The Aims of Ethnology (1889) 1982:636.

3 In Eskimo,. . . we find one word [for snow], *aput*, expressing SNOW ON THE GROUND; another one, *qana*, FALLING SNOW; a third one, *piqsirpoq*, DRIFTING SNOW; and a fourth one, *qimuqsuq*, A SNOWDRIFT. . .

It seems fairly evident that the selection of such simple terms must to a certain extent depend upon the chief interests of a people; and where it is necessary to distinguish a certain phenomenon in many aspects, which in the life of the people each play an entirely independent rôle, many independent words may develop, while in other cases modifications of a single term may suffice.

Thus it happens that each language, from the point of view of another language, may be arbitrary in its classifications; that what appears as a single simple idea in one language may be characterized by a series of distinct phonetic groups in another.

Introduction to Handbook of American Indian Languages (1911) 1966:21–22.

4 The occurrence of the most fundamental grammatical concepts in all languages must be considered as proof of the unity of fundamental psychological processes.

Introduction to Handbook of American Indian Languages (1911) 1966:67.

5 If we knew the whole biological, geographical, and cultural setting of a society completely, and if we understood in detail the ways of reacting of the members of the society and of society as a whole to these conditions, we should not need historical knowledge of the origin of the society to understand its behavior.

Some Problems of Methodology in the Social Sciences (1930) 1940:269.

6 There is no fundamental difference in the ways of thinking of primitive and civilized man. A close connection between race and personality has never been established.

The Mind of Primitive Man (1911) 1963:17. → From the preface to the 1938 edition.

Jean Bodin 1529 or 1530–1596
French political economist

1 Commonweale is a lawfull government of many families, and of that which unto them in common belongeth, with

a puissant soveraigntie. This definition omitted by them which have written of a Commonweale, wee have placed in the first place: for that in all arts and actions, it behoveth us first to behold the end, and afterward the meanes to attaine therunto.

The Six Bookes of a Commonweale (1576) 1962:1.

2 Majestie or Soveraigntie is the most high, absolute, and perpetuall power over the citizens and subjects in a Commonweale.

The Six Bookes of a Commonweale (1576) 1962:84.

Eugen von Böhm-Bawerk 1851–1914
Austrian economist

1 A greater result is obtained by producing goods in roundabout ways than by producing them directly. Where a good can be produced in either way, we have the fact that, by the indirect way, a greater product can be got with equal labour, or the same product with less labour. But, beyond this, the superiority of the indirect way manifests itself in being the only way in which certain goods can be obtained. . . That roundabout methods lead to greater results than direct methods is one of the most important and fundamental propositions in the whole theory of production.

The Positive Theory of Capital (1888) 1923:19–20. → The theory of "roundabout" or time-consuming production asserts that the longer the process of production, from the first use of land and labor until the completion of consumer goods, the larger and better is the final product. See Emil Kauder, "Böhm-Bawerk, Eugen von" (1968).

2 Present goods are, as a rule, worth more than future goods of like kind and number. This proposition is the kernel and centre of the interest theory which I have to present.

The Positive Theory of Capital (1888) 1923:237.

3 What will be the final judgment of the world? Of that I have no manner of doubt. The Marxian system has a past and a present, but no abiding future.

Karl Marx (1896) 1984:117.

4 In the domain of natural science such a work as Marx's would even now be impossible. In the very young social sciences it was able to attain influence, great influence, and it will probably only lose it very slowly, and that because it has its most powerful support not in the convinced intellect of its disciples, but in their hearts, their wishes, and their desires.

Unresolved Contradiction in the Marxian Economic System (1896) 1962:300.

Lord Bolingbroke 1678–1751
[Henry St. John]
British statesman

1 A king of Great Britain is that supreme magistrate who has a negative voice in the legislature. He is entrusted with the executive power, and several other powers and privileges, which we call prerogatives, are annexed to this trust. The two houses of parliament have their rights and privileges; some of which are common to both, others particular to each. They prepare, they pass bills, or they refuse to pass such as are sent to them. They address, represent, advise, remonstrate. . .

If the legislative as well as the executive power was wholly in the king, as in some countries, he would be absolute; if in the lords, our government would be an aristocracy; if in the commons, a democracy. It is this division of power, these distinct privileges attributed to the king, to the lords, and to the commons, which constitute a limited monarchy.

Remarks on the History of England (1730) 1841:332.

2 First, a king is really nothing more than a supreme magistrate, instituted for the service of the community, which requires that the executive power should be vested in a single person. He hath, indeed, a crown on his head, a sceptre in his hand, and velvet robes on his back, and he sits elevated in a throne, whilst others stand on the ground about him; and all this to denote that he is a king, and to draw the attention and reverence of the vulgar. . . The king, when he commands, discharges a trust, and performs a duty, as well as the subject, when he obeys. Notwithstanding which, kings are apt to see themselves in another light, and experience shews us, that even they who made them what they are, are apt to take them for what they are not. . . In the second place, besides this constant desire of incroaching, there is another reason why concessions to the crown are more to be guarded against than others, in limited monarchies. The regal power resides in one person. . . A king cannot be tempted to give up the interest of the crown, because he cannot give up this public interest, without giving up his private interest; whereas the members of such assemblies may promote their private interest, by sacrificing to it that of the public.

A Dissertation upon Parties (1734) 1777:188–189.

Napoleon Bonaparte
See Napoleon I.

Charles Booth 1840–1916
British businessman and social scientist

1 East London lay hidden from view behind a curtain on which were painted terrible pictures: — Starving children, suffering women, overworked men; horrors of drunkenness and vice; monsters and demons of inhumanity; giants of disease and despair. Did these pictures truly represent what lay behind, or did they bear to the facts a relation similar to that which the pictures outside a booth at some country fair bear to the performance or the show within? This curtain we have tried to lift.

Life and Labour of the People in London (1889) 1904:172.

2 Seen from without, the same habits of life, amount of income, method of expenditure, difficulties, occupations, amusements, will strike the mind of the on-looker with

an entirely different meaning according as they are viewed as part of a progress towards a better and higher life, or of a descent towards a more miserable and debased existence. Felt from within, a position will be acceptable and even happy on the upward road, which on the downward path may be hardly endurable.

Life and Labour of the People in London (1889) 1904:172–173.

3 Facts are still needed. But the spirit of patient inquiry is abroad; my attempt is only one of its children.

Life and Labour of the People in London 1903:214.

4 As to methods of inquiry, I think I should say that the statistical method was needed to give bearings to the results of personal observation and personal observation to give life to statistics. . . It is this relative character, or the proportion of facts to each other, to us, to others, to society at large, and to possible remedies, that must be introduced if they are to be of any value at all in social diagnosis. Both single facts, and strings of statistics *may* be true, and demonstrably true, and yet entirely misleading in the way they are used.

Unpublished letter to Beatrice [Potter] Webb. Quoted in T. S. Simey and M. B. Simey, *Charles Booth: Social Scientist* 1960:78. → The date of this letter is not given by the Simeys.

Giuseppe Antonio Borgese 1882–1952
Italian-born U.S. literary scholar

1 Not a single prophet, during more than a century of prophecies. . . ever imagined anything like fascism. There was, in the lap of the future, communism and syndicalism and what not; there was anarchism, and legitimism, and even all-papacy; war, peace, deluge, pan-Germanism, pan-Slavism, Yellow Peril, signals to the planet Mars; there was no fascism. It came as a surprise to all, and to themselves too.

The Intellectual Origins of Fascism 1934:475–476.

Edwin G. Boring 1886–1968
U.S. psychologist

1 A knowledge of the "probability that a difference is not due to chance" is distinctly worth while on the descriptive side; but this measure of significance does not necessarily apply to the general class for which a sample stands. In certain cases it may so apply, but ordinarily there is a constant factor operative in the selection of human material which must be taken into account and which frequently offsets a demonstrably "significant" difference that has been made out between the samples. It is for this reason that mathematical measures of difference are apt to be too high and may need to be discounted in arriving at a scientific conclusion. The case is one of many where statistical ability, divorced from a scientific intimacy with the fundamental observations, leads nowhere.

Mathematical vs. Scientific Significance 1919:337–338.

2 There is no alchemy of probabilities that will change ignorance into knowledge. Expectations must be founded upon cogent rather than insufficient reasons.

The Logic of the Normal Law of Error in Mental Measurement 1920:3.

3 Scientific truth, like juristic truth, must come about by controversy. Personally this view is abhorrent to me. It seems to mean that scientific truth must transcend the individual, that the best hope of science lies in its greatest minds being often brilliantly and determinedly wrong, but in opposition, with some third, eclectically minded, middle-of-the-road nonentity seizing the prize while the great fight for it, running off with it, and sticking it into a textbook for sophomores written from no point of view and in defense of nothing whatsoever. I hate this view, for it is not dramatic and it is not fair; and yet I believe that it is the verdict of the history of science.

The Psychology of Controversy 1929:99.

4 Today we hear less about theories and more about models. What is the difference? The theory claims to be true, even though we all know that assurance about the validity of these claims varies greatly from theory to theory and from time to time for the same theory. The theory is an *as*, whereas the model is an *as-if*. The theory is indicative; the model, subjunctive. The model is a pattern to be abandoned easily at the demand of progress.

When Is Human Behavior Predetermined? 1957:191.

Raymond Boudon 1934–
French sociologist

1 There is no reason whatsoever why [the aggregation of action model] should not play an important role in sociology. . . After all it is crucial in the work of one of the greatest pioneers of sociology, Jean-Jacques Rousseau. The basic idea of the *Social Contract* derives from the fact that when everybody acts freely without consulting each other the result can be disastrous for all, even if one introduces the assumption that men are basically friendly to one another. In other words, as shown by W.G. Runciman and A.K. Sen, the crucial intuition upon which the *Social Contract* rests is nothing other than what was later called the "Prisoner's Dilemma."

The Three Basic Paradigms of Macrosociology (1975) 1980:59–60 → See RAPOPORT:1.

2 Economists are familiar with perverse effects. In a period of inflation it is in my interest to buy a product that will only be of use to me in the coming month, for I am almost certain that its price will then be higher. In doing this I help to perpetuate inflation. My behaviour has only an infinitesimal influence in this respect, but the logic of the situation dictates that many people should behave just as I do. Together these infinitesimal individual influences generate a social effect.

Effects of this kind, often termed perverse effects or effects of composition, do not only appear in the sphere of economic life. There is no reason, after all, why they should be limited to this sphere. In fact it would not be at all excessive to assert that they are present everywhere in social life and that they represent one of the fundamental causes of social imbalances and of social change.

The Unintended Consequences of Social Action (1977) 1982:1.

Kenneth E. Boulding 1910–
British-born U.S. economist

1 The proposition that the meek (that is, the adaptable and serviceable) inherit the earth is not merely a wishful sentiment of religion, but an iron law of evolution.

The Organizational Revolution 1953:252. → See DOBZHANSKY:2.

2 There is a famous character in one of Oscar Wilde's plays who knew the price of everything and the value of nothing. An economist wonders uneasily if the reference is not to him.

Some Contributions of Economics to the General Theory of Value 1956:1.

3 Equality is a luxury of rich societies. If poor societies are to maintain any kind of peak achievement or civilization, they simply cannot afford it. Without sharp inequalities, we would not have had the Parthenon or the cathedrals or the great cultural achievements of any of the past civilizations.

Social Justice in Social Dynamics 1962:92.

4 It has always amused me that what the economist calls an equilibrium of behavior, psychologists tend to call frustration.

The Welfare Economics of Grants (1973) 1981:122.

5 The law. . . is only necessary at the edges of society where custom crumbles, and where the taboos that enable us to live together begin to break down. Thus, one sees the law not so much as the walls of the human household as the weatherstripping and the roof repair.

Reflections on Law and Justice 1978:12.

Pierre Bourdieu 1930–
French sociologist

1 The inheritance of cultural wealth which has been accumulated and bequeathed by previous generations only really belongs (although it is *theoretically* offered to everyone) to those endowed with the means of appropriating it for themselves. In view of the fact that the apprehension and possession of cultural goods as symbolic goods. . . are possible only for those who hold the code making it possible to decipher them. . . it is sufficient to give free play to the laws of cultural transmission for cultural capital to be added to cultural capital and for the structure of the distribution of cultural capital between social classes to be thereby reproduced.

Cultural Reproduction and Social Reproduction (1973) 1977:488.

2 Taste classifies, and it classifies the classifier.

Distinction (1979) 1984:6.

3 A [social] class is defined as much by its *being-perceived* as by its *being*, by its consumption — which need not be conspicuous in order to be symbolic — as much as by its position in the relations of production.

Distinction (1979) 1984:483.

4 Scientific discourse demands a scientific reading, capable of reproducing the operations of which it is itself the product.

Homo academicus (1984) 1988:21.

Pierre Bourdieu 1930–
and
Jean-Claude Passeron 1930–
French sociologists

1 One of the least noticed effects of compulsory schooling is that it succeeds in obtaining from the dominated classes a recognition of legitimate knowledge and know-how (e.g. in law, medicine, technology. . .), entailing the devaluation of the knowledge and know-how they effectively command (e.g. customary law, home medicine, craft techniques. . .) and so providing a market for material and especially symbolic products of which the means of production (not least, higher education) are virtually monopolized by the dominant classes.

Reproduction in Education, Society and Culture (1970) 1977:42.

George E. P. Box 1919–
British-born U.S. statistician

1 To find out what happens to a system when you interfere with it you have to interfere with it (not just passively observe it).

Use and Abuse of Regression 1966:629.

Louis Dembitz Brandeis 1856–1941
U.S. jurist

1 The constitutional right of free speech has been declared to be the same in peace and in war. In peace, too, men may differ widely as to what loyalty to our country demands; and an intolerant majority, swayed by passion or by fear, may be prone in the future, as it has often been in the past, to stamp as disloyal opinions with which it disagrees.

Schaefer v. *United States*, 251 U.S. 495, 1920.

2 The doctrine of the separation of powers was adopted by the Convention of 1787, not to promote efficiency but to preclude the exercise of arbitrary power. The purpose was, not to avoid friction, but, by means of the inevitable friction incident to the distribution of the governmental powers among three departments, to save the people from autocracy.

Myers v. *United States*, 272 U.S. 293, 1926.

3 Those who won our independence believed. . . that fear breeds repression; that repression breeds hate; that hate menaces stable government; that the path of safety lies in the opportunity to discuss freely supposed grievances and proposed remedies; and that the fitting remedy for evil counsels is good ones.

Whitney v. *California*, 274 U.S. 375, 1927.

4 Fear of serious injury cannot alone justify suppression of free speech and assembly. Men feared witches and burnt women. It is the function of speech to free men from the bondage of irrational fears.

Whitney v. *California*, 274 U.S. 376, 1927.

5 The makers of our Constitution undertook to secure conditions favorable to the pursuit of happiness. They recognized the significance of man's spiritual nature, of his feelings and of his intellect. They knew that only a part of the pain, pleasure and satisfactions of life are to be found in material things. They sought to protect Americans in their beliefs, their thoughts, their emotions and their sensations. They conferred, as against the Government, the right to be let alone — the most comprehensive of rights and the right most valued by civilized man.

Olmstead et al. v. *United States*, 277 U.S. 478, 1928. → In his dissenting opinion in *Olmstead*, Brandeis held that wiretapping is an unconstitutional search or seizure. Holmes, on the other hand, dissented on the lesser-of-two-evils theory. Both were vindicated in 1967 when the Supreme Court overruled Olmstead. See HOLMES:17.

6 If the Government becomes a law-breaker, it breeds contempt for law; it invites every man to become a law unto himself; it invites anarchy. To declare that in the administration of the criminal law the end justifies the means — to declare that the Government may commit crimes in order to secure the conviction of a private criminal — would bring terrible retribution.

Olmstead et al. v. *United States*, 277 U.S. 485, 1928.

7 This Court has the power to prevent an experiment. We may strike down the statute which embodies it on the ground that, in our opinion, the measure is arbitrary, capricious or unreasonable. We have power to do this, because the due process clause has been held by the Court applicable to matters of substantive law as well as to matters of procedure. But in the exercise of this high power, we must be ever on our guard, lest we erect our prejudices into legal principles.

New State Ice Co. v. *Leibmann*, 285 U.S. 311, 1932.

8 Able, discerning scholars have pictured for us the economic and social results of. . . removing all limitations upon the size and activities of business corporations and of vesting in their managers vast powers once exercised by stockholders — results not designed by the States and long unsuspected. They show that size alone gives to giant corporations a social significance not attached ordinarily to smaller units of private enterprise. Through size, corporations, once merely an efficient tool employed by individuals in the conduct of private business, have become an institution — an institution which has brought such concentration of economic power that so-called private corporations are sometimes able to dominate the State. . . Such is the Frankenstein monster which States have created by their corporation laws.

Louis K. Liggett Co. et al. v. *Lee, Comptroller, et al.* 288 U.S. 564–565, 567, 1933.

Fernand Braudel 1902–1985
French historian

1 When discussing the rise and fall of empires, it is as well to mark closely their rate of growth, avoiding the temptation to telescope time and discover too early signs of greatness in a state which we know will one day be great, or to predict too early the collapse of an empire which we know will one day cease to be. The life-span of empires cannot be plotted by events, only by careful diagnosis and auscultation — and as in medicine there is always room for error.

The Mediterranean (1949) 1973:Vol. 2, 661.

2 The fundamental reality of any civilization must be its geographical cradle. Geography dictates its vegetational growth and lays down often impassable frontiers. Civilizations are regions, zones not merely as anthropologists understand them when they talk about the zone of the two-headed axe or the feathered arrow; they are areas which both confine man and undergo constant change through his efforts.

The Mediterranean (1949) 1973:Vol. 2, 773.

3 We shall not allow ourselves to repeat the often-voiced opinion that "civilizations are mortal." Mortal perhaps are their ephemeral blooms, the intricate and short-lived creations of an age, their economic triumphs and their social trials, in the short term. But their foundations remain. They are not indestructible, but they are many times more solid than one might imagine.

The Mediterranean (1949) 1973:Vol. 2, 775.

4 If the history of human aggression in the Mediterranean in the sixteenth century is neither fictitious nor illusory, war in its metamorphoses, revivals, Protean disguises and degenerate forms, reasserts its perennial nature: its red lines did not all break at once. *Bellum omnium pater,* the old adage was familiar to the men of the sixteenth century. War, the begetter of all things, the creature of all things, the river with a thousand sources, the sea without a shore: begetter of all things except peace, so ardently longed for, so rarely attained.

The Mediterranean (1949) 1973:Vol. 2, 891.

5 Events are the ephemera of history; they pass across its stage like fireflies, hardly glimpsed before they settle back into darkness and as often as not into oblivion. Every event, however brief, has to be sure a contribution to make, lights up some dark corner or even some wide vista of history. Nor is it only political history which benefits most, for every historical landscape — political, eco-

nomic, social, even geographical — is illumined by the intermittent flare of the event. The preceding chapters have drawn heavily on this concrete evidence, without which we should often find it hard to see anything at all. I am by no means the sworn enemy of the event.

The Mediterranean (1949) 1973:Vol. 2, 901.

6 When I think of the individual, I am always inclined to see him imprisoned within a destiny in which he himself has little hand, fixed in a landscape in which the infinite perspectives of the long term stretch into the distance both behind him and before. In historical analysis as I see it, rightly or wrongly, the long run always wins in the end. Annihilating innumerable events — all those which cannot be accommodated in the main ongoing current and which are therefore ruthlessly swept to one side — it indubitably limits both the freedom of the individual and even the role of chance.

The Mediterranean (1949) 1973:Vol. 2, 1244.

7 Social science virtually abhors the event. Not without reason: the short-term is the most capricious and deceptive form of time.

History and the Social Sciences (1958) 1972:15.

8 The world economy is an expression applied to the whole world. It corresponds, as Sismondi puts it, to "the market of the universe," to "the human race, or that part of the human race which is engaged in trade, and which today in a sense makes up a single market."

A world-economy. . . only concerns a fragment of the world, an economically autonomous section of the planet able to provide for most of its own needs, a section to which its internal links and exchanges give a certain organic unity.

The Perspective of the World (1979) 1984:21–22.

9 The chief privilege of capitalism, today as in the past, remains the ability to *choose*. . . And since it does have the freedom to choose, capitalism can always change horses in mid-stream — the secret of its vitality.

The Perspective of the World (1979) 1984:622.

Franz Brentano 1838–1917
German philosopher

1 Just as the natural sciences study the properties and laws of physical bodies, which are the objects of our external perception, psychology is the science which studies the properties and laws of the soul, which we discover within ourselves directly by means of inner perception, and which we infer, by analogy, to exist in others.

Psychology from an Empirical Standpoint (1874) 1973:5.

Josef Breuer 1842–1925
Austrian physician and physiologist
and
Sigmund Freud 1856–1939
Austrian psychoanalyst

1 Each individual hysterical symptom immediately and permanently disappeared when we had succeeded in bringing clearly to light the memory of the event by which it was provoked and in arousing its accompanying affect, and when the patient had described that event in the greatest possible detail and had put the affect into words. . . Hysterics suffer mainly from reminiscences.

Studies on Hysteria (1893–1895) 1955:6–7.

[*See also* SIGMUND FREUD.]

C. Crane Brinton 1898–1968
U.S. historian

1 Who now reads Spencer? It is difficult for us to realize how great a stir he made in the world. The *Synthetic Philosophy* penetrated to many a bookshelf which held nothing else quite so heavy. It lay beside the works of Buckle and Mill on the shelf of every Englishman of a radical turn of mind. It was read, discussed, fought over. And now it is a drug on the second-hand market, and hardly stirs the interest of the German or American aspirant to the doctorate in philosophy. We are more indifferent to this modern *summa* than to the *summa* of Thomas Aquinas. The completeness of Spencer's downfall is almost sufficient to disarm the critic, and it certainly should predispose him to mercy. But Spencer himself was never merciful, not merciful intellectually at least. He seems never to have harboured any kind of doubt. In a century surely not predisposed to scepticism, few thinkers surpass him in cock-sureness and intolerance. He was the intimate confidant of a strange and rather unsatisfactory God, whom he called the principle of Evolution. His God has betrayed him. We have evolved beyond Spencer.

English Political Thought (1933) 1962:226–227. → Much of this passage is quoted by Talcott Parsons at the beginning of *The Structure of Social Action* (1937).

Charlotte Brontë 1816–1855
British novelist

1 Misery generates hate: these sufferers hated the machines which they believed took their bread from them: they hated the buildings which contained those machines; they hated the manufacturers who owned those buildings.

Shirley (1849) 1965:22. → "Misery generates hate" is the epigram on the title page of the so-called Beveridge Report, *Full Employment in a Free Society* (1944). See WILLIAM HENRY BEVERIDGE:2.

C. Harold Brown

See CHARLES TILLY AND C. HAROLD BROWN.

Roger Brown 1925–
and
David McNeill 1933–
U.S. psychologists

1 The "tip of the tongue" (TOT) phenomenon is a state in which one cannot quite recall a familiar word but can recall words of similar form and meaning. . . The class of cases defined by the conjunction of knowledge and a fail-

ure of recall is a large one. The (TOT) state, which James described, seems to be a small subclass in which recall is felt to be imminent.

The "Tip of the Tongue" Phenomenon 1966:325. → See JAMES:12.

Jerome S. Bruner 1915–
U.S. psychologist

1 It is curiously difficult to recapture preconceptual innocence. Having learned a new language, it is almost impossible to recall the undifferentiated flow of voiced sounds that one heard before one learned to sort the flow into words and phrases. Having mastered the distinction between odd and even numbers, it is a feat to remember what it was like in a mental world where there was no such distinction. In short, the attainment of a concept has about it something of a quantal character. It is as if the mastery of a conceptual distinction were able to mask the preconceptual memory of the things now distinguished.

A Study of Thinking 1956:50. → Written with Jacqueline J. Goodnow and George A. Austin.

2 The shrewd guess, the fertile hypothesis, the courageous leap to a tentative conclusion — these are the most valuable coin of the thinker at work, whatever his line of work.

The Process of Education 1960:14.

3 We begin with the hypothesis that any subject can be taught effectively in some intellectually honest form to any child at any stage of development. It is a bold hypothesis and an essential one in thinking about the nature of a curriculum. No evidence exists to contradict it; considerable evidence is being amassed that supports it.

The Process of Education 1960:33.

4 There is, perhaps, one universal truth about all forms of human cognition: the ability to deal with knowledge is hugely exceeded by the potential knowledge contained in man's environment. To cope with this diversity, man's perception, his memory, and his thought processes early become governed by strategies for protecting his limited capacities from the confusion of overloading. We tend to perceive things schematically, for example, rather than in detail, or we represent a class of diverse things by some sort of averaged "typical instance."

Art as a Mode of Knowing 1962:65.

5 A culture of poverty gets to the young early — in how they learn to set goals, mobilize means, delay or fail to delay gratification. Very early too they learn in-group talk and thinking, and just as their language use reflects less long-range goal analysis, it tends toward a parochialism that makes it increasingly difficult to move or work outside the poverty neighborhood and the group. Make no mistake about it: it is a rich culture, intensely personalized and full of immediate rather than remote concerns. The issue is certainly not cultural deprivation, to be handled, like avitaminosis, with a massive dose of compensatory enrichment.

The Relevance of Education (1970) 1971:160. → See LEWIS:1.

James Bryce 1838–1922
British statesman and historian

1 We have seen that the American Constitution has changed, is changing, and by the law of its existence must continue to change, in its substance and practical working even when its words remain the same.

The American Commonwealth (1888) 1910:Vol. 1, 401.

2 It may seem a paradox to observe that a millionaire has a better and easier social career open to him in England than in America. . . In America, if his private character be bad, if he be mean, or openly immoral, or personally vulgar, or dishonest, the best society may keep its doors closed against him. In England great wealth, skilfully employed, will more readily force these doors to open. . . The existence of a system of artificial rank enables a stamp to be given to base metal in Europe which cannot be given in a thoroughly republican country.

The American Commonwealth (1888) 1910:Vol. 2, 815.

3 Is there. . . no other way in which the people can express their mind and exert their power? Can any means be found of supplying that which elections fail to give? Is the judgment delivered by polling [voting], *i.e.* the counting of heads, the same thing as public opinion? Polling is the only explicit and palpable mode yet devised of expressing the people's will. But does a judgment so delivered necessarily convey the opinion of the thoughtful element among those who vote, and may not that opinion be able to exert a moral authority at times when no legal opportunity is provided for the delivery of a judgment at the polls?

Modern Democracies 1921:Vol. 1, 153.

Zbigniew K. Brzezinski

See CARL T. FRIEDRICH AND ZBIGNIEW K. BRZEZINSKI.

Martin Buber 1878–1965
German-born Israeli philosopher and theologian

1 We may speak of social phenomena wherever the life of a number of men, lived with one another, bound up together, brings in its train shared experiences and reactions. But to be thus bound up together means only that each individual existence is enclosed and contained in a group existence. It does not mean that between one member and another of the group there exists any kind of personal relation. They do feel that they belong together in a way that is, so to speak, fundamentally different from every possible belonging together with someone outside the group. And there do arise, especially in the life of smaller groups, contacts which frequently favour the birth of individual relations, but, on the other hand, frequently make it more difficult. In no case, however, does membership in a group necessarily involve an existential relation between one member and another.

Elements of the Interhuman (1957) 1965:72–73.

James M. Buchanan 1919–
U.S. economist

Why does Camelot lie in ruins? Intellectual error of monumental proportion has been made, and not exclusively by the politicians. Error also lies squarely with the economists. The "academic scribbler" who must bear substantial responsibility is Lord Keynes, whose thinking was uncritically accepted by establishment economists in both America and Britain. The mounting historical evidence of the ill-effects of Keynes's ideas cannot continue to be ignored. Keynesian economics has turned the politicians loose; it has destroyed the effective constraint on politicians' ordinary appetites to spend and spend without the apparent necessity to tax.

The Consequences of Mr Keynes 1978:27. → Written with Richard E. Wagner and John Burton. See KEYNES:24.

Public choice theory has been the avenue through which a romantic and illusory set of notions about the workings of governments and the behavior of persons who govern has been replaced by a set of notions that embody more skepticism about what governments can do and what governors will do, notions that are surely more consistent with the political reality that we may all observe about us.

Politics without Romance (1979) 1984:11.

Opportunity cost is the anticipated value of "that which might be" if choice were made differently. Note that it is not the value of "that which might have been" without the qualifying reference to choice. In the absence of choice, it may be sometimes meaningful to discuss values of events that might have occurred but did not. It is not meaningful to define these values as opportunity costs, since the alternative scenario does not represent a lost or sacrificed opportunity.

Opportunity Cost 1987:719.

Henry Thomas Buckle 1821–1862
British historian

Suicide is merely the product of the general condition of society, and. . . the individual felon only carries into effect what is a necessary consequence of preceding circumstances. In a given state of society, a certain number of persons must put an end to their own life. This is the general law; and the special question as to who shall commit the crime depends of course upon special laws; which, however, in their total action, must obey the large social law to which they are all subordinate. And the power of the larger law is so irresistible, that neither the love of life nor the fear of another world can avail any thing towards even checking its operation.

History of Civilization in England (1857) 1913:Vol. 1, 20.

Georges-Louis Leclerc, comte de Buffon 1707–1788
French naturalist

[Buffon had sent a definition of moral certainty to Daniel Bernoulli, whom he describes as "one of the greatest mathematicians of our century, and the one most knowledgable about the science of probability." Buffon argued that a chance of 0.9999 could be regarded as a moral certainty, it being the probability that a man of 56 will live through a day. What follows is Bernoulli's response of 19 March 1762 and Buffon's comment on it.]

"I strongly approve, Sir, of your method of estimating the limits of moral probabilities; you seek the nature of man from his actions, and you suppose it true that no one worries in the morning that he will die that very day. There being, according to you, one chance in ten thousand that he will die, you conclude that one ten-thousandth of probability makes no impression on the spirit of man, and in consequence that this one ten-thousandth can be regarded as absolutely nothing. This is without doubt to reason as a mathematical philosopher, but this ingenious principle seems to me to lead to a smaller quantity, because the exemption from fear does not extend to those who are already ill. I do not dispute your principle, but it appears to lead to $\frac{1}{100{,}000}$ rather than $\frac{1}{10{,}000}$."

I grant to M. Bernoulli that since the one ten-thousandth was taken from the tables of mortality which represent only the mortality of the *average man*, that is to say, of men in general, in good health or ill, sound or infirm, vigorous or weak, it would be perhaps a little more than ten thousand to one that a man who is healthy, sound, and vigorous will not die in the next twenty-four hours, but it would be wrong to increase this probability to a hundred thousand. Nevertheless, this difference, even if quite large, would not change the main consequences that I drew from my principle.

Essai d'arithmétique morale 1777:57n. → Unpublished translation by Stephen M. Stigler. Buffon's use of *average man* was possibly the inspiration of Quetelet's subsequent usage. See QUETELET:3.

Ralph J. Bunche 1904–1971
U.S. political scientist and diplomat

1 It is to maintain forced inferior status for the Negro that the South, and to only a lesser extent the North, keep the races separate by both legal and extra-legal devices. This separation is not based on any essential repulsion as a result of the physical types of the two races. The Negro is permitted plenty of opportunity for close proximity to the white, if only he carries the identifying badge of inferior status. . . Race, when translated realistically for the American Negro, means that there must never be equality between white and black.

A World View of Race (1936) 1968:88–89.

Jacob Burckhardt 1818–1897
Swiss historian

1 [In the Italian city states] for the first time we detect the modern political spirit of Europe, surrendered freely to its own instincts, often displaying the worst features of an unbridled egoism, outraging every right, and killing every germ of a healthier culture. But wherever this vicious tendency is overcome or in any way compensated a new fact appears in history — the State as the outcome of

reflection and calculation, the State as a work of art.

The Civilization of the Renaissance in Italy (1860) 1958:Vol. 1, 22.

2 In the Middle Ages both sides of human consciousness — that which was turned within as that which was turned without — lay dreaming or half awake beneath a common veil. The veil was woven of faith, illusion, and childish prepossession, through which the world and history were seen clad in strange hues. Man was conscious of himself only as member of a race, people, party, family, or corporation — only through some general category. In Italy this veil first melted into air; an *objective* treatment and consideration of the State and of all the things of this world became possible. The *subjective* side at the same time asserted itself with corresponding emphasis; man became a spiritual *individual,* and recognized himself as such.

The Civilization of the Renaissance in Italy (1860) 1958:Vol. 1, 143.

3 We must leave those who find pleasure in passing sweeping censures on whole nations to do so as they like. The peoples of Europe can maltreat, but happily not judge, one another. A great nation, interwoven by its civilization, its achievements, and its fortunes with the whole life of the modern world, can afford to ignore both its advocates and its accusers. It lives on with or without the approval of theorists.

The Civilization of the Renaissance in Italy (1860) 1975:Vol. 2, 426.

4 We shall study the *recurrent, constant,* and *typical* as echoing in us and intelligible through us.

Reflections on History (1905) 1979:34.

5 History. . . is the breach with nature caused by the awakening of consciousness.

Reflections on History (1905) 1979:56.

6 The arrogant belief in the moral superiority of the present. . . has only fully developed of late years; it makes no exceptions, even in favor of classical antiquity. The secret mental reservation is that money-making is today easier and safer than ever. Were that menaced, the exaltation it engenders would collapse.

Reflections on History (1905) 1979:104.

7 History is the record of what one age finds worthy of note in another.

Quoted in H. R. Trevor-Roper, Introduction to Jacob Burckhardt, *Judgments on History and Historians* 1958:xi.

Ernest W. Burgess

See Robert E. Park and Ernest W. Burgess.

Edmund Burke 1729–1797

Irish-born British political writer and statesman

1 When bad men combine, the good must associate; else they will fall, one by one, an unpitied sacrifice in a contemptible struggle.

Thoughts on the Cause of the Present Discontents (1770) 1865:526.

2 Here this extraordinary man [Charles Townsend], then Chancellor of the Exchequer, found himself in great straits. To please universally was the object of his life; but to tax and to please, no more than to love and to be wise, is not given to men. However, he attempted it.

Speech on American Taxation, 19 April 1774. 1904:67.

3 Your representative owes you, not his industry only, but his judgment; and he betrays, instead of serving you, if he sacrifices it to your opinion.

Speech to the Electors of Bristol, 3 November 1774. 1904:95.

4 All government, indeed every human benefit and enjoyment, every virtue and every prudent act, is founded on compromise and barter. We balance inconveniences; we give and take; we remit some rights, that we may enjoy others; and we choose rather to be happy citizens than subtle disputants.

Speech on Moving His Resolutions for Conciliation with the Colonies, 22 March 1775. 1904:169.

5 Bad laws are the worst sort of tyranny.

Speech at the Guildhall in Bristol (1780) 1904:395.

6 A state without the means of some change is without the means of its conservation.

Reflections on the Revolution in France (1790) 1865:259.

7 People will not look forward to posterity, who never look backward to their ancestors.

Reflections on the Revolution in France (1790) 1865:274.

8 To be attached to the subdivision, to love the little platoon we belong to in society, is the first principle (the germ, as it were) of public affections. It is the first link in the series by which we proceed towards a love to our country and to mankind.

Reflections on the Revolution in France (1790) 1865:292.

9 It is said that twenty-four millions ought to prevail over two hundred thousand. True; if the constitution of a kingdom be a problem of arithmetic.

Reflections on the Revolution in France (1790) 1865:299.

10 I thought ten thousand swords must have leaped from their scabbards to avenge even a look that threatened [the queen] with insult. But the age of chivalry is gone. That of sophisters, economists, and calculators has succeeded; and the glory of Europe is extinguished forever.

Reflections on the Revolution in France (1790) 1865:331.

11 Prejudice is of ready application in the emergency; it previously engages the mind in a steady course of wisdom and virtue, and does not leave the man hesitating in the moment of decision, skeptical, puzzled, and unresolved.

Prejudice renders a man's virtue his habit, and not a series of unconnected acts. Through just prejudice, his duty becomes a part of his nature.

Reflections on the Revolution in France (1790) 1865:347.

12 Society is, indeed, a contract. . . But the state ought not to be considered as nothing better than a partnership agreement in a trade of pepper and coffee, calico or tobacco, or some other such low concern, to be taken up for a little temporary interest, and to be dissolved by the fancy of the parties. . . It is a partnership in all science, a partnership in all art, a partnership in every virtue and in all perfection.

Reflections on the Revolution in France (1790) 1865:359.

13 It cannot at this time be too often repeated, line upon line, precept upon precept, until it comes into the currency of a proverb, — *To innovate is not to reform*. The French revolutionists complained of everything; they refused to reform anything; and they left nothing, no, nothing at all, *unchanged*. The consequences are *before* us, — not in remote history, not in future prognostication: they are about us, they are upon us.

Letter to a Noble Lord (1796) 1904:187.

14 Manners are of more importance than laws. Upon them, in a great measure, the laws depend. The law touches us but here and there, and now and then. Manners are what vex or soothe, corrupt or purify, exalt or debase, barbarize or refine us, by a constant, steady, uniform, insensible operation, like that of the air we breathe in. They give their whole form and color to our lives. According to their quality, they aid morals, they supply them, or they totally destroy them.

Three Letters to a Member of Parliament (1796–1797) 1904:310.

Kenneth Burke 1897–

U.S. philosopher and literary critic

1 One adopts measures in keeping with his past training — and the very soundness of this training may lead him to adopt the wrong measures. People may be unfitted by being fit in an unfit fitness.

Permanence and Change 1935:18.

2 The mere fact that something is to a man's interests is no guaranty that he will be interested in it. It is tremendously to the people's interests that they should understand the causes of war — but it is very hard to get them interested in the subject.

Permanence and Change 1935:55.

3 Any performance is discussible either from the standpoint of what it *attains* or what it *misses*. Comprehensiveness can be discussed as superficiality, intensiveness as stricture, tolerance as uncertainty — and the poor-*pedestrian* abilities of a fish are clearly explainable in terms of his excellence as a *swimmer*. A way of seeing is also a way of not seeing — a focus upon object A involves a neglect of object B.

Permanence and Change 1935:70. → The last sentence has come to be known as "the Burke theorem."

Arthur F. Burns 1904–1987

Austrian-born U.S. economist

1 It is reasonable to expect that contracyclical policy will moderate the amplitude and abbreviate the duration of business contractions in the future, so that our children will be spared the sort of economic collapse that blighted lives in the early thirties. . . But there are no adequate grounds, as yet, for believing that business cycles will soon disappear, or that the government will resist inflation with as much tenacity as depression, or that deep but brief contractions such as occurred in 1920–21 and 1937–38 will never again take place.

Business Cycle Research and the Needs of Our Times 1953:8.

Cyril Burt 1883–1971

British psychologist

1 Tests, infinitely more scientific than those set out below, can still be but the beginning, never the end, of the examination of the child. To take a young mind as it is, and delicately one by one to sound its notes and stops, to detect the smaller discords and appreciate the subtler harmonies, is more of an art than a science. The scientist may standardise the method; to apply that method and to appraise the results, needs the tact, the experience, the imaginative insight of the teacher born and trained.

Mental and Scholastic Tests 1921:xv.

J. B. Bury 1861–1927

British historian

1 [The historian's] view is conditioned by the mentality of his own age; the focus of his vision is determined within narrow limits by the conditions of contemporary civilisation. There can therefore be nothing final about his judgments, and their permanent interest lies in the fact that they are judgments pronounced at a given epoch and are characteristic of the tendencies and ideas of that epoch.

The Ancient Greek Historians (1909) 1958:252.

2 The Progress of humanity belongs to the same order of ideas as Providence or personal immortality. It is true or it is false, and like them it cannot be proved either true or false. Belief in it is an act of faith.

The Idea of Progress (1920) 1955:4.

3 Evolution. . . does not necessarily mean, applied to society, the movement of man to a desirable goal. It is a neutral, scientific conception, compatible either with optimism or with pessimism. According to different estimates it may appear to be a cruel sentence or a guarantee of steady amelioration. And it has been actually interpreted in both ways.

The Idea of Progress (1920) 1955:335–336.

Robert R. Bush

See Frederick Mosteller and Robert R. Bush.

Joseph Butler 1692–1752
British theologian

1 Probable evidence, in its very nature, affords but an imperfect kind of information, and is to be considered as relative only to beings of limited capacities. For nothing which is the possible object of knowledge, whether past, present, or future, can be probable to an infinite Intelligence; . . . to us, probability is the very guide of life.

The Analogy of Religion (1736) 1892:50–51.

Herbert Butterfield 1900–1979
British historian

1 "The whig interpretation of history". . . is the tendency in many historians to write on the side of Protestants and Whigs, to praise revolutions provided they have been successful, to emphasise certain principles of progress in the past and to produce a story which is the ratification if not the glorification of the present.

The Whig Interpretation of History (1931) 1965:v.

2 The study of the past with one eye, so to speak, upon the present is the source of all sins and sophistries in history. . . It is the essence of what we mean by the word "unhistorical."

The Whig Interpretation of History (1931) 1965:31–32.

3 There is something in the nature of historical events which twists the course of history in a direction that no man ever intended.

The Englishman and His History 1944:103.

4 [The scientific revolution] outshines everything since the rise of Christianity and reduces the Renaissance and Reformation to the rank of mere episodes, mere internal displacements, within the system of medieval Christendom.

The Origins of Modern Science 1949:viii.

5 Of all forms of mental activity the most difficult to induce, even in the minds of the young who may be presumed not to have lost their flexibility, is the art of handling the same bundle of data as before, but placing them in a new system of relations with one another by giving them a different framework, all of which virtually means putting on a different kind of thinking-cap for the moment.

The Origins of Modern Science 1949:1.

C

John Elliott Cairnes 1823–1875
Irish economist

What Astronomy does for the phenomena of the heavenly bodies; what Dynamics does for the phenomena of motion; what Chemistry does for the phenomena of chemical combination; what Physiology does for the phenomena of the functions of organic life; that Political Economy does for the phenomena of wealth: it expounds the laws according to which those phenomena co-exist with or succeed each other; that is to say, it expounds the laws of the phenomena of wealth.

The Character and Logical Method of Political Economy (1857) 1875:18.

All industrial progress consists in altering the proportion between these two things; in increasing the remuneration in relation to the cost, or in diminishing the cost in relation to the remuneration. Cost and remuneration are thus economic antitheses of each other; so completely so, that a small cost and a large remuneration are exactly equivalent expressions.

Some Leading Principles of Political Economy Newly Expounded 1874:49.

Donald T. Campbell 1916–
U.S. psychologist

In true experiments the treatment is applied independently of the prior state of the units. In natural experiments exposure to treatment is often a cosymptom of the treated group's condition. The treatment is apt to be an *effect* rather than, or in addition to being, a cause. Psychotherapy is such a cosymptom treatment, as is any other in which the treated group is self-selected or assigned on the basis of need.

Reforms as Experiments 1969:413.

The political stance furthering social experimentation. . . is the recognition of randomization as the most democratic and moral means of allocating scarce resources (and scarce hazardous duties), plus the moral imperative to further utilize the randomization so that society may indeed learn [the] true value of the supposed boon. This is the ideology that makes possible "true experiments" in a large class of social reforms.

Reforms as Experiments 1969:419.

Joseph Campbell 1904–1987
U.S. writer

1 In his life-form the individual is necessarily only a fraction and distortion of the total image of man. He is limited either as male or as female; at any given period of his life he is again limited as child, youth, mature adult, or ancient; furthermore, in his life-role he is necessarily specialized as craftsman, tradesman, servant, or thief, priest, leader, wife, nun, or harlot; he cannot be all. Hence, the totality — the fullness of man — is not in the separate member, but in the body of the society as a whole; the individual can be only an organ.

The Hero with a Thousand Faces 1949:382–383.

Edwin Cannan 1861–1935
British economist

1 The really fundamental questions of economics are why all of us, taken together, are as well off — or as ill off, if that way of putting it be preferred — as we are, and why some of us are much better off and others much worse off than the average.

Wealth (1914) 1928:v.

Richard Cantillon 1680?–1734
Irish economist and merchant

1 By doubling the quantity of money in a State the prices of products and merchandise are not always doubled. A River which runs and winds about in its bed will not flow with double the speed when the amount of its water is doubled.

The proportion of the dearness which the increased quantity of money brings about in the State will depend on the turn which this money will impart to consumption and circulation.

Essai sur la nature du commerce en général (1775) 1931:177, 179.

Karel Čapek 1890–1938
Czech playwright and journalist

1 [*Radius*]: You will work. You will build. . . You will serve them. . . Robots of the world. . . The power of man has fallen. . . A new world has arisen. The rule of the Robots. . . March!

R.U.R. (1923) 1961:89–90. → This play introduced the word "robot" into the world's languages. The word *robota* in Czech means compulsory labor; in the play it refers to a new working class of automatons.

Benjamin Nathan Cardozo 1870–1938
U.S. jurist

1 The legislature, informed only casually and intermittently of the needs and problems of the courts, without expert or responsible or disinterested or systematic advice as to the workings of one rule or another, patches the fabric here and there, and mars often when it would mend. Legislature and courts move on in proud and silent isolation. Some agency must be found to mediate between them.

A Ministry of Justice 1921:113–114.

2 Law never *is*, but is always about to be. It is realized only when embodied in a judgment, and in being realized, expires. There are no such things as rules or principles: there are only isolated dooms.

The Nature of the Judicial Process (1921) 1949:126.

3 Law accepts as the pattern of its justice the morality of the community whose conduct it assumes to regulate.

The Paradoxes of Legal Science 1928:37.

4 Of. . . freedom [of thought and speech] one may say that it is the matrix, the indispensable condition, of nearly every other form of freedom.

Palko v. *Connecticut*, 302 U.S. 327, 1937.

Thomas Carlyle 1795–1881
Scottish historian and social critic

1 A witty statesman said, you might prove anything by figures. We have looked into various statistic works, Statistic-Society Reports, Poor-Law Reports, Reports and Pamphlets not a few, with a sedulous eye to this question of the Working Classes and their general condition in England; we grieve to say, with as good as no result whatever. Assertion swallows assertion; according to the old Proverb, "as the *statist* thinks, the bell clinks"! Tables are like cobwebs, like the sieve of the Danaides; beautifully reticulated, orderly to look upon, but which will hold no conclusion. Tables are abstractions, and the object a most concrete one, so difficult to read the essence of. There are innumerable circumstances; and one circumstance left out may be the vital one on which all turned. Statistics is a science which ought to be honourable, the basis of many most important sciences; but it is not to be carried on by steam, this science, any more than others are; a wise head is requisite for carrying it on. Conclusive facts are inseparable from inconclusive except by a head that already understands and knows.

Chartism (1839) 1904:124.

2 Statistics, one may hope, will improve gradually, and become good for something. Meanwhile, it is to be feared the crabbed satirist was partly right, as things go: "A judicious man," says he, "looks at Statistics, not to get knowledge, but to save himself from having ignorance foisted on him."

Chartism (1839) 1904:125.

3 It is not what a man outwardly has or wants that constitutes the happiness or misery of him. Nakedness, hunger, distress of all kinds, death itself have been cheerfully suffered, when the heart was right. It is the feeling of *injustice* that is insupportable to all men.

Chartism (1839) 1904:144–145.

4 In these complicated times, with Cash Payment as the sole nexus between man and man, the toiling Classes of mankind declare, in their confused but most emphatic way, to the Untoiling, that they will be governed; that they must, — under penalty of Chartisms, Thuggeries, Rick-burnings, and even blacker things than those. . . Cash Payment the sole nexus; and there are so many things which cash will not pay!

Chartism (1839) 1904:168–169.

5 In all epochs of the world's history, we shall find the Great Man to have been the indispensable saviour of his epoch; — the lightning, without which the fuel never would have burnt. The History of the World, I said already, was the Biography of Great Men.

On Heroes, Hero-Worship and the Heroic in History (1841) 1903:13.

6 Burke said there were Three Estates in Parliament; but, in the Reporters' Gallery yonder, there sat a *Fourth Estate* more important far than they all.

On Heroes, Hero-Worship and the Heroic in History (1841) 1903:164.

7 It is not to die, or even to die of hunger, that makes a man wretched; many men have died; all men must die, — the last exit of us all is in a Fire-Chariot of Pain. But it is to live miserable we know not why; to work sore and yet gain nothing; to be heart-worn, weary, yet isolated, unrelated, girt-in with a cold universal Laissez-faire: it is to die slowly all our life long, imprisoned in a deaf, dead, Infinite Injustice, as in the accursed iron belly of a Phalaris' Bull! This is and remains forever intolerable to all men whom God has made.

Past and Present (1843) 1903:210–211.

8 [Economics is] not a "gay science," I should say, like some we have heard of; no, a dreary, desolate, and indeed quite abject and distressing one; what we might call, by way of eminence, the *dismal science*.

The Nigger Question (1849) 1904:354.

Andrew Carnegie 1835–1919
Scottish-born U.S. industrialist and philanthropist

1 While the law [of competition] may be sometimes hard for the individual, it is best for the race, because it insures the survival of the fittest in every department. We accept and welcome, therefore, as conditions to which we must accommodate ourselves, great inequality of environment, the concentration of business, industrial and commercial, in the hands of a few, and the law of competition between these, as being not only beneficial, but essential for the future progress of the race.

Wealth 1899:655. → An example of how readily Herbert Spencer's concept of "the survival of the fittest" was adopted in the United States in the nineteenth century. See DARWIN:4, MAYR:2, and SPENCER:8.

E. H. Carr 1892–1982
British historian

1 It used to be said that facts speak for themselves. This is, of course, untrue. The facts speak only when the historian calls on them: it is he who decides to which facts to give the floor, and in what order or context.

What Is History? 1961:9.

2 In a group or a nation which is riding in the trough, not on the crest, of historical events, theories that stress the role of chance or accident in history will be found to prevail. The view that examination results are all a lottery will always be popular among those who have been placed in the third class.

What Is History? 1961:132.

3 History properly so-called can be written only by those who find and accept a sense of direction in history itself. The belief that we have come from somewhere is closely linked with the belief that we are going somewhere. A society which has lost belief in its capacity to progress in the future will quickly cease to concern itself with its progress in the past.

What Is History? 1961:176.

John B. Carroll 1916–
U.S. psychologist

1 *Psycholinguistics*, as we propose to define the term, is concerned with the processes of encoding and decoding, i.e., the relations which the message bears to intentive behavior, on the one hand, and to interpretive behavior, on the other.

The Interdisciplinary Summer Seminar on Linguistics and Psychology 1951:41. → The term "psycholinguistics" was first used at this 1951 seminar.

Carl Gustav Carus 1789–1869
German physician, psychologist, and philosopher

1 *Der Schlüssel zur Erkenntnis vom Wesen des bewussten Seelenlebens liegt in der Region des Unbewusstseins* [The key to the understanding of the character of the conscious lies in the region of the unconscious].

Psyche 1846:1.

Ernst Cassirer 1874–1945
German philosopher

1 Man has... discovered a new method of adapting himself to his environment. Between the receptor system and the effector system, which are to be found in all animal species, we find in man a third link which we may describe as the *symbolic system*.

An Essay on Man (1944) 1975:24.

James McKeen Cattell 1860–1944
U.S. psychologist and educator

1 It seems to me that most of the research work that has been done by me or in my laboratory is nearly as independent of introspection as work in physics or in zoology. The time of mental processes, the accuracy of perception and movement, the range of consciousness, fatigue and practise, the motor accompaniments of thought, memory, the association of ideas, the perception of space, color-vision, preferences, judgments, individual differences, the behavior of animals and of children, these and other topics I have investigated without requiring the slightest introspection on the part of the subject or undertaking such on my own part during the course of the experiments. It is usually no more necessary for the subject to be a psychologist than it is for the vivisected frog to be a physiologist.

The Conceptions and Methods of Psychology 1904:180.

Raymond B. Cattell 1905–
British-born U.S. psychologist

1 Poetry, religion, drama — the arts of emotionality and of love — come into their own. Indeed adolescence is the time when even the dullest clod knows that he possesses a soul; and it has been said of the genius that he lives in a perpetual adolescence.

An Introduction to Personality Study 1950:215.

Gerald J. Cavanaugh
See PETER GAY AND GERALD J. CAVANAUGH.

René de Chateaubriand 1768–1848
French statesman and writer

1 The past is a fact, a fact that cannot be destroyed; while the future, which is so dear to us, does not exist.

Quoted in Trygve R. Tholfsen, *Historical Thinking* 1967:188.

Colin Cherry 1914–1979
U.S. electrical engineer

1 Communication renders true social life practicable, for communication means organization. Communications have enabled the social unit to grow, from the village to the town, to the modern city-state, until today we see organized systems of mutual dependence grown to cover whole hemispheres. Communication engineers have altered the size and shape of the world.

On Human Communication 1957:4.

2 The human senses (above all, that of hearing) do not possess one set of constant parameters, to be measured independently, one at a time. It is even questionable whether the various "senses" are to be regarded as separate, independent detectors. The human organism is one integrated whole, stimulated into response by physical signals; it is not to be thought of as a box, carrying various independent pairs of terminals labeled "ears," "eyes," "nose," et cetera.

On Human Communication 1957:127–128.

G. K. Chesterton 1874–1936
British author and journalist

1 [*Father Brown*]: Have you ever noticed this — that people never answer what you say? They answer what you mean — or what they think you mean. Suppose one lady says to another in a country house, "Is anybody staying with you?" the lady doesn't answer "Yes; the butler, the three footmen, the parlourmaid, and so on," though the parlourmaid may be in the room, or the butler behind her chair. She says "There is *nobody* staying with us," meaning nobody of the sort you mean. But suppose a doctor inquiring into an epidemic asks, "Who is staying in the house?" then the lady will remember the butler, the parlourmaid, and the rest. All language is used like that; you never get a question answered literally, even when you get it answered truly.

The Invisible Man (1911) 1983:98.

Noam Chomsky 1928–
U.S. linguist

1 The notion "grammatical" cannot be identified with "meaningful" or "significant" in any semantic sense. Sentences (1) and (2) are equally nonsensical, but any speaker of English will recognize that only the former is grammatical.
(1) Colorless green ideas sleep furiously.
(2) Furiously sleep ideas green colorless.

Syntactic Structures (1957) 1964:15.

2 The fact that all normal children acquire essentially comparable grammars of great complexity with remarkable rapidity suggests that human beings are somehow specially designed to do this, with data-handling or "hypothesis-formulating" ability of unknown character and complexity.

A review of B. F. Skinner, *Verbal Behavior* (1959) 1964:577.

3 Linguistic theory is concerned primarily with an ideal speaker-listener, in a completely homogeneous speech-community, who knows its language perfectly and is unaffected by such grammatically irrelevant conditions as memory limitations, distractions, shifts of attention and interest, and errors (random or characteristic) in applying his knowledge of the language in actual performance. This seems to have been the position of the founders of modern general linguistics, and no cogent reason for modifying it has been offered. To study actual linguistic performance, we must consider the interaction of a variety of factors, of which the underlying competence of the speaker-hearer is only one. In this respect, study of language is no different from empirical investigation of other complex phenomena.

Aspects of the Theory of Syntax 1965:3–4.

4 [In sociology] one finds observations, intuitions, impressions, some valid generalizations perhaps. All very valuable, no doubt, but not at the level of explanatory principles. . . Sociolinguistics is. . . a discipline that seeks to apply principles of sociology to the study of language; but I suspect that it can draw little from sociology, and I wonder whether it is likely to contribute much to it. . . You can also collect butterflies and make many observations. If you like butterflies, that's fine; but such work must not be confused with research, which is concerned to discover explanatory principles of some depth and fails if it does not do so.

Language and Responsibility (1977) 1979:56–57.

Winston Churchill 1874–1965
British statesman and historical writer

1 Nothing is more dangerous in wartime than to live in the temperamental atmosphere of a Gallup Poll, always feeling one's pulse and taking one's temperature.

The War Situation, 30 September 1941. 1974:6495.

2 On the night of 10th May, 1941, with one of the last bombs of the last serious raid, our House of Commons was destroyed by the violence of the enemy, and we have now to consider whether we should build it up again, and how, and when. We shape our buildings, and afterwards our buildings shape us.

A Sense of Crowd and Urgency (1943) 1974:6869. → The opening lines in a speech delivered in the House of Commons on October 28, 1943. The editor of Churchill's speeches, Robert Rhodes James, asserts in a headnote to the speech that although historians may question Churchill's assertion that the shape of the House of Commons played a major part in the evolution of the two-party system, "this speech is probably the best description of the particular characteristics of the House of Commons that has ever been made."

3 From Stettin in the Baltic to Trieste in the Adriatic, an iron curtain has descended across the Continent. Behind that line lie all the capitals of the ancient states of Central and Eastern Europe. Warsaw, Berlin, Prague, Vienna, Budapest, Belgrade, Bucharest and Sofia, all these famous cities and the populations around them lie in what I must call the Soviet sphere, and all are subject in one form or another, not only to Soviet influence but to a very high and, in many cases, increasing measure of control from Moscow.

The Sinews of Peace (1946) 1974:7290. → The phrase "iron curtain" was used in the Soviet context as early as 1920, but Churchill's use of it in 1946 made it a part of the language.

4 Many forms of Government have been tried, and will be tried in this world of sin and woe. No one pretends that democracy is perfect or all-wise. Indeed, it has been said that democracy is the worst form of Government except all those other forms that have been tried from time to time.

Parliament Bill, 11 November 1947. 1974:7566.

Marcus Tullius Cicero 106–43 B.C.

Roman statesman and philosopher

1 You understand, then, that the function of a magistrate is to govern, and to give commands which are just and beneficial and in conformity with the law. For as the laws govern the magistrate, so the magistrate governs the people, and it can truly be said that the magistrate is a speaking law, and the law a silent magistrate.

De legibus:Book 3, 459, 461.

2 Diagoras, named the Atheist, once came to Samothrace, and a certain friend said to him, "You who think that the gods disregard men's affairs, do you not remark all the votive pictures that prove how many persons have escaped the violence of the storm, and come safe to port, by dint of vows to the gods?" "That is so," replied Diagoras; "it is because there are nowhere any pictures of those who have been shipwrecked and drowned at sea."

De natura deorum:Book 3, 375. → An early call for the use of a control group in social experiments. As noted in detail by William H. Kruskal and Frederick Mosteller, Representative Sampling, II: Scientific Literature, Excluding Statistics. *International Statistical Review* 1979:Vol. 45, 117, this anecdote with its methodological moral has since been retold often. See, for example, BACON:5 and LAPLACE:4.

3 Who does not know history's first law to be that an author must not dare to tell anything but the truth? And its second that he must make bold to tell the whole truth? That there must be no suggestion of partiality anywhere in his writings? Nor of malice?

De oratore:Vol. 2, 243, 245.

4 *Cui bono*? [Who stood to gain?]

On Behalf of Milo:Par. 32.

John Bates Clark 1847–1938

U.S. economist

1 The picture of a stationary state presented by John Stuart Mill as the goal of competitive industry is the one thing needed to complete the impression of dismalness made by the political economy of the early period. A state could not be so good that the lack of progress would not blight it; nor could it be so bad that the fact of progress would not redeem it. . . The decisive test of an economic system is the rate and direction of its movement.

The Theory of Economic Progress 1896:5.

2 The modern world regards business cycles much as the ancient Egyptians regarded the overflowings of the Nile. The phenomenon recurs at intervals; it is of great importance to everyone, and natural causes of it are not in sight.

Introduction to Karl Rodbertus, *Overproduction and Crises* 1898:1.

3 The welfare of the laboring classes depends on whether they get much or little; but their attitude toward other classes — and, therefore, the stability of the social state — depends chiefly on the question, whether the amount they get, be it large or small, is what they produce. If they create a small amount of wealth and get the whole of it, they may not seek to revolutionize society; but if it were to appear that they produce an ample amount and get only a part of it, many of them would become revolutionists, and all would have the right to do so.

The Distribution of Wealth (1899) 1965:4.

4 The last tool adds less to man's efficiency than do earlier tools. If capital be used in increasing quantity by a fixed working force, it is subject to a law of diminishing productivity. . . What we have now to note is the fact that the diminishing productivity of labor, when it is used in connection with a fixed amount of capital, is a universal phenomenon. . . This action of the general law. . . becomes the basis of a theory of distribution.

The Distribution of Wealth (1899) 1965:48–50.

5 As real as gravitation is the force that draws the actual pay of men *toward* a standard that is set by the final productivity law. This law is universal and permanent: everywhere it will outlive the local and changeful influences that modify its operation. We are to get what we produce — such is the dominant rule of life; and what we are able to produce by means of labor, is determined by what a final unit of mere labor can add to the product that can be created without its aid. *Final productivity governs wages*.

The Distribution of Wealth (1899) 1965:180.

6 The entire study of wealth is, indeed, meaningless unless there be a unit for measuring it; for the questions to be answered are quantitative. How great is the wealth of a nation?

The Distribution of Wealth (1899) 1965:375.

7 No description could exaggerate the evil which is in store for a society given hopelessly over to a régime of private monopoly.

Essentials of Economic Theory (1907) 1968:375.

John Maurice Clark 1884–1963
U.S. economist

1 The machines originally made bargains with man, in which they offered him things he much desired, and in exchange bound him to serve and maintain them, to eliminate the unfit among them and promote their racial progress, and to alter his own social and political arrangements in whatever ways might be necessary in keeping pace with the increasingly complex social organization of the machines themselves, and in keeping the children of man faithful to the service the machines require. The full nature of the terms of these bargains was not, however, revealed to man at the first. Some of the terms became evident only after generations had passed, and of some we cannot yet be sure.

The Empire of Machines 1922:136.

Kenneth B. Clark 1914–
U.S. psychologist

1 America has contributed to the concept of the ghetto the restriction of persons to a special area and the limiting of their freedom of choice on the basis of skin color. The dark ghetto's invisible walls have been erected by the white society, by those who have power, both to confine those who have *no* power and to perpetuate their powerlessness. The dark ghettos are social, political, educational, and — above all — economic colonies. Their inhabitants are subject peoples, victims of the greed, cruelty, insensitivity, guilt, and fear of their masters.

Dark Ghetto (1965) 1989:11.

2 The Negro alone cannot win this fight that transcends the "civil rights struggle." White and Negro must fight together for the rights of human beings to make mistakes and to aspire to human goals. Negroes will not break out of the barriers of the ghetto unless whites transcend the barriers of their own minds, for the ghetto is to the Negro a reflection of the ghetto in which the white lives imprisoned. The poetic irony of American race relations is that the rejected Negro must somehow also find the strength to free the privileged white.

Dark Ghetto (1965) 1989:240.

Karl von Clausewitz 1780–1831
German military theorist

1 War is nothing but a duel on an extensive scale.

On War (1832–1834) 1962:1.

2 The War of a community — of whole Nations, and particularly of civilised Nations — always starts from a political condition, and is called forth by a political motive. It is, therefore, a political act.

On War (1832–1834) 1962:22.

3 We see. . . that War is not merely a political act, but also a real political instrument, a continuation of political commerce, a carrying out of the same by other means.

On War (1832–1834) 1962:23.

William G. Cochran 1909–1980
Scottish-born U.S. statistician

1 In 1905, a physicist measuring the thermal conductivity of copper would have faced, unknowingly, a very small systematic error due to the heating of his equipment and sample by the absorption of cosmic rays, then unknown to physics. In early 1946, an opinion poller, studying Japanese opinion as to who won the war, would have faced a very small systematic error due to the neglect of the 17 Japanese holdouts, who were discovered later north of Saipan. These cases are entirely parallel. Social, biological and physical scientists all need to remember that they have the same problems, the main difference being the decimal place in which they appear.

Principles of Sampling 1954:31. → Written with Frederick Mosteller and John W. Tukey.

I. Bernard Cohen 1914–
U.S. historian of science

1 History without the history of science, to alter slightly an apothegm of Lord Bacon, resembles a statue of Polyphemus without his eye — that very feature being left out which most marks the spirit and life of the person. My own thesis is complementary: science taught. . . without a sense of history is robbed of those very qualities that make it worth teaching to the student of the humanities and the social sciences.

General Education in Science 1952:71.

2 Although few expressions are more commonly used in writing about science than "scientific revolution," there is a continuing debate as to the propriety of applying the concept and term "revolution" to scientific change. There is, furthermore, a wide difference of opinion as to what may constitute a revolution. And although almost all historians would agree that a genuine alteration of an exceptionally radical nature (*the* Scientific Revolution) occurred in the sciences at some time between the late fifteenth (or early sixteenth) century and the end of the seventeenth century, the question of exactly when this revolution occurred arouses as much scholarly disagreement as the cognate question of precisely what it was.

The Newtonian Revolution 1980:3.

3 All revolutionary advances in science may consist less of sudden and dramatic revelations than a series of transformations, of which the revolutionary significance may not be seen (except afterwards, by historians) until the last great step. In many cases the full potentiality and force of a most radical step in such a sequence of transformations may not even be manifest to its author.

The Newtonian Revolution 1980:162.

Morris R. Cohen 1880–1947
Russian-born U.S. philosopher

1 It is interesting to note how many fundamental terms which the social sciences are trying to adopt from physics have as a matter of historical fact originated in the social field. Take, for instance, the notion of *cause*. The Greek *aitia* or the Latin *causa* was originally a purely legal term. It was taken over into physics, developed there, and in the 18th century brought back as a foreign-born king for the adoration of the social sciences. The same is true of the concept of *law of nature*. Originally a strict anthropomorphic conception, it was gradually depersonalized or dehumanized in the natural sciences and then taken over by the social sciences in an effort to eliminate final causes or purposes from the study of human affairs. It is therefore not anomalous to find similar transformations in the history of such fundamental concepts of statistics as *average* and *probability*. The concept of *average* was developed in the Rhodian laws as to the distribution of losses in maritime risks. After astronomers began to use it in correcting their observations, it spread to other physical sciences; and the prestige which it thus acquired has given it vogue in the social field. The term *probability*, as its etymology indicates, originates in practical and legal considerations of probing and proving.

The Statistical View of Nature 1936:327–328.

Edward Coke 1552–1634
British jurist

1 I cannot conjecture that the general communicating of these laws in the English tongue can work any inconvenience, but introduce great profit, seeing that *Ignorantia juris non excusat*, Ignorance of the law excuseth not. And herein I am justified by the wisdom of a parliament.

The First Part of the Institutes of the Laws of England (1628) 1832:Vol. 1, xxxviii–xxxix.

2 And yet in some case a man may not onely use force and armes, but assemble company also. As any may assemble his friends and neighbours, to keep his house against those that come to rob, or kill him, or to offer him violence in it, and is by construction excepted out of this act: and the sherif, &c. ought not to deal with him upon this act; for a mans house is his castle, *et domus sua cuique est tutissimum refugium*; for where shall a man be safe, if it be not in his house?

The Third Part of the Institutes of the Laws of England (1644) 1809:161.

G. D. H. Cole 1889–1959
British historian, economist, and sociologist

1 Sidney Webb's first thought, in dealing with any question that he took up, was to find an administratively workable solution; and apart from a very few essentially simple ideas he did not trouble himself much about any underlying philosophy. . . He had what is sometimes called a "civil service" mind — that is, a habit of translating every idea into terms of the machinery needed to give it effect; and, save concerning the trend, he was quite unaffected by doubts or spiritual hesitations.

The Second International 1956:210.

Margaret Cole 1893–1980
British writer

1 Beatrice in conversation in her middle and later years, was fond of describing herself and her husband as belonging to "the B's of the world," who, she explained, were "bourgeois, bureaucratic, and benevolent," in contrast to the "A's" — as for example Bertrand Russell, G. D. H. Cole, and a good many others, who were "aristocratic, anarchist, and artistic."

Beatrice Webb (1945) 1946:69.

James S. Coleman 1926–
U.S. sociologist

1 Like the *nouveau riche*, a newly rich society looks to the simple solutions which can be purchased with money. But neither the status problems of the *nouveau riche* nor the educational problems of a newly rich society can be so easily solved. The solutions are more costly in effort and in reorganization, though sometimes less costly in dollars. To put the matter briefly, if secondary education is to be successful, it must successfully compete with cars and sports and social activities for the adolescents' attention, in an open market. The adolescent is no longer a child, but will spend his energy in the ways he sees fit. It is up to the adult society to so structure secondary education that it captures this energy.

The Adolescent Society 1961:329.

2 Schools bring little influence to bear on a child's achievement that is independent of his background and general social context; and. . . this very lack of an independent effect means that the inequalities imposed on children by their home, neighborhood, and peer environment are carried along to become the inequalities with which they confront adult life at the end of school. For equality of educational opportunity through the schools must imply a strong effect of schools that is independent of the child's immediate social environment, and that strong independent effect is not present in American schools.

Equality of Educational Opportunity 1966:325. → Written with Ernest Q. Campbell, Carol J. Hobson, James McPartland, Alexander M. Mood, Frederic D. Weinfeld, and Robert L. York. Often called "The Coleman Report."

3 [Consider] the power relations between two kinds of actors in social systems: persons as actors, and the corporate actors (or as the law sometimes terms them, "fictional persons") created when two or more persons combine some portions of their resources to create an acting entity that is distinct from any one of them. As corporate actors have proliferated in modern society, and have come to take on many different forms (including

corporations, conglomerates, communes, trade unions, secret societies, associations), the question of how they can continue to be under the control of persons becomes an important one. The dilemma is a serious one: if a corporate actor is too extensively restrained by the wills of the natural persons from whom its resources originally came, then it cannot exercise its power toward the outside; if it is insufficiently constrained by these persons, it can use its resources against them, exercising its power to subvert their purposes.

Introduction to *Individual Interests and Collective Action* 1986:7–8.

4 There is a broadly perpetrated fiction in modern society, which is compatible with the development of the political philosophy of natural rights, with classical and neoclassical economic theory, and with many of the intellectual developments (and the social changes which generated them) that have occurred since the seventeenth century. This fiction is that society consists of a set of independent individuals, each of whom acts to achieve goals that are independently arrived at, and that the functioning of the social system consists of the combination of these actions of independent individuals. This fiction is expressed in the economic theory of perfect competition in a market, most graphically in Adam Smith's imagery of an "invisible hand."

Foundations of Social Theory 1990:300. → See ADAM SMITH:1.

5 Probably the most important and most original development in the economics of education in the past thirty years has been the idea that the concept of physical capital, as embodied in tools, machines, and other productive equipment, can be extended to include human capital as well. Just as physical capital is created by making changes in materials so as to form tools that facilitate production, human capital is created by changing persons so as to give them skills and capabilities that make them able to act in new ways.

Social capital, in turn, is created when the relations among persons change in ways that facilitate action. Physical capital is wholly tangible, being embodied in observable material form; human capital is less tangible, being embodied in the skills and knowledge acquired by an individual; social capital is even less tangible, for it is embodied in the *relations* among persons. Physical capital and human capital facilitate productive activity, and social capital does so as well.

Foundations of Social Theory 1990:304.

6 A new kind of social science has begun to emerge. . . This social science is not only a search for knowledge for the aesthetic pleasure of discovery or for the sake of knowing, but a search for knowledge for the reconstruction of society. As horizons become wider and possible directions of social progress multiply, knowledge about the self and society, and their relation, gains a new importance and immediacy.

Foundations of Social Theory 1990:651.

7 The theory of formal organizations has been impeded by a fixation on Max Weber's theory of bureaucracy, a theoretical orientation that recognizes purpose only at the apex of an organization and ignores the problem of connecting extrinsic interests of an employee to job performance. Also ignored are the free-rider problems created as externalities when government provides goods and services not contingent on an individual's own contribution. The fixation on bureaucratic theory is part of a broader problem: Theoretical questions concerning social organization have seldom been couched in terms of how to best organize action in order to accomplish a specific task without generating undesirable externalities.

Foundations of Social Theory 1990:654. → See MAX WEBER:21.

R. G. Collingwood 1889–1943
British philosopher and historian

1 To the scientist, nature is always and merely a "phenomenon," not in the sense of being defective in reality, but in the sense of being a spectacle presented to his intelligent observation; whereas the events of history are never mere phenomena, never mere spectacles for contemplation, but things which the historian looks, not at, but through, to discern the thought within them.

The Idea of History (1946) 1956:214.

2 When an historian asks "Why did Brutus stab Caesar?" he means "What did Brutus think, which made him decide to stab Caesar?" The cause of the event, for him, means the thought in the mind of the person by whose agency the event came about: and this is not something other than the event, it is the inside of the event itself.

The Idea of History (1946) 1956:214–215.

3 The history of thought, and therefore all history, is the reenactment of past thought in the historian's own mind.

The Idea of History (1946) 1956:215.

Auguste Comte 1798–1857
French philosopher and sociologist

1 In the last resort, all resolves itself into establishing, through the combined efforts of European men of science, a positive Theory in Politics, distinct from Practice, and one which shall bring our social system into harmony with the present stage of knowledge. Pursuing this course of reflection, we shall perceive that the above conclusions may be resumed in a single conception: *scientific men ought in our day to elevate politics to the rank of a science of observation.*

Plan for the Scientific Operations Necessary for Reorganizing Society (1822) 1911:130.

2 This expression [*social physics*] and the equally indispensable term *positive philosophy* were coined 17 years ago during my early work in political philosophy. Although new, these two essential terms have been rather spoiled by vicious attempts at appropriation by various writers who have not understood their true meaning at

all. This, despite the fact that, from the very beginning, I have established their basic meaning by my scrupulously consistent usage. Above all, I must lay the abuse of the term *social physics* at the door of a Belgian scholar [Adolphe Quetelet] who adopted it recently as the title of a book [*Physique sociale,* 1835] that at best deals with elementary statistics.

Cours de philosophie positive (1830–1842) 1839:Vol. 4, 7n. → Unpublished translation by Yole G. Sills.

3 I think I should risk introducing this new term [sociology]. It is exactly equivalent to *social physics,* a term I introduced previously to designate by a special name this complementary part of natural philosophy which deals with the positive study of the fundamental laws governing social phenomena. The necessity for this coinage to correspond to the special objectives of this volume will, I hope, excuse this last exercise of a legitimate right which I believe I have always used with proper caution and without ceasing to experience a deep feeling of repugnance for the systematic use of neologisms.

Cours de philosophie positive (1830–1842) 1839:Vol. 4, 252. → Unpublished translation by Yole G. Sills.

4 From the study of the development of human intelligence, in all directions, and through all times, the discovery arises of a great fundamental law, to which it is necessarily subject, and which has a solid foundation of proof, both in the facts of our organization and in our historical experience. The law is this: that each of our leading conceptions — each branch of our knowledge — passes successively through three different theoretical conditions: the theological, or fictitious; the metaphysical, or abstract; and the scientific, or positive.

The Positive Philosophy (1830–1842) 1983:71.

5 In the final, the positive, state, the mind has given over the vain search after absolute notions, the origin and destination of the universe, and the causes of phenomena, and applies itself to the study of their laws — that is, their invariable relations of succession and resemblance. Reasoning and observation, duly combined, are the means of this knowledge. What is now understood when we speak of an explanation of facts is simply the establishment of a connection between single phenomena and some general facts.

The Positive Philosophy (1830–1842) 1983:72.

6 It cannot be necessary to prove to anybody who reads this work that ideas govern the world, or throw it into chaos — in other words, that all social mechanism rests upon opinions.

The Positive Philosophy (1830–1842) 1983:83.

7 The means of exploration are three: direct observation, observation by experiment, and observation by comparison. In the first case, we look at the phenomenon before our eyes; in the second, we see how it is modified by artificial circumstances to which we have subjected it; and in the third, we contemplate a series of analogous cases, in which the phenomenon is more and more simplified.

The Positive Philosophy (1830–1842) 1983:132.

Arthur Conan Doyle

See ARTHUR CONAN DOYLE.

Étienne Bonnot de Condillac 1714–1780

French philosopher

1 I have distinguished three sorts of signs; accidental, natural, and instituted. A child nursed by bears has only the former. True it is that we cannot refuse him those sounds which are natural to each passion: but how could he imagine that they are the proper signs of the sensations he feels! If he lived in human society, he would so often hear them utter sounds like those which he makes himself, that some time or other he would connect those sounds with the sensations which they are designed to express. As to the bears, they cannot furnish him with the same opportunity; their roar hath not a sufficient analogy to the human voice. By the communication which these animals have with each other, probably they connect their cries with the perceptions which they signify: and this is what the boy here mentioned could not do. Therefore, for conducting themselves by the impression of natural cries, they have helps which he cannot have; and there is a probability that they have acquired a stronger habit of attention, reminiscence, and imagination than he: but this is the utmost limit of all the operations of the soul of brutes.

An Essay on the Origin of Human Knowledge (1746) 1971:133. → A facsimile of the 1756 translation by Thomas Nugent.

2 We may conclude that brutes have no memory; and that they have only an imagination which they cannot command as they please. They represent to themselves an absent object, only because the image of it in their brain is closely connected with the object present. It is not their memory that directs them to a place, where the day before they met with nourishment: but it is because the sensation of hunger is so strongly connected with the ideas of that place and of the road leading to it, that these ideas are revived, as soon as they feel the sensation. . .

But as soon as a man comes to connect ideas with signs of his own choosing, we find his memory is formed. When this is done, he begins of himself to dispose of his imagination, and to give it a new habit. For by means of the signs which he is able to recall at pleasure, he revives, or at least is often capable of reviving the ideas which are connected with them.

Essai 1746:I, 2, 4.

3 Languages are. . . more or less perfect relative to their adequacy for analysis. The more they facilitate analysis, the more they give assistance to the mind. In effect, we judge and reason with words, just as we calculate with numerals; and languages are for ordinary people what algebra is for geometricians.

Grammaire 1780:286–287.

Condorcet 1743–1794
[Marie Jean Antoine Nicholas Caritat, marquis de Condorcet]
French mathematician and philosopher

1 If man can, with almost complete assurance, predict phenomena when he knows their laws, and if, even when he does not, he can still, with great expectation of success, forecast the future on the basis of his experience of the past, why, then, should it be regarded as a fantastic undertaking to sketch, with some pretence to truth, the future destiny of man on the basis of his history?

Sketch for a Historical Picture of the Progress of the Human Mind (1795) 1955:173.

2 [All phenomena] are equally susceptible of being calculated, and all that is necessary, to reduce the whole of nature to laws similar to those which Newton discovered with the aid of the calculus, is to have a sufficient number of observations and a mathematics that is complex enough.

Unpublished manuscript. Quoted in Frank E. Manuel, *The Prophets of Paris* (1962) 1965:65.

3 The very passions of men, their interests falsely understood, lead them to spread enlightenment, liberty, happiness, to do good despite themselves.

Unpublished manuscript. Quoted in Frank E. Manuel, *The Prophets of Paris* (1962) 1965:73.

Charles H. Cooley 1864–1929
U.S. sociologist

1 I conclude. . . that the imaginations which people have of one another are the *solid facts* of society, and that to observe and interpret these must be a chief aim of sociology.

Human Nature and the Social Order (1902) 1964:121.

2 A man may be regarded as the point of intersection of an indefinite number of circles representing social groups, having as many arcs passing through him as there are groups. This diversity is connected with the growth of communication, and is another phase of the general enlargement and variegation of life.

Human Nature and the Social Order (1902) 1964:148.

3 A social self of this sort might be called the reflected or looking-glass self:

"Each to each a looking-glass
Reflects the other that doth pass."

As we see our face, figure, and dress in the glass, and are interested in them because they are ours, and pleased or otherwise with them according as they do or do not answer to what we should like them to be; so in imagination we perceive in another's mind some thought of our appearance, manners, aims, deeds, character, friends, and so on, and are variously affected by it.

Human Nature and the Social Order (1902) 1964:184.

4 The group to which we give allegiance, and to whose standards we try to conform, is determined by our own selective affinity, choosing among all the personal influences accessible to us; and so far as we select with any independence of our palpable companions, we have the appearance of non-conformity.

Human Nature and the Social Order (1902) 1964:301.
→ The group described by Cooley is part of what has been called a person's "reference group" since Hyman introduced the term in 1942. See HYMAN:1.

5 Self and society are twin-born, we know one as immediately as we know the other, and the notion of a separate and independent ego is an illusion.

Social Organization (1909) 1962:5.

6 By primary groups I mean those characterized by intimate face-to-face associations and coöperation. They are primary in several senses, but chiefly in that they are fundamental in forming the social nature and ideals of the individual.

Social Organization (1909) 1962:23.

7 Public opinion is no mere aggregate of separate individual judgments, but an organization, a coöperative product of communication and reciprocal influence. It may be as different from the sum of what the individuals could have thought out in separation as a ship built by a hundred men is from a hundred boats built by one man.

Social Organization (1909) 1962:121.

8 Conflict and co-operation are not separable things, but phases of one process which always involves something of both. Life, seen largely, is an onward struggle in which now one of these phases and now another may be more conspicuous, but from which neither can be absent.

Social Process (1918) 1966:39.

Carleton S. Coon 1904–1981
U.S. anthropologist

1 The essence of the quantitative approach in cultural anthropology lies in the thesis that the main stream or streams of human culture must have proceeded from simpler to more complex. The evidence of archaeology and of history supports this thesis, which in turn accords with all that we know of life in general. It must be equally apparent that the living cultures of the world vary in degrees of complexity, and that whole cultures can be listed and studied with greatest profit on the basis of such a progressive scheme.

A Reader in General Anthropology (1948) 1958:vii.

Lewis A. Coser 1913–
German-born U.S. sociologist

1 Insofar as conflict is the resolution of tension between antagonists it has stabilizing functions and becomes an integrating component of the relationship. However, not all conflicts are positively functional for the relationship,

but only those which concern goals, values or interests that do not contradict the basic assumptions upon which the relation is founded. Loosely structured groups and open societies, by allowing conflicts, institute safeguards against the type of conflict which would endanger basic consensus and thereby minimize the danger of divergences touching core values. The interdependence of antagonistic groups and the crisscrossing within such societies of conflicts, which serve to "sew the social system together" by cancelling each other out, thus prevent disintegration along one primary line of cleavage.

The Functions of Social Conflict 1956:80. → See Ross:1.

2 *Celibacy and promiscuity, though opposed sexual practices, fulfill identical sociological functions.* From a structural point of view, they are but variants on the same theme — the prevention of particularistic, dyadic attachments.

Greedy Institutions 1974:139.

Antoine Augustin Cournot 1801–1877

French mathematician, economist, and philosopher

1 Those skilled in mathematical analysis know that its object is not simply to calculate numbers, but that it is also employed to find the relations between magnitudes which cannot be expressed in numbers and between *functions* whose law is not capable of algebraic expression. Thus the theory of probabilities furnishes a demonstration of very important propositions, although, without the help of experience, it is impossible to give numerical values for contingent events, except in questions of mere curiosity, such as arise from certain games of chance.

Researches into the Mathematical Principles of the Theory of Wealth (1838) 1971:3.

2 I am far from having thought of writing in support of any system, and from joining the banners of any party; I believe that there is an immense step in passing from theory to governmental applications; I believe that theory loses none of its value in thus remaining preserved from contact with impassioned polemics; and I believe, if this essay is of any practical value, it will be chiefly in making clear how far we are from being able to solve, with full knowledge of the case, a multitude of questions which are boldly decided every day.

Researches into the Mathematical Principles of the Theory of Wealth (1838) 1971:5.

3 Property, power, the distinctions between masters, servants and slaves, abundance, and poverty, rights and privileges, all these are found among the most savage tribes, and seem to flow necessarily from the natural laws which preside over aggregations of individuals and of families; but such an idea of wealth as we draw from our advanced state of civilization, and such as is necessary to give rise to a theory, can only be slowly developed as a consequence of the progress of commercial relations, and of the gradual reaction of those relations on civil institutions.

Researches into the Mathematical Principles of the Theory of Wealth (1838) 1971:7–8.

4 By showing what determinate relations exist between unknown quantities, analysis reduces these unknown quantities to the smallest possible number, and guides the observer to the best observations for discovering their values. It reduces and coördinates statistical documents; and it diminishes the labour of statisticians.

Researches into the Mathematical Principles of the Theory of Wealth (1838) 1971:48–49.

5 Through education, each generation transmits to the one immediately following, a certain groundwork of ideas; and while this act of education or transmission is in operation, the *educating generation* is still present; unexpected, moreover, is the influence of the survivors of a preceding generation who have not ceased taking a notable part in the government of the society, on the movement of ideas and affairs.

Considérations sur la marche des idées et des événements dans les temps modernes (1872) 1934:Vol. 1, chap. 8.

Victor Cousin 1792–1867

French philosopher

1 Give me the map of any country, its configuration, its climate, its waters, its winds, and the whole of its physical geography; give me its natural productions, its flora, its zoology, &c., and I pledge myself to tell you, *à priori*, what will be the quality of man in that country, and what part its inhabitants will act in history; — not accidentally, but necessarily; not at any particular epoch, but in all; in short, — what idea he is called to represent.

Introduction to the History of Philosophy (1828) 1832:240.

Lawrence A. Cremin 1925–1990

U.S. historian

1 [There have been] three abiding characteristics of American education — first, *popularization*, the tendency to make education widely available in forms that are increasingly accessible to diverse peoples; second, *multitudinousness*, the proliferation and multiplication of institutions to provide that wide availability and that increasing accessibility; and third, *politicalization*, the effort to solve certain social problems indirectly through education instead of directly through politics. None of these characteristics has been uniquely American... and yet the three in tandem have marked American education uniquely.

Popular Education and Its Discontents 1990:vii–viii.

J. Hector St. John de Crèvecoeur 1735–1830
[Michel Guillaume Jean de Crèvecoeur]
French-born U.S. writer

1 What, then, is the American, this new man? He is neither an European nor the descendent of an European; hence that strange mixture of blood, which you will find in no other country. . . Here individuals of all nations are melted into a new race of men, whose labours and posterity will one day cause great changes in the world.

Letters from an American Farmer (1782) 1981:69–70. → An early formulation of the "melting pot" metaphor. See ZANGWILL:1 for the origin and GLAZER AND MOYNIHAN:1 for a contemporary evaluation.

Benedetto Croce 1866–1952
Italian philosopher and historian

1 Historical writing does not elaborate concepts, but reproduces particular events in their concreteness; and for that reason we have denied it the character of a science. It is therefore easy. . . to conclude that if history is not science it must be art.

La storia ridotta sotto il concetto generale dell'arte 1919:24.

2 The practical requirements which underlie every historical judgment give to all history the character of "contemporary history" because, however remote in time events there recounted may seem to be, the history in reality refers to present needs and present situations wherein those events vibrate.

History as the Story of Liberty (1938) 1970:19.

D

Robert A. Dahl 1915–
U.S. political scientist

1 The classic assumptions about the need for total citizen participation in democracy were, at the very least, inadequate. If one regards political equality in the making of decisions as a kind of limit to be achieved, then it is axiomatic that this limit could only be arrived at with the complete participation of every adult citizen. Nevertheless, what we call "democracy" — that is, a system of decision-making in which leaders are more or less responsive to the preferences of non-leaders — does seem to operate with a relatively low level of citizen participation. Hence it is inaccurate to say that one of the necessary conditions for "democracy" is extensive citizen participation.

Hierarchy, Democracy, and Bargaining in Politics and Economics (1955) 1956:87.

2 If there is anything to be said for the processes that actually distinguish democracy (or polyarchy) from dictatorship, it is not discoverable in the clear-cut distinction between government by a majority and government by a minority. The distinction comes much closer to being one between government by a minority and government by *minorities*. As compared with the political processes of a dictatorship, the characteristics of polyarchy greatly extend the number, size, and diversity of the minorities whose preferences will influence the outcome of governmental decisions.

A Preface to Democratic Theory (1956) 1963:133.

3 My intuitive idea of power. . . is something like this: *A* has power over *B* to the extent that he can get *B* to do something that *B* would not otherwise do.

The Concept of Power 1957:202–203. → See MAX WEBER:20.

4 *Homo civicus* is not, by nature, a political animal.

Who Governs? (1961) 1967:225. → See ARISTOTLE:7.

Ralf Dahrendorf 1929–
German sociologist

1 The proposition that implicitly or explicitly underlies all research and theoretical work in modern sociology [is]: *Man behaves in accordance with his roles*. Thus man figures in sociological analyses only to the extent that he complies with all the expectations associated with his social positions. This abstraction, the scientific unit of sociology, may be called *homo sociologicus*.

Sociology and Human Nature (1958) 1973:72–73.

2 Democratic man exercises freedom by displaying his personal preferences and idiosyncrasies in a framework of norms and rights shared with everybody else. Democratic man is the man who agrees to differ.

Democracy without Liberty 1961:187.

3 Some speak of hegemony, others simply of power. In the grammar which is used here, the old distinction between a "contract of association" and a "contract of domination" is at best of analytical usefulness. In practice it is difficult to think of human association without an element of domination. Where there is society there is power.

The Modern Social Conflict 1988:26.

Robert Darnton 1939–
U.S. historian

1 The reconstruction of worlds is one of the historian's most important tasks. He undertakes it, not from some strange urge to dig up archives and sift through old paper, but because he wants to talk with the dead. By putting questions to documents and listening for replies, he can sound dead souls and take the measure of the societies they inhabited. If we lost all contact with the worlds we have lost, we would be condemned to live in a two-dimensional, time-bound present, and our own world would turn flat.

The Literary Underground of the Old Regime 1982:v.

2 One thing seems clear to everyone who returns from field work: other people are other. They do not think the way we do. And if we want to understand their way of thinking, we should set out with the idea of capturing otherness. Translated into the terms of the historian's craft, that may merely sound like the familiar injunction against anachronism. It is worth repeating, nonetheless; for nothing is easier than to slip into the comfortable assumption that Europeans thought and felt two centuries

ago just as we do today — allowing for the wigs and wooden shoes. We constantly need to be shaken out of a false sense of familiarity with the past, to be administered doses of culture shock.

The Great Cat Massacre 1984:12.

3 Every age creates its own Rousseau. We have had Rousseau the Robespierrist, the romantic, the progressive, the totalitarian, and the neurotic. I would like to propose Rousseau the anthropologist. He invented anthropology as Freud invented psychoanalysis, by doing it to himself.

The Social Life of Rousseau 1985:69.

Charles Darwin 1809–1882
British naturalist

1 Origin of man now proved. — Metaphysic must flourish. — He who understands baboon <will> would do more towards metaphysics than Locke.

Notebooks, 16 August 1838. 1987:539.

2 At last gleams of light have come, & I am almost convinced (quite contrary to opinion I started with) that species are not (it is like confessing a murder) immutable. Heaven forfend me from Lamarck nonsense of a "tendency to progression" "adaptations from the slow willing of animals" &c, — but the conclusions I am led to are not widely different from his — though the means of change are wholly so — I think I have found out (here's presumption!) the simple way by which species become exquisitely adapted to various ends.

Letter to Joseph Dalton Hooker, 11 January 1844. 1987:2.

3 Without speculation there is no good and original observation.

Letter to A. R. Wallace, 22 December 1857. 1896:465.

4 Owing to this struggle for life, any variation, however slight and from whatever cause proceeding, if it be in any degree profitable to an individual of any species, in its infinitely complex relations to other organic beings and to external nature, will tend to the preservation of that individual, and will generally be inherited by its offspring. The offspring, also, will thus have a better chance of surviving, for, of the many individuals of any species who are periodically born, but a small number can survive. I have called this principle, by which each slight variation, if useful, is preserved, by the term of Natural Selection, in order to mark its relation to man's power of selection. [But the expression often used by Mr. Herbert Spencer of the Survival of the Fittest is more accurate, and is sometimes equally convenient.]

On the Origin of Species (1859) 1964:61. → The sentence within brackets was added by Darwin to the fifth edition of 1869. See SPENCER:8.

5 Nothing is easier than to admit in words the truth of the universal struggle for life, or more difficult — at least I have found it so — than constantly to bear this conclusion in mind.

On the Origin of Species (1859) 1964:62.

6 There is no exception to the rule that every organic being naturally increases at so high a rate, that if not destroyed, the earth would soon be covered by the progeny of a single pair. Even slow-breeding man has doubled in twenty-five years, and at this rate, in a few thousand years, there would literally not be standing room for his progeny.

On the Origin of Species (1859) 1964:64.

7 From the war of nature, from famine and death, the most exalted object which we are capable of conceiving, namely, the production of the higher animals, directly follows. There is grandeur in this view of life, with its several powers, having been originally breathed into a few forms or into one; and that, whilst this planet has gone cycling on according to the fixed law of gravity, from so simple a beginning endless forms most beautiful and most wonderful have been, and are being, evolved.

On the Origin of Species (1859) 1964:490.

8 The same language never has two birth-places. Distinct languages may be crossed or blended together. We see variability in every tongue, and new words are continually cropping up; but as there is a limit to the powers of the memory, single words, like whole languages, gradually become extinct. . . The survival or preservation of certain favoured words in the struggle for existence is natural selection.

The Descent of Man (1871) 1981:Chap. 2, 60–61.

9 False facts are highly injurious to the progress of science, for they often long endure; but false views, if supported by some evidence, do little harm, as every one takes a salutary pleasure in proving their falseness; and when this is done, one path towards error is closed and the road to truth is often at the same time opened.

The Descent of Man (1871) 1981:Chap. 21, 385.

10 For my own part I would as soon be descended from that heroic little monkey, who braved his dreaded enemy in order to save the life of his keeper; or from that old baboon, who, descending from the mountains, carried away in triumph his young comrade from a crowd of astonished dogs — as from a savage who delights to torture his enemies, offers up bloody sacrifices, practises infanticide without remorse, treats his wives like slaves, knows no decency, and is haunted by the grossest superstitions.

The Descent of Man (1871) 1981:Chap. 21, 404–405.

11 Man with all his noble qualities, with sympathy which feels for the most debased, with benevolence which extends not only to other men but to the humblest living creature, with his god-like intellect which has penetrated into the movements and constitution of the solar system — with all these exalted powers — Man still bears in his bodily frame the indelible stamp of his lowly origin.

The Descent of Man (1871) 1981:Chap. 21, 405.

12 Fifteen months after I had begun my systematic enquiry, I happened to read for amusement Malthus on *Population,* and being well prepared to appreciate the struggle for existence which everywhere goes on from long-

continued observations of the habits of animals and plants, it at once struck me that under these circumstances favourable variations would tend to be preserved and unfavourable ones to be destroyed. The result of this would be new species. Here, then, I had at last got a theory by which to work.

Autobiography (1876) 1958:42–43. → Contemporary Darwin scholars believe that Darwin greatly exaggerated Malthus's influence on his thinking. See, for example, Ernst Mayr, *The Growth of Biological Thought* (1982:491–495).

Charles Davenant 1656–1714
British economic and political writer

1 By Political Arithmetick, we mean the Art of Reasoning, by Figures, upon Things relating to Government.

Discourses on the Publick Revenues 1698:Part 1, 2.

2 There is hardly a Society of Merchants, that would not have thought the whole prosperity of the Kingdom depends upon their single Traffick. So that at any time, when they come to be Consulted, their Answers are dark and partial; and when they deliberate themselves in Assemblies, 'tis generally with a Bypass, and a secret Eye to their own Advantage.

Discourses on the Publick Revenues 1698:Part 1, 30.

James C. Davies 1918–
U.S. political scientist

1 Revolutions are most likely to occur when a prolonged period of objective economic and social development is followed by a short period of sharp reversal. The all-important effect on the minds of people in a particular society is to produce, during the former period, an expectation of continued ability to satisfy needs — which continue to rise — and, during the latter, a mental state of anxiety and frustration when manifest reality breaks away from anticipated reality.

Toward a Theory of Revolution (1962) 1969:86. → A statement of the "revolution of rising expectations." See TOCQUEVILLE:28 and 29.

Kingsley Davis 1908–
U.S. sociologist and demographer

1 Viewed in long-run perspective, the growth of the earth's population has been like a long, thin powder fuse that burns slowly and haltingly until it finally reaches the charge and then explodes. For a million or more years our species increased with infinitesimal slowness, flourishing temporarily in some areas, hardly getting started at all in others. Throughout at least 99 per cent of its history it remained extremely sparse.

The World Demographic Transition 1945:1.

2 In Europe, and in Europe overseas, the sociocultural transition known as the Industrial Revolution has been accompanied by an intimately related demographic transition, representing an astounding gain in human efficiency. Under the old regime of high fertility and high mortality, women frequently experienced the drain and danger of pregnancy to no purpose, because a large proportion of the offspring died. Furthermore, energy was spent on the surviving offspring, only to find that many of them died before or during early maturity. Thus too much effort was spent in trying to bring each new generation to full productive maturity. Too much energy was lost in sickness, malnutrition, and preoccupation with death. The new type of demographic balance released a great amount of energy from the eternal chain of reproduction — energy that could be spent on other aspects of life.

The World Demographic Transition 1945:5.

3 Most discussions of the population crisis lead logically to zero population growth as the ultimate goal, because *any* growth rate, if continued, will eventually use up the earth. . . Turning to the actual measures taken, we see that the very use of family planning as the means for implementing population policy poses serious but unacknowledged limits on the intended reduction in fertility. The family-planning movement, clearly devoted to the improvement and dissemination of contraceptive devices, states again and again that its purpose is that of enabling couples to have the number of children they want.

Population Policy 1967:732. → With the publication of this article, "zero population growth" and the acronym "ZPG" came into general use.

Kingsley Davis 1908–
U.S. sociologist and demographer
and
Wilbert E. Moore 1914–1988
U.S. sociologist

1 Social inequality is. . . an unconsciously evolved device by which societies insure that the most important positions are conscientiously filled by the most qualified persons.

Some Principles of Stratification 1945:248.

Natalie Zemon Davis 1928–
U.S. historian

1 Even in the extreme case of religious violence, crowds do not act in a mindless way. They will to some degree have a sense that what they are doing is legitimate, the occasions will relate somehow to the defense of their cause, and their violent behavior will have some structure to it. . . But the rites of violence are not the rights of violence in any *absolute* sense. They simply remind us that if we try to increase safety and trust within a community, try to guarantee that the violence it generates will take less destructive and cruel forms, then we must think less about pacifying "deviants" and more about changing the central values.

The Rites of Violence (1973) 1975:187.

2 The female sex was thought the disorderly one par excellence in early modern Europe. . . Female disorderliness was already seen in the Garden of Eden, when Eve had been the first to yield to the serpent's temptation and incite Adam to disobey the Lord. To be sure, the men of the lower orders were also believed to be especially prone to riot and seditious unrest. But the defects of the males were thought to stem not so much from nature as from nurture; the ignorance in which they were reared, the brutish quality of life and conversation in the peasant's hut or the artisan's shop, and their poverty, which led to envy.

Women on Top 1975:124.

J.D.B. DeBow 1820–1867
U.S. government official

1 Statistics are far from being the barren array of figures ingeniously and laboriously combined into columns and tables, which many persons are apt to suppose them. They constitute rather the ledger of a nation, in which, like the merchant in his books, the citizen can read, at one view, all of the results of a year or of a period of years, as compared with other periods, and deduce the profit or the loss which has been made, in morals, education, wealth or power.

Introduction to *Statistical View of the United States* 1854:9.

Augustus De Morgan 1806–1871
British mathematician and logician

1 [Writing of the theory of probability:] No part of mathematics or mathematical physics involves considerations so strange or so difficult to handle correctly, and there is no subject upon which opinions have been more freely hazarded by the ignorant, or rational dissent more unambiguously expressed by the learned.

Theory of Probabilities 1845:393.

James Steuart Denham
See JAMES STEUART DENHAM.

René Descartes 1596–1650
French mathematician and philosopher

1 Good sense is of all things in the world the most equitably distributed; for everyone thinks himself so amply provided with it, that even those most difficult to please in everything else do not commonly desire more of it than they already have.

Discourse on Method (1637) 1958:Part I, 93.

2 Already in my college days I had been brought to recognize that there is no opinion, however strange, and however difficult of belief, which has not been upheld by one or other of the philosophers. Afterwards, too, in the course of my travels, I observed that those whose sentiments are very contrary to ours are not on this account barbarous and savage, and that many of them make as good or, it may be, better use of reason than we do ourselves. Bearing also in mind how the selfsame man, with the mental equipment proper to him, if nurtured from infancy among the French or the Germans, would come to be different from what he would have been had he lived always among the Chinese or the cannibals; and how, in respect of fashions in dress, what pleased us ten years ago, and which will again please ten years hence, appears to us at the present moment extravagant and ridiculous. Thus I came to see that custom and example have a much more persuasive power than any certitude obtained by way of inquiry.

Discourse on Method (1637) 1958:Part 2, 104–105.

3 I then proceeded to consider, in a general manner, what is requisite to the truth and certainty of a proposition. Having found one — I think, therefore I am [*cogito ergo sum*] — which I knew to be true and certain, I thought that I ought also to know in what this certainty consists; and having noted that in this proposition nothing assures me of its truth save only that I see very clearly that in order to think it is necessary to be, I judged that I could take as being a general rule, that the things we apprehend very clearly and distinctly are true — bearing in mind, however, that there is some difficulty in rightly determining which are those we apprehend distinctly.

Discourse on Method (1637) 1958:Part 4, 119–120.

George Devereux 1908–
Hungarian-born French psychiatrist

1 *The substantive thesis* [of this book is] that, were anthropologists to draw up a complete list of all known types of cultural behavior, this list would overlap, point by point, with a similarly complete list of impulses, wishes, fantasies, etc., obtained by psychoanalysts in a clinical setting, thus demonstrating, by identical means and simultaneously, the psychic unity of mankind and the validity of psychoanalytic interpretations of culture, both of which have hitherto been validated only empirically.

A Study of Abortion in Primitive Societies 1955:vii-viii.

John Dewey 1859–1952
U.S. philosopher

1 Ends are not compromised when referred to the means necessary to realize them. Values do not cease to be values when they are minutely and accurately measured. Acts are not destroyed when their operative machinery is made manifest. . . The simple fact is still too obvious: the more thorough-going and complete the mechanical and causal statement, the more controlled, the more economical are the discovery and realization of human aims.

Psychology and Social Practice 1900:117–118.

2 Grammar expresses the unconscious logic of the popular mind. *The chief intellectual classifications that constitute the working capital of thought have been built up for us by our mother tongue.* Our very lack of explicit consciousness, when using language, that we are then em-

ploying the intellectual systematizations of the race shows how thoroughly accustomed we have become to its logical distinctions and groupings.

How We Think (1910) 1933:235.

3 Learning by doing does not. . . mean the substitution of manual occupations or handwork for text-book studying. At the same time, allowing the pupils to do handwork, whenever there is opportunity for it, is a great aid in holding the child's attention and interest.

Schools of To-Morrow (1915) 1979:255. → The phrase "learning by doing" seems to have been created by others as a summary expression of Dewey's repeated emphasis upon the importance of "experience" and "activity" in education. He rarely used the phrase in his writings.

4 The term "pragmatic" means only the rule of referring all thinking, all reflective considerations, to *consequences* for final meaning and test. Nothing is said about the nature of the consequences; they may be aesthetic, or moral, or political, or religious in quality.

An Added Note as to the "Practical" (1916) 1980:366.

5 Certainly nothing can justify or condemn means except ends, results. But we have to include consequences impartially. . . It is wilful folly to fasten upon some single end or consequence which is liked, and permit the view of that to blot from perception all other undesired and undesirable consequences.

Human Nature and Conduct 1922:228–229.

6 The suggestion that pragmatism is the intellectual equivalent of commercialism need not, however, be taken too seriously. It is of that order of interpretation which would say that English neorealism is a reflection of the aristocratic snobbery of the English; the tendency of French thought to dualism an expression of an alleged Gallic disposition to keep a mistress in addition to a wife; and the idealism of Germany a manifestation of an ability to elevate beer and sausage into a higher synthesis with the spiritual values of Beethoven and Wagner.

Pragmatic America (1922) 1983:307.

7 The Great Society created by steam and electricity may be a society, but it is no community.

The Public and Its Problems 1927:98. → See WALLAS:1.

8 Men hoist the banner of the ideal, and then march in the direction that concrete conditions suggest and reward.

The Quest for Certainty (1929) 1984:224.

9 The office of intelligence in every problem that either a person or a community meets is to effect a working connection between old habits, customs, institutions, beliefs, and new conditions.

Liberalism and Social Action (1935) 1987:37.

10 The moment philosophy supposes it can find a final and comprehensive solution, it ceases to be inquiry and becomes either apologetics or propaganda.

Logic (1938) 1986:42.

11 Law is through and through a social phenomenon; social in origin, in purpose or end, and in application.

My Philosophy of Law (1941) 1988:117.

Persi Diaconis 1945–
U.S. mathematician
and
Frederick Mosteller 1916–
U.S. statistician

1 The law of truly large numbers states: With a large enough sample, any outrageous thing is likely to happen. The point is that truly rare events, say events that occur only once in a million. . . are bound to be plentiful in a population of 250 million people. If a coincidence occurs to one person in a million each day, then we expect 250 occurrences a day and close to 100,000 such occurrences a year.

Methods for Studying Coincidences 1989:859. → See R.A. FISHER:6.

Denis Diderot 1713–1784
French philosopher and encyclopedist

1 There is no more inequality between the different stations in life than there is among the different characters in a comedy: the end of the play finds all the players once again in a common position, and the brief period for which their play lasted did not and could not convince any two of them that one was really above or below the other.

Société 1765.

Wilhelm Dilthey 1833–1911
German philosopher

1 As the human sciences have developed, they have come to contain, besides the knowledge of what is, a consciousness of a system of value judgments and imperatives wherein values, ideals, rules, and the aim to shape the future are connected. A political judgment that condemns an institution is not true or false but rather correct or incorrect insofar as that institution's tendency, its goal, is being appraised; on the other hand, a political judgment which describes the connections of this institution with other institutions can be true or false.

Introduction to the Human Sciences (1883) 1989: 78–79.

2 Man as a fact prior to history and society is a fiction of genetic explanation; the human being which a sound analytic science takes as its object is the individual as a component of society. The difficult problem which psychology must solve is how to attain analytic knowledge of the universal characteristics of man.

Introduction to the Human Sciences (1883) 1989:83.

3 The present is filled with pasts and carries the future in itself.

Gesammelte Schriften (1905–1910) 1927:Vol. 7, 73.

Benjamin Disraeli 1804–1881
[1st earl of Beaconsfield]
British statesman and novelist

1 The Utilitarians in Politics are like the Unitarians in Religion. Both omit Imagination in their systems, and Imagination governs Mankind.

Letters 1833:447. → An entry in Disraeli's so-called "Mutilated Diary."

2 "Well, society may be in its infancy," said Egremont slightly smiling; "but, say what you like, our Queen reigns over the greatest nation that ever existed."

"Which nation?" asked the younger stranger, "for she reigns over two."

The stranger paused; Egremont was silent, but looked inquiringly.

"Yes," resumed the stranger after a moment's interval. "Two nations; between whom there is no intercourse and no sympathy; who are as ignorant of each other's habits, thoughts and feelings, as if they were dwellers in different zones, or inhabitants of different planets; who are formed by a different breeding, are fed by a different food, are ordered by different manners, and are not governed by the same laws."

"You speak of — " said Egremont, hesitatingly.

"THE RICH AND THE POOR."

Sybil (1845) 1980:96.

3 We have sought to offer [this Reform Bill] to the country, in the hope that it will meet with its calm and serious approval, what we believe to be a just and — I will not say final — but conclusive statement. Finality, Sir, is not the language of politics.

Reform Bill, 28 February 1859. 1867:201. → From a speech delivered in the House of Commons while Disraeli was chancellor of the exchequer and parliamentary leader. The Reform Bill was finally passed in 1867.

4 There are three kinds of lies: lies, damned lies, and statistics.

Attributed to Disraeli in *Mark Twain's Autobiography* 1924:Vol. 1, 246. → The editors know of no evidence beyond this attribution that Disraeli ever made this statement.

Maurice H. Dobb 1900–1976
British economist

1 If all that is postulated is simply that men *choose*, without anything being stated even as to how they choose or what governs their choice, it would seem impossible for economics to provide us with any more than a sort of algebra of human choice.

Political Economy and Capitalism (1937) 1975:171.

2 "Exploitation" is neither something "metaphysical" nor simply an ethical judgment (still less "just a noise") as has sometimes been depicted: it is a factual description of a socio-economic relationship, as much as is Marc Bloch's apt characterisation of Feudalism as a system where feudal lords "lived on the labour of other men."

Theories of Value and Distribution since Adam Smith (1973) 1979:145.

Theodosius Dobzhansky 1900–1975
Russian-born U.S. geneticist

1 The adaptive advantage of the ability to acquire even the most rudimentary forms of culture must have been so great in the early stages of human evolution that natural selection rapidly propagated the genotypes which permitted the acquisition of culture throughout the human species. The gene-controlled capacity to learn, absorb, and use new techniques and tools was, then, developed, intensified, and diffused by means of biological evolution, making our species more and more human.

Evolution, Genetics, and Man 1955:339–340.

2 Nature's stern discipline enjoins mutual help at least as often as warfare. The fittest may also be the gentlest.

Mankind Evolving (1962) 1967:134. → See BOULDING:1.

John Dollard 1900–1980
U.S. anthropologist, psychologist, and sociologist

1 *Aggression is always a consequence of frustration.* More specifically the proposition is that the occurrence of aggressive behavior always presupposes the existence of frustration and, contrariwise, that the existence of frustration always leads to some form of aggression.

Frustration and Aggression 1939:1. → Written with Leonard W. Doob, Neal E. Miller, O. H. Mowrer, and Robert R. Sears.

[*See also* NEAL E. MILLER AND JOHN DOLLARD.]

Fyodor Mikhaylovich Dostoyevsky 1821–1881
Russian novelist

1 Who has ever, in all these millennia, seen men acting solely for the sake of advantage? What's to be done with the millions of facts that attest to their *knowingly* — that is, with full awareness of their true interests — dismissing these interests as secondary and rushing off in another direction, at risk, at hazard, without anyone or anything compelling them to do so, but as if solely in order to reject the designated road, and stubbornly, willfully carving out another — a difficult, absurd one — seeking it out virtually in the dark?

Evidently, then, this stubbornness and willfulness has really pleased them more than any advantage. . . Advantage! What is advantage?

Notes from Underground (1864) 1981:22.

2 If someday they should really discover the formula for all our whims and wishes — I mean, what causes them, what laws they're governed by, how they develop and where they lead in one case or another, and so on and so forth; in other words, an actual mathematical formula —

why, then man will perhaps immediately stop wishing; indeed, he'll surely stop wishing. Who wants to wish according to graphs?

Notes from Underground (1864) 1981:29.

Mary Douglas 1921–
British anthropologist

1 Dirt is essentially disorder. There is no such thing as absolute dirt: it exists in the eye of the beholder. If we shun dirt, it is not because of craven fear, still less dread or holy terror. Nor do our ideas about disease account for the range of our behaviour in cleaning or avoiding dirt. Dirt offends against order. Eliminating it is not a negative movement, but a positive effort to organise the environment.

Purity and Danger 1966:2.

2 Dirt. . . is never a unique, isolated event. Where there is dirt there is system. Dirt is the by-product of a systematic ordering and classification of matter, in so far as ordering involves rejecting inappropriate elements.

Purity and Danger 1966:35.

3 If food is treated as a code, the messages it encodes will be found in the pattern of social relations being expressed. The message is about different degrees of hierarchy, inclusion and exclusion, boundaries and transactions across the boundaries. Like sex, the taking of food has a social component, as well as a biological one. Food categories therefore encode social events.

Deciphering a Meal 1971:61.

4 [Evans-Pritchard] was once described as the Stendhal of anthropology. But he showed the way to do something different from fiction. By systematically attending to people's response to misfortune, he justified the distinctive claims of his chosen profession.

Evans-Pritchard 1980:124.

Arthur Conan Doyle 1859–1930
British writer and physician

1 [*Holmes*]: You see, but you do not observe. The distinction is clear. For example, you have frequently seen the steps which lead up from the hall to this room.
[*Watson*]: Frequently.
[*Holmes*]: How often? [*Watson*]: Well, some hundreds of times. [*Holmes*]: Then how many are there? [*Watson*]: How many! I don't know. [*Holmes*]: Quite so! You have not observed. And yet you have seen. That is just my point. Now, I know that there are seventeen steps, because I have both seen and observed.

A Scandal in Bohemia (1891) 1986:349.

2 [*Ross*]: Is there any point to which you would wish to draw my attention?
[*Holmes*]: To the curious incident of the dog in the night-time.
[*Ross*]: The dog did nothing in the night-time.
[*Holmes*]: That was the curious incident.

Silver Blaze (1894) 1953:347.

3 [*Holmes*]: The temptation to form premature theories upon insufficient data is the bane of our profession.

The Valley of Fear (1914) 1953:779.

John Dryden 1631–1700
British poet

1 [*Almanz*]: I am as free as Nature first made man
'Ere the base Laws of Servitude began
When wild in woods the noble Savage ran.

The Conquest of Granada (1672) 1978:Part 1, act 1, scene 1, 30. → This seems to be the origin of "the noble savage."

W. E. B. DuBois 1868–1963
U.S. sociologist

1 Even more than the rest of the race [members of the Negro middle class] feel the difficulty of getting on in the world by reason of their small opportunities for remunerative and respectable work. On the other hand their position as the richest of their race — though their riches is insignificant compared with their white neighbors — makes unusual social demands upon them. A white Philadelphian with $1500 a year can call himself poor and live simply. A Negro with $1500 a year ranks with the richest of his race and must usually spend more in proportion than his white neighbor in rent, dress and entertainment.

The Philadelphia Negro 1899:178.

2 After the Egyptian and Indian, the Greek and Roman, the Teuton and Mongolian, the Negro is a sort of seventh son, born with a veil, and gifted with second-sight in this American world, — a world which yields him no true self-consciousness, but only lets him see himself through the revelation of the other world. It is a peculiar sensation, this double-consciousness, this sense of always looking at one's self through the eyes of others, of measuring one's soul by the tape of a world that looks on in amused contempt and pity.

The Souls of Black Folk (1903) 1953:3.

3 The problem of the twentieth century is the problem of the color-line, — the relation of the darker to the lighter races of men in Asia and Africa, in America and the islands of the sea.

The Souls of Black Folk (1903) 1953:13.

4 Herein lies the tragedy of the age: not that men are poor, — all men know something of poverty; not that men are wicked — who is good? not that men are ignorant — what is Truth? Nay, but that men know so little of men.

The Souls of Black Folk (1903) 1953:226–227.

5 The cost of liberty is less than the price of repression, even though that cost be blood.

John Brown 1909:395.

6 What, then, is this dark world thinking? It is thinking that as wild and awful as this shameful war was, *it is nothing to compare with that fight for freedom which black and brown and yellow men must and will make unless their oppression and humiliation and insult at the hands of the White World cease.* The dark world is going to submit to its present treatment just as long as it must and not one moment longer.

Darkwater (1920) 1969:49.

7 No matter how degraded the factory hand, he is not real estate. The tragedy of the black slave's position was precisely this: his absolute subjection to the individual will of an owner.

Black Reconstruction (1935) 1956:10.

8 In order to paint the South as a martyr to inescapable fate, to make the North the magnanimous emancipator, and to ridicule the Negro as the impossible joke in the whole development, we have in fifty years, by libel, innuendo and silence, so completely misstated and obliterated the history of the Negro in America and his relation to its work and government that today it is almost unknown. This may be fine romance, but it is not science. It may be inspiring, but it is certainly not the truth. And beyond this it is dangerous.

Black Reconstruction (1935) 1956:723.

Otis Dudley Duncan 1921–
U.S. demographer and sociologist

1 One very constructive function of the ability measured by intelligence tests is that it serves as a kind of springboard, launching many men into achievements removing them considerable distances from the social class of their birth. IQ, in an achievement-oriented society, is the primary leaven preventing the classes from hardening into castes.

Ability and Achievement 1968:11.

2 There is hardly any social problem confronting this nation whose solution would be easier if our population were larger. There are few, if any, sectors of the economy whose efficiency would be greater if numbers were larger than they now are.

Observations on Population (1970) 1971:243.

3 A mature science, with respect to the matter of errors in variables, is not one that measures its variables without error, for this is impossible. It is, rather, a science which properly manages its errors, controlling their magnitudes and correctly calculating their implications for substantive conclusions.

Introduction to Structural Equation Models 1975:114.

4 The antiquity of several basic concepts and procedures of social measurements (such as voting, counting people, money, social rank, contests, rewards and punishments, and randomization) suggests that their roots are in the social process itself, broadly conceived, and not specifically in the scientific method as it developed in the seventeenth and later centuries. Where social measurement has relied heavily on methods borrowed from psychophysics, psychometrics, and economic index numbers, rather than methods well suited to the population sciences, it has encountered seemingly intractable difficulties, which are only exacerbated by adherence to an inadequate doctrine of scale types. A sociology of measurement, allied with an expanded historical metrology, is needed not less for the improvement of measurement technique than for an understanding of the role of quantification in society.

Notes on Social Measurement 1984:xiii.

Émile Durkheim 1858–1917
French sociologist

1 Science cannot describe individuals, but only types. If human societies cannot be classified, they must remain inaccessible to scientific description.

Montesquieu's Contribution to the Rise of Social Science (1892) 1960:9.

2 We are. . . led to consider the division of labor in a new light. . . The economic services that it can render are picayune compared to the moral effect that it produces, and its true function is to create in two or more persons a feeling of solidarity.

The Division of Labor in Society (1893) 1964:56.

3 We must not say that an action shocks the common conscience because it is criminal, but rather that it is criminal because it shocks the common conscience. We do not reprove it because it is a crime, but it is a crime because we reprove it.

The Division of Labor in Society (1893) 1964:81.

4 Man is a moral being only because he lives in society, since morality consists in being solidary with a group and varying with this solidarity. Let all social life disappear, and moral life will disappear with it, since it would no longer have any objective.

The Division of Labor in Society (1893) 1964:399.

5 [There] is a category of facts [social facts] with very distinctive characteristics: it consists of ways of acting, thinking, and feeling, external to the individual, and endowed with a power of coercion, by reason of which they control him.

The Rules of Sociological Method (1895) 1958:3.

6 A social fact is every way of acting, fixed or not, capable of exercising on the individual an external constraint; or again, every way of acting which is general throughout a given society, while at the same time existing in its own right independent of its individual manifestations.

The Rules of Sociological Method (1895) 1958:13.

7 The first and most fundamental rule is: *Consider social facts as things.*

The Rules of Sociological Method (1895) 1958:14.

8 In order that the originality of the idealist whose dreams transcend his century may find expression, it is necessary that the originality of the criminal, who is below the level of his time, shall also be possible. One does not occur without the other.

The Rules of Sociological Method (1895) 1958:71.

9 Even one well-made observation will be enough in many cases, just as one well-constructed experiment often suffices for the establishment of a law.

The Rules of Sociological Method (1895) 1958:80.

10 We use the word "function," in preference to "end" or "purpose," precisely because social phenomena do not generally exist for the useful results they produce.

The Rules of Sociological Method (1895) 1958:95.

11 We must. . . seek the explanation of social life in the nature of society itself. It is quite evident that, since it infinitely surpasses the individual in time as well as in space, it is in a position to impose upon him ways of acting and thinking which it has consecrated with its prestige. This pressure, which is the distinctive property of social facts, is the pressure which the totality exerts on the individual.

The Rules of Sociological Method (1895) 1958:102.

12 Society is not a mere sum of individuals. Rather, the system formed by their association represents a specific reality which has its own characteristics. . . The group thinks, feels, and acts quite differently from the way in which its members would were they isolated. If, then, we begin with the individual, we shall be able to understand nothing of what takes place in the group.

The Rules of Sociological Method (1895) 1958:103–104.

13 With increased prosperity desires increase. At the very moment when traditional rules have lost their authority, the richer prize offered these appetites stimulates them and makes them more exigent and impatient of control. The state of de-regulation or anomy is thus further heightened by passions being less disciplined, precisely when they need more disciplining.

Suicide (1897) 1966:253.

14 Egoistic suicide results from man's no longer finding a basis for existence in life; altruistic suicide, because this basis for existence appears to man situated beyond life itself. The third sort of suicide. . . results from man's activity's lacking regulation and his consequent sufferings. By virtue of its origin we shall assign this last variety the name of *anomic suicide*.

Suicide (1897) 1966:258.

15 The proof that the reality of collective tendencies is no less than that of cosmic forces is that this reality is demonstrated in the same way, by the uniformity of effects. When we find that the number of deaths varies little from year to year, we explain this regularity by saying that mortality depends on the climate, the temperature, the nature of the soil, in brief on a certain number of material forces which remain constant through changing generations because independent of individuals. Since, therefore, moral acts such as suicide are reproduced not merely with an equal but with a greater uniformity, we must likewise admit that they depend on forces external to individuals. Only, since these forces must be of a moral order and since, except for individual men, there is no other moral order of existence in the world but society, they must be social.

Suicide (1897) 1966:309.

16 Individual and society are certainly beings with different natures. But far from there being some inexpressible kind of antagonism between the two, far from its being the case that the individual can identify himself with society only at the risk of renouncing his own nature either wholly or in part, the fact is that he is not truly himself, he does not fully realize his own nature, except on the condition that he is involved in society.

Moral Education (1902–1906) 1973:67–68.

17 From the fact that the ideas of time, space, class, cause or personality are constructed out of social elements, it is not necessary to conclude that they are devoid of all objective value. On the contrary, their social origin rather leads to the belief that they are not without foundation in the nature of things.

The Elementary Forms of the Religious Life (1912) 1965:31–32.

18 Sacred things are those which the interdictions protect and isolate; profane things, those to which these interdictions are applied and which must remain at a distance from the first.

The Elementary Forms of the Religious Life (1912) 1965:56.

19 A religion is a unified system of beliefs and practices relative to sacred things, that is to say, things set apart and forbidden — beliefs and practices which unite into one single moral community called a Church, all those who adhere to them.

The Elementary Forms of the Religious Life (1912) 1965:62.

20 God is only a figurative expression of the society.

The Elementary Forms of the Religious Life (1912) 1965:258.

21 There is something eternal in religion which is destined to survive all the particular symbols in which religious thought has successively enveloped itself. There can be no society which does not feel the need of upholding and reaffirming at regular intervals the collective sentiments and the collective ideas which make its unity and its personality.

The Elementary Forms of the Religious Life (1912) 1965:474–475.

22 Socialism is not a science, a sociology in miniature: it is a cry of pain.

Le socialisme: Sa définition, ses débuts, la doctrine saint-simonienne 1928.

23 It is the State that has rescued the child from patriarchal domination and from family tyranny; it is the State that has freed the citizen from feudal groups and later from communal groups; it is the State that has liberated the craftsman and his master from guild tyranny. . . [The State] must even permeate all those secondary groups of family, trade and professional association, Church, regional areas and so on. . . which tend. . . to absorb the personality of their members. It must do this, in order to prevent this absorption and free these individuals, and so as to remind these partial societies that they are not alone and that there is a right that stands above their own rights.

Professional Ethics and Civic Morals (1950) 1957:64–65. → Based on lectures given by Durkheim in the years 1898–1912.

E

Richard A. Easterlin 1926–
U.S. economist and demographer

1 The Easterlin, or "cohort size," hypothesis posits that, other things constant, the economic and social fortunes of a cohort (those born in a given year) tend to vary inversely with its relative size, approximately by the crude birth rate in the period surrounding the cohort's birth.

Easterlin Hypothesis 1987:1.

Hermann Ebbinghaus 1850–1909
German psychologist

1 What is true [in psychology] is alas not new, the new not true.

Über die hartmannsche Philosophie des Unbewussten 1873:67.

2 *De subjecto vetustissimo novissimam promovemus scientiam* [From the most ancient subject we shall produce the newest science].

Selected by Ebbinghaus as the epigraph to *Memory* (1885) 1913.

3 It is with something of a struggle that past states of feeling are realized; when realized, and this is often only through the instrumentality of the movements which accompanied them, they are but pale shadows of themselves. Emotionally true singing is rarer than technically correct singing.

Memory (1885) 1913:3.

4 Psychology has a long past, yet its real history is short.

Psychology 1908:3.

Francis Ysidro Edgeworth 1845–1926
Irish-born British economist and statistician

1 He that will not verify his conclusions as far as possible by mathematics, as it were bringing the ingots of common sense to be assayed and coined at the mint of sovereign science, will hardly realize the full value of what he holds, will want a measure of what it will be worth in however slightly altered circumstances, a means of conveying and making it current.

Mathematical Psychics 1881:3.

2 For moral calculus a further dimension is required; to compare the happiness of one person with the happiness of another, and generally the happiness of groups of different members and different average happiness.

Mathematical Psychics 1881:7.

3 *Atoms of pleasure* are not easy to distinguish and discern; more continuous than sand, more discrete than liquid; as it were nuclei of the just-perceivable, embedded in circumambient semi-consciousness.

We cannot *count* the golden sands of life; we cannot *number* the "innumerable smile" of seas of love; but we seem to be capable of observing that there is here a *greater*, there a *less*, multitude of pleasure-units, mass of happiness; and that is enough.

Mathematical Psychics 1881:8–9.

4 "Mécanique Sociale" may one day take her place along with "Mécanique Celeste," throned each upon the double-sided height of one maximum principle, the supreme pinnacle of moral as of physical science. As the movements of each particle, constrained or loose, in a material cosmos are continually subordinated to one maximum sum-total of accumulated energy, so the movements of each soul, whether selfishly isolated or linked sympathetically, may continually be realising the maximum energy of pleasure, the Divine love of the universe.

Mathematical Psychics 1881:12.

5 The first principle of Economics is that every agent is actuated only by self-interest.

Mathematical Psychics 1881:16.

6 Observations and statistics agree in being quantities grouped about a Mean; they differ, in that the Mean of observations is real, of statistics is fictitious. The mean of

observations is a cause, as it were the source from which diverging errors emanate. The mean of statistics is a description, a representative quantity put for a whole group, the best representative of the group, that quantity which, if we must in practice put one quantity for many, minimizes the error unavoidably attending such practice. Thus measurements by the reduction of which we ascertain a real time, number, distance, are observations. Returns of prices, exports and imports, legitimate and illegitimate marriages or births and so forth, the averages of which constitute the premises of practical reasoning, are statistics. In short observations are different copies of one original; statistics are different originals affording one "generic portrait." Different measurements of the same man are observations; but measurements of different men, grouped round l'homme moyen, are primâ facie at least statistics.

Observations and Statistics 1885:139–140.

7 The Calculus of Probabilities is an instrument which requires the living hand to direct it.

Metretike 1887:18.

8 International trade meaning in plain English trade between nations, it is not surprising that the term should mean something else in Political Economy.

The Pure Theory of International Values (1894) 1925:5.

Albert Einstein 1879–1955
German-born U.S. physicist

1 The description of me and my circumstances in the *Times* shows an amusing feat of imagination on the part of the writer. By an application of the theory of relativity to the taste of readers, to-day in Germany I am called a German man of science, and in England I am represented as a Swiss Jew. If I come to be regarded as a *bête noire* the descriptions will be reversed, and I shall become a Swiss Jew for the Germans and a German man of science for the English!

Einstein on His Theory 1919:14.

2 *Raffiniert ist der Herr Gott, aber boshaft ist er nicht* [The Lord is subtle, but he is not malicious].

Comment, April 1921. Quoted in Abraham Pais, "*Subtle Is the Lord. . .*" (1982) 1983:113. → On his first visit to the United States in 1921, Einstein lectured at Princeton University. While there, he heard that a "nonzero aether drift" had been found at Mount Wilson observatory. This was his comment. It is carved in stone over a fireplace in the building at Princeton that formerly housed the Department of Mathematics.

S.N. Eisenstadt 1923–
Polish-born Israeli sociologist

1 For the social system [age] serves as a category according to which various roles are allocated to various people; for the individual, the awareness of his own age becomes an important integrative element, through its influence on his self-identification. The categorization of oneself as a member of a given age stage serves as an important basis for one's self-perception and role expectations towards others.

From Generation to Generation (1956) 1971:28.

2 The most general traits of political modernization are, on the one hand, continuous development of a high extent of differentiation, unification, and centralization of the political system, and, on the other hand, continuous development of a high extent of "free-floating" . . . political power and resources.

Political Modernization (1964) 1973:74.

Elizabeth L. Eisenstein 1923–
U.S. historian

1 By paying more attention to the duplication of pictorial statements, we might see more clearly why the life sciences no less than the physical ones were placed on a new footing and how the authority of Pliny, no less than that of Galen and Ptolemy, was undermined. Even while acknowledging the importance of the empirical movement and of the slogan "from books to nature" it should be noted that dissatisfaction with literature inherited from scribes coincided with the development of new forms of data collection. The advent of printing made it possible for more of nature to be put into books.

The Printing Press as an Agent of Change 1979: Vol. 2, 686–687.

2 Intellectual and spiritual life. . . were profoundly transformed by the multiplication of the new tools for duplicating books in fifteenth century Europe. The communications shift altered the way Western Christians viewed their sacred book and the natural world. It made the words of God appear more multiform and His handiwork more uniform. The printing press laid the basis for both literal fundamentalism and for modern science. It remains indispensible for humanistic scholarship. It is still responsible for our museum-without-walls.

The Printing Press as an Agent of Change 1979: Vol. 2, 704.

Mircea Eliade 1907–1986
Romanian-born U.S. historian of religion

1 Myths serve as models for ceremonies that periodically reactualize the tremendous events that occurred at the beginning of time. The myths preserve and transmit the paradigms, the exemplary models, for all the responsible activities in which men engage. By virtue of these paradigmatic models revealed to men in mythical times, the Cosmos and society are periodically regenerated.

The Myth of the Eternal Return (1949) 1971:xiv. → From the preface to the English edition.

2 As the rite always consists in the repetition of an archetypal action performed *in illo tempore* (before "history" began) by ancestors or by gods, man is trying, by means of the hierophany, to give "being" to even his most ordi-

nary and insignificant acts. By its repetition, the act coincides with its archetype, and time is abolished.

Patterns in Comparative Religion (1949) 1958:32.

Norbert Elias 1897–1990
German-born British sociologist

1 [Out of] the interweaving of innumerable individual interests and intentions — be they compatible, or opposed and inimical — something eventually emerges that, as it turns out, has neither been planned nor intended by any single individual. And yet it has been brought about by the intentions and actions of many individuals. And this is actually the whole secret of social interweaving — of its compellingness, its regularity, its structure, its processual nature, and its development; this is the secret of sociogenesis and social dynamics.

Über den Prozess der Zivilisation 1969:Vol.2,221.

2 The concept of figuration draws attention to people's interdependencies. What actually binds people together into figurations? Questions like this cannot be answered if we start by considering all individual people on their own, as if each were a *Homo clausus*. . . There is a tacit assumption that societies — figurations formed by interdependent people — are fundamentally no more than congeries of individual atoms. . . The atomic view of society is certainly based in part on an inability to see that these structures, be they marriages or parliaments, economic crises or wars, can be neither understood nor explained by reducing them to the behaviour of their separate participants.

What Is Sociology? (1970) 1978:132–133.

Havelock Ellis 1859–1939
British psychologist

1 I regard sex as the central problem of life. And now that the problem of religion has practically been settled, and that the problem of labor has at least been placed on a practical foundation, the question of sex — with the racial questions that rest on it — stands before the coming generations as the chief problem for solution. Sex lies at the root of life, and we can never learn to reverence life until we know how to understand sex.

Studies in the Psychology of Sex (1897) 1936:Vol. 1, xxx.

Jacques Ellul 1912–
French legal historian

1 "Detechnicization" is impossible. The scope of the system is such that we cannot hope to go back. If we attempted a detechnicization, we would be like primitive forest-dwellers setting fire to their native environment.

The Technological System (1977) 1980:82.

Jon Elster 1940–
Norwegian political scientist, sociologist, and philosopher

1 [By the term counterfinality I] understand *unintended consequences that arise when each individual in a group acts upon an assumption about his relations to others that, when generalized, yields the contradiction in the consequent of the fallacy of composition, the antecedent of that fallacy being true*. It is clear that counterfinality thus defined is a species of real contradictions. . . The requirement that the antecedent of the inference be true, i.e. that there be nothing contradictory in the individual assumptions taken separately guarantees individual rationality. The collective irrationality arises only from the incompatibility of the belief systems.

Logic and Society 1978:106.

2 Given certain structural conditions, such as spatial proximity between group members or low turnover rates in the group, contradictions tend to generate collective action for the purpose of overcoming the contradictions. This collective action may have the effect of reversing or halting the process of change, viz. if the contradiction to be overcome is itself a vehicle of change. If, on the other hand, the contradictions are stable configurations of society, the political process will bring about a change if successful. As collective action, therefore, may both prevent and generate change, the conditions for such action may function both as conditions for stability and as conditions for change. In this sense, I am proposing a *dual* theory of social change.

Logic and Society 1978:134.

3 In the older body of literature rational-choice models were often associated with the assumption that behaviour is motivated merely by egoistic, hedonistic or narrowly self-interested purposes, and the phenomena of altruistic behaviour were either denied or believed to create an insuperable anomaly for these models. At a superficial level this link between rationality and narrowly conceived self-interest can no longer be upheld. Economists of most persuasions agree that the consumption (or even the utility) of other people can enter as an argument in my utility function. My utility may go down as a result of an increase in other people's consumption (as in envy) or it may go up (as in altruism). My welfare may depend in part upon the consumption of some specific person or persons (as in love) or upon the average level of consumption (as in the search for status.). In altruistic gift-giving, the very act of giving may be evaluated positively, over and above the positive evaluation of the pleasure taken in the gift by the recipient.

Ulysses and the Sirens [1979] 1984:141–142.

4 [A] category of paradoxes is paradigmatically given by Groucho Marx's saying "I would not dream of belonging to a club that is willing to have me as a member." . . . Someone willing to recognize *me* must obviously be unworthy of recognition, and his recognition of me equally worthless. (In the master-slave paradox the worthless-

ness of the recognizer, i.e. the slave, is the starting point, while the lack of worth of the recognition, and thus of the recognized, is the conclusion. It can truly be said, therefore, that Marx stood Hegel on his head.) Anyone observing small children at play will have seen this paradox, when one refuses to accept an object that he has solicited because he reckons that it must be pretty worthless if the other is willing to part with it. I also believe that writers sometimes fall victim to this fallacy: if anyone praises their work this automatically disqualifies him from being a serious critic. This, of course, is a form of hubris rather than of excessive modesty, for if anyone fails to praise their work this is seen as equally disqualifying.

Ulysses and the Sirens [1979] 1984:152–153.

5 The most fundamental reason why the Soviet rulers are unable to achieve their goals is found in the lack of reliable information. The omnipotence-cum-impotence of despotism in this respect is classically captured by Tocqueville: "the sovereign can punish immediately any faults he discovers, but he cannot flatter himself into supposing that he sees all the faults he should punish." In the Soviet Union reliable information does not exist, or if it does, cannot be reliably distinguished from the unreliable. The flaw of the system is that all acts tend to have an immediate political significance, which means that information degenerates into informing and so becomes worthless for planning purposes. Or else the information is offered that the informant believes his superiors want to hear, even if they insist on information that reflects the world as it is rather than the world as they would like it to be. The tradition of punishing or at least not rewarding the bearer of bad news is too ingrained for such insistence to be taken seriously. Both the KGB and Gosplan suffer accordingly.

Sour Grapes 1983:88.

6 I would like to suggest that social systems are more malleable than the individuals that make them up, and that great changes will occur [in the Soviet Union] once the lid is taken off. Perhaps one could even hope for a drift towards freedom.

Sour Grapes 1983:89.

Geoffrey Rudolph Elton

See ROBERT WILLIAM FOGEL AND GEOFFREY RUDOLPH ELTON.

Ralph Waldo Emerson 1803–1882

U.S. philosopher and poet

1 All history becomes subjective; in other words there is properly no history, only biography.

History (1841) 1950:127.

2 A man Caesar is born, and for ages after we have a Roman Empire. Christ is born, and millions of minds so grow and cleave to his genius that he is confounded with virtue and the possible of man. An institution is the lengthened shadow of one man.

Self-Reliance (1841) 1940:154.

3 Men are what their mothers made them.

Fate (1860) 1979:10.

Ernst Engel 1821–1896

German statistician and economist

1 *Je ärmer eine Familie ist, einen desto grösseren Antheil von der Gesamtausgabe muss zur Beschaffung der Nahrung aufgewendet werden* [The poorer a family, the greater the proportion of its total expenditure that must be devoted to the provision of food].

Die Productions- und Consumtionsverhältnisse des Königreichs Sachsen (1857) 1895:28–29. → Known as Engel's law of consumption. George J. Stigler (1954:98) has described the research into the expenditures of working-class families that led to this law as "the first and most famous of all statistical analyses of [family] budgets."

Friedrich Engels 1820–1895

German economist, sociologist, and revolutionary

1 Economics is not concerned with things but with relations between persons, and in the final analysis between classes; these relations, however, are always *bound to things* and *appear as things*. Some economists had an inkling of this connection in isolated instances, but Marx was the first to reveal its significance for the whole of economics, thus making the most difficult problems so simple and clear that even bourgeois economists will now be able to grasp them.

Review of *A Contribution to the Critique of Political Economy*, by Karl Marx (1859) 1980:476.

2 The first act by virtue of which the state really constitutes itself the representative of the whole of society — the taking possession of the means of production in the name of society — this is, at the same time, its last independent act as a state. State interference in social relations becomes, in one domain after another, superfluous, and then dies out of itself; the government of persons is replaced by the administration of things, and by the conduct of processes of production. The state is not "abolished." *It dies out*.

Anti-Dühring (1878) 1987:268. → "It dies out" is often translated as "it withers away."

3 [The stock exchange is the] highest vocation for a capitalist, where property merges directly with theft.

Letter to Eduard Bernstein, 10 February 1883. 1956:430.

4 Just as Darwin discovered the law of development of organic nature, so Marx discovered the law of development of human history: the simple fact, hitherto concealed by an overgrowth of ideology, that mankind must first of all eat, drink, have shelter and clothing, before it can pursue politics, science, art, [and] religion.

Speech at the Graveside of Karl Marx (1883) 1950:153.

5 The modern individual family is based on the open or disguised domestic enslavement of the woman; and mod-

ern society is a mass composed solely of individual families as its molecules. Today, in the great majority of cases, the man has to be the earner, the breadwinner of the family, at least among the propertied classes, and this gives him a dominating position which requires no special legal privileges. In the family, he is the bourgeois; the wife represents the proletariat.

The Origin of the Family, Private Property and the State (1884) 1950:211–212.

6 The democratic republic does not abolish the antagonism between the two classes; on the contrary, it provides the field on which it is fought out. And, similarly, the peculiar character of man's domination over woman in the modern family, and the necessity, as well as the manner, of establishing real social equality between the two, will be brought out into full relief only when both are completely equal before the law. It will then become evident that the first premise for the emancipation of women is the reintroduction of the entire female sex into public industry; and that this again demands that the quality possessed by the individual family of being the economic unit of society be abolished.

The Origin of the Family, Private Property and the State (1884) 1950:212.

7 What I contributed — at any rate with the exception of my work in a few special fields — Marx could very well have done without me. What Marx accomplished I would not have achieved. Marx stood higher, saw farther, and took a wider and quicker view than all the rest of us. Marx was a genius; we others were at best talented. Without him the theory would not be by far what it is today. It therefore rightly bears his name.

Ludwig Feuerbach and the End of Classical German Philosophy (1888) 1950:349n.

8 According to the materialist conception of history, the *ultimately* determining element in history is the production and reproduction of real life. More than this neither Marx nor I have ever asserted. Hence if somebody twists this into saying that the economic element is the *only* determining one, he transforms that proposition into a meaningless, abstract, senseless phrase.

Letter to Joseph Bloch, 21–22 September 1890. 1956:498.

9 Ideology is a process accomplished by the so-called thinker consciously, it is true, but with a false consciousness.

Letter to Franz Mehring, 14 July 1893. 1956:541.

[*See also* Karl Marx and Friedrich Engels.]

Erik H. Erikson 1902–

German-born U.S. psychologist and psychoanalyst

1 We do not consider all development a series of crises: we claim only that psychosocial development proceeds by critical steps — "critical" being a characteristic of turning points, of moments of decision between progress and regression, integration and retardation.

Childhood and Society (1950) 1963:270–271.

2 The study of identity. . . becomes as strategic in our time as the study of sexuality was in Freud's time.

Childhood and Society (1950) 1963:282.

3 *Psychosocial Crises in the Life Cycle*

Old Age	Integrity versus Despair
Adulthood	Generativity versus Stagnation
Young Adulthood	Intimacy versus Isolation
Adolescence	Identity versus Confusion
School Age	Industry versus Inferiority
Play Age	Initiative versus Guilt
Early Childhood	Autonomy versus Shame, Doubt
Infancy	Basic Trust versus Basic Mistrust

Life Cycle (1950) 1968:287.

4 What was Freud's Galapagos, what species fluttered what kinds of wings before his searching eyes? It has often been pointed out derisively: his creative laboratory was the neurologist's office, the dominant species hysterical ladies.

The First Psychoanalyst 1957:83.

5 Ideological leaders. . . are subject to excessive fears which they can master only by reshaping the thoughts of their contemporaries; while those contemporaries are always glad to have their thoughts shaped by those who so desperately care to do so. Born leaders seem to fear only more consciously what in some form everybody fears in the depths of his inner life; and they convincingly claim to have an answer.

Young Man Luther (1958) 1962:110.

6 Am I saying. . . that "anatomy is destiny"? Yes, it is destiny, insofar as it determines not only the range and configuration of physiological functioning and its limitation but also, to an extent, personality configurations.

Identity: Youth and Crisis 1968:285. → See Freud:20.

7 [For his associates], Freud had created simultaneously a training institute, a clientele, a publishing house, and, of course, a new professional identity.

"Identity Crisis" in Autobiographic Perspective (1970) 1975:23.

8 It would seem almost self-evident now how the concepts of "identity" and "identity crisis" emerged from my per-

sonal, clinical, and anthropological observations in the thirties and forties. I do not remember when I started to use these terms; they seemed naturally grounded in the experience of emigration, immigration, and Americanization.

"Identity Crisis" in Autobiographic Perspective (1970) 1975:43.

9 Psychohistory. . . is the study of individual and collective life with the combined methods of psychoanalysis and history. In spite of, or because of, the very special and conflicting demands made on the practitioners of these two fields, bridgeheads must be built on each side in order to make a true span possible. But the completed bridge should permit unimpeded two-way traffic; and once this is done, history will simply be history again, but now a history aware of the fact that it has always indulged in a covert and circuitous traffic with psychology which can now be direct, overt, and aware. By the same token, psychoanalysis will have become conscious of its own historical determinants, and *case history* and *life history* will no longer be manners of speaking. The way you "take history" is also a way of "making history."

Dimensions of a New Identity 1974:13.

Kai T. Erikson 1931–
U.S. sociologist

1 It is the *community* that cushions pain, the *community* that provides a context for intimacy, the *community* that represents morality and serves as the repository for old traditions.

Everything in Its Path 1976:193–194.

Euripides c. 484–406 B.C.
Greek playwright

1 [*Menelaus*]: As with sailing,
so with politics: make your cloth too taut,
and your ship will dip and keel, but slacken off
and trim your sails, and things head up again.
The gods, you know, resent being importuned
too much; in the same way the people dislike
being pushed or hustled. Too much zeal offends
where indirection works.

Orestes:232.

E. E. Evans-Pritchard 1902–1973
British anthropologist

1 If Pareto for civilized peoples, and Lévy-Bruhl for savages, had given us a detailed account of their real life during an ordinary day we would be able to judge whether their non-logical behaviour is as qualitatively and quantitatively important as the writers' selective methods would lead us to suppose. Actually, I would contend, non-logical conduct plays a relatively minor part in the behaviour of either primitive or civilized man and is relatively of minor importance.

Science and Sentiment 1936:184.

2 Just as the linguist does not merely learn to understand, speak and translate a native language but seeks to reveal its phonological and grammatical systems, so the social anthropologist is not content merely to observe and describe the social life of a primitive people but seeks to reveal its underlying structural order, the patterns which, once established, enable him to see it as a whole, as a set of interrelated abstractions.

Social Anthropology (1948) 1964:61–62.

3 The thesis I have put before you, that social anthropology is a kind of historiography, and therefore ultimately of philosophy or art, implies that it studies societies as moral systems and not as natural systems, that it is interested in design rather than in process, and that it therefore seeks patterns and not scientific laws, and interprets rather than explains.

Social Anthropology: Past and Present (1950) 1964:152.

4 Just as we can understand the anatomy and physiology of a horse without requiring to know anything about its descent from its five-toed ancestor, so we can understand the structure of a society and the functioning of its institutions without knowing anything about its history. But a society, however defined, in no way resembles a horse, and, mercifully, horses remain horses — or at least they have done so in historic times — and do not turn into elephants or pigs, whereas a society may change from one type to another, sometimes with great suddenness and violence.

Anthropology and History (1961) 1964:181.

5 Any claim to universality demands in the nature of things a historical or psychological, rather than a sociological, explanation, and thereby defeats the sociological purpose, which is to explain differences rather than similarities.

The Comparative Method in Social Anthropology 1963:16.

6 It has sometimes been said that we will be able to establish the laws of social life when we know more and better attested facts, but the contrary appears to be the case. It was easy for anthropologists to speculate about primitive institutions when little was known about them. It is not so easy now, when negative instances, vouched for by competent professional research, crop up everywhere to dispute any general theory.

The Comparative Method in Social Anthropology 1963:25.

F

Frantz Fanon 1925–1961
Martinique-born Algerian psychiatrist and revolutionary

At the level of individuals, violence is a cleansing force. It frees the native from his inferiority complex and from his despair and inaction; it makes him fearless and restores his self-respect. . . When the people have taken violent part in the national liberation, they will allow no one to set themselves up as "liberators." They show themselves to be jealous of the results of their action and take good care not to place their future, their destiny or the fate of their country in the hands of a living god. Yesterday they were completely irresponsible; today they mean to understand everything and make all decisions. Illuminated by violence, the consciousness of the people rebels against any pacification.

The Wretched of the Earth (1961) 1966:73–74.

It is within this mass of humanity, this people of the shanty towns, at the core of the *lumpen-proletariat* that the rebellion will find its urban spearhead. For the *lumpen-proletariat,* that horde of starving men, uprooted from their tribe and from their clan, constitutes one of the most spontaneous and the most radically revolutionary forces of a colonised people.

The Wretched of the Earth (1961) 1966:103.

Lucien Febvre 1878–1956
French historian

There are no necessities, but everywhere possibilities; and man, as master of the possibilities, is the judge of their use. This, by the reversal which it involves, puts man in the first place — man, and no longer the earth, nor the influence of climate, nor the determinant conditions of localities.

A Geographical Introduction to History (1922) 1966:236.

It is never a waste of time to study the history of a word.

Civilisation (1930) 1973:219.

Leon Festinger 1919–1989
U.S. psychologist

1 The basic hypotheses I wish to state are as follows:

1. The existence of dissonance, being psychologically uncomfortable, will motivate the person to try to reduce the dissonance and achieve consonance.

2. When dissonance is present, in addition to trying to reduce it, the person will actively avoid situations and information which would likely increase the dissonance.

A Theory of Cognitive Dissonance 1957:3.

2 The inclination to engage in behavior after extrinsic rewards are removed is not so much a function of past rewards themselves. Rather, and paradoxically, such persistence in behavior is increased by a history of nonrewards or inadequate rewards. I sometimes like to summarize all this by saying that rats and people come to love things for which they have suffered.

The Psychological Effects of Insufficient Rewards 1961:11.

Ludwig Andreas Feuerbach 1804–1872
German philosopher

1 Theology is Anthropology. . . The distinction which is made, or rather supposed to be made, between the theological and anthropological predicates resolves itself into an absurdity.

The Essence of Christianity (1841) 1957:xxxvii.

2 In place of the illusory, fantastic, heavenly position of man which in actual life necessarily leads to the degradation of man, I substitute the tangible, actual, and consequently also the political and social position of mankind. The question concerning the existence or non-existence of God is for me nothing but the question concerning the existence or non-existence of man.

Sämtliche Werke 1846:Vol. 1, xiv–xv.

Paul Feyerabend 1924–
Austrian-born U.S. philosopher of science

1 The idea of a fixed method, or of a fixed theory of rationality, rests on too naive a view of man and his social surroundings. To those who look at the rich material provided by history, and those who are not intent on impoverishing it in order to please their lower instincts, their craving for intellectual security in the form of clarity, precision, "objectivity," "truth," it will become clear that there is only *one* principle that can be defended under *all* circumstances and in *all* stages of human development. It is the principle: *anything goes.*

Against Method (1975) 1988:19. → In a preface written for the revised edition, Feyerabend notes that "anything goes" is not a principle that he holds but rather "the terrified exclamation of a rationalist who takes a closer look at history" (page vii).

2 Unanimity of opinion may be fitting for a church, for the frightened or greedy victims of some (ancient, or modern) myth, or for the weak and willing followers of some tyrant. Variety of opinion is necessary for objective knowledge. And a method that encourages variety is also the only method that is compatible with a humanitarian outlook.

Against Method (1975) 1988:32.

Quentin Fiore

See MARSHALL MCLUHAN AND QUENTIN FIORE.

J. R. Firth 1890–1960
British linguist

1 Most of the give-and-take of conversation in our everyday life is stereotyped and very narrowly conditioned by our particular type of culture. It is a sort of roughly prescribed social ritual, in which you generally say what the other fellow expects you, one way or the other, to say.

The Technique of Semantics (1935) 1957:31. → This resembles what Malinowski termed "phatic communion." See MALINOWSKI:7.

Raymond Firth 1901–
New Zealand-born British anthropologist

1 In the practice of the magic itself there are normally three elements: the things used; the things done; the things spoken. The first element is represented by the *instruments* or *medicines*; the second is the *rite*; the third is the *spell.*

Human Types (1938) 1958:126.

2 As in magic, the rites of a religion are a means of bringing belief and desire together by a set procedure. Ritual is the bridge between faith and action.

Human Types (1938) 1958:144.

Irving Fisher 1867–1947
U.S. economist

1 The so-called "quantity theory," *i.e.* that prices vary proportionately to money, has often been incorrectly formulated, but. . . the theory is correct in the sense that the level of prices varies directly with the quantity of money in circulation, provided the velocity of circulation of that money and the volume of trade which it is obliged to perform are not changed.

The Purchasing Power of Money (1911) 1922:14.

2 Spending and investing differ only in degree, depending on the length of time elapsing between the expenditure and the enjoyment.

The Theory of Interest (1930) 1954:9.

3 Other things being equal, the smaller the income, the higher the preference for present over future income; that is, the greater the impatience to acquire income as early as possible.

The Theory of Interest (1930) 1954:72.

4 Man is the most versatile of all forms of capital, and among the wide range of choices as to the disposition of his energies is the choice between using them for immediate or for remote returns.

The Theory of Interest (1930) 1954:200.

5 The uncertainty of life itself casts a shadow on every business transaction into which time enters.

The Theory of Interest (1930) 1954:216.

R. A. Fisher 1890–1962
British statistician and geneticist

1 If one in twenty does not seem high enough odds, we may, if we prefer it, draw the line at one in fifty (the 2 per cent. point), or one in a hundred (the 1 per cent. point). Personally, the writer prefers to set a low standard of significance at the 5 per cent. point, and ignore entirely all results which fail to reach this level. A scientific fact should be regarded as experimentally established only if a properly designed experiment *rarely fails* to give this level of significance.

The Arrangement of Field Experiments (1926) 1972:85.

2 No aphorism is more frequently repeated in connection with field trials, than that we must ask Nature few questions, or, ideally, one question, at a time. The writer is convinced that this view is wholly mistaken. Nature, he suggests, will best respond to a logical and carefully thought out questionnaire; indeed, if we ask her a single question, she will often refuse to answer until some other topic has been discussed.

The Arrangement of Field Experiments (1926) 1972:92.

3 The statistician cannot excuse himself from the duty of getting his head clear on the principles of scientific inference, but equally no other thinking man can avoid a like obligation.

The Design of Experiments (1935) 1971:2.

4 Inductive inference is the only process known to us by which essentially new knowledge comes into the world.

The Design of Experiments (1935) 1971:7.

5 Men have always been capable of some mental processes of the kind we call "learning by experience." Doubtless this experience was often a very imperfect basis, and the reasoning processes used in interpreting it were very insecure; but there must have been in these processes a sort of embryology of knowledge, by which new knowledge was gradually produced. Experimental observations are only experience carefully planned in advance, and designed to form a secure basis of new knowledge; that is, they are systematically related to the body of knowledge already acquired, and the results are deliberately observed, and put on record accurately.

The Design of Experiments (1935) 1971:8.

6 No isolated experiment, however significant in itself, can suffice for the experimental demonstration of any natural phenomenon; for the "one chance in a million" will undoubtedly occur, with no less and no more than its appropriate frequency, however surprised we may be that it should occur to *us*.

The Design of Experiments (1935) 1971:13–14. → See DIACONIS AND MOSTELLER:1.

Frederick Gard Fleay 1831–1909
British Shakespearian scholar

1 Our analysis, which has hitherto been qualitative, must become quantitative; we must cease to be empirical, and become scientific: in criticism as in other matters, the test that decides between science and empiricism is this: "Can you say, not only of what kind, but how much? If you cannot weigh, measure, number your results, however you may be convinced yourself, you must not hope to convince others, or claim the position of an investigator; you are merely a guesser, a propounder of hypotheses."

On Metrical Tests as Applied to Dramatic Poetry 1874:3. → See KELVIN:1.

Ludwik Fleck 1896–1961
Polish microbiologist and sociologist of science

1 If we define "thought collective" as a community of persons mutually exchanging ideas or maintaining intellectual interaction, we will find by implication that it also provides the special "carrier" for the historical development of any field of thought, as well as for the given stock of knowledge and level of culture. This we have designated thought style.

Genesis and Development of a Scientific Fact (1935) 1979:39. → Thomas S. Kuhn notes in the Preface to his consequential work, *The Structure of Scientific Revolutions* (1962), that Fleck's "almost unknown monograph. . . anticipates many of my own ideas."

2 The individual within the collective is never, or hardly ever, conscious of the prevailing thought style, which almost always exerts an absolutely compulsive force upon his thinking and with which it is not possible to be at variance.

Genesis and Development of a Scientific Fact (1935) 1979:41.

3 The following state of affairs [*Sachverhalt*] is therefore firmly established and can be regarded as a paradigm of many discoveries. *From false assumptions and irreproducible initial experiments an important discovery has resulted after many errors and detours.* The principal actors in the drama cannot tell us how it happened, for they rationalize and idealize the development. Some among the eyewitnesses talk about a lucky accident, and the well-disposed about the intuition of a genius. It is quite clear that the claims of both parties are of no scientific value.

Genesis and Development of a Scientific Fact (1935) 1979:76.

4 This is how *a fact* arises. *At first there is a signal of resistance in the chaotic initial thinking, then a definite thought constraint, and finally a form to be directly perceived.* A fact always occurs in the context of the history of thought and is always the result of a definite thought style.

Genesis and Development of a Scientific Fact (1935) 1979:95.

Robert William Fogel 1926–
U.S. economic historian

1 Political forces, not economic ones, were the overriding factors in the destruction of slavery. If the foes of slavery had waited for economic forces to do their work for them, America might still be a slave society, and democracy, as we know it, might have been a subject only for history books.

Without Consent or Contract 1989:11.

Robert William Fogel 1926–
U.S. economic historian
and
Geoffrey Rudolph Elton 1921–
German-born British historian

1 Among the current discussions, the impact of new and sophisticated methods in the study of the past occupies an important place. The new "scientific" or "cliometric" history — born of the marriage contracted between historical problems and advanced statistical analysis, with economic theory as bridesmaid and the computer as best man — has made tremendous advances in the last generation.

Which Road to the Past? 1983:3.

Robert William Fogel 1926–
and
Stanley L. Engerman 1936–
U.S. economic historians

1 Time on the cross did not come to an end for American blacks with the downfall of the peculiar institution. For

they were held on the cross not just by the chains of slavery but also by the spikes of racism. It is one of the bitterest ironies of history that the antislavery critics who worked so hard to break these chains probably did as much as any other group, perhaps more, to fasten the spikes that have kept blacks in the agony of racial discrimination during their century of freedom.

Time on the Cross 1974:263.

Mary Parker Follett 1868–1933
U.S. social philosopher

1 [The individual] is in himself the whole of society. It is not that the whole is divided up into pieces; the individual is the whole at one point. This is the incarnation.

The New State (1918) 1920:66.

2 We must remember that most people are not for or against anything; the first object of getting people together is to make them respond somehow, to overcome inertia. To disagree, as well as to agree, with people brings you closer to them. I always feel intimate with my enemies. It is not opposition but indifference which separates men.

The New State (1918) 1920:212.

Henry Ford 1863–1947
U.S. industrialist

1 History is more or less bunk. It's tradition. We want to live in the present and the only history that is worth a tinker's damn is the history we make today.

Quoted in Carol Gelderman, *Henry Ford* 1981:177. → From a 1916 interview with Charles Wheeler of the *Chicago Tribune*.

Meyer Fortes 1906–1983
South African-born British anthropologist

1 When we describe structure we are already dealing with general principles far removed from the complicated skein of behaviour, feelings, beliefs, &c., that constitute the tissue of actual social life. We are, as it were, in the realm of grammar and syntax, not of the spoken word. We discern structure in the "concrete reality" of social events only by virtue of having first established structure by abstraction from "concrete reality."

Time and Social Structure (1949) 1963:56.

Michel Foucault 1926–1984
French philosopher

1 In its raw, historical sixteenth-century being, language is not an arbitrary system; it has been set down in the world and forms a part of it, both because things themselves hide and manifest their own enigma like a language and because words offer themselves to men as things to be deciphered. The great metaphor of the book that one opens, that one pores over and reads in order to know nature, is merely the reverse and visible side of another transference, and a much deeper one, which forces language to reside in the world, among the plants, the herbs, the stones, and the animals.

The Order of Things (1966) 1973:35.

2 To seek in the great accumulation of the already-said the text that resembles "in advance" a later text, to ransack history in order to rediscover the play of anticipations or echoes, to go right back to the first seeds or to go forward to the last traces, to reveal in a work its fidelity to tradition or its irreducible uniqueness, to raise or lower its stock of originality, to say that the Port-Royal grammarians invented nothing, or to discover that Cuvier had more predecessors than one thought, these are harmless enough amusements for historians who refuse to grow up.

The Archeology of Knowledge (1969) 1976:144.

3 "Effective" history differs from traditional history in being without constants. Nothing in man — not even his body — is sufficiently stable to serve as the basis for self-recognition or for understanding other men. The traditional devices for constructing a comprehensive view of history and for retracing the past as a patient and continuous development must be systematically dismantled. . . History becomes "effective" to the degree that it introduces discontinuity into our very being — as it divides our emotions, dramatizes our instincts, multiplies our body and sets it against itself.

Nietzsche, Genealogy, History (1971) 1977:153–154.

4 One of the great innovations in the techniques of power in the eighteenth century was the emergence of "population" as an economic and political problem: population as wealth, population as manpower or labor capacity, population balanced between its own growth and the resources it commanded. Governments perceived that they were not dealing simply with subjects, or even with a "people," but with a "population."

The History of Sexuality (1976) 1978:Vol. 1, 25.

5 Power is not something that is acquired, seized, or shared, something that one holds on to or allows to slip away; power is exercised from innumerable points, in the interplay of nonegalitarian and mobile relations. . . Power comes from below; that is, there is no binary and all-encompassing opposition between rulers and ruled at the root of power relations, and serving as a general matrix — no such duality extending from the top down and reacting on more and more limited groups to the very depths of the social body.

The History of Sexuality (1976) 1978:Vol. 1, 94.

6 Let us not. . . ask why certain people want to dominate, what they seek, what is their overall strategy. Let us ask, instead, how things work at the level of on-going subjugation, at the level of those continuous and uninterrupted processes which subject our bodies, govern our gestures, dictate our behaviours etc. In other words, rather than ask ourselves how the sovereign appears to us in his lofty isolation, we should try to discover how it is that subjects are gradually, progressively, really and materially constituted through a multiplicity of organisms, forces, energies, materials, desires, thoughts etc. We should try to

grasp subjection in its material instance as a constitution of subjects. This would be the exact opposite of Hobbes' project in *Leviathan*.

Two Lectures (1976) 1980:97.

Each society has its régime of truth, its "general politics" of truth: that is, the types of discourse which it accepts and makes function as true; the mechanisms and instances which enable one to distinguish true and false statements, the means by which each is sanctioned; the techniques and procedures accorded value in the acquisition of truth; the status of those who are charged with saying what counts as true.

Truth and Power (1977) 1980:131.

"Truth" is to be understood as a system of ordered procedures for the production, regulation, distribution, circulation and operation of statements.

"Truth" is linked in a circular relation with systems of power which produce and sustain it, and to effects of power which it induces and which extend it. A "régime" of truth.

This régime is not merely ideological or superstructural; it was a condition of the formation and development of capitalism.

Truth and Power (1977) 1980:133.

Power relations are rooted deep in the social nexus, not reconstituted "above" society as a supplementary structure whose radical effacement one could perhaps dream of. In any case, to live in society is to live in such a way that action upon other actions is possible — and in fact ongoing. A society without power relations can only be an abstraction.

The Subject and Power (1982) 1983:222–223.

Anatole France 1844–1924
[Jacques Anatole François Thibault]
French novelist, poet, and playwright

[*Choulette*]: We in France are soldiers and we are citizens. Our citizenship is another occasion for pride! For the poor it consists in supporting and maintaining the rich in their power and their idleness. At this task they must labour in the face of the majestic equality of the laws, which forbid rich and poor alike to sleep under bridges, to beg in the streets, and to steal their bread. This equality is one of the benefits of the Revolution.

The Red Lily (1894) 1917?:75.

Felix Frankfurter 1882–1965
Austrian-born U.S. jurist

The history of liberty has largely been the history of the observance of procedural safeguards.

McNabb v. *United States,* 318 U.S. 347, 1943.

As judges we are neither Jew nor Gentile, neither Catholic nor agnostic. We owe equal attachment to the Constitution and are equally bound by our obligations whether we derive our citizenship from the earliest or the latest immigrants to these shores.

West Virginia State Board of Education et al. v. *Barnette et al.,* 319, U.S. 624,1943.

3 It was a wise man who said that there is no greater inequality than the equal treatment of unequals.

Dennis v. *United States* 339 U.S. 184, 1950.

4 In a democratic society like ours, relief must come through an aroused popular conscience that sears the conscience of the people's representatives.

Baker v. *Carr,* 369 U.S. 270, 1962.

Benjamin Franklin 1706–1790
U.S. statesman and scientist

1 Historians relate, not so much what is done, as what they would have believed.

Poor Richard's Almanack (1739) 1987:1212.

2 Our new Constitution is now established, and has an appearance that promises permanency; but in this world nothing can be said to be certain, except death and taxes.

Letter to Jean Baptiste Le Roy, 13 November 1789. 1907:69.

James George Frazer 1854–1941
British anthropologist

1 There is more liberty in the best sense — liberty to think our own thoughts and to fashion our own destinies — under the most absolute despotism, the most grinding tyranny, than under the apparent freedom of savage life, where the individual's lot is cast from the cradle to the grave in the iron mould of hereditary custom.

The Golden Bough (1890) 1922:55.

2 By religion. . . I understand a propitiation or conciliation of powers superior to man which are believed to direct and control the course of nature and of human life. Thus defined, religion consists of two elements, a theoretical and a practical, namely, a belief in powers higher than man and an attempt to propitiate or please them.

The Golden Bough (1890) 1922:57–58.

3 The awe and dread with which the untutored savage contemplates his mother-in-law are amongst the most familiar facts of anthropology.

The Golden Bough (1890) 1922:221.

4 Of the benefactors whom we are bound thankfully to commemorate, many, perhaps most, were savages. For when all is said and done our resemblances to the savage are still far more numerous than our differences from him; and what we have in common with him, and deliberately retain as true and useful, we owe to our savage forefathers who slowly acquired by experience and trans-

mitted to us by inheritance those seemingly fundamental ideas which we are apt to regard as original and intuitive.

The Golden Bough (1890) 1922:307.

5 [Buddhism and Christianity] in exact proportions to their growing popularity, absorbed more and more of those baser elements which they had been instituted for the very purpose of suppressing. Such spiritual decadences are inevitable. The world cannot live at the level of its great men. Yet it would be unfair to the generality of our kind to ascribe wholly to their intellectual and moral weakness the gradual divergence of Buddhism and Christianity from their primitive patterns. For it should never be forgotten that by their glorification of poverty and celibacy both these religions struck straight at the root not merely of civil society but of human existence.

The Golden Bough (1890) 1922:420.

6 The history of thought should warn us against concluding that because the scientific theory of the world is the best that has yet been formulated, it is necessarily complete and final. We must remember that at bottom the generalisations of science or, in common parlance, the laws of nature are merely hypotheses devised to explain that ever-shifting phantasmagoria of thought which we dignify with the high-sounding names of the world and the universe. In the last analysis magic, religion, and science are nothing but theories of thought.

The Golden Bough (1890) 1922:825–826.

7 The idea of regarding the religions of the world not dogmatically but historically — in other words, not as systems of truth or falsehood to be demonstrated or refuted, but as phenomena of consciousness to be studied like any other aspects of human nature — is one which seems hardly to have suggested itself before the nineteenth century.

William Robertson Smith (1894) 1927:281–282. → Frazer's comment on Robertson Smith's contribution to the comparative study of religion.

8 It is the fate of theories to be washed away. . . and I am not so presumptuous as to expect or desire for mine an exemption from the common lot. I hold them all very lightly and have used them chiefly as convenient pegs on which to hang my collection of facts.

The Golden Bough. Quoted in Abram Kardiner and Edward Preble, *They Studied Man* 1961:90–91.

E. Franklin Frazier 1894–1962
U.S. sociologist

1 The evolution of the Negro family in the United States has a special significance for the science of culture. Within the short space of one hundred and fifty years, the Negro family has telescoped the age-long evolution of the human family. On the basis of concrete factual materials it is possible to trace the evolution of the Negro family from its roots in human nature to a highly institutionalized form of human association.

The Negro Family 1949:142.

Edward Augustus Freeman 1823–1892
British historian

1 History is past politics and. . . politics are present history.

The Methods of Historical Study 1886:44.

2 To write about history or language is supposed to be within the reach of every man. To write about natural science is allowed to be within the reach only of those who have mastered the subjects on which they write.

The Methods of Historical Study 1886:91.

Else Frenkel-Brunswik 1908–1958
Austro-Hungarian born U.S. psychologist

1 Intolerance of emotional and cognitive ambiguity seems not only to be a characteristic of the personality of the ethnically prejudiced; it also appears as part of the explicitly stated ego-ideal of exponents of the Nazi ideology in professional psychology. The most notable case is that of E. R. Jaensch with his programatic glorification of a personality type characterized by fixed relationships between stimuli and perceptual responses, and with his rejection of the school of Gestalt psychology mainly on the ground of its stress on the concept of ambiguity.

Dynamic and Cognitive Personality Organization as Seen through the Interviews 1949:464.

Sigmund Freud 1856–1939
Austrian psychoanalyst

1 Charcot, who is one of the greatest of physicians and a man whose common sense borders on genius, is simply wrecking all my aims and opinions. I sometimes come out of his lectures as from out of Notre-Dame, with an entirely new idea about perfection.

Letter to Martha Bernays, 24 November 1885. 1961:196.

2 I have often felt as though I had inherited all the defiance and all the passions with which our ancestors defended their Temple and could gladly sacrifice my life for one great moment in history.

Letter to Martha Bernays, 2 February 1886. 1961:215.

3 I am inclined to suppose that children cannot find their way to acts of sexual aggression unless they have been seduced previously. The foundation for a neurosis would accordingly always be laid in childhood by adults.

The Aetiology of Hysteria (1896) 1962:208–209.

4 The wish-fulfilment theory gives only the psychological and not the biological, or rather metapsychological explanation. . . Biologically dream-life seems to me to proceed directly from the residue of the prehistoric stage of life (one to three years), which is the source of the unconscious and alone contains the aetiology of all the psychoneuroses; the stage which is normally obscured by an amnesia similar to hysteria.

Letter to Wilhelm Fliess, 10 March 1898. 1954:246.

5 It would be one of the greatest triumphs of humanity, one of the most tangible liberations from the constraints of nature to which mankind is subject, if we could succeed in raising the responsible act of procreating children to the level of a deliberate and intentional activity and in freeing it from its entanglement with the necessary satisfaction of a natural need.

Sexuality in the Aetiology of the Neuroses (1898) 1962:277.

6 Reality — wish-fulfillment: it is from this contrasting pair that our mental life springs.

Letter to Wilhelm Fliess, 19 February 1899. 1954:277.

7 *The Interpretation of Dreams*. . . contains. . . the most valuable of all the discoveries it has been my good fortune to make. Insight such as this falls to one's lot but once in a lifetime.

The Interpretation of Dreams (1900) 1958:xxxii. → From the preface to the 1932 English edition.

8 Being in love with the one parent and hating the other are among the essential constituents of the stock of psychical impulses which is formed at that time and which is of such importance in determining the symptoms of the later neurosis. . . This discovery is confirmed by a legend that has come down to us from classical antiquity: a legend whose profound and universal power to move can only be understood if the hypothesis I have put forward in regard to the psychology of children has an equally universal validity. What I have in mind is the legend of King Oedipus and Sophocles' drama which bears his name.

The Interpretation of Dreams (1900) 1958:260–261.

9 Every attempt that has hitherto been made to solve the problem of dreams has dealt directly with their *manifest* content as it is presented in our memory. . . We have introduced a new class of psychical material between the manifest content of dreams and the conclusions of our enquiry: namely, their *latent* content, or (as we say) the "dream-thoughts," arrived at by means of our procedure. It is from these dream-thoughts and not from a dream's manifest content that we disentangle its meaning.

The Interpretation of Dreams (1900) 1958:277.

10 It is my experience, and one to which I have found no exception, that every dream deals with the dreamer himself. Dreams are completely egoistic.

The Interpretation of Dreams (1900) 1958:322.

11 The act of birth is the first experience of anxiety, and thus the source and prototype of the affect of anxiety.

The Interpretation of Dreams (1900) 1958:400–401. → A footnote added in 1909.

12 Dreams, which fulfil their wishes along the short path of regression, have merely preserved for us in that respect a sample of the psychical apparatus's primary method of working, a method which was abandoned as being inefficient. What once dominated waking life, while the mind was still young and incompetent, seems now to have been banished into the night — just as the primitive weapons, the bows and arrows, that have been abandoned by adult men, turn up once more in the nursery. *Dreaming is a piece of infantile mental life that has been superseded.*

The Interpretation of Dreams (1900) 1958:567.

13 When I described one of the psychical processes occurring in the mental apparatus as the "primary" one, what I had in mind was not merely considerations of relative importance and efficiency; I intended also to choose a name which would give an indication of its chronological priority. . . The primary processes are present in the mental apparatus from the first, while it is only during the course of life that the secondary processes unfold, and come to inhibit and overlay the primary ones.

The Interpretation of Dreams (1900) 1958:603.

14 The interpretation of dreams is the royal road to a knowledge of the unconscious activities of the mind.

The Interpretation of Dreams (1900) 1958:608.

15 The unconscious is the true psychical reality; *in its innermost nature it is as much unknown to us as the reality of the external world, and it is as incompletely presented by the data of consciousness as is the external world by the communications of our sense organs.*

The Interpretation of Dreams (1900) 1958:613.

16 There is a great deal of symbolism. . . in life, but as a rule we pass it by without heeding it. When I set myself the task of bringing to light what human beings keep hidden within them, not by the compelling power of hypnosis, but by observing what they say and what they show, I thought the task was a harder one than it really is. He that has eyes to see and ears to hear may convince himself that no mortal can keep a secret. If his lips are silent, he chatters with his finger-tips; betrayal oozes out of him at every pore.

Fragment of an Analysis of a Case of Hysteria (1905) 1953:77–78.

17 The most striking distinction between the erotic life of antiquity and our own no doubt lies in the fact that the ancients laid the stress upon the instinct itself, whereas we emphasize its object. The ancients glorified the instinct and were prepared on its account to honour even an inferior object; while we despise the instinctual activity in itself, and find excuses for it only in the merits of the object.

Three Essays on the Theory of Sexuality (1905) 1953:149. → From a footnote added in 1910.

18 No one who has seen a baby sinking back satiated from the breast and falling asleep with flushed cheeks and a blissful smile can escape the reflection that this picture persists as a prototype of the expression of sexual satisfaction in later life.

Three Essays on the Theory of Sexuality (1905) 1953:182.

19 [Transference] provides the impulsion for comprehending and translating the unconscious; where it refuses to act, the patient does not take this trouble, or does not listen when we present the translation we have found. It is essentially a cure through love.

Letter to Carl Gustav Jung, 6 December 1906. → Translated by Peter Gay.

20 The excremental is all too intimately and inseparably bound up with the sexual; the position of the genitals — *inter urinas et faeces* — remains the decisive and unchangeable factor. One might say here, varying a well-known saying of the great Napoleon: "Anatomy is destiny."

On the Universal Tendency to Debasement in the Sphere of Love (1912) 1957:189. → See NAPOLEON I:1 and ERIK H. ERIKSON:6.

21 I cannot advise my colleagues too urgently to model themselves during psycho-analytic treatment on the surgeon, who puts aside all his feelings, even his human sympathy, and concentrates his mental forces on the single aim of performing the operation as skilfully as possible.

Recommendations to Physicians Practising Psycho-Analysis (1912) 1958:115.

22 The doctor should be opaque to his patients and, like a mirror, should show them nothing but what is shown to him.

Recommendations to Physicians Practising Psycho-Analysis (1912) 1958:118.

23 Even in the later stages of analysis one must be careful not to give a patient the solution of a symptom or the translation of a wish until he is already so close to it that he has only one short step more to make in order to get hold of the explanation for himself.

On Beginning the Treatment (1913) 1958:140.

24 One day the brothers who had been driven out came together, killed and devoured their father and so made an end of the patriarchal horde. United, they had the courage to do and succeeded in doing what would have been impossible for them individually. (Some cultural advance, perhaps, command over some new weapon, had given them a sense of superior strength.) Cannibal savages as they were, it goes without saying that they devoured their victim as well as killing him. The violent primal father had doubtless been the feared and envied model of each one of the company of brothers: and in the act of devouring him they accomplished their identification with him, and each one of them acquired a portion of his strength. The totem meal, which is perhaps mankind's earliest festival, would thus be a repetition and a commemoration of this memorable and criminal deed, which was the beginning of so many things — of social organization, of moral restrictions and of religion.

Totem and Taboo (1913) 1958:141–142.

25 The very deed in which the son offered the greatest possible atonement to the father brought him at the same time to the attainment of his wishes *against* the father. He himself became God, beside, or, more correctly, in place of, the father. A son-religion displaced the father-religion. As a sign of this substitution the ancient totem meal was revived in the form of communion, in which the company of brothers consumed the flesh and blood of the son — no longer the father — obtained sanctity thereby and identified themselves with him. . . The Christian communion, however, is essentially a fresh elimination of the father, a repetition of the guilty deed.

Totem and Taboo (1913) 1958:154–155.

26 Sexual love is undoubtedly one of the chief things in life, and the union of mental and bodily satisfaction in the enjoyment of love is one of its culminating peaks. Apart from a few queer fanatics, all the world knows this and conducts its life accordingly; science alone is too delicate to admit it.

Observations on Transference-Love (1915) 1958:169–170.

27 The strongest egotists as children can become the most helpful citizens, those most capable of self-sacrifice. Most enthusiasts for compassion — *Mitleidsschwärmer* — friends of humanity, protectors of animals, have evolved from little sadists and animal tormentors.

Thoughts for the Times on War and Death (1915) 1957:282. → Translation by Peter Gay.

28 It would be a mistake to suppose that a science consists entirely of strictly proved theses, and it would be unjust to require this. Only a disposition with a passion for authority will raise such a demand, someone with a craving to replace his religious catechism by another, though it is a scientific one. Science has only a few apodeictic propositions in its catechism: the rest are assertions promoted by it to some particular degree of probability. It is actually a sign of a scientific mode of thought to find satisfaction in these approximations to certainty and to be able to pursue constructive work further in spite of the absence of final confirmation.

Introductory Lectures on Psycho-Analysis (1916-1917) 1961:51.

29 The ego is not master in its own house.

A Difficulty in the Path of Psycho-Analysis (1917) 1955:143. → This is Freud's metaphor to describe the blow to human narcissism struck by psychoanalysis.

30 Let us keep before our eyes the nature of the emotional relations which hold between men in general. According to Schopenhauer's famous simile of the freezing porcupines no one can tolerate a too intimate approach to his neighbour.

Group Psychology and the Analysis of the Ego (1921) 1955:101. → In *Parerga und Paralipomena* (1851) 1988 [Vol. 2, 559–560], Schopenhauer tells of porcupines who huddle together in the winter to keep warm, but separate as they feel each other's quills, until they discover "a mean distance at which they could most tolerably exist."

31 I named this process *repression*; it was a novelty, and nothing like it had ever before been recognized in mental life.

An Autobiographical Study (1925) 1959:30.

32 We know less about the sexual life of little girls than of boys. But we need not feel ashamed of this distinction; after all, the sexual life of adult women is a "dark continent" for psychology.

The Question of Lay Analysis (1926) 1959:212. → The phrase "dark continent" is in English in the original.

33 The poets and philosophers before me discovered the unconscious. . . What I discovered was the scientific method by which the unconscious can be studied.

Remark, 1926. Quoted in Lionel Trilling, Freud and Literature (1940) 1950:34. → A remark made on the occasion of the celebration of his 70th birthday.

34 Before the problem of the creative writer, analysis must lay down its arms.

Dostoevsky and Parricide (1928) 1961:177. → Translation by Peter Gay.

35 In what was at first my utter perplexity, I took as my starting-point a saying of the poet-philosopher, Schiller, that "hunger and love are what moves the world."

Civilization and Its Discontents (1930) 1961:117.

36 People [without superegos] habitually allow themselves to do any bad thing which promises them enjoyment, so long as they are sure that the authority will not know anything about it or cannot blame them for it; they are afraid only of being found out.

Civilization and Its Discontents (1930) 1961:125.

37 A child's super-ego is in fact constructed on the model not of its parents but of its parents' super-ego; the contents which fill it are the same and it becomes the vehicle of tradition and of all the time-resisting judgements of value which have propagated themselves in this manner from generation to generation.

New Introductory Lectures on Psycho-Analysis (1933) 1964:67.

38 Where id was, there ego shall be.

New Introductory Lectures on Psycho-Analysis (1933) 1964:80.

39 Homosexuality is assuredly no advantage, but it is nothing to be ashamed of, no vice, no degradation; it cannot be classified as an illness; we consider it to be a variation of the sexual function, produced by a certain arrest of sexual development. Many highly respectable individuals of ancient and modern times have been homosexuals, several of the greatest men among them (Plato, Michelangelo, Leonardo da Vinci, etc.). It is a great injustice to persecute homosexuality as a crime — and a cruelty, too. If you do not believe me, read the books of Havelock Ellis.

Letter to Mrs. . . . 9 April 1935. 1961:419–420.

40 Every normal person, in fact, is only normal on the average. His ego approximates to that of the psychotic in some part or other and to a greater or lesser extent.

Analysis Terminable and Interminable (1937) 1964:235.

41 We know two kinds of things about what we call our psyche (or mental life): firstly, its bodily organ and scene of action, the brain (or nervous system) and, on the other hand, our acts of consciousness, which are immediate data and cannot be further explained by any sort of description. Everything that lies between is unknown to us, and the data do not include any direct relation between these two terminal points of our knowledge.

An Outline of Psycho-Analysis (1940) 1964:144.

42 After long hesitancies and vacillations we have decided to assume the existence of only two basic instincts, *Eros* and *the destructive instinct*. . . The aim of the first of these basic instincts is to establish ever greater unities and to preserve them thus — in short, to bind together; the aim of the second is, on the contrary, to undo connections and so to destroy things. In the case of the destructive instinct we may suppose that its final aim is to lead what is living into an inorganic state. For this reason we also call it the *death instinct*.

An Outline of Psycho-Analysis (1940) 1964:148.

43 The great question that has never been answered and which I have not yet been able to answer, despite my thirty years of research into the feminine soul, is "What does a woman want?" [*Was will das Weib?*]

Remark to Marie Bonaparte. Quoted in Ernest Jones, *The Life and Work of Sigmund Freud* 1955:Vol.2,421.

[*See also* Josef Breuer and Sigmund Freud.]

Gilberto Freyre 1900–1987
Brazilian sociologist

1 Every Brazilian, even the light-skinned fair-haired one, carries about with him on his soul, when not on soul and body alike — for there are many in Brazil with the mongrel mark of the *genipap* — the shadow, or at least the birthmark, of the aborigine or the Negro. . .

In our affections, our excessive mimicry, our Catholicism, which so delights the senses, our music, our gait, our speech, our cradle songs — in everything that is a sincere expression of our lives, we almost all of us bear the mark of that influence. Of the female slave or "mammy" who rocked us to sleep. Who suckled us. Who fed us, mashing our food with her own hands. The influence of the old woman who told us our first tales of ghost and *bicho*. Of the mulatto girl who relieved us of our first *bicho de pé*, of a pruriency that was so enjoyable. Who initiated us into physical love and, to the creaking of a canvas cot, gave us our first complete sensation of being a man. Of the Negro lad who was our first playmate.

The Masters and the Slaves (1933) 1963:278.

Betty Friedan 1921–
U.S. writer

1 The problem that has no name stirring in the minds of so many American women today is not a matter of loss of femininity or too much education, or the demands of domesticity. It is far more important than anyone recognizes. It is the key to these other new and old problems which have been torturing women and their husbands and children, and puzzling their doctors and educators for years. It may well be the key to our future as a nation and a culture. We can no longer ignore that voice within women that says: "I want something more than my husband and my children and my home."

The Feminine Mystique (1963) 1983:32.

2 Who knows what women can be when they are finally free to become themselves? Who knows what women's intelligence will contribute when it can be nourished without denying love? Who knows of the possibilities of love when men and women share not only children, home, and garden, not only the fulfillment of their biological roles, but the responsibilities and passions of the work that creates the human future and the full human knowledge of who they are? It has barely begun, the search of women for themselves. But the time is at hand when the voices of the feminine mystique can no longer drown out the inner voice that is driving women to become complete.

The Feminine Mystique (1963) 1983:378.

3 I think the energy locked up in. . . obsolete masculine and feminine roles is the social equivalent of the physical energy locked up in the realm of $E = MC^2$ — the force that unleashed the holocaust of Hiroshima. I believe the locked-up sexual energies have helped to fuel, more than anyone realizes, the terrible violence erupting in the nation and the world during these past ten years. If I am right, the sex-role revolution will liberate these energies from the service of death and will make it really possible for men and women to "make love, not war."

The Feminine Mystique (1963) 1983:395. → From the epilogue to the 1983 edition.

Milton Friedman 1912–
U.S. economist

1 The role of the economist in discussions of public policy seems to me to be to prescribe what should be done in the light of what can be done, politics aside, and not to predict what is "politically feasible" and then to recommend it.

Comments on Monetary Policy (1951) 1953:264.

2 History suggests only that capitalism is a necessary condition for political freedom. Clearly it is not a sufficient condition. . . It is. . . clearly possible to have economic arrangements that are fundamentally capitalist and political arrangements that are not free.

Capitalism and Freedom 1962:10.

3 Fundamentally, there are only two ways of co-ordinating the economic activities of millions. One is central direction involving the use of coercion — the technique of the army and of the modern totalitarian state. The other is voluntary co-operation of individuals — the technique of the market place.

Capitalism and Freedom 1962:13.

4 The greater part of the new ventures undertaken by government in the past few decades have failed to achieve their objectives. The United States has continued to progress; its citizens have become better fed, better clothed, better housed, and better transported; class and social distinctions have narrowed; minority groups have become less disadvantaged; popular culture has advanced by leaps and bounds. All this has been the product of the initiative and drive of individuals co-operating through the free market. Government measures have hampered not helped this development. We have been able to afford and surmount these measures only because of the extraordinary fecundity of the market. The invisible hand has been more potent for progress than the visible hand for retrogression.

Capitalism and Freedom 1962:199–200. → Adam Smith's "invisible hand" and the counter-formulation "visible hand" are in frequent use by social scientists, e.g., Peter Reuter's *Disorganized Crime: The Economics of the Visible Hand* (1983). See ADAM SMITH:1.

5 Inflation is always and everywhere a monetary phenomenon.

Inflation: Causes and Consequences (1963) 1968:39.

6 Sir: You quote me [Dec. 31] as saying: "We are all Keynesians now." The quotation is correct, but taken out of context. As best I can recall it, the context was: "In one sense, we are all Keynesians now; in another, nobody is any longer a Keynesian." The second half is at least as important as the first.

Letter to the Editor, *Time*, 4 February 1966:13.

7 There is a far better way to guarantee a minimum annual income to all than our present grab bag of programs. That way is to use the mechanism by which we collect the bulk of our taxes, namely, the personal income tax. At one time, citizens were required to contribute to the support of the commonwealth by payments in kind — forced collections of food or timber or forced labor on public projects. That is still the rule in many backward areas and is widely practiced in all totalitarian countries. Both freedom and efficiency were fostered by substituting taxes in money for taxes in kind. . .

I have termed this device for helping the poor a negative income tax in order to stress its identity in concept and operation with the present income tax. The essential idea is to extend the income tax by supplementing the income of the poor by a *fraction* of their unused income tax exemptions and deductions.

The Case for the Negative Income Tax (1968) 1987:57–58.

8 I know of no economist of any standing. . . who has favored a legal limit on the rate of interest that borrowers could pay or lenders receive — though there must have been some. I know of no country that does not limit by law the rates of interest — and I doubt that there are any. As Bentham wrote, "in great political questions, wide indeed is the distance between conviction and practice."

Defense of Usury 1970:79.

9 In both social and natural sciences, the body of positive knowledge grows by the failure of a tentative hypothesis to predict phenomena the hypothesis professes to explain; by the patching up of that hypothesis until someone suggests a new hypothesis that more elegantly or simply embodies the troublesome phenomena, and so on ad infinitum. In both, experiment is sometimes possible, sometimes not (witness meteorology). In both, no experiment is ever completely controlled, and experience often offers evidence that is the equivalent of controlled experiment. In both, there is no way to have a self-contained closed system or to avoid interaction between the observer and the observed. The Gödel theorem in mathematics, the Heisenberg uncertainty principle in physics, the self-fulfilling or self-defeating prophecy in the social sciences all exemplify these limitations.

Inflation and Unemployment (1976) 1987:348.

Carl J. Friedrich 1901–1984
German-born U.S. political scientist
and
Zbigniew K. Brzezinski 1928–
Polish-born U.S. political scientist

1 The "syndrome," or pattern of interrelated traits, of the totalitarian dictatorship consists of an ideology, a single party typically led by one man, a terroristic police, a communications monopoly, a weapons monopoly, and a centrally directed economy.

Totalitarian Dictatorship and Autocracy (1956) 1961:9.

Ragnar Frisch 1895–1973
Norwegian economist

1 Experience has shown that each of these three viewpoints, that of statistics, economic theory, and mathematics, is a necessary, but not by itself a sufficient, condition for a real understanding of the quantitative relations in modern economic life. It is the *unification* of all three that is powerful. And it is this unification that constitutes econometrics.

Editorial in *Econometrica* 1933:2.

Erich Fromm 1900–1980
German-born U.S. psychoanalyst

1 The family is the medium through which the society or the social class stamps its specific structure on the child, and hence on the adult. *The family is the psychological agency of society.*

The Method and Function of an Analytic Social Psychology (1932) 1978:483.

2 Modern man, freed from the bonds of pre-individualistic society, which simultaneously gave him security and limited him, has not gained freedom in the positive sense of the realization of his individual self; that is, the expression of his intellectual, emotional and sensuous potentialities. Freedom, though it has brought him independence and rationality, has made him isolated and, thereby, anxious and powerless.

Escape from Freedom 1941:viii.

3 Man is not only made by history — history is made by man. The solution of this seeming contradiction constitutes the field of social psychology. Its task is to show not only how passions, desires, anxieties change and develop as a *result* of the social process, but also how man's energies thus shaped into specific forms in their turn become *productive forces, molding the social process.*

Escape from Freedom 1941:13–14.

4 Man does not only sell commodities, he sells himself and feels himself to be a commodity.

Escape from Freedom 1941:119.

5 In order that any society may function well, its members must acquire the kind of character which makes them *want* to act in the way they *have* to act as members of the society or of a special class within it. They have to *desire* what objectively is *necessary* for them to do.

Individual and Social Origins of Neurosis 1944:381.

Robert Frost 1874–1963
U.S. poet

1 Why abandon a belief
Merely because it ceases to be true.
Cling to it long enough, and not a doubt
It will turn true again, for so it goes.
Most of the change we think we see in life
Is due to truths being in and out of favour.

The Black Cottage (1914) 1939:77.

François Furet 1927–
French historian and sociologist

1 Politics is the quintessential realm of chance, and so of freedom. It gives history the structure of a novel, except that its plot must be composed of authentic facts verified according to the rules; and this history is indeed the true novel of nations.

In the Workshop of History (1982) 1984:9.

Numa Denis Fustel de Coulanges 1830–1889
French historian

1 The history of Greece and Rome is a witness and an example of the intimate relation which always exists between men's ideas and their social state. Examine the institutions of the ancients without thinking of their religious notions, and you find them obscure, whimsical, and inexplicable.

The Ancient City (1864) 1979:12.

2 Fortunately, the past never completely dies for man. Man may forget it, but he always preserves it within him. For, take him at any epoch, and he is the product, the epitome, of all the earlier epochs. Let him look into his own soul, and he can find and distinguish these different epochs by what each of them has left within him.

The Ancient City (1864) 1979:14.

3 We shall always be powerless to understand the ancients if we continue to study them in thinking of ourselves. It is in themselves, and without any comparison with us that we must observe them.

Questions historiques 1893:406.

4 In order to search for some great truth one has almost always first of all to refute some great error.

Quoted in James Westfall Thompson, *A History of Historical Writing* (1942) 1967:Vol. 2, 371.

5 It is not I who speak, but History which speaks through me.

Quoted in James Westfall Thompson, *A History of Historical Writing* (1942) 1967:Vol. 2, 456. → Said as a rebuke to some students who applauded him.

6 Patriotism is a virtue and history a science, and the two should not be confounded.

Quoted in Fritz Stern, *The Varieties of History* 1956:178.

G

Hans Georg von der Gabelentz 1840–1893
German philologist

1 Every language is a system, all parts of which organically cohere and interact. As one can imagine, no component can be absent or even different, without transforming the whole.

Die Sprachwissenschaft (1891) 1901:481. → Unpublished translation by Michael Silverstein.

John Kenneth Galbraith 1908–
Canadian-born U.S. economist

1 New restraints on private power did appear to replace competition. They were nurtured by the same process of concentration which impaired or destroyed competition. But they appeared not on the same side of the market but on the opposite side, not with competitors but with customers and suppliers. It will be convenient to have a name for this counterpart of competition and I shall call it countervailing power.

American Capitalism (1952) 1980:111.

2 Private economic power is held in check by the countervailing power of those who are subject to it. The first begets the second. The long trend toward concentration of industrial enterprise in the hands of a relatively few firms has brought into existence not only strong sellers, as economists have supposed, but also strong buyers as they have failed to see. The two develop together, not in precise step but in such manner that there can be no doubt that the one is in response to the other.

American Capitalism (1952) 1980:111.

3 Nothing in economics so quickly marks an individual as incompetently trained as a disposition to remark on the legitimacy of the desire for more food and the frivolity of the desire for a more elaborate automobile.

The Affluent Society 1958:147.

4 The notion of independently determined wants still survives [and is] the ultimate triumph of the conventional wisdom in its resistance to the evidence of the eyes.

The Affluent Society 1958:157.

5 A society which sets as its highest goal the production of private consumer goods will continue to reflect such attitudes in all its public decisions. It will entrust public decisions to men who regard any other goal as incredible — or radical.

The Affluent Society 1958:352.

6 Keynes had long been suspect among his colleagues for the clarity of his writing and thought, the two often going together. In *The General Theory* he redeemed his academic reputation. It is a work of profound obscurity, badly written and prematurely published.

Money 1975:217–218.

7 It was with Malthus and Ricardo that economics became the dismal science.

The Age of Uncertainty 1977:35. → See CARLYLE:8.

Ferdinando Galiani 1728–1787
Italian economist

1 In the immense machinery of society, everything hangs together, is connected, and linked. Nothing must disturb the equilibrium lest the whole mechanism overturn. That is why I recommend nothing more strongly than the avoidance of shocks and sudden moves. The shocks break the contacts and springs, and the mechanism is destroyed.

Dialogues sur le commerce des blés 1770:279.

Francis Galton 1822–1911
British statistician and biometrician

1 Exercising the right of occasional suppression and slight modification, it is truly absurd to see how plastic a limited number of observations become, in the hands of men with preconceived ideas.

Meteorographica 1863:5.

2 The processes concerned in simple descent are those of Family Variability and Reversion. It is well to define these words clearly. By family variability is meant the departure of the children of the same or similarly descended families from the ideal mean type of all of them. Reversion is the tendency of that ideal mean type to depart from the parent type, "reverting" towards what may be roughly and perhaps fairly described as the average ancestral type. If family variability had been the only process in simple descent, the dispersion of the race would indefinitely increase with the number of the generations, but reversion checks this increase, and brings it to a standstill.

Typical Laws of Heredity 1877:513. → Although Galton introduced the concept of regression in 1877, it was not until 1885 that he adopted the term in place of his initial term, "reversion."

3 It must be clearly understood that my inquiry is primarily into the inheritance of different degrees of tallness and shortness. That is to say, of measurements made from the crown of the head to the level of mediocrity, upwards or downwards as the case may be, and not from the crown of the head to the ground. In the population with which I deal, the level of mediocrity is 68¼ inches (without shoes). The same law, applying with sufficient closeness both to tallness and shortness, we may include both under the single head of deviations, and I shall call any particular deviation a "deviate." By the use of this word and that of "mid-parentage," we can define the law of regression very briefly. It is that the height-deviate of the offspring is, on the average, two-thirds of the height-deviate of its mid-parentage.

Section H: Anthropology; Opening Address 1885:508.

4 Two variable organs are said to be co-related when the variation of the one is accompanied on the average by more or less variation of the other, and in the same direction. Thus the length of the arm is said to be co-related with that of the leg, because a person with a long arm has usually a long leg, and conversely. If the co-relation be close, then a person with a very long arm would usually have a very long leg; if it be moderately close, then the length of his leg would usually be only long, not very long; and if there were no co-relation at all then the length of his leg would on the average be mediocre. It is easy to see that co-relation must be the consequence of the variations of the two organs being partly due to common causes. If they were wholly due to common causes, the co-relation would be perfect, as is approximately the case with the symmetrically disposed parts of the body. If they were in no respect due to common causes, the co-relation would be *nil*. Between these two extremes are an endless number of intermediate cases, and it will be shown how the closeness of co-relation in any particular case admits of being expressed by a simple number.

Co-relations and Their Measurement 1888:135–136. → This is Galton's first explicit discussion of his invention, correlation. Here he introduced what he called the "index of co-relation," later called the correlation coefficient.

5 *The Charms of Statistics.* — It is difficult to understand why statisticans commonly limit their inquiries to Averages, and do not revel in more comprehensive views. Their souls seem as dull to the charm of variety as that of the native of one of our flat English counties, whose retrospect of Switzerland was that, if its mountains could be thrown into its lakes, two nuisances would be got rid of at once. An Average is but a solitary fact, whereas if a single other fact be added to it, an entire Normal Scheme, which nearly corresponds to the observed one, starts potentially into existence.

Some people hate the very name of statistics, but I find them full of beauty and interest. Whenever they are not brutalised, but delicately handled by the higher methods, and are warily interpreted, their power of dealing with complicated phenomena is extraordinary. They are the only tools by which an opening can be cut through the formidable thicket of difficulties that bars the path of those who pursue the Science of man.

Natural Inheritance 1889:62–63.

6 Whenever you can, count.

Quoted in James R. Newman, Commentary on Sir Francis Galton 1956:1169.

Mohandas K. Gandhi 1869–1948
Indian political leader

1 Satyagraha largely appears to the public as Civil Disobedience or Civil Resistance. It is civil in the sense that it is not criminal. The lawbreaker . . . openly and civilly breaks [unjust laws] and quietly suffers the penalty for their breach. . . In my opinion, the beauty and efficacy of Satyagraha are so great and the doctrine so simple that it can be preached even to children.

Non-violent Resistance (1951) 1961:6–7.

Harold Garfinkel 1917–
U.S. sociologist

1 [Ethnomethodological] studies seek to treat practical activities, practical circumstances, and practical sociological reasoning as topics of empirical study, and by paying to the most commonplace activities of daily life the attention usually accorded extraordinary events, seek to learn about them as phenomena in their own right.

Studies in Ethnomethodology 1967:1.

2 *Routine* [*is*] *a necessary condition of rational action.* . . . Sociological inquiry accepts almost as a truism that the ability of a person to act "rationally" — that is the ability of a person in *conducting his everyday affairs* to calculate; to act deliberately; to project alternative plans of action; to select before the actual fall of events the conditions under which he will follow one plan or another; to give priority in the selection of means to their technical efficacy; to be much concerned with predictability and desirous of "surprise in small amounts"; to prefer the analysis of alternatives and consequences prior to action in preference of improvisation; to be much concerned with questions of what is to be done and how it is to be

done. . . This ability depends upon the person being able to take for granted, to take under trust, a vast array of features of the social order.

Studies in Ethnomethodology 1967:172–173.

Peter Gay 1923–
German-born U.S. historian

1 Macaulay's most discriminating readers found his style wearisome and ultimately profoundly irritating, the style of an orator who smuggles onto the printed page tricks suitable to a debate in the House of Commons, if there. As a committed public speaker, he exaggerates his points, constructs false antitheses, grows heated beyond measure, expands immense ingenuity underlining the obvious and proving the self-evident. He argues all the time: he is always making a case, and sounds as sure of it as only a debater can. His airs and graces, his acrobatic pirouettes, far from concealing, only advertise the essential corruptness of his historical work: he is an advocate rather than a historian, and, to make things worse, a Whig advocate. He professes to detest — and, worse, he really detests — what he is too limited to grasp: the subtler points of philosophy, the mysteries of poetry, the sheer historical interest of personages or causes he does not find sympathetic. Matthew Arnold called Macaulay a philistine, in fact the "Prince of Philistines," a verdict with which Leslie Stephen, with all due caution, concurred; Gladstone called him vulgar — in Greek. All his critics conceded Macaulay the quality of clarity, but he seemed to them clear with illegitimate means and for illegitimate purposes. With Macaulay, clarity somehow becomes a vice.

Macaulay: Intellectual Voluptuary 1974:97–98.

2 It is no accident that Freud should have called the reward one obtains from looking or reading or listening by a name — forepleasure — he borrowed from the most earthy of gratifications. To his mind, aesthetic work, much like the making of love or war, of laws or constitutions, is a way of mastering the world, or of disguising one's failure to master it.

Freud 1988:322.

3 The papers making up *Totem and Taboo* were weapons in Freud's competition with Jung. Freud was displaying in his own struggles an aspect of the oedipal wars often scanted — the father's efforts to best the son. Above all the last and most militant of his four papers, published after his break with Jung, was sweet revenge on the crown prince who had proved so brutal to him and so treacherous to psychoanalysis.

Freud 1988:326.

Peter Gay 1923–
German-born U.S. historian
and
Gerald J. Cavanaugh 1930–
U.S. historian

1 "To namierize" means to establish through close analysis of family identity, party status, and political loyalties the processes of political and social change and the workings of parliamentary systems.

Lewis B. Namier 1975:272.

Clifford Geertz 1926–
U.S. anthropologist

1 It is true that without men there would be no cultural forms; but it is also true that without cultural forms there would be no men.

The Growth of Culture and the Evolution of Mind 1962:736.

2 A pattern of behavior shaped by a certain set of forces turns out, by a plausible but nevertheless mysterious coincidence, to serve ends but tenuously related to those forces. A group of primitives sets out, in all honesty, to pray for rain and ends up by strengthening its social solidarity; a ward politician sets out to get or remain near the trough and ends up mediating between unassimilated immigrant groups and an impersonal government bureaucracy.

Ideology as a Cultural System 1964:56.

3 The road to the general, to the revelatory simplicities of science, lies through a concern with the particular, the circumstantial, the concrete, but a concern organized and directed in terms of the sort of theoretical analyses that I have touched upon — analyses of physical evolution, of the functioning of the nervous system, of social organization, of psychological process, of cultural patterning, and so on — and, most especially, in terms of the interplay among them. That is to say, the road lies, like any genuine Quest, through a terrifying complexity.

The Impact of the Concept of Culture on the Concept of Man (1966) 1973:53–54.

4 A religion is: (1) a system of symbols which acts to (2) establish powerful, pervasive, and long-lasting moods and motivations in men by (3) formulating conceptions of a general order of existence and (4) clothing these conceptions with such an aura of factuality that (5) the moods and motivations seem uniquely realistic.

Religion as a Cultural System (1966) 1973:90.

5 As a religious problem, the problem of suffering is, paradoxically, not how to avoid suffering but how to suffer, how to make of physical pain, personal loss, worldly defeat, or the helpless contemplation of others' agony something bearable, supportable — something, as we say, sufferable.

Religion as a Cultural System (1966) 1973:104.

6 [Culture] no longer has the grandiose, all-promising scope, the infinite versatility of apparent application, it once had. The second law of thermodynamics, or the principle of natural selection, or the notion of unconscious motivation, or the organization of the means of production does not explain everything, not even everything human, but it still explains something; and our attention shifts to isolating just what that something is, to disentangling ourselves from a lot of pseudoscience to

which, in the first flush of its celebrity, it has also given rise.

Thick Description 1973:4.

7 From one point of view, that of the textbook, doing ethnography is establishing rapport, selecting informants, transcribing texts, taking genealogies, mapping fields, keeping a diary, and so on. But it is not these things, techniques and received procedures, that define the enterprise. What defines it is the kind of intellectual effort it is: an elaborate venture in, to borrow a notion from Gilbert Ryle, "thick description."

Thick Description 1973:6.

8 A repertoire of very general, made-in-the-academy concepts and systems of concepts — "integration," "rationalization," "symbol," "ideology," "ethos," "revolution," "identity," "metaphor," "structure," "ritual," "world view," "actor," "function," "sacred," and, of course, "culture" itself — is woven into the body of thick-description ethnography in the hope of rendering mere occurrences scientifically eloquent. The aim is to draw large conclusions from small, but very densely textured facts; to support broad assertions about the role of culture in the construction of collective life by engaging them with complex specifies.

Thick Description 1973:28.

9 In New Guinea and the Trobriand Islands [Malinowski carried out] what is, all in all, probably the most famous, and certainly the most mythicized, stretch of field work in the history of the discipline: the paradigm journey to the paradigm elsewhere.

Works and Lives 1988:75.

Ernest Gellner 1925–
British anthropologist and philosopher

1 Philosophy is explicitness, generality, orientation and assessment. That which one would insinuate, thereof one must speak.

Words and Things (1959) 1979:287. → A parody of Wittgenstein. See WITTGENSTEIN:2.

2 Industrial Society is not merely one containing "industry," large-scale productive units capable of supplying man's material needs in a way which can eliminate poverty: it is also a society in which knowledge plays a part wholly different from that which it played in earlier social forms, and which indeed possesses a quite different type of knowledge. Modern science is inconceivable outside an industrial society: but modern industrial society is equally inconceivable without modern science. Roughly, science is the mode of cognition of industrial society, and industry is the ecology of science.

Thought and Change (1964) 1965:179.

3 Language is the tool of trade for the humanist intellectual, but it is far more than that. Language is, as Vico saw, more than a tool of culture, it *is* culture. Who would love had he not heard of love, asked La Rochefoucauld. And how many things would we do altogether, if the concepts of those things were not built into the language of our culture?

Thought and Change (1964) 1965:195.

4 Power, belief, wealth: the questions about human society are clustered around these notions. They concern the manner in which a society controls its members; the manner in which it forms their thought, and in which their thinking sustains it; and the manner in which it keeps alive and uses its resources.

Saints of the Atlas 1969:1.

Arnold van Gennep 1873–1957
French anthropologist

1 The life of an individual in any society is a series of passages from one age to another and from one occupation to another.

The Rites of Passage (1908) 1966:2–3.

2 Our interest lies not in the particular rites but in their essential significance and their relative positions within ceremonial wholes — that is, their order. For this reason, some rather lengthy descriptions have been included in order to demonstrate how rites of preliminary or permanent separation, transition, and incorporation are placed in relation to one another for a specific purpose. Their positions may vary, depending on whether the occasion is birth or death, initiation or marriage, but the differences lie only in matters of detail. The underlying arrangement is always the same. Beneath a multiplicity of forms, either consciously expressed or merely implied, a typical pattern always recurs: *the pattern of the rites of passage.*

The Rites of Passage (1908) 1966:191.

Henry George 1839–1897
U.S. economist

1 As Produce = Rent + Wages + Interest,
Therefore, Produce – Rent = Wages + Interest.

Thus wages and interest do not depend upon the produce of labor and capital, but upon what is left after rent is taken out; or, upon the produce which they could obtain without paying rent — that is, from the poorest land in use. And hence, no matter what be the increase in productive power, if the increase in rent keeps pace with it, neither wages nor interest can increase.

Progress and Poverty (1879) 1942:144.

2 What I, therefore, propose, as the simple yet sovereign remedy, which will raise wages, increase the earnings of capital, extirpate pauperism, abolish poverty, give remunerative employment to whoever wishes it, afford free scope to human powers, lessen crime, elevate morals, and taste, and intelligence, purify government and carry civilization to yet nobler heights, is — *to appropriate rent by taxation.*

Progress and Poverty (1879) 1942:340.

Edward Gibbon 1737–1794
British historian

1 The policy of the emperors and the senate, as far as it concerned religion, was happily seconded by the reflections of the enlightened, and by the habits of the superstitious, part of their subjects. The various modes of worship which prevailed in the Roman world were all considered by the people as equally true; by the philosopher as equally false; and by the magistrate as equally useful. And thus toleration produced not only mutual indulgence, but even religious concord.

Decline and Fall of the Roman Empire (1776-1788) 1974:Vol. 1, chap 2, 31.

2 It was scarcely possible that the eyes of contemporaries should discover in the public felicity the latent causes of decay and corruption. This long peace, and the uniform government of the Romans, introduced a slow and secret poison into the vitals of the empire. The minds of men were gradually reduced to the same level, the fire of genius was extinguished, and even the military spirit evaporated. . . The name of Poet was almost forgotten; that of Orator was usurped by the sophists. A cloud of critics, of compilers, of commentators, darkened the face of learning, and the decline of genius was soon followed by the corruption of taste.

Decline and Fall of the Roman Empire (1776–1788) 1974:Vol. 1, chap. 2, 61–63.

3 Titus Antoninus Pius has been justly denominated a second Numa. . . His reign is marked by the rare advantage of furnishing very few materials for history, . . . the register of the crimes, follies, and misfortunes of mankind.

Decline and Fall of the Roman Empire (1776–1788) 1974:Vol. 1, chap. 3, 84.

4 If a man were called to fix the period in the history of the world during which the condition of the human race was most happpy and prosperous, he would, without hesitation, name that which elapsed from the death of Domitian to the accession of Commodus. The vast extent of the Roman empire was governed by absolute power, under the guidance of virtue and wisdom. The armies were restrained by the firm but gentle hand of four successive emperors, whose characters and authority commanded involuntary respect. The forms of the civil administration were carefully preserved by Nerva, Trajan, Hadrian, and the Antonines, who delighted in the image of liberty, and were pleased with considering themselves as the accountable ministers of the laws. Such princes deserved the honour of restoring the republic, had the Romans of their days been capable of enjoying a rational freedom.

Decline and Fall of the Roman Empire (1776–1788) 1974:Vol. 1, chap. 3, 85–86.

5 The pure and genuine influence of Christianity may be traced in its beneficial, though imperfect, effects on the Barbarian proselytes of the North. If the decline of the Roman empire was hastened by the conversion of Constantine, his victorious religion broke the violence of the fall, and mollified the ferocious temper of the conquerors.

Decline and Fall of the Roman Empire (1776–1788) 1974:Vol. 4, chap. 38, 175.

6 Experience had shewn him [Pope Gregory the Great] the efficacy of these solemn and pompous rites, to soothe the distress, to confirm the faith, to mitigate the fierceness, and to dispel the dark enthusiasm of the vulgar, and he readily forgave their tendency to promote the reign of priesthood and superstition.

Decline and Fall of the Roman Empire (1776–1788) 1974:Vol. 5, chap. 45, 38.

7 A victorious line of march had been prolonged above a thousand miles from the rock of Gibraltar to the banks of the Loire; the repetition of an equal space would have carried the Saracens to the confines of Poland and the Highlands of Scotland: the Rhine is not more impassable than the Nile or Euphrates, and the Arabian fleet might have sailed without a naval combat into the mouth of the Thames. Perhaps the interpretation of the Koran would now be taught in the schools of Oxford, and her pulpits might demonstrate to a circumcised people the sanctity and truth of the revelation of Mahomet.

From such calamities was Christendom delivered by the genius and fortune of one man [Charles Martel].

Decline and Fall of the Roman Empire (1776–1788) 1974:Vol. 6, chap. 52, 16.

8 If we contrast the rapid progress of this mischievous discovery [gunpowder] with the slow and laborious advances of reason, science, and the arts of peace, a philosopher, according to his temper, will laugh or weep at the folly of mankind.

Decline and Fall of the Roman Empire (1776–1788) 1974:Vol. 7, chap. 65, 86.

9 It was at Rome, on the 15th of October 1764, as I sat musing amid the ruins of the Capitol, while the barefoot friars were singing vespers in the temple of Jupiter, that the idea of writing the decline and fall of the city first started to my mind.

Autobiography (1796) 1961:154.

10 I am at a loss how to describe the success of the work without betraying the vanity of the writer. The first impression was exhausted in a few days; a second and third edition were scarcely adequate to the demand; and the bookseller's property was twice invaded by the pirates of Dublin. My book was on every table, and almost on every toilette; the historian was crowned by the taste or fashion of the day; nor was the general voice disturbed by the barking of any profane critic.

Autobiography (1796) 1961:175. → For another reaction to the publication of *The Decline and Fall* ("Always scribble, scribble, scribble! Eh! Mr. Gibbon?"), see BESTE:1.

Anthony Giddens 1938–
British sociologist

1 The best and most interesting ideas in the social sciences (a) participate in fostering the climate of opinion and the social processes which give rise to them, (b) are in greater or lesser degree entwined with theories-in-use which help to constitute those processes and (c) are thus unlikely to be clearly distinct from considered reflection which lay actors may bring to bear in so far as they discursively articulate, or improve upon, theories-in-use.

The Constitution of Society 1984:xxxiv.

2 From the point of view of the social sciences, it is hard to exaggerate the importance of the unintended consequences of intentional conduct.

The Constitution of Society 1984:11–12.

3 One of the distinctive things about human beings, which separates us from the animals, is that normally we know what we are doing in our activities, and why. That is to say, human beings are concept-bearing agents, whose concepts in some part constitute what it is that they are up to, not contingently, but as an inherent element of what it is that they are up to. In addition, human actors have reasons for their actions, reasons that consistently inform the flow of day-to-day activities.

Social Theory and Modern Sociology 1987:2–3.

Franklin H. Giddings 1855–1931
U.S. sociologist

1 The original and elementary subjective fact in society is *the consciousness of kind.* By this term I mean a state of consciousness in which any being, whether low or high in the scale of life, recognizes another conscious being as of like kind with itself.

The Principles of Sociology (1896) 1970:17.

2 Pluralistic behavior is the subject-matter of the psychology of society, otherwise called sociology, a science statistical in method, which attempts, first, to factorize pluralistic behavior, and second, to explain its genesis, integration, differentiation, and functioning.

Studies in the Theory of Human Society (1922) 1926:252.

Joseph Glanvill 1636–1680
British clergyman and philosopher

1 They that never peep't beyond the common belief in which their easie understandings were at first indoctrinated, are indubitably assur'd of the Truth, and comparative excellency of their receptions, while the larger Souls, that have travell'd the divers *Climates of Opinions,* are more cautious in their *resolves,* and more sparing to determine.

The Vanity of Dogmatizing (1661) 1970:226–227. → Here Glanvill coins the meteorological metaphor which has since entered the language. See AUDEN:3.

Nathan Glazer 1925–
U.S. sociologist
and
Daniel Patrick Moynihan 1927–
U.S. political scientist and politician

1 The notion that the intense and unprecedented mixture of ethnic and religious groups in American life was soon to blend into a homogenous end product has outlived its usefulness, and also its credibility. . . The point about the melting pot . . . is that it did not happen.

Beyond the Melting Pot 1963:v. → See CRÈVECOEUR:1 and ZANGWILL:1 for the origins of the "melting pot" metaphor.

William Godwin 1756–1836
British political philosopher

1 Government can have no more than two legitimate purposes, the suppression of injustice against individuals within the community, and the common defence against external invasion.

An Enquiry Concerning Political Justice (1793) 1926:Vol. 2, book 5, chap. 22, 60.

2 Commerce never really flourishes so much as when it is delivered from the guardianship of legislators and ministers.

An Enquiry Concerning Political Justice (1793) 1926:Vol. 2, book 6, 81.

Johann Wolfgang von Goethe 1749–1832
German poet, dramatist, novelist, and scientist

1 [*Faust*]: With birds like you one can usually tell the nature by the name, and tell it only too clearly, if your name happens to be lord of the flies, or liar, or destroyer. Well, who are you?
[*Mephistopheles*]: A part of the force that always tries to do evil and always does good [*Ein Theil von jener Kraft, die stets das Böse will, und stets das Gute schafft*].

Faust, Part 1 (1808) 1970:20–21.

2 It has been asserted that the world is governed by figures. I do know this: figures tell us whether it is being governed well or badly.

[*Man hat behauptet, die Welt werde durch Zahlen regiert: das aber weiss ich, dass die Zahlen uns belehren, ob sie gut oder schlecht regiert werde.*]

Remark made on Sunday, 31 January 1830. Quoted in J.P. Eckermann, *Conversations with Goethe* (1836–1848) 1964:169. → This remark, in German, has been printed on the page facing the title page of *The Statesman's Year-Book* since its first issue in 1864.

3 No one can take from us the joy of the first becoming aware of something, the so-called discovery. But if we also demand the honor, it can be utterly spoiled for us, for we are usually not the first.

What does discovery mean, and who can say that he has discovered this or that? After all it's pure idiocy to brag about priority; for it's simply unconscious conceit, not to admit frankly that one is a plagiarist.

Epigraph to Lancelot Law Whyte, *The Unconscious before Freud* (1960). → See WHITEHEAD:2.

Erving Goffman 1922–1982
Canadian-born U.S. sociologist

1 Among those who mingle with one another as colleagues in the profession of dentistry, it is possible to find some who have failed to become physicians and others who have succeeded at not becoming pharmacists or optometrists. No doubt there are few positions in life that do not throw together some persons who are there by virtue of failure and other persons who are there by virtue of success. In this sense, the dead are sorted but not segregated, and continue to walk among the living.

On Cooling the Mark Out 1952:463.

2 A character staged in a theater is not in some ways real, nor does it have the same kind of real consequences as does the thoroughly contrived character performed by a confidence man; but the *successful* staging of either of these types of false figures involves use of *real* techniques — the same techniques by which everyday persons sustain their real social situations. Those who conduct face to face interactions on a theater's stage must meet the key requirement of real situations; they must expressively sustain a definition of the situation: but this they do in circumstances that have facilitated their developing an apt terminology for the interactional tasks that all of us share.

The Presentation of Self in Everyday Life (1956) 1973:254–255. → See THOMAS AND THOMAS:2.

3 Three grossly different types of stigma may be mentioned. First there are abominations of the body — the various physical deformities. Next there are blemishes of individual character perceived as weak will, domineering or unnatural passions, treacherous and rigid beliefs, and dishonesty, these being inferred from a known record of, for example, mental disorder, imprisonment, addiction, alcoholism, homosexuality, unemployment, suicidal attempts, and radical political behaviour. Finally there are the tribal stigma of race, nation, and religion, these being stigma that can be transmitted through lineages and equally contaminate all members of a family.

Stigma (1963) 1968:14.

4 The realm of activity that is generated by face-to-face interaction and organized by norms of co-mingling — a domain containing weddings, family meals, chaired meetings, forced marches, service encounters, queues, crowds, and couples — has never been sufficiently treated as a subject matter in its own right. In fact, a convenience has often been made of it. Whenever a concrete illustration has been needed of how it is with a social establishment, or a bit of social structure, or even a society, interaction vignettes have been fetched in to provide vivid evidence and, incidentally, a little obeisance to the fact that there are people out there moving about. Thus interaction practices have been used to illuminate other things, but themselves are treated as though they did not need to be defined or were not worth defining. Yet the nicest use for these events is the explication of their own generic character.

Relations in Public 1971:ix.

5 The individual is linked to society through two principal social bonds: to collectivities through membership and to other individuals through social relationships. He in turn helps make a network of society by linking through himself the social units linked to him.

Relations in Public 1971:188.

6 In our society the very significant assumption is generally made that all events — without exception — can be contained and managed within the conventional system of beliefs. We tolerate the unexplained but not the inexplicable.

Frame Analysis 1974:30.

7 Once individuals — for whatever reason — come into one another's immediate presence, a fundamental principle of social life becomes enormously pronounced, namely, its promissory, evidential character. It is not only that our appearance and manner provide evidence of our statuses and relationships. It is also that the line of our visual regard, the intensity of our involvement, and the shape of our initial actions, allow others to glean our immediate intent and purpose, and all this whether or not we are engaged in talk with them at the time.

The Interaction Order 1983:3. → From a 1982 presidential address to the American Sociological Association.

8 A critical feature of face-to-face gatherings is that in them and them alone we can fit a shape and dramatic form to matters that aren't otherwise palpable to the senses. Through costume, gesture, and bodily alignment we can depict and represent a heterogeneous list of immaterial things, sharing only the fact that they have a significance in our lives and yet do not cast a shadow: notable events in the past, beliefs about the cosmos and our place in it, ideals regarding our various categories of persons, and of course social relationships and larger social structures. These embodiments are centered in ceremonies (in turn embedded in celebrative social occasions) and presumably allow the participants to affirm their affiliation and commitment to their collectivities, and revive their ultimate beliefs.

The Interaction Order 1983:9.

William J. Goode 1917–
U.S. sociologist

1 *All* courtship systems are market or exchange systems. They differ from one another with respect to *who* does the buying and selling, which characteristics are more or less valuable in that market, and how open or explicit the bargaining is.

World Revolution and Family Patterns 1963:8.

2 The ideology of the conjugal family proclaims the right of the individual to choose his or her own spouse, place to live, and even which kin obligations to accept, as against the acceptance of others' decisions. It asserts the worth of the *individual* as against the inherited elements of wealth or ethnic group. The *individual* is to be evaluated, not his lineage.

World Revolution and Family Patterns 1963:19.

William Sealy Gosset 1876–1937
["Student"]
British statistician

1 I fancy you give me credit for being a more systematic sort of cove than I really am in the matter of limits of significance. What would actually happen would be that I should make out P_t (normal) and say to myself "that would be about 50:1; pretty good but as it may not be normal we'd best not be too certain," or "100:1; even allowing that it may not be normal it seems good enough" and whether one would be content with that or would require further work would depend on the importance of the conclusion and the difficulty of obtaining suitable experience.

Letter to E. S. Pearson, 18 May 1929. 1938:244. → All of Gosset's papers except one appeared under the pseudonym "Student."

2 Suppose there are two treatments to be randomized. . . and suppose that by the luck of the draw they come to be arranged in a very *un*balanced manner, say AAAABBBB: is it seriously contended that the risk should be accepted of spoiling the experiment owing to the bias which will affect the mean if there is the usual fertility slope? . . . Not only will the mean be biased, but the apparent precision will tend to be high, and misleading conclusions drawn much more often than the 1 or 5% of the tables.

It is of course perfectly true that *in the long run*, taking all possible arrangements, exactly as many misleading conclusions will be drawn as are allowed for in the tables, and anyone prepared to spend a blameless life in repeating an experiment would doubtless confirm this; nevertheless it would be pedantic to continue with an arrangement of plots known beforehand to be likely to lead to a misleading conclusion.

Comparison between Balanced and Random Arrangements of Field Plots (1938) 1943:202.

Stephen Jay Gould 1941–
U.S. paleontologist and biologist

1 Biological determinism is, in essence, a *theory of limits*. It takes the current status of groups as a measure of where they should and must be. . . We inhabit a world of human differences and predilections, but the extrapolation of these facts to theories of rigid limits is ideology.

The Mismeasure of Man 1981:28–29.

2 *Human equality is a contingent fact of history*. Equality is not true by definition; it is neither an ethical principle (though equal treatment may be) nor a statement about norms of social action. It just worked out that way. A hundred different and plausible scenarios for human history would have yielded other results (and moral dilemmas of enormous magnitude). They didn't happen.

The Flamingo's Smile 1985:186.

3 Asian *Homo erectus* died without issue and does not enter our immediate ancestry (for we evolved from African populations); Neanderthal people were collateral cousins, perhaps already living in Europe while we emerged in Africa. . . In other words, we are an improbable and fragile entity, fortunately successful after precarious beginnings as a small population in Africa, not the predictable end result of a global tendency. We are a thing, an item of history, not an embodiment of general principles.

Wonderful Life 1989:319.

Alvin W. Gouldner 1920–1980
U.S. sociologist

1 The coming crisis of Western Sociology . . . is manifested: (1) by the drift of the dominant Functionalist and Parsonian models toward a convergence with Marxism, . . . previously one of its main polemical targets; (2) by the emerging alienation of young sociologists from Functionalism; (3) by the tendency of such individual expressions of alienation to develop collective and organized forms; (4) by the growing technical criticism of Functional theory; (5) by the transition from such negative criticism to the development of positive and alternative theories. . . ; and (6) by the development of a middle-range "social problems" research and theory that are often oriented to values of "freedom" and "equality" rather than of "order," as Functionalism tends to be.

The Coming Crisis of Western Sociology 1970:410.

Antonio Gramsci 1891–1937
Italian political theorist

1 The actual process of the proletarian revolution cannot be identified with the development and activity of revolutionary organizations of a voluntary and contractual nature, such as political parties and trade unions. These organizations arise in the sphere of bourgeois democracy and political liberty, as affirmations and developments of this political liberty. . . The revolutionary process takes place in the sphere of production, in the factory, where the relations are those of oppressor to oppressed, exploiter to exploited, where freedom for the worker does not exist, and democracy does not exist.

The Factory Council (1920) 1977:260–261.

2 Politics becomes permanent action and gives birth to permanent organisations precisely in so far as it identifies itself with economics.

Prison Notebooks (1933–1934) 1971:139–140.

3 State = political society + civil society, in other words hegemony protected by the armour of coercion.

Prison Notebooks (1933–1934) 1971:263.

4 Illusion is the most tenacious weed in the collective consciousness, history teaches but it has no students.

Quoted in Joseph V. Femia, The Gramsci Phenomenon 1979:483.

Mark Granovetter 1943–
U.S. sociologist

1 Our acquaintances ("weak ties") are less likely to be socially involved with one another than are our close friends ("strong ties"). . . Weak ties, far from being productive of alienation. . . are actually vital for an individual's integration into modern society.

The Strength of Weak Ties 1982:105, 107. → The strength-of-weak-ties theory, first posited by Granovetter in 1973 as a mechanism through which people obtain employment, has been used by him and others to explain such phenomena as the diffusion of innovations in society, recruitment into voluntary associations, and social integration within large organizations.

John Graunt 1620–1674
British statistician and demographer

1 Now having (I know not by what accident) engaged my thoughts upon the *Bills of Mortality*, and so far succeeded therein, as to have reduced several great confused *Volumes* into a few perspicuous *Tables*, and abridged such *Observations* as naturally flowed from them, into a few succinct *Paragraphs*, without any long Series of *multiloquious Deductions*, I have presumed to sacrifice these my small, but first publish'd, *Labours* unto your Lordship, as unto whose benign acceptance of some other of my *Papers*, even the birth of these is due; hoping (if I may without vanity say it) they may be of as much use to persons in your Lordships place, as they are of little or none to me, which is no more than the fairest *Diamonds* are to the *Journeymen Jeweller* that works them, or the poor *Labourer* that first dig'd them from the Earth.

Observations upon the Bills of Mortality (1662) 1899:320. → An early account of quantitative social science research.

T. H. Green 1836–1882
British philosopher and social theorist

1 To uphold the sanctity of contracts is doubtless a prime business of government, but it is no less its business to provide against contracts being made, which, from the helplessness of one of the parties to them, instead of being a security for freedom, become an instrument of disguised oppression.

Lecture on Liberal Legislation and Freedom of Contract (1881) 1888:382.

Thomas Gresham 1519–1579
British merchant and banker

1 [Gresham's Law]: Bad money drives out good money.

Quoted in C. Alexander Harris, Gresham's Law (1896) 1906:262. → Harris reports that Gresham took a prominent part in advising Queen Elizabeth on the reform of the currency, but notes that there is no evidence that he actually formulated Gresham's Law, as mistakenly reported by Henry Dunning Macleod in 1858. See MACLEOD:1.

Howard E. Gruber 1922–
U.S. psychologist

1 Piaget's penchant for children's toys and games did not mean that he had any love for untrammeled spontaneity. On the contrary, research was conducted under conditions controlled enough to permit observation of the progression of intellectual stages in the growth of the child. Moreover, Switzerland is a very proper country. Interest lies in taming the savage mind, not in adoring it. Piaget's innovation was the idea that the child tames himself.

Piaget's Mission 1982:247. → See PIAGET:12.

Emile Grunberg 1905–1988
Austrian-born U.S. economist
and
Franco Modigliani 1918–
Italian-born U.S. economist

1 The expectation function, rather blithely assumed to be known along with the other functions of the system, offers particular methodological difficulties and is actually different from the other functions encountered in economic theory. *Expectations are themselves predictions*, ranging from the elaborate scientific forecast of the large business enterprise to primitive guesses and dark hunches.

The Predictability of Social Events 1954:470–471.

H

Jürgen Habermas 1929–
German philosopher and sociologist

1 As our civilization has become increasingly scientific, the dimension within which theory was once directed toward praxis has become correspondingly constructed. The laws of self-reproduction demand of an industrially advanced society that it look after its survival on the escalating scale of a continually expanded technical control over nature and a continually refined administration of human beings and their relations to each other by means of social organization. In this system, science, technology, industry, and administration interlock in a circular process. In this process the relationship of theory to praxis can now only assert itself as the purposive-rational application of techniques assured by empirical science.

Theory and Practice (1963) 1973:254.

2 Positivism stands or falls with the principle of scientism, that is that the meaning of knowledge is defined by what the sciences do and can thus be adequately explicated through the methodological analysis of scientific procedures.

Knowledge and Human Interests (1968) 1971:67.

3 The grammar of ordinary language governs not only the connection of symbols but also the interweaving of linguistic elements, action patterns, and expressions. In the normal case, these three categories of expressions are complementary, so that linguistic expressions "fit" interactions and both language and action "fit" experiential expressions; of course, their integration is imperfect, which makes possible the latitude necessary for indirect communications. In the limiting case, however, a language game can disintegrate to the point where the three categories of expressions no longer agree. Then actions and nonverbal expressions belie what is expressly stated.

Knowledge and Human Interests (1968) 1971:217–218.

4 What raises us out of nature is the only thing whose nature we can know: *language*. Through its structure, autonomy and responsibility are posited for us. Our first sentence expresses unequivocally the intention of universal and unconstrained consensus.

Knowledge and Human Interests (1968) 1971:314.

5 Violation of a rule has a different consequence according to type. *Incompetent* behavior, which violates valid technical rules or strategies, is condemned per se to failure through lack of success; the "punishment" is built, so to speak, into its rebuff by reality. *Deviant* behavior, which violates consensual norms, provokes sanctions that are connected with the rules only externally, that is by convention. Learned rules of purposive-rational actions supply us with *skills*, internalized norms with *personality structures*. Skills put us in a position to solve problems; motivations allow us to follow norms.

Toward a Rational Society (1969) 1971:92.

6 The mediation of theory and praxis can only be clarified if to begin with we distinguish three functions, which are measured in terms of different criteria: the formation and extension of critical theorems, which can stand up to scientific discourse; the organization of processes of enlightenment, in which such theorems are applied and can be tested in a unique manner by the initiation of processes of reflection carried on within certain groups toward which these processes have been directed; and the selection of appropriate strategies, the solution of tactical questions, and the conduct of the political struggle. On the first level, the aim is true statements, on the second, authentic insights, and on the third, prudent decisions.

Introduction to *Theory and Practice* (1963) 1973:32. → First published in the fourth edition of 1971.

7 In everyday communication, cognitive meanings, moral expectations, subjective expressions and evaluations must relate to one another. Communication processes need a cultural tradition covering all spheres — cognitive, moral-practical and expressive. A rationalized everyday life, therefore, could hardly be saved from cultural impoverishment through breaking open a single cultural sphere — art — and so providing access to just

one of the specialized knowledge complexes. The surrealist revolt would have replaced only one abstraction.

Modernity (1981) 1983:11.

Andrew Hacker 1929–
U.S. political scientist

1 "Old" Americans possess, for the most part, some common characteristics. First of all, they are "WASPs" — in the cocktail party jargon of the sociologists. That is, they are white, they are Anglo-Saxon in origin, and they are Protestant.

Liberal Democracy and Social Control 1957:1010–1011. → This seems to be the first appearance of the term "WASP" in print. However, it was Digby Baltzell's *The Protestant Establishment* (1964) that brought the term into general use.

Ian Hacking 1936–
Canadian philosopher

1 Etymologically, a theory is a collection of speculations. Logicians have revived this usage, and mean by a theory the set of truths about some subject. Thus arithmetic is the theory of numbers, and geology, I suppose, is the theory of rocks. Statistics is the theory of chance.

Logic of Statistical Inference 1965:34.

Alfred Cort Haddon
See JULIAN HUXLEY AND ALFRED CORT HADDON.

F. H. Hahn 1925–
German-born British economist

1 The achievements of economic theory in the last two decades are both impressive and in many ways beautiful. But it cannot be denied that there is something scandalous in the spectacle of so many people refining the analysis of economic states which they give no reason to suppose will ever, or have ever, come about.

Some Adjustment Problems 1970:1.

2 Many people like quoting Keynes's dictum that economics should be like dentistry. Few of them note the singular lack of dentists who have written "General Theories."

The Winter of Our Discontent 1973:323. → See KEYNES:11 and GOFFMAN:1.

3 I have for much of the time been arguing that the emperor's clothes are not quite as fine as is often supposed. Although I have not been as precise and detailed as a more leisurely account would have permitted, I nonetheless hope to have shown that, both on purely logical considerations as well as on the basis of quite simple observations, the invisible hand is likely to be unsure in its operation and occasionally downright arthritic. However, as I have already warned, it is an unwarranted inference from this that there is some social device which will perform more satisfactorily or that we should cut off the hand altogether.

Reflections on the Invisible Hand 1982:16. → See ADAM SMITH:1.

[*See also* KENNETH J. ARROW AND F. H. HAHN.]

Élie Halévy 1870–1937
French historian

1 The economic doctrine of Adam Smith is the doctrine of Mandeville set out in a form which is no longer paradoxical and literary, but rational and scientific. The principle of the identity of interests is not perhaps a principle which is true to the exclusion of all others, but it is a principle which can always be applied, in a general if not in a universal way, in the sphere of political economy.

The Growth of Philosophic Radicalism (1901–1904) 1955:90.

2 I shall not dwell upon the story of the last week before the war, dramatic as it is. I shall disregard the suggestions made retrospectively by a host of well-meaning critics, as to what such and such a sovereign, or prime minister, or foreign secretary, should, on this particular day, at this or that particular hour, have done or not done, said or not said, in order to prevent the war. Pills to cure an earthquake! The object of my study is the earthquake itself. I shall attempt to define the collective forces, the collective feelings and movements of public opinion, which, in the early years of the twentieth century, made for strife.

The World Crisis of 1914–1918 (1930) 1966:210–211.

G. Stanley Hall 1844–1924
U.S. psychologist

1 All possible *truth* is practical. To ask whether our conception of chair or table corresponds to the real chair or table apart from the uses to which they may be put, is as utterly meaningless and vain as to inquire whether a musical tone is red or yellow. No other conceivable relation than this between ideas and things can exist. The *unknowable is what I cannot react upon*. The active part of our nature is not only an essential part of cognition itself, but it always has a voice in determining what shall be believed and what rejected.

The Muscular Perception of Space 1878:446.

2 The early stages of growth are telescoped into each other almost indistinguishably, so that phylogenetically the embryo lives a thousand years in a day, and the higher the species the more rapid relatively is the transit through the lower stages. This law of tachygenesis may perhaps be expressed somewhat as follows: Heredity, which slowly appears as a substitute for the external causes that have produced a given series of characters, tends to produce that succession with increasing economy and speed and also to become in a way more independent of the causes which originally determined it.

Adolescence (1904) 1911:Vol. 1, 3.

3 The ordered, regular life of maturity involves necessarily more or less degeneration for simple tendencies. Indeed, the best definition of genius is intensified and prolonged adolescence, to which excessive or premature systematization is fatal.

Adolescence (1904) 1911:Vol. 2, 90–91.

Alexander Hamilton 1757?–1804
West Indian-born U.S. statesman

1 Laws are a dead letter without courts to expound and define their true meaning and operation.

Federalist 22 (1787) 1961:150.

2 Though it cannot be pretended that the principles of moral and political knowledge have, in general, the same degree of certainty with those of the mathematics, yet they have much better claims in this respect than to judge from the conduct of men in particular situations we should be disposed to allow them. The obscurity is much oftener in the passions and prejudices of the reasoner than in the subject. Men, upon too many occasions, do not give their own understandings fair play; but, yielding to some untoward bias, they entangle themselves in words and confound themselves in subtleties.

Federalist 31 (1788) 1961:194.

3 Though we cannot acquiesce in the political heresy of the poet who says:

"For forms of government let fools contest —
That which is best administered is best," —

yet we may safely pronounce that the true test of a good government is its aptitude and tendency to produce a good administration.

Federalist 68 (1788) 1961:414. → "The poet" is Alexander Pope. See POPE:2.

Learned Hand 1872–1961
U.S. jurist

1 I shall ask no more than that you agree with Dean [Charles Ralph] Inge that even though counting heads is not an ideal way to govern, at least it is better than breaking them.

Democracy (1932) 1953:92.

2 Risk for risk, for myself I had rather take my chance that some traitors will escape detection than spread abroad a spirit of general suspicion and distrust, which accepts rumor and gossip in place of undismayed and unintimidated inquiry.

A Plea for the Open Mind and Free Discussion (1952) 1959:216. → From a speech on 24 October 1952 during the period of so-called "McCarthyism" in U.S. political life.

Garrett Hardin 1915–
U.S. biologist

1 The tragedy of the commons develops in this way. Picture a pasture open to all. It is to be expected that each herdsman will try to keep as many cattle as possible on the commons. Such an arrangement may work reasonably satisfactorily for centuries because tribal wars, poaching, and disease keep the numbers of both man and beast well below the carrying capacity of the land. Finally, however, comes the day of reckoning, that is, the day when the long-desired goal of social stability becomes a reality. At this point, the inherent logic of the commons remorselessly generates tragedy.

As a rational being, each herdsman seeks to maximize his gain. Explicitly or implicitly, more or less consciously, he asks; "What is the utility *to me* of adding one more animal to my herd?" This utility has one negative and one positive component.

1) The positive component is a function of the increment of one animal. Since the herdsman receives all the proceeds from the sale of the additional animal, the positive utility is nearly +1.

2) The negative component is a function of the additional overgrazing created by one more animal. Since, however, the effects of overgrazing are shared by all the herdsmen, the negative utility for any particular decision-making herdsman is only a fraction of −1.

Adding together the component partial utilities, the rational herdsman concludes that the only sensible course for him to pursue is to add another animal to his herd. And another; and another. . . But this is the conclusion reached by each and every rational herdsman sharing a commons. Therein is the tragedy. Each man is locked into a system that compels him to increase his herd without limit — in a world that is limited. Ruin is the destination toward which all men rush, each pursuing his own best interest in a society that believes in the freedom of the commons. Freedom in a commons brings ruin to all.

The Tragedy of the Commons 1968:1244. → For the origin of this metaphor, see LLOYD:1.

Michael Harrington 1928–1989
U.S. political scientist and socialist

1 The other America, the America of poverty, is hidden today in a way that it never was before. Its millions are socially invisible to the rest of us.

The Other America 1962:3.

2 For the middle class, the police protect property, give directions, and help old ladies. For the urban poor, the police are those who arrest you. In almost any slum there is a vast conspiracy against the forces of law and order.

The Other America 1962:16.

3 There is the fundamental paradox of the welfare state: that it is not built for the desperate, but for those who are already capable of helping themselves.

The Other America 1962:161.

David Hartley 1705–1757
British psychologist

1 The influence of *Association* over our Opinions and Affections, and its Use in explaining those Things in an accurate and precise Way, which are commonly referred to the Power of Habit and Custom, is a general and indeterminate one.

Observations on Man (1749) 1966:5–6.

Heinz Hartmann 1894–1970
Austrian-born U.S. psychoanalyst

1 Contrasts in the ego there are many: the ego has from its start the tendency to oppose the drives, but one of its main functions is also to help them toward gratification; it is a place where insight is gained, but also of rationalization; it promotes objective knowledge of reality, but at the same time, by way of identification and social adjustment, takes over in the course of its development the conventional prejudices of the environment; it pursues its independent aims, but it is also characteristic of it to consider the demands of the other substructures of personality.

Comments on the Psychoanalytic Theory of the Ego (1950) 1964:138–139.

William Harvey 1578–1657
British physician and anatomist

1 I profess both to learn and to teach anatomy, not from books but from dissections; not from the positions of philosophers but from the fabric of nature.

The Circulation of the Blood (1628) 1923:8. → For a paraphrase of Harvey's famous remark, see WILLIAM HENRY BEVERIDGE:1.

Edward R. Hawkins 1908–1963
and
Willard W. Waller 1899–1945
U.S. sociologists

1 The prostitute, the pimp, the peddler of dope, the operator of the gambling hall, the vendor of obscene pictures, the bootlegger, the abortionist, all are productive, all produce goods or services which people desire and for which they are willing to pay. It happens that society has put these goods and services under the ban, but people go on producing them and people go on consuming them, and an act of the legislature does not make them any less a part of the economic system.

Critical Notes on the Cost of Crime 1936:684–685.

Friedrich A. von Hayek 1899–1992
Austrian-born British economist

1 That [the social scientist] systematically starts from the concepts which guide individuals in their actions and not from the results of their theorising about their actions, is the characteristic feature of that methodological individualism which is closely connected with the subjectivism of the social sciences.

Scientism and the Study of Society 1942:286. → This seems to be the first appearance in print of the term "methodological individualism." See POPPER:1.

2 The various kinds of collectivism, communism, fascism, etc., differ among themselves in the nature of the goal toward which they want to direct the efforts of society. But they all differ from liberalism and individualism in wanting to organize the whole of society and all its resources for this unitary end and in refusing to recognize autonomous spheres in which the ends of the individuals are supreme.

The Road to Serfdom (1944) 1972:56.

3 The system of private property is the most important guaranty of freedom, not only for those who own property, but scarcely less for those who do not.

The Road to Serfdom (1944) 1972:103–104.

4 Planning in the specific sense in which the term is used in contemporary controversy necessarily means central planning — direction of the whole economic system according to one unified plan. Competition, on the other hand, means decentralized planning by many separate persons. The halfway house between the two, about which many people talk but which few like when they see it, is the delegation of planning to organized industries, or, in other words, monopolies.

The Use of Knowledge in Society (1945) 1948:79.

5 We must look at the price system as. . . a mechanism for communicating information if we want to understand its real function.

The Use of Knowledge in Society (1945) 1948:86.

6 Many of the greatest things man has achieved are not the result of consciously directed thought, and still less the product of a deliberately co-ordinated effort of many individuals, but of a process in which the individual plays a part which he can never fully understand. They are greater than any individual precisely because they result from the combination of knowledge more extensive than a single mind can master.

The Counter-Revolution of Science (1952) 1964:84.

7 Neither the Greeks of the fifth century B.C. nor their successors for the next two thousand years developed a systematic social theory which explicitly dealt with [the] unintended consequences of human action or accounted for the manner in which an order or regularity could form itself among those actions which none of the acting persons had intended. It therefore never became clear that what was really required was a three-fold division which inserted between the phenomena which were natural in the sense that they were wholly independent of human action, and those which were artificial or conventional in the sense that they were the product of human design, a distinct middle category comprising all those unintended patterns and regularities which we find to exist in human society and which it is the task of social theory to explain.

Studies in Philosophy, Politics and Economics 1967:97.

8 The aim for which the successful entrepreneur wants to use his profits may well be to provide a hospital or an art gallery for his home town. But quite apart from the question of what he wants to do with his profits after he has earned them, he is led to benefit more people by aiming at the largest gain than he could if he concentrated on

the satisfaction of the needs of known persons. He is led by the invisible hand of the market to bring the succour of modern conveniences to the poorest homes he does not even know.

Law, Legislation and Liberty (1976) 1978:Vol. 2, 145. → See ADAM SMITH:1.

Georg Wilhelm Friedrich Hegel 1770–1831

German philosopher

1 Poverty in itself does not make men into a rabble; a rabble is created only when there is joined to poverty a disposition of mind, an inner indignation against the rich, against society, against the government, &c.

Philosophy of Right (1821) 1952:277.

2 When we walk the streets at night in safety, it does not strike us that this might be otherwise. This habit of feeling safe has become second nature, and we do not reflect on just how this is due solely to the working of special institutions. Commonplace thinking often has the impression that force holds the state together, but in fact its only bond is the fundamental sense of order which everybody possesses.

Philosophy of Right (1821) 1952:282.

3 Public opinion contains all kinds of falsity and truth, but it takes a great man to find the truth in it. The great man of the age is the one who can put into words the will of his age, tell his age what its will is, and accomplish it. What he does is the heart and the essence of his age, he actualizes his age. The man who lacks sense enough to despise public opinion expressed in gossip will never do anything great.

Philosophy of Right (1821) 1952:295.

4 Rulers, Statesmen, Nations, are wont to be emphatically commended to the teaching which experience offers in history. But what experience and history teach is this — that peoples and governments never have learned anything from history, or acted on principles deduced from it. Each period is involved in such peculiar circumstances, exhibits a condition of things so strictly idiosyncratic, that its conduct must be regulated by considerations connected with itself, and itself alone.

The Philosophy of History (1837) 1956:6. → See SANTAYANA:1.

5 In history an additional result is commonly produced by human actions beyond that which they aim at and obtain — that which they immediately recognize and desire. They gratify their own interest; but something further is thereby accomplished, latent in the actions in question, though not present to their consciousness, and not included in their design. . . This may be called the *cunning of reason [List der Vernunft]*.

The Philosophy of History (1837) 1956:27, 33.

6 The East knew and to the present day knows only that *One* is Free; the Greek and the Roman world, that *some* are free; the German World knows that *All* are free. The first political form therefore which we observe in History, is *Despotism*, the second *Democracy* and *Aristocracy*, the third *Monarchy*.

The Philosophy of History (1837) 1956:104.

7 The History of the World is nothing but the development of the Idea of Freedom.

The Philosophy of History (1837) 1956:456.

8 Reason is just as cunning as she is powerful. Her cunning consists principally in her mediating activity, which, by causing objects to act and re-act on each other in accordance with their own nature, in this way, without any direct interference in the process, carries out reason's intentions.

Die Logik 1840:382.

Robert L. Heilbroner 1919–

U.S. economist

1 [The great economists] can be called the worldly philosophers, for they sought to embrace in a scheme of philosophy the most worldly of all of man's activities — his drive for wealth. It is not, perhaps, the most elegant kind of philosophy, but there is no more intriguing or more important one.

The Worldly Philosophers (1953) 1980:14.

2 In an age which no longer waits patiently through this life for the rewards of the next, it is a crushing spiritual blow to lose one's sense of participation in mankind's journey, and to see only a huge milling-around, a collective living-out of lives with no larger purpose than the days which each accumulates. When we estrange ourselves from history we do not enlarge, we diminish ourselves, even as individuals. We subtract from our lives one meaning which they do in fact possess, whether we recognize it or not. We cannot help living in history. We can only fail to be aware of it.

The Future as History 1960:209.

3 The neoclassical model has rigor, but alas, also mortis. The Marxian model has relevance, but alas, also mistakes.

Putting Marx to Work 1968:10.

4 While history forces on us a salutary agnosticism with regard to the long-term prospects for capitalism, it is interesting to note that all the great economists have envisaged an eventual end to the capitalist period of history. Smith describes the accumulation process as ultimately reaching a plateau when the attainment of riches will be "complete," followed by a lengthy and deep decline. Ricardo and Mill anticipate the arrival of a "stationary state," which Mill foresees as the staging ground for a kind of associationist socialism. Marx anticipates a series of worsening crises, each crisis serving a temporary rejuvenating function but bringing closer the day when the system will no longer be able to manage its internal contradictions. Keynes foresees "a somewhat comprehensive

socialization of investment"; Schumpeter, an evolution into a kind of bureaucratic socialism.

Capitalistic and Acapitalistic Production 1987:353.

5 Less than seventy-five years after it officially began, the contest between capitalism and socialism is over: capitalism has won.

Reflections: The Triumph of Capitalism 1989:98.

Carl G. Hempel 1905–
German-born U.S. philosopher

1 General laws have quite analogous functions in history and in the natural sciences. . . They form an indispensable instrument of historical research, and. . . they even constitute the common basis of various procedures which are often considered as characteristic of the social in contradistinction to the natural sciences.

The Function of General Laws in History 1942:35. → This article sets forth what is often called the "covering-law" theory of historical explanation.

L. J. Henderson 1878–1942
U.S. biochemist and sociologist

1 A. . . difference between most system-building in the social sciences and systems of thought and classification of the natural sciences is to be seen in their evolution. In the natural sciences both theories and descriptive systems grow by adaptation to the increasing knowledge and experience of the scientists. In the social sciences, systems often issue fully formed from the mind of one man. Then they may be much discussed if they attract attention, but progressive adaptive modification as a result of the concerted efforts of great numbers of men is rare.

The Study of Man 1941:19–20.

Heraclitus c. 540–c. 480 B.C.
Greek philosopher

1 You could not step twice into the same rivers; for other waters are ever flowing on to you.

On the Universe:483.

Johann Gottfried von Herder 1744–1803
German philosopher and historian

1 We always live in a world we ourselves create.

Uebers Erkennen und Empfinden in der menschlichen Seele (1774) 1892:252. → Unpublished translation by Edward J. Doherty.

2 Since man is no independent substance, but is connected with all the elements of nature. . . shall not he also be changed by it? It is far too little, to compare him to the absorbing sponge, the sparking tinder: he is a multitudinous harmony, a living self, on whom the harmony of all the powers that surround him operates.

Reflections on the Philosophy of the History of Mankind (1784–1791) 1968:4.

3 *How transitory all human structures are, nay how oppressive the best institutions become in the course of a few generations.* The plant blossoms, and fades: your fathers have died, and mouldered into dust: your temple is fallen: your tabernacle, the tables of your law, are no more: language itself, that bond of mankind, becomes antiquated: and shall a political constitution, shall a system of government or religion, that can be erected solely on these, endure for ever?

Reflections on the Philosophy of the History of Mankind (1784–1791) 1968:163–164.

4 Some. . . have thought fit to employ the term *races* for four or five divisions, according to regions of origin or complexion. I see no reason for employing this term. Race refers to a difference of origin, which. . . either does not exist or which comprises in each of these regions or complexions the most diverse "races." For every distinct community is a *nation*, having its own national culture as it has its own language.

Ideen zur Philosophie der Geschichte der Menschheit (1785) 1887:Part 2, 257–258.

5 "Millions" of people on the globe live without states. . . father and mother, man and wife, child and brother, friend and man — these are natural relationships through which we become happy; what the *state* can give us is an artificial contrivance; unfortunately it can also deprive us of something far more important — rob us of ourselves.

Ideen zur Philosophie der Geschichte der Menschheit (1785) 1887:Part 2, 341.

Herodotus 5th century B.C.
Greek historian

1 I, Herodotus of Halicarnassus, am here setting forth my history, that time may not draw the color from what man has brought into being, nor those great and wonderful deeds, manifested by both Greeks and barbarians, fail of their report, and, together with all this, the reason why they fought one another.

The History:33. → The first sentence of what is in effect the first book of history in the Western world.

John F. W. Herschel 1792–1871
British astronomer

1 Whether statistics be an art or a science. . .or a scientific art, we concern ourselves little. It is the basis of social and political dynamics, and affords the only secure ground on which the truth or falsehood of the theories and hypotheses of that complicated science can be brought to the test.

Quetelet on Probabilities (1850) 1857:434–435.

Melville Jean Herskovits 1895–1963
U.S. anthropologist

1 The proverb gives us an excellent example of how revealing the analysis of social context can be. In African socie-

ties it is a mark of elegance to be able to interlard one's speech with these aphorisms. Proverbs are cited in the native courts in much the same way as our lawyers cite precedent. It is held boorish for a younger man to employ proverbs in discussions with an elder. The morals they point give insights into the basic values of society; they teach us what is held to be right and wrong. They are, indeed, an index to accepted canons of thought and action.

The Study of African Oral Art 1961:453.

J. H. Hexter 1910–
U.S. historian

1 It is well to focus on decision because of a peculiarity of historical vocabulary — one which for decades has affected the language of history. . . Fully to describe it is unnecessary; it is sufficiently revealed by the words in which it is imbedded: *tended, grew out of, developed, evolved; trend, development, tendency, evolution, growth.* In the historical writing of the past half- century these simple words have enabled historians to conceal their ignorance from others and from themselves.

Reappraisals in History (1961) 1963:213.

2 If physicists could not quote in the text, they would not feel that much was lost with respect to advancement of knowledge of the natural world. If historians could not quote, they would deem it a disastrous impediment to the communication of knowledge about the past. A luxury for physicists, quotation is a necessity for historians, indispensable to historiography.

Historiography 1968:385.

John R. Hicks 1904–1989
British economist

1 Casual labour is often badly paid, not because it gets less than it is worth, but because it is worth so appallingly little.

The Theory of Wages (1932) 1968:82.

2 [The economist always seeks to refer his analysis of a problem] back to some "datum," that is to say, to something which is extra-economic. This something may be apparently very remote from the problem which was first taken up, for the chains of economic causation are often very long. But he always wants to hand over the problem in the end to some sociologist or other — if there is a sociologist waiting for him. Very often there isn't.

Economic Theory and the Social Sciences 1936:135.

3 Whether it is a rule of economic affairs that "to him that hath shall be given" may be disputed; but there can be no doubt that it is a rule of borrowing and lending that *to him that hath shall be lent.*

The Social Framework (1942) 1943:89.

4 One must assume that the people in one's models do not know what is going to happen, and know that they do not know just what is going to happen. As in history!

Economic Perspectives 1977:vii.

Gertrude Himmelfarb 1922–
U.S. historian

1 Intellectual revolutions. . . are like political revolutions, only more so, political revolutions tending to vanish under the cold eye of the historian, until the new régime is only the legalization and continuation of a movement begun in the old, and intellectual revolutions often reducing themselves to little more than the synthesizing and popularizing of ideas long current.

Darwin and the Darwinian Revolution 1959:369.

2 It is not only political history that the social historian denies or belittles. It is reason itself: the reason embodied in the polity, in the constitutions and laws that permit men to order their affairs in a rational manner — or, on occasion, in an irrational manner, which other men perceive as such and rationally, often heroically, struggle against. It is the reason transmitted to the present by way of constitutions and laws, which themselves specify the means for their amendment and reform. And it is the reason inherent in the historical enterprise itself, in the search for an objective truth that always eludes the individual historian but that always (or so it was once thought) informs and inspires his work.

"History with the Politics Left Out" (1984) 1987:21.

3 After several decades of the new history, we can better appreciate what we are in danger of losing if we abandon the old. We will lose not only the unifying theme that has given coherence to history, not only the notable events, individuals, and institutions that have constituted our historical memory and our heritage, not only the narrative that has made history readable and memorable — not only, in short, a meaningful past — but also a conception of man as a rational, political animal. And that loss is even more difficult to sustain, for it involves a radical redefinition of human nature.

"History with the Politics Left Out" (1984) 1987:25.

Albert O. Hirschman 1915–
German-born U.S. economist

1 Since we necessarily underestimate our creativity, it is desirable that we underestimate to a roughly similar extent the difficulties of the tasks we face so as to be tricked by these two offsetting underestimates into undertaking tasks that we can, but otherwise would not dare, tackle. The principle is important enough to deserve a name: since we are apparently on the trail here of some sort of invisible or hidden hand that beneficially hides difficulties from us, I propose *the Hiding Hand.*

Development Projects Observed 1967:13.

2 The customer who, dissatisfied with the product of one firm, shifts to that of another, uses the market to defend his welfare or to improve his position; and he also sets in motion market forces which may induce recovery on the part of the firm that has declined in comparative performance. This is the sort of mechanism economics thrives on. It is neat — one either exits or one does not; it is impersonal — any face-to-face confrontation between

customer and firm with its imponderable and unpredictable elements is avoided and success and failure of the organization are communicated to it by a set of statistics; and it is indirect — any recovery on the part of the declining firm comes by courtesy of the Invisible Hand, as an unintended by-product of the customer's decision to shift.

Exit, Voice, and Loyalty 1970:15–16.

3 There are two main types of activist reactions to discontent with organizations to which one belongs or with which one does business: either to *voice* one's complaints, while continuing as a member or customer, in the hope of improving matters; or to *exit* from the organization, to take one's business elsewhere.

Exit, Voice, and the State (1978) 1981:246.

4 Modern political science owes a great deal to Machiavelli's shocking claim that ordinary notions of moral behavior for individuals may not be suitable as rules of conduct for states. More generally, it appeared, as a result of the wealth of insights discovered by Machiavelli, that the traditional concentration on the "ought," on the manner in which princes and statesmen ought to behave, interferes with the fuller understanding of the "is" that can be achieved when attention is closely and coldly riveted on the ways in which statecraft is in fact carried on.

Morality and the Social Sciences (1980) 1981:294–295.

5 Love, benevolence, and civic spirit neither are scarce factors in fixed supply nor do they act like skills and abilities that improve and expand more or less indefinitely with practice. Rather, they exhibit a complex, composite behavior: they atrophy when not adequately practiced and appealed to by the ruling socioeconomic regime, yet will once again make themselves scarce when preached and relied on to excess.

Against Parsimony (1984) 1986:157.

6 The thesis of the perverse effect. . . asserts not merely that a movement or policy will fall short of its goal or will occasion unexpected costs or negative side effects but that *the attempt to push society in a certain direction will result in its moving in the opposite direction*. . . Like many other elements of reactionary thinking, the thesis of the perverse effect was first put forward in the wake of the French Revolution.

Reactionary Rhetoric 1989:64. → See BOUDON:2.

Thomas Hobbes 1588–1679

British philosopher and political theorist

1 For what is the *heart*, but a *spring*; and the *nerves*, but so many *strings*; and the *joints*, but so many *wheels*, giving motion to the whole body, such as was intended by the artificer? *Art* goes yet further, imitating that rational and most excellent work of nature, *man*. For by art is created that great LEVIATHAN called a COMMONWEALTH, or STATE, in Latin CIVITAS, which is but an artificial man; though of greater stature and strength than the natural, for whose protection and defence it was intended; and in which the *sovereignty* is an artificial *soul*, as giving life and motion to the whole body.

Leviathan (1651) 1946:5.

2 The most noble and profitable invention of all other was that of SPEECH, consisting of *names* or *appellations*, and their connexion; whereby men register their thoughts; recall them when they are past; and also declare them one to another for mutual utility and conversation; without which, there had been amongst men, neither commonwealth, nor society, nor contract, nor peace, no more than amongst lions, bears, and wolves.

Leviathan (1651) (1946) Part 1, chap. 4, 18.

3 The manner how speech serveth to the remembrance of the consequence of causes and effects, consisteth in the imposing of *names*, and the *connexion* of them.

Of names, some are *proper*, and singular to one only thing, as *Peter, John, this man, this tree*; and some are *common* to many things, *man, horse, tree*; every of which, though but one name, is nevertheless the name of divers particular things; in respect of all which together, it is called an *universal*; there being nothing in the world universal but names; for the things named are every one of them individual and singular.

Leviathan (1651) 1946:Part 1, chap. 4, 19.

4 Nature itself cannot err; and as men abound in copiousness of language, so they become more wise, or more mad than ordinary. Nor is it possible without letters for any man to become either excellently wise, or, unless his memory be hurt by disease or ill constitution of organs, excellently foolish. For words are wise men's counters, they do but reckon by them; but they are the money of fools, that value them by the authority of an Aristotle, a Cicero, or a Thomas, or any other doctor whatsoever, if but a man.

Leviathan (1651) 1946:Part 1, chap. 4, 22.

5 To govern well a family, and a kingdom, are not different degrees of prudence; but different sorts of business; no more than to draw a picture in little, or as great, or greater than the life, are different degrees of art.

Leviathan (1651) 1946:Part 1, chap. 8, 45.

6 The thoughts are to the desires, as scouts, and spies, to range abroad, and find the way to the things desired.

Leviathan (1651) 1946:Part 1, chap. 8, 46.

7 The power *of a man*, to take it universally, is his present means, to obtain some future apparent good; and is either *original* or *instrumental*. . . Reputation of power, is power.

Leviathan (1651) 1946:Part 1, chap. 10, 56.

8 In the first place, I put for a general inclination of all mankind, a perpetual and restless desire of power after power, that ceaseth only in death.

Leviathan (1651) 1946:Part 1, chap. 11, 64.

9 And in these four things, opinion of ghosts, ignorance of second causes, devotion towards what men fear, and taking of things casual for prognostics, consisteth the natural seed of *religion*; which by reason of the different fancies, judgments, and passions of several men, hath grown up into ceremonies so different, that those which are used by one man, are for the most part ridiculous to another.

Leviathan (1651) 1946:Part 1, chap. 12, 72.

10 During the time men live without a common power to keep them all in awe, they are in that condition which is called war; and such a war, as is of every man, against every man.

Leviathan (1651) 1946:Part 1, chap. 13, 82.

11 Whatsoever therefore is consequent to a time of war, where every man is enemy to every man; the same is consequent to the time, wherein men live without other security, than what their own strength, and their own invention shall furnish them withal. In such condition, there is no place for industry; because the fruit thereof is uncertain: and consequently no culture of the earth; no navigation, nor use of the commodities that may be imported by sea; no commodious building; no instruments of moving, and removing, such things as require much force; no knowledge of the face of the earth; no account of time; no arts; no letters; no society; and which is worst of all, continual fear, and danger of violent death; and the life of man, solitary, poor, nasty, brutish, and short.

Leviathan (1651) 1946:Part 1, chap. 13, 82.

12 To this war of every man, against every man, this also is consequent; that nothing can be unjust. The notions of right and wrong, justice and injustice have there no place. Where there is no common power, there is no law: where no law, no injustice. Force, and fraud, are in war the two cardinal virtues.

Leviathan (1651) 1946:Part 1, chap. 13, 83.

13 Because the condition of man. . . is a condition of war of every one against every one; in which case every one is governed by his own reason; and there is nothing he can make use of, that may not be a help unto him, in preserving his life against his enemies; it followeth, that in such a condition, every man has a right to every thing; even to one another's body. And therefore, as long as this natural right of every man to every thing endureth, there can be no security to any man, how strong or wise soever he be, of living out the time, which nature ordinarily alloweth men to live. And consequently it is a precept, or general rule of reason, *that every man, ought to endeavour peace, as far as he has hope of obtaining it; and when he cannot obtain it, that he may seek, and use, all helps, and advantages of war*. The first branch of which rule, containeth the first, and fundamental law of nature; which is, *to seek peace, and follow it*. The second, the sum of the right of nature; which is, *by all means we can, to defend ourselves*.

Leviathan (1651) 1946:Part 1, chap. 14, 85.

14 The skill of making, and maintaining commonwealths, consisteth in certain rules, as doth arithmetic and geometry; not, as tennis-play, on practice only: which rules, neither poor men have the leisure, nor men that have had the leisure, have hitherto had the curiosity, or the method to find out.

Leviathan (1651) 1946:Part 2, chap. 20, 136.

15 Of systems subordinate, some are *political* and some *private*. *Political*, otherwise called *bodies politic*, and *persons in law*, are those, which are made by authority from the sovereign power of the commonwealth. *Private*, are those, which are constituted by subjects amongst themselves, or by authority from a stranger. For no authority derived from foreign power, within the dominion of another, is public there, but private.

Leviathan (1651) 1946:Part 2, chap. 22, 146. → An early use of the term "body politic."

John A. Hobson 1858–1940
British economist

1 A completely socialist State which kept good books and presented regular balance-sheets of expenditure and assets would soon discard Imperialism; an intelligent *laissez-faire* democracy which gave duly proportionate weight in its policy to all economic interests alike would do the same.

Imperialism (1902) 1965:47.

2 Everywhere appear excessive powers of production, excessive capital in search of investment. It is admitted by all business men that the growth of the powers of production in their country exceeds the growth in consumption, that more goods can be produced than can be sold at a profit, and that more capital exists than can find remunerative investment.

It is this economic condition of affairs that forms the taproot of Imperialism.

Imperialism (1902) 1965:81.

3 We are well aware that most British missionaries are quite untainted by admixture of political and commercial motives, and that they set about their work in a single spirit of self-sacrifice, eager to save the souls of the heathen, and not a whit concerned to push British trade or "sanctify the spirit of Imperialism."

Imperialism (1902) 1965:203.

A. M. Hocart 1883–1939
British anthropologist

1 We are so used to being governed that we think it the most natural thing in the world, sometimes self-evident. Yet, from Hobbes on, Moderns have always felt that some explanation was needed, that man was not created governed, and that he must at some time have acquired government.

Kings and Councillors (1936) 1970:128.

Thomas Hodgskin 1787–1869
British social theorist and journalist

1 One is almost tempted to believe that capital is a sort of cabalistic word, like Church or State, or any other of those general terms which are invented by those who fleece the rest of mankind to conceal the hand that shears them.

Labour Defended against the Claims of Capital (1825) 1963:60.

2 There is no state of society, probably, in which division of labour between the sexes does not take place. It is and *must* be practised the instant *a family* exists. Among even the most barbarous tribes, *war* is the exclusive business of the males; and they are in general, the principal hunters and fishers. The man takes to himself the perils and pleasures of the chase, and the woman labours in and about the hut. Different employments for the *sexes* may be traced in all communities, in every age of the world, and in every history, whether fabulous or true. In modern as well as ancient times, in the most civilized as well as in the most barbarous societies, we find the men, as the rule, taking the out-door work to themselves, and leaving to the women most of the domestic occupations. This primary division of labour springs from sexual difference of organization, it has its foundation in the difference of our physical constitution, in the different parental duties required of the sexes, and is co-extensive with the existence of our race.

Popular Political Economy 1827:111–112. → An early, biologistic formulation of the sexual division of labor.

Richard Hofstadter 1916–1970
U.S. historian

1 Such biological ideas as the "survival of the fittest," whatever their doubtful value in natural science; are utterly useless in attempting to understand society. . . The life of a man in society, while it is incidentally a biological fact, has characteristics that are not reducible to biology and must be explained in the distinctive terms of a cultural analysis;. . . the physical well-being of men is a result of their social organization and not vice versa. . . Social improvement is a product of advances in technology and social organization, not of breeding or selective elimination. . . Judgments as to the value of competition between men or enterprises or nations must be based upon social and not allegedly biological consequences; and. . . there is nothing in nature or a naturalistic philosophy of life to make impossible the acceptance of moral sanctions that can be employed for the common good.

Social Darwinism in American Thought (1944) 1955:204.

2 Almost the entire span of American history under the present Constitution has coincided with the rise and spread of modern industrial capitalism. In material power and productivity the United States has been a flourishing success. Societies that are in such good working order have a kind of mute organic consistency. They do not foster ideas that are hostile to their fundamental working arrangements. Such ideas may appear, but they are slowly and persistently insulated, as an oyster deposits nacre around an irritant.

The American Political Tradition 1948:viii–ix.

3 We have, at all times, two kinds of processes going on in inextricable connection with each other: *interest politics*, the clash of material aims and needs among various groups and blocs; and *status politics*, the clash of various projective rationalizations arising from status aspirations and other personal motives. In times of depression and economic discontent — and by and large in times of acute national emergency — politics is more clearly a matter of interests, although of course status considerations are still present. In times of prosperity and general well-being on the material plane, status considerations among the masses can become much more influential in our politics.

The Pseudo-conservative Revolt — 1954 (1954) 1965:53.

4 There is a great difference between locating conspiracies *in* history and saying that history *is*, in effect, a conspiracy, between singling out those conspiratorial acts that do on occasion occur and weaving a vast fabric of social explanation out of nothing but skeins of evil plots.

The Age of Reform (1955) 1956:71–72.

5 [Frederick Jackson Turner] is perhaps most reminiscent of Lord Acton — a man whose high repute, resting on a long and imposing shelf of unwritten books, might well have been considerably diminished if he had ever taken the trouble to do them.

The Progressive Historians (1968) 1970:94.

Lancelot Hogben 1895–1975
British biologist

1 With full responsibility for my words as a professional biologist, I do not hesitate to say that all existing and genuine knowledge about the way in which the physical characteristics of human communities are related to their cultural capabilities can be written on the back of a postage stamp.

Preface on Prejudices 1937:9.

2 The tireless versatility and consuming curiosity of men like William Petty and Robert Hooke can only prosper when social circumstances sustain high hopes in those whose brains have not been addled by a cloistered sophistication. If Petty is justly claimed as the father of Political Economy, the character and interests of no man could differ more conspicuously from those of a university professor of economics. He had the first desideratum of a genuine man of science — the itch to discover things for himself.

Prolegomena to Political Arithmetic 1938:23.

Oliver Wendell Holmes 1841–1935
U.S. jurist

1 The life of the law has not been logic: it has been experience. The felt necessities of the time, the prevalent moral and political theories, intuitions of public policy, avowed or unconscious, even the prejudices which judges share with their fellow-men, have had a good deal more to do than the syllogism in determining the rules by which men should be governed. The law embodies the story of a nation's development through many centuries, and it cannot be dealt with as if it contained only the axioms and corollaries of a book of mathematics.

The Common Law (1881) 1967:5.

2 The first requirement of a sound body of law is, that it should correspond with the actual feelings and demands of the community, whether right or wrong.

The Common Law (1881) 1967:36.

3 The law, as far as it depends on learning, is indeed. . . the government of the living by the dead. To a very considerable extent no doubt it is inevitable that the living should be so governed. The past gives us our vocabulary and fixes the limits of our imagination; we cannot get away from it. . . But the present has a right to govern itself so far as it can; and it ought always to be remembered that historic continuity with the past is not a duty, it is only a necessity.

Speech at Harvard Law School, 25 June 1895. 1913:67–68.

4 For the rational study of the law the black-letter man may be the man of the present, but the man of the future is the man of statistics and the master of economics.

The Path of the Law (1897) 1943:83.

5 Great cases like hard cases make bad law. For great cases are called great, not by reason of their real importance in shaping the law of the future, but because of some accident of immediate overwhelming interest which appeals to the feelings and distorts the judgment. These immediate interests exercise a kind of hydraulic pressure which makes what previously was clear seem doubtful, and before which even well settled principles of law will bend.

Northern Securities Co. v. *United States,* 193 U.S. 400–401, 1904.

6 The Fourteenth Amendment does not enact Mr. Herbert Spencer's Social Statics. . . A constitution is not intended to embody a particular economic theory.

Lochner v. *New York,* 198 U.S. 75, 1905. → The Fourteenth Amendment to the U.S. Constitution, ratified by the states between 1865 and 1866, contains — among others — provisions for "due process of law" and "equal protection of the laws."

7 General propositions do not decide concrete cases. The decision will depend on a judgment or intuition more subtle than any articulate major premise.

Lochner v. *New York,* 198 U.S. 76, 1905.

8 A State cannot be expected to move with the celerity of a private business man; it is enough if it proceeds, in the language of the English Chancery, with all deliberate speed.

Virginia v. *West Virginia,* 222 U.S. 19–20, 1911.

9 The common law is not a brooding omnipresence in the sky, but the articulate voice of some sovereign or quasi-sovereign that can be identified.

Southern Pacific Company v. *Jensen,* 244 U.S. 222, 1917.

10 It is not necessarily true that income means the same thing in the Constitution and the act. A word is not a crystal, transparent and unchanged, it is the skin of a living thought and may vary greatly in color and content according to the circumstances and the time in which it is used.

Towne v. *Eisner,* 245 U.S. 425, 1918.

11 The character of every act depends upon the circumstances in which it is done. . . The most stringent protection of free speech would not protect a man in falsely shouting fire in a theatre and causing a panic. It does not even protect a man from an injunction against uttering words that may have all the effect of force. . . The question in every case is whether the words used are used in such circumstances and are of such a nature as to create a clear and present danger that they will bring about the substantive evils that Congress has a right to prevent. It is a question of proximity and degree.

Schenck v. *United States,* 249 U.S. 52, 1919.

12 I do not doubt for a moment that by the same reasoning that would justify punishing persuasion to murder, the United States constitutionally may punish speech that produces or is intended to produce a clear and imminent danger that it will bring about forthwith certain substantive evils that the United States constitutionally may seek to prevent. . . It is only the present danger of immediate evil or an intent to bring it about that warrants Congress in setting a limit to the expression of opinion where private rights are not concerned.

Abrams et al. v. *United States,* 250 U.S. 627–628, 1919.

13 Persecution for the expression of opinions seems to me perfectly logical. If you have no doubt of your premises or your power and want a certain result with all your heart you naturally express your wishes in law and sweep away all opposition. To allow opposition by speech seems to indicate that you think the speech impotent, as when a man says that he has squared the circle, or that you do not care whole-heartedly for the result, or that you doubt either your power or your premises. But when men have realized that time has upset many fighting faiths, they may come to believe even more than they believe the very foundations of their own conduct that the ultimate good desired is better reached by free trade in ideas — that the best test of truth is the power of the thought to get itself

accepted in the competition of the market, and that truth is the only ground upon which their wishes safely can be carried out. That at any rate is the theory of our Constitution. It is an experiment, as all life is an experiment. Every year if not every day we have to wager our salvation upon some prophecy based upon imperfect knowledge. While that experiment is part of our system I think that we should be eternally vigilant against attempts to check the expression of opinions that we loathe and believe to be fraught with death, unless they so imminently threaten immediate interference with the lawful and pressing purposes of the law that an immediate check is required to save the country. . . Only the emergency that makes it immediately dangerous to leave the correction of evil counsels to time warrants making any exception to the sweeping command, "Congress shall make no law. . . abridging the freedom of speech."

Abrams et al. v. *United States,* 250 U.S. 630–631, 1919.

4 When we are dealing with words that also are a constituent act, like the Constitution of the United States, we must realize that they have called into life a being the development of which could not have been foreseen completely by the most gifted of its begetters. It was enough for them to realize or to hope that they had created an organism; it has taken a century and has cost their successors much sweat and blood to prove that they created a nation. The case before us must be considered in the light of our whole experience and not merely in that of what was said a hundred years ago.

State of Missouri v. *Holland, United States Game Warden,* 252 U.S. 433, 1920.

5 Taxes are what we pay for civilized society.

Compañía General de Tabacos de Filipinas v. *Collector of Internal Revenue,* 275 U.S. 100, 1927.

6 The power to tax is not the power to destroy while this Court sits.

Panhandle Oil Co. v. *Knox,* 277 U.S. 223, 1928.

7 We have to choose, and for my part I think it a less evil that some criminals should escape than that the government should play an ignoble part.

Olmstead et al. v. *United States,* 277 U.S. 470, 1928.

8 If there is any principle of the Constitution that more imperatively calls for attachment than any other it is the principle of free thought — not free thought for those who agree with us but freedom for the thought that we hate.

United States v. *Schwimmer,* 279 U.S. 654–655, 1929.

9 The law is the calling of thinkers. But to those who believe with me that not the least godlike of man's activities is the large survey of causes, that to know is not less than to feel, I say. . . that a man may live greatly in the law as well as elsewhere.

The Profession of the Law (1934) 1962:28–29. → From a 17 February 1886 lecture to Harvard undergraduates.

Gerald Holton 1922–

German-born U.S. physicist and historian of science

1 As a result of the phenomenally rapid change and growth of physics, the men and women who did their great work one or two generations ago may be our distant predecessors in terms of the state of the field, but they are our close neighbors in terms of time and tastes. This may be an unprecedented state of affairs among professions; one can perhaps be forgiven if one characterizes it epigrammatically with a disastrously mixed metaphor: in the sciences, we are now uniquely privileged to sit side-by-side with the giants on whose shoulders we stand.

On the Recent Past of Physics 1961:807. → See NEWTON:1.

2 [Consider] those fundamental presuppositions . . . that show up in the motivation of the scientist's actual work, as well as in the end-product for which he strives . . . I call them *themata* (singular *thema*, from the Greek θέμα, that which is laid down, proposition, primary word). . . The scientist is generally not, and need not be, conscious of the themata he uses, but the historian of science can chart the growth of a given thema in the work of an individual over time, and show its power upon his scientific imagination. Thematic analysis, then, is in the first instance the identification of the particular map of themata which, like the lines in a fingerprint, can characterize a scientist or a part of the scientific community at a given time.

Thematic Presuppositions and the Direction of Scientific Advance (1981) 1986:18.

3 To this day, we see all around us the Promethean drive to *omnipotence through technology* and to *omniscience through science*. The effecting of all things possible and the knowledge of all causes are the respective primary imperatives of technology and of science. But the motivating imperative of society continues to be the very different one of its physical and spiritual survival. It is now far less obvious than it was in Francis Bacon's world how to bring the three imperatives into harmony, and how to bring all three together to bear on problems where they superpose.

Science, Technology, and the Fourth Discontinuity (1982) 1986:183. → See BACON:11.

George C. Homans 1910–1989

U.S. sociologist

1 It is really intolerable that we can say only one thing at a time; for social behavior displays many features at the same time, and so in taking them up one by one we necessarily do outrage to its rich, dark, organic unity.

Social Behavior: Its Elementary Forms 1961:114.

2 If a serious effort is made to construct theories that will even begin to explain social phenomena, it turns out that

their general propositions are not about the equilibrium of societies but about the behavior of men.

Bringing Men Back In 1964:818.

3 Propositions of behavioral psychology are the general explanatory propositions in the field of human behavior, that is, the field of social science. . . We shall never be able to explain many things because we have, and can get, no adequate information about the given conditions within which the general propositions are to be applied. I argue only that when we think we can explain, our general principles turn out to be psychological.

The Nature of Social Science 1967:54–55.

4 The reason why people with similar backgrounds behave in similar ways here and now — so far as they do behave in similar ways — is that they are likely to have had similar past experiences. But it is also history that makes our findings even at the level closest to individual behavior only statistically true.

The Nature of Social Science 1967:90.

Earnest A. Hooton 1887–1954
U.S. anthropologist

1 Primitive peoples are probably not race-conscious to the deplorable or laudable extent which is characteristic of civilized populations. I mean that they are rather naïvely free from race prejudice until they have learned it from bitter experience. The American Indian was quite ready to take the European literally to his arms until he found out that a civilized embrace was inevitably throttling.

The Biology of Primitive Human Societies (1934) 1937:143.

2 Man is a predatory mammal which has achieved dominance over all vertebrates by a ruthless use of superior intelligence. From prehistoric times this ingeniously selfish biped has realized that the greatest gain of power and booty lies in preying upon his own species. It is easier to seize wealth than to create it.

Plain Statements about Race (1936) 1937:150.

Karen Horney 1885–1952
German-born U.S. psychoanalyst

1 When we realize the great import of cultural conditions on neuroses, the biological and physiological conditions, which are considered by Freud to be their root, recede into the background. The influence of these latter factors should be considered only on the basis of well established evidence. . . I believe that a strict adherence to all of Freud's theoretical interpretations entails the danger of tending to find in neuroses what Freud's theories lead one to expect to find. It is the danger of stagnation.

The Neurotic Personality of Our Time 1937:viii–ix.

2 For good reasons every culture clings to the belief that its own feelings and drives are the one normal expression of "human nature," and psychology has not made an exception to this rule. Freud, for example, concludes from his observations that woman is more jealous than man, and then tries to account for this presumably general phenomenon on biological grounds.

The Neurotic Personality of Our Time 1937:16–17.

3 [The] contradictions embedded in our culture are precisely the conflicts which the neurotic struggles to reconcile: his tendencies toward aggressiveness and his tendencies toward yielding; his excessive demands and his fear of never getting anything; his striving toward self-aggrandizement and his feeling of personal helplessness. The difference from the normal is merely quantitative. While the normal person is able to cope with the difficulties without damage to his personality, in the neurotic all the conflicts are intensified to a degree that makes any satisfactory solution impossible.

The Neurotic Personality of Our Time 1937:289.

4 There is no such thing as an isolated repetition of isolated experiences; but the entirety of infantile experiences combines to form a certain character structure, and it is this structure from which later difficulties emanate.

New Ways in Psychoanalysis (1939) 1966:9.

5 Compulsive drives are specifically neurotic; they are born of feelings of isolation, helplessness, fear and hostility, and represent ways of coping with the world despite these feelings; they aim primarily not at satisfaction but at safety; their compulsive character is due to the anxiety lurking behind them.

Our Inner Conflicts 1945:12–13.

Fred W. Householder 1913–
U.S. linguist

1 On the metaphysics of linguistics there are two extreme positions, which may be termed (and have been) the "God's truth" position and the "hocus-pocus" position. The theory of the "God's truth" linguists (and I regret to say I am one) is that a language *has* a structure, and the job of the linguist is (a) to find out what that structure is, and (b) to describe it as clearly, economically, and elegantly as he can, without at any point obscuring the God's truth structure of the language. The hocus-pocus linguist believes (or professes to believe — words and behavior are not always in harmony) that a language (better, a corpus, since we describe only the corpus we know) is a mass of incoherent, formless data, and the job of the linguist is somehow to arrange and organize this mass, imposing on it some sort of structure (which must not, of course, be in any striking or obvious conflict with anything in the data).

Review of Zellig S. Harris, *Methods in Structural Linguistics* 1952:260.

Everett C. Hughes 1897–1983
U.S. sociologist

1 I have already used the term *ethnic group,* a colorless catch-all much used by anthropologists and sociologists;

it is a term likely to be taken up by a larger public, and consequently likely to take on color that will compel the sociologists to get a new one, for it is one of the risks of our trade that our words lose the scientifically essential virtue of neutrality as they acquire the highly desirable virtue of being commonly used.

The Study of Ethnic Relations (1948) 1971:153.

H. Stuart Hughes 1916–
U.S. historian

1 To learn something of how humanity in past ages saw and heard and felt and smelled, we historians must be eternally on the alert for the casual reference, the apparently trivial clue, that will suddenly open up a whole unsuspected realm of understanding.

History as Art and as Science 1964:29.

Johan Huizinga 1872–1945
Dutch historian

1 To the world when it was half a thousand years younger, the outlines of all things seemed more clearly marked than to us. The contrast between suffering and joy, between adversity and happiness, appeared more striking. All experience had yet to the minds of men the directness and absoluteness of the pleasure and pain of child-life. Every event, every action, was still embodied in expressive and solemn forms, which raised them to the dignity of a ritual.

The Waning of the Middle Ages (1919) 1952:1.

2 The excesses and abuses resulting from an extreme familiarity with things holy, as well as the insolent mingling of pleasure with religion, are generally characteristic of periods of unshaken faith and of a deeply religious culture. The same people who in their daily life mechanically follow the routine of a rather degraded sort of worship will be capable of rising suddenly, at the ardent word of a preaching monk, to unparalleled heights of religious emotion. Even the stupid sin of blasphemy has its roots in a profound faith.

The Waning of the Middle Ages (1919) 1952:145–146.

3 The true character of the spirit of an age is better revealed in its mode of regarding and expressing trivial and commonplace things than in the high manifestations of philosophy and science. For all scholarly speculation, at least in Europe, is affiliated in a very complicated way to Greek, Hebrew, even Babylonian and Egyptian origins, whereas in everyday life the spirit of a race or of an epoch expresses itself naïvely and spontaneously.

The Waning of the Middle Ages (1919) 1952:206.

4 The fifteenth century in France and the Netherlands is still medieval at heart. The diapason of life had not yet changed. Scholastic thought, with symbolism and strong formalism, the thoroughly dualistic conception of life and the world still dominated. The two poles of the mind continued to be chivalry and hierarchy. Profound pessimism spread a general gloom over life. The gothic principle prevailed in art. But all these forms and modes were on the wane. A high and strong culture is declining, but at the same time and in the same sphere new things are being born. The tide is turning, the tone of life is about to change.

The Waning of the Middle Ages (1919) 1952:308.

5 The spirit of playful competition is, as a social impulse, older than culture itself and pervades all life like a veritable ferment. Ritual grew up in sacred play; poetry was born in play and nourished on play; music and dancing were pure play. Wisdom and philosophy found expression in words and forms derived from religious contests. The rules of warfare, the conventions of noble living were built up on play-patterns. We have to conclude, therefore, that civilization is, in its earliest phases, played. It does not come *from* play like a babe detaching itself from the womb: it arises *in* and *as* play, and never leaves it.

Homo ludens (1938) 1955:173.

6 Real civilization cannot exist in the absence of a certain play-element, for civilization presupposes limitation and mastery of the self, the ability not to confuse its own tendencies with the ultimate and highest goal, but to understand that it is enclosed within certain bounds freely accepted. Civilization will, in a sense, always be played according to certain rules, and true civilization will always demand fair play.

Homo ludens (1938) 1955:211.

Clark L. Hull 1884–1952
U.S. psychologist

1 The greatest problem confronting a mechanistic psychology at the present time is to discover the mechanism by means of which certain generalized habits or dispositions can act as selecting agents and particularly control and evoke other habit units. *If I can solve this problem I can found a new school of psychology*. The naive behaviorism of the present has not even appreciated the problem, to say nothing of having solved it.

Diary entry, March 1927. 1962:823.

2 The moral of the whole thing is that innumerable attempts to derive a satisfactory (i.e., scientific) theory of knowledge and of thought and reason from conscious experience as such have failed. In the place of this I propose to develop a system which starts from exactly the opposite end. I shall invert the whole historical system. I shall start with action — habit — and proceed to deduce all the rest, including conscious experience, from action, i.e., habit.

Diary entry, 26 June 1930. 1962:837.

3 A theory is a systematic deductive derivation of the secondary principles of observable phenomena from a relatively small number of primary principles or postulates, much as the secondary principles or theorems of geometry are all ultimately derived as a logical hierarchy from a

few original definitions and primary principles called axioms.

Principles of Behavior 1943:2.

Wilhelm von Humboldt 1767–1835
German statesman and philologist

1 Language is the formative organ of *thought. Intellectual activity,* entirely mental, entirely internal, and to some extent passing without trace, becomes, through *sound,* externalized in speech and perceptible to the senses. Thought and language are therefore one and inseparable from each other. But the former is also intrinsically bound to the necessity of entering into a *union* with the verbal sound; thought cannot otherwise achieve clarity, nor the idea become a concept.

On Language (1836) 1988:54–55.

2 Regardless of communication between man and man, speech is a necessary condition for the thinking of the individual in solitary seclusion. In appearance, however, language develops only *socially,* and man understands himself only once he has tested the intelligibility of his words by trial upon others.

On Language (1836) 1988:56.

3 Words well up freely from the breast, without necessity or intent, and there may well have been no wandering horde in any desert that did not already have its own songs. For man, as a species, is a singing creature, though the notes, in his case, are also coupled with thought.

On Language (1836) 1988:60.

David Hume 1711–1776
Scottish philosopher, political economist, and historian

1 All the sciences have a relation, greater or less, to human nature; and. . . however wide any of them may seem to run from it, they still return back by one passage or another. Even *Mathematics, Natural Philosophy, and Natural Religion,* are in some measure dependent on the science of MAN; since they lie under the cognizance of men, and are judged of by their powers and faculties.

A Treatise of Human Nature (1739–1740) 1975:xv.

2 As the science of man is the only solid foundation for the other sciences, so the only solid foundation we can give to this science itself must be laid on experience and observation.

A Treatise of Human Nature (1739–1740) 1975:xvi.

3 Reason is, and ought only to be the slave of the passions, and can never pretend to any other office than to serve and obey them.

A Treatise of Human Nature (1739–1740) 1975:Book 2, 415.

4 Of all the animals with which this globe is peopled, there is none towards whom nature seems, at first sight, to have exercis'd more cruelty than towards man, in the numberless wants and necessities, with which she has loaded him, and in the slender means, which she affords to the relieving these necessities.

A Treatise of Human Nature (1739–1740) 1975:Book 3, 484.

5 'Tis by society alone [man] is able to supply his defects, and raise himself up to an equality with his fellow-creatures, and even acquire a superiority above them.

A Treatise of Human Nature (1739–1740) 1975:Book 3, 485.

6 When every individual person labours a-part, and only for himself, his force is too small to execute any considerable work; his labour being employ'd in supplying all his different necessities, he never attains a perfection in any particular art; and as his force and success are not at all times equal, the least failure in either of these particulars must be attended with inevitable ruin and misery. Society provides a remedy for these *three* inconveniences.

A Treatise of Human Nature (1739–1740) 1975:Book 3, 485.

7 It is evident that all reasonings concerning *matter of fact* are founded on the relation of cause and effect, and that we can never infer the existence of one object from another unless they be connected together, either mediately or immediately. . . Here is a billiard ball lying on the table, and another ball moving toward it with rapidity. They strike; and the ball which was formerly at rest now acquires a motion.

An Abstract of a Treatise of Human Nature (1740) 1955:186.

8 Nothing appears more surprizing to those, who consider human affairs with a philosophical eye, than the easiness with which the many are governed by the few; and the implicit submission, with which men resign their own sentiments and passions to those of their rulers. . . The governors have nothing to support them but opinion. It is therefore, on opinion only that government is founded; and this maxim extends to the most despotic and most military governments, as well as to the most free and most popular.

Of the First Principles of Government (1741) 1985:32.

9 In contriving any system of government, and fixing the several checks and controuls of the constitution, every man ought to be supposed a *knave,* and to have no other end, in all his actions, than private interest.

Of the Independency of Parliament (1741) 1985:42.

10 Men are generally more honest in their private than in their public capacity, and will go greater lengths to serve a party, than when their own private interest is alone concerned. Honour is a great check upon mankind.

Of the Independency of Parliament (1741) 1985:43.

11 There is nothing, in itself, valuable or despicable, desirable or hateful, beautiful or deformed; but that these at-

tributes arise from the particular constitution and fabric of human sentiment and affection.

The Skeptic (1742) 1985:162.

The great end of all human industry, is the attainment of happiness. For this were arts invented, sciences cultivated, laws ordained, and societies modelled, by the most profound wisdom of patriots and legislators. Even the lonely savage, who lies exposed to the inclemency of the elements, and the fury of wild beasts, forgets not, for a moment, this grand object of his being. Ignorant as he is of every art of life, he still keeps in view the end of all those arts, and eagerly seeks for felicity amidst that darkness with which he is environed.

The Stoic (1742) 1985:148.

That the sun will not rise tomorrow is no less intelligible a proposition and implies no more contradiction than the affirmation *that it will rise*. We should in vain, therefore, attempt to demonstrate its falsehood.

An Inquiry Concerning Human Understanding (1748) 1955:40.

If. . . the past may be no rule for the future, all experience becomes useless and can give rise to no inference or conclusion.

An Inquiry Concerning Human Understanding (1748) 1955:51.

Custom. . . is the great guide of human life. It is that principle alone which renders our experience useful to us and makes us expect, for the future, a similar train of events with those which have appeared in the past. Without the influence of custom we should be entirely ignorant of every matter of fact beyond what is immediately present to the memory and senses. We should never know how to adjust means to ends or to employ our natural powers in the production of any effect. There would be an end at once of all action as well as of the chief part of speculation.

An Inquiry Concerning Human Understanding (1748) 1955:58–59.

Though there be no such thing as *chance* in the world, our ignorance of the real cause of any event has the same influence on the understanding and begets a like species of belief or opinion.

An Inquiry Concerning Human Understanding (1748) 1955:69.

When we run over libraries, persuaded of these principles, what havoc must we make? If we take in our hand any volume — of divinity or school metaphysics, for instance — let us ask, *Does it contain any abstract reasoning concerning quantity or number*? No. *Does it contain any experimental reasoning concerning matter of fact and existence*? No. Commit it then to the flames, for it can contain nothing but sophistry and illusion.

An Inquiry Concerning Human Understanding (1748) 1980:173.

18 The propensity to company and society is strong in all rational creatures; and the same disposition, which gives us this propensity, makes us enter deeply into each other's sentiments, and causes like passions and inclinations to run, as it were, by contagion, through the whole club or knot of companions.

Of National Characters (1748) 1985:202.

19 The tenth legion of CAESAR and the regiment of PICARDY in FRANCE were formed promiscuously from among the citizens; but having once entertained a notion, that they were the best troops in the service, this very opinion really made them such.

Of National Characters (1748) 1985:212.

20 Money is not, properly speaking, one of the subjects of commerce; but only the instrument which men have agreed upon to facilitate the exchange of one commodity for another. It is none of the wheels of trade: It is the oil which renders the motion of the wheels more smooth and easy.

Of Money (1752) 1955:33.

21 Every thing in the world is purchased by labour; and our passions are the only causes of labour.

Of Commerce (1754) 1985:261.

22 The encrease of riches and commerce in any one nation, instead of hurting, commonly promotes the riches and commerce of all its neighbours; and. . . a state can scarcely carry its trade and industry very far, where all the surrounding states are buried in ignorance, sloth, and barbarism.

On the Jealousy of Trade (1758)1985:328.

23 Look round the world, contemplate the whole and every part of it: you will find it to be nothing but one great machine, subdivided into an infinite number of lesser machines, which again admit of subdivisions to a degree beyond what human senses and faculties can trace and explain. All these various machines, and even their most minute parts, are adjusted to each other with an accuracy which ravishes into admiration all men who have ever contemplated them. The curious adapting of means to ends, throughout all nature, resembles exactly, though it much exceeds, the productions of human contrivance — of human design, thought, wisdom, and intelligence.

Dialogues Concerning Natural Religion (1779) 1948:Part 2, 17.

Ellsworth Huntington 1876–1947

U.S. geographer

1 Civilization and climatic energy appear to go hand in hand. This suggests the far-reaching hypothesis that a stimulating climate is an essential condition for civilization.

Weather and Civilizations 1916:14.

Samuel P. Huntington 1927–
U.S. political scientist

1 As society changes, so does the role of the military. In the world of oligarchy, the soldier is a radical; in the middle-class world he is a participant and arbiter; as the mass society looms on the horizon he becomes the conservative guardian of the existing order. Thus, paradoxically but understandably, the more backward a society is, the more progressive the role of its military; the more advanced a society becomes, the more conservative and reactionary becomes the role of its military.

Political Order in Changing Societies 1968:221.

Francis Hutcheson 1694–1746
Scottish philosopher

1 As the natural Consequences of our Actions are various, some *good* to our selves, and *evil* to the Publick; and others *evil* to our selves, and *good* to the Publick; or either *useful* both to our selves and others, or *pernicious* to both; the entire Motive to good Actions is not always *Benevolence alone*; or Motive to Evil, *Malice alone*; (nay, this last is seldom any Motive at all) but in most Actions we must look upon *Self-Love* as another Force, sometimes conspiring with *Benevolence,* and assisting it, when we are excited by Views of *private Interest,* as well as *publick Good*; and sometimes opposing *Benevolence,* when the good Action is any way *difficult* or *painful* in the Performance.

Inquiry Concerning Moral Good and Evil (1725) 1726:184.

Julian Huxley 1887–1975
British biologist
and
Alfred Cort Haddon 1855–1940
British anthropologist

1 The popular and scientific views of "race" no longer coincide. The word "race," as applied scientifically to human groupings, has lost any sharpness of meaning. To-day it is hardly definable in scientific terms, except as an abstract concept which *may,* under certain conditions, very different from those now prevalent, have been realized approximately in the past, and *might,* under certain other but equally different conditions, be realized in the distant future.

We Europeans 1935:107.

T. H. Huxley 1825–1895
British biologist

1 Science is, I believe, nothing but *trained and organised common sense,* differing from the latter only as a veteran may differ from a raw recruit: and its methods differ from those of common sense only so far as the guardsman's cut and thrust differ from the manner in which a savage wields his club.

On the Educational Value of the Natural History Sciences (1854) 1971:53.

2 Our reverence for the nobility of manhood will not be lessened by the knowledge that Man is, in substance and in structure, one with the brutes; for, he alone possesses the marvellous endowment of intelligible and rational speech, whereby, in the secular period of his existence, he has slowly accumulated and organized the experience which is almost wholly lost with the cessation of every individual life in other animals; so that now he stands raised upon it as on a mountain top, far above the level of his humble fellows, and transfigured from his grosser nature by reflecting, here and there, a ray from the infinite source of truth.

Man's Place in Nature (1863) 1959:132.

3 The great tragedy of Science — the slaying of a beautiful hypothesis by an ugly fact.

Biogenesis and Abiogenesis (1870) 1896:244. → From his presidential address to the British Association for the Advancement of Science.

4 M. Comte's philosophy in practice might be compendiously described as Catholicism *minus* Christianity.

On the Physical Basis of Life 1871:140. → From a lecture given in Edinburgh in 1868.

5 History warns us. . .that it is the customary fate of new truths to begin as heresies and to end as superstitions; and, as matters now stand, it is hardly rash to anticipate that, in another twenty years, the new generation, educated under the influences of the present day, will be in danger of accepting the main doctrines of the "Origin of Species," with as little reflection, and it may be with as little justification, as so many of our contemporaries, twenty years ago, rejected them.

The Coming of Age of "The Origin of Species" (1880) 1896:229.

6 [On reading *The Origin of Species*]: How extremely stupid not to have thought of that.

Quoted in Ernst Mayr, Introduction to Charles Darwin, *On the Origin of Species* (1859) 1964:xv.

Herbert H. Hyman 1918–1985
U.S. psychologist and sociologist

1 In shaping their attitudes men may orient themselves to groups other than their own. If the groups to which individuals refer themselves, their reference groups, are empirically determined, knowledge and predictions of attitude, self-evaluation, and conduct will be enhanced; the cherished principles about group influences can be protected; and an understanding of the complex pro-

cesses by which men relate themselves to groups can be enriched.

Reference Groups 1968:354. → The concept of "reference group" was coined by Hyman in *The Psychology of Status* (1942).

Dell Hymes 1927–

U.S. anthropologist and linguist

1 *There is a fundamental difference. . . between what is not said because there is no occasion to say it, and what is not said because one has not and does not find a way to say it*. For the language to be used to say such things, the language must change.

Why Linguistics Needs the Sociologist (1967) 1974:72.

2 There are rules of use without which the rules of grammar would be useless. Just as rules of syntax can control aspects of phonology, and just as semantic rules perhaps control aspects of syntax, so rules of speech acts enter as a controlling factor for linguistic form as a whole.

On Communicative Competence (1971) 1972:278.

I

Ibn Khaldûn 1332–1406
Tunisian historian, sociologist, and philosopher

1 All records, by their very nature, are liable to error — nay, they contain factors which make for error. The first of these is *partisanship* towards a creed or opinion. . . The second factor conducive to error is *over-confidence* in one's sources. . . A third factor is the *failure to understand* what is intended. . . A fourth source of error is a *mistaken belief in the truth*. . . A fifth factor is the inability rightly to *place an event in its real context*, owing to the obscurity and complexity of the situation. The chronicler contents himself with reporting the event as he saw it, thus distorting its significance. A sixth factor is the very common desire to *gain the favour* of those of high rank, by praising them, by spreading their fame, by flattering them, by embellishing their doings and by interpreting in the most favourable way all their actions. . . The seventh cause of error, and the most important of all, is *the ignorance of the laws* governing the transformation of human society. For every single thing, whether it be an object or an action, is subject to a law governing its nature and any changes that may take place in it.

An Arab Philosophy of History (1377) 1950:27–28. → Selections from *The Muqaddimah*.

2 Another cause of error is *exaggeration*. . . Thus we find that most of our contemporaries give free rein to their imagination, follow the whisperings of exaggeration, and transgress the limitations of customary experience, when speaking of the armies of contemporary states, or of states which existed in the recent past; or when discussing the troops of Muslim or Christian nations; or when enumerating the revenues of kings, or the taxes or dues levied by them; or when estimating the expenditure of the wealthy, or the fortunes of the rich. Should we, however, check up these figures by asking the responsible officials for the number of their troops, or the rich for a statement of their wealth, profits, and expenditures, the result is apt to come to less than a tenth of the popular estimate.

An Arab Philosophy of History (1377) 1950:29. → An early recognition of "response bias."

3 Another hidden source of error in historical writing is the *ignoring of the transformations* that occur in the condition of epochs and peoples with the passage of time and the changes of periods. Such changes occur in such an unnoticeable way and take so long to make themselves felt, that they are very difficult to discern and are observed only by a small number of men.

An Arab Philosophy of History (1377) 1950:29–30.

4 History is a discipline widely cultivated among nations and races. It is eagerly sought after. The men in the street, the ordinary people, aspire to know it. Kings and leaders vie for it.

Both the learned and the ignorant are able to understand it. For on the surface history is no more than information about political events, dynasties, and occurrences of the remote past, elegantly presented and spiced with proverbs. It serves to entertain large, crowded gatherings and brings to us an understanding of human affairs. (It shows) how changing conditions affected (human affairs), how certain dynasties came to occupy an ever wider space in the world, and how they settled the earth until they heard the call and their time was up.

The inner meaning of history, on the other hand, involves speculation and an attempt to get at the truth, subtle explanation of the causes and origins of existing things, and deep knowledge of the how and why of events. (History,) therefore, is firmly rooted in philosophy. It deserves to be accounted a branch of (philosophy).

The Muqaddimah (1377) 1958:Vol. 1, 6.

5 Historiography [has come] to be considered a domain of the common people. Therefore, today, the scholar in this field needs to know the principles of politics, the (true) nature of existent things, and the differences among nations, places, and periods with regard to ways of life, character, qualities, customs, sects, schools, and everything else. He further needs a comprehensive knowledge of present conditions in all these respects. He must compare similarities or differences between the present and the past (or distantly located) conditions. He must know how the causes of the similarities in certain cases and of

the differences in others. He must be aware of the differing origins and beginnings of (different) dynasties and religious groups, as well as of the reasons and incentives that brought them into being and the circumstances and history of the persons who supported them. His goal must be to have complete knowledge of the reasons for every happening, and to be acquainted with the origin of every event. Then, he must check transmitted information with the basic principles he knows. If it fulfills their requirements, it is sound. Otherwise, the historian must consider it as spurious and dispense with it. It was for this reason alone that historiography was highly considered by the ancients. . . Most scholars, however, forgot this, the (real) secret of historiography, with the result that it became a stupid occupation. Ordinary people as well as (scholars) who had no firm foundation of knowledge considered it a simple matter to study and know history, to delve into it and sponge on it. Strays got into the flock, bits of shell were mixed with the nut, truth was adulterated with lies.

The Muqaddimah (1377) 1958:Vol. 1, 55–56.

6 Such is the purpose of this first book of our work. (The subject) is in a way an independent science. (This science) has its own peculiar object — that is, human civilization and social organization. It also has its own peculiar problems — that is, explaining the conditions that attach themselves to the essence of civilization, one after the other. Thus, the situation is the same with this science as it is with any other science, whether it be a conventional or an intellectual one.

The Muqaddimah (1377) 1958:Vol. 1, 77.

7 Social organization is necessary to the human species. Without it, the existence of human beings would be incomplete. God's desire to settle the world with human beings and to leave them as His representatives on earth would not materialize. This is the meaning of civilization, the object of the science under discussion.

The Muqaddimah (1377) 1958:Vol. 1, 91.

8 One knows from philosophical works the statement that "man is political by nature." The philosophers cite that statement in connection with establishing the existence of prophecy and other things. The adjective "political" refers to the "town" (*polis*) which they use as another word for human social organization.

The statement means that a single human being cannot live by himself, and his existence can materialize only in association with his fellow men. (Alone) he would be unable to have a complete existence and lead a complete life. By his very nature, he needs the co-operation of others to satisfy all his needs. Such co-operation requires, firstly, consultation, and, then, association and the things that follow after it. Dealings with other people, when there is oneness of purpose may lead to mutual affection, and when the purposes differ, they may lead to strife and altercation. Thus, mutual dislike and mutual affection, friendship and hostility, originate. This leads to war and peace among nations and tribes.

The Muqaddimah (1377) 1958:Vol. 2, 417. → See ARISTOTLE:7.

J

Roman Jakobson 1896–1982
Russian-born U.S. linguist

1 Were we to comprise the leading idea of present-day science in its most various manifestations, we could hardly find a more appropriate designation than *structuralism*. Any set of phenomena examined by contemporary science is treated not as a mechanical agglomeration but as a structural whole, and the basic task is to reveal the inner, whether static or developmental, laws of this system. What appears to be the focus of scientific preoccupations is no longer the outer stimulus, but the internal premises of the development; now the mechanical conception of processes yields to the question of their functions.

Retrospect (1929) 1971:711.

2 There are messages primarily serving to establish, to prolong, or to discontinue communication, to check whether the channel works ("Hello, do you hear me?"), to attract the attention of the interlocutor or to confirm his continued attention ("Are you listening?" or in Shakespearean diction, "Lend me your ears!" — and on the other end of the wire "Um-hum!"). This set for CONTACT, or in Malinowski's terms PHATIC function, may be displayed by a profuse exchange of ritualized formulas, by entire dialogues with the mere purport of prolonging communication.

Linguistics and Poetics 1960:355. → See MALINOWSKI:7.

3 Jeremy Bentham, who was perhaps the first to disclose the manifold "linguistic fictions" which underlie the grammatical structure and which are used throughout the whole field of language as a "necessary resource," arrived in his *Theory of Fictions* at a challenging conclusion: "to language, then — to language alone — it is, that fictitious entities owe their existence; their impossible, yet indispensable existence." Linguistic fictions should neither be "mistaken for realities" nor be ascribed to the creative fancy of linguists: they "owe their existence" actually "to language alone" and particularly to the "grammatical form of the discourse," in Bentham's terms.

Poetry of Grammar and Grammar of Poetry (1961) 1987:123. → See BENTHAM:12.

4 [How many languages do you speak?] This is very difficult to answer, this question. It depends what means "speak." I can improvise lectures in Russian, Czech, Polish, French, German, and English — six languages. Kurylowicz, the leading Polish linguist, once said, "Jakobson is a peculiar man. He speaks fluently Russian in six languages."

Quoted in Ved Mehta, *John Is Easy to Please* 1971:229.

William James 1842–1910
U.S. psychologist and philosopher

1 Every thought you now have and every act and intention owes its complexion to the acts of your dead and living brothers. *Everything* we know and are is through men. We have no revelation but through man. Every sentiment that warms your gizzard, every brave act that ever made your pulse bound and your nostril open to a confident breath was a man's act. However mean a man may be, man is *the best we know*; and your loathing as you turn from what you probably call the vulgarity of human life — your homesick yearning for a *Better*, somewhere — is furnished by your manhood; your ideal is made up of traits suggested by past men's words and actions.

Letter to Thomas W. Ward, January 1868. 1920:131–132.

2 The best way to define a man's character would be to seek out the particular mental or moral attitude in which, when it came upon him, he felt himself most deeply and intensely active and alive. At such moments there is a voice inside which speaks and says: "*This* is the real me!"

Letter to Mrs. James (1878) 1920:199.

3 Not every "man" fits every "hour." Some incompatibilities there are. A given genius may come either too early or too late. Peter the Hermit would now be sent to a luna-

tic asylum. John Mill in the tenth century would have lived and died unknown. Cromwell and Napoleon need their revolutions, Grant his civil war. An Ajax gets no fame in the day of telescopic-sighted rifles; and, to express differently an instance which Spencer uses, what could a Watt have effected in a tribe which no precursive genius had taught to smelt iron or to turn a lathe?

Great Men and Their Environment (1880) 1910:229–230.

4 Evolution is a change from a no-howish untalkaboutable all-alikeness to a somehowish and in general talkaboutable not-all-alikeness by continuous sticktogetherations and somethingelseifications.

Lecture Notes 1880–1897. → James gave a course at Harvard on "The Philosophy of Evolution," using Herbert Spencer's *First Principles* (1862) as a text. He wrote this parody of Spencer's verbose definition of evolution to read to his students. See SPENCER:6.

5 A Beethoven string-quartet is truly, as some one has said, a scraping of horses' tails on cats' bowels, and may be exhaustively described in such terms; but the application of this description in no way precludes the simultaneous applicability of an entirely different description.

The Sentiment of Rationality (1882) 1910:76.

6 I can well understand why [Wilhelm] Wundt should make his compatriots impatient. Foreigners can afford to be indifferent for he doesn't *crowd* them so much. He aims at being a sort of Napoleon of the intellectual world. Unfortunately he will never have a Waterloo, for he is a Napoleon without genius and with no central idea which, if defeated, brings down the whole fabric in ruin. . . Cut him up like a worm, and each fragment crawls; there is no *noeud vital* in his medulla oblongata, so that you can't kill him all at once.

Letter to Carl Stumpf, 6 February 1887. 1920:263.

7 Habit is. . . the enormous fly-wheel of society, its most precious conservative agent. It alone is what keeps us all within the bounds of ordinance, and saves the children of fortune from the envious uprisings of the poor. It alone prevents the hardest and most repulsive walks of life from being deserted by those brought up to tread therein. It keeps the fishermen and the deck-hand at sea through the winter; it holds the miner in his darkness, and nails the countryman to his log-cabin and his lonely farm through all the months of snow; it protects us from invasion by the natives of the desert and the frozen zone. It dooms us all to fight out the battle of life upon the lines of our nurture or our early choice, and to make the best of a pursuit that disagrees, because there is no other for which we are fitted, and it is too late to begin again. It keeps different social strata from mixing. Already at the age of twenty-five you see the professional mannerism settling down on the young commercial traveller, on the young doctor, on the young minister, on the young counsellor-at-law. You see the little lines of cleavage running through the character, the tricks of thought, the prejudices, the ways of the "shop," in a word, from which the man can by-and-by no more escape than his coat-sleeve can suddenly fall into a new set of folds. On the whole, it is best he should not escape. It is well for the world that in most of us, by the age of thirty, the character has set like plaster, and will never soften again.

The Principles of Psychology (1890) 1950:Vol. 1, 121.

8 The great thing. . . in all education, is to *make our nervous system our ally instead of our enemy*. It is to fund and capitalize our acquisitions, and live at ease upon the interest of the fund. *For this we must make automatic and habitual, as early as possible, as many useful actions as we can*, and guard against the growing into ways that are likely to be disadvantageous to us, as we should guard against the plague.

The Principles of Psychology (1890) 1950:Vol. 1, 122.

9 The drunken Rip Van Winkle, in [Joseph] Jefferson's play, excuses himself for every fresh dereliction by saying, "I won't count this time"! Well! he may not count it, and a kind Heaven may not count it; but it is being counted none the less. Down among his nerve-cells and fibres the molecules are counting it, registering and storing it up to be used against him when the next temptation comes. Nothing we ever do is, in strict literalness, wiped out. Of course, this has its good side as well as its bad one. As we become permanent drunkards by so many separate drinks, so we become saints in the moral, and authorities and experts in the practical and scientific spheres, by so many separate acts and hours of work.

The Principles of Psychology (1890) 1950:Vol. 1, 127.

10 If pleasures and pains have no efficacy, one does not see. . . why the most noxious acts, such as burning, might not give thrills of delight, and the most necessary ones, such as breathing, cause agony.

The Principles of Psychology (1890) 1950:Vol. 1, 144.

11 Consciousness. . . does not appear to itself chopped up in bits. Such words as "chain" or "train" do not describe it fitly as it presents itself in the first instance. It is nothing jointed; it flows. A "river" or a "stream" are the metaphors by which it is most naturally described. *In talking of it hereafter, let us call it the stream of thought, of consciousness, or of subjective life.*

The Principles of Psychology (1890) 1950:Vol. 1, 239. → The origin of the phrase "stream of consciousness."

12 Suppose we try to recall a forgotten name. The state of our consciousness is peculiar. There is a gap therein; but no mere gap. It is a gap that is intensely active. A sort of wraith of the name is in it, beckoning us in a given direction, making us at moments tingle with the sense of our closeness, and then letting us sink back without the longed-for term. If wrong names are proposed to us, this singularly definite gap acts immediately so as to negate them. They do not fit into its mould. And the gap of one word does not feel like the gap of another, all empty of

content as both might seem necessarily to be when described as gaps.

The Principles of Psychology (1890) 1950:Vol. 1, 251. → See BROWN AND MCNEILL:1 on the "tip of the tongue" phenomenon.

13 *In its widest possible sense. . . a man's Self is the sum total of all that he* CAN *call his,* not only his body and his psychic powers, but his clothes and his house, his wife and children, his ancestors and friends, his reputation and works, his lands and horses, and yacht and bank-account. All these things give him the same emotions. If they wax and prosper, he feels triumphant; if they dwindle and die away, he feels cast down, — not necessarily in the same degree for each thing, but in much the same way for all.

The Principles of Psychology (1890) 1950:Vol. 1, 291–292.

14 *A man has as many social selves as there are individuals who recognize him* and carry an image of him in their mind. To wound any one of these his images is to wound him. But as the individuals who carry the images fall naturally into classes, we may practically say that he has as many different social selves as there are distinct *groups* of persons about whose opinion he cares. He generally shows a different side of himself to each of these different groups.

The Principles of Psychology (1890) 1950:Vol. 1, 294. → James implicitly uses the concept of "reference group" developed in 1942 by Herbert H. Hyman. See HYMAN:1.

15 The whole feeling of reality, the whole sting and excitement of our voluntary life, depends on our sense that in it things are *really being decided* from one moment to another, and that it is not the dull rattling off of a chain that was forged innumerable ages ago.

The Principles of Psychology (1890) 1950:Vol. 1, 453.

16 In the practical use of our intellect, forgetting is as important a function as recollecting.

The Principles of Psychology (1890) 1950:Vol. 1, 679.

17 Genius. . . means little more than the faculty of perceiving in an unhabitual way.

The Principles of Psychology (1890) 1950:Vol. 2, 110.

18 My theory. . . is that *the bodily changes follow directly the perception of the exciting fact, and that our feeling of the same changes as they occur* IS *the emotion.* Common-sense says, we lose our fortune, are sorry and weep; we meet a bear, are frightened and run; we are insulted by a rival, are angry and strike. The hypothesis here to be defended says that this order of sequence is incorrect, that the one mental state is not immediately induced by the other, that the bodily manifestations must first be interposed between, and that the moral rational statement is that we feel sorry because we cry, angry because we strike, afraid because we tremble, and not that we cry, strike, or tremble, because we are sorry, angry, or fearful, as the case may be. Without the bodily states following on the perception, the latter would be purely cognitive in form, pale, colorless, destitute of emotional warmth. We might then see the bear, and judge it best to run, receive the insult and deem it right to strike, but we should not actually *feel* afraid or angry.

The Principles of Psychology (1890) 1950:Vol. 2, 449–450. → This is a formulation of the James-Lange theory of emotion, developed independently in the 1880s by James and the Danish thinker C. G. Lange.

19 Mental facts cannot be properly studied apart from the physical environment of which they take cognizance.

Psychology (1892) 1928:3.

20 A man's social me is the recognition which he gets from his mates. We are not only gregarious animals, liking to be in sight of our fellows, but we have an innate propensity to get ourselves noticed, and noticed favorably, by our kind.

Psychology (1892) 1928:179.

21 Objective evidence and certitude are doubtless very fine ideals to play with, but where on this moonlit and dream-visited planet are they found?

The Will to Believe (1896) 1910:14.

22 Science can tell us what exists; but to compare the *worths,* both of what exists and of what does not exist, we must consult not science, but what Pascal calls our heart.

The Will to Believe (1896) 1910:22.

23 No one need be too much cast down by the discovery of his deficiency in any elementary faculty of the mind. What tells in life is the whole mind working together, and the deficiencies of any one faculty can be compensated by the efforts of the rest. You can be an artist without visual images, a reader without eyes, a mass of erudition with a bad elementary memory. In almost any subject your passion for the subject will save you. If you only care enough for a result, you will almost certainly attain it.

Talks to Teachers on Psychology (1899) 1923:136–137.

24

THE TENDER-MINDED.	THE TOUGH-MINDED.
Rationalistic (going by "principles"),	Empiricist (going by "facts"),
Intellectualistic,	Sensationalistic,
Idealistic,	Materialistic,
Optimistic,	Pessimistic,
Religious,	Irreligious,
Free-willist,	Fatalistic,
Monistic,	Pluralistic,
Dogmatical.	Sceptical.

Pragmatism (1907) 1946:12. → This is James's famous dichotomy of intellectual temperaments.

25 A glance at the history of the idea will show you still better what pragmatism means. The term is derived from the same Greek word (πράγμα), meaning action, from

which our words "practice" and "practical" come. . . The tangible fact at the root of all our thought-distinctions, however subtle, is that there is no one of them so fine as to consist in anything but a possible difference of practice. To attain perfect clearness in our thoughts of an object, then, we need only consider what conceivable effects of a practical kind the object may involve — what sensations we are to expect from it, and what reactions we must prepare. Our conception of these effects, whether immediate or remote, is then for us the whole of our conception of the object, so far as that conception has positive significance at all.

This is the principle of [Charles Sanders] Peirce, the principle of pragmatism. It lay entirely unnoticed by any one for twenty years, until I. . . brought it forward again and made a special application of it to religion. By that date (1898) the times seemed ripe for its reception. The word "pragmatism" spread, and at present it fairly spots the pages of the philosophic journals. . . It is evident that the term applies itself conveniently to a number of tendencies that hitherto have lacked a collective name, and that it has "come to stay."

Pragmatism (1907) 1946:46–47 → See PEIRCE:5.

26 First. . . a new theory is attacked as absurd; then it is admitted to be true, but obvious and insignificant; finally it is seen to be so important that its adversaries claim that they themselves discovered it.

Pragmatism (1907) 1946:198.

27 Pragmatism. . . asks its usual question. "Grant an idea or belief to be true," it says, "what concrete difference will its being true make in any one's actual life? How will the truth be realized? What experiences will be different from those which would obtain if the belief were false? What, in short, is the truth's cash-value in experiential terms?"

The moment pragmatism asks this question, it sees the answer: *True ideas are those that we can assimilate, validate, corroborate, and verify. False ideas are those that we can not.* That is the practical difference it makes to us to have true ideas; that, therefore, is the meaning of truth, for it is all that truth is known-as.

Pragmatism (1907) 1946:200–201.

28 The truth of an idea is not a stagnant property inherent in it. Truth *happens* to an idea. It *becomes* true, is *made* true by events. Its verity *is* in fact an event, a process: the process namely of its verifying itself, its veri-*fication*. Its validity is the process of its valid-*ation*.

Pragmatism (1907) 1946:201.

29 If now — and this is my idea — there were, instead of military conscription a conscription of the whole youthful population to form for a certain number of years a part of the army enlisted against *Nature*, the injustice would tend to be evened out, and numerous other goods to the commonwealth would follow. The military ideals of hardihood and discipline would be wrought into the growing fibre of the people; no one would remain blind as the luxurious classes now are blind, to man's relations to the globe he lives on, and to the permanently sour and hard foundations of his higher life.

The Moral Equivalent of War (1910) 1911:263.

Elizabeth Janeway 1913–

U.S. social critic and novelist

1 The usual definition of power as being a quality possessed by the powerful. . . won't do in the present case. To understand the workings of power as a relationship one must also consider the situation of the weak, the other, second member of the process by which society at once exists and changes. And women are the oldest, largest, and most central group of human creatures in the wide category of the weak and the ruled. The adjustments that women have made to life over centuries spent as subordinate partners in a power relationship illuminate the whole range of power situations.

Powers of the Weak 1980:4.

Morris Janowitz 1919–1988

U.S. sociologist

1 Those organizational and professional qualities which make it possible for the military of a new nation to accumulate political power, and even to take over political power, are the same as those which limit its ability to rule effectively.

The Military in the Political Development of New Nations 1964:1.

Thomas Jefferson 1743–1826

U.S. statesman and political philosopher

1 We hold these truths to be self-evident, that all men are created equal, that they are endowed by their Creator with certain unalienable Rights, that among these are Life, Liberty and the pursuit of Happiness. That to secure these rights, Governments are instituted among Men, deriving their just powers from the consent of the governed. That whenever any Form of Government becomes destructive of these ends, it is the Right of the People to alter or to abolish it, and to institute new Government, laying its foundation on such principles, and organizing its powers in such form, as to them shall seem most likely to effect their Safety and Happiness.

The Declaration of Independence 1776.

2 All the powers of government, legislative, executive, and judiciary, result to the legislative body. The concentrating these in the same hands is precisely the definition of despotic government. It will be no alleviation that these powers will be exercised by a plurality of hands, and not by a single one. 173 despots would surely be as oppressive as one. Let those who doubt it turn their eyes on the republic of Venice.

Notes on the State of Virginia (1785) 1984:245.

3 I am safe in affirming that the proofs of genius given by the Indians of North America, place them on a level with

whites in the same uncultivated states. The North of Europe furnishes subjects enough for comparison with them, and for a proof of their equality. I have seen some thousands myself, and conversed much with them, and have found in them a masculine, sound understanding.

Letter to General Chastellux, 7 June 1785. 1830:230.

4 The legitimate powers of government extend to such acts only as are injurious to others. But it does me no injury for my neighbour to say there are twenty gods, or no god. It neither picks my pocket nor breaks my leg.

Notes on the State of Virginia (1785) 1984:285.

5 The Newtonian principle of gravitation is now more firmly established, on the basis of reason, than it would be were the government to step in, and to make it an article of necessary faith. Reason and experiment have been indulged, and error has fled before them. It is error alone which needs the support of government. Truth can stand by itself.

Notes on the State of Virginia (1785) 1984:286.

6 The basis of our governments being the opinion of the people, the very first object should be to keep that right; and were it left to me to decide whether we should have a government without newspapers, or newspapers without a government, I should not hesitate a moment to prefer the latter.

Letter to Edward Carrington, 16 January 1787. 1984:880.

7 I hold it that a little rebellion now and then is a good thing, & as necessary in the political world as storms in the physical.

Letter to James Madison, 30 January 1787. 1984:882.

8 God forbid we should ever be 20 years without such a rebellion [Shays's Rebellion]. . . We have had 13. states independent 11. years. There has been one rebellion. That comes to one rebellion in a century & a half for each state. . . What signify a few lives lost in a century or two? The tree of liberty must be refreshed from time to time with the blood of patriots & tyrants. It is its natural manure.

Letter to William S. Smith, 13 November 1787. 1984:911.

9 The question Whether one generation of men has a right to bind another, seems never to have been started either on this or our side of the water. Yet it is a question of such consequences as not only to merit decision, but place also, among the fundamental principles of every government. The course of reflection in which we are immersed here on the elementary principles of society has presented this question to my mind; and that no such obligation can be transmitted I think very capable of proof. I set out on this ground which I suppose to be self evident, "*that the earth belongs in usufruct to the living*;" that the dead have neither powers nor rights over it. The portion occupied by an individual ceases to be his when himself ceases to be, and reverts to the society.

Letter to James Madison, 6 September 1789. 1984:959.

10 It is proper you should understand what I deem the essential principles of our Government. . . Equal and exact justice to all men, of whatever state or persuasion, religious or political; peace, commerce, and honest friendship, with all nations; entangling alliances with none; the support of the State governments in all their rights, as the most competent administrations for our domestic concerns and the surest bulwarks against antirepublican tendencies; the preservation of the General Government in its whole constitutional vigor, as the sheet anchor of our peace at home and safety abroad; a jealous care of the right of election by the people — a mild and safe corrective of abuses which are lopped by the sword of revolution where peaceable remedies are unprovided; absolute acquiescence in the decisions of the majority, the vital principles of republics, from which is no appeal but to force, the vital principle and immediate parent of despotism; a well-disciplined militia, our best reliance in peace and for the first moments of war till regulars may relieve them; the supremacy of the civil over the military authority; economy in the public expense, that labor may be lightly burthened; the honest payment of our debts and sacred preservation of the public faith; encouragement of agriculture, and of commerce as its handmaid; the diffusion of information and arraignment of all abuses at the bar of the public reason; freedom of religion; freedom of the press, and freedom of person under the protection of the habeas corpus, and trial by juries impartially selected.

First Inaugural Address, 4 March 1801. 1984:494–495.

11 Believing that religion is a matter which lies solely between man and his God, that he owes account to none other for his faith or his worship, that the legislative powers of government reach actions only, and not opinions, I contemplate with sovereign reverence that act of the whole American people which declared that their Legislature should "make no law respecting an establishment of religion, or prohibiting the free exercise thereof," thus building a wall of separation between Church and State.

Letter to the Danbury [Connecticut] Baptist Association, 1 January 1802. 1967:142.

12 I agree with you that there is a natural aristocracy among men. The grounds of this are virtue and talents.

Letter to John Adams, 28 October 1813. 1984:1305.

13 I know no safe depository of the ultimate powers of the society but the people themselves; and if we think them not enlightened enough to exercise their control with a wholesome discretion, the remedy is not to take it from them, but to inform their discretion by education.

Letter to William Charles Jarvis, September 28, 1820. 1905:163.

14 Our first and fundamental maxim should be, never to entangle ourselves in the broils of Europe. Our second, never to suffer Europe to intermeddle with cis-Atlantic affairs. America, North and South, has a set of interests distinct from those of Europe, and peculiarly her own.

Letter to James Monroe, 24 October 1823. 1984:1481.

15 The object of the Declaration of Independence [was] not to find out new principles, or new arguments, never before thought of, not merely to say things which had never been said before; but to place before mankind the common sense of the subject, in terms so plain and firm as to command their assent, and to justify ourselves in the independent stand we are compelled to take. Neither aiming at originality of principle or sentiment, nor yet copied from any particular and previous writing, it was intended to be an expression of the American mind, and to give to that expression the proper tone and spirit called for by the occasion. All its authority rests then on the harmonizing sentiments of the day, whether expressed in conversation, in letters, printed essays, or the elementary books of public right, as Aristotle, Cicero, Locke, Sidney, &c.

Letter to Henry Lee, 8 May 1825. 1984:1501.

16 All eyes are opened, or opening, to the rights of man. The general spread of the light of science has already laid open to every view the palpable truth, that the mass of mankind has not been born with saddles on their back, nor a favored few booted and spurred, ready to ride them legitimately, by the grace of God.

Letter to Roger C. Weightman, 24 June 1826. 1984:1517. → Jefferson's last letter before his death on the Fourth of July, the fiftieth anniversary of the adoption of the Declaration of Independence. In this letter, he sent his regrets that he could not attend the Fourth of July ceremonials in Washington.

17 Here was buried
Thomas Jefferson
Author of the Declaration of American Independence
of the Statute of Virginia for religious freedom
& Father of the University of Virginia.

Epitaph (1826) 1984:706. → Jefferson requested that his epitaph should be this inscription "& not a word more," in order to emphasize his intellectual accomplishments rather than his political career.

Otto Jespersen 1860–1943
Danish linguist

1 Man is a classifying animal: in one sense it may be said that the whole process of speaking is nothing but distributing phenomena, of which no two are alike in every respect, into different classes on the strength of perceived similarities and dissimilarities. In the name-giving process we witness the same ineradicable and very useful tendency to see likenesses and to express similarity in the phenomena through similarity in name.

Language (1922) 1964:388–389.

William Stanley Jevons 1835–1882
British economist

1 During the last session I have worked a good deal at political economy; in the last few months I have fortunately struck out what I have no doubt is *the true Theory of Economy*, so thorough-going and consistent, that I cannot read other books on the subject without indignation.

Letter to Herbert Jevons, 1 June 1860. 1886:151.

2 The alternatives before us are simple. . . If we lavishly and boldly push forward in the creation and distribution of our riches, it is hard to over-estimate the pitch of beneficial influence to which we may attain in the present. *But the maintenance of such a position is physically impossible. We have to make the momentous choice between brief but true greatness and longer continued mediocrity.*

The Coal Question (1865) 1866:375–376.

3 I have attempted to treat Economy as a Calculus of Pleasure and Pain.

The Theory of Political Economy (1871) 1957:vi.

4 Repeated reflection and inquiry have led me to the somewhat novel opinion, that *value depends entirely upon utility*.

The Theory of Political Economy (1871) 1957:1.

5 It is clear that Economics, if it is to be a science at all, must be a mathematical science. There exists much prejudice against attempts to introduce the methods and language of mathematics into any branch of the moral sciences. Many persons seem to think that the physical sciences form the proper sphere of mathematical method, and that the moral sciences demand some other method, — I know not what.

The Theory of Political Economy (1871) 1957:3.

6 Exchange is so important a process in the maximising of utility. . . that some economists have regarded their science as treating of this operation alone. . . I am perfectly willing to agree with the high importance attributed to exchange.

It is impossible to have a correct idea of the science of Economics without a perfect comprehension of the Theory of Exchange.

The Theory of Political Economy (1871) 1957:75–76.

7 There must be perfectly free competition, so that any one will exchange with any one else upon the slightest apparent advantage. There must be no conspiracies for absorbing and holding supplies to produce unnatural ratios of exchange. . . A market, then, is theoretically perfect only when all traders have perfect knowledge of the conditions of supply and demand, and the consequent ratio of exchange.

The Theory of Political Economy (1871) 1957:86–87.

8 The keystone of the whole Theory of Exchange, and of the principal problems of Economics, lies in this proposi-

tion — *The ratio of exchange of any two commodities will be the reciprocal of the ratio of the final degrees of utility of the quantities of commodity available for consumption after the exchange is completed.* When the reader has reflected a little upon the meaning of this proposition, he will see, I think, that it is necessarily true, if the principles of human nature have been correctly represented in previous pages.

The Theory of Political Economy (1871) 1957:95.

9 The fact is, that *labour once spent has no influence on the future value of any article*: it is gone and lost for ever. In commerce bygones are for ever bygones; and we are always starting clear at each moment, judging the values of things with a view to future utility.

The Theory of Political Economy (1871) 1957:164.

10 But though labour is never the cause of value, it is in a large proportion of cases the determining circumstance, and in the following way: *Value depends solely on the final degree of utility. How can we vary this degree of utility? — By having more or less of the commodity to consume. And how shall we get more or less of it? — By spending more or less labour in obtaining a supply.* According to this view, then, there are two steps between labour and value. Labour affects supply, and supply affects the degree of utility, which governs value, or the ratio of exchange. In order that there may be no possible mistake about this all-important series of relations, I will restate it in a tabular form, as follows: —

Cost of production determines supply;
Supply determines final degree of utility;
Final degree of utility determines value.

The Theory of Political Economy (1871) 1957:165. → See KEYNES:25.

11 A free labourer. . . will cease to labour just at the point when the pain becomes equal to the corresponding pleasure gained.

The Theory of Political Economy (1871) 1957:176.

12 The problem of Economics may, as it seems to me, be stated thus: — *Given, a certain population, with various needs and powers of production, in possession of certain lands and other sources of material: required, the mode of employing their labour which will maximise the utility of the produce.*

The Theory of Political Economy (1871) 1957:267.

John of Salisbury d.1180
British prelate and scholar

1 Between a tyrant and a prince there is this single or chief difference, that the latter obeys the law and rules the people by its dictates, accounting himself as but their servant.

Policraticus (1476?) 1979:Book 4, 44.

Samuel Johnson 1709–1784
British lexicographer and literary critic

1 [*Johnson*]: Great abilities are not requisite for an Historian; for in historical composition, all the greatest powers of the human mind are quiescent. He has facts ready to his hand; so there is no exercise of invention. Imagination is not required in any high degree; only about as much as is used in the lower kinds of poetry. [6 July 1763]

Quoted in James Boswell, *Life of Johnson* (1791) 1980:301.

2 [*Johnson*]: Levellers wish to level *down* as far as themselves; but they cannot bear levelling *up* to themselves. They would all have some people under them; why not then have some people above them? [21 July 1763]

Quoted in James Boswell, *Life of Johnson* (1791) 1980:317.

3 [*Boswell*]: Sir Alexander Dick tells me, that he remembers having a thousand people in a year to dine at his house: that is, reckoning each person as one, each time that he dined there. [*Johnson*]: That, Sir, is about three a day. [*Boswell*]: How your statement lessens the idea. [*Johnson*]: That, Sir, is the good of counting. It brings every thing to a certainty, which before floated in the mind indefinitely. [18 April 1783]

Quoted in James Boswell, *Life of Johnson* (1791) 1980:1221–1222.

James Joll 1918–
British historian

1 All doctrines, whether religious or anarchist, which wholly deny the value of the existing order of things may produce either puritans or libertines; and a single one of the latter quickly makes the public forget the far greater number of the former.

The Anarchists (1964) 1966:19.

Ernest Jones 1879–1958
British psychoanalyst

1 [Freud's] great strength, though sometimes also his weakness, was the quite extraordinary respect he had for the *singular fact*. . . When he got hold of a simple but significant fact he would feel, and know, that it was an example of something general or universal, and the idea of collecting statistics on the matter was quite alien to him.

The Life and Work of Sigmund Freud 1953:Vol. 1, 96–97.

Martin Joos 1907–1978
U.S. linguist

1 In the long run, then, it had to be Bloomfield that served as the Newton of American Linguistics, while Sapir was its Leibniz.

Preface to *Readings in Linguistics* (1957) 1958:v.

Carl Gustav Jung 1875–1961
Swiss psychologist

1 We ought to be particularly grateful to [Henri] Bergson for having broken a lance in defence of the irrational.

The Structure of the Unconscious (1916) 1953:283.

2 The great problems of life, including of course sex, are always related to the primordial images of the collective unconscious. These images are balancing or compensating factors that correspond to the problems which life confronts us with in reality.

This is no matter for astonishment, since these images are deposits of thousands of years of experience of the struggle for existence and for adaptation.

Psychological Types (1921) 1971:220–221.

3 When orientation by the object predominates in such a way that decisions and actions are determined not by subjective views but by objective conditions, we speak of an extraverted attitude. When this is habitual, we speak of an extraverted type. If a man thinks, feels, acts, and actually lives in a way that is *directly* correlated with the objective conditions and their demands, he is extraverted.

Psychological Types (1921) 1971:333.

4 We should not pretend to understand the world only by the intellect; we apprehend it just as much by feeling. Therefore the judgment of the intellect is, at best, only a half-truth, and must, if it is honest, also admit its inadequacy.

Psychological Types (1921) 1971:495.

5 Identification with one's office or one's title is very attractive indeed, which is precisely why so many men are nothing more than the decorum accorded to them by society. In vain would one look for a personality behind this husk. Underneath all the padding one would find a very pitiable little creature. That is why the office — or whatever this outer husk may be — is so attractive: it offers easy compensation for personal deficiencies.

The Relations between the Ego and the Unconscious (1928) 1953:142.

6 Dream analysis stands or falls with [the hypothesis of the unconscious]. Without it the dream appears to be merely a freak of nature, a meaningless conglomerate of memory-fragments left over from the happenings of the day.

Dream Analysis in Its Practical Application (1930) 1956:1–2.

7 As was customary throughout antiquity, primitive people today make a free use of phallic symbols, yet it never occurs to them to confuse the phallus, as a ritualistic symbol, with the penis. They always take the phallus to mean the creative *mana*, the power of healing and fertility, "that which is unusually potent"... Its equivalents in mythology and in dreams are the bull, the ass, the pomegranate, the *yoni*, the he-goat, the lightning, the horse's hoof, the dance, the magical cohabitation in the furrow, and the menstrual fluid, to mention only a few of many. That which underlies all of these images — and sexuality itself — is an archetypal content that is hard to grasp, and that finds its best psychological expression in the primitive *mana* symbol.

Dream Analysis in Its Practical Application (1930) 1956:22.

8 The great decisions of human life have as a rule far more to do with the instincts and other mysterious unconscious factors than with conscious will and well-meaning reasonableness. The shoe that fits one person pinches another; there is no recipe for living that suits all cases. Each of us carries his own life-form — an indeterminable form which cannot be superseded by any other.

The Aims of Psychotherapy (1931) 1956:60–61.

9 Every civilized human being, whatever his conscious development, is still an archaic man at the deeper levels of his psyche. Just as the human body connects us with the mammals and displays numerous relics of earlier evolutionary stages going back even to the reptilian age, so the human psyche is likewise a product of evolution which, when followed up to its origins, shows countless archaic traits.

Archaic Man (1931) 1956:126.

10 Man's unconscious... contains all the patterns of life and behaviour inherited from his ancestors, so that every human child, prior to consciousness, is possessed of a potential system of adapted psychic functioning.

The Basic Postulates of Analytical Psychology (1931) 1956:185.

11 It seems to us as if the collective unconscious, which appears to us in dreams, had no consciousness of its own contents — though of course we cannot be sure of this, any more than we are in the case of insects. The collective unconscious, moreover, seems not to be a person, but something like an unceasing stream or perhaps an ocean of images and figures which drift into consciousness in our dreams or in abnormal states of mind.

The Basic Postulates of Analytical Psychology (1931) 1956:186.

12 Complexes are psychic contents which are outside the control of the conscious mind. They have been split off from consciousness and lead a separate existence in the unconscious, being at all times ready to hinder or to reinforce the conscious intentions.

A Psychological Theory of Types (1931) 1956:79.

13 The dream is a little hidden door in the innermost and most secret recesses of the soul, opening into that cosmic night which was psyche long before there was any ego-consciousness, and which will remain psyche no matter how far our ego-consciousness extends.

The Meaning of Psychology for Modern Man (1933) 1964:144–145.

14 I can still recall vividly how Freud said to me, "My dear Jung, promise me never to abandon the sexual theory. That is the most essential thing of all. You see, we must make a dogma of it, an unshakable bulwark". . . In some astonishment I asked him, "A bulwark — against what?" To which he replied, "Against the black tide of mud" — and here he hesitated for a moment, then added — "of occultism."

Memories, Dreams, Reflections (1961) 1963:150.

15 One does not dream: one is dreamed. We "undergo" the dream, we are the objects.

Quoted in Jolan Jacobi, *The Psychology of Jung* 1943:69.

K

Immanuel Kant 1724–1804
German philosopher

1 *The means employed by Nature to bring about the development of all the capacities of men is their antagonism in society, so far as this is, in the end, the cause of a lawful order among men.*

By "antagonism" I mean the unsocial sociability of men, i.e., their propensity to enter into society, bound together with a mutual opposition which constantly threatens to break up the society.

Idea for a Universal History from a Cosmopolitan Point of View (1784) 1963:15.

2 If it were possible to have so profound an insight into a man's mental character as shown by internal as well as external actions, as to know all its motives, even the smallest, and likewise all the external occasions that can influence them, we could calculate a man's conduct for the future with as great certainty as a lunar or solar eclipse; and nevertheless we may maintain that the man is free.

Critique of Practical Reason (1785) 1909:193. → See LAPLACE:2.

3 There is. . . only one categorical imperative. It is: Act only according to that maxim by which you can at the same time will that it should become a universal law.

Foundations of the Metaphysics of Morals (1785) 1959:39.

4 Now, I say, man and, in general, every rational being exists as an end in himself and not merely as a means to be arbitrarily used by this or that will. In all his actions, whether they are directed to himself or to other rational beings, he must always be regarded at the same time as an end. All objects of inclinations have only a conditional worth, for if the inclinations and the needs founded on them did not exist, their object would be without worth. The inclinations themselves as the sources of needs, however, are so lacking in absolute worth that the universal wish of every rational being must be indeed to free himself completely from them.

Foundations of the Metaphysics of Morals (1785) 1959:46.

5 The character of the human race. . . is that of. . . a multitude of persons living one after another and one beside another, unable to *do without* peaceful coexistence, yet also unable to *avoid* being constantly hateful to one another. . . ; a coalition always threatened with dissolution, but on the whole progressing towards a world-wide *civil society*.

Anthropologie in pragmatischer Hinsicht (1798) 1964:687.

Abraham Kaplan

See HAROLD D. LASSWELL AND ABRAHAM KAPLAN.

Abram Kardiner 1891–1981
U.S. psychoanalyst

1 When an ethnographer reports that in a given society divorces are frequent; that the accounts of religious dogmas are inaccurate and inconsistent; that when people are ill they just lie down and die; that they have little interest in permanent structures; that they have no conscience or tendency to depressive reactions — all these may be unrelated events, or may be deeply interconnected. . . The contribution that psychodynamics makes is to demonstrate that these traits are related, and, by the very fact that they are so, a special direction is given to the adaptation of the society as a whole, and a special imprint is left on the individual exposed to this particular social process.

The Psychological Frontiers of Society 1945:xviii.

Alphonse Karr 1808–1890
French novelist

1 *Plus ça change — plus c'est la même chose* [The more things change, the more they remain the same].

Les Guêpes (1849) 1853:428. → This sentence soon became an aphorism, and in 1875 Karr published a book entitled *Plus ça change*. . . . For three contemporary reversals of the aphorism, see BATESON:4, LAZARSFELD:4, and SILVERSTEIN:1.

Daniel Katz 1903–
and
Floyd H. Allport 1890–1978
U.S. psychologists

1 In nearly every instance in which [college students] express their feelings to one another, this illusion of "what the group feels" enters to distort their expression. An inaccurate estimate of the "group opinion" is therefore universally accepted. This situation, which we may speak of as "pluralistic ignorance," has made possible an exaggerated impression of the universality of the attitudes in question.

Students' Attitudes 1931:152.

Elihu Katz 1926–
U.S. and Israeli sociologist
and
Paul F. Lazarsfeld 1901–1976
Austrian-born U.S. psychologist and sociologist

1 Who or what influences the influentials? Here is where the mass media re-entered the picture. For the leaders [in this survey] reported much more than the non-opinion leaders that for them, the mass media were influential. Pieced together this way, a new idea emerged — the suggestion of a "two-step flow of communication." The suggestion basically was this: that ideas, often, seem to flow *from* radio and print *to* opinion leaders and *from them* to the less active sections of the population.

Personal Influence 1955:32.

Karl Kautsky 1854–1938
Austro-Hungarian born German socialist

1 Few things are. . . more childish than to demand of the socialist that he draw a picture of the commonwealth which he strives for. . . Never yet in the history of mankind has it happened that a revolutionary party was able to foresee, let alone determine, the forms of the new social order which it strove to usher in.

The Class Struggle (1892) 1971:122–123.

2 The method is what is decisive in Marxian socialism, not the results. . . The results discovered by Marx and Engels are not the last word of science. Society is in flux, in constant development, and not only new facts appear but also new methods of observation and research. Some of what Marx and Engels asserted becomes untenable, some of it needs to be modified, some gaps they left open must be filled.

Bernstein und das Sozialdemokratische Programm (1899) 1979:17, 20. → Unpublished translation by John H. Kautsky.

3 What is new in society is in the last analysis always traceable to a new technology that produces new economic conditions and social relations. In society and its economy there is no moving force through which it could by itself continue to develop without the impetus of technical innovations.

Natur und Gesellschaft 1929:499. → Unpublished translation by John H. Kautsky.

Albert Galloway Keller

See WILLIAM GRAHAM SUMNER AND ALBERT GALLOWAY KELLER.

Hansfried Kellner

See PETER L. BERGER AND HANSFRIED KELLNER.

Hans Kelsen 1881–1973
Austro-Hungarian born U.S. legal theorist

1 Every political ideology has its root in volition, not in cognition; in the emotional, not in the rational, element of our consciousness; it arises from certain interests, or, rather, from interests other than the interest in truth.

General Theory of Law and State 1945:xvi.

2 Legal independence of parliament from the people means that the principle of democracy is, to a certain extent, replaced by that of the division of labor. In order to conceal this shifting from one principle to another, the fiction is used that parliament "represents" the people.

General Theory of Law and State 1945:292.

Lord Kelvin 1824–1907
[William Thomson, 1st baron Kelvin]
British physicist

1 I often say that when you can measure what you are speaking about and express it in numbers you know something about it; but when you cannot measure it, when you cannot express it in numbers, your knowledge is of a meagre and unsatisfactory kind: it may be the beginning of knowledge, but you have scarcely, in your thoughts, advanced to the stage of *science,* whatever the matter may be.

Electrical Units of Measurement (1883) 1891:80–81. → Known as the "Kelvin Dictum." The economist Jacob Viner reportedly replied that "even when we can measure a thing, our knowledge will be meager and unsatisfactory." For another reply, see KNIGHT:8. On the diffusion of the dictum, see Robert K. Merton et al., "The Kelvin Dictum and Social Science" (1984).

George F. Kennan 1904–
U.S. diplomat and historian

1 [The Soviet Union's] main concern is to make sure that it has filled every nook and cranny available to it in the basin of world power. . . In these circumstances it is clear that the main element of any United States policy toward the Soviet Union must be that of a long-term, patient but firm and vigilant containment of Russian expansive tendencies.

The Sources of Soviet Conduct 1947:575. → This article, published in *Foreign Affairs* under the pseudonym "X," was first written as a memorandum to Secretary of the Navy James F. Forrestal. A highly influential article, urging a policy of containment, it established Kennan as the leading U.S. authority on contemporary Soviet affairs when he was revealed to be its author.

2 The conduct of foreign relations ought not to be conceived as a purpose in itself for a political society, and

particularly a democratic society, but rather as one of the means by which some higher and more comprehensive purpose is pursued. . . A political society does not live to conduct foreign policy; it would be more correct to say that it conducts foreign policy in order to live.

The Two Planes of International Reality 1954:4.

3 Many of the present relationships of international life are only the eroded remnants of ones which, at one time, were relationships of uncompromising hostility. Every government is in some respects a problem for every other government, and it will always be this way so long as the sovereign state, with its supremely self-centered rationale, remains the basis of international life.

Russia and the West under Lenin and Stalin 1961:393.

4 History shows that belief in the inevitability of war with a given power affects behavior in such a way as to cripple all constructive policy approaches towards that power, leaves the field open for military compulsions, and thus easily takes on the character of a self-fulfilling prophecy. A war regarded as inevitable or even probable, and therefore much prepared for, has a very good chance of eventually being fought.

The Cloud of Danger 1977:201–202. → See FRIEDMAN:9; MERTON:2.

Robert F. Kennedy 1925–1968
U.S. lawyer and politician

1 The gross national product [GNP] does not allow for the health of our children, the quality of their education or the joy of their play. It does not include the beauty of our poetry, or the strength of our marriages, the intelligence of our public debate or the integrity of our public officials.

It measures neither our wit nor our courage, neither our wisdom nor our devotion to our country. It measures everything, in short, except that which makes life worthwhile, and it can tell us everything about America except why we are proud that we are Americans.

Campaign speech (1968) 1987:B12.

Otto Kerner 1908–1976
U.S. lawyer and politician

1 This is our basic conclusion: Our Nation is moving toward two societies, one black, one white — separate and unequal.

Introduction to the report of the Kerner Commission 1968:1. → See DISRAELI:2.

William Kessen
See GEORGE MANDLER AND WILLIAM KESSEN.

Nathan Keyfitz 1913–
Canadian-born U.S. demographer

1 Numbers provide the rhetoric of our age. . . What rounded periods and flourishes were to Victorian eloquence, what Latin tags did for the eighteenth century, numbers contribute to eloquence now; they testify to the seriousness and trustworthiness of the speaker, as well as to his proper education.

The Social and Political Context of Population Forecasting 1987:235.

John Maynard Keynes 1883–1946
British economist

1 If I let you have a halfpenny and you kept it for a very long time, you would have to give me back that halfpenny and another too. That's interest.

Quoted in R. F. Harrod, *The Life of John Maynard Keynes* 1951:8. → Keynes's reply, at age 4 1/2, when asked what "interest" is; quoted from his father's diary.

2 There is no subtler, no surer means of overturning the existing basis of society than to debauch the currency. The process engages all the hidden forces of economic law on the side of destruction, and does it in a manner which not one man in a million is able to diagnose.

The Economic Consequences of the Peace (1919) 1971:149.

3 This *long run* is a misleading guide to current affairs. *In the long run we are all dead.* Economists set themselves too easy, too useless a task if in tempestuous seasons they can only tell us that when the storm is long past the ocean is flat again.

A Tract on Monetary Reform (1923) 1971:65.

4 The study of economics does not seem to require any specialised gifts of an unusually high order. Is it not, intellectually regarded, a very easy subject compared with the higher branches of philosophy and pure science? Yet good, or even competent, economists are the rarest of birds. An easy subject, at which very few excel! The paradox finds its explanation, perhaps, in that the master-economist must possess a rare *combination* of gifts. He must reach a high standard in several different directions and must combine talents not often found together. He must be mathematician, historian, statesman, philosopher — in some degree. He must understand symbols and speak in words. He must contemplate the particular in terms of the general, and touch abstract and concrete in the same flight of thought. He must study the present in the light of the past for the purposes of the future. No part of man's nature or his institutions must lie entirely outside his regard. He must be purposeful and disinterested in a simultaneous mood; as aloof and incorruptible as an artist, yet sometimes as near the earth as a politician.

Alfred Marshall: 1842–1924 (1924) 1951:140–141.

5 Professor [Max] Planck, of Berlin, the famous originator of the Quantum Theory, once remarked to me that in early life he had thought of studying economics, but had found it too difficult! Professor Planck could easily master the whole corpus of mathematical economics in a few days. He did not mean that! But the amalgam of logic and intuition and the wide knowledge of facts, most of which are not precise, which is required for economic interpre-

tation in its highest form is, quite truly, overwhelmingly difficult for those whose gift mainly consists in the power to imagine and pursue to their furthest points the implications and prior conditions of comparatively simple facts which are known with a high degree of precision.

Alfred Marshall 1842–1924 (1924) 1951:158n.

6 Marshall was the first great economist *pur sang* that there ever was; the first who devoted his life to building up the subject as a separate science, standing on its own foundations, with as high standards of scientific accuracy as the physical or the biological sciences.

Alfred Marshall: 1842–1924 (1924) 1951:205.

7 The Labour Party. . . is a class party, and the class is not my class. . . The *class* war will find me on the side of the educated *bourgeoisie*.

Am I a Liberal? (1925) 1972:297.

8 The Principle of the Survival of the Fittest could be regarded as one vast generalisation of the Ricardian economics. Socialistic interferences became, in the light of this grander synthesis, not merely inexpedient, but impious, as calculated to retard the onward movement of the mighty process by which we ourselves had risen like Aphrodite out of the primeval slime of Ocean.

The End of Laissez-Faire 1926:17. → See SPENCER:7.

9 Marxian Socialism must always remain a portent to the historians of Opinion — how a doctrine so illogical and so dull can have exercised so powerful and enduring an influence over the minds of men, and through them, the events of history.

The End of Laissez-Faire 1926:47–48.

10 The important thing for Government is not to do things which individuals are doing already, and to do them a little better or a little worse; but to do those things which at present are not done at all.

The End of Laissez-Faire 1926:67.

11 Do not let us overestimate the importance of the economic problem, or sacrifice to its supposed necessities other matters of greater and more permanent significance. It should be a matter for specialists — like dentistry. If economists could manage to get themselves thought of as humble, competent people, on a level with dentists, that would be splendid!

Economic Possibilities for Our Grandchildren (1930) 1972:332. → See GOFFMAN:1; HAHN:1.

12 Monetary theory, when all is said and done, is little more than a vast elaboration of the truth that "it all comes out in the wash." But to show this to us and to make it convincing, we must have a complete inventory. That the amount of money taken by the shops over the counter is equal, in the aggregate, to the amount of money spent by their customers; that the expenditure of the public is equal, in the aggregate, to the amount of their incomes *minus* what they have put on one side; these simple truths and the like are those, apparently, the bearing and significance of which it is most difficult to comprehend.

A Treatise on Money (1930) 1971:Vol. 2, 366–367.

13 A "sound" banker, alas! is not one who foresees danger and avoids it, but one who, when he is ruined, is ruined in a conventional and orthodox way along with his fellows, so that no one can really blame him.

The Consequences to the Banks of the Collapse of Money Values (1932) 1972:156.

14 To understand my state of mind. . . you have to know that I believe myself to be writing a book on economic theory, which will largely revolutionise — not, I suppose, at once but in the course of the next ten years — the way the world thinks about economic problems.

Letter to George Bernard Shaw, New Year's Day, 1935. 1982:42. → Written the year before the publication of *The General Theory of Employment, Interest and Money*.

15 The composition of this book has been for the author a long struggle of escape, and so must the reading of it be for most readers if the author's assault upon them is to be successful, — a struggle of escape from habitual modes of thought and expression. The ideas which are here expressed so laboriously are extremely simple and should be obvious. The difficulty lies, not in the new ideas, but in escaping from the old ones, which ramify, for those brought up as most of us have been, into every corner of our minds.

The General Theory of Employment, Interest and Money (1936) 1973:xxiii.

16 The postulates of classical theory are applicable to a special case only and not to the general case, the situation which it assumes being a limiting point of the possible positions of equilibrium. Moreover, the characteristics of the special case assumed by the classical theory happen not to be those of the economic society in which we actually live, with the result that its teaching is misleading and disastrous if we attempt to apply it to the facts of experience.

The General Theory of Employment, Interest and Money (1936) 1973:3.

17 Since Malthus was unable to explain clearly (apart from an appeal to the facts of common observation) how and why effective demand could be deficient or excessive, he failed to furnish an alternative construction; and Ricardo conquered England as completely as the Holy Inquisition conquered Spain.

The General Theory of Employment, Interest and Money (1936) 1973:32.

18 In short —

Income = value of output = consumption + investment.

Saving = income − consumption.

Therefore saving = investment.

The General Theory of Employment, Interest and Money (1936) 1973:63.

19 The fundamental psychological law, upon which we are entitled to depend with great confidence both *a priori* from our knowledge of human nature and from the detailed facts of experience, is that men are disposed, as a rule and on the average, to increase their consumption as their income increases, but not by as much as the increase in their income.

The General Theory of Employment, Interest and Money (1936) 1973:96.

20 If the Treasury were to fill old bottles with banknotes, bury them at suitable depths in disused coalmines which are then filled up to the surface with town rubbish, and leave it to private enterprise on well-tried principles of *laissez-faire* to dig the notes up again... there need be no more unemployment... It would, indeed, be more sensible to build houses and the like; but if there are political and practical difficulties in the way of this, the above would be better than nothing.

The General Theory of Employment, Interest and Money (1936) 1973:129.

21 Ancient Egypt was doubly fortunate, and doubtless owed to this its fabled wealth, in that it possessed *two* activities, namely, pyramid-building as well as the search for the precious metals, the fruits of which, since they could not serve the needs of man by being consumed, did not stale with abundance. The Middle Ages built cathedrals and sang dirges. Two pyramids, two masses for the dead, are twice as good as one; but not so two railways from London to York.

The General Theory of Employment, Interest and Money (1936) 1972:131.

22 The energies and skill of the professional investor and speculator are mainly occupied... not with making superior long-term forecasts of the probable yield of an investment over its whole life, but with foreseeing changes in the conventional basis of valuation a short time ahead of the general public. They are concerned, not with what an investment is really worth to a man who buys it "for keeps," but with what the market will value it at, under the influence of mass psychology, three months or a year hence... The social object of skilled investment should be to defeat the dark forces of time and ignorance which envelop our future. The actual, private object of the most skilled investment to-day is "to beat the gun," as the Americans so well express it, to outwit the crowd, and to pass the bad, or depreciating, half-crown to the other fellow... It is, so to speak, a game of Snap, of Old Maid, of Musical Chairs — a pastime in which he is victor who says *Snap* neither too soon nor too late, who passes the Old Maid to his neighbour before the game is over, who secures a chair for himself when the music stops...

Or, to change the metaphor slightly, professional investment may be likened to those newspaper competitions in which the competitors have to pick out the six prettiest faces from a hundred photographs, the prize being awarded to the competitor whose choice most nearly corresponds to the average preferences of the competitors as a whole; so that each competitor has to pick, not those faces which he himself finds prettiest, but those which he thinks likeliest to catch the fancy of the other competitors, all of whom are looking at the problem from the same point of view. It is not a case of choosing those which, to the best of one's judgment, are really the prettiest, nor even those which average opinion genuinely thinks the prettiest. We have reached the third degree where we devote our intelligences to anticipating what average opinion expects the average opinion to be. And there are some, I believe, who practise the fourth, fifth and higher degrees.

The General Theory of Employment, Interest and Money (1936) 1973:154–156.

23 The importance of money essentially flows from its being a link between the present and the future.

The General Theory of Employment, Interest and Money (1936) 1973:293.

24 The ideas of economists and political philosophers, both when they are right and when they are wrong, are more powerful than is commonly understood. Indeed the world is ruled by little else. Practical men, who believe themselves to be quite exempt from any intellectual influences, are usually the slaves of some defunct economist. Madmen in authority, who hear voices in the air, are distilling their frenzy from some academic scribbler of a few years back... In the field of economic and political philosophy there are not many who are influenced by new theories after they are twenty-five or thirty years of age, so that the ideas which civil servants and politicians and even agitators apply to current events are not likely to be the newest. But, soon or late, it is ideas, not vested intersts, which are dangerous for good or evil.

The General Theory of Employment, Interest and Money (1936) 1973:383–384. → From the final paragraph of the book. See BUCHANAN:1.

25 The first modern book on economics [Jevons's *Theory of Political Economy*] has proved singularly attractive to all bright minds newly attacking the subject; — simple, lucid, unfaltering, chiselled in stone where Marshall knits in wool.

William Stanley Jevons 1951:284–285. → From a lecture at the Royal Statistical Society, 21 April 1936. Keynes quoted a passage from Jevons which includes the famous tabular sentence:

Cost of production determines supply;
Supply determines final degree of utility;
Final degree of utility determines value.

See JEVONS:10.

Ibn Khaldûn

See IBN KHALDÛN.

Søren Kierkegaard 1813–1855

Danish philosopher

1 It is in Socrates that the concept of irony has its inception in the world. Concepts, like individuals, have their histories and are just as incapable of withstanding the ravages of time as are individuals. But in and through all this they retain a kind of homesickness for the scenes of their childhood. As philosophy cannot be indifferent to the

subsequent history of this concept, so neither can it content itself with the history of its origin, though it be ever so complete and interesting a history as such. Philosophy always requires something more, requires the eternal, the true, in contrast to which even the fullest existence as such is but a happy moment.

The Concept of Irony (1841) 1971:47–48.

Martin Luther King, Jr. 1929–1968
U.S. clergyman and civil rights leader

1 There is more power in socially organized masses on the march than there is in guns in the hands of a few desperate men.

The Social Organization of Nonviolence (1959) 1986:33.

2 Much has been made of the willingness of. . . devotees of nonviolent social action to break the law. Paradoxically, although they have embraced Thoreau's and Gandhi's civil disobedience on a scale dwarfing any past experience in American history, they do respect law. They feel a moral responsibility to obey just laws. But they recognize that there are also unjust laws.

The Time for Freedom Has Come (1961) 1986:164.

3 Life is breathed into a judicial decision by the persistent exercise of legal rights until they become usual and ordinary in human experience.

The Case against "Tokenism" (1962) 1986:109.

4 Let us not seek to satisfy our thirst for freedom by drinking from the cup of bitterness and hatred. We must forever conduct our struggle on the high plane of dignity and discipline. We must not allow our creative protest to degenerate into physical violence. Again and again we must rise to the majestic heights of meeting physical force with soul force.

I Have a Dream (1963) 1986:218. → Delivered before the Lincoln Memorial on 28 August 1963 as the keynote address of the March on Washington, D.C., for Civil Rights.

5 I still have a dream. It is a dream deeply rooted in the American dream that one day this nation will rise up and live out the true meaning of the creed — we hold these truths to be self-evident, that all men are created equal.

I Have a Dream (1963) 1986:219.

6 Softmindedness is one of the basic causes of race prejudice. The toughminded person always examines the facts before he reaches conclusions; in short, he postjudges. The tenderminded person reaches a conclusion before he has examined the first fact; in short, he prejudges and is prejudiced.

The Strength to Love (1963) 1986:493. → See JAMES:24.

Melanie Klein 1882–1960
Austrian-born British psychoanalyst

1 Symbolism is the foundation of all sublimation and of every talent, since it is by way of symbolic equation that things, activities and interests become the subject of libidinal phantasies.

The Importance of Symbol-formation in the Development of the Ego (1930) 1948:237.

Clyde Kluckhohn 1905–1960
U.S. anthropologist

1 My basic postulate. . . is that no cultural forms survive unless they constitute responses which are adjustive or adaptive.

Navaho Witchcraft 1944:46.

2 A given bit of culture is "functional" insofar as it defines a mode of response which is adaptive from the standpoint of the society or adaptive and adjustive from the standpoint of the individual.

Navaho Witchcraft 1944:47.

Clyde Kluckhohn 1905–1960
U.S. anthropologist
and
Henry A. Murray 1893–1988
U.S. psychologist

1 Every man is in certain respects
a. like all other men,
b. like some other man,
c. like no other man.

Personality Formation (1944) 1967:53.

2 Without the discovery of uniformities there can be no concepts, no classifications, no formulations, no principles, no laws; and without these no science can exist.

Personality Formation (1944) 1967:55–56.

[*See also* HENRY A. MURRAY; HENRY A. MURRAY AND CLYDE KLUCKHOHN; ALFRED L. KROEBER AND CLYDE KLUCKHOHN.]

Frank H. Knight 1885–1972
U.S. economist

1 The "personal" interests which our rich and powerful business men work so hard to promote are not personal interests at all in the conventional economic sense of a desire to consume commodities. They consume in order to produce rather than produce in order to consume, in so far as they do either. The real motive is the desire to excel, to win at a game, the biggest and most fascinating game yet invented, not excepting even statecraft and war.

Risk, Uncertainty and Profit (1921) 1971:360.

2 The chief thing which the common-sense individual actually wants is not satisfactions for the wants he has, but more, and *better* wants.

Ethics and the Economic Interpretation (1922) 1935:22.

3 The "economic man". . . has been much mistreated by both friends and foes, but such a conception, explicit or implicit, underlies all economic speculation. The economic man is the individual who obeys economic laws,

which is merely to say that he obeys *some* laws of conduct, it being the task of the science to find out what the laws are. He is the *rational* man, the man who knows what he wants and orders his conduct intelligently with a view to getting it. In no other sense can there be laws of conduct or a science of conduct; the only possible "science" of conduct is that which treats of the behaviour of the economic man.

Ethics and the Economic Interpretation (1922) 1935:35.

4 Economic activity is *at the same time* a means of want-satisfaction, an agency for want-and-character-formation, a field of creative self-expression, and a competitive sport. While men are "playing the game" of business, they are also moulding their own and other personalities, and creating a civilization whose worthiness to endure cannot be a matter of indifference.

The Ethics of Competition (1923) 1935:47.

5 Where the family is the social unit, the inheritance of wealth, culture, educational advantages, and economic opportunities tend toward the progressive increase of inequality, with bad results for personality at both ends of the scale.

The Ethics of Competition (1923) 1935:50.

6 Between business and politics, it is as easy and as reasonable to assert that corruption goes one way as the other. The conspicuous differences, it may be remarked, are in the matter of frankness. Both finally "give the people what they want," after doing their utmost to make them want what they want to give.

The Newer Economics and the Control of Economic Activity 1932:476.

7 The Economic man neither competes nor higgles — nor does he co-operate, psychologically speaking; he treats other human beings as if they were slot machines.

Ethics and Economic Reform (1939) 1947:66.

8 The saying often quoted from Lord Kelvin. . . that "where you cannot measure your knowledge is meagre and unsatisfactory," as applied in mental and social science, is misleading and pernicious. This is another way of saying that these sciences are not sciences in the sense of physical science and cannot attempt to be such without forfeiting their proper nature and function. Insistence on a concretely quantitative economics means the use of statistics of physical magnitudes, whose economic meaning and significance is uncertain and dubious. (Even wheat is approximately homogeneous only if measured in economic terms.) And a similar statement would apply even more to other social sciences. In this field, the Kelvin dictum very largely means in practice, "if you cannot measure, measure anyhow!"

"What is Truth" in Economics? (1940) 1956:166. → See KELVIN:1.

9 A humorist once popular in this country stated my favorite "principle" in education: "It ain't ignorance that does the most damage, it's knowin' so derned much that ain't so."

The Role of Principles in Economics and Politics (1951) 1958:256.

10 The right principle is to respect all the principles, take them fully into account, and then use *good judgment* as to how far to follow one or another in the case in hand. All principles are false, because all are true — in a sense and to a degree; hence, none is true in a sense and to a degree which would deny to others a similarly qualified truth.

The Role of Principles in Economics and Politics (1951) 1958:256.

11 The supreme and inestimable merit of the exchange mechanism is that it enables a vast number of people to co-operate in the use of means to achieve ends as far as their interests are mutual, without arguing or in any way agreeing about either the ends or the methods of achieving them.

The Role of Principles in Economics and Politics (1951) 1956:267.

12 Liberals hold that men are not to be trusted, beyond necessity, with arbitrary power. As Lord Acton said, power corrupts — corrupts the initially good — and absolute power corrupts absolutely. But weakness in the face of power corrupts equally and apart from consequences, both the power-seeking attitude and that of servility are inherently to be condemned.

Intelligence and Democratic Action 1960:14. → See ACTON:3.

13 A society made up of economic men, even as consumers, would be a fantastic monstrosity and a physical impossibility. Nor have I mentioned the worst limitations.

Intelligence and Democratic Action 1960:107.

14 The Perfect Christian and the Economic Man would have one thing in common: neither one would have any friends.

Oral tradition. Quoted in George J. Stigler, personal communication, 9 June 1987.

Arthur Koestler 1905–1983
Hungarian-born British writer

1 [*Ivanov*]: The principle that the end justifies the means is and remains the only rule of political ethics; anything else is just vague chatter and melts away between one's fingers.

Darkness at Noon (1940) 1941:156. → In this novel based upon the Moscow Trials of the 1930s, the accused Rubashov is confronted with two examining magistrates: Gletkin, the fanatic, and Ivanov, the cynic.

Kurt Koffka 1886–1941
German-born U.S. psychologist

1 The Gestalt category wherever it is applied in science signifies the attempt to find within the mass of phenomena

coherent functional wholes, to treat them as full primary realities and to understand the behavior of these wholes as well as of their parts, from whole rather than from part laws. To apply the category of cause and effect means to find out which parts of nature stand in the cause–effect relation. Similarly, to apply the Gestalt category means to find out which parts of nature belong as parts to functional wholes, to discover their position in these wholes, their degree of relative independence and the articulation of larger wholes into subwholes.

Gestalt 1931:645.

2 A psychology which has no place for the concepts of meaning and value cannot be a complete psychology. At best it can give a sort of understructure, treating of the animal side of man, on which the main building, harbouring his cultural side, must be erected.

Principles of Gestalt Psychology 1935:19.

3 If one compares the behaviour of the bird at the top of the pecking list, the despot, with that of one very far down, the second or third from the last, then one finds the latter much more cruel to the few others over whom he lords it than the former in his treatment of all members. As soon as one removes from the group all members above the penultimate, his behaviour becomes milder and may even become very friendly. . . It is not difficult to find analogies to this in human societies, and therefore one side of such behaviour must be primarily the effects of the social groupings, and not of individual characteristics.

Principles of Gestalt Psychology 1935:669.

Wolfgang Köhler 1887–1967

Estonian-born U.S. psychologist

1 It is hardly an exaggeration to say that a chimpanzee kept in solitude is not a real chimpanzee at all.

The Mentality of Apes (1917) 1925:293.

2 If we wish to imitate the physical sciences, we must not imitate them in their contemporary, most developed form; we must imitate them in their historical youth, when their state of development was comparable to our own at the present time. Otherwise we should behave like boys who try to copy the imposing manners of full-grown men.

Gestalt Psychology 1929:43.

3 *Gestalt* psychology is said by some critics to repeat the word "whole" continually, to neglect the existence of parts and therefore to sacrifice that wonderful tool of all scientific procedure, analysis. Nothing could be a more misleading statement, as may be judged from the fact that we found it necessary to mention *segregation* wherever we were dealing with a unit or a definite whole.

Gestalt Psychology 1929:182.

4 In the German language. . . the noun "gestalt" has two meanings: besides the connotation of "shape" or "form" as a *property* of things, it has the meaning of a concrete individual and characteristic entity, existing as something detached and *having* a shape or form as one of its attributes. Following this tradition, in *gestalt theorie* the word "gestalt" means any segregated whole, and the consideration of *gestaltqualitäten* has become a more special side of the *gestaltproblem*, the prevailing idea being that the same general type of dynamical process which leads to the formation and segregation of extended wholes will also explain their specific properties.

Gestalt Psychology 1929:192–193.

5 Man has no direct access to the physical world. The phenomenal world contains all the material which is directly given to him. Thus, our approach to the physical domain will under all circumstances consist of inferences which we draw from the observation of certain percepts or, perhaps, also from other experiences; it will always be a procedure of *construction*. For this construction no building material is available but what we find in the phenomenal world.

The Place of Value in a World of Facts 1938:142.

6 Our present knowledge of human perception leaves no doubt as to the general form of any theory which is to do justice to such knowledge: a theory of perception must be a *field theory*. By this we mean that the neural functions and processes with which the perceptual facts are associated in each case are located in a continuous medium; and that the events in one part of this medium influence the events in other regions in a way that depends directly on the properties of both in their relation to each other. This is the conception with which all physicists work.

Dynamics in Psychology 1940:55.

7 It would be interesting to inquire how many times essential advances in science have first been made possible by the fact that the boundaries of special disciplines were *not* respected. . . Trespassing is one of the most successful techniques in science.

Dynamics in Psychology 1940:115–116.

Leszek Kolakowski 1927–

Polish-born British philosopher

1 The simplest improvements in social conditions require so huge an effort on the part of society that full awareness of this disproportion would be most discouraging and would thereby make any social progress impossible. The effort must be prodigally great if the result is to be at all visible. . . It is not at all peculiar then that this terrible disproportion must be quite weakly reflected in human consciousness if society is to generate the energy required to effect changes in social and human relations. For this purpose, one exaggerates the prospective results into a myth so as to make them take on dimensions which correspond a bit more to the immediately felt effort. . . [The myth acts like] a Fata Morgana which makes beautiful lands arise before the eyes of the members of a caravan and thus increases their efforts to the point

where, in spite of all their sufferings, they reach the next tiny waterhold. Had such tempting mirages not appeared, the exhausted caravan would inevitably have perished in the sandstorm, bereft of hope.

Der Mensch ohne Alternative 1961:127–128.

2 Positivism stands for a certain philosophical attitude to human knowledge; strictly speaking, it does not prejudge questions about how men arrive at knowledge. . . It is a collection of rules and evaluative criteria referring to human knowledge: it tells us what kind of contents in our statements about the world deserve the name of knowledge and supplies us with norms that make it possible to distinguish between that which may and that which may not reasonably be asked.

Positivist Philosophy (1966) 1972:10–11.

3 Positivists do not object to inquiry into the immediately invisible causes of any observed phenomenon, they object only to any accounting for it in terms of occult entities that are by definition inaccessible to human knowledge.

Positivist Philosophy (1966) 1972:12.

Mirra Komarovsky 1906–
Russian-born U.S. sociologist

1 Women became a "social problem" because technological and social changes over the past century and a half have disturbed an old equilibrium without as yet replacing it with another. As a result, our society is a veritable crazy quilt of contradictory practices and beliefs. Some old attitudes persist stubbornly in the face of a new reality which has long since rendered them meaningless. New conditions have arisen which have not as yet been defined by public opinion — leaving human beings without guidance and protection. New goals have emerged without the social machinery required for their attainment. The old and the new moralities exist side by side dividing the heart against itself.

Women in the Modern World 1953:48.

2 There is no profit in minimizing the radical transformations in contemporary value systems and in several social institutions that the realization of the goal of sex equality would require. Real options for men and women will be available only when our society includes — along with economic success, creative professional achievement, athletic prowess, and political power — esteem for nurturant socialization of children not as a task for women only. If men believed for a moment that building bridges, or managing a corporation, or writing books was no more essential to society than helping to shape the personality of a child, they would demand more of a hand in this endeavor too.

Women in College 1965:317.

N. D. Kondratieff 1892–c. 1931
Russian economist and statistician

1 *On the basis of the available data, the existence of long waves of cyclical character is very probable.*

At the same time, we believe ourselves justified in saying that the long waves, if existent at all, are a very important and essential factor in economic development, a factor the effects of which can be found in all the principal fields of social and economic life. . . We are also of the opinion that the long waves arise out of causes which are inherent in the essence of the capitalistic economy.

The Long Waves in Economic Life (1925) 1935:115.

Alexandre Koyré 1892–1964
Russian-born French and U.S. historian of science

1 What the founders of modern science, among them Galileo, had to do, was not to criticize and to combat certain faulty theories, and to correct or to replace them by better ones. They had to do something quite different. They had to destroy one world and to replace it by another. They had to reshape the framework of our intellect itself, to restate and to reform its concepts, to evolve a new approach to Being, a new concept of knowledge, a new concept of science — and even to replace a pretty natural approach, that of common sense, by another which is not natural at all.

Galileo and Plato 1943:405.

2 It is possible that the deepest meaning and aim of Newtonianism, or rather, of the whole scientific revolution of the seventeenth century, of which Newton is the heir and the highest expression, is just to abolish the world of the "more or less," the world of qualities and sense perception, the world of appreciation of our daily life, and to replace it by the (Archimedean) universe of precision, of exact measures, of strict determination. . . This revolution [is] one of the deepest, if not the deepest, mutations and transformations accomplished — or suffered — by the human mind since the invention of the cosmos by the Greeks, two thousand years before.

The Significance of the Newtonian Synthesis (1950) 1965:4–5.

3 We must not forget. . . that "influence" is not a simple, but on the contrary, a very complex, bilateral relation. We are not influenced by everything we read or learn. In one sense, and perhaps the deepest, we ourselves determine the influences we are submitting to; our intellectual ancestors are by no means given to, but are freely chosen by, us.

From the Closed World to the Infinite Universe (1957) 1958:5–6.

Siegfried Kracauer 1889–1966
German-born U.S. sociologist and historian

1 Marx once pithily. . . declared that he himself was no Marxist. Is there any influential thinker who would not have to protect his thoughts from what his followers — or his enemies, for that matter — make of them? Every idea is coarsened, flattened, and distorted on its way through the world. The world which takes possession of it does so according to its own lights and needs. Once a vision be-

comes an institution, clouds of dust gather about it, blurring its contours and contents. The history of ideas is a history of misunderstandings.

History 1969:6–7. → See MARX:24.

Alfred L. Kroeber 1876–1960
U.S. anthropologist

1 All civilization in a sense exists only in the mind. Gunpowder, textile arts, machinery, laws, telephones are not themselves transmitted from man to man or from generation to generation, at least not permanently. It is the perception, the knowledge and understanding of them, their *ideas* in the Platonic sense, that are passed along. Everything social can have existence only through mentality.

The Superorganic (1917) 1952:38.

2 When we cease to look upon invention or discovery as some mysterious inherent faculty of individual minds which are randomly dropped in space and time by fate; when we center our attention on the plainer relation of one such advancing step to the others; when, in short, interest shifts from individually biographic elements — which can be only dramatically artistic, didactically moralizing, or psychologically interpretable — and attaches whole heartedly to the social or civilizational, evidence on this point will be infinite in quantity, and the presence of majestic forces or sequences pervading civilization will be irresistibly evident.

The Superorganic (1917) 1952:45.

3 "Structure" appears to be just a yielding to a word that has perfectly good meaning but suddenly becomes fashionably attractive for a decade or so — like "streamlining" — and during its vogue tends to be applied indiscriminately because of the pleasurable connotations of its sound. Of course a typical personality can be viewed as having a structure. But so can a physiology, any organism, all societies and all cultures, crystals, machines — in fact everything that is not wholly amorphous has a structure. So what "structure" adds to the meaning of our phrase seems to be nothing, except to provoke a degree of pleasant puzzlement.

Anthropology (1923) 1948:325.

4 The kite, the manner of manipulating the marbles, the cut of a garment, the tipping of the hat, remain as cultural facts after every physiological and psychological consideration of the individuals involved has been exhausted.

Sub-human Culture Beginnings (1928) 1931:476.

5 I see no evidence of any true law in the phenomena dealt with; nothing cyclical, regularly repetitive, or necessary. There is nothing to show either that every culture must develop patterns within which a florescence of quality is possible, or that, having once so flowered, it must wither without chance of revival.

Configurations of Culture Growth 1944:761.

6 Geniuses are the indicators of the realization of coherent pattern growths of cultural value.

Configurations of Culture Growth 1944:839.

7 It is culture that is at once the precondition of all human history and its abiding and growing precipitate. It is the hereditary faculty for culture that is the most distinctive feature of man as an animal. It is that part of the larger whole of culture which we ordinarily call "speech" that makes the accumulation of the remaining part of culture possible; and it is this remainder — culture in the more specific sense — that gives speech most of its content, gives us human beings something to talk about.

Introduction to *Anthropology Today* 1953:xiv.

8 That the members of our civilization and of others are very little aware of total style need not discourage us much. Every human language has such a patterned style — we call it its grammar — of which the speakers are unaware while speaking, but which can be discovered by analysis and can be formulated.

Style and Civilizations 1957:106.

Alfred L. Kroeber 1876–1960 and Clyde Kluckhohn 1905–1960
U.S. anthropologists

1 Culture consists of patterns, explicit and implicit, of and for behavior acquired and transmitted by symbols, constituting the distinctive achievement of human groups, including their embodiments in artifacts; the essential core of culture consists of traditional (i.e., historically derived and selected) ideas and especially their attached values; culture systems may, on the one hand, be considered as products of action, on the other as conditioning elements of further action.

Culture 1952:181.

P'etr Kropotkin 1842–1921
Russian social philosopher and anarchist

1 After having discussed the importance of mutual aid in various classes of animals, I was evidently bound to discuss the importance of the same factor in the evolution of man. This was the more necessary as there are a number of evolutionists who may not refuse to admit the importance of mutual aid among animals, but who, like Herbert Spencer, will refuse to admit it for man. For primitive man — they maintain — war of each against all was *the* law of life.

Mutual Aid (1902) 1972:22–23.

2 Sociability is as much a law of nature as mutual struggle [and] mutual aid is as much a law of animal life as mutual struggle.

Mutual Aid (1902) 1972:30.

Thomas S. Kuhn 1922–
U.S. historian of science

1 The transition from a paradigm in crisis to a new one from which a new tradition of normal science can emerge is far from a cumulative process, one achieved by an articulation or extension of the old paradigm. Rather it is a

reconstruction of the field from new fundamentals, a reconstruction that changes some of the field's most elementary theoretical generalizations as well as many of its paradigm methods and applications. During the transition period there will be a large but never complete overlap between the problems that can be solved by the old and by the new paradigm. But there will also be a decisive difference in the modes of solution. When the transition is complete, the profession will have changed its view of the field, its methods, and its goals.

The Structure of Scientific Revolutions (1962) 1970:84–85.

2 Examining the record of past research from the vantage of contemporary historiography, the historian of science may be tempted to exclaim that when paradigms change, the world itself changes with them. Led by a new paradigm, scientists adopt new instruments and look in new places. Even more important, during revolutions scientists see new and different things when looking with familiar instruments in places they have looked before. It is rather as if the professional community had been suddenly transported to another planet where familiar objects are seen in a different light and are joined by unfamiliar ones as well.

The Structure of Scientific Revolutions (1962) 1970:111.

3 The resolution of revolutions is selection by conflict within the scientific community of the fittest way to practice future science. The net result of a sequence of such revolutionary selections, separated by periods of normal research, is the wonderfully adapted set of instruments we call modern scientific knowledge.

The Structure of Scientific Revolutions (1962) 1970:172.

4 Scientific development depends in part on a process of non-incremental or revolutionary change. Some revolutions are large, like those associated with the names of Copernicus, Newton, or Darwin, but most are much smaller, like the discovery of oxygen or the planet Uranus. The usual prelude to changes of this sort is, I believe, the awareness of anomaly, of an occurrence or set of occurrences that does not fit existing ways of ordering phenomena. The changes that result therefore require "putting on a different kind of thinking-cap," one that renders the anomalous lawlike but that, in the process, also transforms the order exhibited by some other phenomena, previously unproblematic.

The Essential Tension 1977:xvii. → See BUTTERFIELD:5.

L

Jacques Lacan 1901–1981
French psychoanalyst

1 Symbols in fact envelop the life of man in a network so total that they join together, before he comes into the world, those who are going to engender him "by flesh and blood"; so total that they bring to his birth, along with the gifts of the stars, if not with the gifts of the fairies, the shape of his destiny; so total that they give the words that will make him faithful or renegade, the law of the acts that will follow him right to the very place where he *is* not yet and even beyond his death; and so total that through them his end finds its meaning in the last judgement, where the Word absolves his being or condemns it— unless he attain the subjective bringing to realization of being-for-death.

Écrits (1966) 1977:68.

2 If Freud had brought to man's knowledge nothing more than the truth that there is such a thing as the true, there would be no Freudian discovery. Freud would belong to the line of moralists in whom a whole tradition of humanist analysis is embodied, a milky way to the heavens of European culture in which Balthazar Gracian and La Rochefoucauld shine as stars of the first order, and in which Nietzsche features as a nova as dazzling as it is short-lived.

Écrits (1966) 1977:119.

3 [In Freud's] "The Interpretation of Dreams" every page deals with what I call the letter of the discourse, in its texture, its usage, its immanence in the matter in question. For it is with this work that the work of Freud begins to open the royal road to the unconscious. And Freud gave us notice of this; his confidence at the time of launching this book in the early days of this century only confirms what he continued to proclaim to the end: that he had staked the whole of his discovery on this essential expression of his message.

Écrits (1966) 1977:159. → See Freud:14.

4 If I have said that the unconscious is the discourse of the Other (with a capital O), it is in order to indicate the beyond in which the recognition of desire is bound up with the desire for recognition.

In other words this other is the Other that even my lie invokes as a guarantor of the truth in which it subsists.

By which we can also see that. . . with the appearance of language the dimension of truth emerges.

Écrits (1966) 1977:172.

Karl Lamprecht 1856–1915
German historian

1 History is primarily a socio-psychological science. In the conflict between the old and the new tendencies in historical investigation. . . we are at the turn of the stream, the parting of the ways in historical science.

Historical Development and Present Character of the Science of History 1906:111.

Oskar Lange 1904–1965
Polish economist

1 [The] superiority of Marxian economics is only a partial one. There are some problems before which Marxian economics is quite powerless, while "bourgeois" economics solves them easily. What can Marxian economics say about monopoly prices? What has it to say on the fundamental problems of monetary and credit theory? What apparatus has it to offer for analysing the incidence of a tax, or the effect of a certain technical innovation on wages? And (irony of Fate!) what can Marxian economics contribute to the problem of the optimum contribution of productive resources in a socialist economy?

Marxian Economics and Modern Economic Theory 1934-1935:191. → Joseph A. Schumpeter noted that Lange's paper makes it "very clear" that "economic theory is a technique of reasoning" and that "the literary defense of the cause of socialism stands to lose efficiency by clinging to outworn tools" of economic analysis. See his *History of Economic Analysis* (1954:884).

2 The really important point in discussing the economic merits of socialism is not that of comparing the equilibrium position of a socialist and of a capitalist economy with respect to social welfare. Interesting as such a comparison is for the economic theorist, it is not the real issue in the discussion of socialism. The real issue is *whether the further maintenance of the capitalist system is compatible with economic progress.*

On the Economic Theory of Socialism (1936–1937) 1938:110.

3 The *principle of economic rationality*. . . asserts that the maximum degree of realization of the end is achieved by proceeding in such a way that either for a given outlay of means the maximum degree of realization of the end is achieved, or that for a given degree of realization of the end the outlay of the means is minimal. The first variant of this procedure is called *the principle of greatest effect* or *the principle of greatest efficiency*. The second variant is called *the principle of the minimum outlay of means* or *the principle of economy of means*. . . These are thus two equivalent variants of the principle of economic rationality.

Political Economy (1959) 1963:Vol. 1, 167–168.

Susanne K. Langer 1895–1985
U.S. philosopher

1 An animal's environment consists of the things that act on his senses. . . He does not live in a world of unbroken space and time, filled with events even when he is not present or when he is not interested; his "world" has a fragmentary, intermittent existence, arising and collapsing with his activities. A human being's world hangs together, its events fit into each other; no matter how devious their connections, there always are connections, in one big framework of space and time. . . *The world* is something human.

The Growing Center of Knowledge (1956) 1962:146.

Pierre Simon de Laplace 1749–1827
French mathematician

1 I present here without the aid of analysis [mathematics] the principles and general results of this theory, applying them to the most important questions of life, which are indeed for the most part only problems of probability. Strictly speaking it may even be said that nearly all our knowledge is problematical [only probable]; and in the small number of things which we are able to know with certainty, even in the mathematical sciences themselves, the principal means for ascertaining truth — induction and analogy — are based on probabilities; so that the entire system of human knowledge is connected with the theory set forth in this essay.

A Philosophical Essay on Probabilities (1814) 1951: 1–2.

2 If an intelligence, at a given instant, knew all the forces that animate nature and the position of each constituent being; if, moreover, this intelligence were sufficiently great to submit these data to analysis, it could embrace in the same formula the movements of the greatest bodies of the universe and those of the smallest atoms: to this intelligence nothing would be uncertain, and the future, as the past, would be present to its eyes.

Essai philosophique sur les probabilités. (1814) 1986:31. → Unpublished translation by Stephen M. Stigler. See KANT:2.

3 The regularity which astronomy shows us in the movements of the comets doubtless occurs in all phenomena. The curve described by a simple molecule of air or water vapor is regulated in a manner just as certain as the orbits of the planets; the only difference between these is that introduced by our ignorance. Probability is relative in part to this ignorance, and in part to our knowledge.

Essai philosophique sur les probabilités (1814) 1986:34. → Unpublished translation by Stephen M. Stigler. This statement, reconciling probability with determinism, was first made in Laplace's 1795 lectures at the École Normale.

4 The wish to see into the future, and the consonance of many remarkable events with the predictions of astrologers, fortunetellers, and soothsayers, with premonitions and dreams, and with numbers and days reputed to be lucky or unlucky, has given birth to a multitude of widespread prejudices. People do not reflect upon the large number of noncoincidences which have made no impression, or which are unknown. However, it is necessary to know these in order to judge the probability of the causes they attribute to the coincidences. Such knowledge would doubtless confirm what reason tells us regarding these prejudices. Thus, the philosopher of antiquity, upon entering a temple built to glorify the power of a god and being shown the votive offerings of all those who were saved from shipwreck after having invoked that god, made a remark in accord with the calculus of probabilities when he observed that he did not see inscribed the names of those who perished despite such an invocation.

Essai philosophique sur les probabilités (1814) 1986:169. → Unpublished translation by Stephen M. Stigler. Laplace's version of the story of the shipwrecked sailors first appeared in the 4th edition of 1819. See CICERO:2 for an earlier version.

5 The theory of probabilities is essentially only common sense reduced to calculation; it helps us to judge accurately what sound minds perceive by a sort of instinct, often without being able to give a reason.

Essai philosophique sur les probabilités (1814) 1986:206. → Unpublished translation by Stephen M. Stigler.

6 *Je n'avais pas besoin de cette hypothèse-là* [I have no need for this hypothesis].

Quoted in Augustus De Morgan, *A Budget of Paradoxes* (1872) 1915:Vol. 2, 2. → De Morgan reports that Laplace once went to present an edition of his *Sys-*

tème du monde to Napoleon. The emperor, who was fond of putting embarrassing questions, received it, saying, "M. Laplace, they tell me you have written this large book on the system of the universe, and have never even mentioned its Creator." Laplace gave the blunt reply quoted above. Napoleon, greatly amused, told the story to the mathematician Joseph Louis Lagrange, who exclaimed, "Ah! It is a beautiful hypothesis; it explains many things" [*Ah! c'est une belle hypothèse; ça explique beaucoup de choses*].

François de La Rochefoucauld 1613–1680
French moralist

1 It is easier to know mankind in general than any particular man.

Maxim No. 436 (1665) 1959:113.

Karl S. Lashley 1890–1958
U.S. psychologist

1 The phenomena of behavior and of mind are ultimately describable in the concepts of the mathematical and physical sciences.

The Problem of Serial Order in Behavior 1951:112.

Harold J. Laski 1893–1950
British political scientist

1 Social legislation has the incurable habit of tending towards paternalism; and paternalism, however wide be the basis of consent upon which it is erected, is the subtlest form of poison to the democratic state.

The Problem of Administrative Areas (1918) 1968:43.

2 It is today a commonplace that the real source of authority in any state is with the holders of economic power. The will that is effective is their will; the commands that are obeyed are their commands.

The Problem of Administrative Areas (1918) 1968:62.

3 In the processes of politics what, broadly speaking, gets registered is not a will that is at each moment in accord with the state-purpose, but the will of those who in fact operate the machine of government.

Authority in the Modern State 1919:37.

4 The whole theory of the state. . . is contained in the idea of public need.

Introduction to Leon Duguit, *Law in the Modern State* (1913) 1919:xx. → From the introduction to the 1919 edition.

5 Within the State, [men] meet as persons. Their claims are equal claims. They are not barristers or miners, Catholics or Protestants, employers or workers. They are, as a matter of social theory, simply persons who need certain services they cannot themselves produce if they are to realise themselves. Clearly, a function of this kind, however it is organised, involves a pre-eminence over other functions. The State controls the level at which men are to live as men.

A Grammar of Politics (1925) 1938:70.

6 My property is, from the standpoint of political justice, the measure of economic worth placed by the State upon my personal effort towards the realisation of its end.

A Grammar of Politics (1925) 1938:87–88.

7 Liberty in a laissez faire society is attainable only by those who have the wealth or opportunity to purchase it; and these are always a negligible minority. Experience accordingly drove the state to interfere; and the liberal state of the nineteenth century was gradually replaced by the social service state of the twentieth. This may be described by saying that it again joins the ideal of liberty to that of equality, and this in the name of social justice.

Liberty 1933:443.

Peter Laslett 1915–
British historian

1 Time was when the whole of life went forward in the family, in a circle of loved, familiar faces, known and fondled objects, all to human size. That time has gone for ever. It makes us very different from our ancestors.

The World We Have Lost (1965) 1973:22.

2 People and nations and cultures vary in the extent to which they wish to understand themselves in time. . . but to claim that there has ever been a generation anywhere with no sense of history is to go too far. . . All historical knowledge is knowledge with a view to ourselves as we are here and now. . . Historical knowledge. . . is in fact almost always of greater intrinsic interest than Jupiter's moons, or the wingspan of fly populations, because it is knowledge about people with whom we can identify ourselves.

The World We Have Lost Further Explored 1983:275.

Ferdinand Lassalle 1825–1864
German socialist and labor leader

1 [*Franz*]: *Das Ziel nicht zeige, zeige auch den Weg.*
Denn so verwachsen ist hienieden Weg und Ziel,
Dass eines sich stets ändert mit dem andern
Und andrer Weg auch andres Ziel erzeugt.
[Show us not the aim without the way,
For ends and means on earth are so entangled
That changing one, you change the other too:
Each different path brings other ends in view.]

Franz von Sickingen 1859:93. → From Lassalle's five-act play, which takes place during the Thirty Years War. Franz and his friend Ulrich von Hutten — to whom these lines are spoken — are struggling for freedom of conscience against the Papacy.

2 Wages. . . cannot fall with anything like permanence below the ordinary rate of living; as from it would flow emigration, celibacy, restraint in the number of births; circumstances in the end lessening the number of laborers; an equilibrium is thus secured, keeping wages generally uniform; the wages being at all times in obedience to the vibrations. There is no gain saying the assurance that the wages of a people are regulated by their ordinary

habits of living, those habits conforming to the limits of existence and propagation. This is the cruel, rigorous law that governs wages under the present system.

Open Letter to the National Labor Association of Germany (1862) 1879:14. → This is the "iron law of wages" which Lassalle took from Ricardo and did much to popularize.

Harold D. Lasswell 1902–1978
U.S. political scientist

Political science without biography is a form of taxidermy.

Psychopathology and Politics (1930) 1960:1.

In a sense politics proceeds by the creation of fictitious values.

Psychopathology and Politics (1930) 1960:195.

Politics is the study of *who gets what, when, and how*.

World Politics and Personal Insecurity (1935) 1950:3.

It is thinkable that men will some day face a common disaster which is capable of uniting them in concerted efforts to survive.

World Politics and Personal Insecurity (1935) 1950:252.

The study of politics is the study of influence and the influential. The science of politics states conditions; the philosophy of politics justifies preferences. This book, restricted to political analysis, declares no preferences. It states conditions.

Politics (1936) 1951:295.

The influential are those who get the most of what there is to get. Available values may be classified as *deference, income, safety*. Those who get most are *elite*; the rest are *mass*.

Politics (1936) 1951:295.

A convenient way to describe an act of communication is to answer the following questions:

Who
Says What
In Which Channel
To Whom
With What Effect?

The Structure and Function of Communication in Society (1948) 1964:37. → This question served as a major paradigm for the field of mass communications research as it developed in the United States in the 1950s and 1960s.

The language of politics is the language of power. It is the language of decision. It registers and modifies decision. It is battle cry, verdict and sentence, statute, ordinance and rule, oath of office, controversial news, comment and debate.

The Language of Power 1949:8.

If the world holds together, political scientists will concern themselves with doing what they can to illuminate the impact of the arts on politics and of politics on architecture, literature, music, graphics, plastics, and the dance. More than this — the aesthetic interest will find creative expression in the criticism of power, rectitude, and in fact of all values.

The Future of Political Science 1963:185.

Harold D. Lasswell 1902–1978
U.S. political scientist
and
Abraham Kaplan 1918–
U.S. philosopher

1 The analysis of political symbols often requires. . . a distinction between manifest and latent content. The manifest content — the literal, direct, or obvious significance — may be far removed from power practices and relations. The symbol may purport to state a nonsocial fact or express a nonpower demand; but its latent content may be directly political.

Power and Society 1950:104.

Eighth Earl of Lauderdale
See JAMES MAITLAND.

John Law 1671–1729
Scottish economist and banker

1 Goods have a Value from the Uses they are apply'd to; and their Value is Greater or Lesser, not so much from their more or less valuable, or necessary Uses; as from the greater or lesser Quantity of them in proportion to the Demand for them. *Example.* Water is of great use, yet of little Value; because the Quantity of Water is much greater than the Demand for it. Diamonds are of little use, yet of great Value, because the Demand for Diamonds is much greater, than the Quantity of them.

Money and Trade Consider'd (1705) 1720:4.

Paul F. Lazarsfeld 1901–1976
Austrian-born U.S. psychologist and sociologist

1 In the last analysis, more than anything else people can move other people. From an ethical point of view this is a hopeful aspect in the serious social problem of propaganda. The side which has the more enthusiastic supporters and which can mobilize grass-root support in an expert way has great chances of success.

The People's Choice (1944) 1948:158. → Written with Bernard Berelson and Hazel Gaudet.

2 The mixture of contempt and anxiety which the term "methodology" so often evokes should be replaced by a better understanding of its intent. T. S. Eliot has caught it well: ". . . the end of all our exploring/Will be to arrive where we started/And know the place for the first time."

Problems in Methodology (1959) 1982:208.

3 It is the tragic story of the cultural crusader in a mass society that he cannot win, but that we would be lost without him.

The Mass Media and the Intellectual Community (1961) 1972:154.

4 Let me. . . stress. . . the need to focus on the specific procedures of the social scientist. I obviously want to

deny the unity of science as little as I would speak out for sin. But just as I believe that basically scientific work has a unifying rationality, I am also convinced that each subject matter has its own problems which need special attention. We should be guided by the inversion of a French proverb: the more it is the same, the more it is different. In my opinion, at this moment, the detailed explication of the *differential* aspects of empirical social research badly needs the attention of the philosopher of science.

Philosophy of Science and Empirical Social Research (1962) 1972:275. → For the origin of the French proverb, see KARR:1.

5 When we deal with nature, many objects, like trees or stones or animals, force themselves on us visually. Social entities are much more the product of creative intelligence. The notion of a clique, for instance, or of a reference group, the inner gallery for which so many of us play the drama of our lives, or the distinction between an introverted and an extroverted personality are real conceptual inventions. In social observations we are often in the position of a bird which flies across the sky with a flock of other birds. For the external observer, the flock has a clearly visible geometric shape; but does the bird within the flock even know about the shape of his "group"? By what social interrelations among the birds is the form of the group maintained?

The Obligations of the 1950 Pollster to the 1984 Historian (1964) 1972:288. → First published in 1950.

6 I remember a formula I created at the time [after World War I]: a fighting revolution requires economics (Marx); a victorious revolution requires engineers (Russia); a defeated revolution calls for psychology (Vienna).

An Episode in the History of Social Research (1968) 1982:13. → Lazarsfeld's explanation for having established a psychological research institute in Vienna as Austrian nationalism overcame socialism in the 1920s.

7 The organization man is a special case of a well-known sociological notion of the marginal man who is part of two different cultures. He lives under cross pressures that move him in a number of directions. According to his gifts and external circumstances he may become a revolutionary, a surrealist, a criminal. In some cases his marginality may become the driving force for institutional efforts; the institution he creates shelters him and at the same time helps him crystallize his own identity.

Interview with Paul Lazarsfeld 1976. → The word "organization" is translated as "institution" in the source cited in the bibliography. See PARK:4 and WILLIAM H. WHYTE:1 for formulations of "the marginal man" and "the organization man."

Paul F. Lazarsfeld 1901–1976
Austrian-born U.S. psychologist and sociologist
and
Morris Rosenberg 1922–1992
U.S. sociologist

1 There is a well-known story about the centipede who lost his ability to walk when he was asked in which order he moved his feet. But other details of the story are buried in conspiratorial silence. First of all, there is no mention of the fact that the inquiry came from a methodologist who wanted to improve the walking efficiency of the centipede community. Then, little attention is paid to the other centipedes who participated in the investigation. Not all of them reacted with such disastrous effects. Some were able to give rather reasonable answers; from these the investigator worked diligently to arrive at general principles of walking behavior.

When the methodologist finally published his findings, there was a general outcry that he had only reported facts which everyone already knew. Nevertheless, by his formulating this knowledge clearly, and by adding hitherto unobserved facts at various points, the average centipede in the community was eventually able to walk better. After a generation or so, this knowledge was incorporated into textbooks, and so filtered down to students on a lower level of scholarship. In retrospect this was the outstanding result. Of course, the great centipede ballet dancer and other creative walking artists continued to depend on hereditary endowments, and could not be produced by the school system. But the general level of walking, characteristic of the centipede in the street, was improved. In this way, individuals endowed with great personal gifts started out at a higher level, and achieved creative performances unparalleled in the past.

General Introduction to *The Language of Social Research* 1955:1.

Paul F. Lazarsfeld 1901–1976
Austrian-born U.S. psychologist and sociologist
and
Wagner Thielens, Jr. 1925–
U.S. sociologist

1 What we call the effective scope of a man's world characterizes. . . what he perceives, what he has contact with, and what he reaches for through his interests or his expectations. Partly still a metaphor and partly a step toward a precise concept, the term is backed by a broad array of empirical data.

The Academic Mind 1958:264.
[*See also* ELIHU KATZ AND PAUL F. LAZARSFELD.]

Edmund R. Leach 1910–1989
British anthropologist

1 The fervour that Functionalism aroused among a limited intellectual circle was not based in reasoned analysis. Malinowski had many of the qualities of a prophet. . . He claimed to be the creator of an entirely new academic discipline. A whole generation of his followers were brought up to believe that social anthropology began in the Trobriand islands in 1914.

The Epistemological Background to Malinowski's Empiricism (1957) 1970:124.

2 Custom is what men do, normal men, average men. . . Custom "makes sense" not in terms of some external, logically ordered, moral system, but in terms of the private

self-interest of the average man in that particular cultural situation.

Pul Eliya (1961) 1968:298.

3 In a strictly scientific sense it is silly to pretend that death and birth are the same thing, yet without question many religious dogmas purport to maintain precisely that. Moreover, the make-believe that birth follows death is not confined to beliefs about the hereafter, it comes out also in the pattern of religious ritual itself. It appears not only in *rites de passage*. . . but also in a high proportion of sacrificial rites of a sacramental character. . . The rite as a whole falls into sections, a symbolic death, a period of ritual seclusion, a symbolic rebirth.

Time and False Noses 1961:133.

4 We talk of measuring time, as if time were a concrete thing waiting to be measured; but in fact we *create time* by creating intervals in social life. Until we have done this there is no time to be measured.

Time and False Noses 1961:135.

5 The environment is not a natural thing; it is a set of interrelated percepts, a product of culture. It yields food to the aborigine but none to the white traveller because the former perceives food where the latter sees only inedible insects. . . What this environment is, is not discoverable objectively; it is a matter of perception. The relation between a society and its environment can be understood only when we see how the environment is organized in terms of the verbal categories of those who use it.

Culture and Social Cohesion 1965:25, 38.

6 There are no "laws" of historical process; there are no "laws" of sociological probability. The fundamental characteristic of human culture is its endless diversity. It is not a chaotic diversity but it is not a predestined diversity either. Anthropologists who imagine that, by the exercise of reason, they can reduce the observations of the ethnographers to a nomothetic natural science are wasting their time.

Social Anthropology 1982:51–52.

Gustave Le Bon 1841–1931
French psychologist

1 Under certain given circumstances, and only under those circumstances, an agglomeration of men presents new characteristics very different from those of the individuals composing it. The sentiments and ideas of all the persons in the gathering take one and the same direction, and their conscious personality vanishes. A collective mind is formed, doubtless transitory, but presenting very clearly defined characteristics. The gathering has thus become what, in the absence of a better expression, I will call an organized crowd, or, if the term is considered preferable, a psychological crowd. It forms a single being and is subject to the *law of the mental unity of crowds*.

The Crowd (1895) 1979:58–59.

2 The characteristics of the reasoning of crowds are the association of dissimilar things possessing a merely apparent connection. . . and the immediate generalization of particular cases.

The Crowd (1895) 1979:70.

Georges-Louis Leclerc, comte de Buffon
See GEORGES-LOUIS LECLERC, COMTE DE BUFFON.

Lenin 1870–1924
[Vladimir Il'ich Ul'ianov]
Russian revolutionary leader

1 Without revolutionary theory there can be no revolutionary movement.

What Is to Be Done? (1902) 1961:369.

2 (1) No revolutionary movement can endure without a stable organisation of leaders maintaining continuity; (2) . . . the broader the popular mass drawn spontaneously into the struggle, which forms the basis of the movement and participates in it, the more urgent the need for such an organisation, and the more solid this organisation must be (for it is much easier for all sorts of demagogues to side-track the more backward sections of the masses); (3) . . . such an organisation must consist chiefly of people professionally engaged in revolutionary activity; (4) . . . in an autocratic state, the more we *confine* the membership of such an organisation to people who are professionally engaged in revolutionary activity and who have been professionally trained in the art of combating the political police, the more difficult will it be to unearth the organisation; and (5) the *greater* will be the number of people from the working class and from the other social classes who will be able to join the movement and perform active work in it.

What Is to Be Done? (1902) 1961:464.

3 *Every* question "runs in a vicious circle" because political life as a whole is an endless chain consisting of an infinite number of links. The whole art of politics lies in finding and taking as firm a grip as we can of the link that is least likely to be struck from our hands, the one that is most important at the given moment, the one that most of all guarantees its possessor the possession of the whole chain.

What Is to Be Done? (1902) 1961:502.

4 Imperialism is capitalism at that stage of development at which the dominance of monopolies and finance capital is established; in which the export of capital has acquired pronounced importance; in which the division of the world among the international trusts has begun, in which the division of all territories of the globe among the biggest capitalist powers has been completed.

Imperialism, the Highest Stage of Capitalism (1916) 1964:266–267.

5 Politics begin where the masses are, not where there are thousands, but where there are millions, that is where serious politics begin.

Report Delivered to the Seventh Congress of the Russian Communist Party (Bolsheviks), 7 March 1918. 1937:295.

6 Anyone who has carefully observed life in the countryside, as compared with life in the cities, knows that we have not torn up the roots of capitalism and have not undermined the foundation, the basis, of the internal enemy. The latter depends on small-scale production, and there is only one way of undermining it, namely, to place the economy of the country, including agriculture, on a new technical basis, that of modern large-scale production. Only electricity provides that basis.

Communism is Soviet power plus the electrification of the whole country.

Report on the Work of the Council of People's Commissars, 22 December 1920. 1966:516.

A. N. Leont'ev 1903–1979
Russian psychologist

1 American researchers are constantly seeking to discover how the child came to be what he is; we in the USSR are striving to discover not how the child came to be what he is, but how he can become what he not yet is.

Quoted in Urie Bronfenbrenner, Toward an Experimental Ecology of Human Development 1977:528.

Wassily Leontief 1906–
Russian-born U.S. economist

1 Direct factual study and quantitative descriptions of the structural properties of the economic system, detailed in content, comprehensive in coverage, and systematically designed to fill the specific requirement of an appropriate theoretical scheme, seem to offer the only promising approach to empirically significant understanding of the operational characteristics of the modern economy.

The task thus imposed on the collector of primary factual information exceeds by far anything demanded hitherto from quantitative empirical research in economics or any other social science. It is only reasonable to suggest that the theorist should meet him half way by redesigning his analytical scheme so as to take advantage of the strengths and mitigate the weaknesses of the observational data to which it will have to be applied.

Gibbs and Mathematical Economics (1954) 1985:40.

2 Our free enterprise system has rightly been compared to a gigantic computing machine capable of solving its own problems automatically. But any one who has had some practical experience with large computers knows that they do break down and can't operate unattended.

Theoretical Assumptions and Nonobserved Facts 1971:6.

3 Throughout the history of their discipline. . . economists have had to work with very little data and, therefore, have developed methods for reaching conclusions with a minimum of information. Economic theory is constructed in such a way as to extract the most from very little data; it is a theory that uses averages, general index numbers, and very general arguments. In the past thirty years, as many more data have become available, economists have found themselves in the situation of a man stranded on an island with nothing to eat, who, when he is rescued and given food, gets indigestion. The challenge for economics at the present time is to develop a theory that can absorb data without ruining them, and that, at the same time, will permit us to utilize detailed information instead of arguing in broad generalities.

Natural Resources, Environmental Disruption, and Growth Prospects of the Developed and Less Developed Countries 1977:21.

Frédéric Le Play 1806–1882
French sociologist

1 The surest way an outside observer has to know the spiritual and moral life of people is very similar to the procedure which a chemist uses to understand the nature of minerals. The mineral is known when the analysis has isolated all the elements which enter into its composition and when one has verified that the weight of all these elements adds up exactly to that of the mineral under analysis. A similar numerical verification is always available to the student who analyses systematically the social unit represented by the family.

Les ouvriers européens (1855) 1877–1879:Vol. 1, 224.

2 Every fact about the existence of a worker's family ends up more or less directly in a receipt or an expenditure. There is scarcely a sentiment or an action worthy of mention which does not leave a clear trace in the budget of receipts or that of expenses.

Les ouvriers européens (1855) 1877–1879:Vol. 1, 237.

Max Lerner 1902–1992
Russian-born U.S. political scientist and journalist

1 Power politics existed before Machiavelli was ever heard of; it will exist long after his name is only a faint memory. What he did, like Harvey, was to recognize its existence and subject it to scientific study.

Introduction to Niccolò Machiavelli, *The Prince* (1532) 1950:xliii.

Primo Levi 1919–1987
Italian chemist and writer

1 The great technological breakthroughs of the last two centuries (the new metallurgies, steam engine, electrical energy, and internal-combustion engine) have brought about profound sociological changes but have not shaken humanity at its foundations; on the contrary, at least for the big innovations of the last thirty years (nuclear energy, solid-state physics, insecticides, fungicides, and detergents), they have led to consequences which have a much greater scope and different nature from what anyone dared expect.

The Moon and Us (1985) 1989:36.

Donald N. Levine 1931–
U.S. sociologist

1 There are benefits to be gained from the ambiguities of scientific discourse. Of the four. . . functions served by

ambiguity, two remain outside the boundaries of scientific work. The function of attaining enlightenment through the intuition of indeterminacy belongs to mysticism, or perhaps to philosophy and poetry, not to the disciplined activity of science. And the protection of one's meanings and intentions through ambiguously opaque utterance. . . cannot be sanctioned as appropriate conduct for a scientific enquirer.

Through its two other functions, however — the evocative representation of complex meanings and the bonding of a community through diffuse symbols — ambiguity has long served and will continue to serve the general objectives of scientific activity. It is useful for scientific formulations to express an abundance of meanings, for these can ignite a cluster of insights that in turn lead to novel explorations.

The Flight from Ambiguity 1985:218.

Claude Lévi-Strauss 1908–
French anthropologist

Mauss sait tout [Mauss knows everything].

French Sociology 1945:527. → This is Lévi-Strauss' report on a frequent remark of Mauss' students; he had been one.

In my mind, models are reality, and I would even say that they are the only reality.

Discussion in *An Appraisal of* Anthropology Today. 1953:115.

Today I sometimes wonder if anthropology did not attract me, without my realizing this, because of a structural affinity between the civilizations it studies and my particular way of thinking. I have no aptitude for prudently cultivating a given field and gathering in the harvest year after year: I have a neolithic kind of intelligence.

Tristes tropiques (1955) 1974:53.

Following Rousseau, and in what I consider to be a definitive manner, Marx established that social science is no more founded on the basis of events than physics is founded on sense data: the object is to construct a model and to study its property and its different reactions in laboratory conditions in order later to apply the observations to the interpretation of empirical happenings, which may be far removed from what had been forecast.

Tristes tropiques (1955) 1974:57.

Both history and ethnography are concerned with societies *other* than the one in which we live. Whether this *otherness* is due to remoteness in time (however slight), or to remoteness in space, or even to cultural heterogeneity, is of secondary importance compared to the basic similarity of perspective. . . All that the historian or ethnographer can do, and all that we can expect of either of them, is to enlarge a specific experience to the dimensions of a more general one, which thereby becomes accessible *as experience* to men of another country or another epoch. And in order to succeed, both historian and ethnographer must have the same qualities: skill, precision, a sympathetic approach, and objectivity.

Structural Anthropology (1958) 1967:17.

6 In anthropology as in linguistics. . . it is not comparison that supports generalization, but the other way around. If, as we believe to be the case, the unconscious activity of the mind consists in imposing forms upon content, and if these forms are fundamentally the same for all minds — ancient and modern, primitive and civilized. . . — it is necessary and sufficient to grasp the unconscious structure underlying each institution and each custom, in order to obtain a principle of interpretation valid for other institutions and other customs.

Structural Anthropology (1958) 1967:21–22.

7 Because they are symbolic systems, kinship systems offer the anthropologist a rich field, where his efforts can almost (and we emphasize the "almost") converge with those of the most highly developed of the social sciences, namely, linguistics. But to achieve this convergence, from which it is hoped a better understanding of man will result, we must never lose sight of the fact that, in both anthropological and linguistic research, we are dealing strictly with symbolism.

Structural Anthropology (1958) 1967:49.

8 For centuries the humanities and the social sciences have resigned themselves to contemplating the world of the natural and exact sciences as a kind of paradise which they will never enter. And all of a sudden there is a small door which is being opened between the two fields, and it is linguistics which has done it.

Structural Anthropology (1958) 1967:69.

9 Anthropology found its Galileo in Rivers, its Newton in Mauss.

Structural Anthropology (1958) 1967:159.

10 Myth and action form a pair always associated with the duality of patient and healer. In the schizophrenic cure the healer performs the actions and the patient produces his myth; in the shamanistic cure the healer supplies the myth and the patient performs the actions.

Structural Anthropology (1958) 1967:196.

11 The unconscious. . . is always empty — or, more accurately, it is as alien to mental images as is the stomach to the foods which pass through it.

Structural Anthropology (1958) 1967:198.

12 Language is the most perfect of all those cultural manifestations which, in one respect or another, constitute systems, and if we want to understand art, religion or law, and perhaps even cooking or the rules of politeness, we must imagine them as being codes formed by articulated signs, following the pattern of linguistic communication.

Culture and Language (1959) 1969:150–151.

13 I therefore claim to show, not how men think in myths, but how myths operate in men's minds without their being aware of the fact.

The Raw and the Cooked (1964) 1983:Vol. 1, 12.

14 If the final aim of anthropology is to contribute to a better knowledge of objectified thought and its mechanisms, it is in the last resort immaterial whether in this book the thought processes of the South American Indians take shape through the medium of my thought, or whether mine take place through the medium of theirs.

The Raw and the Cooked (1964) 1983:Vol. 1, 13.

15 Anthropology. . . is the outcome of a historical process which has made the larger part of mankind subservient to the other, and during which millions of innocent human beings have had their resources plundered and their institutions and beliefs destroyed, whilst they themselves were ruthlessly killed, thrown into bondage, and contaminated by diseases they were unable to resist. Anthropology is daughter to this era of violence: its capacity to assess more objectively the facts pertaining to the human condition reflects, on the epistemological level, a state of affairs in which 1 part of mankind treated the other as an object.

Anthropology 1966:126.

16 Native cultures are disintegrating faster than radioactive bodies; and the Moon, Mars, and Venus will still be at the same distance from the Earth when that mirror which other civilizations still hold up to us will have so receded from our eyes that, however costly and elaborate the instruments at our disposal, we may never again be able to recognize and study this image of ourselves.

Anthropology 1966:127.

Lucien Lévy-Bruhl 1857–1939
French anthropologist

1 The individual is only himself by virtue of being at the same time something other than himself. Viewed in this fresh aspect, far from being one unit, as we conceive him to be, he is one and yet several, at the same time. Thus he is. . . a veritable "centre of participation."

The "Soul" of the Primitive (1927) 1966:202.

2 Let us expressly rectify what I believed correct in 1910: there is not a primitive mentality distinguishable from the other by *two* characteristics which are peculiar to it (mystical and prelogical). There is a mystical mentality which is more marked and more easily observable among "primitive peoples" than in our own societies, but it is present in every human mind.

The Notebooks on Primitive Mentality (1949) 1975:100–101. → Written in August–September 1938 and published posthumously.

Kurt Lewin 1890–1947
German-born U.S. psychologist

1 Times of political change show very impressively the high degree to which education, in nearly all of its aspects, depends upon the social structure of the group. *It seems to be easier for society to change education than for education to change society.*

Some Social-psychological Differences between the United States and Germany (1936) 1948:4.

2 To the psychologist who has observed the historical development of the concept of "whole," or Gestalt, in psychology, most of the argumentation about the group mind sounds strangely familiar. It took psychology many steps before it discovered that a dynamic whole has properties which are different from the properties of their parts or from the sum of their parts.

Field Theory and Experiment in Social Psychology (1939) 1976:146.

3 In general terms, behavior *(B)* is a function *(F)* of the person *(P)* and of his environment *(E)*, $B = F(P, E)$. This statement is correct for emotional outbreaks as well as for "purposive" directed activities; for dreaming, wishing, and thinking, as well as for talking and acting.

Behavior and Development as a Function of the Total Situation (1946) 1976:239.

4 Experience in leadership training, in changing of food habits, work production, criminality, alcoholism, prejudices, all indicate that it is usually easier to change individuals formed into a group than to change any one of them separately.

Group Decision and Social Change 1947:472.

Oscar Lewis 1914–1970
U.S. anthropologist

1 One can speak of a culture of poverty, for it has its own modalities and distinctive social and psychological consequences for its members. It seems to me that the culture of poverty cuts across regional, rural-urban and even national boundaries.

The Culture of the Vecindad in Mexico City 1958:387.

2 Poverty in modern nations. . . is a way of life, remarkably stable and persistent, passed down from generation to generation along family lines.

The Children of Sanchez 1961:xxiv.

Abraham Lincoln 1809–1865
U.S. statesman

1 As I would not be a *slave*, so I would not be a *master*. This expresses my idea of democracy. Whatever differs from this, to the extent of the difference, is no democracy.

Speech on Slavery and Democracy (1858?) 1989:484.

2 I hold, that in contemplation of universal law, and of the Constitution, the Union of these States is perpetual. Per-

petuity is implied, if not expressed, in the fundamental law of all national governments. It is safe to assert that no government proper, ever had a provision in its organic law for its own termination.

First Inaugural Address, 4 March 1861. 1989:217.

3 Fellow-citizens, *we* cannot escape history. We of this Congress and this administration, will be remembered in spite of ourselves. . . In giving freedom to the *slave*, we *assure* freedom to the *free* — honorable alike in what we give, and what we preserve. We shall nobly save, or meanly lose, the last, best hope of earth.

Annual Message to Congress, 1 December 1862. 1989:415.

Charles E. Lindblom 1917–
U.S. political scientist

1 "Muddling through" — or incrementalism as it is more usually labeled — is and ought to be the usual method of policy making.

Still Muddling, Not Yet Through 1979:517.

2 Incrementalism in politics is not, in principle, slow moving. It is not necessarily, therefore, a tactic of conservatism. A fast-moving sequence of small changes can more speedily accomplish a drastic alteration of the *status quo* than can an only infrequent major policy change.

Still Muddling, Not Yet Through 1979:520.

Gardner Lindzey 1920–
U.S. psychologist

1 If the biological necessity of outbreeding led to the evolution of a set of prohibitions against this powerful tendency [incest], the operation of these negative sanctions against an almost equally strong countertendency could well constitute a psychological dilemma of enormous consequence. . . If the incest taboo has indeed created a basic conflict and consequent developmental frailty that characterizes all mankind, and if only Freud successfully identified this state of affairs, it should come as no surprise that psychoanalytic theory possesses a kind of transcendental vigor that guarantees wide applicability, pertinence, and impact.

Some Remarks Concerning Incest, the Incest Taboo, and Psychoanalytic Theory 1967:1056–1057.

Ralph Linton 1893–1953
U.S. anthropologist

1 Every civilized group of which we have record has been a hybrid group, a fact which disposes effectively of the theory that hybrid peoples are inferior to pure-bred ones.

The Study of Man (1936) 1964:34.

2 The growth and spread of civilization has gone on with a serene indifference to racial lines. All groups who have had an opportunity to acquire civilization have not only acquired it but also added to its content. Conversely, no group has been able to develop a rich or complex culture when it was isolated from outside contacts.

The Study of Man (1936) 1964:54.

3 A status, as distinct from the individual who may occupy it, is simply a collection of rights and duties.

The Study of Man (1936) 1964:113.

4 A *rôle* represents the dynamic aspect of a status. The individual is socially assigned to a status and occupies it with relation to other statuses. When he puts the rights and duties which constitute the status into effect, he is performing a rôle. Rôle and status are quite inseparable, and the distinction between them is of only academic interest. There are no rôles without statuses or statuses without rôles.

The Study of Man (1936) 1964:114.

5 Our solid American citizen. . . throws back covers made from cotton domesticated in India and wool from sheep domesticated in the Near East. . . He slips into moccasins, invented by the Indians of the Eastern Woodlands, and goes to the bathroom, whose fixtures are a mixture of European and American inventions. . . He takes off his pajamas, a garment invented in India, and washes with soap invented by the ancient Gauls. He then shaves, a masochistic rite which seems to have been derived from either Sumer or Ancient Egypt. . . When our friend has finished eating he settles back to smoke, an American Indian habit, consuming a plant domesticated in Brazil, in either a pipe derived from the Indians of Virginia, or a cigarette derived from Mexico. . . While smoking he reads the news of the day, imprinted in characters invented by the ancient Semites upon a material invented in China by a process invented in Germany. As he absorbs the accounts of foreign troubles he will, if he is a good conservative citizen, thank a Hebrew deity in an Indo-European language that he is 100 percent American.

One Hundred Per Cent American 1937. → From a frequently reprinted essay that began as an ad lib reply to a student's question after a lecture on diffusion.

6 The need for eliciting favorable responses from others is an almost constant component of [personality]. Indeed, it is not too much to say that there is very little organized human behavior which is not directed toward its satisfaction in at least some degree.

The Cultural Background of Personality 1945:91.

Gabriel Lippmann 1845–1921
French physicist

1 Everyone believes in the normal law, the experimenters because they imagine that it is a mathematical theorem, and the mathematicians because they think it is an experimental fact.

Conversation with Henri Poincaré. Quoted in Poincaré, *Calcul des probabilités* (1896) 1912:171. → Unpublished translation by Stephen M. Stigler.

Walter Lippmann 1889–1974
U.S. political journalist

1 The newspaper is in all literalness the bible of democracy, the book out of which a people determines its conduct. It is the only serious book most people read. It is the only book they read every day.

Liberty and the News 1920:47.

2 Democracy in its original form never seriously faced the problem which arises because the pictures inside people's heads do not automatically correspond with the world outside.

Public Opinion (1922) 1965:19.

3 The subtlest and most pervasive of all influences are those which create and maintain the repertory of stereotypes. We are told about the world before we see it. We imagine most things before we experience them. And those preconceptions, unless education has made us acutely aware, govern deeply the whole process of perception. They mark out certain objects as familiar or strange, emphasizing the difference, so that the slightly familiar is seen as very familiar, and the somewhat strange as sharply alien. They are aroused by small signs, which may vary from a true index to a vague analogy. Aroused, they flood fresh vision with older images, and project into the world what has been resurrected in memory.

Public Opinion (1922) 1965:59–60. → This book introduced the word "stereotype" first into the vocabulary of the social sciences and then into the vernacular.

4 The study of error is not only in the highest degree prophylactic, but it serves as a stimulating introduction to the study of truth. As our minds become more deeply aware of their own subjectivism, we find a zest in objective method that is not otherwise there. We see vividly, as normally we should not, the enormous mischief and casual cruelty of our prejudices.

Public Opinion (1922) 1965:256.

5 The press is no substitute for institutions. It is like the beam of a searchlight that moves restlessly about, bringing one episode and then another out of darkness into vision. Men cannot do the work of the world by this light alone. They cannot govern society by episodes, incidents and eruptions.

Public Opinion (1922) 1965:229.

6 A nation has security when it does not have to sacrifice its legitimate interests to avoid war and is able, if challenged, to maintain them by war.

U.S. Foreign Policy 1943:51.

Seymour Martin Lipset 1922–
U.S. sociologist and political scientist

1 The average large trade union contains only one formal organization, the union apparatus itself, and a mass of individual members. There are no autonomous suborganizations which can function as centers of opposition or as independent sources of organizational communication. It is perhaps paradoxical that the very organizations which allow workers to act collectively in their relations with employers are ordinarily so constructed that *within* them the members are usually unable to act collectively in dealing with their leaders.

Union Democracy 1956:77. → Written with Martin A. Trow and James S. Coleman.

2 The study of the conditions encouraging democracy must. . . focus on the sources of both cleavage and consensus.

Cleavage — where it is legitimate — contributes to the integration of societies and organizations. Trade-unions, for example, help to integrate their members in the larger body politic and give them a basis for loyalty to the system. . . Consensus on the norms of tolerance which a society or organization accepts has often developed only as a result of basic conflict, and requires the continuation of conflict to sustain it.

The Sociology of Politics (1960) 1981:1–2.

3 There have been three uniquely American stances: conscientious objection to unjust wars, nonrecognition of "evil" foreign regimes, and the insistence that wars must end with the "unconditional surrender" of the Satanic enemy. Linked to Protestant sectarianism, conscientious objection to military service was until recently largely an American phenomenon. To decry wars, to refuse to go, is at least as American as apple pie.

The First New Nation (1963) 1979:xxxvii.

Friedrich List 1789–1846
German-born U.S. economist

1 The errors and contradictions of the prevailing school [i.e., J. B. Say and Adam Smith] can be easily corrected from the standpoint of *the theory of the productive powers*. Certainly those who fatten pigs or prepare pills are productive, but the instructors of youths and of adults, virtuosos, musicians, physicians, judges, and administrators, are productive in a much higher degree. The former *produce values of exchange*, and the latter *productive powers*.

The National System of Political Economy (1841) 1966:143.

Karl N. Llewellyn 1893–1962
U.S. legal scholar

1 The theory that rules decide cases seems for a century to have fooled, not only library-ridden recluses, but judges. . . The theory flew in the face of common sense and professional experience. If rules decided cases, one judge would be as good as another, provided only the rules had been adduced before him.

The Constitution as an Institution 1934:7.

William Forster Lloyd 1795–1852
British mathematician and political economist

1 Why are the cattle on a common so puny and stunted? Why is the common itself so bare-worn, and cropped so differently from the adjoining inclosures? No inequality, in respect of natural or acquired fertility, will account for the phenomenon. The difference depends on the difference of the way in which an increase of stock in the two cases affects the circumstances of the author of the increase. If a person puts more cattle into his own field, the amount of the subsistence which they consume is all deducted from that which was at the command, of his original stock; and if, before, there was no more than a sufficiency of pasture, he reaps no benefit from the additional cattle, what is gained in one way being lost in another. But if he puts more cattle on a common, the food which they consume forms a deduction which is shared between all the cattle, as well that of others as his own, in proportion to their number, and only a small part of it is taken from his own cattle.

Two Lectures on the Checks to Population (1837) 1968:30–31. → This passage is the origin of Garrett Hardin's influential metaphor of "the tragedy of the commons." See HARDIN:1.

John Locke 1632–1704
British philosopher and political theorist

1 The care of the salvation of men's souls cannot belong to the magistrate; because, though the rigour of laws and the force of penalties were capable to convince and change men's minds, yet would not that help at all to the salvation of their souls. . . These considerations, to omit many others that might have been urged to the same purpose, seem unto me sufficient to conclude that all the power of civil government relates only to men's civil interests, is confined to the care of the things of this world, and hath nothing to do with the world to come.

A Letter Concerning Toleration (1689) 1963:21, 23.

2 Suppose this business of religion were let alone, and that there were some other distinction made between men and men upon account of their different complexions, shapes, and features, so that those who have black hair (for example) or grey eyes should not enjoy the same privileges as other citizens. . . Can it be doubted but these persons, thus distinguished from others by the colour of their hair and eyes, and united together by one common persecution, would be as dangerous to the magistrate as any others that had associated themselves merely upon the account of religion?

A Letter Concerning Toleration (1689) 1963:97, 99.

3 Truth scarce ever yet carried it by vote anywhere at its first appearance: new opinions are always suspected, and usually opposed, without any other reason but because they are not already common.

An Essay Concerning Human Understanding (1690) 1959:Vol. 1, 4.

4 The senses at first let in *particular* ideas, and furnish the yet empty cabinet, and the mind by degrees growing familiar with some of them, they are lodged in the memory, and names got to them.

An Essay Concerning Human Understanding (1690) 1959:Vol. 1, book 1, chap. 1, 48–49.

5 Had you or I been born at the Bay of Soldania, possibly our thoughts and notions had not exceeded those brutish ones of the Hottentots that inhabit there. And had the Virginia king Apochancana been educated in England, he had been perhaps as knowing a divine, and as good a mathematician as any in it; the difference between him and a more improved Englishman lying barely in this, that the exercise of his faculties was bounded within the ways, modes, and notions of his own country, and never directed to any other or further inquiries.

An Essay Concerning Human Understanding (1690) 1959:Vol. 1, book 1, chap. 3, 103.

6 When men have found some general propositions that could not be doubted of as soon as understood, it was, I know, a short and easy way to conclude them innate. This being once received, it eased the lazy from the pains of search, and stopped the inquiry of the doubtful concerning all that was once styled innate. And it was of no small advantage to those who affected to be masters and teachers, to make this the principle of principles, — *that principles must not be questioned*. For, having once established this tenet, — that there are innate principles, it put their followers upon a necessity of receiving *some* doctrines as such; which was to take them off from the use of their own reason and judgment, and put them on believing and taking them upon trust without further examination: in which posture of blind credulity, they might be more easily governed by, and made useful to some sort of men, who had the skill and office to principle and guide them.

An Essay Concerning Human Understanding (1690) 1959:Vol. 1, book 1, chap. 3, 116.

7 Let us. . . suppose the mind to be, as we say, white paper, void of all characters, without any ideas: — How comes it to be furnished? Whence comes it by that vast store which the busy and boundless fancy of man has painted on it with an almost endless variety? Whence has it all the *materials* of reason and knowledge? To this I answer, in one word, from EXPERIENCE. In that all our knowledge is founded; and from that it ultimately derives itself.

An Essay Concerning Human Understanding (1690) 1959:Vol. 1, book 2, chap. 1, 121–122.

8 Things. . . are good or evil, only in reference to pleasure or pain. That we call *good*, which is apt to cause or increase pleasure, or diminish pain in us; or else to procure or preserve us the possession of any other good or absence of any evil. And, on the contrary, we name that *evil* which is apt to produce or increase any pain, or diminish any pleasure in us: or else to procure us any evil, or deprive us of any good.

An Essay Concerning Human Understanding (1690) 1959:Vol. 1, book 2, chap. 20, 303.

9 Every man has so inviolable a liberty to make words stand for what ideas he pleases, that no one hath the power to make others have the same ideas in their minds that he has, when they use the same words that he does.

An Essay Concerning Human Understanding (1690) 1959:Vol. 2, book 3, chap. 2, 12.

10 Language being the great conduit, whereby men convey their discoveries, reasonings, and knowledge, from one to another, he that makes an ill use of it, though he does not corrupt the fountains of knowldege, which are in things themselves, yet he does, as much as in him lies, break or stop the pipes whereby it is distributed to the public use and advantage of mankind.

An Essay Concerning Human Understanding (1690) 1959:Vol. 2, book 3, chap. 11, 149.

11 If the opinions and persuasions of others, whom we know and think well of, be a ground of assent, men have reason to be Heathens in Japan, Mahometans in Turkey, Papists in Spain, Protestants in England, and Lutherans in Sweden.

An Essay Concerning Human Understanding (1690) 1959:Vol. 2, book 4, chap. 15, 368.

12 Religion, which should most distinguish us from beasts, and ought most peculiarly to elevate us, as rational creatures, above brutes, is that wherein men often appear most irrational, and more senseless than beasts themselves. *Credo, quia impossible est*: I believe, because it is impossible, might, in a good man, pass for a sally of zeal; but would prove a very ill rule for men to choose their opinions or religion by.

An Essay Concerning Human Understanding (1690) 1959:Vol. 2, book 4, chap. 18, 426–427.

13 A Man can never be oblig'd in Conscience to submit to any Power, unless he can be satisfied who is the Person, who has a Right to Exercise that Power over him. If this were not so, there would be no distinction between Pirates and Lawful Princes, he that has Force is without any more ado to be obey'd, and Crowns and Scepters would become the Inheritance only of Violence and Rapine.

Two Treatises of Government (1690) 1965:240.

14 The great Question which in all Ages has disturbed mankind, and brought on them the greatest part of those Mischiefs which have ruin'd Cities, depopulated Countries, and disordered the Peace of the world, has been, Not whether there be Power in the World, nor whence it came, but who should have it.

Two Treatises of Government (1690) 1965:257.

15 He that is nourished by the Acorns he pickt up under an Oak, or the Apples he gathered from the Trees in the Wood, has certainly appropriated them to himself. No Body can deny but the nourishment is his. I ask then, When did they begin to be his? When he digested? Or when he eat? Or when he boiled? Or when he brought them home? Or when he pickt them up? And 'tis plain, if the first gathering made them not his, nothing else could. That *labour* put a distinction between them and common. That added something to them more than Nature, the common Mother of all, had done; and so they became his private right.

Two Treatises of Government (1690) 1965:329–330.

16 Those who are united into one Body, and have a common establish'd Law and Judicature to appeal to, with Authority to decide Controversies between them, and punish Offenders, *are in Civil Society* one with another.

Two Treatises of Government (1690) 1965:367.

17 Every Man, by consenting with others to make one Body Politick under one Government, puts himself under an Obligation to every one of that Society, to submit to the determination of the *majority*, and to be concluded by it; or else this *original Compact*, whereby he with others incorporates into *one Society*, would signify nothing, and be no Compact, if he be left free, and under no other ties, than he was in before in the State of Nature.

Two Treatises of Government (1690) 1965:376.

18 Submitting to the Laws of any Country, living quietly, and enjoying Priviledges and Protection under them, *makes not a Man a Member of that Society*: This is only a local Protection and Homage due to, and from all those, who, not being in a state of War, come within the Territories belonging to any Government, to all parts whereof the force of its Law extends. But this no more *makes a Man a Member of that Society*, a perpetual Subject of that Commonwealth, than it would make a Man a Subject to another in whose Family he found it convenient to abide for some time; though, whilst he continued in it, he were obliged to comply with the Laws, and submit to the Government he found there. And thus we see, that *Foreigners*, by living all their Lives under another Government, and enjoying the Priviledges and Protection of it, though they are bound, even in Conscience, to submit to its Administration, as far forth as any Denison; yet do not thereby come to be *Subjects or Members of that Commonwealth*. Nothing can make any Man so, but his actually entering into it by positive Engagement, and express Promise and Compact. This is that, which I think, concerning the beginning of Political Societies, and that *Consent which makes any one a Member* of any Commonwealth.

Two Treatises of Government (1690) 1965:394.

19 The great and *chief end* therefore, of Mens uniting into Commonwealths, and putting themselves under Government, *is the Preservation of their Property*.

Two Treatises of Government (1690) 1965:395.

20 Where-ever Law ends Tyranny begins.

Two Treatises of Government (1690) 1965:448.

Jacques Loeb 1859–1924
German-born U.S. biophysiologist

1 Since Pawlow [Pavlov] and his pupils have succeeded in causing the secretion of saliva in the dog by means of optic and acoustic signals, it no longer seems strange to us that what the philosopher terms an "idea" is a process which can cause chemical changes in the body.

The Significance of Tropisms for Psychology 1912:62.

Arthur O. Lovejoy 1873–1963
U.S. philosopher and historian of ideas

1 Through the Middle Ages and down to the late eighteenth century, many philosophers, most men of science, and, indeed, most educated men, were to accept without question — the conception of the universe as a "Great Chain of Being," composed of an immense, or — by the strict but seldom rigorously applied logic of the principle of continuity — of an infinite number of links ranging in hierarchical order from the meagerest kind of existents, which barely escape non-existence, through "every possible" grade up to the *ens perfectissimum* — or, in a somewhat more orthodox version, to the highest possible kind of creature, between which and the Absolute Being the disparity was assumed to be infinite — every one of them differing from that immediately above and that immediately below it by the "least possible" degree of difference.

The Great Chain of Being (1936) 1960:59.

2 The history of the idea of the Chain of Being — in so far as that idea presupposed such a complete rational intelligibility of the world — is the history of a failure; more precisely and more justly, it is the record of an experiment in thought carried on for many centuries by many great and lesser minds, which can now be seen to have had an instructive negative outcome. The experiment, taken as a whole, constitutes one of the most grandiose enterprises of the human intellect. But as the consequences of this most persistent and most comprehensive of hypotheses became more and more explicit, the more apparent became its difficulties; and when they are fully drawn out, they show the hypothesis of the absolute rationality of the cosmos to be unbelievable.

The Great Chain of Being (1936) 1960:329.

A. Lawrence Lowell 1856–1943
U.S. political scientist and educator

1 To William Morton Wheeler, profound student of insects, who has shown that they too can conduct complex communities without the use of reason.

Quoted in Jeffries Wyman and Stanley J. Gill, Conversations with Jeffries Wyman 1987:11. → Lowell, while president of Harvard University, used this citation in presenting an honorary degree to Wheeler.

Leo Lowenthal 1900–
German-born U.S. sociologist and literary critic

1 A large proportion of the heroes [in biographies in popular magazines in the early 1900s] are idols of production. . . There is not a single hero from the world of sports and. . . few artists and entertainers. . . Present day magazine heroes [are] "idols of consumption." Indeed, almost every one of them is directly, or indirectly, related to the sphere of leisure time.

The Triumph of Mass Idols (1944) 1984:206, 208. → An early classic of the content analysis of the mass media.

2 The academic disciplines which have been traditionally charged with the history and analysis of literature have been caught unaware by the impact of mass literature. . . and they have maintained an attitude of haughty indifference to the lower depths of the imagination in print. A field and a challenge have thus been left open and the sociologist will have to do something about them.

On Sociology of Literature (1948) 1984:257.

3 Empirical social science has become a kind of applied asceticism. It stands clear of any entanglements with foreign powers and thrives in an atmosphere of rigidly enforced neutrality. It refuses to enter the sphere of meaning. . . [It] takes the phenomena of modern life, including the mass media, at face value. It rejects the task of placing them in a historical and moral context.

Historical Perspectives of Popular Culture (1950) 1984:10.

4 Man is born, strives, loves, suffers, and dies in any society, but it is the portrayal of *how* he reacts to these common human experiences that matters, since they almost invariably have a social nexus. Precisely because great literature presents the whole man in depth, the artist tends to justify or defy society rather than be its passive chronicler.

Social Meanings in Literature 1986:2.

Robert H. Lowie 1883–1957
Austrian-born U.S. anthropologist

1 One fact. . . encountered at every stage and in every phase of society, by itself lays the axe to the root of any theory of historical laws — the extensive occurrence of diffusion. Creating nothing, this factor nevertheless makes all other agencies taper almost into nothingness beside it in its effect on the total growth of human civilization.

Primitive Society (1920) 1961:434.

2 To that planless hodgepodge, that thing of shreds and patches called civilization, its historian can no longer yield superstitious reverence. He will realize better than others the obstacles to infusing design into the amorphous product; but in thought at least he will not grovel

before it in fatalistic acquiescence but dream of a rational scheme to supplant the chaotic jumble.

Primitive Society (1920) 1961:441.

3 The basic problem of the state is. . . not that of explaining the somersault by which ancient peoples achieved the step from a government by personal relations to one by territorial contiguity only. The question is rather to show what processes strengthened the local tie which must be recognized as not less ancient than the rival principle.

The Origin of the State 1927:27.

4 Since biological change occurs slowly and cultural changes occur in every generation, it is futile to try to explain the fleeting phenomena of culture by a racial constant. We can often explain them — in terms of contact with other peoples, of individual genius, of geography — but not by *racial* differences.

An Introduction to Cultural Anthropology (1934) 1940:9.

Lucian 2nd century A.D.
Greek essayist and historian

1 The historian's one task is to tell the thing as it happened. This he cannot do, if he is Artaxerxes's physician, trembling before him, or hoping to get a purple cloak, a golden chain, a horse of the Nisaean breed in payment for his laudations. A fair historian, a Xenophon, a Thucydides, will not accept that position. He may nurse some private dislikes, but he will attach far more importance to the public good, and set the truth high above his hate; he may have his favourites, but he will not spare their errors. For history, I say again, has this and this only for its own; if a man will start upon it, he must sacrifice to no God but Truth; he must neglect all else; his sole rule and unerring guide is this — to think not of those who are listening to him now, but of the yet unborn who shall seek his converse.

The Way to Write History:129. → See RANKE:1.

Thomas Luckmann

See PETER L. BERGER AND THOMAS LUCKMANN.

Niklas Luhmann 1927–
German sociologist

1 Historical facts embody selections: that is the key to establishing a connection between social structures and temporal horizons. History is a process in which selections are made from a horizon of possibilities.

World-Time and System History (1975) 1982:294.

2 I propose to define time as *the social interpretation of reality with respect to the difference between past and future.*

The Future Cannot Begin (1976) 1982:274.

3 General systems theory and cybernetics supplanted the classical conceptual model of a whole made out of parts and relations between parts with a model emphasizing the *difference* between systems and environments. This new paradigm made it possible to relate both the structures (including forms of differentiation) and processes of systems to the environment.

The Differentiation of Society (1977) 1982:229.

4 Stratification is. . . compatible with functional differentiation, certainly at the level of special roles, but also of role systems — for example, bureaucracies, religious temples, or labor organizations. It channels access to these roles. It approaches its limits, however, if subsystems define their clientele in universalistic terms. Society as a whole shifts in the direction of functional differentiation if society introduces compulsory education for everyone, if *every* person (whether nobleman or commoner, Christian, Jewish or Muslim, infant or adult) has the same legal status, if "the public" is provided with a political function as an electorate, if every individual is acknowledged as choosing or not choosing a religious commitment, and if everybody given the necessary resources can buy anything and pursue any occupation.

The Differentiation of Society (1977) 1982:243.

5 For any system the environment is always more complex than the system itself. No system can maintain itself by means of a point-for-point correlation with its environment, i.e., can summon enough "requisite variety" to match its environment. So each one has to reduce environmental complexity — primarily by restricting the environment itself and perceiving it in a categorically preformed way. On the other hand, the difference of system and environment is a prerequisite for the reduction of complexity because reduction can be performed only *within the system*, both for the system itself *and* its environment.

Ecological Communication (1986) 1989:11–12.

6 The wealth of historical facts which historians are able to dig up from their sources never fails to dash all attempts at theoretical treatment, unless one concedes from the outset that any theory has to be selective in approach. Moreover, historians and sociologists customarily have their own different ways of treating empirical data, and thus both professions can justifiably accuse each other of making unwarranted generalizations. Finally, sociological theory — or so it seems to me, at any rate — is nowhere near complex enough, and above all is not elaborated in sufficiently abstract terms as to be able really to tackle the wealth of historical data. The only possible path one can take in order to uncover the details (or, as in the present case, the boring, old-fashioned pedantry of a body of often mediocre literature) leads via the detour of theoretical abstraction.

Preface to the English edition of *Love as Passion* (1982) 1986:1–2. → First published in the 1986 edition.

György Lukács 1885–1971
Hungarian literary critic and social theorist

1 Let us assume for the sake of argument that recent research had disproved once and for all every one of Marx's

individual theses. Even if this were to be proved, every serious "orthodox" Marxist would still be able to accept all such modern findings without reservation and hence dismiss all of Marx's theses *in toto* — without having to renounce his orthodoxy for a single moment. . . Orthodoxy refers exclusively to *method*.

History and Class Consciousness (1923) 1971:1.

2 It is not the primacy of economic motives in historical explanation that constitutes the decisive difference between Marxism and bourgeois thought, but the point of view of totality. The category of totality, the all-pervasive supremacy of the whole over the parts is the essence of the method which Marx took over from Hegel. . . *The primacy of the category of totality is the bearer of the principle of revolution in science.*

History and Class Consciousness (1923) 1971:27.

3 Nature is a societal category. That is to say, whatever is held to be natural at any given stage of social development, however this nature is related to man and whatever form his involvement with it takes, i.e. nature's form, its content, its range and its objectivity are all socially conditioned.

History and Class Consciousness (1923) 1971:234.

Rosa Luxemburg 1870–1919

Polish-born German economic theorist and revolutionary

1 It is absolutely false and totally unhistorical to represent work for reforms as a drawn-out revolution, and revolution as a condensed series of reforms. A social transformation and a legislative reform do not differ according to their *duration* but according to their *essence*. The whole secret of historical transformations through the utilization of political power consists precisely in the change of simple quantitative modification into a new quality, or to speak more concretely, in the transition from one historical period, one social order, to another.

He who pronounces himself in favor of the method of legal reforms *in place of and as opposed to* the conquest of political power and social revolution does not really choose a more tranquil, surer and slower road to the *same* goal. He chooses a *different* goal.

Social Reform or Revolution (1899) 1971:115–116.

2 No law obliges the proletariat to submit itself to the yoke of capitalism. Need, the lack of means of production, are responsible for this submission. And, within the framework of bourgeois society, no law in the world can give to the proletariat these means, for not laws but economic development have stolen them.

Social Reform or Revolution (1899) 1971:117.

3 Historically, the errors committed by a truly revolutionary movement are infinitely more fruitful than the infallibility of the cleverest Central Committee.

Leninism or Marxism? (1904) 1961:108.

4 If the vulgar scheme sees the connection between mass strike and revolution only in bloody street encounters with which the mass strikes conclude, a somewhat deeper look into the Russian events shows an exactly opposite connection: in reality the mass strike does not produce the revolution, but the revolution produces the mass strike.

The Mass Strike (1906) 1971:51.

5 Capitalism must. . . always and everywhere fight a battle of annihilation against every historical form of natural economy that it encounters, whether this is slave economy, feudalism, primitive communism, or patriarchal peasant economy. The principal methods in this struggle are political force (revolution, war), oppressive taxation by the state, and cheap goods; they are partly applied simultaneously, and partly they succeed and complement one another.

The Accumulation of Capital (1913) 1968:369.

Helen Merrell Lynd

See ROBERT S. LYND AND HELEN MERRELL LYND.

Robert S. Lynd 1892–1970

U.S. sociologist

1 Elderly people in our culture are frequently oriented toward the past, the time of their vigor and power, and resist the future as a threat. It is probable that a whole culture in an advanced stage of loss of relative power and of disintegration may thus have a dominant orientation toward a lost golden age, while life is lived sluggishly along in the present.

Knowledge for What? (1939) 1946:88n.

2 Social science is confined neither to practical politics nor to things whose practicality is demonstrable this afternoon or tomorrow morning. Nor is its rôle merely to stand by, describe, and generalize, like a seismologist watching a volcano. There is no other agency in our culture whose rôle it is to ask long-range and, if need be, abruptly irreverent questions of our democratic institutions; and to follow these questions with research and the systematic charting of the way ahead. The responsibility is to keep everlastingly challenging the present with the question: But what is it that we human beings want, and what things would have to be done, in what ways and in what sequence, in order to change the present so as to achieve it?

Knowledge for What? (1939) 1946:250.

Robert S. Lynd 1892–1970 and **Helen Merrell Lynd** 1896–1982

U.S. sociologists

1 It is. . . this division into working class and business class that constitutes the outstanding cleavage in Middletown. The mere fact of being born upon one or the other side of the watershed roughly formed by these two groups is the most significant single cultural factor tending to influence what one does all day long throughout one's life;

whom one marries; when one gets up in the morning; whether one belongs to the Holy Roller or Presbyterian church; or drives a Ford or a Buick; whether or not one's daughter makes the desirable high school Violet Club; or one's wife meets with the Sew We Do Club or with the Art Students' league; whether one belongs to the Odd Fellows or to the Masonic Shrine; whether one sits about evenings with one's necktie off; and so on indefinitely throughout the daily comings and goings of a Middletown man, woman, or child.

Middletown 1929:23–24.

2 At no point is one brought up more sharply against the impossibility of studying Middletown as a self-contained, self-starting community than when one watches these space-binding leisure-time inventions imported from without — automobile, motion picture, and radio — reshaping the city.

Middletown 1929:271.

3 It is characteristic of mankind to make as little adjustment as possible in customary ways in the face of new conditions; the process of social change is epitomized in the fact that the first Packard car body delivered to the manufacturers had a whipstock on the dashboard.

Middletown 1929:498n.

4 In a pecuniary culture politically committed to the minimizing of class lines there tend to be relatively few plateaus of sheltered "arrival." Democracy under private capitalism has shaved off the edges of these plateaus and the whole population moves, according to the ethos of our culture, endlessly and breathlessly up one long unbroken sandy slope of acquisition.

Middletown in Transition (1937) 1965:317.

Jean François Lyotard 1924–
French philosopher

1 The postmodern would be that which, in the modern, puts forward the unpresentable in presentation itself; that which denies itself the solace of good forms, the consensus of a taste which would make it possible to share collectively the nostalgia for the unattainable; that which searches for new presentations, not in order to enjoy them but in order to impart a stronger sense of the unpresentable.

What Is Postmodernism? (1982) 1984:81.

M

Thomas Babington Macaulay 1800–1859
British historian and statesman

1 No war ought ever to be undertaken but under circumstances which render all interchange of courtesy between the combatants impossible. It is a bad thing that men should hate each other, but it is far worse that they should contract the habit of cutting one anothers throats without hatred. War is never lenient but where it is wanton; when men are compelled to fight in self-defence, they must hate and avenge; this may be bad, but it is human nature, it is the clay as it came from the hand of the potter.

On Mitford's History of Greece (1824) 1843:392–393.

2 Many politicians of our time are in the habit of laying it down as a self-evident proposition, that no people ought to be free till they are fit to use their freedom. The maxim is worthy of the fool in the old story, who resolved not to go into the water till he had learnt to swim! If men are to wait for liberty till they become wise and good in slavery, they may indeed wait forever.

Milton (1825) 1843:51.

3 We doubt whether any name in literary history be so generally odious as that of the man whose character and writings we now propose to consider. The terms in which he is commonly described would seem to import that he was the Tempter, the Evil Principle, the discoverer of ambition and revenge, the original inventor of perjury: that, before the publication of his fatal *Prince*, there had never been a hypocrite, a tyrant, or a traitor, a simulated virtue or a convenient crime. One writer gravely assures us, that Maurice of Saxony learned all his fraudulent policy from that execrable volume. Another remarks, that, since it was translated into Turkish, the Sultans have been more addicted than formerly to the custom of strangling their brothers. Our own foolish Lord Lyttleton charges the poor Florentine with the manifold treasons of the House of Guise, and the massacre of St. Bartholomew. Several authors have hinted that the Gunpowder Plot is to be primarily attributed to his doctrines, and seem to think that his effigy ought to be substituted for that of Guy Fawkes, in those processions by which the ingenuous youth of England annually commemorate the preservation of the Three Estates. The Church of Rome has pronounced his works accursed things. Nor have our own countrymen been backward in testifying their opinion of his merits. Out of his surname they have coined an epithet for a knave — and out of his Christian name a synonyme for the Devil.

Machiavelli (1827) 1843:68–69.

4 Facts are the mere dross of history. It is from the abstract truth which interpenetrates them, and lies latent among them, like gold in the ore, that the mass derives its whole value; and the precious particles are generally combined with the baser in such a manner that the separation is a task of the utmost difficulty.

History (1828) 1843:163–164.

5 The Fire of London, it has been observed, was a blessing. It burned down the city, but it burned out the plague. The same may be said of the tremendous devastation of the Roman dominions. It annihilated the noisome recesses in which lurked the seeds of great moral maladies; it cleared an atmosphere fatal to the health and vigour of the human mind. It cost Europe a thousand years of barbarism to escape the fate of China.

History (1828) 1843:184.

6 We are inclined to think that, with respect to every great addition which has been made to the stock of human knowledge, the case has been similar; that without Copernicus we should have been Copernicans — that without Columbus America would have been discovered — that without Locke we should have possessed a just theory of the origin of human ideas.

Review of *The Poetical Works of John Dryden* (1828) 1880:110.

7 How. . . are we to arrive at just conclusions on a subject so important to the happiness of mankind? Surely by that method which, in every experimental science to which it has been applied, has signally increased the power and knowledge of our species, — by that method for which

our new philosophers would substitute quibbles scarcely worthy of barbarous respondents and opponents of the middle ages, — by the method of induction; — by observing the present state of the world, — by assiduously studying the history of past ages, — by sifting the evidence of facts, — by carefully combining and contrasting those which are authentic, — by generalizing with judgment and diffidence, — by perpetually bringing the theory which we have constructed to the test of new facts, — by correcting, or altogether abandoning it, according as those new facts prove it to be partially or fundamentally unsound. . . This is that noble science of politics.

Mill's *Essay on Government* (1829) 1844:366–367.

8 Formerly, according to [Robert Southey], the laws governed; now public opinion governs. What are laws but expressions of the opinion of some class which has power over the rest of the community? By what was the world ever governed, but by the opinion of some person or persons? By what else can it ever be governed?

Southey's Colloquies on Society (1830) 1843:308.

9 No particular man is necessary to the State. We may depend on it that, if we provide the country with popular institutions, those institutions will provide it with great men.

Speech Delivered in the House of Commons, 2 March 1831. 1898:421.

10 The Church of Rome. . . thoroughly understands, what no other Church has ever understood, how to deal with enthusiasts. In some sects — particularly in infant sects — enthusiasm is suffered to be rampant. In other sects — particularly in sects long established and richly endowed — it is regarded with aversion. The Catholic Church neither submits to enthusiasm nor proscribes it, but uses it.

Ranke's *History of the Popes* (1840) 1843:344.

11 It will be my endeavor to relate the history of the people as well as the history of the government, to trace the progress of useful and ornamental arts, to describe the rise of religious sects and the changes of literary taste, to portray the manners of successive generations, and not to pass by with neglect even the revolutions which have taken place in dress, furniture, repasts, and public amusements.

The History of England (1848) 1901:Vol. 1, 3.

12 The Puritan hated bear-baiting, not because it gave pain to the bear, but because it gave pleasure to the spectators.

The History of England (1848) 1901:Vol. 1, 159.

13 [Charles Montagu, 1st earl of Halifax] was the chief of those politicians whom the two great parties contemptuously called Trimmers. Instead of quarrelling with this nickname, he assumed it as a title of honor, and vindicated, with great vivacity, the dignity of the appellation. Everything good, he said, trims between extremes.

The History of England (1848) 1901:Vol. 1, 240- 241.

Mc-

Names beginning with this prefix are alphabetized as if spelled Mac-.

William McDougall 1871–1938
British-born U.S. psychologist

1 Psychologists must cease to be content with the sterile and narrow conception of their science as the science of consciousness, and must boldly assert its claim to be the positive science of the mind in all its aspects and modes of functioning, or, as I would prefer to say, the positive science of conduct or behaviour.

An Introduction to Social Psychology (1908) 1928:13.

2 Take away these instinctive dispositions with their powerful impulses, and the organism would become incapable of activity of any kind; it would lie inert and motionless like a wonderful clockwork whose mainspring had been removed or a steam-engine whose fires had been drawn.

An Introduction to Social Psychology (1908) 1928:38.

3 The striving to achieve an end is. . . the mark of behaviour; and behaviour is the characteristic of living things.

Psychology 1912:20.

Richard McGahey 1950–
U.S. economist

1 "Underclass" is a misleading and destructive label that lumps together distinct people with distinct problems. . . "Underclass" is the latest in a long line of labels that stigmatize poor people for their poverty by focusing exclusively on individual characteristics. Older terms include the "undeserving poor," the "*lumpenproletariat*," and the "culture of poverty."

Poverty's Voguish Stigma 1982:29.

Niccolò Machiavelli 1469–1527
Italian political theorist and statesman

1 On the coming of evening, I return to my house and enter my study; and at the door I take off the day's clothing, covered with mud and dust, and put on garments regal and courtly; and reclothed appropriately, I enter the ancient courts of ancient men, where, received by them with affection, I feed on that food which only is mine and which I was born for, where I am not ashamed to speak with them and to ask them the reason for their actions; and they in their kindness answer me; and for four hours of time I do not feel boredom, I forget every trouble, I do not dread poverty, I am not frightened by death; entirely I give myself over to them.

Letter to Francesco Vettori, 10 December 1513. 1961:142.

2 [I] have composed a little work *On Princedoms*, where I go as deeply as I can into considerations on this subject, debating what a princedom is, of what kinds they are, how they are gained, how they are kept, why they are lost.

Letter to Francesco Vettori, 10 December 1513. 1961:142.

3 In constituting and legislating for a commonwealth it must needs be taken for granted that all men are wicked and that they will always give vent to the malignity that is in their minds when opportunity offers. That evil dispositions often do not show themselves for a time is due to a hidden cause which those fail to perceive who have had no experience of the opposite; but in time — which is said to be the father of all truth — it reveals itself.

The Discourses (1532) 1974:111–112.

4 Rarely, if ever, does it happen that a state, whether it be a republic or a kingdom, is either well-ordered at the outset or radically transformed *vis-à-vis* its old institutions unless this be done by one person. It is likewise essential that there should be but one person upon whose mind and method depends any similar process of organization.

The Discourses (1532) 1974:132.

5 As the observance of divine worship is the cause of greatness in republics, so the neglect of it is the cause of their ruin. Because, where the fear of God is wanting, it comes about either that a kingdom is ruined, or that it is kept going by the fear of a prince, which makes up for the lack of religion.

The Discourses (1532) 1974:141.

6 When the safety of one's country wholly depends on the decision to be taken, no attention should be paid either to justice or injustice, to kindness or cruelty, or to its being praiseworthy or ignominious. On the contrary, every other consideration being set aside, that alternative should be wholeheartedly adopted which will save the life and preserve the freedom of one's country.

The Discourses (1532) 1974:515.

7 Men ought either to be caressed or destroyed, since they will seek revenge for minor hurts but will not be able to revenge major ones. Any harm you do to a man should be done in such a way that you need not fear his revenge.

The Prince (1532) 1977:Chap. 3, 7.

8 Men almost always prefer to walk in paths marked out by others and pattern their actions through imitation. Even if he cannot follow other people's paths in every respect, or attain to the merit [*virtù*] of his originals, a prudent man should always follow the footsteps of the great and imitate those who have been supreme. His own talent [*virtù*] may not come up to theirs, but at least it will have a sniff of it. Thus he will resemble skilled archers who, seeing how far away the target lies, and knowing the strength [*virtù*] of their bow, aim much higher than the real target, not because they expect the arrow to fly that far, but to accomplish their real end by aiming beyond it.

The Prince (1532) 1977:Chap. 6, 16.

9 Nothing is harder to manage, more risky in the undertaking, or more doubtful of success than to set up as the introducer of a new order. Such an innovator has as enemies all the people who were doing well under the old order, and only halfhearted defenders in those who hope to profit from the new.

The Prince (1532) 1977:Chap. 6, 17.

10 Armed prophets always win and unarmed prophets lose. Apart from all [other] factors. . . it is the nature of people to be fickle; to persuade them of something is easy, but to make them stand fast in that conviction is hard. Hence things must be arranged so that when they no longer believe they can be compelled to believe by force.

The Prince (1532) 1977:Chap. 6, 18.

11 The prince can earn the good will of his subjects in many ways, but as they vary according to circumstances, I can give no fixed rules and will say nothing of them. One conclusion only can be drawn: the prince must have people well disposed toward him; otherwise in times of adversity there's no hope.

The Prince (1532) 1977:Chap. 9, 30.

12 A prince should never count on what he sees in times of quiet, when the citizens find the state useful to them, and everyone pushes forward, making big promises and professing readiness to die for the prince — as long as death is far away; but when times are tough, when the state really needs its citizens, few are to be found. And a crisis of this sort is particularly dangerous, as a prince never experiences it a second time. Thus a wise prince will think of ways to keep his citizens of every sort and under every circumstance dependent on the state and on him; and then they will always be trustworthy.

The Prince (1532) 1977:Chap. 9, 31.

13 A prince. . . should have no other object, no other thought, no other subject of study, than war, its rules and disciplines; this is the only art for a man who commands, and it is of such value [*virtù*] that it not only keeps born princes in place, but often raises men from private citizens to princely fortune.

The Prince (1532) 1977:Chap. 14, 42.

14 A great many men have imagined states and princedoms such as nobody ever saw or knew in the real world, for there's such a difference between the way we really live and the way we ought to live that the man who neglects the real to study the ideal will learn how to accomplish his ruin, not his salvation. Any man who tries to be good all the time is bound to come to ruin among the great number who are not good. Hence a prince who wants to keep his post must learn how not to be good, and use that knowledge, or refrain from using it, as necessity requires.

The Prince (1532) 1977:Chap. 15, 44.

15 Is it better to be loved than feared, or vice versa? I don't doubt that every prince would like to be both; but since it is hard to accommodate these qualities, if you have to

make a choice, to be feared is much safer than to be loved.

The Prince (1532) 1977:Chap. 17, 47.

16 Since a prince must know how to use the character of beasts, he should pick for imitation the fox and the lion. As the lion cannot protect himself from traps, and the fox cannot defend himself from wolves, you have to be a fox in order to be wary of traps, and a lion to overawe the wolves.

The Prince (1532) 1977:Chap. 18, 50.

17 I think it may be true that Fortune governs half of our actions, but that even so she leaves the other half more or less, in our power to control. I would compare her to one of those torrential streams which, when they overflow, flood the plains, rip up trees and tear down buildings, wash the land away here and deposit it there; everyone flees before them, everyone yields to their onslaught, unable to stand up to them in any way. This is how they are; yet this does not mean that men cannot take countermeasures while the weather is still fine, shoring up dikes and dams, so that when the waters rise again, they are either carried off in a channel or confined where they do no harm. So with Fortune, who exerts all her power where there is no strength [*virtù*] prepared to oppose her, and turns to smashing things up wherever there are no dikes and restraining dams.

The Prince (1532) 1977:Chap. 25, 70.

18 It is better to be rash than timid, for Fortune is a woman, and the man who wants to hold her down must beat and bully her.

The Prince (1532) 1977:Chap. 25, 72.

Robert M. MacIver 1882–1970
Scottish-born U.S. sociologist and political theorist

1 Many a vain and specious formula has been set forward in the name of sociology, many a hollow generalisation has been declared an eternal social law, and too frequently the invention of terms has taken the place of the discovery of principles.

Community (1917) 1924:viii.

2 We are apt to think we know what time is because we can measure it, but no sooner do we reflect upon it than that illusion goes.

So it appears that the range of the measurable is not the range of the knowable. There are things we can measure, like time, but yet our minds do not grasp their meaning. There are things we cannot measure, like happiness or pain, and yet their meaning is perfectly clear to us.

The Elements of Social Science (1921) 1931:15–16.

3 The notion that force is the creator of government is one of those part-truths that beget total errors.

The Web of Government (1947) 1965:12.

4 Custom is always at work turning example into precedent and precedent into institution.

The Web of Government (1947) 1965:26.

5 Everywhere men weave a web of relationships with their fellows, as they buy and sell, as they worship, as they rejoice and mourn. This greater web of relationships is society, and a community is a delimited area of society. Within this web of community are generated many controls that are not governmental controls, many associations that are not political associations, many usages and standards of behavior that are in no sense the creation of the state. In the community develops the law behind law, the multi-sanctioned law that existed before governments began and that the law of government can never supersede. Without the prior laws of the community all the laws of the state would be empty formulas. Custom, the first "king of men," still rules. The *mores* still prescribe. Manners and modes still flourish. The laws made by governments cannot rescind them, cannot long defy them or deeply invade them.

The Web of Government (1947) 1965:145.

6 Anomy signifies the state of mind of one who has been pulled up from his moral roots, who has no longer any standards but only disconnected urges, who has no longer any sense of continuity, of folk, of obligation. The anomic man has become spiritually sterile, responsive only to himself, responsible to no one. He derides the values of other men. His only faith is the philosophy of denial. He lives on the thin line of sensation between no future and no past.

The Ramparts We Guard 1950:84.

Halford Mackinder 1861–1947
British geographer

1 When our statesmen are in conversation with the defeated enemy, some airy cherub should whisper to them from time to time this saying:

Who rules East Europe commands the Heartland:
Who rules the Heartland commands the World-Island:
Who rules the World-Island commands the World.

Democratic Ideals and Reality (1919) 1942:150.

Henry Dunning Macleod 1821–1902
Scottish economist

1 No sooner had Queen Elizabeth ascended the throne, than she turned her attention to the state of the currency, being moved thereto by the illustrious Gresham, who has the great merit of being as far as we can discover, the first who discerned the great fundamental law of the currency, that good and bad money cannot circulate together. The fact had been repeatedly observed before, as we have seen, but no one, that we are aware, had discovered the necessary relation between the facts, before Sir Thomas Gresham.

The Elements of Political Economy 1858:475–476. → See GRESHAM:1.

Marshall McLuhan 1911–1980
Canadian mass communications theorist

1 In a culture like ours, long accustomed to splitting and dividing all things as a means of control, it is sometimes a bit of a shock to be reminded that, in operational and practical fact, the medium is the message. This is merely to say that the personal and social consequences of any medium — that is, of any extension of ourselves — result from the new scale that is introduced into our affairs by each extension of ourselves, or by any new technology.

Understanding Media 1964:7.

Marshall McLuhan 1911–1980
Canadian mass communications theorist
and
Quentin Fiore 1920–
U.S. graphics designer

1 Ours is a brand-new world of allatonceness [all-at-onceness]. "Time" has ceased, "space" has vanished. We now live in a *global village*. . . a simultaneous happening. . . The new electronic interdependence recreates the world in the image of a global village.

The Medium Is the Massage 1967:63, 67.

David McNeill
See Roger Brown and David McNeill.

William H. McNeill 1917–
Canadian-born U.S. historian

1 Myth and history are close kin inasmuch as both explain how things got to be the way they are by telling some sort of story. But our common parlance reckons myth to be false while history is, or aspires to be, true. Accordingly, a historian who rejects someone else's conclusions calls them mythical, while claiming that his own views are true. But what seems true to one historian will seem false to another, so one historian's truth becomes another's myth, even at the moment of utterance.

Mythistory 1986:1.

James Madison 1751–1836
U.S. statesman and political philosopher

1 By a faction I understand a number of citizens, whether amounting to a majority or minority of the whole, who are united and actuated by some common impulse of passion, or of interest, adverse to the rights of other citizens, or to the permanent and aggregate interests of the community.

Federalist No. 10 (1787) 1961:78.

2 Liberty is to faction what air is to fire, an aliment without which it instantly expires. But it could not be a less folly to abolish liberty, which is essential to political life, because it nourishes faction than it would be to wish the annihilation of air, which is essential to animal life, because it imparts to fire its destructive agency.

Federalist No. 10 (1787) 1961:78.

3 The most common and durable source of factions has been the various and unequal distribution of property. Those who hold and those who are without property have ever formed distinct interests in society.

Federalist No. 10 (1787) 1961:79.

4 To secure the public good and private rights against the danger of. . . faction, and at the same time to preserve the spirit and the form of popular government, is then the great object to which our inquiries are directed.

Federalist No. 10 (1787) 1961:80.

5 The accumulation of all powers, legislative, executive, and judiciary, in the same hands, whether of one, a few, or many, and whether hereditary, self-appointed, or elective, may justly be pronounced the very definition of tyranny.

Federalist No. 47 (1788) 1961:301.

6 If it be true that all governments rest on opinion, it is no less true that the strength of opinion in each individual, and its practical influence on his conduct, depend much on the number which he supposes to have entertained the same opinion.

Federalist No. 49 (1788) 1961:314–315.

7 What is government itself but the greatest of all reflections on human nature? If men were angels, no government would be necessary. If angels were to govern men, neither external nor internal controls on government would be necessary. In framing a government which is to be administered by men over men, the great difficulty lies in this: you must first enable the government to control the governed; and in the next place, oblige it to control itself.

Federalist No. 51 (1788) 1961:322.

8 In every political society, parties are unavoidable. A difference of interests, real or supposed is the most natural and fruitful source of them. . . The great art of politicians lies in making them checks and balances to each other.

Parties (1792) 1906:86.

9 The Constitution supposes, what the History of all Govts demonstrates, that the Ex. is the branch of power most interested in war, & most prone to it. It has accordingly, with studied care, vested the question of war in the Legisl.

Letter to Thomas Jefferson, 2 April 1798. 1906:312.

Alfred Thayer Mahan 1840–1914
U.S. naval historian

1 The history of Sea Power is largely, though by no means solely, a narrative of contests between nations, of mutual rivalries, of violence frequently culminating in war. . . The history of sea power, while embracing in its broad sweep all that tends to make a people great upon the sea or by the sea, is largely a military history.

The Influence of Sea Power upon History (1890) 1918:1.

2 The surer of himself an admiral is, the finer the tactical development of his fleet, the better his captains, the more reluctant must he necessarily be to enter into a *mêlée* with equal forces, in which all these advantages will be thrown away, chance reign supreme, and his fleet be placed on terms of equality with an assemblage of ships which have never before acted together. History has lessons as to when *mêlées* are, or are not, in order.

The Influence of Sea Power upon History (1890) 1918:4.

Henry Sumner Maine 1822–1888
British legal historian

1 The lofty contempt which a civilised people entertains for barbarous neighbors has caused a remarkable negligence in observing them, and this carelessness has been aggravated at times by fear, by religious prejudice, and even by the use of these very terms — civilisation and barbarism — which convey to most persons the impression of a difference not merely in degree but in kind.

Ancient Law (1861) 1917:71.

2 Nor is it difficult to see what is the tie between man and man which replaces by degrees those forms of reciprocity in rights and duties which have their origin in the Family. It is Contract. Starting, as from one terminus of history, from a condition of society in which all the relations of Persons are summed up in the relations of Family, we seem to have steadily moved towards a phase of social order in which all these relations arise from the free agreement of Individuals.

Ancient Law (1861) 1917:99.

3 All the forms of Status taken notice of in the Law of Persons were derived from, and to some extent are still coloured by, the powers and privileges anciently residing in the Family. If then we employ Status, agreeably with the usage of the best writers, to signify these personal conditions only, and avoid applying the term to such conditions as are the immediate or remote result of agreement, we may say that the movement of the progressive societies has hitherto been a movement from Status to Contract.

Ancient Law (1861) 1917:100.

4 To the Romans belongs pre-eminently the credit of inventing the Will, the institution which, next to the Contract, has exercised the greatest influence in transforming human society.

Ancient Law (1861) 1917:114.

5 The mistake of judging the men of other periods by the morality of our own day has its parallel in the mistake of supposing that every wheel and bolt in the modern social machine had its counterpart in more rudimentary societies.

Ancient Law (1861) 1917:182–183.

6 Except the blind forces of Nature, nothing moves in this world which is not Greek in its origin.

Village Communities in the East and West (1871) 1880:238.

7 No geniuses of an equally high order so completely divorced themselves from history as Hobbes and Bentham, or appear, to me at all events, so completely under the impression that the world had always been more or less as they saw it.

Lectures on the Early History of Institutions 1875:396.

8 Almost all the civilised States derive their national unity from common subjection, past or present, to royal power; the Americans of the United States, for example, are a nation because they once obeyed a king.

Prospects of Popular Government (1885) 1918:28.

Frederic William Maitland 1850–1906
British jurist and legal historian

1 It seems to be assumed that *the* history of *the* family can be written and that it will come out in some such form as this: We start with promiscuity, the next stage is "mother right," the next "father right," and so forth. Or again take the history of property — land is owned first by the tribe or horde, then by the house-community, then by the village-community, then by the individual.

Now I will not utterly deny the possibility of some such science of the very early stages in human progress. . . But even in this region I think it plain that our scientific people have been far too hasty with their laws. . . Our cases, all told, are not very many and very rarely indeed have we any direct evidence of the passage of a barbarous nation from one state to another. My own belief is that by and by anthropology will have the choice between being history and being nothing.

The Body Politic (1911) 1968:248–249. → From a speech read at the Eranus Club about 1899.

[*See also* Frederick Pollock and Frederic William Maitland.]

James Maitland 1759–1839
[8th earl of Lauderdale]
British economist and statesman

1 Nothing but the impossibility of general combination protects the public wealth against the rapacity of private avarice.

An Inquiry into the Nature and Origin of Public Wealth 1804:54.

Bronislaw Malinowski 1884–1942
Polish-born British anthropologist

1 In the field one has to face a chaos of facts, some of which are so small that they seem insignificant; others loom so large that they are hard to encompass with one synthetic glance. But in this crude form they are not scientific facts at all; they are absolutely elusive, and can be fixed only by interpretation, by seeing them *sub specie aeternitatis*,

by grasping what is essential in them and fixing this. *Only laws and generalizations are scientific facts,* and field work consists only and exclusively in the interpretation of the chaotic social reality, in subordinating it to general rules.

Baloma (1916) 1954:238.

2 I began to take part. . . in the village life, to look forward to the important or festive events, to take personal interest in the gossip and the developments of the small village occurrences; to wake up every morning to a day, presenting itself to me more or less as it does to the native. . . With this, and with the capacity of enjoying their company and sharing some of their games and amusements, I began to feel that I was indeed in touch with the natives, and this is certainly the preliminary condition of being able to carry on successful field work.

Argonauts of the Western Pacific (1922) 1961:7–8.

3 It is a very far cry from the famous answer given long ago by a representative authority who, asked, what are the manners and customs of the natives, answered, "Customs none, manners beastly," to the position of the modern Ethnographer!

Argonauts of the Western Pacific (1922) 1961:10.

4 The time when we could tolerate accounts presenting us the native as a distorted, childish caricature of a human being are gone. This picture is false, and like many other falsehoods, it has been killed by Science.

Argonauts of the Western Pacific (1922) 1961:11.

5 What appears to us an extensive, complicated, and yet well ordered institution is the outcome of ever so many doings and pursuits, carried on by savages, who have no laws or aims or charters definitely laid down. They have no knowledge of the *total outline* of any of their social structure. They know their own motives, know the purpose of individual actions and the rules which apply to them, but how, out of these, the whole collective institution shapes, this is beyond their mental range.

Argonauts of the Western Pacific (1922) 1961:83.

6 The emotional attitude of man has a greater sway over custom than has reason. The main attitude of a native to other, alien groups is that of hostility and mistrust. The fact that to a native every stranger is an enemy, is an ethnographic feature reported from all parts of the world.

Argonauts of the Western Pacific (1922) 1961:345.

7 There can be no doubt that we have here a new type of linguistic use — *phatic communion* I am tempted to call it, actuated by the demon of terminological invention — a type of speech in which ties of union are created by a mere exchange of words. Let us look at it from the special point of view with which we are here concerned; let us ask what light it throws on the function or nature of language. Are words in Phatic Communion used primarily to convey meaning, the meaning which is symbolically theirs? Certainly not! They fulfil a social function and that is their principal aim, but they are neither the result of intellectual reflection, nor do they necessarily arouse reflection in the listener. Once again we may say that language does not function here as a means of transmission of thought.

The Problem of Meaning in Primitive Languages (1923) 1953:315.

8 There are no peoples however primitive without religion and magic. Nor are there, it must be added at once, any savage races lacking either in the scientific attitude or in science, though this lack has been frequently attributed to them.

Magic, Science and Religion (1925) 1954:17.

9 The festive and public character of the ceremonies of cult is a conspicuous feature of religion in general. Most sacred acts happen in a congregation; indeed, the solemn conclave of the faithful united in prayer, sacrifice, supplication, or thanksgiving is the very prototype of a religious ceremony. Religion needs the community as a whole so that its members may worship in common its sacred things and its divinities, and society needs religion for the maintenance of moral law and order.

Magic, Science and Religion (1925) 1954:54.

10 The spell is that part of magic which is occult, handed over in magical filiation, known only to the practitioner. To the natives knowledge of magic means knowledge of spell, and in an analysis of any act of witchcraft it will always be found that the ritual centers round the utterance of the spell. The formula is always the core of the magical performance.

Magic, Science and Religion (1925) 1954:73.

11 [Magic] enables man to carry out with confidence his important tasks, to maintain his poise and his mental integrity in fits of anger, in the throes of hate, of unrequited love, of despair and anxiety. The function of magic is to ritualize man's optimism, to enhance his faith in the victory of hope over fear. Magic expresses the greater value for man of confidence over doubt, of steadfastness over vacillation, of optimism over pessimism.

Magic, Science and Religion (1925) 1954:90.

12 The functional view of culture insists. . . upon the principle that in every type of civilisation, every custom, material object, idea and belief fulfils some vital function.

Anthropology 1926:133.

13 When the native is asked what he would do in such and such a case, he answers what he *should* do; he lays down the pattern of best possible conduct. When he acts as informant to a field-anthropologist, it costs him nothing to retail the Ideal of the law. His sentiments, his propensities, his bias, his self-indulgences as well as tolerance of others' lapses, he reserves for his behaviour in real life. And even then, though he acts thus, he would be unwilling to admit often even to himself, that he ever acts below the standard of law.

Crime and Custom in Savage Society (1926) 1951:120.

14 Myth fulfils in primitive culture an indispensable function: it expresses, enhances, and codifies belief; it safeguards and enforces morality; it vouches for the efficiency of ritual and contains practical rules for the guidance of man. Myth is thus a vital ingredient of human civilization; it is not an idle tale, but a hard-worked active force; it is not an intellectual explanation or an artistic imagery, but a pragmatic charter of primitive faith and moral wisdom.

Myth in Primitive Psychology (1926) 1971:19.

15 The anthropologist must relinquish his comfortable position in the long chair on the verandah of the missionary compound, Government station, or planter's bungalow, where, armed with pencil and notebook and at times with a whisky and soda, he has been accustomed to collect statements from informants, write down stories, and fill out sheets of paper with savage texts. He must go out into the villages, and see the natives at work in gardens, on the beach, in the jungle; he must sail with them to distant sandbanks and to foreign tribes, and observe them in fishing, trading, and ceremonial overseas expeditions. Information must come to him full-flavoured from his own observations of native life, and not be squeezed out of reluctant informants as a trickle of talk. Field-work can be done first, or second-hand even among savages, in the middle of pile-dwellings, not far from actual cannibalism and head-hunting.

Myth in Primitive Psychology (1926) 1971:92–93.

16 The meaning of a word is not mysteriously contained in it but is rather an active effect of the sound uttered within a context of situation. The utterance of sound is a significant act indispensable in all forms of human concerted action. It is a type of behavior strictly comparable to the handling of a tool, the wielding of a weapon, the performance of a ritual or the concluding of a contract. The use of words is in all these forms of human activity an indispensable correlate of manual and bodily behavior.

Culture 1931:622.

17 No culture could survive if its arts and crafts, its weapons and economic pursuits were based on mystical, non-empirical conceptions and doctrines. When human culture is approached from the pragmatic, technological side, it is found that primitive man is capable of exact observation, of sound generalizations and of logical reasoning in all those matters which affect his normal activities and are at the basis of his production. Knowledge is then an absolute derived necessity of culture.

Culture 1931:634.

18 Coastal sailing as long as it is perfectly safe and easy commands no magic. Overseas expeditions are invariably bound up with ceremonies and ritual. Man resorts to magic only where chance and circumstances are not fully controlled by knowledge.

Culture 1931:636.

19 I have been speaking of the *functional method* as if it were an old-established school of anthropology. Let me confess at once: the magnificent title of the Functional School of Anthropology has been bestowed by myself, in a way on myself, and to a large extent out of my own sense of irresponsibility.

The Sexual Life of Savages in North-Western Melanesia (1929) 1932:xxix. → From the Special Foreword to the third edition.

20 Functionalism differs from other sociological theories more definitely, perhaps, in its conception and definition of the individual than in any other respect. The functionalist includes in his analysis not merely the emotional as well as the intellectual side of mental processes, but also insists that man in his full biological reality has to be drawn into our analysis of culture. The bodily needs and environmental influences, and the cultural reactions to them, have thus to be studied side by side.

The Group and the Individual in Functional Analysis 1939:939–940.

21 Rivers is the Rider Haggard of anthropology; I shall be the Conrad.

Quoted in Raymond Firth, Malinowski as Scientist and as Man (1957) 1964:6. → Haggard (1856–1925) was a popular British novelist.

Thomas Robert Malthus 1766–1834
British economist

1 I think I may fairly make two postulata.

First, That food is necessary to the existence of man.

Secondly, That the passion between the sexes is necessary and will remain nearly in its present state.

These two laws, ever since we have had any knowledge of mankind, appear to have been fixed laws of our nature, and, as we have not hitherto seen any alteration in them, we have no right to conclude that they will ever cease to be what they now are, without an immediate act of power in that Being who first arranged the system of the universe, and for the advantage of his creatures, still executes, according to fixed laws, all its various operations.

An Essay on the Principle of Population (1798) 1970:Chap. 1, 70–71.

2 Population, when unchecked, increases in a geometrical ratio. Subsistence increases only in an arithmetical ratio. A slight acquaintance with numbers will shew the immensity of the first power in comparison of the second.

An Essay on the Principle of Population (1798) 1970:Chap. 1, 71.

3 A foresight of the difficulties attending the rearing of a family acts as a preventive check, and the actual distresses of some of the lower classes, by which they are disabled from giving the proper food and attention to their children, act as a positive check to the natural increase of population.

An Essay on the Principle of Population (1798) 1970:Chap. 4, 89.

4 Many of the questions both in morals and politics seem to be of the nature of the problems de maximis and minimis in Fluxions [Newton's term for the rate at which variables change]; in which there is always a point where a certain effect is the greatest, while on either side of this point it gradually diminishes.

Observations on the Effects of the Corn Laws 1814:30.

5 Moral restraint, in application to the present subject, may be defined to be, abstinence from marriage, either for a time or permanently, from prudential considerations, with a strictly moral conduct towards the sex in the interval. And this is the only mode of keeping population on a level with the means of subsistence which is perfectly consistent with virtue and happiness. All other checks, whether of the preventive or the positive kind, though they may greatly vary in degree, resolve themselves into some form of vice or misery.

A Summary View of the Principle of Population (1830) 1970:250.

Bernard Mandeville 1670?-1733
Dutch-born British political writer

1 Vast Numbers throng'd the fruitful Hive;
Yet those vast Numbers made 'em thrive;
Millions endeavoring to supply
Each other's Lust and Vanity.

The Grumbling Hive (1705) 1924:Vol. 1, 18.

2 Then leave Complaints: Fools only strive
To make a Great an Honest Hive
T'enjoy the World's Conveniences,
Be fam'd in War, yet live in Ease,
Without great Vices, is a vain
Eutopia seated in the Brain.
Fraud, Luxury, and Pride must live,
While we the Benefits receive:
Hunger's a dreadful Plague, no doubt,
Yet who digests or thrives without?
Do we not owe the Growth of Wine
To the dry shabby crooked Vine?
Which, while its Shoots neglected stood,
Chok'd other Plants, and ran to Wood;
But blest us with its noble Fruit,
As soon as it was ty'd and cut:
So Vice is beneficial found,
When it's by Justice lopt and bound;
Nay, where the People would be great,
As necessary to the State,
As Hunger is to make 'em eat.
Bare Virtue can't make Nations live
In Splendor; they, that would revive
A Golden Age, must be as free,
For Acorns, as for Honesty.

The Grumbling Hive (1705) 1924:Vol. 1, 36–37.

3 Pride and Vanity have built more Hospitals than all the Virtues together.

The Fable of the Bees (1714) 1924:Vol. 1, 261.

4 It is in Morality as it is in Nature, there is nothing so perfectly Good in Creatures that it cannot be hurtful to any one of the Society, nor any thing so entirely Evil, but it may prove beneficial to some part or other of the Creation: So that things are only Good and Evil in reference to something else, and according to the Light and Position they are placed in.

The Fable of the Bees (1714) 1924:Vol. 1, 367.

5 I am sorry if the Words Private Vices, Publick Benefits, have ever given any Offence to a well-meaning Man. The Mystery of them is soon unfolded when once they are rightly understood; but no Man of Sincerity will question the Innocence of them, that has read the last Paragraph, where I take my Leave of the Reader, *and conclude with repeating the seeming Paradox, the Substance of which is advanced in the Title Page; that private Vices by the dextrous Management of a skilful Politician, may be turn'd into publick Benefits.*

A Vindication of the Book (1723) 1924:Vol. 1, 411–412. → This appendix was added by Mandeville to the third edition of *The Fable of the Bees* in 1723. Defenders of Mandeville's assertion that "private vices" lead to "publick benefits" have often overlooked Mandeville's caveat that the management of a skilled politician may be required if these benefits are to be received.

6 The whole Superstructure [of Civil Society] is made up of the reciprocal Services, which Men do to each other. How to get these Services perform'd by others, when we have Occasion for them, is the grand and almost constant Sollicitude in Life of every individual Person. To expect, that others should serve us for nothing, is unreasonable; therefore all Commerce, that Men can have together, must be a continual bartering of one thing for another.

The Fable of the Bees (1729) 1924:Vol. 2, 349. → Volume 2 was first published in 1729.

George Mandler 1924–
Austrian-born U.S. psychologist
and
William Kessen 1925–
U.S. psychologist

1 [Benjamin] Franklin and [Michael] Faraday were both asked "What good is it?" by curious and puzzled friends who were watching the demonstration of a new device. Franklin's famous reply "What good is a new-born child?" was a pointed recognition of our ignorance of future utilities, but Faraday expressed more accurately the disdain of the pure scientist for questions of applicability when he responded to [William] Gladstone, "Why, sir, there is every probability that you will soon be able to tax it."

The Language of Psychology 1959:253.

Marya Mannes 1904–1990
U.S. writer

1 What is asserted by a man is an opinion; what is asserted by a woman is opinionated. A woman with ideas and the

ability to express them is something of a social embarrassment.

The Problems of Creative Women 1963:127.

Karl Mannheim 1893–1947
Hungarian-born German sociologist

1 Generation location is based on the existence of biological rhythm in human existence — the factors of life and death, a limited span of life, and ageing. Individuals who belong to the same generation, who share the same year of birth, are endowed, to that extent, with a common location in the historical dimension of the social process.

The Problem of Generations (1927) 1952:290. → See ORTEGA Y GASSET:2.

2 Romantic-conservative youth, and the liberal-rationalist group, belong to the same actual generation but form separate "generation units" within it. The *generation unit* represents a much more concrete bond than the actual generation as such. *Youth experiencing the same concrete historical problems may be said to be part of the same actual generation; while those groups within the same actual generation which work up the material of their common experiences in different specific ways, constitute separate generation units.*

The Problem of Generations (1927) 1952:304.

3 [Men living in groups] do not confront the objects of the world from the abstract levels of a contemplating mind as such, nor do they do so exclusively as solitary beings. On the contrary they act with and against one another in diversely organized groups, and while doing so they think with and against one another.

Ideology and Utopia (1929–1931) 1946:3.

4 The concept "ideology" reflects the one discovery which emerged from political conflict, namely, that ruling groups can in their thinking become so intensively interest-bound to a situation that they are simply no longer able to see certain facts which would undermine their sense of domination. There is implicit in the word "ideology" the insight that in certain situations the collective unconscious of certain groups obscures the real condition of society both to itself and to others and thereby stabilizes it.

Ideology and Utopia (1929–1931) 1946:36.

5 The concept of utopian thinking reflects the opposite discovery of the political struggle, namely that certain oppressed groups are intellectually so strongly interested in the destruction and transformation of a given condition of society that they unwittingly see only those elements in the situation which tend to negate it. Their thinking is incapable of correctly diagnosing an existing condition of society. They are not at all concerned with what really exists; rather in their thinking they already seek to change the situation that exists. Their thought is never a diagnosis of the situation; it can be used only as a direction for action. In the utopian mentality, the collective unconscious, guided by a wishful representation and the will to action, hides certain aspects of reality. It turns its back on everything which would shake its belief or paralyse its desire to change things.

Ideology and Utopia (1929–1931) 1946:36.

6 With the emergence of the general formulation of the total conception of ideology, the simple theory of ideology develops into the sociology of knowledge. What was once the intellectual armament of a party is transformed into a method of research in social and intellectual history generally.

Ideology and Utopia (1929–1931) 1946:69.

7 It is no accident that the one group regards history as a circulation of *elites*, while for the others, it is a transformation of the historical-social structure. Each gets to see primarily only that aspect of the social and historical totality towards which it is oriented by its purpose.

Ideology and Utopia (1929–1931) 1946:127.

8 An experimental outlook, unceasingly sensitive to the dynamic nature of society and to its wholeness, is not likely to be developed by a class occupying a middle position but only by a relatively classless stratum which is not too firmly situated in the social order. . . This unanchored, *relatively* classless stratum is, to use Alfred Weber's terminology, the "socially unattached intelligentsia" *(freischwebende Intelligenz).* It is impossible in this connection to give even the sketchiest outline of the difficult sociological problem raised by the existence of the intellectual.

Ideology and Utopia (1929–1931) 1946:137–138. → See Alfred Weber, *Der dritte oder der vierte Mensch* (1953:59), for a formulation of his concept of a "free-floating" intelligentsia.

9 A state of mind is utopian when it is incongruous with the state of reality within which it occurs. . . .Such an incongruent orientation became utopian only when in addition it tended to burst the bonds of the existing order. Consequently representatives of a given order have not in all cases taken a hostile attitude towards orientations transcending the existing order. . . Not until certain social groups embodied these wish-images into their actual conduct, and tried to realize them, did these ideologies become utopian.

Ideology and Utopia (1929–1931) 1946:173–174.

10 If we look into the past, it seems possible to find a fairly adequate criterion of what is to be regarded as ideological and what as utopian. This criterion is their realization. Ideas which later turned out to have been only distorted representations of a past or potential social order were ideological, while those which were adequately realized in the succeeding social order were relative utopias.

Ideology and Utopia (1929–1931) 1946:184.

11 The sociology of knowledge is closely related to, but increasingly distinguishable from, the theory of ideology, which has also emerged and developed in our own time. The study of ideologies has made it its task to unmask the

more or less conscious deceptions and disguises of human interest groups, particularly those of political parties. The sociology of knowledge is concerned not so much with distortions due to a deliberate effort to deceive as with the varying ways in which objects present themselves to the subject according to the differences in social settings. Thus, mental structures are inevitably differently formed in different social and historical settings.

Ideology and Utopia (1929–1931) 1946:238.

12 [Sociological interpretation does not imply] that mind and thought are nothing but the expression and reflex of various "locations" in the social fabric, and that there exist only quantitatively determinable functional correlations and no potentiality of "freedom" grounded in mind; it merely means that even within the sphere of the intellectual, there are processes amenable to rational analysis, and that it would be an ill-advised mysticism which would shroud things in romantic obscurity at a point where rational cognition is still practicable. Anyone who wants to drag in the irrational where the lucidity and acuity of reason still must rule by right merely shows that he is afraid to face the mystery at its legitimate place.

Competition as a Cultural Phenomenon 1952:228–229. → From a lecture delivered at the Sixth Congress of German Sociologists in 1928.

Frank E. Manuel 1910– and **Fritzie P. Manuel** 1914–
U.S. historians

1 Every utopia, rooted as it is in time and place, is bound to reproduce the stage scenery of its particular world as well as its preoccupation with contemporary social problems. . . Often a utopian foresees the later evolution and consequences of technological developments already present in an embryonic state; he may have antennae sensitive to the future. His gadgets, however, rarely go beyond the mechanical potentialities of his age. Try as he may to invent something new, he cannot make a world out of nothing.

Utopian Thought in the Western World 1979:23.

Mao Zedong 1893–1976
Chinese revolutionary leader

1 Where do correct ideas come from? Do they drop from the skies? No. Are they innate in the minds? No. They come from social practice, and from it alone; they come from three kinds of social practice, the struggle for production, the class struggle and scientific experiment.

Quotations from Chairman Mao Tse-Tung 1967:116.

Herbert Marcuse 1898–1979
German-born U.S. philosopher

1 The theory of alienation demonstrated the fact that man does not realize himself in his labor, that his life has become an instrument of labor, that his work and its products have assumed a form and power independent of him as an individual. But the liberation from this state seems to require, not the arrest of alienation, but its consummation, not the reactivation of the repressed and productive personality but its abolition. The elimination of human potentialities from the world of (alienated) labor creates the preconditions for the elimination of labor from the world of human potentialities.

Eros and Civilization (1955) 1966:105.

2 Free election of masters does not abolish the masters or the slaves. Free choice among a wide variety of goods and services does not signify freedom if these goods and services sustain social controls over a life of toil and fear — that is, if they sustain alienation. And the spontaneous reproduction of superimposed needs by the individual does not establish autonomy; it only testifies to the efficacy of the controls.

One-Dimensional Man (1964) 1966:7–8.

3 The so-called consumer economy and the politics of corporate capitalism have created a second nature of man which ties him libidinally and aggressively to the commodity form. The need for possessing, consuming, handling, and constantly renewing the gadgets, devices, instruments, engines, offered to and imposed upon the people, for using these wares even at the danger of one's own destruction, has become a "biological" need in the sense just defined. The second nature of man thus militates against any change that would disrupt and perhaps even abolish this dependence of man on a market ever more densely filled with merchandise — abolish his existence as a consumer consuming himself in buying and selling. The needs generated by this system are thus eminently stabilizing, conservative needs: the counterrevolution anchored in the instinctual structure.

An Essay on Liberation 1969:11.

Robert Ranulph Marett 1866–1943
British anthropologist

1 None of Darwin's particular doctrines will necessarily endure the test of time and trial. Into the melting-pot must they go as often as any man of science deems it fitting. But Darwinism as the touch of nature that makes the whole world kin can hardly pass away.

Anthropology 1912:11. → "One touch of nature makes the whole world kin" is spoken by Ulysses in Shakespeare's *Troilus and Cressida*.

Alfred Marshall 1842–1924
British economist

1 Economic doctrine. . . is not a body of concrete truth, but an engine for the discovery of concrete truth, similar to, say, the theory of mechanics.

The Present Position of Economics (1885) 1956:159.

2 Experience in controversies such as these [over wages] brings out the impossibility of learning anything from facts till they are examined and interpreted by reason;

and teaches that the most reckless and treacherous of all theorists is he who professes to let facts and figures speak for themselves, who keeps in the background the part he has played, perhaps unconsciously, in selecting and grouping them, and in suggesting the argument *post hoc ergo propter hoc.*

The Present Position of Economics (1885) 1956:167–168.

3 Political Economy or Economics is a study of mankind in the ordinary business of life.

Principles of Economics (1890) 1961:Vol. 1, 1.

4 The study of the causes of poverty is the study of the causes of the degradation of a large part of mankind.

Principles of Economics (1890) 1961:Vol. 1, 3.

5 As with the demand of one person so with that of a whole market. And we may say generally: — The *elasticity* (or *responsiveness) of demand* in a market is great or small according as the amount demanded increases much or little for a given fall in price, and diminishes much or little for a given rise in price.

Principles of Economics (1890) 1961:Vol. 1, 102.

6 Human nature being what it is, we are justified in speaking of the interest on capital as the reward of the sacrifice involved in the waiting for the enjoyment of material resources, because few people would save much without reward; just as we speak of wages as the reward of labour, because few people would work hard without reward.

Principles of Economics (1890) 1961:Vol. 1, 232.

7 We might as reasonably dispute whether it is the upper or the under blade of a pair of scissors that cuts a piece of paper, as whether value is governed by utility or cost of production. It is true that when one blade is held still, and the cutting is effected by moving the other, we may say with careless brevity that the cutting is done by the second; but the statement is not strictly accurate, and is to be excused only so long as it claims to be merely a popular and not a strictly scientific account of what happens.

Principles of Economics (1890) 1961:Vol. 1, 348. → See SIMON:8.

8 If we compare one country of the civilized world with another, or one part of England with another, or one trade in England with another, we find that the degradation of the working classes varies almost uniformly with the amount of rough work done by women.

Principles of Economics (1890) 1961:Vol. 1, 564.

9 [Auguste] Comte's attack on [John Stuart] Mill illustrates the general rule that in discussions on method and scope, a man is nearly sure to be right when affirming the usefulness of his own procedure, and wrong when denying that of others.

Principles of Economics (1890) 1961:Vol. 1, 771n.

10 I had a growing feeling in the later years of my work at the subject that a good mathematical theorem dealing with economic hypotheses was very unlikely to be good economics: and I went more and more on the rules — (1) Use mathematics as a shorthand language, rather than as an engine of inquiry. (2) Keep to them till you have done. (3) Translate into English. (4) Then illustrate by examples that are important in real life. (5) Burn the mathematics. (6) If you can't succeed in 4, burn 3. This last I did often.

Letter to A. L. Bowley, 27 February 1906. 1956:427.

11 Government creates scarcely anything. . . A Government could print a good edition of Shakespeare's works, but it could not get them written.

The Social Possibilities of Economic Chivalry 1907:21–22.

12 Money or "currency" is desired as a means to an end; but yet it does not conform to the general rule that, the larger the means toward a certain end, the better will that end be attained. It may indeed be compared to oil used to enable a machine to run smoothly. A machine will not run well unless oiled; and a novice may infer that the more oil he supplies, the better the machine will run: but in fact oil in excess will clog the machine. In like manner an excessive increase of currency, causes it to lose credit, and perhaps even to cease to be "current."

Money, Credit & Commerce (1923) 1960:38.

13 Wealth is distributed in a manner less conducive to the well-being of mankind than it would be if the rich were somewhat less rich, and the poor were somewhat less poor: and real wealth would be greatly increased, even though there were no change in the aggregate of bricks and houses and clothes and other material things, if only it were possible to effect that change without danger to freedom and to social order; and without impairing the springs of initiative, enterprise and energy.

Undated Fragment 1956:366.

John Marshall 1755–1835
U.S. jurist

1 The power to tax involves the power to destroy.

McCulloch v. *Maryland,* U.S. 431, 1819.

2 The people made the constitution, and the people can unmake it. It is the creature of their will, and lives only by their will.

Cohens v. *Virginia,* U.S. 389, 1821.

T.H. Marshall 1893–1981
British sociologist

1 Wide generalizations and the interpretation of concrete social phenomena lie far apart. From whichever end one starts, the journey is long and arduous, and the travellers are sorely tempted, in their impatience to arrive, to take at some point or other a bold leap over intervening space, landing on the other side dazed and bewildered, having

lost a large part of their baggage in their flight. What they need is. . . stepping stones in the middle distance.

Sociology at the Crossroads (1946) 1964:12.

2 Citizenship is a status bestowed on those who are full members of a community. All who possess the status are equal with respect to the rights and duties with which the status is endowed. . . Social class, on the other hand, is a system of inequality. . . How is it that these two opposing principles could grow and flourish side by side in the same soil? What made it possible for them to be reconciled with one another and to become, for a time at least, allies instead of antagonists? The question is a pertinent one, for it is clear that, in the twentieth century, citizenship and the capitalist class system have been at war.

Citizenship and Social Class (1950) 1964:84.

3 The more you look on wealth as conclusive proof of merit, the more you incline to regard poverty as evidence of failure — but the penalty for failure may seem to be greater than the offence warrants. In such circumstances it is natural that the more unpleasant features of inequality should be treated, rather irresponsibly, as a nuisance, like the black smoke that used to pour unchecked from our factory chimneys. And so in time, as the social conscience stirs to life, class-abatement, like smoke-abatement, becomes a desirable aim to be pursued as far as is compatible with the continued efficiency of the social machine.

Citizenship and Social Class (1950) 1964:86.

4 Citizenship is itself becoming the architect of social inequality.

Citizenship and Social Class (1950) 1964:106.

Marsilius of Padua c. 1275–c. 1343
Italian political theorist

1 The living and living well which are appropriate to men fall into two kinds, of which one is temporal or earthly, while the other is usually called eternal or heavenly. However, this latter kind of living, the eternal, the whole body of philosophers were unable to prove by demonstration, nor was it self-evident, and therefore they did not concern themselves with the means thereto. But as to the first kind of living and living well or good life, that is, the earthly, and its necessary means, this the glorious philosophers comprehended almost completely through demonstration. Hence for its attainment they concluded the necessity of the civil community, without which this sufficient life cannot be obtained.

Defensor pacis (1324) 1980:12–13.

2 The legislator, or the primary and proper efficient cause of the law, is the people or the whole body of citizens, or the weightier part thereof, through its election or will expressed by words in the general assembly of the citizens, commanding or determining that something be done or omitted with regard to human civil acts, under a temporal pain or punishment.

Defensor pacis (1324) 1980:45.

Harriet Martineau 1802–1876
British social, economic, and political journalist

1 Wealth and opinion were practically worshipped before Washington opened his eyes on the sun which was to light him to his deeds; and the worship of Opinion is, at this day, the established religion of the United States.

Society in America 1837:Vol. 2, 153.

2 The grand secret of wise inquiry into Morals and Manners is to begin with the study of THINGS, using the DISCOURSE OF PERSONS as a commentary upon them.

Though the facts sought by travellers relate to Persons, they may most readily be learned from Things. The eloquence of Institutions and Records, in which the action of the nation is embodied and perpetuated, is more comprehensive and more faithful than that of any variety of individual voices. The voice of a whole people goes up in the silent workings of an institution; the condition of the masses is reflected from the surface of a record. The Institutions of a nation, — political, religious or social, — put evidence into the observer's hands as to its capabilities and wants, which the study of individuals could not yield in the course of a lifetime. The records of any society, be they what they may, whether architectural remains, epitaphs, civic registers, national music, or any other of the thousand manifestations of the common mind which may be found among every people, afford more information on Morals in a day than converse with individuals in a year.

How to Observe 1838:73–74.

2 Manners have not been treated of separately from Morals in any of the preceding divisions of the objects of the traveller's observation. The reason is, that manners are inseparable from morals, or, at least, cease to have meaning when separated. Except as manifestations of morals, they have no interest, and can have no permanent existence. A traveller who should report of them exclusively is not only no philosopher, but does not merit the name of an observer.

How to Observe 1838:222.

4 To him, and to him only, who has studied the principles of morals, and thus possessed himself of a key to the mysteries of all social weal and wo, will manners be an index answering as faithfully to the internal movements, harmonious or discordant, of society, as the human countenance to the workings of the human heart.

How to Observe 1838:222.

Karl Marx 1818–1883
German economist, sociologist, and revolutionary

1 Religion is the sigh of the oppressed creature, the heart of a heartless world, just as it is the spirit of spiritless conditions. It is the *opium* of the people.

Contribution to the Critique of Hegel's Philosophy of Law (1844) 1975:175.

2 Theory is capable of gripping the masses as soon as it demonstrates *ad hominem*, and it demonstrates *ad*

hominem as soon as it becomes radical. To be radical is to grasp the root of the matter. But for man the root is man himself.

Contribution to the Critique of Hegel's Philosophy of Law (1844) 1975:182.

3 Labour is *external* to the worker, i.e., it does not belong to his intrinsic nature. . . In his work, therefore, he does not affirm himself but denies himself, does not feel content but unhappy, does not develop freely his physical and mental energy but mortifies his body and ruins his mind. The worker therefore only feels himself outside his work, and in his work feels outside himself. He feels at home when he is not working, and when he is working he does not feel at home. . . As a result, therefore, man (the worker) only feels himself freely active in his animal functions — eating, drinking, procreating, or at most in his dwelling and in dressing-up, etc.; and in his human functions he no longer feels himself to be anything but an animal. What is animal becomes human and what is human becomes animal.

Economic and Philosophic Manuscripts of 1844 (1844) 1975:274–275. → Written in 1844 but first published in full in 1932.

4 Natural science will in time incorporate into itself the science of man, just as the science of man will incorporate into itself natural science: there will be *one* science.

Economic and Philosophic Manuscripts of 1844 (1844) 1975:304.

5 The philosophers have only *interpreted* the world in various ways; the point is to *change* it.

Theses on Feuerbach (1845) 1976:5. → Epitaph on Marx's tombstone in Highgate Cemetery, London. The "Theses" was written in 1845 and first published as an appendix to the 1888 edition of Friedrich Engels, *Ludwig Feuerbach and the End of Classical German Philosophy*.

6 Hegel remarks somewhere that all facts and personages of great importance in world history occur, as it were, twice. He forgot to add: the first time as tragedy, the second as farce.

The Eighteenth Brumaire of Louis Bonaparte (1852) 1963:15.

7 Men make their own history, but they do not make it just as they please; they do not make it under circumstances chosen by themselves, but under circumstances directly encountered, given and transmitted from the past. The tradition of all the dead generations weighs like a nightmare on the brain of the living.

The Eighteenth Brumaire of Louis Bonaparte (1852) 1963:15.

8 The small-holding peasants form a vast mass, the members of which live in similar conditions but without entering into manifold relations with one another. . . Each individual peasant family is almost self-sufficient; it itself directly produces the major part of its consumption and thus acquires its means of life more through exchange with nature than in intercourse with society. A small holding, a peasant and his family; alongside them another small holding, another peasant and another family. A few score of these make up a village, and a few score of villages make up a Department. In this way, the great mass of the French nation is formed by simple addition of homologous magnitudes, much as potatoes in a sack form a sack of potatoes.

The Eighteenth Brumaire of Louis Bonaparte (1852) 1963:123–124.

9 Now as for myself, I do not claim to have discovered either the existence of classes in modern society or the struggle between them. Long before me, bourgeois historians had described the historical development of this struggle between the classes, as had bourgeois economists their economic anatomy. My own contribution was 1. to show that the *existence of classes* is merely bound up with *certain historical phases in the development of production*; 2. that the class struggle necessarily leads to the *dictatorship of the proletariat*; 3. that this dictatorship itself constitutes no more than a transition to the *abolition of all classes* and to a *classless society*.

Letter to Joseph Weydemeyer, 5 March 1852. 1983:62, 65.

10 The individual and isolated hunter or fisher who forms the starting point with Smith and Ricardo belongs to the insipid illusions of the eighteenth century. They are adventure stories which do not by any means represent, as students of the history of civilisation imagine, a reaction against over-refinement and a return to a misunderstood natural life.

The Grundrisse (1857–1858) 1971:16. → Written in 1857–1858; first published in 1903.

11 Society does not consist of individuals; it expresses the sum of connections and relationships in which individuals find themselves.

The Grundrisse (1857–1858) 1971:77.

12 The mode of production of material life conditions the general process of social, political and intellectual life. It is not the consciousness of men that determines their existence, but their social existence that determines their consciousness.

A Contribution to the Critique of Political Economy (1859) 1970:20–21.

13 It is remarkable how Darwin rediscovers, among the beasts and plants, the society of England with its division of labour, competition, opening up of new markets, "inventions" and Malthusian "struggle for existence." It is Hobbes' "*bellum omnium contra omnes*" and is reminiscent of Hegel's *Phenomenology*, in which civil society figures as an "intellectual animal kingdom," whereas, in Darwin, the animal kingdom figures as civil society.

Letter to Friedrich Engels, 18 June 1862. 1985:381.

14 The country that is more developed industrially only shows, to the less developed, the image of its own future.

Capital (1867) 1987:Vol. 1, 19.

15 The mystification which dialectic suffers at Hegel's hands, by no means prevents him from being the first to present its general form of working in a comprehensive and conscious manner. With him it is standing on its head. It must be turned right side up again, if you would discover the rational kernel within the mystical shell.

Capital (1867) 1967:Vol. 1, 20. → From the Afterword to the second German edition.

16 Labour is not the only source of material wealth, of use-values produced by labour. As William Petty puts it, labour is its father and the earth its mother.

Capital (1867) 1967:Vol. 1, 50. → See PETTY:2.

17 So far no chemist has ever discovered exchange-value either in a pearl or a diamond.

Capital (1867) 1967:Vol. 1, 87.

18 Capital is money: Capital is commodities. . . Because it is value, it has acquired the occult quality of being able to add value to itself. It brings forth living offspring, or, at the least, lays golden eggs.

Capital (1867) 1967:Vol. 1, 152

19 A critical history of technology would show how little any of the inventions of the 18th century are the work of a single individual. Hitherto there is no such book. Darwin has interested us in the history of Nature's Technology, *i.e.,* in the formation of the organs of plants and animals, which organs serve as instruments of production for sustaining life. Does not the history of the productive organs of man, of organs that are the material basis of all social organisation, deserve equal attention? And would not such a history be easier to compile, since, as Vico says, human history differs from natural history in this, that we have made the former, but not the latter? Technology discloses man's mode of dealing with Nature, the process of production by which he sustains his life, and thereby also lays bare the mode of formation of his social relations, and of the mental conceptions that flow from them.

Capital (1867) 1987:Vol. 1, 352n. → See VICO:5.

20 [The effect of capitalist development is to] mutilate the labourer into a fragment of a man, degrade him to the level of an appendage of a machine, destroy every remnant of charm in his work and turn it into a hated toil.

Capital (1867) 1967:Vol. 1, 604.

21 Centralisation of the means of production and socialisation of labour at last reach a point where they become incompatible with their capitalist integument. Thus integument is burst asunder. The knell of capitalist private property sounds. The expropriators are expropriated.

Capital (1867) 1967:Vol. 1, 715.

22 In a higher phase of communist society, after the enslaving subordination of individuals under division of labour, and therewith also the antithesis between mental and physical labour, has vanished; after labour, from a mere means of life, has itself become the prime necessity of life; after the productive forces have also increased with the all-round development of the individual, and all the springs of co-operative wealth flow more abundantly — only then can the narrow horizon of bourgeois right be fully left behind and society inscribe on its banners: from each according to his ability, to each according to his needs!

Critique of the Gotha Programme (1875) 1938:10. → Written by Marx in 1875; first published, with notes by Engels, in 1891.

23 *Ce qu'il y a de certain, c'est que moi je ne suis pas Marxiste* [What's certain is that I'm no Marxist].

Quoted in a letter from Friedrich Engels to Eduard Bernstein, 2–3 November 1882. 1967:93. → Unpublished translation by Yole G. Sills. Engels quoted Marx in French because he was recalling what Marx had said to his son-in-law, the French socialist Paul Lafargue, in rejecting the French "Marxists" of the late 1870s. Later, in a 5 August 1890 letter to Conrad Schmidt (and perhaps in other letters), Engels quoted Marx to much the same effect.

Karl Marx 1818–1883
and
Friedrich Engels 1820–1895

German economists, sociologists, and revolutionaries

1 *History* does *nothing,* it "possesses *no* immense wealth," it "wages *no* battles." It is *man,* real, living man who does all that, who possesses and fights; "history" is not, as it were, a person apart, using man as a means to achieve *its own* aims; history is *nothing but* the activity of man pursuing his aims.

The Holy Family (1845) 1975:93. → Engels wrote the first part of *The Holy Family* and is listed as the senior author of the 1845 edition. Marx, however, wrote most of the book, and is listed as the senior author of the edition in his collected works from which this selection is taken.

2 Language is as old as consciousness, language *is* practical, real consciousness that exists for other men as well, and only therefore does it also exist for me; language, like consciousness, only arises from the need, the necessity, of intercourse with other men. Where there exists a relationship, it exists for me: the animal does not *"relate"* itself to anything, it does not *"relate"* itself at all. For the animal its relation to others does not exist as a relation. Consciousness is, therefore, from the very beginning a social product, and remains so as long as men exist at all.

The German Ideology (1845–1846) 1976:44. → Written in the years 1845–1846, the full text was first published in 1932 as *Die deutsche Ideologie.*

3 [Man] is a hunter, a fisherman, a shepherd, or a critical critic, and must remain so if he does not want to lose his means of livelihood; whereas in communist society, where nobody has one exclusive sphere of activity but

each can become accomplished in any branch he wishes, society regulates the general production and thus makes it possible for me to do one thing today and another tomorrow, to hunt in the morning, fish in the afternoon, rear cattle in the evening, criticise after dinner, just as I have a mind, without ever becoming hunter, fisherman, shepherd or critic.

The German Ideology (1845–1846) 1976:47.

4 A spectre is haunting Europe, the spectre of Communism.

The Communist Manifesto (1848) 1964:1.

5 The history of all hitherto existing society is the history of class struggles.

Freeman and slave, patrician and plebeian, lord and serf, guild-master and journeyman, in a word, oppressor and oppressed, stood in constant opposition to one another, carried on an uninterrupted, now hidden, now open fight, a fight that each time ended either in a revolutionary reconstitution of society at large, or in the common ruin of the contending classes.

The Communist Manifesto (1848) 1964:2.

6 The executive of the modern State is but a committee for managing the common affairs of the whole bourgeoisie.

The Communist Manifesto (1848) 1964:5.

7 The bourgeoisie, wherever it has got the upper hand, has put an end to all feudal, patriarchal, idyllic relations. It has pitilessly torn asunder the motley feudal ties that bound man to his "natural superiors," and has left remaining no other bond between man and man than naked self-interest, than callous "cash payment." It has drowned the most heavenly ecstacies of religious fervor, of chivalrous enthusiasm, of philistine sentimentalism, in the icy water of egotistical calculation. It has resolved personal worth into exchange value, and in place of the numberless indefeasible chartered freedoms, has set up that single, unconscionable freedom, Free Trade. In one word, for exploitation, veiled by religious and political illusions, it has substituted naked, shameless, direct, brutal exploitation.

The Communist Manifesto (1848) 1964:5–6. → See CARLYLE:4.

8 The bourgeoisie has subjected the country to the rule of the towns. It has created enormous cities, has greatly increased the urban population as compared with the rural, and has thus rescued a considerable part of the population from the idiocy of rural life.

The Communist Manifesto (1848) 1964:9.

9 What else does the history of ideas prove, than that intellectual production changes in character in proportion as material production is changed? The ruling ideas of each age have ever been the ideas of its ruling class.

The Communist Manifesto (1848) 1964:37.

10 The Communists disdain to conceal their views and aims. They openly declare that their ends can be attained only by the forcible overthrow of all existing social conditions. Let the ruling classes tremble at a Communistic revolution. The proletarians have nothing to lose but their chains. They have a world to win.

Working men of all countries, unite!

The Communist Manifesto (1848) 1964:62.

Abraham H. Maslow 1908–1970
U.S. psychologist

1 It is quite true that man lives by bread alone — when there is no bread. But what happens to man's desires when there *is* plenty of bread and when his belly is chronically filled?

At once other (and higher) needs emerge and these, rather than physiological hungers, dominate the organism. And when these in turn are satisfied, again new (and still higher) needs emerge, and so on. This is what we mean by saying that the basic human needs are organized into a hierarchy of relative prepotency.

Motivation and Personality 1954:83.

2 Most behavior is multimotivated. Within the sphere of motivational determinants any behavior tends to be determined by several or *all* of the basic needs simultaneously rather than by only one of them. Eating may be partially for the sake of filling the stomach, and partially for the sake of comfort and amelioration of other needs. One may make love not only for pure sexual release, but also to convice oneself of one's masculinity, or to make a conquest, to feel powerful, to win more basic affection. . . It would be possible (theoretically if not practically) to analyze a single act of an individual and see in it the expression of his physiological needs, his safety needs, his love needs, his esteem needs, and self-actualization.

Motivation and Personality 1954:102.

Marcel Mauss 1872–1950
French sociologist and anthropologist

1 There are no uncivilized people, only peoples with different civilizations.

L'enseignement de l'histoire des religions des peuples non-civilisés à l'École des Hautes Études 1902:43.

2 Linguistic facts are effects rather than causes. On the one hand, the categories of collective thought are not necessarily expressed in the categories of language, and, on the other hand, those which are expressed by language are not necessarily those which are the most conscious or most important.

On Language and Primitive Forms of Classification 1923:944–947.

3 We intend. . . to isolate one important set of phenomena: namely, prestations which are in theory voluntary, disinterested and spontaneous, but are in fact obligatory and interested. The form usually taken is that of the gift generously offered; but the accompanying behaviour is for-

mal pretence and social deception, while the transaction itself is based on obligation and economic self-interest.

The Gift (1925) 1967:1.

4 Total prestation not only carries with it the obligation to repay gifts received, but it implies two others equally important: the obligation to give presents and the obligation to receive them.

The Gift (1925) 1967:10–11.

5 To refuse to give, or to fail to invite, is — like refusing to accept — the equivalent of a declaration of war; it is a refusal of friendship and intercourse.

The Gift (1925) 1967:11.

6 It is only our Western societies that quite recently turned man into an economic animal. But we are not yet all animals of the same species. In both lower and upper classes pure irrational expenditure is in current practice: it is still characteristic of some French noble houses. *Homo oeconomicus* is not behind us, but before, like the moral man, the man of duty, the scientific man and the reasonable man. For a long time man was something quite different; and it is not so long now since he became a machine — a calculating machine.

The Gift (1925) 1967:74.

7 The study of the concrete, which is the study of the whole, is made more readily, is more interesting and furnishes more explanations in the sphere of sociology than the study of the abstract.

The Gift (1925) 1967:78.

Friedrich Max Müller

See FRIEDRICH MAX MÜLLER.

James Clerk Maxwell 1831–1879

Scottish physicist

1 If we betake ourselves to the statistical method, we do so confessing that we are unable to follow the details of each individual case, and expecting that the effects of widespread causes, though very different in each individual, will produce an average result on the whole nation, from a study of which we may estimate the character and propensities of an imaginary being called the Mean Man.

Quoted in Lewis Campbell and William Garnett, *The Life of James Clerk Maxwell* (1882) 1969:439. → See QUETELET:2.

Rollo May 1909–

U.S. psychologist

1 The chief problem of people in the middle decade of the twentieth century is *emptiness*. By that I mean not only that many people do not know what they want; they often do not have any clear idea of what they feel.

Man's Search for Himself 1953:14.

2 Memory is not just the imprint of the past time upon us; it is the keeper of what is meaningful for our deepest hopes and fears. As such, memory is another evidence that we have a flexible and creative relation to time, the guiding principle being not the clock but the qualitative significance of our experiences.

Man's Search for Himself 1953:258.

Elton Mayo 1880–1949

Australian-born U.S. industrial psychologist

1 The problem *is not that of the sickness of an acquisitive society; it is that of the acquisitiveness of a sick society.*

The Human Problems of an Industrial Civilization (1933) 1946:153. → Mayo's reference is to Tawney's *The Acquisitive Society* (1920). See TAWNEY:2.

2 The difference between a good observer and one who is not good is that the former is quick to take a hint from the facts, from his early efforts to develop skill in handling them, and quick to acknowledge the need to revise or alter the conceptual framework of his thinking. The other — the poor observer — continues dogmatically onward with his original thesis, lost in a maze of correlations, long after the facts have shrieked in protest against the interpretation put upon them.

The Social Problems of an Industrial Civilization 1945:116.

Ernst Mayr 1904–

U.S. biologist and historian of science

1 The assumptions of population thinking are diametrically opposed to those of the typologist. The populationist stresses the uniqueness of everything in the organic world. What is true for the human species, — that no two individuals are alike, — is equally true for all other species of animals and plants. . . All organisms and organic phenomena are composed of unique features and can be described collectively only in statistical terms. Individuals, or any kind of organic entities, form populations of which we can determine the arithmetic mean and the statistics of variation. Averages are merely statistical abstractions, only the individuals of which the populations are composed have reality. The ultimate conclusions of the population thinker and of the typologist are precisely the opposite. For the typologist, the type (*eidos*) is real and the variation an illusion, while for the populationist the type (average) is an abstraction and only the variation is real. No two ways of looking at nature could be more different.

Darwin and the Evolutionary Theory in Biology 1959:2.

2 Spencer's ideas contributed nothing positive to Darwin's thinking; on the contrary, they became a source of considerable subsequent confusion. It was Spencer who suggested substituting for natural selection the term "survival of the fittest," which is so easily considered tautological; it was likewise he who became the chief proponent in England of the importance of the inheritance of acquired characters (in his famous controversy with Weismann). Worst of all, it was he who became the principal spokesman for a social theory based on a brutal

struggle for existence, misleadingly termed social Darwinism.

The Growth of Biological Thought 1982:386.

George Herbert Mead 1863–1931

U.S. social psychologist, sociologist, and philosopher

1 The attitude of hostility toward the lawbreaker has the unique advantage of uniting all members of the community in the emotional solidarity of aggression. While the most admirable of humanitarian efforts are sure to run counter to the individual interests of very many in the community, or fail to touch the interest and imagination of the multitude and to leave the community divided or indifferent, the cry of thief or murder is attuned to profound complexes, lying below the surface of competing individual effort, and citizens who have separated by divergent interests stand together against the common enemy.

The Psychology of Punitive Justice 1918:591.

2 The self can exist for the individual only if he assumes the roles of the others. The presence in the conduct of the individual of the tendencies to act as others act may be, then, responsible for the appearance in the experience of the individual of a social object, i.e., an object answering to complex reactions of a number of individuals, and also for the appearance of the self. Indeed, these two appearances are correlative.

The Genesis of the Self and Social Control (1921–1925) 1964:284.

3 Social control depends. . . upon the degree to which the individuals in society are able to assume the attitudes of the others who are involved with them in common endeavor.

The Genesis of the Self and Social Control (1921–1925) 1964:291.

4 In a human society, a language gesture is a stimulus that reverberates and calls out the same attitude in the individual who makes it as it does in others who respond to it; we hear what we say to others as well as what others say to us.

1927 Class Lectures in Social Psychology (1927) 1982:136.

5 Consciousness is both the difference which arises in the environment because of its relation to the organism in its organic process of adjustment, and also the difference in the organism because of the change which has taken place in the environment. We refer to the first as meaning, and to the second as ideation.

The Philosophy of the Present 1932:4.

6 Social psychology has, as a rule, dealt with various phases of social experience from the psychological standpoint of individual experience. The point of approach which I wish to suggest is that of dealing with experience from the standpoint of society, at least from the standpoint of communication as essential to the social order. Social psychology, on this view, presupposes an approach to experience from the standpoint of the individual, but undertakes to determine in particular that which belongs to this experience because the individual himself belongs to a social structure, a social order.

Mind, Self, and Society (1934) 1962:1.

7 We are unconsciously putting ourselves in the place of others and acting as others act. . . We are, especially through the use of the vocal gestures, continually arousing in ourselves those responses which we call out in other persons, so that we are taking the attitudes of the other persons into our own conduct.

Mind, Self, and Society (1934) 1962:69.

8 The self has a character which is different from that of the physiological organism proper. The self is something which has a development; it is not initially there, at birth, but arises in the process of social experience and activity, that is, develops in the given individual as a result of his relations to that process as a whole and to other individuals within that process.

Mind, Self, and Society (1934) 1962:135.

9 Man's behavior is such in his social group that he is able to become an object to himself, a fact which constitutes him a more advanced product of evolutionary development than are the lower animals. Fundamentally it is this social fact — and not his alleged possession of a soul or mind with which he, as an individual, has been mysteriously and supernaturally endowed, and with which the lower animals have not been endowed — that differentiates him from them.

Mind, Self, and Society (1934) 1962:137n.

10 The individual experiences himself as such, not directly, but only indirectly, from the particular standpoints of other individual members of the same social group, or from the generalized standpoint of the social group as a whole to which he belongs. For he enters his own experience as a self or individual, not directly or immediately, not by becoming a subject to himself, but only in so far as he first becomes an object to himself just as other individuals are objects to him or in his experience; and he becomes an object to himself only by taking the attitudes of other individuals toward himself within a social environment or context of experience and behavior in which both he and they are involved.

Mind, Self, and Society (1934) 1962:138.

11 If we contrast play with the situation in an organized game, we note the essential difference that the child who plays in a game must be ready to take the attitude of everyone else involved in that game, and that these different rôles must have a definite relationship to each other.

Mind, Self, and Society (1934) 1962:151.

12 The organized community or social group which gives to the individual his unity of self may be called "the general-

ized other." The attitude of the generalized other is the attitude of the whole community.

Mind, Self, and Society (1934) 1962:154.

It is in the form of the generalized other that the social process influences the behavior of the individuals involved in it. . . For it is in this form that the social process or community enters as a determining factor into the individual's thinking.

Mind, Self, and Society (1934) 1962:155.

What we mean by self-consciousness is an awakening in ourselves of the group of attitudes which we are arousing in others, especially when it is an important set of responses which go to make up the members of the community. It is unfortunate to fuse or mix up consciousness, as we ordinarily use that term, and self-consciousness. Consciousness, as frequently used, simply has reference to the field of experience, but self-consciousness refers to the ability to call out in ourselves a set of definite responses which belong to the others of the group. Consciousness and self-consciousness are not on the same level. A man alone has, fortunately or unfortunately, access to his own toothache, but that is not what we mean by self-consciousness.

Mind, Self, and Society (1934) 1962:163.

Truth is valuable only in a community where it has universal acceptance. If a thing is not recognized as true, then it does not function as true in the community. People have to recognize it if they are going to act on it.

Movements of Thought in the Nineteenth Century 1936:29. → See Thomas and Thomas:2.

Margaret Mead 1901–1978

U.S. anthropologist

As the traveller who has been once from home is wiser than he who has never left his own door step, so a knowledge of one other culture should sharpen our ability to scrutinise more steadily, to appreciate more lovingly, our own.

Coming of Age in Samoa (1928) 1939:13.

The child is not born wanting a father, he is taught his need by the social blessedness of others. No Samoan child, in a society where the parent-child relationship is diffused over dozens of adults, would dream of creating an ideal father; nor do the Samoans, finding such quiet satisfaction among their uncritical equals, build a heaven which reverberates on earth.

Growing Up in New Guinea (1930) 1939:255.

When we look about us among different civilisations and observe the vastly different styles of life to which the individual has been made to conform, to the development of which he has been made to contribute, we take new hope for humanity and its potentialities. But these potentialities are passive not active, helpless without a cultural milieu in which to grow.

Growing Up in New Guinea (1930) 1939:271.

4 Historically our own culture has relied for the creation of rich and contrasting values upon many artificial distinctions, the most striking of which is sex. It will not be by the mere abolition of these distinctions that society will develop patterns in which individual gifts are given place instead of being forced into an ill-fitting mould. If we are to achieve a richer culture, rich in contrasting values, we must recognize the whole gamut of human potentialities, and so weave a less arbitrary social fabric, one in which each diverse human gift will find a fitting place.

Sex and Temperament (1935) 1939:322.

5 Simple peoples and civilized peoples, mild peoples and violent, assertive peoples, will all go to war if they have the invention, just as those peoples who have the custom of dueling will have duels and peoples who have the pattern of vendetta will indulge in vendetta. . . Warfare. . . is just an invention, older and more widespread than the jury system, but none the less an invention.

Warfare Is Only an Invention 1940:403–404.

6 The way in which people behave is all of a piece, their virtues and their sins, the way they slap the baby, handle their court cases, and bury their dead. It would be impossible suddenly to introduce "democracy" which is a word for a type of behavior and an attitude of mind which runs through our whole culture, through our selection of candidates for office, our behavior in street cars, our schools and our newspapers, into an undemocratic society — as it would suddenly to introduce feudalism into a modern American city.

And Keep Your Powder Dry (1942) 1949:20.

7 We know of no culture that has said, articulately, that there is no difference between men and women except in the way they contribute to the creation of the next generation.

Male and Female 1949:8.

8 Anthropologists learn, by doing field-work, to think of many things together that most students of human behaviour are not accustomed to thinking of together. This way of thinking, which refers a whole series of apparently disparate acts — the way a child is fed, a house-post carved, a prayer recited, a poem composed, or a deer stalked — to one whole, which is the way of life of a people, this is a habit of mind that we carry over into work we do in our own cultures too.

Male and Female 1949:24.

9 Between the layman's "*Naturally* no human society" and the anthropologist's "No *known* human society" lie thousands of detailed and painstaking studies, made by hurricane-lamp and firelight, by explorer and missionary and modern scientists, in many parts of the world.

Male and Female 1949:34.

10 The anthropologist. . . does not want to understand the culture *so that* he can get a house built, a garden dug, carriers for his gear, labourers on a new air-field, or converts for his religion. He does not even, as a doctor would, want to cure them of their diseases or change their ideas of public health, persuade them to bury their dead in a neat little cemetery instead of under the house, "where

they will be less lonely." He does not want to improve them, convert them, govern them, trade with them, recruit them, or heal them. He wants only to understand them, and by understanding them to add to our knowledge of the limitations and the potentialities of human beings.

Male and Female 1949:39.

11 Samoa culture demonstrates how much the tragic or the easy solution of the Oedipus situation depends upon the inter-relationship between parents and children, and is not created out of whole cloth by the young child's biological impulses.

Male and Female 1949:119.

12 Any member of a group, provided that his position within that group is properly specified, is a perfect sample of the group-wide pattern on which he is acting as an informant. So a twenty-one-year-old boy born of Chinese-American parents in a small upstate New York town who has just graduated *summa cum laude* from Harvard and a tenth-generation Boston-born deaf mute of United Kingdom stock are equally perfect examples of American national character, *provided that their individual position and individual characteristics are taken fully into account.*

National Character 1953:648.

13 Female animals defending their young are notoriously ferocious and lack the playful delight in combat which characterizes the mock combats of males of the same species. There seems very little ground for claiming that the mother of young children is more peaceful, more responsible, and more thoughtful for the welfare of the human race than is her husband or brother.

Male and Female (1949) 1964:xxiv. → From an introduction dated October 1954.

Gardiner C. Means

See ADOLF A. BERLE AND GARDINER C. MEANS.

Franz Mehring 1846–1919

German historian and socialist

1 In one sense Marx was certainly Lassalle's teacher and in another sense he was not. From one point of view Marx might have said of Lassalle what Hegel is alleged to have said on his deathbed about his own pupils: only one of them understood me, and he misunderstood me.

Karl Marx (1918) 1935:335.

Antoine Meillet 1866–1936

French linguist

1 The totally arbitrary character of the sign alone makes possible the comparative method in historical linguistics.

La méthode comparative en linguistique historique 1925:2. → Unpublished translation by Michael Silverstein.

2 Every linguistic fact reveals a fact of civilization.

Linguistique historique et linguistique générale 1936:Vol. 2, 168. → Unpublished translation by Michael Silverstein.

Friedrich Meinecke 1862–1954

German historian

1 The struggles among nations. . . threaten to become like the rivalries of student corporations, distinguished from one another only by the colors of their caps and armbands. . . The ideas that fill the minds of French, Italian, German, English and Russian chauvinists are so similar as to be identical.

Die deutsche Erhebung von 1914 1915:93–94. → Unpublished translation by Richard W. Sterling.

2 The German school of history has always held to the doctrine that war and power politics are not invariably destructive forces but can also be creative forces. Evil can produce good, and spiritual values may emerge from base materials. But this is a process that must not be idealized. It does not prove [Hegel's] cunning of reason. It confirms instead the impotence of reason.

Die Idee der Staatsräson in der neueren Geschichte 1924:505. → Unpublished translation by Richard W. Sterling. See GOETHE:1 and HEGEL:5.

Carl Menger 1840–1921

Austrian economist

1 Value is the importance that goods acquire for economizing individuals when these individuals are aware of being dependent on command of them for the satisfaction of their needs.

Principles of Economics (1871) 1950:228.

2 Language, religion, law, even the state itself, and, to mention a few economic social phenomena, the phenomena of markets, of competition, of money, and numerous other social structures are already met with in epochs of history where we cannot properly speak of a purposeful activity of the community as such directed at establishing them. . . We are confronted here with the appearance of social institutions which to a high degree serve the welfare of society. . . and yet are not the result of communal social activity. It is here that we meet a noteworthy, perhaps the most noteworthy, problem of the social sciences:

How can it be that institutions which serve the common welfare and are extremely significant for its development come into being without a common will [*Gemeinwellen*] *directed toward establishing them?*

Problems of Economics and Sociology (1883) 1963:146.

3 The historians have stepped upon the territory of our science like foreign conquerors, in order to force upon us their language and their customs, their terminology and their methods, and to fight intolerantly every branch of enquiry which does not correspond with their special method.

Die Irrthümer des Historismus in der deutschen Nationalökonomie 1884:Preface. Quoted in John Neville Keynes, *The Scope and Method of Political Economy* (1891) 1955:324. → Menger is attacking Gustav Schmoller, a leader of the historical school of economics, during the controversy called the *Methodenstreit* or "Dispute on Methods."

Charles E. Merriam 1874–1953
U.S. political scientist

1 Some day we may take another angle of approach than the formal, as other sciences tend to do, and begin to look at political behavior as one of the essential objects of inquiry. Government, after all, is not made up merely of documents containing laws and rules, or of structures of a particular form, but is fundamentally based upon patterns of action in types of situations.

Progress in Political Research 1926:7. → From the presidential address to the American Political Science Association by the man often called the father of the behavioral study of politics.

2 Power does not lie in the guns, or the ships, or the walls of stone, or the lines of steel. Important as these are, the real political power lies in a definite common pattern of impulse. If the soldiers choose to disobey or even shoot their officers, if the guns are turned against the government, if the citizenry connives at disobedience of the law, and makes of it even a virtue, then authority is impotent and may drag its bearer down to doom.

Political Power (1934) 1964:21.

3 "Civil disobedience" is a phenomenon of private as well as of public government. In the family, in the school, in the church, and in industry methods of neutralizing authority may be found in profusion. One may see children at a very immature age finding ingenious ways and means of evading the rigors of parental discipline. Overworked or discontented slaves have lines of protest. Prisoners even may strike, and workers of high and lowly status may defy and obstruct the policies of authority. It is not necessary to disobey; a literal execution of a wrong order may be even more successful as a protest.

Systematic Politics 1945:218.

Robert K. Merton 1910–
U.S. sociologist

1 Four sets of institutional imperatives — universalism [truth-claims are to be subjected to preestablished impersonal criteria], communism [scientific property is a heritage held in common], disinterestedness, organized skepticism — are taken to comprise the ethos of modern science.

The Normative Structure of Science (1942) 1973:270.

2 The self-fulfilling prophecy is, in the beginning, a *false* definition of the situation evoking a new behavior which makes the originally false conception come *true*. The specious validity of the self-fulfilling prophecy perpetuates a reign of error. For the prophet will cite the actual course of events as proof that he was right from the very beginning. . . Such are the perversities of social logic.

The Self-Fulfilling Prophecy (1948) 1968:477.

3 The *distinctive* intellectual contributions of the sociologist are found primarily in the study of unintended consequences (among which are latent functions) of social practices as well as in the study of anticipated consequences (among which are manifest functions).

Manifest and Latent Functions (1949) 1968:120. → For a more extensive discussion of unanticipated consequences, see Merton's 1936 paper, "The Unanticipated Consequences of Purposive Social Action," reprinted in his *Sociological Ambivalence* (Free Press, 1976).

4 [The] complex pattern of the misallocation of credit for scientific work must quite evidently be described as "the Matthew effect," for, as will be remembered, the Gospel According to St. Matthew puts it this way:

> For unto every one that hath shall be given, and he shall have abundance: but from him that hath not shall be taken away even that which he hath.

Put in less stately language, the Matthew effect consists of the accruing of greater increments of recognition for particular scientific contributions to scientists of considerable repute and the withholding of such recognition from scientists who have not yet made their mark.

The Matthew Effect in Science (1968) 1973:445–446.

John Theodore Merz 1840–1922
British historian

1 In spite of the wonderful increase of scientific knowledge and the general diffusion of scientific thought in the course of the century, uncertainty is still the main and dominant characteristic of our life in nature and society. . . Thus has arisen the science of large numbers or statistics, and the many methods of which it is possessed.

A History of European Thought in the Nineteenth Century 1903:Vol. 2, 552, 555.

Robert Michels 1876–1936
German-born Italian political scientist and sociologist

1 Organization implies the tendency to oligarchy. In every organization, whether it be a political party, a professional union, or any other association of the kind, the aristocratic tendency manifests itself very clearly. The mechanism of the organization, while conferring a solidity of structure, induces serious changes in the organized mass, completely inverting the respective position of the leaders and the led. As a result of organization, every party or professional union becomes divided into a minority of directors and a majority of directed.

Political Parties (1911) 1949:32.

2 The social revolution would not effect any real modification of the internal structure of the mass. The socialists might conquer, but not socialism, which would perish in the moment of its adherents' triumph.

Political Parties (1911) 1949:391.

3 It is organization which gives birth to the dominion of the elected over the electors, of the mandataries over the

mandators, of the delegates over the delegators. Who says organization, says oligarchy.

Political Parties (1911) 1949:401. → Michels' summary of his "iron law of oligarchy."

4 The defects inherent in democracy are obvious. It is none the less true that as a form of social life we must choose democracy as the least of evils.

Political Parties (1911) 1949:407. → See CHURCHILL:4.

5 The democratic currents of history resemble successive waves. They break ever on the same shoal. They are ever renewed. This enduring spectacle is simultaneously encouraging and depressing. When democracies have gained a certain stage of development, they undergo a gradual transformation, adopting the aristocratic spirit, and in many cases also the aristocratic forms, against which at the outset they struggled so fiercely.

Political Parties (1911) 1949:408.

6 Our consistent knowledge of the political life of the principal civilized nations of the world authorizes us to assert that the tendency toward oligarchy constitutes one of the historic necessities, one of the iron laws of history, from which the most democratic modern societies and, within those societies, the most advanced parties, have been unable to escape.

The Sociological Character of Political Parties (1927) 1949:141–142.

7 Whether authority is of personal or institutional origin it is created and maintained by public opinion, which in its turn is conditioned by sentiment, affection, reverence or fatalism. Even when authority rests on mere physical coercion it is accepted by those ruled, although the acceptance may be due to a fear of force.

Authority 1930:319.

James Mill 1773–1836
Scottish philosopher and economist

1 If nature had produced spontaneously all the objects which we desire, and in sufficient abundance for the desires of all, there would have been no source of dispute or of injury among men, nor would any man have possessed the means of ever acquiring authority over another.

An Essay on Government (1820) 1955:48.

2 Wealth, Power, and Dignity, derive a great portion of their efficacy, from their comparative amount; that is, from their being possessed in greater quantity than most other people possess them. In contemplating them with the satisfaction with which powerful causes of pleasure are contemplated, we seldom fail to include the comparison. And the state of consciousness, formed by the contemplation and comparison taken together, is called Pride.

Analysis of the Phenomena of the Human Mind (1829) 1967:Vol. 2, 213.

3 That which constitutes a Party, or class, is always some community of Interest: in other words, some thing or things, to be obtained, secured, or augmented, by the common endeavours of the class, and operating as a cause of pleasure to all of them.

Analysis of the Phenomena of the Human Mind (1829) 1967:Vol. 2, 227.

4 We have already remarked, that, of all the Causes of our Pleasures and Pains, none are to be compared in point of magnitude, with the actions of ourselves, and our Fellow-creatures. From this class of causes, a far greater amount of Pleasures and Pains proceed, than from all other causes taken together.

Analysis of the Phenomena of the Human Mind (1829) 1967:Vol. 2, 280.

John Stuart Mill 1806–1873
British economist and political philosopher

1 History is not the foundation, but the verification, of the social science; it corroborates, and often suggests, political truths, but cannot prove them. The proof of them is drawn from the laws of human nature; ascertained through the study of ourselves by reflection, and of mankind by actual intercourse with them.

Sedgwick's Discourse (1835) 1969:45.

2 Nothing is more true than that it is produce which constitutes the market for produce, and that every increase of production, if distributed without miscalculation among all kinds of produce in the proportion which private interest would dictate, creates, or rather constitutes, its own demand.

Of the Influence of Consumption on Production (1844) 1967:278.

3 The laws and conditions of the production of wealth partake of the character of physical truths. There is nothing optional or arbitrary in them. . . It is not so with the Distribution of Wealth. That is a matter of human institution solely. The things once there, mankind, individually or collectively, can do with them as they like.

Principles of Political Economy (1848) 1965:Book 2, 199.

4 If. . . the choice were to be made between Communism with all its chances, and the present state of society with all its sufferings and injustices; if the institution of private property necessarily carried with it as a consequence, that the produce of labour should be apportioned as we now see it, almost in an inverse ratio to the labour — the largest portions to those who have never worked at all, the next largest to those whose work is almost nominal, and so in a descending scale, the remuneration dwindling as the work grows harder and more disagreeable, until the most fatiguing and exhausting bodily labour cannot count with certainty on being able to earn even the necessaries of life; if this or Communism were

the alternative, all the difficulties, great or small, of Communism would be but as dust in the balance.

Principles of Political Economy (1848) 1965:Book 2, 207.

No man made the land. It is the original inheritance of the whole species. Its appropriation is wholly a question of general expediency. When private property in land is not expedient, it is unjust.

Principles of Political Economy (1848) 1965:Book 2, 230.

Only through the principle of competition has political economy any pretension to the character of a science. So far as rents, profits, wages, prices, are determined by competition, laws may be assigned for them. Assume competition to be their exclusive regulator, and principles of broad generality and scientific precision may be laid down, according to which they will be regulated.

Principles of Political Economy (1848) 1965:Book 2, 239.

Exchange is not the fundamental law of the distribution of produce, no more than roads and carriages are the essential laws of motion, but merely a part of the machinery for effecting it. To confound these ideas, seems to me, not only a logical, but a practical blunder.

Principles of Political Economy (1848) 1965:Book 3, 455.

Happily, there is nothing in the laws of Value which remains for the present or any future writer to clear up; the theory of the subject is complete.

Principles of Political Economy (1848) 1965:Book 3, 456.

Money. . . is a machine for doing quickly and commodiously, what would be done, though less quickly and commodiously, without it: and like many other kinds of machinery, it only exerts a distinct and independent influence of its own when it gets out of order.

Principles of Political Economy (1848) 1965:Book 3, 506.

It is hardly possible to overrate the value, in the present low state of human improvement, of placing human beings in contact with persons dissimilar to themselves, and with modes of thought and action unlike those with which they are familiar. . . Such communication has always been, and is peculiarly in the present age, one of the primary sources of progress.

Principles of Political Economy (1848) 1965:Book 3, 594.

Society. . . practises a social tyranny more formidable than many kinds of political oppression, since, though not usually upheld by such extreme penalties, it leaves fewer means of escape, penetrating much more deeply into the details of life, and enslaving the soul itself. Protection, therefore, against the tyranny of the magistrate is not enough: there needs protection also against the tyranny of the prevailing opinion and feeling; against the tendency of society to impose, by other means than civil penalties, its own ideas and practices as rules of conduct on those who dissent from them; to fetter the development, and, if possible, prevent the formation, of any individuality not in harmony with its ways, and compel all characters to fashion themselves upon the model of its own.

On Liberty (1859) 1977:220.

12 The only purpose for which power can be rightfully exercised over any member of a civilized community, against his will, is to prevent harm to others. His own good, either physical or moral, is not a sufficient warrant.

On Liberty (1859) 1977:223.

13 If all mankind minus one, were of one opinion, and only one person were of the contrary opinion, mankind would be no more justified in silencing that one person, than he, if he had the power, would be justified in silencing mankind.

On Liberty (1859) 1977:229.

14 We can never be sure that the opinion we are endeavouring to stifle is a false opinion; and if we were sure, stifling it would be an evil still.

On Liberty (1859) 1977:229.

15 Trade is a social act.

On Liberty (1859) 1977:293.

16 Opinion is itself one of the greatest active social forces. One person with a belief, is a social power equal to ninety-nine who have only interests.

Considerations on Representative Government (1861) 1977:381.

17 [While participating in public functions, the private citizen] is called upon. . . to weigh interests not his own; to be guided, in case of conflicting claims, by another rule than his private partialities; to apply, at every turn, principles and maxims which have for their reason of existence the common good: and he usually finds associated with him in the same work minds more familiarized than his own with these ideas and operations, whose study it will be to supply reasons to his understanding, and stimulation to his feeling for the general interest. He is made to feel himself one of the public, and whatever is for their benefit to be for his benefit.

Considerations on Representative Government (1861) 1977:412.

18 It is evident, that the only government which can fully satisfy all the exigencies of the social state, is one in which the whole people participate; that any participation, even in the smallest public function, is useful; that the participation should everywhere be as great as the general degree of improvement of the community will allow; and that nothing less can be ultimately desirable, than the admission of all to a share in the sovereign power of the state. But since all cannot, in a community exceeding a single small town, participate personally in

any but some very minor portions of the public business, it follows that the ideal type of a perfect government must be representative.

Considerations on Representative Government (1861) 1977:412.

19 The very principle of constitutional government requires it to be assumed, that political power will be abused to promote the particular purposes of the holder; not because it is always so, but because such is the natural tendency of things, to guard against which is the especial use of free institutions.

Considerations on Representative Government (1861) 1977:505.

20 It is in general a necessary condition of free institutions, that the boundaries of governments should coincide in the main with those of nationalities.

Considerations on Representative Government (1861) 1977:548.

21 It is better to be a human being dissatisfied than a pig satisfied; better to be Socrates dissatisfied than a fool satisfied.

Utilitarianism (1861) 1969:212.

22 The principle which regulates the existing social relations between the two sexes — the legal subordination of one sex to the other — is wrong in itself, and now one of the chief hindrances to human improvement; and. . . it ought to be replaced by a principle of perfect equality, admitting no power or privilege on the one side, nor disability on the other.

The Subjection of Women (1869) 1984:259.

23 So true is it that unnatural generally means only uncustomary, and that everything which is usual appears natural. The subjection of women to men being a universal custom, any departure from it quite naturally appears unnatural.

The Subjection of Women (1869) 1984:270.

24 What is now called the nature of women is an eminently artificial thing — the result of forced repression in some directions, unnatural stimulation in others. It may be asserted without scruple, that no other class of dependents have had their character so entirely distorted from its natural proportions by their relation with their masters; for, if conquered and slave races have been, in some respects, more forcibly repressed, whatever in them has not been crushed down by an iron heel has generally been let alone, and if left with any liberty of development, it has developed itself according to its own laws; but in the case of women, a hot-house and stove cultivation has always been carried on of some of the capabilities of their nature, for the benefit and pleasure of their masters.

The Subjection of Women (1869) 1984:276.

25 Laws and institutions require to be adapted, not to good men, but to bad. Marriage is not an institution designed for a select few. Men are not required, as a preliminary to the marriage ceremony, to prove by testimonials that they are fit to be trusted with the exercise of absolute power.

The Subjection of Women (1869) 1984:287.

George A. Miller 1920–
U.S. psychologist

1 There is a clear and definite limit to the accuracy with which we can identify absolutely the magnitude of a unidimensional stimulus variable. I would propose to call this limit the *span of absolute judgment,* and I maintain that for unidimensional judgments this span is usually somewhere in the neighborhood of seven.

The Magical Number Seven, Plus or Minus Two (1956) 1967:32.

2 What about the magical number seven? What about the seven wonders of the world, the seven seas, the seven deadly sins, the seven daughters of Atlas in the Pleiades, the seven ages of man, the seven levels of hell, the seven primary colors, the seven notes of the musical scale, and the seven days of the week? What about the seven-point rating scale, the seven categories for absolute judgment, the seven objects in the span of attention, and the seven digits in the span of immediate memory? For the present I propose to withhold judgment. Perhaps there is something deep and profound behind all these sevens, something just calling out for us to discover it. But I suspect that it is only a pernicious, Pythagorean coincidence.

The Magical Number Seven, Plus or Minus Two (1956) 1967:42–43.

3 Some men's mistakes are more seminal than other men's valid insights.

Review of Benjamin Lee Whorf, *Language, Thought, and Reality* 1978:96. → See AUBREY:2.

Neal E. Miller 1909–
U.S. psychologist
and
John Dollard 1900–1980
U.S. anthropologist, psychologist, and sociologist

1 Culture, as conceived by social scientists, is a statement of the design of the human maze, of the type of reward involved, and of what responses are to be rewarded. It is in this sense a recipe for learning.

Social Learning and Imitation (1941) 1953:5.

C. Wright Mills 1916–1962
U.S. sociologist

1 If we took the one hundred most powerful men in America, the one hundred wealthiest, and the one hundred most celebrated away from the institutional positions they now occupy, away from their resources of men and women and money, away from the media of mass communication that are now focused upon them — then they would be powerless and poor and uncelebrated. For

power is not of a man. Wealth does not center in the person of the wealthy. Celebrity is not inherent in any personality. To be celebrated, to be wealthy, to have power requires access to major institutions, for the institutional positions men occupy determine in large part their chances to have and to hold these valued experiences.

The Power Elite (1956) 1959:10–11.

2 Neither the very top nor the very bottom of modern society is a normal part of the world of those who read and write books: we are more familiar with the middle ranks. To understand the middle classes we have only to *see* what is actually around us, but to understand the very top or the very bottom, we must first seek to discover and describe. And that is very difficult to do: the very top of modern society is often inaccessible, the very bottom often hidden.

The Power Elite (1956) 1959:362.

3 Fate has to do with events in history that are the summary and unintended results of innumerable decisions of innumerable men. Each of their decisions is minute in consequence and subject to cancellation or reinforcement by other such decisions. There is no link between any one man's intention and the summary result of the innumerable decisions. Events are beyond human decisions: history is made behind men's backs.

Culture and Politics (1959) 1963:243.

4 The sociological imagination enables us to grasp history and biography and the relations between the two within society. That is its task and its promise. To recognize this task and this promise is the mark of the classic social analyst.

The Sociological Imagination 1959:6.

5 [The sociological] imagination is the capacity to shift from one perspective to another — from the political to the psychological; from examination of a single family to comparative assessment of the national budgets of the world; from the theological school to the military establishment; from considerations of an oil industry to studies of contemporary poetry. It is the capacity to range from the most impersonal and remote transformations to the most intimate features of the human self — and to see the relations between the two.

The Sociological Imagination 1959:7.

6 No one who does not come to grips with the ideas of marxism can be an adequate social scientist; no one who believes that marxism contains the last word can be one either.

The Marxists (1962) 1963:11.

Wesley C. Mitchell 1874–1948
U.S. economist

1 An incipient revival of activity. . . develops into full prosperity, prosperity gradually breeds a crisis, the crisis merges into depression, depression becomes deeper for a while, but ultimately engenders a fresh revival of activity, which is the beginning of another cycle. A theory of business cycles must therefore be a descriptive analysis of the cumulative changes by which one set of business conditions transforms itself into another set.

Business Cycles and Their Causes (1913) 1941:ix.

2 Because it. . . rationalizes economic life itself, the use of money lays the foundation for a rational theory of that life. Money may not be the root of *all* evil, but it is the root of economic science.

The Role of Money in Economic Theory (1916) 1937:171.

3 It is a misconception to suppose that consumers guide their course by ratiocination — they don't think except under stress. There is no way of deducing from certain principles what they will do, just because their behavior is not itself rational. One has to find out what they do. That is a matter of observation, which the economic theorists had taken all too lightly. Economic theory became a fascinating subject — the orthodox types particularly — when one began to take the mental operations of the theorists as the problem, instead of taking their theories seriously.

Letter to John Maurice Clark, 9 August 1928. 1952:95.

4 [Veblen] investigated a variety of institutions, or institutional complexes, from the leisure class to the machine process, business enterprise and absentee ownership. . . Even when he dealt with questions which have a place in standard treatises on economics — such as credit, business combinations, profits, socialism — he drew little from, and he contributed little to, the standard discussions. . . We shall have no more of [his] investigations, with their curious erudition, their irony, their dazzling phrases, their bewildering reversals of problems and values.

Obituary: Thorstein Veblen: 1857–1929 1929:649.

Franco Modigliani 1918–
Italian-born U.S. economist

1 Is the rate of interest determined by the demand for and supply of cash? Or is it determined by those "real factors," psychological and technological, that can be subsumed under the concepts of propensity to save and marginal efficiency of investment?. . . We can answer both questions affirmatively. We do not have to choose between these two alternatives any more than between the following two: Is the price of fish determined by the daily demand and the daily supply; or is it determined by the average yearly demand and the cost of fishing?

Liquidity Preference and the Theory of Interest and Money 1944:86.

2 As I look at the work accomplished and that still to be done, I sometimes feel that my only regret is that I have but one life cycle to give to the life cycle hypothesis.

The Life Cycle Hypothesis of Saving Twenty Years Later 1975:33.

3 The study of individual thrift and aggregate saving and wealth has long been central to economics because national saving is the source of the supply of capital, a major factor of production controlling the productivity of labor and its growth over time. It is because of this relation between saving and productive capital that thrift has traditionally been regarded as a virtuous, socially beneficial act.

Life Cycle, Individual Thrift, and the Wealth of Nations (1985) 1986:297. → From Modigliani's 1985 Nobel lecture delivered in Stockholm.

[*See also* EMILE GRUNBERG AND FRANCO MODIGLIANI.]

Theodor Mommsen 1817–1903
German historian

1 Those who have lived through historical events, as I have. . . begin to see that history is neither written nor made without love or hate.

Quoted in G. P. Gooch, *History and Historians* (1913) 1959:462.

Ashley Montagu 1905–
British-born U.S. anthropologist and social biologist

1 The idea of "race" represents one of the most dangerous myths of our time, and one of the most tragic. Myths are most effective and dangerous when they remain unrecognized for what they are. Many of us are happy in the complacent belief that myths are what primitive people believe in, but of which we ourselves are completely free. We may realize that a myth is a faulty explanation leading to social delusion and error, but we do not usually realize that we ourselves share in the mythmaking faculty with all men of all times and places, that each of us has his own store of myths which have been derived from the traditional stock of the society in which we live. In earlier days we believed in magic, possession, and exorcism, in good and evil supernatural powers, and until recently we believed in witchcraft. Today many of us believe in "race." "Race" is the witchcraft of our time. The means by which we exorcise demons. It is the contemporary myth. Man's most dangerous myth.

Man's Most Dangerous Myth: The Fallacy of Race (1942) 1964:23.

Montesquieu 1689–1755
[Charles Louis de Secondat, baron de la Brède et de Montesquieu]
French social and political theorist

1 I have laid down the first principles, and have found that the particular cases follow naturally form them; that the histories of all nations are only consequences of them; and that every particular law is connected with another law, or depends on some other of a more general extent.

The Spirit of the Laws (1748) 1949:Vol. 1, lxvii.

2 Laws, in their most general signification, are the necessary relations arising from the nature of things. In this sense all beings have their laws: the Deity His laws, the material world its laws, the intelligences superior to man their laws, the beasts their laws, man his laws.

The Spirit of the Laws (1748) 1949:Vol. 1, book 1, 1.

3 Now, a government is like every thing else: to preserve it we must love it.

The Spirit of the Laws (1748) 1949:Vol. 1, book 4, 34.

4 In the state of nature, indeed, all men are born equal, but they cannot continue in this equality. Society makes them lose it, and they recover it only by the protection of the laws.

The Spirit of the Laws (1748) 1949:Vol. 1, book 8, 111.

5 When the legislative and executive powers are united in the same person, or in the same body of magistrates, there can be no liberty; because apprehensions may arise, lest the same monarch or senate should enact tyrannical laws, to execute them in a tyrannical manner.

Again, there is no liberty, if the judiciary power be not separated from the legislative and executive. Were it joined with the legislative, the life and liberty of the subject would be exposed to arbitrary control; for the judge would then be the legislator. Were it joined to the executive power, the judge might behave with violence and oppression.

The Spirit of the Laws (1748) 1949:Vol. 1, book 11, 151–152. → See JEFFERSON:4 and MADISON:5.

6 The laws do not take upon them to punish any other than overt acts.

The Spirit of the Laws (1748) 1949:Vol. 1, book 12, 193.

7 Politics are a smooth file, which cuts gradually, and attains its end by a slow progression.

The Spirit of the Laws (1748) 1949:Vol. 1, book 14, 232. → See MAX WEBER:14; his metaphor was "politics is a strong and slow boring of hard boards."

8 Mankind are influenced by various causes: by the climate, by the religion, by the laws, by the maxims of government, by precedents, morals, and customs; whence is formed a general spirit of nations.

The Spirit of the Laws (1748) 1949:Vol. 1, book 19, 293.

9 Solon being asked if the laws he had given to the Athenians were the best, he replied, "I have given them the best they were able to bear" — a fine expression that ought to be perfectly understood by all legislators!

The Spirit of the Laws (1748) 1949:Vol.1,book 19,305.

Wilbert E. Moore

See KINGSLEY DAVIS AND WILBERT E. MOORE.

Jacob L. Moreno 1889–1974
Romanian-born U.S. psychiatrist

1 An instrument to measure the amount of organization shown by social groups is called [a] *sociometric test*. The sociometric test requires an individual to choose his associates for any group of which he is or might become a

member. He is expected to make his choices without restraint and whether the individuals chosen are members of the present group or outsiders.

Who Shall Survive? 1934:11. → Sociometry was developed in post-1918 Europe; Moreno brought it to the United States with this strange and innovative book.

C. Lloyd Morgan 1852–1936
British psychologist and philosopher

1 In no case may we interpret an action [of an animal] as the outcome of the exercise of a higher psychical faculty, if it can be interpreted as the outcome of the exercise of one which stands lower in the psychological scale.

An Introduction to Comparative Psychology 1894:53. → Known as Morgan's canon, the principle of parsimony in animal research.

Lewis Henry Morgan 1818–1881
U.S. anthropologist

1 The several nations of the Iroquois, united, constituted one Family, dwelling together in one Long House; and these ties of family relationship were carried throughout their civil and social system, from individuals to tribes, from tribes to nations, and from the nations to the League itself, and bound them together in one common, indissoluble brotherhood.

League of the Iroquois (1851) 1972:60.

2 This great passion of civilized man [for gain], in its use and abuse his blessing and his curse, never roused the Indian mind. It was doubtless the great reason of his continuance in the hunter state; for the desire of gain is one of the earliest manifestations of progressive mind, and one of the most powerful passions of which the mind is susceptible. It clears the forest, rears the city, builds the merchantman — in a word, it has civilized our race.

League of the Iroquois (1851) 1972:139.

3 With the rise of property, considered as an institution, with the settlement of its rights, and above all, with the established certainty of its transmission to lineal descendants, came the first possibility among mankind of the true family in its modern acceptation. . . It is impossible to separate property, considered in the concrete, from civilization, or for civilization to exist without its presence, protection, and regulated inheritance. Of property in this sense, all barbarous nations are necessarily ignorant.

Systems of Consanguinity and Affinity 1870:492.

4 When the discoverers of the New World bestowed upon its inhabitants the name of *Indians*, under the impression that they had reached the Indies, they little suspected that children of the same original family, although upon a different continent, stood before them. By a singular coincidence error was truth.

Systems of Consanguinity and Affinity 1870:508.

5 The great antiquity of mankind upon the earth has been conclusively established. It seems singular that the proofs should have been discovered as recently as within the last thirty years, and that the present generation should be the first called upon to recognize so important a fact. . .

This knowledge changes materially the views which have prevailed respecting the relations of savages to barbarians, and of barbarians to civilized men. It can now be asserted upon convincing evidence that savagery preceded barbarism in all the tribes of mankind, as barbarism is known to have preceded civilization. The history of the human race is one in source, one in experience, and one in progress.

Ancient Society (1877) 1964:5.

6 [The working of iron] must be held the greatest event in human experience, preparatory to civilization. . . Furnished with iron tools, capable of holding both an edge and a point, mankind were certain of attaining to civilization. The production of iron was the event of events in human experience, without a parallel, and without an equal, beside which all other inventions and discoveries were inconsiderable, or at least subordinate.

Ancient Society (1877) 1964:43.

7 When we recognize the duration of man's existence upon the earth, the wide vicissitudes through which he has passed in savagery and in barbarism, and the progress he was compelled to make, civilization might as naturally have been delayed for several thousand years in the future, as to have occurred when it did in the good providence of God. We are forced to the conclusion that it was the result, as to the time of its achievement, of a series of fortuitous circumstances. It may well serve to remind us that we owe our present condition, with its multiplied means of safety and of happiness, to the struggles, the sufferings, the heroic exertions and the patient toil of our barbarous, and more remotely, of our savage ancestors. Their labors, their trials and their successes were a part of the plan of the Supreme Intelligence to develop a barbarian out of a savage, and a civilized man out of this barbarian.

Ancient Society (1877) 1964:468.

Oskar Morgenstern 1902–1977
German-born U.S. economist

1 There is a fundamental difference (in the field of economics) between mere *data* and *observations*. . . *Observations* are deliberately *designed*; other *data* are merely *obtained*.

On the Accuracy of Economic Obervations (1950) 1963:88.

[*See also* JOHN VON NEUMANN AND OSKAR MORGENSTERN.]

Samuel Eliot Morison 1887–1976
U.S. historian

1 America was discovered accidentally by a great seaman who was looking for something else; when discovered it was not wanted; and most of the exploration for the next fifty years was done in the hope of getting through or around it. America was named after a man who discov-

ered no part of the New World. History is like that, very chancy.

The Oxford History of the American People 1965:23.

Gaetano Mosca 1858–1941
Italian political scientist

1 If a new source of wealth develops in a society, if the practical importance of knowledge grows, if an old religion declines or a new one is born, if a new current of ideas spreads, then, simultaneously, far-reaching dislocations occur in the ruling class. One might say, indeed, that the whole history of civilized mankind comes down to a conflict between the tendency of dominant elements to monopolize political power and transmit possession of it by inheritance, and the tendency toward a dislocation of old forces and an insurgence of new forces.

The Ruling Class (1896) 1939:65.

2 History teaches that the class that bears the lance or holds the musket regularly forces its rule upon the class that handles the spade or pushes the shuttle.

The Ruling Class (1896) 1939:228.

Frederick Mosteller 1916–
U.S. statistician

1 Although we often hear that data speak for themselves, their voices can be soft and sly.

Beginning Statistics with Data Analysis 1983:234. → Written with Stephen E. Fienberg and Robert E. K. Rourke.

Frederick Mosteller 1916–
U.S. statistician
and
Robert R. Bush 1920–1971
U.S. psychologist

1 The main purpose of a significance test is to inhibit the natural enthusiasm of the investigator.

Selected Quantitative Techniques 1954:331–332.

Frederick Mosteller 1916–
and
David L. Wallace 1928–
U.S. statisticians

1 People cannot count, at least not very high.

Inference and Disputed Authorship 1964:7.

[*See also* PERSI DIACONIS AND FREDERICK MOSTELLER.]

Daniel Patrick Moynihan

See NATHAN GLAZER AND DANIEL PATRICK MOYNIHAN.

Friedrich Max Müller 1823–1900
German philologist

1 The language which we speak, and the languages that are and that have been spoken in every part of our globe since the first dawn of human life and human thought, supply materials capable of scientific treatment. We can collect them, we can classify them, we can reduce them to their constituent elements, and deduce from them some of the laws that determine their origin, govern their growth, necessitate their decay; we can treat them, in fact, in exactly the same spirit in which the geologist treats his stones and petrifactions, — nay, in some respects, in the same spirit in which the astronomer treats the stars of heaven, or the botanist the flowers of the field. There *is* a Science of Language, as there is a science of the earth, its flowers, and its stars.

Lectures on the Science of Language (1866) 1875:9.

Lewis Mumford 1895–1990
U.S. architectural and cultural critic

1 The city is a fact in nature, like a cave, a run of mackerel or an ant-heap. But it is also a conscious work of art, and it holds within its communal framework many simpler and more personal forms of art. Mind *takes form* in the city; and in turn, urban forms condition mind. For space, no less than time, is artfully reorganized in cities: in boundary lines and silhouettes, in the fixing of horizontal planes and vertical peaks, in utilizing or denying the natural site, the city records the attitude of a culture and an epoch to the fundamental facts of its existence. The dome and the spire, the open avenue and the closed court, tell the story, not merely of different physical accommodations, but of essentially different conceptions of man's destiny. The city is both a physical utility for collective living and a symbol of those collective purposes and unanimities that arise under such favoring circumstance. With language itself, it remains man's greatest work of art.

The Culture of Cities 1938:5.

2 Even historians forget too easily that the largest part of every culture is transmitted, not through a few institutions and a handful of texts, but by a million daily acts and observances and imitations. Remove even a third of the population, and with it will go a multitude of skills, a vast heritage of living knowledge, an abundance of sensitive discriminations, passed from parent to child, from master to apprentice, from neighbor to neighbor. There is no mechanical substitute for a living tradition.

The Condition of Man 1944:154–155.

3 It is not the purity of the orthodox Christian doctrine that has kept the Eastern and Western Churches alive and enabled them to flourish even in a scientific age, but just the opposite: the non-systematic elements, seeping in from other cultures and from contradictory experiences of life: covert heresies that have given the Christian creed a vital buoyancy that seemingly tighter bodies of doctrine have lacked.

The Conduct of Life 1951:177.

4 To withdraw like a monk and live like a prince — this was the purpose of the original creators of the suburb. They proposed in effect to create an asylum, in which they could, as individuals, overcome the chronic defects of

civilization while still commanding at will the privileges and benefits of urban society. This utopia proved to be, up to a point, a realizable one: so enchanting that those who contrived it failed to see the fatal penalty attached to it — the penalty of popularity, the fatal inundation of a mass movement whose very numbers would wipe out the goods each individual sought for his own domestic circle, and, worse, replace them with a life that was not even a cheap counterfeit, but rather the grim antithesis.

The City in History 1961:486. → See HARDIN:1.

Hugo Münsterberg 1863–1916
German-born U.S. psychologist

1 [In America], the feeling of equality will crop out where nature designed none, as for instance between youth and mature years. . . Parents even make it a principle to implore and persuade their children, holding it to be a mistake to compel or punish them; and they believe that the schools should be conducted in the same spirit.

The Americans 1904:28.

George P. Murdock 1897–1985
U.S. anthropologist

1 The nuclear family is a universal human social grouping. Either as the sole prevailing form of the family or as the basic unit from which more complex familial forms are compounded, it exists as a distinct and strongly functional group in every known society. No exception, at least, has come to light in the 250 representative cultures surveyed for the present study.

Social Structure (1949) 1960:2.

2 The evidence from our 250 societies supports the contention of the American historical anthropologists, against the evolutionists, that there is no inevitable sequence of social forms nor any necessary association between particular rules of residence or descent or particular types of kin groups or kinship terms and levels of culture, types of economy, or forms of government or class structure. On the other hand, it supports the evolutionists, against the several schools of historical anthropology, in the conclusion that parallelism or independent invention is relatively easy and common in the field of social organization, and that any structural form can be developed anywhere if conditions are propitious.

Social Structure (1949) 1960:200.

3 It now seems to me distressingly obvious that culture, social system, and all comparable supra-individual concepts, such as collective representations, group mind, and social organism, are illusory conceptual abstractions inferred from observations of the very real phenomena of individuals interacting with one another and with their natural environments. The circumstances of their interaction often lead to similarities in the behaviour of different individuals which we tend to reify under the name of culture, and they cause individuals to relate themselves to others in repetitive ways which we tend to reify as structures or systems. But culture and social structure are actually mere epiphenomena — derivative products of the social interaction of pluralities of individuals.

Anthropology's Mythology 1972:19.

Gardner Murphy 1895–1979
U.S. psychologist

1 It has become accepted doctrine that we must attempt to study the whole man. Actually we cannot study even a whole tree or a whole guinea pig. But it is a whole tree and a whole guinea pig that have survived and evolved, and we must make the attempt.

Personality 1947:5.

2 The case history is frequently merely a "history" that makes too much of bygones; it may obscure the fact that we must be concerned with the present experience of the child. The present situation may be far more important than any past experience.

Personality 1947:868.

Gilbert Murray 1866–1957
Australian-born British classicist

1 Any one who turns from the great writers of classical Athens, say Sophocles or Aristotle, to those of the Christian era must be conscious of a great difference in tone. There is a change in the whole relation of the writer to the world about him. The new quality is not specifically Christian: it is just as marked in the Gnostics and Mithras-worshippers as in the Gospels and the Apocalypse, in Julian and Plotinus as in Gregory and Jerome. It is hard to describe. It is a rise of asceticism, of mysticism, in a sense, of pessimism; a loss of self-confidence, of hope in this life and of faith in normal human effort; a despair of patient inquiry, a cry for infallible revelation; an indifference to the welfare of the state, a conversion of the soul to God. It is an atmosphere in which the aim of the good man is not so much to live justly, to help the society to which he belongs and enjoy the esteem of his fellow creatures; but rather, by means of a burning faith, by contempt for the world and its standards, by ecstasy, suffering, and martyrdom, to be granted pardon for his unspeakable unworthiness, his immeasurable sins. There is an intensifying of certain spiritual emotions; an increase of sensitiveness, a failure of nerve.

Five Stages of Greek Religion 1925:155. → First published in 1912 as *Four Stages of Greek Religion*.

Henry A. Murray 1893–1988
U.S. psychologist

1 Personology. . . is the science of men, taken as gross units, and by definition it encompasses "psycho-analysis" (Freud), "analytical psychology" (Jung), "individual psychology" (Adler) and other terms which stand for meth-

ods of inquiry or doctrines rather than realms of knowledge.

Explorations in Personality 1938:4. → This book was written at the Harvard Psychological Clinic by a group headed by Murray.

2 Man is a "time-binding" organism; which is a way of saying that, by conserving some of the past and anticipating some of the future, a human being can, to a significant degree, make his behaviour accord with events that have happened as well as those that are to come. Man is not a mere creature of the moment, at the beck and call of any stimulus or drive. What he does is related not only to the settled past but also to shadowy preconceptions of what lies ahead.

Explorations in Personality 1938:49.

3 It is possible to become emotionally identified with a single urge if the author animates it to heroic proportions and gives the reader a dramatic account of its vicissitudes, conflicts, frustrations and successes. A volume on the "will-to-power" may be as exciting as a biography of Napoleon. A chronicle of the sexual instinct is as intriguing as the memoirs of Casanova or St. Anthony. But if one has been driven to the view by observed facts that personality is the outcome of numerous forces — now one and now another being of major import — then it is impossible to choose a hero.

Explorations in Personality 1938:143.

4 In my philosophy there are no absolute or inevitable laws, no enduring certainties: every observation, every inference, every explanation, and every prediction is a matter of less or greater probability. To this most psychologists, I trust, would be ready to assent.

Preparations for the Scaffold of a Comprehensive System 1959:50.

5 Personality, as defined by this PS [personological system], has not only a comprehensive scope but a comprehensive span; the history of the personality *is* the personality.

Components of an Evolving Personological System 1968:8.

Henry A. Murray 1893–1988
U.S. psychologist
and
Clyde Kluckhohn 1905–1960
U.S. anthropologist

1 Human personality is a compromise formation, a dynamic resultant of the conflict between the individual's own impulses (as given by biology and modified by culture and by specific situations) and the demands, interests, and impulses of other individuals.

Outline of a Conception of Personality (1948) 1967:46.

[*See also* Clyde Kluckhohn and Henry A. Murray; Alfred L. Kroeber and Clyde Kluckhohn.]

Gunnar Myrdal 1898–1987
Swedish economist and sociologist

1 Not since Reconstruction has there been more reason to anticipate fundamental changes in American race relations, changes which will involve a development toward the American ideals.

An American Dilemma 1944:Vol. 1, xix.

2 The American Negro problem is a problem in the heart of the American. It is there that the interracial tension has its focus. It is there that the decisive struggle goes on. This is the central viewpoint of this treatise. Though our study includes economic, social, and political race relations, at bottom our problem is the moral dilemma of the American — the conflict between his moral valuations on various levels of consciousness and generality. The "American Dilemma," referred to in the title of this book, is the ever-raging conflict between, on the one hand, the valuations preserved on the general plane which we shall call the "American Creed," where the American thinks, talks, and acts under the influence of high national and Christian precepts, and, on the other hand, the valuations on specific planes of individual and group living, where personal and local interests; economic, social, and sexual jealousies; considerations of community prestige and conformity; group prejudice against particular persons or types of people; and all sorts of miscellaneous wants, impulses, and habits dominate his outlook.

An American Dilemma 1944:Vol. 1, xlii.

3 *The white man's rank order of discriminations*. . . held nearly unanimously is the following:

Rank 1. Highest in this order stands the bar against intermarriage and sexual intercourse involving white women.

Rank 2. Next come the several etiquettes and discriminations, which specifically concern behavior in personal relations. (These are the barriers against dancing, bathing, eating, drinking together, and social intercourse generally; peculiar rules as to handshaking, hat lifting, use of titles, house entrance to be used, social forms when meeting on streets and in work, and so forth. These patterns are sometimes referred to as the denial of "social equality" in the narrow meaning of the term.)

Rank 3. Thereafter follow the segregations and discriminations in use of public facilities such as schools, churches and means of conveyance.

Rank 4. Next comes political disfranchisement.

Rank 5. Thereafter come discriminations in law courts, by the police, and by other public servants.

Rank 6. Finally come the discriminations in securing land, credit, jobs, or other means of earning a living, and discriminations in public relief and other social welfare activities. . .

Next in importance to the fact of the white man's rank order of discriminations is the fact that *the Negro's own rank order is just about parallel, but inverse, to that of the white man*. The Negro resists least the discrimination on the ranks placed highest in the white man's evaluation and resents most any discrimination on the lowest level.

An American Dilemma 1944:Vol. 1, 60–61.

4 In [the] magical sphere of the white man's mind, the Negro is inferior, totally independent of rational proofs or disproofs. And he is inferior in a deep and mystical sense. *The "reality" of his inferiority is the white man's own indubitable sensing of it, and that feeling applies to every single Negro.* This is a manifestation of the most primitive form of religion. There is fear of the unknown in this feeling, which is "superstition" in the literal sense of this old word. Fear is only increased by the difficulties in expressing it in rational language and explaining it in such a way that it makes sense. So the Negro becomes a "contrast conception." He is "the opposite race" — an inner enemy, "antithesis of character and properties of the white man."

An American Dilemma 1944:Vol. 1, 100.

5 The Negroes' status in America is so precarious that they simply have to get the support of all possible allies in the white camp. . . The vicious circle keeping Negroes down is so perfected by such interlocking caste controls that the Negroes must attempt to move the whole system by attacking as many points as possible.

An American Dilemma 1944:Vol. 2, 794.

6 The treatment of the Negro is America's greatest and most conspicuous scandal.

An American Dilemma 1944:Vol. 2, 1020.

7 To find the practical formulas for [the] never-ending reconstruction of society is the supreme task of social science. The world catastrophe places tremendous difficulties in our way and may shake our confidence to the depths. Yet we have today in social science a greater trust in the improvability of man and society than we have ever had since the Enlightenment.

An American Dilemma 1944:Vol. 2, 1024. → The concluding paragraph of the text.

8 The social sciences have all received their impetus much more from the urge to improve society than from simple curiosity about its working. Social policy has been primary, social theory secondary.

The Relation between Social Theory and Social Policy 1953:210.

9 The facts about unemployment and its immediate causes are well known in America, owing to its excellent statistical reporting. . .

Less often observed and commented upon is the tendency of the changes under way to trap an "underclass" of unemployed and, gradually, unemployable persons and families of the bottom of a society in which, for the majority of people above that level, the increasingly democratic structure of the educational system creates more and more liberty — real liberty — and equality of opportunity, at least over the course of two generations.

Challenge to Affluence (1962) 1963:40. → This appears to be the first published use of the term "underclass" in this sense. In *Chartism* [(1839) 1904:122], Carlyle mentions the "under classes," presumably referring to the working classes as well as those beneath them.

10 Students in the field of social science have imbibed the ethos of truth-seeking so thoroughly that they often appear particularly happy when they arrive at conclusions different from what they had expected or assumed from the start. By increasing true knowledge and purging opportunistic, false beliefs in this way, social science lays the groundwork for an ever more effective education: making people's beliefs more rational, forcing valuations out in the open, and making it more difficult to retain valuations on the lower level opposing those on the higher level.

Objectivity in Social Research 1969:41.

N

Ernest Nagel 1901–1985
U.S. philosopher of science

1 It is the desire for explanations that are at once systematic and controllable by factual evidence that generates science; and it is the organization and classification of knowledge on the basis of explanatory principles that is the distinctive goal of the sciences.

The Structure of Science 1961:4.

2 The undeniable difficulties that stand in the way of obtaining reliable knowledge of human affairs because of the fact that social scientists differ in their value orientations are practical difficulties. The difficulties are not necessarily insuperable, for since by hypothesis it is not impossible to distinguish between fact and value, steps can be taken to identify a value bias when it occurs, and to minimize if not to eliminate completely its perturbing effects.

The Structure of Science 1961:489.

L. B. Namier 1888–1960
Polish-born British historian

1 One would expect people to remember the past and to imagine the future. But in fact, when discoursing or writing about history, they imagine it in terms of their own experience, and when trying to gauge the future they cite supposed analogies from the past: till, by a double process of repetition, they imagine the past and remember the future.

Symmetry and Repetition (1941) 1942:69–70.

2 States are not created or destroyed, and frontiers redrawn or obliterated, by argument and majority votes; nations are freed, united, or broken by blood and iron, and not by a generous application of liberty and tomato-sauce; violence is the instrument of national movement.

1848 (1946) 1964:36.

3 The crowning attainment of historical study is a historical sense — an intuitive understanding of how things do not happen (how they did happen is a matter of specific knowledge).

History 1952:4.

4 The discussion whether history is an art or a science seems futile: it is like medical diagnosis; a great deal of previous experience and knowledge, and the scientific approach of the trained mind, are required, yet the final conclusions (to be re-examined in the light of evidence) are intuitive: an art. The great historian is like the great artist or doctor: after he has done his work, others should not be able to practise within its sphere in the terms of the preceding era.

History 1952:8–9.

Napoleon I 1769–1821
[Napoleon Bonaparte]
Corsican-born French general and emperor

1 What do they want from fate in our age? Politics is fate.

Quoted in J. Christopher Herold, *The Mind of Napoleon* (1955:149). → From a 1808 conversation with Goethe, whose report, written in German, was that Napoleon had said *"Die Politik ist das Schicksal."* For Freud's famous paraphrase, *"Die Anatomie ist das Schicksal* [Anatomy is destiny]," see FREUD:20.

Franz Neumann 1900–1954
German-born U.S. political scientist

1 Sociology is concerned with description of the factual; political theory is concerned with the truth. The truth of political theory is political freedom. From this follows one basic postulate: Since no political system can realize political freedom fully, political theory must by necessity be critical. It cannot justify and legitimize a concrete political system; it must be critical of it. A conformist political theory is no theory.

The Concept of Political Freedom (1953) 1957:162.

Sigmund Neumann 1904–1962
German-born U.S. political scientist

1 Mob psychology, when it seizes a whole nation, destroys the web of its complex social structure. Like the individual differentiations of its members, so the innumerable associations of the living community are melted into one gray mass. This process of "massification" — the dissolution of free organizations, the flattening of the social pyramid — in a way preceded the rise of modern dictators. They were the product of this disintegration of society which in turn became the basis of their established rule.

Permanent Revolution 1942:115.

Otto Neurath 1882–1945
Austrian philosopher and sociologist

1 That we always have to do with a whole network of concepts and not with concepts that can be isolated, puts any thinker into the difficult position of having unceasing regard for the whole mass of concepts that he cannot even survey all at once, and to let the new grow out of the old. . . We are like sailors who on the open sea must reconstruct their ship but are never able to start afresh from the bottom. Where a beam is taken away a new one must at once be put there, and for this the rest of the ship is used as support. In this way, by using the old beams and driftwood, the ship can be shaped entirely anew, but only by gradual reconstruction.

Anti-Spengler (1921) 1973:198–199. → See PUTNAM:1.

Allan Nevins 1890–1971
U.S. historian

1 We [should] have some organization which made a systematic attempt to obtain, from the lips and papers of living Americans who have led significant lives, a fuller record of their participation in the political, economic, and cultural life of the last sixty years.

The Gateway to History (1938) 1962:8. → This idea led Nevins to establish the Columbia University Oral History project.

2 To arrive at an interpretation, the historian takes a considerable body of problems and events, and so arranges them as to illustrate some dominant idea. That is, he synthesizes his material about some concept which governs the whole of it; he utilizes a series of analyses, which at first may have seemed chaotic and jumbled, and produces a general conclusion which throws them into perspective. This is not anatomy, it is physiology. It breathes the spark of life into dead materials and makes them move as living bodies.

The Gateway to History (1938) 1962:262–263.

3 It is a law of history that whenever peaceful evolution fails to effect a needed set of changes, some revolutionary agency steps in and does so. Change and growth are so indispensable in human affairs that whenever an effort is made to erect an immovable dam, the force of the piling waters finally becomes absolutely irresistible.

Ordeal of the Union (1947) 1975:Vol. 1, 532.

Allen Newell 1927–1992
U.S. psychologist and computer scientist

1 The digital-computer field defined computers as machines that manipulated numbers. The great thing was, adherents said, that everything could be encoded into numbers, even instructions. In contrast, scientists in AI [artificial intelligence] saw computers as machines that manipulated symbols. The great thing was, they said, that everything could be encoded into symbols, even numbers.

Intellectual Issues in the History of Artificial Intelligence 1983:196.

Isaac Newton 1642–1727
British mathematician, astronomer, and physicist

1 If I have seen further it is by standing on ye sholders of Giants.

Letter to Robert Hooke, 5 February 1675/6. 1959:416. → The first known usage of this aphorism is that of Bernard of Chartres. Robert K. Merton's *On the Shoulders of Giants* (1965) traces its divagating history. See BERNARD OF CHARTRES:1.

2 I do not know what I may appear to the world, but to myself I seem to have been only like a boy playing on the seashore, and diverting myself in now and then finding a smoother pebble or a prettier shell than ordinary, whilst the great ocean of truth lay all undiscovered before me.

Attributed in David Brewster, *Memoirs of the Life, Writings, and Discoveries of Sir Isaac Newton* (1855) 1965:Vol. 2, 407.

Jerzy Neyman 1894–1981
Russian-born U.S. statistician

1 Whenever we attempt to test a hypothesis we naturally try to avoid errors in judging it. This seems to indicate the right way of proceeding: when choosing a test we should try to minimize the frequency of errors that may be committed in applying it.

Lectures and Conferences on Mathematical Statistics 1938:44.

Reinhold Niebuhr 1892–1971
U.S. theologian and social philosopher

1 Man's capacity for justice makes democracy possible; but man's inclination to injustice makes democracy necessary.

The Children of Light and the Children of Darkness 1944:xi.

Friedrich Wilhelm Nietzsche 1844–1900
German philosopher

1 In dreams we all resemble the savage.

Human All-Too-Human (1878) 1964:Part 1, 23.

2 Every tradition grows continually more venerable, the farther off lies its origin, the more this is lost sight of; the veneration paid it accumulates from generation to generation, the tradition at last becomes holy and excites awe; and thus in any case the morality of piety is a much older morality than that which requires un-egoistic actions.

Human All-Too-Human (1878) 1964:Part 1, 95.

3 God is dead; but given the way of men, there may still be caves for thousands of years in which his shadow will be shown. — And we — we still have to vanquish his shadow, too.

The Gay Science (1882) 1974:167. → This is the first occurrence of this formulation in Nietzsche's writings.

4 That which can in general be attained through punishment, in men and in animals, is an increase of fear, a heightening of prudence, mastery of the desires: thus punishment *tames* men, but it does not make them "better" — one might with more justice assert the opposite.

On the Genealogy of Morals (1887) 1968:519.

5 Liberal institutions straightway cease from being liberal, the moment they are soundly established: once this is attained no more grievous and more thorough enemies of freedom exist than liberal institutions.

The Twilight of the Idols (1889) 1911:94.

Florence Nightingale 1820–1910
British nursing educator and public health reformer

1 M. Quetelet gave me his *Physique Sociale* and his *Anthropometrie*. He said almost like Sir Isaac Newton: "These are only a few pebbles picked up on the vast seashore of the ocean to be explored. Let the explorations be carried out."

Letter to Francis Galton, 7 February 1891. 1924:418. → See NEWTON:2 and PEARSON:5.

Robert A. Nisbet 1913–
U.S. sociologist

1 The word [community] encompasses all forms of relationships which are characterized by a high degree of personal intimacy, emotional depth, moral commitment, social cohesion, and continuity in time. Community is founded on man conceived in his wholeness rather than in one or another of the roles, taken separately, that he may hold in a social order. It draws its psychological strength from levels of motivation deeper than those of mere volition or interest, and it achieves its fulfillment in a submergence of individual will that is not possible in unions of mere convenience or rational assent. Community is a fusion of feeling and thought, of tradition and commitment, of membership and volition. It may be found in, or be given symbolic expression by, locality, religion, nation, race, occupation, or crusade.

The Sociological Tradition 1966:47–48.

2 Rousseau is the first to justify absolute power in the name of virtue, equality, and freedom. Power is more than power: it is refuge from the inequities and uncertainties of ordinary society.

The Social Philosophers 1973:153.

3 A generally odious form of historiography today, called psychohistory, uses psychoanalytic recall at a distance, to discern Oedipal strivings and castration complexes in a Martin Luther or a Woodrow Wilson. Thus, it is said triumphantly, the assignment of cause is now scientific. Another form of history currently vying with psychohistory is quantitative history or cliometrics. The data, the facts all historians work with, are dug out in vast detail and given computer assimilation. The result, it is said solemnly, is the replacement of such vague words as *few* and *many* with 364 and 13,458, thus giving accuracy and within that accuracy the "true" story.

Historical Necessity 1982:160.

4 Herbert Spencer has often been smiled at for his resounding statement: "Progress is not an accident . . . but a beneficent necessity." Yet he was, in context, merely saying what Marx, Comte and Darwin, among many, were saying: that positivism, or socialism or higher corporeal and mental endowment, was necessary because each was the result of processes internal to and constitutive of the system.

The Making of Modern Society 1986:44. → See SPENCER:1.

Elisabeth Noelle-Neumann 1916–
German communications analyst

1 Restraint [on the part of opponents] made the view that was receiving vocal support appear to be stronger than it really was and the other view weaker. Observations made in one context spread to another and encouraged people either to proclaim their views or to swallow them and keep quiet until, in a spiraling process, the one view dominated the public scene and the other disappeared from public awareness as its adherents became mute. This is the process that can be called a "spiral of silence."

The Spiral of Silence (1980) 1984:5.

2 In attempting to avoid those who think differently from themselves, people lose their quasistatistical ability to assess correctly the views of their environment. The term "pluralistic ignorance," introduced by American sociology, could be applied to this ignorance of how "people" think. It is the condition known as polarization. Society splits; one can speak of divided public opinion. The distinguishing feature is that each camp greatly overestimates itself in what is called a "looking glass perception."

The Spiral of Silence (1980) 1984:124. → See KATZ AND ALLPORT:1.

John T. Noonan, Jr. 1926–
U.S. legal scholar

1 The users of any system — scientific, theological, legal — encounter points where their premises and their practices are inconsistent. These gaps in the system must be bridged or the system changed. To bridge the gaps, those who accept the system employ fictions. . . Fictions are a necessity of law.

Persons and Masks of the Law 1976:25.

William D. Nordhaus
See PAUL A. SAMUELSON AND WILLIAM D. NORDHAUS.

Dudley North 1641–1691
British financier and economist

1 The main spur to Trade, or rather to Industry and Ingenuity, is the exorbitant Appetites of Men, which they will take pains to gratifie, and so be disposed to work, when nothing else will incline them to it; for did Men content themselves with bare Necessaries, we should have a poor World.

Discourses upon Trade (1691) 1822:14.

O

Michael Oakeshott 1901–1990
British philosopher and political theorist

1 History is the historian's experience. It is "made" by nobody save the historian; to write history is the only way of making it.

Experience and Its Modes 1933:99.

2 If the historical past be knowable, it must belong to the present world of experience; if it be unknowable, history is worse than futile, it is impossible. The fact is, then, that the past in history varies with the present, rests upon the present, is the present.

Experience and Its Modes 1933:107.

3 To "fix" a text involves an interpretation; the text is the interpretation and the interpretation is the text.

Experience and Its Modes 1933:113.

4 The strict conception of cause, and all that it involves, when introduced into historical experience, instead of bringing light, brings darkness; instead of order, added chaos.

Experience and Its Modes 1933:132–133.

5 Politics, we know, is a second-rate form of human activity, neither an art nor a science, at once corrupting to the soul and fatiguing to the mind, the activity either of those who cannot live without the illusion of affairs or those so fearful of being ruled by others that they will pay away their lives to prevent it.

Introduction to Thomas Hobbes, *Leviathan* (1651) 1946:1xiv.

William of Ockham c. 1280–c. 1349
[William of Occam]
British philosopher

1 What can be accounted for by fewer assumptions is explained in vain by more.

Quoted in Ernest A. Moody, William of Ockham 1974:173. → Known as Ockham's Razor because of his frequent use of the dictum; there is no evidence that it was original with him. Various versions of the Latin "original" have been published.

William Fielding Ogburn 1886–1959
U.S. sociologist

1 We cannot have a science without measurement. And science will grow in the social studies in direct ratio to the use of measurement.

Bias, Psychoanalysis, and the Subjective in Relation to the Social Sciences 1922:74. → See KELVIN:1.

2 The thesis is that the various parts of modern culture are not changing at the same rate, some parts are changing much more rapidly than others; and that since there is a correlation and interdependence of parts, a rapid change in one part of our culture requires readjustments through other changes in the various correlated parts of culture.

Social Change, With Respect to Culture and Original Nature 1922:200–201. → The first statement of Ogburn's hypothesis of cultural lag.

3 There is in our social organizations an institutional inertia, and in our social philosophies a tradition of rigidity. Unless there is a speeding up of social invention or a slowing down of mechanical invention, grave maladjustments are certain to result.

Recent Social Trends in the United States 1933:Vol. 1, xxviii. → From "A Review of Findings. . . ." *Recent Social Trends* is the report of a massive survey of American life commissioned by President Herbert Hoover but not published until the early months of the Roosevelt Administration. Ogburn served as director of research.

C. K. Ogden 1889–1957
British psychologist and linguist
and
I. A. Richards 1893–1979
British literary critic

1 Words, as everyone now knows, "mean" nothing by themselves, although the belief that they did. . . was once

equally universal. It is only when a thinker makes use of them that they stand for anything, or, in one sense, have "meaning." They are instruments.

The Meaning of Meaning 1923:12–13.

Mancur Olson 1932–
U.S. economist

1 Unless the number of individuals in a group is quite small, or unless there is coercion or some other special device to make individuals act in their common interest, *rational, self-interested individuals will not act to achieve their common or group interests*. In other words, even if all of the individuals in a large group are rational and self-interested, and would gain if, as a group, they acted to achieve their common interest or objective, they will still not voluntarily act to achieve that common or group interest.

The Logic of Collective Action 1965:2. → See HARDIN:1.

2 Organizations for collective action have extraordinarily anti-social incentives; they engage in distributional struggles, even when the excess burden of such struggles is very great, rather than in production. They also will tend to make decisions slowly and thereby retard technological advance and adaptations to macroeconomic and monetary shocks. It follows that societies that have been through catastrophes that have destroyed organizations for collective action, such as Germany, Japan, and Italy, can be expected to enjoy "economic miracles."

Collective Action 1987:476.

J. Robert Oppenheimer 1904–1967
U.S. physicist

1 Despite the vision and the farseeing wisdom of our wartime heads of state, the physicists felt a peculiarly intimate responsibility for suggesting, for supporting, and in the end, in large measure, for achieving, the realization of atomic weapons. Nor can we forget that these weapons, as they were in fact used, dramatized so mercilessly the inhumanity and evil of modern war. In some sort of crude sense which no vulgarity, no humor, no over-statement can quite extinguish, the physicists have known sin; and this is a knowledge which they cannot lose.

Physics in the Contemporary World 1947:11.

Nicole Oresme d. 1382
French mathematician and economist

1 There are three ways in which profit may be made from money, without laying it out for its natural purpose; one is the art of the moneychanger, banking or exchange, another is usury, a third alteration of the coinage. The first way is contemptible, the second bad and the third worse.

A Treatise on the Origin, Nature, Law and Alterations of Money [*De moneta*] (c. 1373) 1956:27.

José Ortega y Gasset 1883–1955
Spanish philosopher

1 I do not deny that there may be other well-founded causes for the hatred which various classes feel toward politicians, but the *main one seems to me that politicians are symbols of the fact that every class must take every other class into account*.

Invertebrate Spain (1921) 1937:51.

2 The changes in vital sensibility which are decisive in history, appear under the form of the generation. A generation is not a handful of outstanding men, nor simply a mass of men; it resembles a new integration of the social body, with its select minority and its gross multitude, launched upon the orbit of existence with a pre-established vital trajectory. The generation is a dynamic compromise between mass and individual, and is the most important conception in history. It is, so to speak, the pivot responsible for the movements of historical evolution.

The Modern Theme (1923) 1961:14–15. → See MANNHEIM:1.

3 Liberalism — it is well to recall this to-day — is the supreme form of generosity; it is the right which the majority concedes to minorities and hence it is the noblest cry that has ever resounded in this planet. It announces the determination to share existence with the enemy; more than that, with an enemy which is weak.

The Revolt of the Masses (1930) 1957:76.

4 A revolution does not last more than fifteen years, the period which coincides with the flourishing of a generation.

The Revolt of the Masses (1930) 1957:93.

George Orwell 1903–1950
[Eric Blair]
British political novelist and journalist

1 For once Benjamin consented to break his rule, and he read out to her what was written on the wall. There was nothing there now except a single Commandment. It ran:

ALL ANIMALS ARE EQUAL
BUT SOME ANIMALS ARE MORE EQUAL
THAN OTHERS.

Animal Farm (1945) 1987:90.

2 Who controls the past. . . controls the future: who controls the present controls the past.

Nineteen Eighty-Four 1949:35. → A slogan of the Party as depicted in Orwell's dystopia.

3 [*O'Brien*]: There will be no loyalty, except loyalty toward the Party. There will be no love, except the love of Big Brother. There will be no laughter, except the laugh of triumph over a defeated enemy. There will be no art, no literature, no science. When we are omnipotent we shall have no more need of science. There will be no distinc-

tion between beauty and ugliness. There will be no curiosity, no enjoyment of the process of life. All competing pleasures will be destroyed. But always — do not forget this, Winston — always there will be the intoxication of power, constantly increasing and constantly growing subtler. Always, at every moment, there will be the thrill of victory, the sensation of trampling on an enemy who is helpless. If you want a picture of the future, imagine a boot stamping on a human face — forever.

Nineteen Eighty-Four 1949:270–271.

John Louis O'Sullivan 1813–1895

U.S. journalist and diplomat

1 The best government is that which governs least.

Introduction (1838) 1967:6. → This slogan, used in the Introduction to Volume 1, Number 1 of *The United States Magazine, and Democratic Review,* was also the magazine's epigraph. It has been attributed to both Thomas Jefferson and Thomas Paine; Henry David Thoreau began his essay on "Civil Disobedience," published in 1849, by quoting it as a motto that he could heartily accept; and Walter Lippmann noted in *A Preface to Politics* (1913:266) that "It is perfectly true that that government is best which governs least." See THOREAU:1.

P

Thomas Paine 1737–1809
British–U.S. political philosopher

1 Society in every state is a blessing, but government, even in its best state, is but a necessary evil; in its worst state an intolerable one; for when we suffer, or are exposed to the same miseries *by a government*, which we might expect in a country *without government*, our calamity is heightened by reflecting that we furnish the means by which we suffer. Government, like dress, is the badge of lost innocence; the palaces of kings are built upon the ruins of the bowers of paradise.

Common Sense (1776) 1942:1.

2 Every age and generation must be as free to act for itself *in all cases* as the ages and generations which preceded it. The vanity and presumption of governing beyond the grave is the most ridiculous and insolent of all tyrannies. Man has no property in man; neither has any generation a property in the generations which are to follow. . . I am contending for the rights of the *living*, and against their being willed away, and controuled and contracted for, by the manuscript assumed authority of the dead; and Mr. [Edmund] Burke is contending for the authority of the dead over the rights and freedom of the living.

The Rights of Man (1791–1792) 1958:12–13.

3 The idea of hereditary legislators is as inconsistent as that of hereditary judges, or hereditary juries; and as absurd as an hereditary mathematician, or an hereditary wise man; and as ridiculous as an hereditary poet-laureate.

The Rights of Man (1791–1792) 1958:62.

R.R. Palmer 1909–
U.S. historian

1 The two nouns, "democrat" and "aristocrat," were coinages of the period, unknown before the 1780's. No "democrats" fought in the American Revolution; and the Age of Aristocracy, as long as it was unchallenged, heard nothing of "aristocrats." Neither word was current in English before 1789; in France, *aristocrate* crops up in the reign of Louis XVI, *démocrate* not until 1789.

The Age of the Democratic Revolution: The Challenge 1959:15.

2 What had happened by 1800, even in countries where it was temporarily suppressed, was the assertion of "equality" as a prime social desideratum. It was an equality that meant a wider diffusion of liberty. That the assurance of some liberties meant the curtailment of others was well understood, so that, more on the continent of Europe than elsewhere, the democratic movement brought a consolidation of public authority, or of the state. It was not an equality that could long accept the surrender of liberty; the solution provided by Bonaparte could not prove to be durable. Nor was it an equality that repudiated the power of government; the world of Thomas Jefferson would also pass.

The Age of the Democratic Revolution: The Struggle 1964:572.

Vilfredo Pareto 1848–1923
Italian economist and sociologist

1 There is a mania on the part of mathematical economists to try and find reasons in support of protection! Cournot, Auspitz, Launhardt, and there are undoubtedly others I don't know. The science is thus going backwards; *it does not progress*. Regarding this argument, Smith, Mill, Ricardo, and Cairnes reason 100 times better *and with greater precision* than these modern economists.

Letter to Maffeo Pantaleoni, 5 January 1892. 1984:152. → Unpublished translation by Yole G. Sills.

2 Human behaviour reveals *uniformities* which constitute *natural laws*. If these uniformities did not exist, then there would be neither social science nor political economy, and even the study of history would largely be useless. In effect, if the future actions of men have nothing in common with their past actions, our knowledge of them, although possibly satisfying our curiosity by way of

an interesting story, would be entirely useless to us as a guide in life.

Cours d'économie politique (1896–1897) 1966:97.

3 Anarchism, which wishes to destroy all forms of tutelage, no more merits serious discussion than a fairy-tale for the nursery. Of course, if we set the imagination free of all restraint, we can certainly envisage a time when men will desire only what is truly advantageous to themselves, their nation and their species. But it is clear that men of this kind will be wholly different from men as we know them; there is no point, therefore, in occupying ourselves with them.

Cours d'économie politique (1896–1897) 1966:109.

4 Above, far above, the prejudices and passions of men soar the laws of nature. Eternal and immutable, they are the expression of the creative power; they represent what is, what must be, what otherwise could not be. Man can come to understand them: he is incapable of changing them. From the infinitely great down to the infinitely small, all things are subject to them. The sun and the planets follow the laws discovered by Newton and Laplace, just as the atoms in their combinations follow the laws of chemistry, as living creatures follow the laws of biology. It is only the imperfections of the human mind which multiply the divisions of the sciences, separating astronomy from physics or chemistry, the natural sciences from the social sciences. In essence, science is one. It is none other than the truth.

Cours d'économie politique (1896–1897) 1966:122.

5 Some authors assume that if one doubles all the factors in production, the product will also double. This may in some cases be approximately true, but not rigorously and in general. . . If one has, for example, a transportation business in Paris, it would be necessary to assume another business and another Paris. Or since this other Paris does not exist, one should consider two businesses in Paris itself. Consequently, one cannot admit that the quantity of factors in production having doubled, the product would also double.

Cours d'économie politique (1896–1897) 1964:Vol. 2, 82–83. → Unpublished translation by Yole G. Sills.

6 Free competition of entrepreneurs yields the same values for the production coefficients as would be obtained by determining them by the condition that commodity outputs should be chosen in such a way that, for some appropriate distribution, maximum ophelimity would be achieved for each individual in society.

Cours d'économie politique 1896–1897:Vol. 2, 94.

7 A sign which almost invariably presages the decadence of an aristocracy is the intrusion of humanitarian feelings and of affected sentimentalising which render the aristocracy incapable of defending its position. Violence, we should note, is not to be confused with force. Often enough one observes cases in which individuals and classes which have lost the force to maintain themselves in power make themselves more and more hated because of their outbursts of random violence. The strong man strikes only when it is absolutely necessary, and then nothing stops him. Trajan was strong, not violent: Caligula was violent, not strong.

Les systèmes socialistes (1902–1903) 1966:135.

8 Human actions display certain uniformities. . . and it is thanks to this property alone that they can be made the subject of a scientific study. These uniformities also have another name. They are called *laws*.

Whoever studies a social science, whoever asserts anything at all on the subject of the effects of such and such an economic, political or social measure, implicitly admits the existence of these uniformities; otherwise his study would not have any subject matter, and there would be no basis for his statements. If there were no uniformities, the budget of a state, of a commune, or even of an industrial company could not be drawn up even approximately.

Manual of Political Economy (1906) 1971:3–4.

9 The great error of the present age is of believing that men can be governed by pure reasoning, without resort to force. Yet force is the foundation of all social organisation.

Le manuel d'économie politique (1906) 1966:157.

10 Logical interpretations of non-logical conduct become in their turn causes of logical conduct and sometimes even of non-logical conduct; and they have to be reckoned with in determining the social equilibrium. From that standpoint, the interpretations of plain people are generally of greater importance than the interpretations of scholars. As regards the social equilibrium, it is of far greater moment to know what the plain man understands by "virtue" than to know what philosophers think about it.

The Mind and Society (1916) 1935:Vol. 1, par. 260, 177.

11 [Various] considerations tend to keep thinkers from the field of non-logical conduct and carry them over into the field of the logical. Most scholars are not satisfied with discovering what is. They are anxious to know, and even more anxious to explain to others, what *ought* to be. In that sort of research, logic reigns supreme; and so the moment they catch sight of conduct that is non-logical, instead of going ahead along that road they turn aside, often seem to forget its existence, at any rate generally ignore it, and beat the well-worn path that leads to logical conduct.

The Mind and Society (1916) 1935:Vol. 1, par. 264, 179.

12 Let us assume that in every branch of human activity each individual is given an index which stands as a sign of his capacity, very much the way grades are given in the various subjects in examinations in school. The highest type of lawyer, for instance, will be given 10. The man who does not get a client will be given 1 — reserving zero for the man who is an out-and-out idiot. To the man who has made his millions — honestly or dishonestly as the

case may be — we will give 10. To the man who has earned his thousands we will give 6; to such as just manage to keep out of the poor-house, 1, keeping zero for those who get in. . . So let us make a class of the people who have the highest indices in their branch of activity, and to that class give the name of *élite*.

The Mind and Society (1916) 1935: Vol. 3, pars. 2057,2031: 1422–1423.

13 The manner in which the various groups in a population intermix has to be considered. In moving from one group to another an individual generally brings with him certain inclinations, sentiments, attitudes, that he has acquired in the group from which he comes, and that circumstance cannot be ignored.

To this mixing, in the particular case in which only two groups, the *élite* and the non-*élite*, are envisaged, the term "circulation of élites" has been applied — in French, *circulation des élites*.

The Mind and Society (1916) 1935:Vol. 3, pars. 2041–2042; 1425–1426.

14 Aristocracies do not last. Whatever the causes, it is an incontestable fact that after a certain length of time they pass away. History is a graveyard of aristocracies.

The Mind and Society (1916) 1935:Vol. 3, par. 2053, 1430.

15 If we examine the many theories about constitutional and parliamentary states that have been expounded in the last century, we find that none is valid for the present: They go in one way and the facts go in another. For example, if we reread John Stuart Mill's *Representative Government* and his *On Liberty* — works which were celebrated at one time — we are taken into the intellectual atmosphere of a society that has nothing in common with contemporary society and that seems quite unreal.

Who cares any more about the balance of power? Or the proper balance between the rights of the state and the rights of the individual? Is the highly-revered "ethical state" still with us? The Hegelian state is a superb concept which has survived for the use and benefit of poetic and metaphysical sociologists; workers prefer the tangible benefits of higher wages, progressive taxation, and more leisure. At the same time, they enjoy myths of their own: the myth of a saintly proletariat, the myth of an inherently evil capitalistic system, the myth of an ideal government under councils of workers and soldiers, and so on.

Trasformazioni della democrazia (1921) 1946:35–36. → Unpublished translation by Yole G. Sills.

Robert E. Park 1864–1944

U.S. sociologist

1 A person is simply an individual who has somewhere, in some society, social status; but status turns out finally to be a matter of distance — social distance. . . It is because social relations are so frequently and so inevitably correlated with spatial relations; because physical distances so frequently are, or seem to be, the indexes of social distances, that statistics have any significance whatever for sociology.

The Urban Community as a Spatial Pattern and a Moral Order (1925) 1952:177. → Park's concept "social distance" was adopted and developed by Emory S. Bogardus in "A Social Distance Scale" (1933), *Sociology and Social Research* 17:265–271.

2 Everyone is always and everywhere, more or less consciously, playing a rôle. . . It is in these rôles that we know each other; it is in these rôles that we know ourselves.

Behind Our Masks 1926:137.

3 In human society every act of every individual tends to become a gesture, since what one does is always an indication of what one intends to do. The consequence is that the individual in society lives a more or less public existence, in which all his acts are anticipated, checked, inhibited, or modified by the gestures and the intentions of his fellows. It is in this social conflict, in which every individual lives more or less in the mind of every other individual, that human nature and the individual may acquire their most characteristic and human traits.

Human Nature and Collective Behavior (1926) 1927:738.

4 One of the consequences of migration is to create a situation in which the same individual — who may or may not be a mixed blood — finds himself striving to live in two diverse cultural groups. The effect is to produce an unstable character — a personality type with characteristic forms of behavior. This is the "marginal man." It is in the mind of the marginal man that the conflicting cultures meet and fuse. It is, therefore, in the mind of the marginal man that the process of civilization is visibly going on, and it is in the mind of the marginal man that the process of civilization may best be studied.

Human Migration and the Marginal Man 1928:881. → Park talked to Everett V. Stonequist in 1928 about "the marginal man," as Stonequist reports in his 1937 book. See STONEQUIST:1.

5 In the city all the secret ambitions and all the suppressed desires find somewhere an expression. The city magnifies, spreads out, and advertises human nature in all its various manifestations. It is this that makes the city interesting, even fascinating. It is this, however, that makes it of all places the one in which to discover the secrets of human hearts, and to study human nature and society.

The City as a Social Laboratory 1929:19.

6 Race consciousness. . . is to be regarded as a phenomenon, like class or caste consciousness, that enforces social distances. Race relations, in this sense, are not so much the relations that exist between individuals of different races as between individuals conscious of these differences.

The Nature of Race Relations (1939) 1974:81.

Robert E. Park 1864–1944
and
Ernest W. Burgess 1886–1966
U.S. sociologists

1 The most important facts that sociologists have to deal with are opinions (attitudes and sentiments), but until students learn to deal with opinions as the biologists deal with organisms, that is, to dissect them — reduce them to their component elements, describe them, and define the situation (environment) to which they are a response — we must not expect very great progress in sociological science.

Introduction to the Science of Sociology (1921) 1924:vi.

2 The city . . . is something more than a congeries of individual men and of social conveniences — streets, buildings, electric lights, tramways, and telephones, etc.; something more, also, than a mere constellation of institutions and administrative devices — courts, hospitals, schools, police, and civil functionaries of various sorts. The city is, rather, a state of mind, a body of customs and traditions, and of the organized attitudes and sentiments that inhere in these customs and are transmitted with this tradition. The city is not, in other words, merely a physical mechanism and an artificial construction. It is involved in the vital processes of the people who compose it; it is a product of nature, and particularly of human nature.

The City 1925:1.

3 The city is rooted in the habits and customs of the people who inhabit it. The consequence is that the city possesses a moral as well as a physical organization, and these two mutually interact in characteristic ways to mold and modify one another. It is the structure of the city which first impresses us by its visible vastness and complexity. But this structure has its basis, nevertheless, in human nature, of which it is an expression. On the other hand, this vast organization which has arisen in response to the needs of its inhabitants, once formed, imposes itself upon them as a crude external fact, and forms them, in turn, in accordance with the design and interests which it incorporates. Structure and tradition are but different aspects of a single cultural complex.

The City 1925:4.

C. Northcote Parkinson 1909–
British historian

1 Work expands so as to fill the time available for its completion.

Parkinson's Law 1957:2.

2 Parkinson's Law is a purely scientific discovery, inapplicable except in theory to the politics of the day. It is not the business of the botanist to eradicate the weeds. Enough for him if he can tell us just how fast they grow.

Parkinson's Law 1957:13.

Elsie Clews Parsons 1875–1941
U.S. anthropologist

1 Women try hard to live down to what is expected of them. In fact deviations from these expectations are not tolerated by either sex. Is not an "unwomanly" woman publicly more disesteemed and berated than a fickle or tricky or petty woman, than an ignoramus, a coward, or a chatterbox?

The Old-Fashioned Woman 1913:210.

2 Even the woman movement we have called feminism has not succeeded by and large in giving women any control over men. It has only changed the distribution of women along the two stated lines of control by men, removing vast numbers of women from the class supported by men to the class working for them.

Social Rule 1916:53–54.

3 To be declassified is very painful to most persons and so the charge of unwomanliness has ever been a kind of whip against the would-be woman rebel. Not until she fully understands how arbitrary it is and how guileful, unwittingly guileful of course, will she cease to fear its crack . . . The *new woman* means the woman not yet classified, perhaps not classifiable, the woman *new* not only to men, but to herself.

Social Rule 1916:55.

Talcott Parsons 1902–1979
U.S. sociologist

1 A scientifically unimportant discovery is one which, however true and however interesting for other reasons, has no consequences for a system of theory with which scientists in that field are concerned.

The Structure of Social Action (1937) 1968:Vol. 1, 7.

2 All empirically verifiable knowledge — even the common-sense knowledge of everyday life — involves implicitly, if not explicitly, systematic theory. . . The importance of this statement lies in the fact that certain persons who write on social subjects vehemently deny it. They say they state merely facts and let them "speak for themselves." But the fact a person denies that he is theorizing is no reason for taking him at his word and failing to investigate what implicit theory is involved in his statements.

The Structure of Social Action (1937) 1968:Vol. 1, 10.
→ See ALFRED MARSHALL:2.

3 The central fact — a fact beyond all question — is that in certain aspects and to certain degrees, under certain conditions, human action is rational. That is, men adapt themselves to the conditions in which they are placed and adapt means to their ends in such a way as to approach the most efficient manner of achieving these ends. And the relations of these means and conditions to the achievement of their ends are "known" to be intrinsically verifiable by the methods of empirical science.

The Structure of Social Action (1937) 1968:Vol. 1, 19.

4 A fact is not itself a phenomenon at all, but a proposition *about* one or more phenomena.

The Structure of Social Action (1937) 1968:Vol. 1, 41.

5 The abstractness of some of the concepts which are employed in the theory of action consists precisely in the fact that they are descriptive not of the actual observable state of affairs of overt action, but of norms toward which it may be regarded as being oriented. . . The only reason for admitting such concepts to a scientific theory is that they are in fact descriptive of an empirical phenomenon, namely the state of mind of the actor. They exist in this state of mind, but not in the actor's "external world." It is, indeed, this circumstance which necessitates resort, on the part of the theory of action, to the subjective point of view.

The Structure of Social Action (1937) 1968:Vol. 1, 295.

6 It is a fact that social existence depends to a large extent on a moral consensus of its members and that the penalty of its too radical breakdown is social extinction. This fact is one which the type of liberal whose theoretical background is essentially utilitarian is all too apt to ignore — with unfortunate practical as well as theoretical consequences. Thus Durkheim is able to offer what this type of liberal theorist entirely lacks — an explanation of why increasing diversity of ethical opinion should be associated with social instability, *anomie*, rather than, as such liberals would tend to assume, an increase of happiness.

The Structure of Social Action (1937) 1968:Vol. 1, 395–396.

7 Ritual actions are not. . . either simply irrational, or pseudo rational, based on prescientific erroneous knowledge, but are of a different character altogether and as such not to be measured by the standards of intrinsic rationality at all.

The Structure of Social Action (1937) 1968:Vol. 1, 431.

8 Sociology should. . .be thought of as a science of action— of the ultimate common value element *in its relations* to the other elements of action.

The Structure of Social Action (1937) 1968:Vol. 1, 440.

9 A generalized social system is a conceptual scheme, not an empirical phenomenon. It is a logically integrated system of generalized concepts of empirical reference in terms of which an indefinite number of concretely differing empirical systems can be described and analyzed.

An Analytical Approach to the Theory of Social Stratification (1940) 1964:71.

10 Psychologists as a group have not treated the individual as a unit *in* a functioning social system, but rather as the concrete human being who was then conceived as proceeding to form social systems. They have thus not adequately taken account of the peculiar sense in which their categories are abstract.

Introduction to Max Weber, *The Theory of Social and Economic Organization* (1922) 1947:27. → From the 1947 edition, translated and edited by Parsons.

11 Veblen was a highly unsophisticated person who demonstrates the typical reaction of a disillusioned idealist in his scientific work. Weber, who it should be remembered was a close contemporary, was on a totally different level of scientific and cultural sophistication. The fact that a Veblen rather than a Weber gathers a school of ardent disciples around him bears witness to the great importance of factors other than the sheer weight of evidence and analysis in the formation of schools of social thought.

Introduction to Max Weber, *The Theory of Social and Economic Organization* (1922) 1947:40n.

12 Reduced to the simplest possible terms. . . a social system consists in a plurality of individual actors interacting with each other in a situation which has at least a physical or environmental aspect, actors who are motivated in terms of a tendency to the "optimization of gratification" and whose relation to their situations, including each other, is defined and mediated in terms of a system of culturally structured and shared symbols.

The Social System 1951:5–6.

Blaise Pascal 1623–1662
French mathematician, physicist, and philosopher

1 The most unreasonable things in the world become most reasonable, because of the unruliness of men. What is less reasonable than to choose the eldest son of a queen to rule a State? We do not choose as captain of a ship the passenger who is of the best family.

This law would be absurd and unjust; but because men are so themselves, and always will be so, it becomes reasonable and just. For whom will men choose, as the most virtuous and able? We at once come to blows, as each claims to be the most virtuous and able. Let us then attach this quality to something indisputable. This is the king's eldest son. That is clear, and there is no dispute. Reason can do no better, for civil war is the greatest of evils.

Pensées (1670) 1958:320, 90.

2 Man is but a reed, the most feeble thing in nature; but he is a thinking reed.

Pensées (1670) 1958:347, 97.

Jean-Claude Passeron

See Pierre Bourdieu and Jean-Claude Passeron.

Louis Pasteur 1822–1895
French chemist and bacteriologist

1 In the fields of observation, chance only favors the prepared mind.

Discours [at Douai] (1854) 1939:131. → Unpublished translation by Yole G. Sills.

Don Patinkin 1922–
U.S. and Israeli economist

1 There are many who see Keynes' trilogy as The Saga of Man's Struggle for Freedom from the Quantity Theory —

and I think there can be little doubt that Keynes himself so saw it.

Keynes' Monetary Thought 1976:18.

2 In studying a man's basic writings we must distinguish between that which was fully integrated into his conceptual framework and that which was not; between the systematic component of his thinking and the random component; between, if you wish, the "signal" — or what I have called the "central message" — the writer wished to convey and the "noise."

Anticipations of the General Theory? 1982:16.

Ivan Petrovich Pavlov 1849–1936
Russian physiologist and psychologist

1 Mankind will possess incalculable advantages and extraordinary control over human behavior when the scientific investigator will be able to subject his fellow men to the same external analysis he would employ for any natural object, and when the human mind will contemplate itself not from within but from without.

Scientific Study of the So-Called Psychical Processes in the Higher Animals (1906) 1967:95.

2 One can truly say that the irresistible progress of natural science since the time of Galileo has made its first halt before the study of the higher parts of the brain, the organ of the most complicated relations of the animal to the external world. And it seems, and not without reason, that now is the really critical moment for natural science; for the brain, in its highest complexity — the human brain — which created and creates natural science, itself becomes the object of this science.

Natural Science and the Brain (1909) 1967:120.

3 Nervous activity consists in general of the phenomena of excitation and inhibition. . . I shall not commit a great error if I liken these two phenomena to positive and negative electricity.

Some Fundamental Laws of the Work of the Cerebral Hemispheres (1910–1911) 1967:156.

4 The science of the conditioned reflexes. . . has to do always with only objective facts — facts existing in time and space.

Some Principles of the Activity of Central Nervous System as Shown from the Study of Conditioned Reflexes (1911–1912) 1967:192.

5 Definite, constant, and inborn reactions of the higher animals to certain influences of the external world, reactions taking place through the agency of the nervous system, have for a long time been the object of strict physiological investigation, and have been named reflexes. We call these unconditioned reflexes.

The Objective Study of the Highest Nervous Activity of Animals (1913) 1967:214.

6 I am convinced that an important stage of human thought will have been reached when the physiological and the psychological, the objective and the subjective, are actually united, when the tormenting conflicts or contradictions between my consciousness and my body will have been factually resolved or discarded.

Physiology of the Higher Nervous Activity (1932) 1941:93–94.

7 The nervous system is the most complex and delicate instrument on our planet, by means of which relations, connections are established between the numerous parts of the organism, as well as between the organism, as a highly complex system, and the innumerable, external influences. If the closing and opening of electric current is now regarded as an ordinary technical device, why should there be any objection to the idea that the same principle acts in this wonderful instrument? On this basis the *constant connection between the external agent and the response of the organism, which it evokes, can be rightly called an unconditioned reflex, and the temporary connection — a conditioned reflex.*

The Conditioned Reflex (1935) 1957:249.

8 As you know, I am an experimenter from head to foot. . . Our government is also an experimenter, only on an incomparably higher plane. I passionately desire to live in order to see the victorious completion of this historical social experiment.

Quoted in W. Horsley Gantt, Introduction to volume 2 of Ivan Petrovich Pavlov, *Lectures on Conditioned Reflexes* (1923) 1941:33. → From a 1935 address to a meeting of physiologists at the Kremlin.

Karl Pearson 1857–1936
British statistician

1 One of the strongest factors of social stability is the inertness, nay, rather active hostility, with which human societies receive all new ideas.

The Grammar of Science 1892:2.

2 "Endow scientific research and we shall know the truth, when and where it is possible to ascertain it"; but the counterblast is at hand: "To endow research is merely to encourage the research for endowment; the true men of science will not be held back by poverty, and if science is of use to us, it will pay for itself." Such are but a few samples of the conflict of opinion which we find raging around us.

The Grammar of Science 1892:5.

3 It may appear. . . that the goddess Chance is only the personification of ignorance — of *inscientia* — and that accurate reasoning cannot, as it certainly does not, play a part in her worship. But for science chance is identical with knowledge, not with ignorance, — with partial knowledge, it is true, but none the less with knowledge.

The Scientific Aspect of Monte Carlo Roulette (1894) 1897:Vol. 1, 43.

4 I am not a member of the Sociological Society, and I must confess myself sceptical as to its power to do effective

work. Frankly, I do not believe in groups of men and women who have each and all their alloted daily task creating a new branch of science. I believe it must be done by some one man who by force of knowledge, of method and of enthusiasm hews out, in rough outline it may be, but decisively, a new block and creates a school to carve out its details. I think you will find on inquiry that this is the history of each great branch of science. The initiative has been given by some one great thinker, a Descartes, a Newton, a Virchow, a Darwin or a Pasteur. A Sociological Society until we have found a great sociologist is a herd without its leader — there is no authority to set bounds to your science or to prescribe its functions.

Discussion of a paper on eugenics 1905:52.

5 [Florence Nightingale] held that the universe — including human communities — was evolving in accordance with a divine plan; that it was man's business to endeavour to understand this plan and guide his actions in sympathy with it. But to understand God's thoughts, she held we must study statistics, for these are the measure of his purpose. Thus the study of statistics was for her a religious duty.

The Life, Letters and Labours of Francis Galton 1924:Vol. 2, 415.

Charles Sanders Peirce 1839–1914

U.S. philosopher of science

1 That is, indeed, the precise and only use or significance of these fractions termed probabilities: they give security in the long run.

Review of John Venn's *The Logic of Chance* (1867) 1966:5.

2 Every work of science great enough to be well remembered for a few generations affords some exemplification of the defective state of the art of reasoning of the time when it was written; and each chief step in science has been a lesson in logic.

The Fixation of Belief (1877) 1960:225.

3 It is a common observation that a science first begins to be exact when it is quantitatively treated. What are called the exact sciences are no others than the mathematical ones.

The Doctrine of Chances (1878) 1923:61.

4 The rudest numerical scales, such as that by which the mineralogists distinguish different degrees of hardness, are found useful. The mere counting of pistils and stamens sufficed to bring botany out of total chaos into some kind of form. It is not, however, so much from *counting* as from *measuring*, not so much from the conception of number as from that of continuous quantity, that the advantage of mathematical treatment comes. Number, after all, only serves to pin us down to a precision in our thoughts which, however beneficial, can seldom lead to lofty conceptions, and frequently descends to pettiness.

The Doctrine of Chances (1878) 1923:61–62.

5 [My] word "pragmatism" has gained general recognition in a generalized sense that seems to argue power of growth and vitality. The famed psychologist, James, first took it up, seeing that his "radical empiricism" substantially answered to the writer's definition of pragmatism. . . The writer, finding his bantling "pragmatism" so promoted, feels that it is time to kiss his child good-by and relinquish it to its higher destiny; while to serve the precise purpose of expressing the original definition, he begs to announce the birth of the word "pragmaticism," which is ugly enough to be safe from kidnappers.

What Pragmatism Is (1905) 1965:276–277. → See JAMES:25.

6 When I gave the doctrine of JAMES pragmatism the name it bears, — and a doctrine of vital significance it is, — I derived the name by which I christened it from πράγμα— "behaviour,"—in order that it should be understood that the doctrine is that the only real significance of a general term lies in the general behaviour which it implies.

Unpublished letter to Howes Norris, May 1912. → Quoted in Carolyn Eisele, Peirce's Pragmaticism 1987:95.

S. J. Perelman 1904–1979

U.S. writer and critic

1 There is nothing like a good, painstaking survey full of decimal points and guarded generalizations to put a glaze like a Sung vase on your eyeball.

Keep It Crisp 1946:173.

William Petersen 1912–

U.S. demographer and sociologist

1 Most . . . analysts of migration. . . [imply] that man is everywhere sedentary, remaining fixed until he is impelled to move by some force. Like most psychological universals, this one can be matched by its opposite: man migrates because of wanderlust. And like all such universals, these cannot explain differential behavior: if all men are sedentary (or migratory) "by nature," why do some migrate and some not? If a simplistic metaphor is used, it should be at least as complex as its mechanical analogue, which includes not only the concept of forces but also that of inertia.

A General Typology of Migration (1958) 1964:274.

William Petty 1623–1687

British economist

1 When a man giveth out his money upon condition that he may not demand it back until a certain time to come. . . he certainly may take a compensation for this inconvenience . . . And this allowance is what we commonly call Usury.

A Treatise of Taxes and Contributions (1662) 1963:47.

2 Labour is the Father and active principle of Wealth, as Lands are the Mother.

A Treatise of Taxes and Contributions (1662) 1963:68.

3 The Gain which is made by *Manufactures,* will be greater, as the Manufacture it self is greater and better. For in so vast a City *Manufactures* will beget one another, and each *Manufacture* will be divided into as many parts as possible, whereby the Work of each *Artisan* will be simple and easie; As for Example. In the making of a *Watch,* If one Man shall make the *Wheels,* another the *Spring,* another shall Engrave the *Dial-plate,* and another shall make the *Cases,* then the *Watch* will be better and cheaper, than if the whole Work be put upon any one Man.

Another Essay in Political Arithmetick Concerning the Growth of the City of London, 1682 (1683) 1963:473. → See ADAM SMITH:4.

4 I have taken the course (as a Specimen of the Political Arithmetick I have longed aimed at) to express my self in Terms of *Number, Weight,* or *Measure*; to use only Arguments of Sense, and to consider only such Causes, as have visible Foundations in Nature; leaving those that depend upon the mutable Minds, Opinions, Appetites, and Passions of particular Men, to the Consideration of others.

Political Arithmetick (1690) 1963:244. → Written c. 1676; first authorized edition published in 1690 by Petty's son.

5 Money is but the Fat of the Body-politick, whereof too much doth as often hinder its Agility, as too little makes it sick. . . As Fat lubricates the motion of the Muscles, feeds in want of Victuals, fills up uneven Cavities, and beautifies the Body, so doth Money in the State quicken its Action, feeds from abroad in the time of Dearth at Home; even accounts by reason of it's divisibility, and beautifies the whole, altho more especially the particular persons that have it in plenty.

Verbum sapienti (1691) 1963:113. → Written in 1665; first published in 1691.

Jean Piaget 1896–1980
Swiss psychologist

1 The child has less verbal continence simply because he does not know what it is to keep a thing to himself. Although he talks almost incessantly to his neighbours, he rarely places himself at their point of view. He speaks to them for the most part as if he were alone, and as if he were thinking aloud. He speaks, therefore, in a language which disregards the precise shade of meaning in things and ignores the particular angle from which they are viewed, and which above all is always making assertions, even in argument, instead of justifying them.

The Language and Thought of the Child (1923) 1969:60.

2 Ego-centrism, while it does not exactly explain the child's incapacity for true causal explanation and logical justification, is nevertheless closely connected with it. And we can understand how, as a result of this, the child's mind is always hovering between these two convergent paths, and is also equally removed from both.

The Language and Thought of the Child (1923) 1969:240.

3 The child's first year of life is unfortunately still an abyss of mysteries for the child. If only we could know what was going on in a baby's mind while observing him in action, we could certainly understand everything there is to psychology.

La première année de l'enfant 1927:97. → Unpublished translation by Howard E. Gruber and Jacques Voneche.

4 Society is nothing but a series (or rather many intersecting series) of generations, each exercising pressure upon the one which follows it, and Auguste Comte was right in pointing to this action of one generation upon the other as the most important phenomenon of sociology.

The Moral Judgment of the Child (1932) 1965:336.

5 Logic is the morality of thought just as morality is the logic of action.

The Moral Judgment of the Child (1932) 1965:398.

6 Chance, . . . in the accommodation peculiar to sensorimotor intelligence, plays the same role as in scientific discovery. It is only useful to the genius and its revelations remain meaningless to the unskilled.

The Origins of Intelligence in Children (1936) 1952:303.

7 To understand how the budding intelligence constructs the external world, we must first ask whether the child, in its first months of life, conceives and perceives things as we do, as objects that have substance, that are permanent and of constant dimensions.

The Construction of Reality in the Child (1937) 1954:3.

8 Every psychological explanation comes sooner or later to lean either on biology or on logic (or on sociology, but this in turn leads to the same alternatives).

The Psychology of Intelligence (1947) 1950:3.

9 I have never, either implicitly or explicitly, expressed the view that knowledge is a copy of reality because such a view is contrary to my position with respect to the nature of intelligence. My whole conception of intellectual operations is based on the premise that to know or to understand is to transform reality and to assimilate it to schemes of transformation.

Response to Brian Sutton-Smith 1966:111.

10 A structure is a system of transformations. Inasmuch as it is a system and not a mere collection of elements and their properties, these transformations involve laws: the structure is preserved or enriched by the interplay of its transformation laws, which never yield results external to the system nor employ elements that are external to it. In

short, the notion of structure is composed of three key ideas: the idea of wholeness, the idea of transformation, and the idea of self-regulation.

Structuralism (1968) 1977:768.

11 In order to know objects, the subject must act upon them, and therefore transform them: he must displace, connect, combine, take apart, and reassemble them.

From the most elementary sensorimotor actions (such as pushing and pulling) to the most sophisticated intellectual operations, which are interiorized actions, carried out mentally (e.g., joining together, putting in order, putting into one-to-one correspondence), knowledge is constantly linked with actions or operations, that is, with *transformations*.

Piaget's Theory (1970) 1983:104.

12 Remember. . . that each time one prematurely teaches a child something he could have discovered for himself, that child is kept from inventing it and consequently from understanding it completely.

Piaget's Theory (1970) 1983:113.

Jean Piaget 1896–1980
Swiss psychologist
and
Alina Szeminska 1907–1986
Polish psychologist

1 Every notion, whether it be scientific or merely a matter of common sense, presupposes a set of principles of conservation, either explicit or implicit. It is a matter of common knowledge that in the field of the empirical sciences the introduction of the principle of inertia (conservation of rectilinear and uniform motion) made possible the development of modern physics. . . Conservation is a necessary condition for all rational activity.

The Child's Conception of Number (1941) 1952:3.

2 The child does not first acquire the notion of quantity and then attribute constancy to it; he discovers true quantification only when he is capable of constructing wholes that are preserved.

The Child's Conception of Number (1941) 1952:5.

Arthur Cecil Pigou 1877–1959
British economist

1 If it were not for the hope that a scientific study of men's social actions may lead, not necessarily directly or immediately, but at some time and in some way, to practical results in social improvement, not a few students of these actions would regard the time devoted to their study as time misspent. That is true of all social sciences, but especially of economics. For economics "is a study of mankind in the ordinary business of life"; and it is not in the ordinary business of life that mankind is most interesting or inspiring. One who desired knowledge of man apart from the fruits of knowledge would seek it in the history of religious enthusiasm, of martyrdom, or of love; he would not seek it in the market-place.

The Economics of Welfare (1920) 1978:4. → See ALFRED MARSHALL:3 for the origin of this famous definition.

2 Any transference of income from a relatively rich man to a relatively poor man of similar temperament, since it enables more intense wants to be satisfied at the expense of less intense wants, must increase the aggregate sum of satisfaction. The old "law of diminishing utility" thus leads securely to the proposition: Any cause which increases the absolute share of real income in the hands of the poor, provided that it does not lead to a contraction in the size of the national dividend from any point of view, will, in general, increase economic welfare.

The Economics of Welfare (1920) 1978:89.

3 The environment of one generation *can* produce a lasting result, because it can affect the environment of future generations. Environments. . . as well as people, have children.

The Economics of Welfare (1920) 1978:113.

4 We have watched an artist firing arrows at the moon. Whatever be thought of his marksmanship, we can all admire his virtuosity.

Mr. J. M. Keynes' *General Theory of Employment, Interest and Money* 1936:132.

Max Planck 1858–1947
German physicist

1 A new scientific truth does not triumph by convincing its opponents and making them see the light, but rather because its opponents eventually die, and a new generation grows up that is familiar with it.

Scientific Autobiography and Other Papers (1948) 1949:33–34.

Plato 427–347 B.C.
Greek philosopher

1 [*Socrates*]: Can we rightly speak of a beauty which is always passing away, and is first this and then that? Must not the same thing be born and retire and vanish while the word is in our mouths?
[*Cratylus*]: Undoubtedly.
[*Socrates*]: Then how can that be a real thing which is never in the same state? For obviously things which are the same cannot change while they remain the same, and if they are always the same and in the same state, and never depart from their original form, they can never change or be moved.
[*Cratylus*]: Certainly they cannot.
[*Socrates*]: Nor yet can they be known by anyone, for at the moment that the observer approaches, then they become other and of another nature, so that you cannot get any further in knowing their nature or state, for you cannot know that which has no state.

Cratylus:473.

2 [*Socrates*]: There are not many very good or very bad people, but the great majority are something between the two. . . Can you think of anything more unusual than coming across a very large or small man, or dog, or any other creature? Or one which is very swift or slow, ugly or beautiful, white or black? Have you never realized that extreme instances are few and rare, while intermediate ones are many and plentiful?

Phaedo:72.

3 [*Socrates*]: If men learn [writing], it will implant forgetfulness in their souls; they will cease to exercise memory because they rely on that which is written, calling things to remembrance no longer from within themselves, but by means of external marks. What you have discovered is a recipe not for memory, but for reminder. And it is no true wisdom that you offer your disciples, but only its semblance, for by telling them of many things without teaching them you will make them seem to know much, while for the most part they know nothing, and as men filled, not with wisdom, but with the conceit of wisdom, they will be a burden to their fellows.

Phaedrus:520. → An early warning of the unanticipated consequences of new technologies.

4 [*Socrates*]: Answer me this. . . The same magnitudes seem greater to the eye from near at hand than they do from a distance. This is true of thickness and also of number, and sounds of equal loudness seem greater near at hand than at a distance. If now our happiness consisted in doing, I mean in choosing, greater lengths and avoiding smaller, where would lie salvation? In the art of measurement or in the impression made by appearances? Haven't we seen that the appearance leads us astray and throws us into confusion so that in our actions and our choices between great and small we are constantly accepting and rejecting the same things, whereas the metric art would have canceled the effect of the impression, and by revealing the true state of affairs would have caused the soul to live in peace and quiet and abide in the truth, thus saving our life? Faced with these considerations, would people agree that our salvation would lie in the art of measurement?

Protagoras:347.

5 [*Thrasymachus*]: I proclaim that justice is nothing else than the interest of the stronger. And now why do you not praise me? But of course you won't.

[*Socrates*]: Let me first understand you. . . Justice, as you say, is the interest of the stronger. What, Thrasymachus, is the meaning of this?

Republic:Book 1, 338, 19.

6 [*Socrates*]: Let us begin and create in idea a State; and yet the true creator is necessity, who is the mother of our invention.

Republic:Book 2, 369, 60. → See VEBLEN:13.

7 [*Socrates*]: Any city, however small, is in fact divided into two, one the city of the poor, the other of the rich; these are at war with one another; and in either there are many smaller divisions, and you would be altogether beside the mark if you treated them all as a single State. But if you deal with them as many, and give the wealth or power or persons of the one to the others, you will always have a great many friends and not many enemies.

Republic:Book 4, 423, 132–133. → See DISRAELI:2.

8 [*Socrates*]: Until philosophers are kings, or the kings and princes of this world have the spirit and power of philosophy, and political greatness and wisdom meet in one, and those commoner natures who pursue either to the exclusion of the other are compelled to stand aside, cities will never have rest from their evils, — no, nor the human race, as I believe, — and then only will this our State have a possibility of life and behold the light of day.

Republic:Book 5, 473, 203.

9 [*Socrates*]: Behold! human beings living in an underground den, which has a mouth open towards the light and reaching all along the den. . . Like ourselves. . . they see only their own shadows, or the shadows of one another, which the fire throws on the opposite wall of the cave?

[*Glaucon*]: True. . . how could they see anything but the shadows if they were never allowed to move their heads?

[*Socrates*]: And of the objects which are being carried in like manner they would only see the shadows?. . . And if they were able to converse with one another, would they not suppose that they were naming what was actually before them?

[*Glaucon*]: Very true.

[*Socrates*]: And suppose further that the prison had an echo which came from the other side, would they not be sure to fancy when one of the passers-by spoke that the voice which they heard came from the passing shadow?

[*Glaucon*]: No question.

[*Socrates*]: To them. . . the truth would be literally nothing but the shadows of the images.

[*Glaucon*]: That is certain.

Republic:Book 7, 514–515, 253–254.

10 [*Socrates*]: You must contrive for your future rulers another and a better life than that of a ruler, and then you may have a well-ordered State; for only in the State which offers this, will they rule who are truly rich, not in silver and gold, but in virtue and wisdom, which are the true blessings of life. Whereas if they go to the administration of public affairs, poor and hungering after their own private advantage, thinking that hence they are to snatch the chief good, order there can never be; for they will be fighting about office, and the civil and domestic broils which thus arise will be the ruin of the rulers themselves and of the whole State.

Republic:Book 7, 521, 262.

11 [*Socrates*]: Have you not observed how, in a democracy, many persons, although they have been sentenced to death or exile, just stay where they are and walk about the world — the gentleman parades like a hero, and nobody sees or cares?

[*Adeimantus*]: Yes. . . many and many a one.

[*Socrates*]: See too. . . the forgiving spirit of democracy, and the "don't care" about trifles, and the disregard which she shows of all the fine principles which we solemnly laid down at the foundation of the city. . .

[*Adeimantus*]: Yes, she is of a noble spirit.

[*Socrates*]: These and other kindred characteristics are proper to democracy, which is a charming form of government, full of variety and disorder, and dispensing a sort of equality to equals and unequals alike.

Republic:Book 8, 558, 312.

12 [*Socrates*]: The ruin of oligarchy is the ruin of democracy; the same disease magnified and intensified by liberty overmasters democracy — the truth being that the excessive increase of anything often causes a reaction in the opposite direction; and this is the case not only in the seasons and in vegetables and animal life, but above all in forms of government.

[*Adeimantus*]: True.

[*Socrates*]: The excess of liberty, whether in States or individuals, seems only to pass into excess of slavery.

[*Adeimantus*]: Yes, the natural order.

[*Socrates*]: And so tyranny naturally arises out of democracy, and the most aggravated form of tyranny and slavery out of the most extreme form of liberty?

[*Adeimantus*]: As we might expect.

Republic:Book 8, 564, 320–321.

13 [*Socrates*]: Perhaps someone may say, But surely, Socrates, after you have left us you can spend the rest of your life in quietly minding your own business.

This is the hardest thing of all to make some of you understand. If I say that this would be disobedience to God, and that is why I cannot "mind my own business," you will not believe that I am serious. If on the other hand I tell you that to let no day pass without discussing goodness and all the other subjects about which you hear me talking and examining both myself and others is really the very best thing that a man can do, and that life without this sort of examination is not worth living, you will be even less inclined to believe me.

Socrates' Defense (Apology):22–23.

14 [*Socrates*]: Now consider whether knowledge is a thing you can possess. . . without having it about you, like a man who has caught some wild birds — pigeons or what not — and keeps them in an aviary he has made for them at home. In a sense, of course, we might say he "has" them all the time inasmuch as he possesses them, mightn't we?

[*Theaetetus*]: Yes.

[*Socrates*]: But in another sense he "has" none of them, though he has got control of them, now that he has made them captive in an enclosure of his own. . .

[*Theaetetus*]: That is so.

[*Socrates*]:. . . Let us suppose that every mind contains a kind of aviary stocked with birds of every sort, some in flocks apart from the rest, some in small groups, and some solitary, flying in any direction among them all.

[*Theaetetus*]: Be it so. What follows?

[*Socrates*]: When we are babies we must suppose this receptacle empty, and take the birds to stand for pieces of knowledge. Whenever a person acquires any piece of knowledge and shuts it up in his enclosure, we must say he has learned or discovered the thing of which this is the knowledge, and that is what "knowing" means.

Theaetetus:904.

William Playfair 1759–1823
British statistician and economist

1 The human mind has been so worked upon for a number of years past, and the same subjects have been so frequently brought forward, that it is necessary to produce novelty, but above all to aim at facility, in communicating information; for the desire of obtaining it has diminished in proportion as disgust and satiety have encreased.

Lineal Arithmetic 1798:8.

2 Statistical accounts are to be referred to as a dictionary by men of riper years, and by young men as a grammar, to teach them the relations and proportions of different statistical subjects, and to imprint them on the mind at a time when the memory is capable of being impressed in a lasting and durable manner, thereby laying the foundation for accurate and valuable knowledge.

The Statistical Breviary 1801:5–6.

3 It is not without some pains and labour that the memory is impressed with the proportion between different quantities expressed in words or figures, many persons never take that trouble; — and there is even, to those that do so, a fresh effort of memory necessary each time the question occurs. It is different with a chart, as the eye cannot look on similar forms without involuntarily as it were comparing their magnitudes. So that what in the usual mode was attended with some difficulty, becomes not only easy, but as it were unavoidable.

The Statistical Breviary 1801:6.

4 No study is less alluring or more dry and tedious than statistics, unless the mind and imagination are set to work, or that the person studying is particularly interested in the subject; which last can seldom be the case with young men in any rank of life.

The Statistical Breviary 1801:16.

Georgy Valentinovich Plekhanov 1857–1918
Russian political philosopher and revolutionary

1 [Hegel] showed that we are free only to the degree that we know the laws of nature and sociohistorical development and to the degree that we, submitting to them, rely upon them. This was a great gain both in the field of philosophy and in the field of social science — a gain that, however, only modern, dialectical, materialism has exploited in full measure.

Izbrannye filosofskie proizvedeniia 1956:Vol. 2, 443. Quoted in Loren R. Graham, *Science, Philosophy, and*

Human Behavior in the Soviet Union 1987:443. → According to Graham (pages 25 and 443) this passage, from a 1891 article by Plekhanov, is believed to be the first printed use of the phrase "dialectical materialism."

J. H. Plumb 1911–
British historian

1 The critical historical process has helped to weaken the past, for by its very nature it dissolves those simple, structural generalizations by which our forefathers interpreted the purpose of life in historical terms. Doubtless this is why totalitarian societies keep such a firm hand on their historians and permit them no freedom, except in the accumulation of erudition. In such societies history is still a social process, a sanctification, and not a quest for truth.

The Death of the Past 1970:14.

2 History . . . is not the past. The past is always a created ideology with a purpose, designed to control individuals, or motivate societies, or inspire classes. Nothing has been so corruptly used as concepts of the past. The future of history and historians is to cleanse the story of mankind from those deceiving visions of a purposeful past. The death of the past can only do good so long as history flourishes. Above all, one hopes that the past will not rise phoenix-like from its own ashes to justify again, as it so often has, the subjection and exploitation of men and women, to torture them with fears, or to stifle them with a sense of their own hopelessness. The past has only served the few; perhaps history may serve the multitude.

The Death of the Past 1970:17.

3 Whether we like it or not, quantification in history is here to stay for reasons which the quantifiers themselves might not actively approve. We are becoming a numerate society: almost instinctively there seems now to be a greater degree of truth in evidence expressed numerically than in any literary evidence, no matter how shaky the statistical evidence, or acute the observing eye.

Is History Sick? 1973:64.

Henri Poincaré 1854–1912
French mathematician, physicist, and philosopher

1 The sociologist is in a more embarrassing position [than the astronomer, the physicist, or biologist]. The elements, which for him are men, are too dissimilar, too variable, too capricious, in a word, too complex themselves. Furthermore, history does not repeat itself; how, then, is he to select the interesting fact, the fact which is repeated? Method is precisely the selection of facts, and accordingly our first care must be to devise a method. Many have been devised because none holds the field undisputed. Nearly every sociological thesis proposes a new method, which, however, its author is very careful not to apply, so that sociology is the science with the greatest number of methods and the least results.

Science and Method (1908) 1952:19–20.

2 *All the scientist creates in a fact is the language in which he enunciates it.* If he predicts a fact, he will employ this language, and for all those who can speak and understand it, his prediction is free from ambiguity. Moreover, this prediction once made, it evidently does not depend upon him whether it is fulfilled or not.

The Value of Science (1911) 1913:332.

Karl Polanyi 1886–1964
Austrian-born U.S. economist

1 *The congenital weakness of nineteenth century society was not that it was industrial but that it was a market society.* Industrial civilization will continue to exist when the utopian experiment of a self-regulating market will be no more than a memory.

The Great Transformation (1944) 1975:250.

2 Power and economic value are a paradigm of social reality. They do not spring from human volition: noncooperation is impossible in regard to them. The function of power is to ensure that measure of conformity which is needed for the survival of the group; its ultimate source is opinion . . . Economic value ensures the usefulness of the goods produced; . . . its source is human wants and scarcity — and how could we be expected not to desire one thing more than another? Any opinion or desire will make us participants in the creation of power and in the constituting of economic value. No freedom to do otherwise is conceivable.

The Great Transformation (1944) 1975:258.

Michael Polanyi 1891–1976
Hungarian-born British chemist and philosopher

1 Nobody knows more than a tiny fragment of science well enough to judge its validity and value at first hand. For the rest he has to rely on views accepted at second hand on the authority of a community of people accredited as scientists. But this accrediting depends in its turn on a complex organization. For each member of the community can judge at first hand only a small number of his fellow members, and yet eventually each is accredited by all. What happens is that each recognizes as scientists a number of others by whom he is recognized as such in return, and these relations form chains which transmit these mutual recognitions at second hand through the whole community. This is how each member becomes directly or indirectly accredited by all. The system extends into the past. Its members recognize the same set of persons as their masters and derive from this allegiance a common tradition, of which each carries on a particular strand.

Personal Knowledge (1958) 1964:163.

2 Almost every major systematic error which has deluded men for thousands of years relied on practical experience. Horoscopes, incantations, oracles, magic, witchcraft, the cures of witch doctors and of medical practitioners before the advent of modern medicine, were all

firmly established through the centuries in the eyes of the public by their supposed practical successes. The scientific method was devised precisely for the purpose of elucidating the nature of things under more carefully controlled conditions and by more rigorous criteria than are present in the situations created by practical problems.

Personal Knowledge (1958) 1964:183.

The amount of knowledge which we can justify from evidence directly available to us can never be large. The overwhelming proportion of our factual beliefs continue therefore to be held at second hand through trusting others, and in the great majority of cases our trust is placed in the authority of comparatively few people of widely acknowledged standing.

Personal Knowledge (1958) 1964:208.

Frederick Pollock 1845–1937
British legal scholar
and
Frederic William Maitland 1850–1906
British legal historian and jurist

Such is the unity of all history that any one who endeavours to tell a piece of it must feel that his first sentence tears a seamless web. The oldest utterance of English law that has come down to us has Greek words in it: words such as *bishop, priest* and *deacon*. If we would search out the origins of Roman law, we must study Babylon: this at least was the opinion of the great Romanist of our own day. A statute of limitations must be set; but it must be arbitrary. The web must be rent; but, as we rend it, we may watch the whence and whither of a few of the severed and ravelling threads which have been making a pattern too large for any man's eye.

The History of English Law (1895) 1968:Vol. 1, 1.

Among the most momentous and permanent effects of [the Norman Conquest]. . . was its effect on the language of English lawyers, for language is no mere instrument which we can control at will; it controls us.

The History of English Law (1895) 1968:Vol. 1, 87.

Our forms of [legal] action are not mere rubrics nor dead categories; they are not the outcome of a classificatory process that has been applied to pre-existing materials. They are institutes of the law; they are — we say it without scruple — living things. Each of them lives its own life, has its own adventures, enjoys a longer or shorter day of vigour, usefulness and popularity, and then sinks perhaps into a decrepit and friendless old age. A few are still-born, some are sterile, others live to see their children and children's children in high places. The struggle for life is keen among them and only the fittest survive.

The History of English Law (1895) 1968:Vol. 2, 561. → See SPENCER:7.

The behaviour which is expected of a judge in different ages and by different systems of law seems to fluctuate between two poles. At one of these the model is the conduct of the man of science who is making researches in his laboratory and will use all appropriate methods for the solution of problems and the discovery of truth. At the other stands the umpire of our English games, who is there, not in order that he may invent tests for the powers of the two sides, but merely to see that the rules of the game are observed. It is towards the second of these ideals that our English medieval procedure is strongly inclined.

The History of English Law (1895) 1968:Vol. 2, 670–671.

Polybius c. 200–c. 118 B.C.
Greek historian

1 Now I would admit that authors should have a partiality for their own country but they should not make statements about it that are contrary to facts. Surely the mistakes of which we writers are guilty and which it is difficult for us, being but human, to avoid are quite sufficient; but if we make deliberate misstatements in the interest of our country or of friends or for favour, what difference is there between us and those who gain their living by their pens?

Fragment of Book 16:29.

Alexander Pope 1688–1744
British poet

1 Know then thyself, presume not God to scan;
The proper study of Mankind is Man.
Plac'd on this isthmus of a middle state,
A being darkly wise, and rudely great:
With too much knowledge for the Sceptic side,
With too much weakness for the Stoic's pride,
He hangs between; in doubt to act, or rest;
In doubt to deem himself a God, or Beast;
In doubt his Mind or Body to prefer,
Born but to die, and reas'ning but to err;
Alike in ignorance, his reason such,
Whether he thinks too little, or too much:
Chaos of Thought and Passion, all confus'd;
Still by himself abus'd, or disabus'd;
Created half to rise, and half to fall;
Great lord of all things, yet a prey to all;
Sole judge of Truth, in endless Error hurl'd:
The glory, jest, and riddle of the world!

An Essay on Man (1733) 1950: Epistle 2, 53–56.

2 For Forms of Government let fools contest;
Whate'er is best administer'd is best.

An Essay on Man (1733) 1950: Epistle 3, 123–124. → See HAMILTON:3.

Karl R. Popper 1902–
Austrian-born British philosopher

1 Psychologism is, I believe, correct only in so far as it insists upon what may be called "methodological individu-

alism" as opposed to "methodological collectivism"; it rightly insists that the "behaviour" and the "actions" of collectives, such as states or social groups, must be reduced to the behaviour and to the actions of human individuals. But the belief that the choice of such an individualist method implies the choice of a psychological method is mistaken.

The Open Society and Its Enemies (1945) 1950:87. → See HAYEK:1.

2 Even those [institutions and traditions] which arise as the result of conscious and intentional human actions are, as a rule, *the indirect, the unintended and often the unwanted by-products of such actions.*

The Open Society and Its Enemies (1945) 1950:Chap. 14, 286.

3 The *"conspiracy theory of society"*. . . is the view that an explanation of a social phenomenon consists in the discovery of the men or groups who are interested in the occurrence of this phenomenon (sometimes it is a hidden interest which has first to be revealed), and who have planned and conspired to bring it about.

The Open Society and Its Enemies (1945) 1950:287.

4 [It is] the main task of the theoretical social sciences . . . to trace the unintended social repercussions of intentional human actions.

Prediction and Prophecy in the Social Sciences (1948) 1968:342.

5 [The holists] insist that the specialist's study of "petty details" must be complemented by an "integrating" or "synthetic" method which aims at reconstructing "the whole process"; and they assert that "sociology will continue to ignore the essential question as long as specialists refuse to see their problems as a whole." But this holistic method necessarily remains a mere programme. Not one example of a scientific description of a whole, concrete social situation is ever cited. And it cannot be cited, since in every such case it would always be easy to point out aspects which have been neglected, aspects that may be important in some context or other.

The Poverty of Historicism 1957:79.

6 We may distinguish the following three worlds or universes: first, the world of physical objects or of physical states; secondly, the world of states of consciousness, or of mental states, or perhaps of behavioural dispositions to act; and thirdly, the world of *objective contents of thought*, especially of scientific and poetic thoughts and of works of art.

Epistemology without a Knowing Subject (1968) 1972:106.

7 The influence (for good or ill) of Plato's work is immeasurable. Western thought, one might say, has been either Platonic or anti-Platonic, but hardly ever non-Platonic.

Plato 1968:163.

8 All languages are theory-impregnated.

Conjectural Knowledge (1971) 1972:30.

Robert P. Porter 1852–1917
U.S. government official

1 Up to and including 1880 the country had a frontier of settlement, but at present the unsettled area has been so broken into by isolated bodies of settlement that there can hardly be said to be a frontier line. In the discussion of its extent and its westward movement it can not, therefore, any longer have a place in the census reports.

Progress of the Nation: 1790 to 1890 1895:xxxiv. In part 1 of *Report on Population of the United States at the Eleventh Census*:1890. → Written with Henry Gannett and William C. Hunt. Although this report was not published until 1895, Frederick Jackson Turner knew of its conclusion and based his "Frontier Thesis" on it. See TURNER:2.

Roscoe Pound 1870–1964
U.S. legal philosopher

1 Justice, which is the end of the law, is the ideal compromise between the activities of each and the activities of all in a crowded world.

The Causes of Popular Dissatisfaction with the Administration of Justice 1906:399.

2 Wealth, in a commercial age, is made up largely of promises.

An Introduction to the Philosophy of Law (1922) 1959:133.

3 In the nature of things [the social sciences] cannot be sciences in the sense of physics or chemistry or astronomy. They have been organized as philosophies, have been worked out on the lines of geometry, have been remade into theories of history, have had their period of positivism, have turned to social psychology, and are now in an era of neo-Kantian methodology in some hands and of economic determinism or psychological realism or relativist skepticism or phenomenological intuitionism in other hands. They do not impart wisdom: they need to be approached with acquired wisdom.

The Humanities in an Absolutist World 1944:22.

Derek J. de Solla Price 1922–1983
British-born U.S. historian of science

1 Using any reasonable definition of a scientist, we can say that 80 to 90 percent of all the scientists that have ever lived are alive now. Alternatively, any young scientist, starting now and looking back at the end of his career upon a normal life span, will find that 80 to 90 percent of all scientific work achieved by the end of the period will have taken place before his very eyes, and that only 10 to 20 percent will antedate his experience.

Little Science, Big Science (1963) 1986:1.

2 It is clear that we cannot go up another two orders of magnitude as we have climbed the last five. If we did, we should have two scientists for every man, woman, child, and dog in the population, and we should spend on them

twice as much money as we had. Scientific doomsday is therefore less than a century distant.

Little Science, Big Science (1963) 1986:17.

3 [Some groups of scientists constitute] invisible colleges in the same sense as did those first unofficial pioneers who later banded together to form the Royal Society in 1660. . . They give each man status in the form of approbation from his peers, they confer prestige, and, above all, they effectively solve a communication crisis by reducing a large group to a small select one.

Little Science, Big Science (1963) 1986:76. → Price adopted and extended Robert Boyle's seventeenth-century term "invisible college" to designate an informal collective of closely interacting scientists.

Pierre Joseph Proudhon 1809–1865
French political theorist

1 If I were asked to answer the following question: *What is slavery?* and I should answer in one word, *It is murder*, my meaning would be understood at once. No extended argument would be required to show that the power to take from a man his thought, his will, his personality, is a power of life and death; and that to enslave a man is to kill him. Why, then, to this other question: What is property? may I not likewise answer, It is robbery, without the certainty of being misunderstood; the second proposition being no other than a transformation of the first?

What Is Property? (1840) 1966:37. → Proudhon's remark is often translated as "Property is theft."

2 Communism is inequality, but not as property is. Property is the exploitation of the weak by the strong. Communism is the exploitation of the strong by the weak.

What Is Property? (1840) 1966:261.

3 Liberty, Equality, Fraternity! I say rather Liberty, Equality, Severity.

Carnets 1843–1846:Vol 1, 169.

4 I vote against the constitution. . . not because it contains things of which I disapprove, and does not contain things of which I approve: I vote against the constitution because it is a constitution.

Statement in the Constituent Assembly of 1848.

5 To be governed is to be watched over, inspected, spied on, directed, legislated at, regulated, docketed, indoctrinated, preached at, controlled, assessed, weighed, censored, ordered about, by men who have neither the right nor the knowledge nor the virtue. To be governed means to be, at each operation, at each transaction, at each movement, noted, registered, controlled, taxed, stamped, measured, valued, assessed, patented, licensed, authorized, endorsed, admonished, hampered, reformed, rebuked, arrested. It is to be, on the pretext of the general interest, taxed, drilled, held to ransom, exploited, monopolized, extorted, squeezed, hoaxed, robbed; then at the least resistance, at the first word of complaint, to be repressed, fined, abused, annoyed, followed, bullied, beaten, disarmed, garotted, imprisoned, machine-gunned, judged, condemned, deported, flayed, sold, betrayed and finally mocked, ridiculed, insulted, dishonoured. That's government, that's its justice, that's its morality!

L'idée générale de la révolution au 19e siècle (1851) 1929:344.

6 What no monarchy, not even that of the Roman emperors, has been able to accomplish; what Christianity, that epitome of the ancient faiths, has been unable to produce, the universal Republic, the economic Revolution, will accomplish, cannot fail to accomplish.

General Idea of the Revolution in the Nineteenth Century (1851) 1923:283.

7 A social fact of incalculable importance is occurring in the heart of society; it is. . . the arrival in political life of the most numerous and poorest class.

De la capacité politique des classes ouvrières 1865.

Hilary Putnam 1926–
U.S. philosopher

1 My picture of our situation is not the famous [Otto] Neurath picture of science as the enterprise of reconstructing a boat while the boat floats on the open ocean . . . First, I would put ethics, philosophy, in fact the whole culture in the boat, and not just "science," for I believe all the parts of the culture are inter-dependent. And, second, my image is not of a single boat but of a *fleet* of boats. The people in each boat are trying to reconstruct their own boat without modifying it so much at any one time that the boat sinks, as in the Neurath image. In addition, people are passing supplies and tools from one boat to another and shouting advice and encouragement (or discouragement) to each other. Finally, people sometimes decide they do not like the boat they are in and move to a different boat altogether. (And sometimes a boat sinks or is abandoned.) It is all a bit chaotic; but since it is a fleet, no one is ever totally out of signalling distance from all the other boats. We are not trapped in individual solipsistic hells (or need not be) but invited to engage in a truly human dialogue; one which combines collectivity with individual responsibility.

Philosophers and Human Understanding 1981:118. → For the Neurath image upon which this picture is based, see NEURATH:1.

François Quesnay 1694–1774
French economist

1 The sovereign and the nation must never forget that land is the only source of wealth and that it is agriculture which multiplies it.

Maximes générales du gouvernement économique d'un royaume agricole (1758) 1888:331. → Unpublished translation by Yole G. Sills.

2 In the case of everything in this world, abuse is a close neighbour of order. . . Change or displace one figure and the whole calculation is thrown into disorder. Introduce one wrong note into the harmony of society, and the whole political mechanism feels the effect and falls apart, and concord is then as difficult to re-establish as it would be for the world to take shape as a result of the accidental concourse of atoms of Epicurus.

Extract from *Rural Philosophy* (1763) 1963:58.

3 Need alone is the father of industry; it makes the worker dedicate himself to it in order to earn his living and it entices all those who can buy to obtain its products.

Réponse au mémoire de M. H. (1766) 1888:391. → Unpublished translation by Yole G. Sills.

Adolphe Quetelet 1796–1874
Belgian statistician and sociologist

1 There is a *budget* which we pay with frightful regularity — it is that of prisons, dungeons, and scaffolds.

A Treatise on Man (1835) 1842:6.

2 It would appear. . . that moral phenomena, when observed on a great scale, are found to resemble physical phenomena; and we thus arrive, in inquiries of this kind, at the fundamental principle, that *the greater the number of individuals observed, the more do individual peculiarities, whether physical or moral, become effaced, and leave in a prominent point of view the general facts, by virtue of which society exists and is preserved.*

A Treatise on Man (1835) 1842:6.

3 [The] determination of the average man is not merely a matter of speculative curiosity; it may be of the most important service to the science of man and the social system. It ought necessarily to precede every other inquiry into social physics, since it is, as it were, the basis. The average man, indeed, is in a nation what the centre of gravity is in a body; it is by having that central point in view that we arrive at the apprehension of all the phenomena of equilibrium and motion.

A Treatise on Man (1835) 1842:96. → See BUFFON:1.

4 *Society prepares crime, and the guilty are only the instruments by which it is executed.* Hence it happens that the unfortunate person who loses his head on the scaffold, or who ends his life in prison, is in some manner an expiatory victim for society.

A Treatise on Man (1835) 1842:108.

5 There is a general law which governs our universe and seems destined to create life here. It gives to everything that breathes an infinite variation, without disturbing the balance of nature [*les principles de conservation*]. This law, which has long been unrecognized by science, and which until now has been put to no practical use, I shall call the *law of accidental causes.*

Du systéme social 1848:16. → Unpublished translation by Stephen M. Stigler.

R

A. R. Radcliffe-Brown 1881–1955
British anthropologist

Every custom and belief of a primitive society plays some determinate part in the social life of the community, just as every organ of a living body plays some part in the general life of the organism. The mass of institutions, customs and beliefs forms a single whole or system that determines the life of the society, and the life of the society is not less real, or less subject to natural laws, than the life of an organism.

The Andaman Islanders (1922) 1948:229–230.

It is not the effects of the sanctions upon the person to whom they are applied that are the most important but rather the general effects within the community applying the sanctions. For the application of any sanction is a direct affirmation of the social sentiments by the community and thereby constitutes an important, possibly essential, mechanism for maintaining these sentiments.

Social Sanction 1934:533.

In human society the social structure as a whole can only be *observed* in its functioning. Some of the features of social structure, such as the geographical distribution of individuals and groups can be directly observed, but most of the social relations which in their totality constitute the structure, such as relations of father and son, buyer and seller, ruler and subject, cannot be observed except in the social activities in which the relations are functioning.

On the Concept of Function in Social Science (1935) 1965:181.

A social system (the total social structure of a society together with the totality of social usages in which that structure appears and on which it depends for its continued existence) has a certain kind of unity, which we may speak of as a functional unity.

On the Concept of Function in Social Science (1935) 1965:181.

5 If we take up the structural point of view, we study these things, not in abstraction or isolation, but in their direct and indirect relations to social structure, i.e., with reference to the way in which they depend upon, or affect the social relations between persons and groups of persons.

On the Concept of Function in Social Science (1935) 1965:195.

6 In studying political organization, we have to deal with the maintenance or establishment of social order, within a territorial framework, by the organized exercise of coercive authority through the use, or the possibility of use, of physical force.

Preface to Meyer Fortes and E. E. Evans-Pritchard (editors), *African Political Systems* (1940) 1970:xiv.

7 You will not. . . say of culture patterns that they act upon an individual, which is as absurd as to hold a quadratic equation capable of commiting a murder.

A Natural Science of Society (1948) 1957:30.

8 Malinowski has explained that he is the inventor of functionalism, to which he gave its name. His definition of it is clear; it is the theory or doctrine that every feature of culture of any people past or present is to be explained by reference to seven biological needs of individual human beings. I cannot speak for the other writers to whom the label functionalist is applied by [Dorothy Gregg and Elgin Williams], though I very much doubt if Redfield or Linton accept this doctrine. As for myself I reject it entirely, regarding it as useless and worse. As a consistent opponent of Malinowski's functionalism I may be called an anti-functionalist.

Functionalism: A Protest 1949:320–321.

Paul Radin 1883–1959
Polish-born U.S. anthropologist

1 Every generation occupies itself with interpreting Trickster anew. No generation understands him fully but no generation can do without him. . . He represents not only the undifferentiated and distant past, but likewise the

undifferentiated present within every individual. This constitutes his universal and persistent attraction. And so he became and remained everything to every man—god, animal, human being, hero, buffoon, he who was before good and evil, denier, affirmer, destroyer and creator. If we laugh at him, he grins at us. What happens to him happens to us.

The Trickster (1956) 1972:168–169.

John Rae 1796–1872
Scottish-born Canadian–U.S. economist

1 The things to which vanity seems most readily to apply itself are those to which the use or consumption is most apparent, and of which the effects are most difficult to discriminate. Articles of which the consumption is not conspicuous are incapable of gratifying this passion.

The Sociological Theory of Capital (1834) 1905:247. → Rae's doctrine of conspicuous consumption, published 65 years before Veblen's *Theory of the Leisure Class* (1899). See VEBLEN:3.

Frank Plumpton Ramsey 1903–1930
British mathematician and philosopher

1 Logic issues in tautologies, mathematics in identities, philosophy in definitions; all trivial, but all part of the vital work of clarifying and organising our thought.

The Foundations of Mathematics (1931) 1965.

2 Where I seem to differ from some of my friends is in attaching little importance to physical size. I don't feel the least humble before the vastness of the heavens. The stars may be large, but they cannot think or love; and these are qualities which impress me far more than size does. I take no credit for weighing nearly seventeen stone.

The Foundations of Mathematics (1931) 1965.

Otto Rank 1884–1939
Austrian-born U.S. psychoanalyst

1 The artist, despite the high intellectual achievement of his sublimation, represents, relative to his affective life, ontogenetically and *phylogenetically* an atavistic stage, a survival from an infantile stage — exactly as Freud had represented regression to the infantile as the determinant of neurosis.

Das Inzestmotiv in Dichtung und Sage 1912:68.

2 Anxiety originally relates to something external, an object or a situation; whereas guilt is, so to say, an inner anxiety, a being afraid of oneself. Anxiety is thus a biological concept, guilt is an ethical concept. So the great problem of the inner and the outer in a scientific sense could be formulated as the problem of biology versus ethics (or the reverse), in other words, as the great conflict between our biological and our purely human Self.

Beyond Psychoanalysis 1929:8.

3 My own life work is completed, the subjects of my former interest, the hero, the artist, the neurotic appear once more upon the stage, not only as participants in the eternal drama of life but after the curtain has gone down, unmasked, undressed, unpretentious, not as punctured illusions, but as human beings who require no interpreter.

Beyond Psychology (1941) 1958:16.

Leopold von Ranke 1795–1886
German historian

1 *Man hat der Historie das Amt, die Vergangenheit zu richten, die Mitwelt zum Nutzen zukünftiger Jahre zu belehren, beigemessen: so hoher Aemter unterwindet sich gegenwartiger Versuch nicht: er will blos zeigen, wie es eigentlich gewesen* [To history has been assigned the office of judging the past, of instructing the present for the benefit of future generations. This work does not have such a lofty ambition. It wants only to show what actually happened].

Geschichten der romanischen und germanischen Völker von 1494 bis 1514 (1824) 1885:vii.

2 The historian must keep his eye on the universal aspect of things. He will have no preconceived ideas as does the philosopher; rather, while he reflects on the particular, the development of the world in general will become apparent to him. This development, however, is not related to universal concepts which might have prevailed at one time or another, but to completely different factors. There is no nation on earth that has not had some contact with other nations. It is through this external relationship, which in turn depends on a nation's peculiar character, that the nation enters on the stage of world history, and universal history must therefore focus on it.

Fragment from the 1830's. → Quoted in Fritz Stern (editor), *The Varieties of History* (1956:59–60).

3 I see a time coming when we shall build modern history no longer on the accounts even of contemporary historians except where they possessed original knowledge, much less on derivative writers, but on the relations of eye-witnesses and the original documents.

Quoted in G. P. Gooch, *History and Historians* (1913) 1959:83–84.

Anatol Rapoport 1911–
Russian-born U.S. mathematical biologist

1 Two prisoners accused of the same crime are kept in separate cells. Only a confession by one or both can lead to conviction. If neither confesses, they can be convicted of a lesser offense, incurring a penalty of one month in prison. If both plead guilty of the major crime, both receive a reduced sentence, five years. If one confesses and the other does not, the first goes free (for having turned State's evidence), while the other receives the full sentence, ten years in prison. Under the circumstances is it rational to admit guilt or to deny it?

If my partner confesses (so each prisoner might reason), I stand to gain by confessing, for in that case, I get five years instead of ten years, if I don't confess. If, on the other hand, my partner does not confess, it is still to my advantage to confess, for a confession sets me free, while otherwise I must serve a month. Therefore I am better off confessing *regardless* of whether my partner does or not.

The "partner," being in the same situation, reasons the same way. Consequently, both confess and are sentenced to five years. Had they not confessed, they would have been sentenced to only one month. In what sense, therefore, can one assert that "to confess" was the prudent (or "rational") course of action?

The anecdote is attributed to A. W. Tucker, and the game depicting the situation has been christened appropriately "Prisoner's Dilemma."

Prisoner's Dilemma — Recollections and Observations 1974:17. → The *Oxford English Dictionary* has in its files a letter from A. W. Tucker reporting upon his 1950 formulation of the Prisoner's Dilemma. He never published it, but he notes that it spread through "the grapevine."

John Rawls 1921–

U.S. philosopher

1 Justice is the first virtue of social institutions, as truth is of systems of thought. A theory however elegant and economical must be rejected or revised if it is untrue; likewise laws and institutions no matter how efficient and well-arranged must be reformed or abolished if they are unjust.

A Theory of Justice 1971:3.

2 A conception of social justice. . . is to be regarded as providing in the first instance a standard whereby the distributive aspects of the basic structure of society are to be assessed. This standard, however, is not to be confused with the principles defining the other virtues, for the basic structure, and social arrangements generally, may be efficient or inefficient, liberal or illiberal, and many other things, as well as just or unjust. A complete conception defining principles for all the virtues of the basic structure, together with the respective weights when they conflict, is more than a conception of justice; it is a social ideal. The principles of justice are but a part, although perhaps the most important part, of such a conception. A social ideal in turn is connected with a conception of society, a vision of the way in which the aims and purposes of social cooperation are to be understood. . . Fully to understand a conception of justice we must make explicit the conception of social cooperation from which it derives.

A Theory of Justice 1971:9–10.

3 The principle of choice for an association of men is interpreted as an extension of the principle of choice for one man. Social justice is the principle of rational prudence applied to an aggregative conception of the welfare of the group.

A Theory of Justice 1971:24.

4 The difference principle represents, in effect, an agreement to regard the distribution of natural talents as a common asset and to share in the benefits of this distribution whatever it turns out to be. Those who have been favored by nature, whoever they are, may gain from their good fortune only on terms that improve the situation of those who have lost out . . . We are led to the difference principle if we wish to set up the social system so that no one gains or loses from his arbitrary place in the distribution of natural assets or his initial position in society without giving or receiving compensating advantages in return.

A Theory of Justice 1971:101–102.

5 In a well-ordered society the need for status is met by the public recognition of just institutions, together with the full and diverse internal life of the many free communities of interests that equal liberty allows. The basis for self-esteem in a just society is not then one's income share but the publicly affirmed distribution of fundamental rights and liberties.

A Theory of Justice 1971:544.

Robert Redfield 1897–1958

U.S. anthropologist

1 [A primitive or folk] society is small, isolated, nonliterate, and homogeneous, with a strong sense of group solidarity. The ways of living are conventionalized into that coherent system which we call "a culture." Behavior is traditional, spontaneous, uncritical, and personal; there is no legislation or habit of experiment and reflection for intellectual ends. Kinship, its relationships and institutions, are the type categories of experience and the familial group is the unit of action. The sacred prevails over the secular; the economy is one of status rather than of market.

The Folk Society 1947:293.

2 In most of social science, human nature is itself a part of the method. One must use one's own humanity as a means to understanding. The physicist need not sympathize with his atoms, nor the biologist with his fruit flies, but the student of people and institutions must employ his natural sympathies in order to discover what people think or feel and what the institution means.

Social Science among the Humanities (1949) 1962:52.

3 "World view" differs from culture, ethos, mode of thought, and national character. It is the picture the members of a society have of the properties and characters upon their stage of action. While "national character" refers to the way these people look to the outsider looking in on them, "world view" refers to the way the world looks to that people looking out. Of all that is connoted by "culture," "world view" attends especially to the way a man, in a particular society, sees himself in relation to all else. It is the properties of existence as distinguished from and related to the self. It is, in short, a man's idea of the universe. It is that organization of ideas

which answers to a man the questions: Where am I? Among what do I move? What are my relations to these things?

The Primitive World View 1952:30.

4 The folk society is that society in which the technical order is subordinated within the moral order.

The Primitive World and Its Transformations 1953:48.

5 The unity and distinctiveness of the little community is felt by everyone who is brought up in it and as part of it. The people of a band or a village or a small town know each of the other members of that community as parts of one another; each is strongly aware of just that group of people, as belonging together: the "we" that each inhabitant uses recognizes the separateness of that band or village from all others.

The Little Community 1955:10.

6 The real structure of tradition, in any civilization or part thereof, is an immensely intricate system of relationships between the levels or components of tradition, which we enormously oversimplify by referring to as "high" or "low" or as "great" and "little."

Civilizations as Cultural Structures? (1958) 1962:394.

7 Myths and ceremonies, like much of art and some of play, are collective and traditional forms in which the people of a society remind themselves of what matters to them and why it matters. They are gestures made by a people to itself.

How Human Society Operates (1960) 1962:438.

David Ricardo 1772–1823
British economist

1 The interest of the landlord is always opposed to the interest of every other class in the community. His situation is never so prosperous, as when food is scarce and dear: whereas, all other persons are greatly benefited by procuring cheap food.

An Essay on the Influence of a Low Price of Corn on the Profits of Stock (1815) 1951:21.

2 Utility. . . is not the measure of exchangeable value, although it is absolutely essential to it. If a commodity were in no way useful — in other words, if it could in no way contribute to our gratification — it would be destitute of exchangeable value, however scarce it might be, or whatever quantity of labour might be necessary to procure it.

The Principles of Political Economy and Taxation (1817) 1963:5.

3 Rent is that portion of the produce of the earth which is paid to the landlord for the use of the original and indestructible powers of the soil.

The Principles of Political Economy and Taxation (1817) 1963:29.

4 The reason. . . why raw produce rises in comparative value, is because more labour is employed in the production of the last portion obtained, and not because a rent is paid to the landlord. The value of corn is regulated by the quantity of labour bestowed on its production on that quality of land, or with that portion of capital, which pays no rent. Corn is not high because a rent is paid, but a rent is paid because corn is high.

The Principles of Political Economy and Taxation (1817) 1963:33–34.

5 Labour, like all other things which are purchased and sold, and which may be increased or diminished in quantity, has its natural and its market price. The natural price of labour is that price which is necessary to enable the labourers, one with another, to subsist and to perpetuate their race, without either increase or diminution.

The Principles of Political Economy and Taxation (1817) 1963:45.

6 The natural price of labour. . . depends on the price of the food, necessaries, and conveniences required for the support of the labourer and his family. With a rise in the price of food and necessaries, the natural price of labour will rise; with the fall in their price, the natural price of labour will fall.

The Principles of Political Economy and Taxation (1817) 1963:45.

7 Under a system of perfectly free commerce, each country naturally devotes its capital and labour to such employments as are most beneficial to each. This pursuit of individual advantage is admirably connected with the universal good of the whole. By stimulating industry, by rewarding ingenuity, and by using most efficaciously the peculiar powers bestowed by nature, it distributes labour most effectively and most economically: while, by increasing the general mass of productions, it diffuses general benefit, and binds together, by one common tie of interest and intercourse, the universal society of nations throughout the civilised world.

The Principles of Political Economy and Taxation (1817) 1963:70.

Stuart A. Rice 1889–1969
U.S. sociologist and statistician

1 It must be kept in mind that an index is a *representative* figure. It stands for some quantity, degree of activity, value, or situation, which cannot itself be expressed directly.

The Historico-Statistical Approach to Social Studies 1930:11.

I. A. Richards
See C. K. Ogden and I. A. Richards.

Lewis Fry Richardson 1881–1953
British meteorologist and student of the causes of war

1 The equations [on the causes of war] are merely a description of what people would do if they did not stop to think. The process described by the ensuing equation is

not to be thought of as inevitable. It is what *would occur if instinct and tradition were allowed to act uncontrolled.*

Arms and Insecurity 1960:12.

Philip Rieff 1922–
U.S. sociologist

1 It is exhilarating and yet terrifying to read Freud as a moralist, to see how compelling can be the judgment of a man who never preaches, leads us nowhere, assures us of nothing except perhaps that, having learned from him, the burden of misery we must find strength to carry will be somewhat lighter.

Freud (1959) 1979:xi.

David Riesman 1909–
U.S. sociologist

1 The society of high growth potential develops in its typical members a social character whose conformity is insured by their tendency to follow tradition: these I shall term tradition-directed people and the society in which they live *a society dependent on tradition-direction.*

The society of transitional population growth develops in its typical members a social character whose conformity is insured by their tendency to acquire early in life an internalized set of goals. These I shall term inner-directed people and the society in which they live *a society dependent on inner-direction.*

Finally, the society of incipient population decline develops in its typical members a social character whose conformity is insured by their tendency to be sensitized to the expectations and preferences of others. These I shall term other-directed people and the society in which they live one *dependent on other-direction.*

The Lonely Crowd 1950:9. → Written in collaboration with Reuel Denney and Nathan Glazer.

2 While all people want and need to be liked by some of the people some of the time, it is only the modern other-directed types who make this their chief source of direction and chief area of sensitivity.

The Lonely Crowd 1950:23.

3 The product now in demand is neither a staple nor a machine; it is a personality.

The Lonely Crowd 1950:46.

4 The idea that men are created free and equal is both true and misleading: men are created different; they lose their social freedom and their individual autonomy in seeking to become like each other.

The Lonely Crowd 1950:373.

Matilda White Riley 1911–
U.S. sociologist

1 There is a dynamic interplay between people growing older and society undergoing change. People age in different ways because society changes; and in turn the ways in which people age are continually shaping society.

Aging and Social Change (1980) 1982:11.

W. H. R. Rivers 1864–1922
British anthropologist

1 Human beings do not pursue the course of their daily lives and perform the complicated actions of social life merely as automata conforming to the institutions and customs into which they have been born. There remains a vast field for study in the ideas, beliefs, emotions, and sentiments which act as the immediate motives of their actions. It is possible, indeed probable, that some of the customs which I suppose to have been brought to Oceania from elsewhere, or to have been the direct product of immigrant ideas, may have arisen much later out of ideas which did not belong to any one culture, but are natural to mankind.

The History of Melanesian Society 1914:Vol. 2, 595.

2 We of this movement [the historical school of ethnology] believe that many customs which were once supposed to be the products of a simple process of evolution among an isolated people have in fact behind them a long and tortuous history. It is held that the first task of the ethnologist is to unravel this history.

History and Ethnology 1922:5.

3 The people say to themselves: "Why should we bring children into the world only to work for the white man?" Measures which, before the coming of the European, were used chiefly to prevent illegitimacy have become the instrument of racial suicide.

The Psychological Factor 1922:104.

Alice M. Rivlin 1931–
U.S. economist

1 Like the medical profession, which also deals with an incredibly complex system, we economists just have to keep applying our imperfect knowledge as carefully as possible and learning from the results. Both doctors and economists need humility, but neither should abandon their patients to the quacks.

Taming the Economic Policy Monster 1987:2. → Concluding statement of her presidential address to the American Economic Association, New Orleans, December 1986.

Lionel Robbins 1898–1984
British economist

1 Economics is the science which studies human behaviour as a relationship between ends and scarce means which have alternative uses.

An Essay on the Nature and Significance of Economic Science (1932) 1984:16.

2 Economics is entirely neutral between ends; . . . in so far as the achievement of *any* end is dependent on scarce

means, it is germane to the preoccupations of the economist.

An Essay on the Nature and Significance of Economic Science (1932) 1984:24.

3 Wealth is not wealth because of its substantial qualities. It is wealth because it is scarce.

An Essay on the Nature and Significance of Economic Science (1932) 1984:47.

William Robertson Smith

See WILLIAM ROBERTSON SMITH.

James Harvey Robinson 1863–1936 and Charles A. Beard 1874–1948

U.S. historians

1 It may well be that men of science, not kings, or warriors, or even statesmen are to be the heroes of the future.

The Development of Modern Europe 1908:Vol. 2, 421.

[*See also* CHARLES A. BEARD; CHARLES A. BEARD AND MARY R. BEARD.]

Joan Robinson 1903–1983

British economist

1 Any government which had both the power and the will to remedy the major defects of the capitalist system would have the will and the power to abolish it altogether, while governments which have the power to retain the system lack the will to remedy its defects.

Review of R. F. Harrod, *The Trade Cycle* 1936:693.

2 The purpose of studying economics is not to acquire a set of ready-made answers to economic questions, but to learn how to avoid being deceived by economists.

Marx, Marshall and Keynes (1955) 1980:17.

3 The whole elaborate structure of the metaphysical justification for profit was blown up when he [Keynes] pointed out that capital yields a return not because it is *productive* but because it is *scarce*.

The Keynesian Revolution (1962) 1963:75.

4 What made the *General Theory* so hard to accept was not its intellectual content, which in a calm mood can easily be mastered, but its shocking implications. Worse than private vices being public benefits, it seemed that the new doctrine was the still more disconcerting proposition that private virtues (of thriftiness and careful husbandry) were public vices. . .

By making it impossible to believe any longer in an automatic reconciliation of conflicting interests into a harmonious whole, the *General Theory* brought out into the open the problem of choice and judgement that the neo-classicals had managed to smother. The ideology to end ideologies broke down. Economics once more became Political Economy. . .

Keynes brought back *time* into economic theory. He woke the Sleeping Princess from the long oblivion to which "equilibrium" and "perfect foresight" had condemned her and led her out into the world here and now.

The Keynesian Revolution (1962) 1963:75–76.

5 Economics limps along with one foot in untested hypotheses and the other in untestable slogans.

Metaphysics, Morals and Science (1962) 1963:25.

6 It is possible to defend our economic system on the ground that, patched up with Keynesian correctives, it is, as he put it, the "best in sight." Or at any rate that it is not too bad, and that change is painful. In short, that our system is the best system that we have got.

Or it is possible to take the tough-minded line that Schumpeter derived from Marx. The system is cruel, unjust, turbulent, but it does deliver the goods, and, damn it all, it's the goods that you want.

Or, conceding its defects, to defend it on political grounds — that democracy as we know it could not have grown up under any other system and cannot survive without it.

What is not possible, at this time of day, is to defend it, in the neo-classical style, as a delicate self-regulating mechanism, that has only to be left to itself to produce the greatest satisfaction for all.

What Are the Rules of the Game? (1962) 1963:138–139.

7 Marx did not have very much to say about the economics of socialism. As Kalecki once remarked, it was not his business to write science fiction.

Economics versus Political Economy (1968) 1980:28.

8 In the natural sciences, controversies are settled in a few months, or at a time of crisis, in a year or two, but in the social so-called sciences, absurd misunderstanding can continue for sixty or a hundred years without being cleared up.

Thinking about Thinking (1979) 1980:60.

F. J. Roethlisberger 1898–1974

U.S. sociologist

1 If one experiments on a stone, the stone does not know it is being experimented upon — all of which makes it simple for people experimenting on stones. But if a human being is being experimented upon, he is likely to know it. Therefore, his attitudes toward the experiment and toward the experimenters become very important factors in determining his responses to the situation.

Now that is what happened in the Relay Assembly Test Room.

Management and Morale 1941:14. → In this book, Roethlisberger published his formulations of the "Hawthorne effect," which is only tacitly recognized in F.J. Roethlisberger and William J. Dixon, *Management and the Worker* (1939).

2 Workers are not isolated, unrelated individuals; they are social animals and should be treated as such.

Management and Morale 1941:26.

Carl R. Rogers 1902–1987

U.S. psychologist

1 Behavior is a reaction to the field as perceived. It would therefore appear that behavior might be best understood by gaining, in so far as possible, the internal frame of reference of the person himself, and seeing the world of experience as nearly as possible through his eyes.

Client-Centered Therapy (1951) 1965:494.

2 *What is most personal is most general*. . . The very feeling which has seemed to me most private, most personal, and hence most incomprehensible by others, has turned out to be an expression for which there is a resonance in many other people.

On Becoming a Person 1961:26.

Géza Róheim 1891–1953

Hungarian-born U.S. anthropologist and psychoanalyst

1 By culture we shall understand the sum of all sublimations, all substitutes or reaction formations, in short, everything in society that inhibits impulses or permits their distorted satisfaction. Thus we are led logically to assume that individual cultures can be derived from typical infantile traumata, and that culture in general (everything which differentiates man from the lower animals) is a consequence of infantile experience.

The Riddle of the Sphinx 1934:216.

Franklin Delano Roosevelt 1882–1945

U.S. lawyer and statesman

1 I see one-third of a nation ill-housed, ill-clad, ill-nourished.

Second Inaugural Address, 20 January 1937. 1946:91.

2 Politics, after all, is only an instrument through which to achieve Government.

Address at the Jackson Day Dinner, 8 January 1940. 1946:195.

3 In the future days, which we seek to make secure, we look forward to a world founded upon four essential human freedoms.

The first freedom is freedom of speech and expression — everywhere in the world.

The second is freedom of every person to worship God in his own way — everywhere in the world.

The third is freedom from want — which, translated into world terms, means economic understandings which will secure to every nation a healthy peace time life for its inhabitants — everywhere in the world.

The fourth is freedom from fear — which, translated into world terms, means a world-wide reduction [in] armaments to such a point and in such a thorough fashion that no nation will be in a position to commit an act of physical aggression against any neighbor — anywhere in the world.

Speech, 6 January 1941. 1946:266.

Richard Rorty 1931–

U.S. philosopher

1 The current movement to make the social sciences "hermeneutical" rather than Galilean makes a reasonable, Deweyan point if it is taken as saying: narratives as well as laws, redescriptions as well as predictions, serve a useful purpose in helping us deal with the problems of society. In this sense, the movement is a useful protest against the fetishism of old-fashioned, "behaviorist" social scientists who worry about whether they are being "scientific." But this protest goes too far when it waxes philosophical and begins to draw a principled distinction between man and nature, announcing that the ontological difference dictates a methodological difference.

Method, Social Science, and Social Hope (1981) 1982:198–199.

2 [The] claim that we need to look for *internal* explanations of people or cultures or texts takes civility as a methodological strategy. But civility is not a method, it is simply a virtue. The reason why we invite the moronic psychopath to address the court before being sentenced is not that we hope for better explanations than expert psychiatric testimony has offered. We do so because he is, after all, one of us. By asking for his own account in his own words, we hope to decrease our chances of acting badly. What we hope for from social scientists is that they will act as interpreters for those with whom we are not sure how to talk. This is the same thing we hope for from our poets and dramatists and novelists.

Method, Social Science, and Social Hope (1981) 1982:202.

Wilhelm Roscher 1817–1894

German economist

1 That which is general in Political Economy has, it must be acknowledged, much that is analogous to the mathematical sciences. Like the latter, it swarms with abstractions. Just as there are, strictly speaking, no mathematical lines or points in nature, and no mathematical lever, there is nowhere such a thing as production or rent, entirely pure and simple.

Principles of Political Economy (1854) 1878:103.

Morris Rosenberg

See Paul F. Lazarsfeld and Morris Rosenberg.

Edward A. Ross 1866–1951

U.S. sociologist

1 A society. . . which is riven by a dozen oppositions along lines running in every direction, may actually be in less danger of being torn with violence or falling to pieces than one split along just one line. For each new cleavage contributes to narrow the cross clefts, so that one might say that society is *sewn together* by its inner conflicts.

The Principles of Sociology 1920:165. → See Coser:1 and Williams:1.

Theodore Roszak 1933–
U.S. historian

1 It would hardly seem an exaggeration to call what we see arising among the young a "counter culture." Meaning: a culture so radically disaffiliated from the mainstream assumptions of our society that it scarcely looks to many as a culture at all, but takes on the alarming appearance of a barbaric intrusion.

The Making of a Counter Culture (1963) 1969:42. → In 1960, the sociologist J. Milton Yinger proposed "contraculture" for this phenomenon, but "counterculture" won out. See his "Contraculture and Subculture" (1960:625–635).

Barbara J. Rothstein 1939–
U.S. jurist

1 In order for the flag to endure as a symbol of freedom in this nation, we must protect with equal vigor the right to destroy it and the right to wave it.

United States of America v. *Mark John Haggerty, et al.*, United States District Court, Western District of Washington at Seattle, February 1990:16. → A decision declaring the Flag Protection Act of 1989 unconstitutional.

Jean Jacques Rousseau 1712–1778
Genevan-born French philosopher and political theorist

1 While government and laws provide for the safety and well-being of assembled men, the sciences, letters, and arts, less despotic and perhaps more powerful, spread garlands of flowers over the iron chains with which men are burdened, stifle in them the sense of that original liberty for which they seemed to have been born, make them love their slavery, and turn them into what is called civilized peoples.

Discourse on the Sciences and Arts (1750) 1964:36.

2 Men are perverse; they would be even worse if they had the misfortune to be born learned.

Discourse on the Sciences and Arts (1750) 1964:47.

3 The first person who, having fenced off a plot of ground, took it into his head to say *this is mine* and found people simple enough to believe him, was the true founder of civil society.

Discourse on the Origin and Foundations of Inequality among Men (1755) 1964:141.

4 From the moment one man needed the help of another, as soon as they observed that it was useful for a single person to have provisions for two, equality disappeared, property was introduced, labor became necessary; and vast forests were changed into smiling fields which had to be watered with the sweat of men, and in which slavery and misery were soon seen to germinate and grow with the crops.

Discourse on the Origin and Foundations of Inequality among Men (1755) 1964:151–152.

5 The savage lives within himself; the sociable man, always outside of himself, knows how to live only in the opinion of others; and it is, so to speak, from their judgment alone that he draws the sentiment of his own existence.

Discourse on the Origin and Foundations of Inequality among Men (1755) 1964:179.

6 Carefully determine what happens in every public deliberation, and it will be seen that the general will is always for the common good; but very often there is a secret division, a tacit confederacy, which, for particular ends, causes the natural disposition of the assembly to be set at naught. In such a case the body of society is really divided into other bodies, the members of which acquire a general will, which is good and just with respect to these new bodies, but unjust and bad with regard to the whole, from which each is thus dismembered.

A Discourse on Political Economy (1755) 1973:122.

7 If it is good to know how to deal with men as they are, it is much better to make them what there is need that they should be. The most absolute authority is that which penetrates into a man's inmost being, and concerns itself no less with his will than with his actions.

A Discourse on Political Economy (1755) 1973:127.

8 I know of only three instruments with which the morals [manners] of a people can be acted upon: the force of the laws, the empire of opinion, and the appeal of pleasure.

Letter to M. d'Alembert on the Theatre (1758) 1982:22.

9 Everything is good as it leaves the hands of the Author of things; everything degenerates in the hands of man. He forces one soil to nourish the products of another, one tree to bear the fruit of another. He mixes and confuses the climates, the elements, the seasons. He mutilates his dog, his horse, his slave. He turns everything upside down; he disfigures everything; he loves deformity, monsters. He wants nothing as nature made it, not even man; for him, man must be trained like a school horse; man must be fashioned in keeping with his fancy like a tree in his garden.

Émile (1762) 1979:37.

10 Civil man is born, lives, and dies in slavery. At his birth he is sewed in swaddling clothes; at his death he is nailed in a coffin. So long as he keeps his human shape, he is enchained by our institutions.

Émile (1762) 1979:42–43.

11 Man is born free; and everywhere he is in chains. One thinks himself the master of others, and still remains a greater slave than they. How did this change come about? I do not know. What can make it legitimate? That question I think I can answer.

Social Contract (1762) 1973:Book 1, chap. 1, 165.

12 The strongest is never strong enough to be always the master, unless he transforms strength into right, and obedience into duty. Hence the right of the strongest,

which, though to all seeming meant ironically, is really laid down as a fundamental principle.

Social Contract (1762) 1973:Book 1, chap. 3, 168.

13 "The problem is to find a form of association which will defend and protect with the whole common force the person and goods of each associate, and in which each, while uniting himself with all, may still obey himself alone, and remain as free as before." This is the fundamental problem of which the social contract provides the solution.

Social Contract (1762) 1973:Book 1, chap. 6, 174.

14 If then we discard from the social compact what is not of its essence, we shall find that it reduces itself to the following terms:

"Each of us puts his person and all his power in common under the supreme direction of the general will, and, in our corporate capacity, we receive each member as an indivisible part of the whole."

Social Contract (1762) 1973:Book 1, chap. 6, 175.

15 Laws are always of use to those who possess and harmful to those who have nothing: from which it follows that the social state is advantageous to men only when all have something and none too much.

Social Contract (1762) 1973:Book 1, chap. 9, 181n.

16 There is often a great deal of difference between the will of all and the general will; the latter considers only the common interest, while the former takes private interest into account, and is no more than a sum of particular wills: but take away from these same wills the pluses and minuses that cancel one another, and the general will remains as the sum of the differences.

Social Contract (1762) 1973:Book 2, chap. 3, 185.

17 If we ask in what precisely consists the greatest good of all, which should be the end of every system of legislation, we shall find it reduces itself to two main objects, liberty and equality — liberty, because all particular dependence means so much force taken from the body of the State, and equality, because liberty cannot exist without it.

Social Contract (1762) 1973:Book 2, chap. 11, 204.

18 If we take the term in the strict sense, there never has been a real democracy, and there never will be. It is against the natural order for the many to govern and the few to be governed. It is unimaginable that the people should remain continually assembled to devote their time to public affairs, and it is clear that they cannot set up commissions for that purpose without the form of administration being changed.

Social Contract (1762) 1973:Book 3, chap. 4, 217.

19 Good laws lead to the making of better ones; bad ones bring about worse. As soon as any man says of the affairs of the State *What does it matter to me?* the State may be given up for lost.

Social Contract (1762) 1973:Book 3, chap. 15, 240.

20 To study men, we must look close by; to study man, we must learn to look afar; if we are to discover essential characteristics, we must first observe differences.

Essai sur l'origine des langues (1781) 1877:384.

Bertrand Russell 1872–1970
British philosopher

1 The essence of language lies, not in the use of this or that special means of communication, but in the employment of fixed associations (however these may have originated) in order that something now sensible — a spoken word, a picture, a gesture, or what not — may call up the "idea" of something else. Whenever this is done, what is now sensible may be called a "sign" or "symbol," and that of which it is intended to call up the "idea" may be called its "meaning." This is a rough outline of what constitutes "meaning."

The Analysis of Mind 1921:191.

2 We are. . . led to a somewhat vague distinction between what we may call "hard" data and "soft" data. This distinction is a matter of degree, and must not be pressed; but if not taken too seriously it may help to make the situation clear. I mean by "hard" data those which resist the solvent influence of critical reflection, and by "soft" data those which, under the operation of this process, become to our minds more or less doubtful.

Our Knowledge of the External World 1929:75. → Based upon the Lowell Lectures delivered in Boston in 1914. So far as we know, this is the first distinction made between "hard" and "soft" data.

S

Marshall Sahlins 1930–
U.S. anthropologist

1 So far as I know, we are the only people who think themselves risen from savages; everyone else believes they descend from gods.

Culture and Practical Reason 1976:52–53.

Henry St. John
See Lord Bolingbroke.

Saint-Simon 1760–1825
[Claude Henri de Rouvroy, comte de Saint-Simon]
French social philosopher

1 Society is a world which is upside down.

The nation holds as a fundamental principle that the poor should be generous to the rich, and that therefore the poorer classes should daily deprive themselves of necessities in order to increase the superfluous luxury of the rich.

The most guilty men, the robbers on a grand scale, who oppress the mass of the citizens, and extract from them three or four hundred millions a year, are given the responsibility of punishing minor offences against society.

Ignorance, superstition, idleness and costly dissipation are the privilege of the leaders of society, and men of ability, hard-working and thrifty, are employed only as inferiors and instruments.

To sum up, in every sphere men of greater ability are subject to the control of men who are incapable. From the point of view of morality, the most immoral men have the responsibility of leading the citizens towards virtue; from the point of view of distributive justice, the most guilty men are appointed to punish minor delinquents.

The Organizer (1819) 1964:74–75.

Saint-Simonians
French followers of Saint-Simon

1 In the absence of any official inventory of ascertained discoveries, the isolated scientists daily run the risk that they may be repeating experiments already made by others. If they were acquainted with other experiments, they would be spared efforts often as laborious as they are useless, and it would be easier for them to obtain means for forging ahead. Let us add here that their security is not complete. They are haunted by the work of a competitor. Possibly someone else is gleaning the same field and may, as the saying goes, "get there first." The scientist has to hide himself and conduct in haste and isolation work requiring deliberation and demanding aid from the association.

The Doctrine of Saint-Simon (1830) 1958:9. → The Saint-Simonians formed a short-lived movement which spread their version of Saint-Simon's doctrine after his death. In addition to its core French members, it attracted the notice of such young intellectuals as Carlyle, Heine, and John Stuart Mill.

John of Salisbury
See John of Salisbury.

Paul A. Samuelson 1915–
U.S. economist

1 I am giving away no secrets when I solemnly aver — upon the basis of vivid personal recollection — that no one else in Cambridge, Massachusetts, really knew what it [Keynes' *General Theory*] was about for some 12 to 18 months after its publication. Indeed, until the appearance of the mathematical models of Meade, Lange, Hicks, and Harrod there is reason to believe that Keynes himself did not truly understand his own analysis.

Lord Keynes and the General Theory 1946:188.

2 *The existence of analogies between central features of various theories implies the existence of a general theory which underlies the particular theories and unifies them with respect to those central features.* This fundamental principle of generalization by abstraction was enunciated by the eminent American mathematician E. H. Moore more than thirty years ago. It is the purpose of the pages that follow to work out its implications for theoretical and applied economics.

An economist of very keen intuition would perhaps have suspected from the beginning that seemingly diverse fields — production economics, consumer's behavior, international trade, public finance, business cycles, income analysis — possess striking formal similarities, and that economy of effort would result from analyzing these common elements.

I can make no claim to such initial insight. Only after laborious work in each of these fields did the realization dawn upon me that essentially the same inequalities and theorems appeared again and again, and that I was simply proving the same theorems a wasteful number of times.

Foundations of Economic Analysis (1947) 1961:3.

3 The further development of analytical economics along the lines of comparative dynamics must rest with the future. It is to be hoped that it will aid in the attack upon diverse problems — from the trivial behavior of a single small commodity, to the fluctuations of important components of the business cycle, and even to the majestic problems of economic development.

Foundations of Economic Analysis (1947) 1961:355.

4 How treacherous are economic "laws" in economic life: e.g., Bowley's Law of constant relative wage share; Long's Law of constant population participation in the labor force; Pareto's Law of unchangeable inequality of incomes; Denison's Law of constant private saving ratio; Colin Clark's Law of a 25 per cent ceiling on government expenditure and taxation; Modigliani's Law of constant wealth-income ratio; Marx's Law of the falling rate of real wage and/or the falling rate of profit; Everybody's Law of a constant capital-output ratio. If these be laws, Mother Nature is a criminal by nature.

A Brief Survey of Post-Keynesian Developments (1963) 1966:1539.

5 You never get something for nothing. From a nonempirical base of axioms you never get empirical results. Deductive analysis cannot determine whether the empirical properties of the stochastic model I posit come at all close to resembling the empirical determinants of today's real-world markets.

Proof That Properly Anticipated Prices Fluctuate Randomly (1965) 1972:783.

6 The theorem [of future prices] is so general that I must confess to having oscillated over the years in my own mind between regarding it as trivially obvious (and almost trivially vacuous) and regarding it as remarkably sweeping. Such perhaps is characteristic of basic results.

Proof That Properly Anticipated Prices Fluctuate Randomly (1965) 1972:786.

7 We are all post-Keynesians now. . . All? Well, almost all. Professor Milton Friedman is an exception. His is a voice that says the rate of growth of the money supply is vastly more important than any changes in tax rates or fiscal expenditures. And Friedman's voice is like the voice of ten.

Monetarism Pure and Neat, No (1968) 1983:325. → First published in the *London Sunday Telegraph* as "Don't Make Too Much of the Quantity Theory." See FRIEDMAN:6.

8 Economics. . . was a sleeping princess waiting for the invigorating kiss of Maynard Keynes. . . but. . . economics was also waiting for the invigorating kiss of mathematical methods.

Economics in a Golden Age (1970) 1972:159–160.

Paul A. Samuelson 1915–
and
William D. Nordhaus 1941–
U.S. economists

1 The *invisible-hand* doctrine is a concept for explaining why the outcome of a market mechanism looks so orderly. Smith's insight about the guiding function of the market mechanism has inspired modern economists — both the admirers and the critics of capitalism. After two centuries of experience and thought, however, we now recognize the scope and realistic limitations of this doctrine. We know that the market sometimes lets us down, that there are "market failures." Two of the most important market failures. . . are the *absence of perfect competition* and the presence of *externalities*.

Economics (1948) 1985:46.

2 People do not live by bread alone. Nor does society live by GNP alone. But on our way to that utopian state of affluence where concern about material well-being will disappear, we do need a summary measure of aggregate economic performance.

Economics (1948) 1985:102. → See KENNEDY:1.

George Santayana 1863–1952
Spanish-born U.S. philosopher

1 Progress, far from consisting in change, depends on retentiveness. When change is absolute there remains no being to improve and no direction is set for possible improvement: and when experience is not retained, as among savages, infancy is perpetual. Those who cannot remember the past are condemned to repeat it.

The Life of Reason (1905–1906) 1953:82.

2 The attempt to speak without speaking any particular language is not more hopeless than the attempt to have a religion that shall be no religion in particular. . . Every living and healthy religion has a marked idiosyncrasy. Its power consists in its special and surprising message and in the bias which that revelation gives to life. The vistas it opens and the mysteries it propounds are another world to live in; and another world to live in — whether we expect ever to pass wholly into it or no — is what we mean by having a religion.

The Life of Reason (1905–1906) 1953:180.

3 History is always written wrong, and so always needs to be rewritten.

The Life of Reason (1905–1906) 1953:397.

Edward Sapir 1884–1939
U.S. anthropologist and linguist

1 Were a language ever completely "grammatical," it would be a perfect engine of conceptual expression. Unfortunately, or luckily, no language is tyrannically consistent. All grammars leak.

Language (1921) 1949:38.

2 Both simple and complex types of language of an indefinite number of varieties may be found spoken at any desired level of cultural advance. When it comes to linguistic form, Plato walks with the Macedonian swineherd, Confucius with the head-hunting savage of Assam.

Language (1921) 1949:219.

3 Everything that we have so far seen to be true of language points to the fact that it is the most significant and colossal work that the human spirit has evolved — nothing short of a finished form of expression for all communicable experience. This form may be endlessly varied by the individual without thereby losing its distinctive contours; and it is constantly reshaping itself as is all art. Language is the most massive and inclusive art we know, a mountainous and anonymous work of unconscious generations.

Language (1921) 1949:219–220.

4 We may say that a language is so constructed that no matter what any speaker of it may desire to communicate, no matter how original or bizarre his idea or his fancy, the language is prepared to do his work. . . The world of linguistic forms, held within the framework of a given language, is a complete system of reference.

The Grammarian and His Language (1924) 1949:153.

5 Linguistics has also that profoundly serene and satisfying quality which inheres in mathematics and in music and which may be described as the creation out of simple elements of a self-contained universe of forms. Linguistics has neither the sweep nor the instrumental power of mathematics, nor has it the universal aesthetic appeal of music. But under its crabbed, technical appearance there lies hidden the same classical spirit, the same freedom in restraint, which animates mathematics and music at their purest. This spirit is antagonistic to the romanticism which is rampant in America today and which debauches so much of our science with its frenetic desire.

The Grammarian and His Language (1924) 1949:159.

6 Poetry I neither read nor write. . . I really think I shall end life's prelude by descending into the fastnesses of a purely technical linguistic erudition. . . I can understand better than ever before what content there may be in pure mathematics.

Letter to Ruth Benedict, 14 June 1925. 1959: 180.

7 Human beings do not live in the objective world alone, nor alone in the world of social activity as ordinarily understood, but are very much at the mercy of the particular language which has become the medium of expression for their society. It is quite an illusion to imagine that one adjusts to reality essentially without the use of language and that language is merely an incidental means of solving specific problems of communication or reflection. The fact of the matter is that the "real world" is to a large extent unconsciously built up on the language habits of the group. No two languages are ever sufficiently similar to be considered as representing the same social reality. The worlds in which different societies live are distinct worlds, not merely the same world with different labels attached.

The Status of Linguistics as a Science (1929) 1949:162.

8 Better than any other social science, linguistics shows by its data and methods, necessarily more easily defined than the data and methods of any other type of discipline dealing with socialized behavior, the possibility of a truly scientific study of society which does not ape the methods nor attempt to adopt unrevised the concepts of the natural sciences.

The Status of Linguistics as a Science (1929) 1949:166.

9 Language is the communicative process par excellence in every known society, and it is exceedingly important to observe that whatever may be the shortcomings of a primitive society judged from the vantage point of civilization its language inevitably forms as sure, complete and potentially creative an apparatus of referential symbolism as the most sophisticated language that we know of.

Communication 1931:78.

10 Fashion is custom in the guise of departure from custom.

Fashion 1931:140.

11 Human beings do not wish to be modest; they want to be as expressive — that is, as immodest — as fear allows; fashion helps them solve their paradoxical problem.

Fashion 1931:143.

12 Cultural anthropology is not valuable because it uncovers the archaic in the psychological sense. It is valuable because it is constantly rediscovering the normal.

Cultural Anthropology and Psychiatry (1932) 1949:515.

13 If a man who has never seen more than a single elephant in the course of his life nevertheless speaks without the slightest hesitation of ten elephants or a million elephants or a herd of elephants or of elephants walking two by two or three by three or of generations of elephants, it is obvious that language has the power to analyze experience into theoretically dissociable elements and to create that world of the potential intergrading with the actual which enables human beings to transcend the immediately given in their individual experiences and to join in a larger common understanding. This common understanding constitutes culture.

Language 1933:156–157.

George Sarton 1884–1956
Belgian-born U.S. historian of science

1 The most ominous conflict of our time is the difference of opinion, of outlook, between men of letters, historians, philosophers, the so-called humanists, on the one side and scientists on the other. The gap cannot but increase because of the intolerance of both and the fact that science is growing by leaps and bounds.

The History of Science and the History of Civilization (1930) 1988:54–55. → See SNOW:2.

2 A great injustice is made when Comte is called the founder of sociology, for Quetelet has better claims to this title . . . Auguste Comte (1798–1857) was probably the first to speak of social physics (as early as 1822) and of sociology (1839) . . . Comte wrote on these matters as on many others with unbearable prolixity and conceit. In the meanwhile Quetelet was not only saying what to do but actually doing it . . . Comte talked, strutted and soared, and apparently ignored the terre-à-terre activity of his fellow worker in "social physics," but that activity was far more creative than his own . . . Comte had no appreciation of the importance of the theory of probability, nor of statistics, nor of the statistical approach to biology and sociology.

Quetelet (1935) 1962:236–237.

3 I like to think of the constant presence in any sound Republic of two guardian angels: the Statistician and the Historian of Science. The former keeps his finger on the pulse of Humanity, and gives the necessary warning when things are not as they should be. . . If the Statistician is like a physician, the Historian is like a priest,— the guardian of man's most precious heritage, of the one treasure which, whatever may happen, can never be taken away from him — for the past is irrevocable.

Quetelet (1935) 1962:241.

Ferdinand de Saussure 1857–1913
Swiss linguist

1 *A science that studies the life of signs within society* is conceivable; it would be a part of social psychology and consequently of general psychology; I shall call it *semiology* (from Greek *sēmeîon* "sign"). Semiology would show what constitutes signs, what laws govern them. Since the science does not yet exist, no one can say what it would be; but it has a right to existence, a place staked out in advance. Linguistics is only a part of the general science of semiology; the laws discovered by semiology will be applicable to linguistics, and the latter will circumscribe a well-defined area within the mass of anthropological facts.

Course in General Linguistics (1916) 1966:16.

2 Language is speech less speaking. It is the whole set of linguistic habits which allow an individual to understand and to be understood.

Course in General Linguistics (1916) 1966:77.

3 Psychologically our thought — apart from its expression in words — is only a shapeless and indistinct mass.

Course in General Linguistics (1916) 1966:111.

4 Language can. . . be compared with a sheet of paper: thought is the front and the sound the back; one cannot cut the front without cutting the back at the same time; likewise in language, one can neither divide sound from thought nor thought from sound; the division could be accomplished only abstractedly, and the result would be either pure psychology or pure phonology.

Course in General Linguistics (1916) 1966:113.

5 Within the same language, all words used to express related ideas limit each other reciprocally. . . The value of just any term is accordingly determined by its environment; it is impossible to fix even the value of the word signifying "sun" without first considering its surroundings: in some languages it is not possible to say "sit in the *sun*."

Course in General Linguistics (1916) 1966:116.

6 A linguistic system is a series of differences of sound combined with a series of differences of ideas.

Course in General Linguistics (1916) 1966:120.

Alfred Sauvy 1898–1990
French economist and demographer

1 This Third World, ignored, exploited and despised, exactly as the Third Estate was before the Revolution, would also like to become something.

General Theory of Population (1966) 1969:204n. → This statement was first published in *L'Observateur*, 14 August 1952. Sauvy believed that this was the first use of the phrase "third world."

2 [An aging society is one comprised of] old people ruminating over old ideas in old houses.

Quoted in Michael S. Teitelbaum, As Societies Age 1979:143. → This remark is quoted frequently; when queried by the editors, Sauvy reported that he had published it somewhere, but he could not recall where.

Jean Baptiste Say 1767–1832
French economist

1 No act of saving subtracts in the least from consumption, provided the thing saved be re-invested or restored to productive employment. On the contrary, it gives rise to a consumption perpetually renovated and recurring; whereas there is no repetition of an unproductive consumption.

A Treatise on Political Economy (1803) 1841:110.

2 It is production which opens a demand for products. . . A product is no sooner created, than it, from that instant, affords a market for other products to the full extent of its own value.

A Treatise on Political Economy (1803) 1841:133–134. → This is Say's celebrated "law of markets."

Isaac Schapera 1905–
South African anthropologist

1 The Aryan is a man with a white skin, a thick skin and a foreskin.

From lectures at the University of Cape Town during World War II. Quoted in Adam Kuper, personal communication, 7 December 1987.

E. E. Schattschneider 1892–1971
U.S. political scientist

1 The most important distinction in modern political philosophy, the distinction between democracy and dictatorship, can be made best in terms of party politics. The parties are not therefore merely appendages of modern government; they are in the center of it and play a determinative and creative role in it.

Party Government 1942:1.

Thomas C. Schelling 1921–
U.S. economist

1 Recall the famous case of [Sherlock] Holmes and Moriarty on separate trains, neither directly in touch with the other, each having to choose whether to get off at the next station. We can consider three kinds of payoff. In one, Holmes wins a prize if they get off at different stations, Moriarty wins it if they get off at the same station; this is the zero-sum game, in which the preferences of the two players are perfectly correlated inversely. In the second case, Holmes and Moriarty will both be rewarded if they succeed in getting off at the same station, whatever station that may be; this is the pure-coordination game, in which the preferences of the players are perfectly correlated positively. The third payoff would show Holmes and Moriarty both being rewarded if they succeed in getting off at the same station, but Holmes gaining more if both he and Moriarty get off at one particular station, Moriarty gaining more if both get off at some other particular station, both losing unless they get off at the same station. This is the usual nonzero-sum game, or "imperfect-correlation-of-preferences" game. This is the mixture of conflict and mutual dependence that epitomizes bargaining situations. By specifying particular communication and intelligence systems for the players, we can enrich the game or make it trivial or provide an advantage to one of the two players in the first and third variants.

The Strategy of Conflict 1960:87.

2 The name of this discipline, "game theory" . . . has frivolous connotations. It is also easily confused with "gaming," as in war gaming, business gaming, crisis gaming — confused, that is, with simulations of decision or conflict . . . If we had a more general name for the subject now known as "game theory," it would be found that a great many parlor games fit the definition. It was this that led the authors of the first great work in the field to call their book, *Theory of Games and Economic Behavior.*

What Is Game Theory? (1967) 1984:240–241. → See Von Neumann and Morgenstern:1.

Friedrich von Schiller 1759–1805
German dramatist, poet, and historian

1 Man only plays when in the full meaning of the word he is a man, and *he is only completely a man when he plays.*

Essays Aesthetical and Philosophical (1795) 1916:71.

Arthur M. Schlesinger, Jr. 1917–
U.S. historian

1 The choice we face is not between progress with conflict and progress without conflict. The choice is between conflict and stagnation. You cannot expel conflict from society any more than you can from the human mind. When you attempt it, the psychic costs in schizophrenia or torpor are the same.

The totalitarians regard the toleration of conflict as our central weakness. So it may appear to be in an age of anxiety. But we know it to be basically our central strength.

The Vital Center (1949) 1962:255.

2 I trust that a graduate student some day will write a doctoral essay on the influence of the Munich analogy on the subsequent history of the twentieth century. Perhaps in the end he will conclude that the multitude of errors committed in the name of "Munich" may exceed the original error of 1938.

The Inscrutability of History (1966) 1967:89.

3 I have often thought that a futurist trying to forecast the next three American Presidents in early 1940 would hardly have named as the first President after Franklin D. Roosevelt an obscure back-bench senator from Missouri, anticipating defeat by the governor of his state in the Democratic primaries; as the second, an unknown lieutenant-colonel in the United States Army; and, as the third, a kid still at college. . . The salient fact about the historical process, so far as the short run is concerned, is its inscrutability.

The Inscrutability of History (1966) 1967:94.

4 It is hardly surprising that the first historian to emphasize the accelerating velocity of history [Henry Adams] should have been an American.

Foreword to *The Cycles of American History* 1986:x.

Arthur Schopenhauer 1788–1860
German philosopher

1 The sciences, since they are systems of conceptions, speak always of species; history speaks of individuals. It would accordingly be a science of individuals, which is a contradiction. It also follows that the sciences all speak of

that which always is: history, on the other hand, of that which is once, and then no more.

On History (1844) 1928:322. → First published as a supplement to the second edition of *The World as Will and Idea*.

2 Before every great truth has been discovered, a previous feeling, a presentiment, a faint outline thereof, as in a fog, is proclaimed, and there is a vain attempt to grasp it just because the progress of the times prepared the way for it. Accordingly, it is precluded by isolated utterances; but he alone is the author of a truth who has recognized it from its grounds and has thought it out to its consequents; who has developed its whole content and has surveyed the extent of its domain; and who, fully aware of its value and importance, has therefore expounded it clearly and coherently. . . Columbus is the discoverer of America, not the first shipwrecked sailor there cast up by the waves.

Parerga and Paralipomena (1851) 1974:Vol. 1, 133. → See WHITEHEAD:2.

E. F. Schumacher 1911–1977

German-born British economist

1 I have no doubt that it is possible to give a new direction to technological development, a direction that shall lead it back to the real needs of man, and that also means: *to the actual size of man*. Man is small, and, therefore, small is beautiful. To go for giantism is to go for self- destruction.

Small Is Beautiful 1973:148.

Joseph A. Schumpeter 1883–1950

Austro-Hungarian born U.S. economist

1 Without development there is no profit, without profit no development. For the capitalist system it must be added further that without profit there would be no accumulation of wealth.

The Theory of Economic Development (1912) 1934:154.

2 The spirit of a people, its cultural level, its social structure, the deeds its policy may prepare — all this and more is written in its fiscal history, stripped of all phrases. He who knows how to listen to its message here discerns the thunder of world history more clearly than anywhere else.

The Crisis of the Tax State (1918) 1954:7.

3 For the duration of its collective life, or the time during which its identity may be assumed, each class resembles a hotel or an omnibus, always full, but always of different people.

Social Classes (1927) 1955:126.

4 This historic and irreversible change in the way of doing things we call "innovation" and we define: innovations are changes in production functions which cannot be decomposed into infinitesimal steps. Add as many mail-coaches as you please, you will never get a railroad by so doing.

The Analysis of Economic Change (1935) 1951:136.

5 On the whole, . . . my opinion is definitely favorable to the publication of [Talcott Parsons' *Structure of Social Action*] which not everyone will appreciate, but which everyone must recognize as a very serious piece of research. Commercial publication seems to me to be pretty much out of the question, but I may be wrong in this. American thought has of late so much turned in these directions that sales may be after all more favorable than I expect.

Unpublished memorandum to the Harvard University Committee on Research in the Social Sciences, December 23, 1936. → *The Structure of Social Action* was published by a commercial publisher in 1937 and remains in print.

6 What distinguishes [Marx] from the economists of his own time and those who preceded him, was precisely a vision of economic evolution as a distinct process generated by the economic system itself. In every other respect he only used and adapted the concepts and propositions of Ricardian economics, but the concept of economic evolution which he put into an unessential Hegelian setting, is quite his own.

Preface to the Japanese edition of *Theorie der wirtschaftlichen Entwicklung* (1937) 1951:160.

7 Analyzing business cycles means neither more nor less than analyzing the economic process of the capitalist era. Most of us discover this truth which at once reveals the nature of the task and also its formidable dimensions. Cycles are not, like tonsils, separable things that might be treated by themselves, but are, like the beat of the heart, of the essence of the organism that displays them.

Business Cycles (1939) 1982:Vol. 1, v.

8 Capitalism is that form of private property economy in which innovations are carried out by means of borrowed money, which in general, though not by logical necessity, implies credit creation.

Business Cycles (1939) 1982:Vol. 1, 223.

9 Marxism *is* a religion. To the believer it presents, first, a system of ultimate ends that embody the meaning of life and are absolute standards by which to judge events and actions; and, secondly, a guide to those ends which implies a plan of salvation and the indication of the evil from which mankind, or a chosen section of mankind, is to be saved.

Capitalism, Socialism, and Democracy (1942) 1975:5.

10 Queen Elizabeth owned silk stockings. The capitalist achievement does not typically consist in providing more silk stockings for queens but in bringing them within the reach of factory girls in return for steadily decreasing amounts of effort.

Capitalism, Socialism, and Democracy (1942) 1975:67.

11 Capitalism. . . is by nature a form or method of economic change and not only never is but never can be stationary. And this evolutionary character of the capitalist process is not merely due to the fact that economic life goes on in a social and natural environment which changes and by its change alters the data of economic action; this fact is important and these changes (wars, revolutions and so on) often condition industrial change, but they are not its prime movers. Nor is this evolutionary character due to a quasi-automatic increase in population and capital or to the vagaries of monetary systems of which exactly the same thing holds true. The fundamental impulse that sets and keeps the capitalist engine in motion comes from the new consumers' goods, the new methods of production or transportation, the new markets, the new forms of industrial organization that capitalist enterprise creates.

Capitalism, Socialism, and Democracy (1942) 1975:82–83.

12 If the monastery gave birth to the intellectual of the medieval world, it was capitalism that let him loose and presented him with the printing press.

Capitalism, Socialism, and Democracy (1942) 1975:147.

13 There is nothing surprising in the habit of economists to invade the sociological field. A large part of their work — practically the whole of what they have to say on institutions and on the forces that shape economic behavior — inevitably overlaps the sociologist's preserves. In consequence, a no-man's land or everyman's land has developed that might conveniently be called economic sociology.

Vilfredo Pareto (1949) 1951:134.

14 The fact is that the *Wealth of Nations* does not contain a single *analytic* idea, principle, or method that was entirely new in 1776.

History of Economic Analysis 1954:184.

15 The word Econometrics is, I think, Professor [Ragnar] Frisch's, and it has been coined by analogy with Biometrics, statistical biology. A distinctive name, embodying a program, is perfectly justified in this case. . . And so we may leave it at that, though the term is exposed to objection on philological grounds: it ought to be either Ecometrics or Economometrics.

History of Economic Analysis 1954:209n. → See FRISCH:1.

Alfred Schutz 1899–1959

Austrian-born U.S. sociologist and philosopher

1 I can understand the acts and motives of Caesar as well as of the cave-man who left no other testimony of his existence than the firestone hatchet exhibited in the showcase of the museum.

Interactional Relationships (1942–1967) 1970:180–181. → Georg Simmel seems to have been the first sociologist to use the metaphor of "understanding Caesar"; Max Weber used it a decade later and attributed it to Simmel. See SIMMEL:11 and MAX WEBER:7.

2 The phenomenologist does not deny the existence of the outer world, but for his analytical purpose he makes up his mind to suspend belief in its existence — that is, to refrain intentionally and systematically from all judgments related directly or indirectly to the existence of the outer world.

Some Leading Concepts of Phenomenology (1944) 1962:104.

Edwin R. A. Seligman 1861–1939

U.S. economist

1 The existence of man depends upon his ability to sustain himself; the economic life is therefore the fundamental condition of all life.

The Economic Interpretation of History (1902) 1903:3.

Philip Selznick 1919–

U.S. sociologist

1 *Coöptation is the process of absorbing new elements into the leadership or policy-determining structure of an organization as a means of averting threats to its stability or existence*. . . The significance of coöptation for organizational analysis is not simply that there is a change in or a broadening of leadership, and that this is an adaptive response, but also *that this change is consequential for the character and role of the organization or governing body*. Coöptation results in some constriction of the field of choice available to the organization or leadership in question. The character of the coöpted elements will necessarily shape the modes of action available to the group which has won adaptation at the price of commitment to outside elements.

TVA and the Grass Roots 1949:13, 15–16.

2 We shall speak of organizations and organizational practices as weapons when they are used by a power-seeking elite *in a manner unrestrained by the constitutional order of the arena within which the contest takes place*. In this usage, "weapon" is not meant to denote *any* political tool, but one torn from its normal context and unacceptable to the community as a legitimate mode of action.

The Organizational Weapon 1952:2.

Nassau William Senior 1790–1864

British economist

1 The instant wages cease to be a bargain — the instant the labourer is paid, not according to his *value*, but his *wants*, he ceases to be a freeman. He acquires the indolence, the improvidence, the rapacity, and the malignity, but not the subordination of a slave.

The Causes and Remedies of the Present Disturbances (1830) 1831:x.

2 The subject treated by the Political Economist. . . is not Happiness, but Wealth; his premises consist of a very few general propositions, the result of observation, or consciousness, and scarcely requiring proof, or even formal statement, which almost every man, as soon as he hears them, admits as familiar to his thoughts, or at least as included in his previous knowledge; and his inferences are nearly as general, and, if he has reasoned correctly, as certain, as his premises.

An Outline of the Science of Political Economy (1836) 1965:2–3.

3 The business of a Political Economist is neither to recommend nor to dissuade, but to state general principles, which it is fatal to neglect, but neither advisable, nor perhaps practicable, to use as the sole, or even the principal, guides in the actual conduct of affairs. . . To decide in each case how far those conclusions are to be acted upon, belongs to the art of government, an art to which Political Economy is only one of many subservient Sciences.

An Outline of the Science of Political Economy (1836) 1965:3.

4 Although Human Labour, and the Agency of Nature, independently of that of man, are the primary Productive Powers, they require the concurrence of a Third Productive Principle to give to them complete efficiency. The most laborious population, inhabiting the most fertile territory, if they devoted all their labour to the production of immediate results, and consumed its produce as it arose, would soon find their utmost exertions insufficient to produce even the mere necessaries of existence.

To the Third Principle, or Instrument of Production, without which the two others are inefficient, we shall give the name of *Abstinence:* a term by which we express the conduct of a person who either abstains from the unproductive use of what he can command, or designedly prefers the production of remote to that of immediate results.

It was to the effects of this Third Instrument of Production that we adverted, when we laid down, as the third of our elementary propositions, that *the Powers of Labour and of the other Instruments which produce Wealth may be indefinitely increased by using their Products as the means of further Production.*

An Outline of the Science of Political Economy (1836) 1965:58. → See SOLOW:1.

William Shakespeare 1564–1616
British dramatist and poet

1 [*Jaques*]: All the world's a stage,
And all the men and women merely players:
They have their exits and their entrances;
And one man in his time plays many parts,
His acts being seven ages. At first the infant,
Mewling and puking in the nurse's arms.
Then the whining school-boy, with his satchel
And shining morning face, creeping like snail
Unwillingly to school. And then the lover,
Sighing like furnace, with a woeful ballad
Made to his mistress' eyebrow. Then a soldier,
Full of strange oaths, and bearded like the pard,
Jealous in honour, sudden and quick in quarrel,
Seeking the bubble reputation
Even in the cannon's mouth. And then the justice,
In fair round belly with good capon lined,
With eyes severe and beard of formal cut,
Full of wise saws and modern instances;
And so he plays his part. The sixth age shifts
Into the lean and slipper'd pantaloon,
With spectacles on nose and pouch on side,
His youthful hose, well saved, a world too wide
For his shrunk shank; and his big manly voice,
Turning again toward childish treble, pipes
And whistles in his sound. Last scene of all,
That ends this strange eventful history,
Is second childishness and mere oblivion,
Sans teeth, sans eyes, sans taste, sans every thing.

As You Like It:Act 2, scene 7, 677.

2 [*Hamlet*]: Madam, how like you this play?
[*Queen*]: The lady doth protest too much, methinks.

Hamlet:Act 3, scene 2, 756.

3 [*Prince*]: I never thought to hear you speak again.
[*King*]: Thy wish was father, Harry, to that thought.

The Second Part of King Henry IV:Act 4, scene 5, 546.

4 [*Miranda*]: O, wonder!
How many goodly creatures are there here!
How beauteous mankind is! O brave new world,
That has such people in't!

The Tempest:Act 5, scene 1, 1323.

George Bernard Shaw 1856–1950
Irish-born British playwright

1 [*Sir Patrick*]: [Medicine is] a very good profession, too, my lad. When you know as much as I know of the ignorance and superstition of the patients, youll wonder that we're half as good as we are.
[*Ridgeon*]: We're not a profession: we're a conspiracy.
[*Sir Patrick*]: All professions are conspiracies against the laity. And we cant all be geniuses like you. Every fool can get ill; but every fool cant be a good doctor: there are not enough good ones to go round.

The Doctor's Dilemma (1906) 1985:116. → See ADAM SMITH:17.

2 [*Liza*]:. . . the difference between a lady and a flower girl is not how she behaves, but how shes treated. I shall always be a flower girl to Professor Higgins, because he always treats me as a flower girl, and always will; but I know I can be a lady to you, because you always treat me as a lady, and always will.

Pygmalion (1912) 1930:197.

Charles Sherrington 1857–1952
British physiologist

1 With the nervous system intact the reactions of the various parts of that system, the "simple reflexes," are ever combined into great unitary harmonies, actions which in their sequence one upon another constitute in their continuity what may be termed the "behaviour."

The Integrative Action of the Nervous System (1906) 1961:238.

Edward Shils 1911–
U.S. sociologist

1 Modern society is no lonely crowd, no horde of refugees fleeing from freedom. It is no *Gesellschaft,* soulless, egotistical, loveless, faithless, utterly impersonal and lacking any integrative forces other than interest or coercion. It is held together by an infinity of personal attachments, moral obligations in concrete contexts, professional and creative pride, individual ambition, primordial affinities, and a civil sense which is low in many, high in some, and moderate in most persons.

Primordial, Personal, Sacred, and Civil Ties (1957) 1975:112.

2 From a distant and almost police-like concern with the "condition of the poor," from a concern with numbers as clues to national wealth and power, from a desire to "unmask" and discredit the hopes and fantasies of the race, sociology has advanced to a fundamental orientation — incipiently present in the classics, and now tentatively elaborated in the prevailing direction of sociological theory — that appreciates not just the animality or mechanical properties of man, but his cognitive, moral, and appreciative humanity.

The Calling of Sociology 1961:1411.

3 Society has a center. There is a central zone in the structure of society [which] is not, as such, a spatially located phenomenon. It almost always has a more or less definite location within the bounded territory in which the society lives. Its centrality has, however, nothing to do with geometry and little with geography.

Center and Periphery (1961) 1975:3.

Judith N. Shklar 1928–
Latvian-born U.S. political scientist

1 Rousseau was the last of the classical utopists. He was the last great political theorist to be utterly uninterested in history, past or future, the last also to judge and condemn without giving any thought to programs of action. His enduring originality and fascination are entirely due to the acute psychological insight with which he diagnosed the emotional diseases of modern civilization. Both the radical new ideas and the tradition of utopianism were essential to his critical task.

Men and Citizens 1969:1.

2 [Rousseau's] *Social Contract* was not meant to be a plan for any future society, but a standard for judging existing institutions. It was a yardstick, not a program.

Men and Citizens 1969:17.

3 If the various possible identification tags were really appropriate, the greatest of political theorists would have nothing to say to us. We would not even bother to "place" them in the first place. A Locke bent on justifying child labor, a Montesquieu glorifying the nobility of the robe, a Machiavelli advising a Medici to scheme and fight, are figures too reduced to be even worth criticizing. Yet one continues to read and to respond to them and to the even more distant Plato and Aristotle with a vigor that few other authors have been able to arouse. In fact, they educate us and that is why they are interpreted and re-interpreted.

Men and Citizens 1969: 217–218.

Michael Silverstein 1945–
U.S. anthropologist and linguist

1 With language. . . we might come most clearly to formulate the social scientist's dilemma of "structure" vs. "action" in a never-ending historical movement. If "structure" is a set of (formalizable) patterns according to which "action" (contextually-situated social behavior) is interpretable, a so-called synchronic statement (or model) of "structure" tells us in what respect "action" remains the same within a social system, in what sense discernible instances of social behavior remain "the same" action. What we find, however, when we attempt to apprehend everything in such structural terms (here we return to Whorf's theme of "indeterminacy"), is that plus c'est la même chose, plus ça change.

Language Structure and Linguistic Ideology 1979:234. → A reversal of Alphonse Karr's 1844 epigram. See KARR:1.

Georg Simmel 1858–1918
German sociologist

1 The actions of a society, compared to those of the individual, possess an unswerving accuracy and expediency. The individual is pushed hither and thither by contradictory impressions, impulses and thoughts and his mind offers at each moment a multitude of possibilities for action, between which he not always knows how to choose with objective accuracy or even merely with subjective certainty. In contrast, the social group is indeed clear who it holds to be its friend and who its enemy.

Über soziale Differenzierung 1890:85.

2 "Pure sociology" . . . abstracts the mere elements of sociation. It isolates it inductively and psychologically from the heterogeneity of its contents and purposes, which, in themselves, are not societal. It thus proceeds like grammar, which isolates the pure forms of language from their contents through which these forms, nevertheless, come to life. In a comparable manner, social groups which are the most diverse imaginable in purpose

and general significance, may nevertheless show identical forms of behavior toward one another on the part of their individual members. We find superiority and subordination, competition, division of labor, formation of parties, representation, inner solidarity coupled with exclusiveness toward the outside, and innumerable similar features in the state, in a religious community, in a band of conspirators, in an economic association, in an art school, in the family.

The Philosophy of Money (1900) 1978:22.

3 The phenomena of valuation and purchase, of exchange and the means of exchange, of the forms of production and the values of possession, which economics views from *one* standpoint, are here viewed from another. . . A single science. . . never exhausts the totality of a reality.

The Philosophy of Money (1900) 1978:54–55.

4 The exchange of the products of labour, or of any other possessions, is obviously one of the purest and most primitive forms of human socialization; not in the sense that "society" already existed and then brought about acts of exchange but, on the contrary, that exchange is one of the functions that creates an inner bond between men — a society, in place of a mere collection of individuals. Society is not an absolute entity which must first exist so that all the individual relations of its members — super- and sub-ordination, cohesion, imitation, division of labour, exchange, common attack and defence, religious community, party formations and many others — can develop within its framework or be represented by it: it is only the synthesis or the general term for the totality of these specific interactions.

The Philosophy of Money (1900) 1978:175.

5 Without the general trust that people have in each other, society itself would disintegrate, for very few relationships are based entirely upon what is known with certainty about another person, and very few relationships would endure if trust were not as strong as, or stronger than, rational proof or personal observation.

The Philosophy of Money (1900) 1978:178–179.

6 Never has an object that owes its value exclusively to its quality as a means, to its convertibility into more definite values [as money], so thoroughly and unreservedly developed into a psychological absolute value, into a completely engrossing final purpose governing our practical consciousness.

The Philosophy of Money (1900) 1978:232.

7 Money, more than any other form of value, makes possible the secrecy, invisibility and silence of exchange. . . Money's formlessness and abstractness makes it possible to invest it in the most varied and most remote values and thereby to remove it completely from the gaze of neighbours. Its anonymity and colourlessness does not reveal the source from which it came.

The Philosophy of Money (1900) 1978:385.

8 In some respects, money may be compared to language, which also lends itself to the most divergent directions of thought and feeling. Money belongs to those forces whose peculiarity lies in a lack of peculiarity, but which, none the less, may colour life very differently because their mere formal, functional and quantitative nature is confronted with qualitatively determined contents and directions of life, and induces them to generate qualitatively new formations.

The Philosophy of Money (1900) 1978:470.

9 Dyads, wholes composed of only two participants, presuppose a greater individualization of their members than larger groups do (other things being equal). . . The essential point is that within a dyad, there can be no majority which could outvote the individual. This majority, however, is made possible by the mere addition of a third member.

The Isolated Individual and the Dyad (1902) 1950:137.

10 The relationships and concerns of the typical metropolitan resident are so manifold and complex that, especially as a result of the agglomeration of so many persons with such differentiated interests, their relationships and activities intertwine with one another into a many-membered organism. In view of this fact, the lack of the most exact punctuality in promises and performances would cause the whole to break down into an inextricable chaos. If all the watches in Berlin suddenly went wrong in different ways even only as much as an hour, its entire economic and commercial life would be derailed for some time.

The Metropolis and Mental Life (1903) 1971:328.

11 *Man kein Cäsar zu sein braucht, um Cäsar wirklich zu verstehen, und kein zweiter Luther, um Luther zu begreifen* [One need not be a Caesar truly to understand Caesar, nor a second Luther to understand Luther].

Die Probleme der Geschichtsphilosophie 1905:57. → As Donald N. Levine has observed (personal communication), Simmel introduced this aphorism to signify the plausibility of reconstructing the experience of historical figures despite their cultural distance from us. For later uses of the aphorism, see MAX WEBER:7 and SCHUTZ:1.

12 A certain amount of discord, inner divergence and outer controversy, is organically tied up with the very elements that ultimately hold the group together.

Conflict (1908) 1955:17–18.

13 Peace does not follow conflict with the same directness [as conflict follows peace]. The ending of conflict is a specific enterprise. It belongs neither to war nor to peace, just as a bridge is different from either bank it connects.

Conflict (1908) 1955:110.

14 [In modern society] a very special type of friendship emerges . . . These differentiated friendships which connect us with one individual in terms of affection, with another, in terms of common intellectual aspects, with a third, in terms of religious impulses, and with a fourth, in terms of common experiences — all these friendships present a very special synthesis in regard to the question

of discretion, of reciprocal revelation and concealment. They require that the friends do not look into those mutual spheres of interest and feeling which, after all, are not included in the relation and which, if touched upon, would make them feel painfully the limits of their mutual understanding.

Friendship and Love (1908) 1950:326.

15 Men regard one another, and men are jealous one of another; they write one another letters or dine together; they meet in sympathy or antipathy quite apart from all tangible interests; their gratitude for altruistic service weaves a chain of consequences never to be sundered; they ask the way of one another and they dress and adorn themselves for one another; — these are instances chosen quite at random from the thousand relations momentary or lasting, conscious or unconscious, transitory or fraught with consequences, which, playing from person to person, knit us incessantly together. Every moment such threads are spun, are dropped and again caught up, replaced by others, woven up with others. These are the reciprocities between the atoms of society, reciprocities that only the piercing vision of psychology can investigate, which determine all the tenacity and elasticity, all the variegation and unity of this so intelligible and yet so mysterious life of society.

Soziologie 1908:19.

16 If wandering is the liberation from every given point in space, and thus the conceptional opposite to fixation at such a point, the sociological form of the "stranger" presents the unity, as it were, of these two characteristics. This phenomenon too, however, reveals that spatial relations are only the condition, on the one hand, and the symbol, on the other, of human relations.

The Stranger (1908) 1950:402.

17 [The stranger] is freer, practically and theoretically; he surveys conditions with less prejudice; his criteria for them are more general and more objective ideals; he is not tied down in his action by habit, piety, and precedent.

The Stranger (1908) 1950:405.

18 Nobody, in general, wishes that his influence completely determine the other individual. He rather wants this influence, this determination of the other, to act back upon *him*. Even the abstract will-to-dominate, therefore, is a case of interaction.

Superordination and Subordination (1908) 1950:181.

19 Without the phenomenon we call faithfulness, society could simply not exist, as it does, for any length of time. The elements which keep it alive — the self-interest of its members, suggestion, coercion, idealism, mechanical habit, sense of duty, love, inertia — could not save it from breaking apart if they were not supplemented by this factor.

Faithfulness and Gratitude (1917) 1950:379.

20 Knowing and not knowing about the consequences of our actions [we] are all like the chess player. . . If he did not know, to a certain extent, what the consequences of a certain move would be, the game would be impossible; but it would also be impossible if this foresight extended indefinitely.

The Transcendent Character of Life (1918) 1971:354.

Herbert A. Simon 1916–

U.S. political scientist, psychologist, and economist

1 It is a fatal defect of the current principles of administration that, like proverbs, they occur in pairs. For almost every principle one can find an equally plausible and acceptable contradictory principle. Although the two principles of the pair will lead to exactly opposite organizational recommendations, there is nothing in the theory to indicate which is the proper one to apply.

Administrative Behavior (1945) 1961:20.

2 Since an organization is not an organism the only memory it possesses, in the proper sense of the term, is the collective memory of its participants. This is insufficient for organization purposes, first, because what is in one man's mind is not necessarily available to other members of the organization, and, second, because when an individual leaves an organization the organization loses that part of its "memory."

Administrative Behavior (1945) 1961:166.

3 *The central concern of administrative theory is with the boundary between the rational and the non-rational aspects of human social behavior.* Administrative theory is peculiarly the theory of intended and bounded rationality — of the behavior of human beings who *satisfice* because they have not the wits to *maximize*.

Introduction to the 1957 edition of *Administrative Behavior* (1945) 1961:xxiv.

4 The capacity of the human mind for formulating and solving complex problems is very small compared with the size of the problems whose solution is required for objectively rational behavior in the real world.

Rationality and Administrative Decision Making 1957:198.

5 A man, viewed as a behaving system, is quite simple. The apparent complexity of his behavior over time is largely a reflection of the complexity of the environment in which he finds himself.

The Sciences of the Artificial 1969:25.

6 There is no contradiction between the intuitive model of thinking and the behavioral model, nor do the two models represent alternative modes of thought residing in different cerebral hemispheres and competing for control over the mind. All serious thinking calls on both modes, both search-like processes and the sudden recognition of familiar patterns. Without recognition based on previous experience, search through complex spaces would proceed in snail-like fashion. Intuition exploits the knowledge we have gained through our past searches. . . In

most problem situations combining aspects of novelty with familiar components, intuition and search will cooperate in reaching solutions.

Reason in Human Affairs 1983:28–29.

7 Fortunately, it is not necessary to surround creativity with mystery and obfuscation. No sparks of genius need be postulated to account for human invention, discovery, creation. These acts are acts of the human brain, the same brain that helps us dress in the morning, arrive at our office, and go through our daily chores, however uncreative most of these chores may be. Today we have a substantial body of empirical evidence about the processes that people use to think and to solve problems, and evidence, as well, that these same processes can account for the thinking and problem solving that is adjudged creative.

What We Know about the Creative Process 1985:4.

8 What distinguishes science from every other form of human intellectual activity is that it disciplines speculation with facts. Theory and data are the two blades of the scissors. But the metaphor is not quite right, for the blades are not symmetric. When theories and facts are in conflict, the theories must yield. Economics has strayed from that simple principle, and must return to it.

Statement in Werner Sichel (editor), *The State of Economic Science* 1989:110. → See ALFRED MARSHALL:7.

Théodore Simon

See ALFRED BINET AND THÉODORE SIMON.

J. C. L. Simonde de Sismondi 1773–1842
Swiss historian and economist

1 I am convinced that one falls into serious error in wishing always to generalize everything connected with the social sciences. It is on the contrary essential to study human conditions in detail. One must get hold now of a period, now of a country, now of a profession, in order to see clearly what a man is and how institutions act upon him.

Études sur l'économie politique 1837:Vol. 1, iv.

Henry C. Simons 1899–1946
U.S. economist

1 There must be outright dismantling of our gigantic corporations, and persistent prosecution of producers who organize, by whatever methods, for price maintenance or output limitation. There must be explicit and unqualified repudiation of the so-called "rule of reason". . . In short, restraint of trade must be treated as a major crime, and prosecuted unremittently by a vigilant administrator.

A Positive Program for Laissez Faire 1934:19.

2 A luxury is something that some people think that others should do without.

Quoted anonymously in George J. Stigler, *The Theory of Price* 1946:86. → Attributed to Simons by Stigler, personal communication, 9 November 1988.

B. F. Skinner 1904–1990
U.S. psychologist

1 The more sophisticated neurological views generally agree with the popular view in contending that behavior is in itself incomprehensible but may be reduced to law if it can be shown to be controlled by an internal system susceptible to scientific treatment. Facts about behavior are not treated in their own right, but are regarded as something to be explained or even explained away by the prior facts of the nervous system.

The Behavior of Organisms 1938:4.

2 Operationism may be defined as the practice of talking about (1) one's observations, (2) the manipulative and calculational procedures involved in making them, (3) the logical and mathematical steps which intervene between earlier and later statements, and (4) *nothing else*.

The Operational Analysis of Psychological Terms 1945:270.

3 "The science of behavior is full of special twists like that," said Frazier. "It's the science of science — a special discipline concerned with talking about talking and knowing about knowing. Well, there's a motivational twist, too. Science in general emerged from a competitive culture. Most scientists are still inspired by competition or at least supported by those who are. But when you come to apply the methods of science to the special study of human behavior, the competitive spirit commits suicide. It discovers the extraordinary fact that in order to survive, we must in the last analysis *not* compete."

Walden Two (1948) 1976:281. → From his utopian novel about a planned community based on behavioral engineering, in which Skinnerian positive reinforcement replaces negative reinforcement.

4 Instead of saying that a man behaves because of the consequences which *are* to follow his behavior, we simply say that he behaves because of the consequences which *have* followed similar behavior in the past. This is, of course, the Law of Effect or operant conditioning.

Science and Human Behavior 1953:87.

5 Operant conditioning shapes behavior as a sculptor shapes a lump of clay. Although at some point the sculptor seems to have produced an entirely novel object, we can always follow the process back to the original undifferentiated lump, and we can make the successive stages by which we return to this condition as small as we wish.

Science and Human Behavior 1953:91.

6 There are many ways of changing the probability that an organism will eat; at the same time, a single kind of deprivation strengthens many kinds of behavior. The concept of hunger as a drive brings these various relations together in a single term.

Science and Human Behavior 1953:144.

7 A man may spend a great deal of time designing his own life — he may choose the circumstances in which he is to live with great care, and he may manipulate his daily

environment on an extensive scale. Such activity appears to exemplify a high order of self-determination. But it is also behavior, and we account for it in terms of other variables in the environment and history of the individual. It is these variables which provide the ultimate control.

Science and Human Behavior 1953:240.

8 The hypothesis that man is not free is essential to the application of scientific method to the study of human behavior. The free inner man who is held responsible for the behavior of the external biological organism is only a prescientific substitute for the kinds of causes which are discovered in the course of a scientific analysis.

Science and Human Behavior 1953:447.

9 An organism learns to react discriminately to the world around it under certain contingencies of reinforcement. Thus, a child learns to name a color correctly when a given response is reinforced in the presence of the color and extinguished in its absence. The verbal community may make the reinforcement of an extensive repertoire of responses contingent on subtle properties of colored stimuli. We have reason to believe that the child will not discriminate among colors — that he will not see two colors as different — until exposed to such contingencies. So far as we know, the same process of differential reinforcement is required if a child is to distinguish among the events occurring within his own skin.

Behaviorism at Fifty 1963:953.

Neil J. Smelser 1930–
U.S. sociologist

1 When comparing a society with its past or with another society, we often employ a dichotomy such as "advanced vs. backward," "developed vs. underdeveloped," "civilized vs. uncivilized," or "complex vs. simple." Sometimes these words yield too little information, because they claim simply that one society is superior to another. Sometimes they yield too much, for terms like "advanced" shroud a galaxy of vague connotations. Hence to use such words may generate conflicts of pride and conflicts of meaning, both of which subvert intelligent discourse.

Social Change in the Industrial Revolution 1959:1.

2 [The editors' interest in work and love] is partly personal, rooted in that cryptic phrase, reportedly uttered by Freud in his mature years, that the definition of maturity was to be found in the capacity to love and to work. The sphinx-like character of that statement has contributed in part to its fascination and the extended exploration devoted to it since it was voiced. Nothing endures like a profound and incomplete utterance of a master.

Issues in the Study of Work and Love in Adulthood 1980:4.

3 There are pockets of hostility toward the behavioral and social sciences on the part of government officials. . . [Hostility takes] the following forms:

Research in the behavioral and social sciences produces trivial, obvious, and unimportant results, and expenditures on that kind of research are wasteful of public funds. . . Is of no use to the government, and therefore should not be funded. . . Is basically unscientific — according to the canons of hard science, and is therefore undeserving of study. . . Is basically dangerous ideologically. . .

It is difficult to conceive how the behavioral and social sciences could be simultaneously trivial, useless, unscientific, and threatening.

Introduction to *Handbook of Sociology* 1988:14.

Adam Smith 1723–1790
Scottish political economist

1 The rich only select from the heap what is most precious and agreeable. They consume little more than the poor, and in spite of their natural selfishness and rapacity, though they mean only their own conveniency, though the sole end which they propose from the labours of all the thousands whom they employ, be the gratification of their own vain and insatiable desires, they divide with the poor the produce of all their improvements. They are led by an invisible hand to make nearly the same distribution of the necessaries of life, which would have been made, had the earth been divided into equal portions among all its inhabitants, and thus without intending it, without knowing it, advance the interest of the society, and afford means to the multiplication of the species.

The Theory of Moral Sentiments (1759) 1982:184–185. → See also ADAM SMITH:21, FRIEDMAN:4, and HAHN:3. The phrase "invisible hand" appears in various contexts. For example, Shakespeare's Macbeth (Act 3, scene 2, 1040) describes Lady Macbeth's "bloody and invisible hand," and in Lewis Carroll's *Through the Looking Glass* [(1872) 1960:188], the White King found himself "held in the air by an invisible hand."

2 [The "man of system"] seems to imagine that he can arrange the different members of a great society with as much ease as the hand arranges the different pieces upon a chess-board. He does not consider that the pieces upon the chess-board have no other principle of motion besides that which the hand impresses upon them; but that, in the great chess-board of human society, every single piece has a principle of motion of its own, altogether different from that which the legislature might chuse to impress upon it.

Theory of Moral Sentiments (1759) 1982:234.

3 The Life which I led at Glasgow was a pleasurable, dissipated life in comparison of that which I lead here at Present. I have begun to write a book in order to pass away the time.

Letter to David Hume, 5 July 1764. 1977:102 → Smith lived in Toulouse and Paris for 18 months as tutor to Henry Scott, the 3rd duke of Buccleuch. The book was to become *The Wealth of Nations*.

4 To take an example. . . from a very trifling manufacture; but one in which the division of labour has been very often taken notice of, the trade of the pin-maker; a workman not educated to this business. . . nor acquainted with the use of the machinery employed in it. . . could scarce, perhaps, with his utmost industry, make one pin in a day, and certainly could not make twenty. But in the way in which this business is now carried on, not only the whole work is a peculiar trade, but it is divided into a number of branches, of which the greater part are likewise peculiar trades. One man draws out the wire, another straights it, a third cuts it, a fourth points it, a fifth grinds it at the top for receiving the head; to make the head requires two or three distinct operations; to put it on, is a peculiar business, to whiten the pins is another; it is even a trade by itself to put them into the paper; and the important business of making a pin is, in this manner, divided into about eighteen distinct operations, which, in some manufactories, are all performed by distinct hands, though in others the same man will sometimes perform two or three of them. I have seen a small manufactory of this kind where ten men only were employed, and where some of them consequently performed two or three distinct operations. But though they were very poor, and therefore but indifferently accommodated with the necessary machinery, they could, when they exerted themselves, make among them. . . upwards of forty-eight thousand pins in a day. Each person, therefore, making a tenth part of forty-eight thousand pins, might be considered as making four thousand eight hundred pins in a day. But if they had all wrought separately and independently, and without any of them having been educated to this peculiar business, they certainly could not each of them made twenty, perhaps not one pin in a day; that is, certainly, not the two hundred and fortieth, perhaps not the four thousand eight hundredth part of what they are at present capable of performing, in consequence of a proper division and combination of their different operations.

The Wealth of Nations (1776) 1937:Book 1, chap. 1, 4–5. → See PETTY:3.

5 It is the great multiplication of the productions of all the arts, in consequence of the division of labour, which occasions, in a well-governed society, that universal opulence which extends itself to the lowest ranks of the people.

The Wealth of Nations (1776) 1937:Book 1, chap. 1, 11.

6 This division of labour, from which so many advantages are derived, is not originally the effect of any human wisdom. . . It is the necessary, though very slow and gradual, consequence of a certain propensity in human nature which has in view no such extensive utility; the propensity to truck, barter, and exchange one thing for another.

The Wealth of Nations (1776) 1937:Book 1, chap. 2, 13.

7 Man has almost constant occasion for the help of his brethren, and it is in vain for him to expect it from their benevolence only. He will be more likely to prevail if he can interest their self-love in his favour, and shew them that it is for their own advantage to do for him what he requires of them. Whoever offers to another a bargain of any kind, proposes to do this. Give me that which I want, and you shall have this which you want, is the meaning of every such offer; and it is in this manner that we obtain from one another the far greater part of those good offices which we stand in need of. It is not from the benevolence of the butcher, the brewer, or the baker, that we expect our dinner, but from their regard to their own interest.

The Wealth of Nations (1776) 1937:Book 1, chap. 2, 14.

8 The word VALUE, it is to be observed, has two different meanings, and sometimes expresses the utility of some particular object, and sometimes the power of purchasing other goods which the possession of that object conveys. The one may be called "value in use"; the other, "value in exchange." The things which have the greatest value in use have frequently little or no value in exchange; and on the contrary, those which have the greatest value in exchange have frequently little or no value in use. Nothing is more useful than water: but it will purchase scarce any thing; scarce any thing can be had in exchange for it. A diamond, on the contrary, has scarce any value in use; but a very great quantity of other goods may frequently be had in exchange for it.

The Wealth of Nations (1776) 1937:Book 1, chap. 4, 28.

9 The real price of every thing, what every thing really costs to the man who wants to acquire it, is the toil and trouble of acquiring it. . . Labour was the first price, the original purchase-money that was paid for all things.

The Wealth of Nations (1776) 1937:Book 1, chap. 5, 30.

10 It was not by gold or by silver, but by labour, that all the wealth of the world was originally purchased; and its value, to those who possess it, and who want to exchange it for some new productions, is precisely equal to the quantity of labour which it can enable them to purchase or command.

The Wealth of Nations (1776) 1937:Book 1, chap. 5, 30–31.

11 It is often difficult to ascertain the proportion between two different quantities of labour. The time spent in two different sorts of work will not always alone determine this proportion. The different degrees of hardship endured, and of ingenuity exercised, must likewise be taken into account. There may be more labour in an hour's hard work than in two hours easy business; or in an hour's application to a trade which it cost ten years labour to learn, than in a month's industry at an ordinary and obvious employment. But it is not easy to find any accurate measure either of hardship or ingenuity. In exchanging indeed the different productions of different sorts of labour for one another, some allowance is commonly made for both. It is adjusted, however, not by any

accurate measure, but by the higgling and bargaining of the market, according to that sort of rough equality which, though not exact, is sufficient for carrying on the business of common life.

The Wealth of Nations (1776) 1937:Book 1, chap. 5, 31.

12 If among a nation of hunters. . . it usually costs twice the labour to kill a beaver which it does to kill a deer, one beaver should naturally exchange for or be worth two deer. It is natural that what is usually the produce of two days or two hours labour, should be worth double of what is usually the produce of one day's or one hour's labour.

The Wealth of Nations (1776) 1937:Book 1, chap. 6, 47.

13 We rarely hear, it has been said, of the combinations of masters, though frequently of those of workmen. But whoever imagines, upon this account, that masters rarely combine, is as ignorant of the world as of the subject. Masters are always and every where in a sort of tacit, but constant and uniform combination, not to raise the wages of labour above their actual rate.

The Wealth of Nations (1776) 1937:Book 1, chap. 8, 66–67.

14 Servants, labourers and workmen of different kinds, make up the far greater part of every great political society. But what improves the circumstances of the greater part can never be regarded as an inconveniency to the whole. No society can surely be flourishing and happy, of which the far greater part of the members are poor and miserable.

The Wealth of Nations (1776) 1937:Book 1, chap. 8, 78–79.

15 The wages paid to journeymen and servants of every kind must be such as may enable them, one with another, to continue the race of journeymen and servants, according as the increasing, diminishing, or stationary demand of the society may happen to require.

The Wealth of Nations (1776) 1937:Book 1, chap. 8, 80.

16 When any expensive machine is erected, the extraordinary work to be performed by it before it is worn out, it must be expected, will replace the capital laid out upon it, with at least the ordinary profits. A man educated at the expence of much labour and time to any of those employments which require extraordinary dexterity and skill, may be compared to one of those expensive machines. The work which he learns to perform, it must be expected, over and above the usual wages of common labour, will replace to him the whole expence of his education, with at least the ordinary profits of an equally valuable capital. It must do this too in a reasonable time, regard being had to the very uncertain duration of human life, in the same manner as to the more certain duration of the machine.

The difference between the wages of skilled labour and those of common labour, is founded upon this principle.

The Wealth of Nations (1776) 1937:Book 1, chap. 10, 101.

17 People of the same trade seldom meet together, even for merriment and diversion, but the conversation ends in a conspiracy against the public, or in some contrivance to raise prices. It is impossible indeed to prevent such meetings, by any law which either could be executed, or would be consistent with liberty and justice.

The Wealth of Nations (1776) 1937:Book 1, chap. 10, 128.

18 It is the highest impertinence and presumption. . . in kings and ministers, to pretend to watch over the oeconomy of private people, and to restrain their expence. . . Let them look well after their own expence, and they may safely trust private people with theirs.

The Wealth of Nations (1776) 1937:Book 2, chap. 3, 329.

19 If. . . capital is divided between two different grocers, their competition will tend to make both of them sell cheaper, than if it were in the hands of one only; and if it were divided among twenty, their competition would be just so much the greater, and the chance of their combining together, in order to raise the price, just so much the less.

The Wealth of Nations (1776) 1937:Book 2, chap. 5, 342.

20 It is not the multitude of ale-houses. . . that occasions a general disposition to drunkenness among the common people; but that disposition arising from other causes necessarily gives employment to a multitude of ale-houses.

The Wealth of Nations (1776) 1937:Book 2, chap. 5, 343.

21 As every individual. . . endeavours as much as he can both to employ his capital in the support of domestic industry, and so to direct that industry that its produce may be of the greatest value; every individual necessarily labours to render the annual revenue of the society as great as he can. He generally, indeed, neither intends to promote the public interest, nor knows how much he is promoting it. By preferring the support of domestic to that of foreign industry, he intends only his own security; and by directing that industry in such a manner as its produce may be of the greatest value, he intends only his own gain, and he is in this, as in many other cases, led by an invisible hand to promote an end which was no part of his intention. Nor is it always the worse for the society that it was no part of it. By pursuing his own interest he frequently promotes that of the society more effectually than when he really intends to promote it. I have never known much good done by those who affected to trade for the public good.

The Wealth of Nations (1776) 1937:Book 4, chap. 2, 423. → For other uses of "the invisible hand," see ADAM SMITH:1.

22 To found a great empire for the sole purpose of raising up a people of customers, may at first sight appear a project fit only for a nation of shopkeepers. It is, however, a project altogether unfit for a nation of shopkeepers; but extremely fit for a nation whose government is influenced by shopkeepers.

The Wealth of Nations (1776) 1937:Book 4, chap. 7, 579.

23 Consumption is the sole end and purpose of all production; and the interest of the producer ought to be attended to, only so far as it may be necessary for promoting that of the consumer.

The Wealth of Nations (1776) 1937:Book 4, chap. 8, 625.

24 In order to make every individual feel himself perfectly secure in the possession of every right which belongs to him, it is not only necessary that the judicial should be separated from the executive power, but that it should be rendered as much as possible independent of that power.

The Wealth of Nations (1776) 1937:Book 5, chap. 1, 681.

William Robertson Smith 1846–1894
Scottish historian of religion

1 As a rule the myth is no explanation of the origin of the ritual to any one who does not believe it to be a narrative of real occurrences, and the boldest mythologist will not believe that. But if it be not true, the myth itself requires to be explained, and every principle of philosophy and common sense demands that the explanation be sought, not in arbitrary allegorical theories, but in the actual facts of ritual or religious custom to which the myth attaches. The conclusion is, that in the study of ancient religions we must begin, not with myth, but with ritual and traditional usage.

Religion of the Semites (1889) 1901:18.

2 Religion was made up of a series of acts and observances, the correct performance of which was necessary or desirable to secure the favour of the gods or to avert their anger; and in these observances every member of society had a share, marked out for him either in virtue of his being born within a certain family and community, or in virtue of the station, within the family and community that he had come to hold in the course of his life. . . Religion did not exist for the saving of souls but for the preservation and welfare of society.

Religion of the Semites (1889) 1901:28–29.

3 A man was born into a fixed relation to certain gods as surely as he was born into relation to his fellowmen; and his religion, that is, the part of conduct which was determined by his relation to the gods, was simply one side of the general scheme of conduct prescribed for him by his position as a member of society.

Religion of the Semites (1889) 1901:30.

4 Ancient religion is but a part of the general social order which embraces gods and men alike.

Religion of the Semites (1889) 1901:32.

C. P. Snow 1905–1980
British physicist and novelist

1 I felt I was moving among two groups [literary intellectuals and scientists] — comparable in intelligence, identical in race, not grossly different in social origin, earning about the same incomes, who had almost ceased to communicate at all, who in intellectual, moral and psychological climate had so little in common that instead of going from Burlington House or South Kensington to Chelsea, one might have crossed an ocean.

The Two Cultures (1959) 1964:2.

2 Literary intellectuals at one pole — at the other scientists, and as the most representative, the physical scientists. Between the two a gulf of mutual incomprehension — sometimes (particularly among the young) hostility and dislike, but most of all lack of understanding.

The Two Cultures (1959) 1964:4.

3 The number 2 is a very dangerous number: that is why the dialectic is a dangerous process. Attempts to divide anything into two ought to be regarded with much suspicion. . . I was searching for something a little more than a dashing metaphor, a good deal less than a cultural map: and for those purposes the two cultures is about right.

The Two Cultures (1959) 1964:9. → The statistician William H. Kruskal (1988:231), in a plea for more cross-disciplinary research, has argued that we need "n cultures of intellectual disciplines, where n lies perhaps between 15 and 20."

Robert M. Solow 1924–
U.S. economist

1 Workers get paid for working; what do capitalists get paid for? For "waiting" while roundabout processes of production percolate, or for "abstaining" from some current consumption in favor of replacing or augmenting the stock of capital and maintaining or increasing future consumption. Since so much of the "waiting" gets done in expensive automobiles and luxurious resorts, while the "abstinence" excites little sympathy in an even slightly cynical observer, the whole apparatus begins to look like a transparent verbal trick. (Indeed, I think "abstinence" is an even more repulsive way of putting it than "waiting," though if one could strip away the moral or moralistic overtones, I think it is an economically more useful description.) But even so, there is no excuse for economists to lose the concept in their resentment at the language. One of the elegant showpieces of economics is its analysis of the resource-allocation implications of a system of prices or shadow prices. We have learned to free this analysis of ethical overtones. All that is necessary in capital theory is to draw a conceptual distinction between the imputed return to capital and the income of capitalists.

Here, as elsewhere in economics, but with rather more irony here, the best way of understanding the economics of capitalism may be to think about a socialist economy.

Capital Theory and the Rate of Return 1963:10- 11.

2 Most of the modern theory of economic growth is devoted to analyzing the properties of steady states and to finding out whether an economy not initially in a steady state will evolve into one if it proceeds under specified rules of the game. It is worth looking at some figures to see if the steady-state picture does actually give a fair shorthand summary of the facts of life in advanced industrial economies. The reason it is worth doing is not simply to say yes or no, to accept or reject the steady state as a theoretical construct. No such simple description will ever fit the facts very well. If it bears no relation at all to what one sees, then obviously one will be suspicious of any theory that clings to the steady state. It is more likely, however, that the data will be neither perfectly consistent nor utterly inconsistent with the "stylized facts." One wants, then, some indication of the importance of having a flexible theory that is capable of explaining approximate steady states but has at the same time a reasonable escape hatch, a way of accounting for systematic divergence from the steady state. Of course one must not go too far; a theory capable of explaining anything that might possibly be observed is hardly a theory at all.

Growth Theory 1970:4–5.

3 The steady state is not a bad place for the theory of growth to start, but may be a dangerous place for it to end.

Growth Theory 1970:7.

4 I am trying to express an attitude towards the building of very simple models. I don't think that models like this lead directly to prescription for policy or even to detailed diagnosis. But neither are they a game. They are more like reconnaissance exercises. If you want to know what it's like out there, it's all right to send two or three fellows in sneakers to find out the lay of the land and whether it will support human life. If it turns out to be worth settling, then that requires an altogether bigger operation. The job of building usable larger-scale econometric models on the basis of whatever analytical insights come from simple models is much more difficult and less glamorous. But it may be what God made graduate students for. Presumably he had something in mind.

Growth Theory 1970:105.

5 My impression is that the Doomsday Models divert attention from remedial public policy by permitting everyone to blame "the predicament of mankind." Who could pay attention to a humdrum affair like legislation to tax sulfur emissions when the date of the Apocalypse has just been announced by a computer?

Notes on "Doomsday Models" 1972:3833.

6 Any successful line of economic analysis is almost certain to be a group product. We attach names to ideas for good and bad reasons, but useful ideas are usually worked out and critically refined by a research community. I have some faith that the ideas of "neoclassical" growth theory are viable just because they have attracted a research community.

Growth Theory and After 1988:316.

Werner Sombart 1863–1941

German economist and economic historian

1 The concept of capitalism and even more clearly the term itself may be traced primarily to the writings of social theoreticians . . . It cannot be said that a clear cut definition has ever been attempted. Even Karl Marx, who virtually discovered the phenomenon, defined only certain aspects of capitalism as the occasion required. When the term is used by socialists in any definite sense it has the character of a political byword with a strong ethical tinge.

Capitalism 1930:195.

2 While individual action under capitalism is informed by the ideal of highest rationality, the capitalistic system as a whole remains irrational, because the other dominant capitalistic idea, that of acquisition . . . leaves the regulation of the total economic process to the uncoordinated discretion of individual economic agents. From this coexistence of well nigh perfect rationality and of the greatest irrationality originate the numerous strains and stresses which are peculiarly characteristic of the economic system of capitalism.

Capitalism 1930:198.

Georges Sorel 1847–1922

French political theorist

1 Hatred can unleash upheavals, destroy a social organization and throw a country into an era of bloody revolutions; but it produces nothing. Our forefathers could afford to believe that after overthrowing power it is enough to allow things to take their natural course for the reign of reason to begin. We have gained too much experience to accept this naïve optimism; the position of authority does not long remain vacant; tyranny quickly succeeds tyranny. Socialists no longer want to leap into the unknown.

The Ethics of Socialism (1899) 1987:100.

2 The final regime imagined by socialists cannot be fixed at a determined date by a sociological prediction; it is in the present. It is not outside us; it is in our own hearts. Socialism is being realized every day, under our very eyes, to the extent that we are able to conceive what socialist conduct is, to the extent that we know how to direct institutions and, consequently, to the extent that the socialist ethic is formed in our consciousness and in life.

The Ethics of Socialism (1899) 1987:108.

3 The dangers which threaten the future of the world may be avoided, if the proletariat hold on with obstinacy to revolutionary ideas, so as to realise as much as possible Marx's conception. . . Proletarian violence, carried on as a pure and simple manifestation of the sentiment of the class war, appears thus as a very fine and very heroic

thing; it is at the service of the immemorial interests of civilisation; it is not perhaps the most appropriate method of obtaining immediate material advantages, but it may save the world from barbarism.

Reflections on Violence (1908) 1961:98.

4 The myth must be judged as a means of acting on the present; any attempt to discuss how far it can be taken literally as future history is devoid of sense. *It is the myth in its entirety which is alone important*: its parts are only of interest in so far as they bring out the main idea.

Reflections on Violence (1908) 1961:126.

5 The general strike is indeed what I have said: the *myth* in which Socialism is wholly comprised, *i.e.* a body of images capable of evoking instinctively all the sentiments which correspond to the different manifestations of the war undertaken by Socialism against modern society. Strikes have engendered in the proletariat the noblest, deepest, and most moving sentiments that they possess; the general strike groups them all in a co-ordinated picture, and, by bringing them together, gives to each one of them its maximum of intensity; appealing to their painful memories of particular conflicts, it colours with an intense life all the details of the composition presented to consciousness.

Reflections on Violence (1908) 1961:127.

6 It is to violence that Socialism owes those high ethical values by means of which it brings *salvation* to the modern world.

Reflections on Violence (1908) 1961:249.

Pitirim A. Sorokin 1889–1968
Russian-born U.S. sociologist

1 Any organized social group is always a stratified social body. There has not been and does not exist any permanent social group which is "flat," and in which all members are equal.

Social Mobility (1927) 1959:12.

2 Each [type of culture: ideational, sensate, idealistic] has its own mentality; its own system of truth and knowledge; its own philosophy and *Weltanschauung*; its own type of religion and standards of "holiness"; its own system of right and wrong; its own forms of art and literature; its own mores, laws, code of conduct; its own predominant forms of social relationships; its own economic and political organization; and, finally, its own type of *human personality*, with a peculiar mentality and conduct.

Social and Cultural Dynamics 1937–1941:Vol. 1, 67.

3 The first implication of the principle of immanent change may be formulated as follows: *As long as it exists and functions, any sociocultural system incessantly generates consequences which are not the results of the external factors to the system, but the consequences of the existence of the system and of its activities.*

Social and Cultural Dynamics 1937–1941:Vol. 4, 600–601.

4 The fundamental social relationships regulated by official law change but slowly, providing the society with a necessary stability and order. An incessant change of such fundamental social relationships as property, the family, and forms of government would mean a continuous revolution — economic, social, and political — which would make stable order in the society impossible. These facts explain why the norms of official law tend to "harden" and in this "hardened" form tend to stay unchanged for decades, even centuries, until a profound change in the law-convictions of the members occurs. . . *Official law, then, always lags somewhat behind unofficial law.*

Society, Culture, and Personality 1947:82.

5 Any science, at any moment of its historical existence, contains not only truth but also much that is half-truth, sham-truth, and plain error. This has been especially true of the social and psychological disciplines, for the complexity of mental and social phenomena allows many a fallacy to be taken for the last word of science, "operationally defined, empirically tested, and precisely measured."

Preface to *Fads and Foibles in Modern Sociology* 1956:v.

Herbert Spencer 1820–1903
British sociologist and philosopher

1 Progress. . . is not an accident, but a necessity. Instead of civilization being artificial, it is a part of nature; all of a piece with the development of the embryo or the unfolding of a flower. The modifications mankind have undergone and are still undergoing result from a law underlying the whole organic creation; and provided the human race continues and the constitution of things remains the same, those modifications must end in completeness. . . As surely as there is any efficacy in educational culture or any meaning in such terms as *habit, custom, practice*; so surely must the human faculties be molded into complete fitness for the social state; so surely must the things we call evil and immortality disappear; so surely must man become perfect.

Social Statics (1850) 1954:60.

2 Those who cavalierly reject the Theory of Evolution as not being adequately supported by facts, seem to forget that their own theory is supported by no facts at all.

The Development Hypothesis (1852) 1966:1.

3 The advance from the simple to the complex, through a process of successive differentiations, is seen alike in the earliest changes of the Universe to which we can reason our way back, and in the earliest changes which we can inductively establish; it is seen in the geologic and climatic evolution of the Earth; it is seen in the unfolding of every single organism on its surface, and in the multiplication of kinds of organisms; it is seen in the evolution of Humanity, whether contemplated in the civilized individual, or in the aggregate of races; it is seen in the evolution of Society in respect alike of its political, its religious, and its economical organization; and it is seen in

the evolution of all those endless concrete and abstract products of human activity which constitute the environment of our daily life. From the remotest past which Science can fathom, up to the novelties of yesterday, that in which Progress essentially consists, is the transformation of the homogeneous into the heterogeneous.

Progress: Its Law and Cause (1857) 1966:35.

4 Every active force produces more than one change — every cause produces more than one effect.

Progress: Its Law and Cause (1857) 1966:37.

5 A leading fact in human progress is that every science is evolved out of its corresponding art. It results from the necessity we are under, both individually and as a race, of reaching the abstract by way of the concrete, that there must be practice and an accruing experience with its empirical generalizations, before there can be science. Science is organized knowledge; and before knowledge can be organized, some of it must be possessed. Every study, therefore, should have a purely experimental introduction; and only after an ample fund of observations has been accumulated, should reasoning begin.

Education 1860:119.

6 Evolution is an integration of matter and concomitant dissipation of motion; during which the matter passes from an indefinite, incoherent homogeneity to a definite, coherent heterogeneity; and during which the retained motion undergoes a parallel transformation.

First Principles (1862) 1888:396. → For a parody of this definition, see JAMES:4.

7 This survival of the fittest, which I have here sought to express in mechanical terms, is that which Mr. Darwin has called "natural selection, or the preservation of favoured races in the struggle for life."

The Principles of Biology (1864–1867) 1966:Vol. 1, 530. → See DARWIN:4.

8 The law is the survival of the *fittest*. . . The law is not the survival of the "better" or the "stronger," if we give to those words any thing like their ordinary meanings. It is the survival of those which are constitutionally fittest to thrive under the conditions in which they are placed; and very often that which, humanly speaking, is inferiority, causes the survival. . . As I am responsible for the phrase, I suppose I am competent to say that the word "fittest" was chosen for this reason.

Mr. Martineau on Evolution (1872) 1966:379. → Spencer's influence on Darwin's thinking is largely discounted by contemporary historians of science. See MAYR:2.

9 What is a society?. . . A society is an organism.

The Principles of Sociology (1876) 1906:Vol. 1, 447,449.

10 A social organism is like an individual organism in these essential traits: — that it grows; that while growing it becomes more complex; that while becoming complex its parts acquire increasing mutual dependence; and that its life is immense in length compared with the lives of its component units. . .In both cases there is increasing integration accompanied by increasing heterogeneity.

An Autobiography 1904:Vol. 2, 55–56.

Oswald Spengler 1880–1936
German historian

1 The "Decline of the West" comprises nothing less than the problem of *Civilization*. We have before us one of the fundamental questions of all higher history. What is Civilization, understood as the organic-logical sequel, fulfillment and finale of a culture? . . . Civilizations are the most external and artificial states of which a species of developed humanity is capable. They are a conclusion . . . death following life, rigidity following expansion, intellectual age and the stone-built, petrifying world-city following mother-earth and the spiritual childhood of Doric and Gothic. They are an end, irrevocable, yet by inward necessity reached again and again.

The Decline of the West (1918) 1926:Vol. 1, 31.

2 There are no longer noblesse and bourgeoisie, freemen and slaves, Hellenes and Barbarians, believers and unbelievers, *but only cosmopolitans and provincials*. All other contrasts pale before this one, which dominates all events, all habits of life, all views of the world.

The Decline of the West (1922) 1928:Vol. 2, 99.

Spinoza 1632–1677
[Baruch, Benedict, or Benedictus de Spinoza]
Dutch philosopher

1 Nothing comes to pass in nature, which can be set down to a flaw therein; for nature is always the same, and everywhere one and the same in her efficacy and power of action; that is, nature's laws and ordinances, whereby all things come to pass and change from one form to another, are everywhere and always the same; so that there should be one and the same method of understanding the nature of all things whatsoever, namely, through nature's universal laws and rules.

The Ethics (1677) 1955:Part 3, 129.

2 I shall consider human actions and desires in exactly the same manner, as though I were concerned with lines, planes, and solids.

The Ethics (1677) 1955:Part 3, 129.

3 In no case do we strive for, wish for, long for, or desire anything, because we deem it to be good, but on the other hand we deem a thing to be good, because we strive for it, wish for it, long for it, or desire it.

The Ethics (1677) 1955:Part 3, 137.

4 An emotion can only be controlled or destroyed by another emotion contrary thereto, and with more power for controlling emotion.

The Ethics (1677) 1955:Part 4, 194.

5 The definition of man as a social animal has met with general assent; in fact, men do derive from social life

much more convenience than injury. Let satirists then laugh their fill at human affairs, let theologians rail, and let misanthropes praise to their utmost the life of untutored rusticity, let them heap contempt on men and praises on beasts; when all is said, they will find that men can provide for their wants much more easily by mutual help, and that only by uniting their forces can they escape from the dangers that on every side beset them: not to say how much more excellent and worthy of our knowledge it is, to study the actions of men than the actions of beasts.

The Ethics (1677) 1955:Part 4, 210.

I have laboured carefully, not to mock, lament, or execrate, but to understand human actions [*Sedulo curavi humanas actiones non ridere, non lugere, neque destari, sed intelligere*].

A Political Treatise (1677) 1955:288.

We cannot even conceive, that every citizen should be allowed to interpret the commonwealth's decrees or laws. For were every citizen allowed this, he would thereby be his own judge, because each would easily be able to give a colour of right to his own deeds.

A Political Treatise (1677) 1955:302.

Piero Sraffa 1898–1983
Italian-born British economist

Money is not only the medium of exchange, but also a store of value, and the standard in terms of which debt, and other legal obligations, habits, opinions, conventions, in short all kinds of relations between men, are more or less rigidly fixed.

Dr. Hayek on Money and Capital 1932:43.

Josiah Stamp 1880–1941
British economist and banker

The Government are very keen on amassing statistics — they collect them, add them, raise them to the *n*th power, take the cube root and prepare wonderful diagrams. But what you must never forget is that every one of those figures comes in the first instance from the *chowty dar* (village watchman), who just puts down what he damn pleases.

Some Economic Factors in Modern Life 1929:258–259. → Often attributed to Stamp. He himself attributes the statement to an English judge in India addressing a young man named Harold Cox.

Herbert Stein 1916–
U.S. economist

Capitalism survived its [1929] crisis and went on to great successes. But the capitalism that survived and succeeded was not the capitalism of 1929. The capitalism that will succeed in the next sixty years may not be the capitalism of 1989. Capitalism succeeded in large part because it adapted.

The Triumph of the Adaptive Society 1989:1.

2 "Supply-side economics" . . . could be interpreted to mean economics supplied to meet the demand of politicians to rationalize what they intend to do.

The Triumph of the Adaptive Society 1989:19.

Fritz Stern 1926–
German-born U.S. historian

1 Liberalism — at its best, the institutionalization of decency — in practice is all too often dull, inadequate, and tolerant of what should be intolerable. Illiberalism, in turn, is often exciting and, in the short run, efficient. It is also the institutionalization of suspicion and the perpetuation of nonage. Even in today's democracy, the Germans occasionally manifest the fact that they never went through a liberal phase. Their history can be read as an object lesson in the failure of illiberalism.

Introduction to Germany Revisited 1972:211–212.

2 It is often asserted that a culture must be judged by its treatment of minorities and deviants; a student of the German past would find this a cogent and, indeed, irrefutable argument. It is a necessary, but not a sufficient criterion. A culture must also recognize, recruit, and, in a sense, form talent; it must know how to coax talent into achievement. This too is a test of its virtue and of its instinct for survival. These are responsibilities that speak most directly to our universities, to every university.

Einstein's Germany 1987:50.

Laurence Sterne 1713–1768
Irish-born British novelist

1 It is the nature of an hypothesis, when once a man has conceived it, that it assimilates every thing to itself, as proper nourishment; and, from the first moment of your begetting it, it generally grows the stronger by every thing you see, hear, read, or understand.

The Life and Opinions of Tristram Shandy (1760) 1819:Book 2, chap. 19, 177–178. → See Bacon:7 and W.I.B. Beveridge:1.

James Steuart Denham 1712–1780
Scottish political economist

1 Public spirit. . . is as superfluous in the governed, as it ought to be all-powerful in the statesman. . . Were every one to act for the public, and neglect himself, the statesmen would be bewildered. . . Were a people to become quite disinterested, there would be no possibility of governing them. Every one might consider the interest of his country in a different light, and many might join in the ruin of it, by endeavouring to promote its advantages.

An Inquiry into the Principles of Political Oeconomy 1767:Vol. 1, 164–165.

2 *Arbitrary* power can never be delegated; for if it be *arbitrary*, it may be turned against the monarch, as well as against the subject.

An Inquiry into the Principles of Political Oeconomy 1767:Vol. 1, 243.

3 If a thousand pounds are bestowed upon making a fire-work, a number of people are thereby employed, and gain a temporary livelihood. If the same sum is bestowed for making a canal for watering the fields of a province, a like number of people may reap the same benefit, and hitherto accounts stand even: but the fire-work played off, what remains, but the smoke and stink of the powder? Whereas the consequence of the canal is a perpetual fertility to a formerly barren soil.

An Inquiry into the Principles of Political Oeconomy 1767:Vol. 1, 519.

Julian H. Steward 1902–1972

U.S. anthropologist

1 Man enters the ecological scene. . . not merely as another organism which is related to other organisms in terms of his physical characteristics. He introduces the super-organic factor of culture, which also affects and is affected by the total web of life.

Theory of Culture Change (1955) 1979:31.

George J. Stigler 1911–1991

U.S. economist

1 The division of labor is not a quaint practice of eighteenth-century pin factories; it is a fundamental principle of economic organization.

The Division of Labor Is Limited by the Extent of the Market (1951) 1986:23. → See ADAM SMITH:4.

2 One should hardly have to tell academicians that information is a valuable resource: knowledge *is* power. And yet it occupies a slum dwelling in the town of economics. Mostly it is ignored: the best technology is assumed to be known; the relationship of commodities to consumer preferences is a datum. And one of the information-producing industries, advertising, is treated with a hostility that economists normally reserve for tariffs or monopolists.

The Economics of Information (1961) 1986:46. → See BACON:1.

3 The innumerable regulatory actions are conclusive proof, not of effective regulation, but of the desire to regulate. And if wishes were horses, one would buy stock in a harness factory.

What Can Regulators Regulate? (1962) 1986:224.

4 What economic tasks can a state perform? I propose a set of rules which bear on the answer to the question. . .
RULE 1: *The state cannot do anything quickly.*
RULE 2: *When the national state performs detailed economic tasks, the responsible political authorities cannot possibly control the manner in which they are performed, whether directly by governmental agencies or indirectly by regulation of private enterprise.*
RULE 3: *The democratic state strives to treat all citizens in the same manner; individual differences are ignored if remotely possible.*
RULE 4: *The ideal public policy, from the viewpoint of the state, is one with identifiable beneficiaries, each of whom is helped appreciably, at the cost of many unidentifiable persons, none of whom is hurt much.*
RULE 5: *The state never knows when to quit.*

The Government of the Economy 1963:7, 9, 10–12.

5 In 1776 our venerable master [Adam Smith] offered clear and emphatic advice to his countrymen on the proper way to achieve economic prosperity. This advice was of course directed also to his countrymen in the American colonies, although at that very moment we were busily establishing what would now be called a major tax loophole. The main burden of Smith's advice, as you know, was that the conduct of economic affairs is best left to private citizens — that the state will be doing remarkably well if it succeeds in its unavoidable tasks of winning wars, preserving justice, and maintaining the various highways of commerce.

The Economist and the State (1965) 1986:99.

6 The *Wealth of Nations* is a stupendous palace erected upon the granite of self-interest.

Smith's Travels on the Ship of State (1971) 1975:237.

7 The discipline that assumes man to be a reasonably efficient utility maximizer is singularly ill suited to assuming that the political activity of men bears little relationship to their desires. . . The failure to analyze the political process — to leave it as a curious mixture of benevolent public interest and unintentional blunders — is most unsatisfactory.

The Economist as Preacher (1981) 1986:309.

8 Without a theory of value the economist can have no theory of international trade nor possibly a theory of money. This central problem of value does not change in its essential content if one seeks to explain values in rural or urban societies, or in agricultural or industrial societies. Indeed, if the problem of value were so chameleonlike as to alter its nature whenever the economic or political system altered, each epoch in economic life would require its own theory, and short epochs would get short-lived theories.

The Process and Progress of Economics (1982) 1986:138.

Stephen M. Stigler 1941–

U.S. statistician

1 Beware of the problem of testing too many hypotheses; the more you torture the data, the more likely they are to confess, but confessions obtained under duress may not be admissible in the court of scientific opinion.

Testing Hypotheses or Fitting Models? 1987:148.

Arthur L. Stinchcombe 1933–

U.S. sociologist

1 A power is legitimate to the degree that, by virtue of the doctrines and norms by which it is justified, the power-

holder can call upon sufficient other centers of power, as reserves in case of need, to make his power effective.

Constructing Social Theories 1968:162.

2 People define situations, but do not define them as they please.

[A] Theory of Social Structure 1975:15. → A synthesis of well-known aphorisms of W.I. Thomas and Karl Marx. See MARX:8 and THOMAS AND THOMAS:2.

3 The question of how to apply social theory to historical materials, as it is usually posed, is ridiculous. One does not apply theory to history; rather one uses history to develop theory.

Theoretical Methods in Social History 1978:1.

Lawrence Stone 1919–
U.S. historian

1 As often as not in history it is the *unintended* consequences that really matter: to mention but one example, it was Louis XVI's belated and half-hearted attempts at reform that provoked the aristocratic reaction, which in turn opened the way to the bourgeois, the peasant, and the sans-culotte revolutions.

The Causes of the English Revolution 1972:11.

2 The movement to narrative by the "new historians" marks the end of an era: the end of the attempt to produce a coherent and scientific explanation of change in the past. Models of historical determinism based on economics, demography or sociology have collapsed in the face of the evidence, but no full-blown deterministic model based on any other social science — politics, psychology or anthropology — has emerged to take its place. Structuralism and functionalism have not turned out much better. Quantitative methodology has proved a fairly weak reed which can only answer a limited set of problems. Forced into a choice between *a priori* statistical models of human behavior, and understanding based on observation, experience, judgment and intuition, some of the "new historians" are now tending to drift back towards the latter mode of interpreting the past.

The Past and the Present Revisited 1987:91–92.

Everett V. Stonequist 1901–1979
U.S. sociologist

1 The individual who through migration, education, marriage, or some other influence leaves one social group or culture without making a satisfactory adjustment to another finds himself on the margin of each but a member of neither. He is a "marginal man."

The Marginal Man 1937:2–3. → Stonequist reported that the concept of "the marginal man" was first used by Park. See PARK:4.

Samuel A. Stouffer 1900–1960
U.S. sociologist

1 There is one crucial fact which could support the prediction that as the younger generation ages, it will still be more tolerant than its elders — given more or less the same external conditions. This fact is *the greater schooling which the younger generation has received.*

In thirty years, America has seen an almost revolutionary uplift in the schooling of its population at both the high school and college levels. Consequently, if education, *independent of age*, makes for tolerance, the present younger generation, when it reaches later years, should be more tolerant than its elders are today.

The Younger Generation Has More Schooling (1955) 1962:121. → Stouffer's main conclusion from a massive survey of the U.S. public's attitudes toward civil liberties.

Lytton Strachey 1880–1932
British biographer and critic

1 The history of the Victorian Age will never be written: we know too much about it. For ignorance is the first requisite of the historian — ignorance, which simplifies and clarifies, which selects and omits, with a placid perfection unattainable by the highest art. Concerning the Age which has just passed, our fathers and our grandfathers have poured forth and accumulated so vast a quantity of information that the industry of a Ranke would be submerged by it, and the perspicacity of a Gibbon would quail before it.

Eminent Victorians 1918:v.

Leo Strauss 1899–1973
German-born U.S. political scientist

1 Present-day American social science, as far as it is not Roman Catholic social science, is dedicated to the proposition that all men are endowed by the evolutionary process or by a mysterious fate with many kinds of urges and aspirations, but certainly with no natural right.

Natural Right and History 1953:2.

2 According to our social science, we can be or become wise in all matters of secondary importance, but we have to be resigned to utter ignorance in the most important respect: we cannot have any knowledge regarding the ultimate principles of our choices, i.e., regarding their soundness or unsoundness; our ultimate principles have no other support than our arbitrary and hence blind preferences.

Natural Right and History 1953:4.

3 Moral obtuseness is the necessary condition for scientific analysis. For to the extent to which we are not yet completely insensitive to moral distinctions, we are forced to make value judgments. The habit of looking at social or human phenomena without making value judgments has a corroding influence on any preferences. The more serious we are as social scientists, the more completely

we develop within ourselves a state of indifference to any goal, or to aimlessness and drifting, a state of what may be called nihilism.

What Is Political Philosophy? (1955) 1973:18–19.

William Stubbs 1825–1901
British historian

1 The History of Institutions cannot be mastered, — can scarcely be approached, — without an effort. It affords little of the romantic incident or of the picturesque grouping which constitute the charm of History in general, and holds out small temptation to the mind that requires to be tempted to the study of Truth. But it has a deep value and an abiding interest to those who have courage to work upon it. It presents, in every branch, a regularly developed series of causes and consequences, and abounds in examples of that continuity of life, the realisation of which is necessary to give the reader a personal hold on the past and a right judgment of the present. For the roots of the present lie deep in the past, and nothing in the past is dead to the man who would learn how the present comes to be what it is.

The Constitutional History of England (1874) 1880:Vol. 1, v.

"Student"
See WILLIAM SEALY GOSSET.

Harry Stack Sullivan 1892–1949
U.S. psychiatrist

1 Man is not a creature of instinct — the view of Aristotle and of William McDougall; of transcendental powers between or among which he may choose his allegiance — the medieval view rather sympathetic to Otto Rank; of logic and its categorical opposite — Bacon and in a way Alfred Adler and Alfred Korzybski; of the evolution of social intellect — Comte and some mental hygienists; of racial fitness — de Gobineau and Führer Hitler; of a conflict of society and one's instincts — Freud; or of a racial unconscious — Jung.

As we survey the present, we can see four significant conceptions. For the general biologist, man is the most complexly integrated organism thus far evolved. For the psychobiologist, man is an individual organism the total-function of which is mentally integrated life. For the social psychologist, man is the human animal transformed by social experience into a human being. For the psychiatrist, a student of interpersonal relations, man is the tangible substrate of human life.

The Human Organism and Its Necessary Environment (1940) 1953:30–31.

2 When the satisfaction or the security of another person becomes as significant to one as is one's own satisfaction or security, then the state of love exists. So far as I know, under no other circumstances is a state of love present, regardless of the popular usage of the word.

The Human Organism and Its Necessary Environment (1940) 1953:42–43.

3 The point is that the self is approved by significant others, that any tendencies of the personality that are not so approved, that are in fact strongly disapproved, are dissociated from personal awareness.

The Human Organism and Its Necessary Environment (1940) 1953:46. → See G. H. MEAD:12.

4 One has information only to the extent to which one has tended to communicate one's experience — through the medium of consensually valid verbal means. Theoretically, this last qualification gives somewhat undue importance to the use of words; by and large, it is a good principle to which to adhere in treatment work. Most patients have for years been acting out conflicts, substitutions, and compromises; the benefits of treatment come in large part from their learning to notice what they are doing, and this is greatly expedited by carefully validated verbal statements as to what seems to be going on.

Therapeutic Conceptions (1940) 1953:222–223.

William Graham Sumner 1840–1910
U.S. sociologist

1 We are born into no right whatever but what has an equivalent and corresponding duty right alongside of it. There is no such thing on this earth as something for nothing.

The Forgotten Man (1883) 1969:472.

2 The Forgotten Man . . . works, he votes, generally he prays — but he always pays — yes, above all, he pays. He does not want an office; his name never gets into the newspaper except when he gets married or dies. He keeps production going on. He contributes to the strength of parties. He is flattered before election. He is strongly patriotic. He is wanted, whenever, in his little circle, there is work to be done . . . He does not frequent the grocery or talk politics at the tavern. Consequently, he is forgotten . . . All the burdens fall on him, or on her, for it is time to remember that the Forgotten Man is not seldom a woman.

The Forgotten Man (1883) 1969:491–492.

3 If we put together all that we have learned from anthropology and ethnography about primitive men and primitive society, we perceive that the first task of life is to live. Men begin with acts, not with thoughts.

Folkways (1906) 1940:2.

4 From the first acts by which men try to satisfy needs, each act stands by itself, and looks no further than the immediate satisfaction. From recurrent needs arise habits for the individual and customs for the group, but these results are consequences which were never conscious, and never foreseen or intended. They are not noticed until they have long existed, and it is still longer before they are appreciated.

Folkways (1906) 1940:3–4.

5 A differentiation arises between ourselves, the we-group, or in-group, and everybody else, or the others-groups,

out-groups. . . Loyalty to the group, sacrifice for it, hatred and contempt for outsiders, brotherhood within, warlikeness without, — all grow together, products of the same situation.

Folkways (1906) 1940:12–13.

[Ethnocentrism is the] view of things in which one's own group is the center of everything and all others are scaled and rated with reference to it. . . Each group nourishes its own pride and vanity, boasts itself superior, exalts its own divinities and looks with contempt on outsiders.

Folkways (1906) 1940:13.

The notion of right is in the folkways. It is not outside of them, of independent origin, and brought to them to test them. In the folkways, whatever is, is right.

Folkways (1906) 1940:28.

The mores come down to us from the past. Each individual is born into them as he is born into the atmosphere, and he does not reflect on them or criticise them any more than a baby analyzes the atmosphere before he begins to breathe it.

Folkways (1906) 1940:76.

The men, women, and children who compose a society at any time are the unconscious depositaries and transmitters of the mores. They inherited them without knowing it; they are molding them unconsciously; they will transmit them involuntarily. The people cannot make the mores. They are made by them.

Folkways (1906) 1940:477.

It would be hard to find a single instance of a direct assault by positive effort upon poverty, vice, and misery which has not either failed or, if it has not failed directly and entirely, has not entailed other evils greater than the one which it removed.

Sociology (1911) 1970:186.

William Graham Sumner 1840–1910 and **Albert Galloway Keller** 1874–1956

U.S. sociologists

If society is to endure, no considerations whatever can take precedence over success in self-maintenance, that is, in the food-quest and in the provision of protection of all kinds of life. "The first task of life is to live."

The Science of Society 1927:Vol. 1, 42.

2 [Religion] has supported the use of the old, in the matter of foods, instruments, processes, and products; has favored both war and peace, wealth and poverty, diligence and idleness, virginity and prostitution, humility and ostentation, indulgence and austerity. It has prescribed game-laws, cannibalism, human sacrifice, the killing of the old, suicide, incest, polyandry, polygyny, slavery, and the levirate; has guaranteed all forms of property-holding, of inheritance, and of government; has both favored and proscribed commerce and the taking of interest; it has been forced to bend to new vices. It has therefore offered no absolute standard of morality, for there is none, but has sanctioned what lay in the mores of the time and place — or, often, what lay in the mores of the place at some previous time.

The Science of Society 1927:Vol. 2, 1463.

Edwin H. Sutherland 1883–1950

U.S. sociologist

1 Violations of law by persons in the upper socioeconomic class are, for convenience, called "white collar crimes." This concept is not intended to be definitive, but merely to call attention to crimes which are not ordinarily included within the scope of criminology. White collar crime may be defined approximately as a crime committed by a person of respectability and high social status in the course of his occupation. Consequently it excludes many crimes of the upper class such as most cases of murder, intoxication, or adultery, since these are not a part of the occupational procedures. Also, it excludes the confidence games of wealthy members of the underworld, since they are not persons of respectability and high social status.

White Collar Crime (1949) 1983:7.

Alina Szeminska

See JEAN PIAGET AND ALINA SZEMINSKA.

T

Hippolyte Adolphe Taine 1828–1893
French historian, philosopher, and critic

1 Let the parentage of creeds be established, or the classification of poems, or the growth of constitutions, or the transformations of idioms, and we have only cleared the ground. True history begins when the historian has discerned beyond the mists of ages the living, active man, endowed with passions, furnished with habits, special in voice, feature, gesture, and costume, distinctive and complete, like anybody that you have just encountered in the street.

History of English Literature (1864) 1900:vol. 1, 2.

2 The Ancient Régime, the Revolution, the Modern Régime, are the three conditions of things which I shall strive to describe with exactitude. I have no hesitation in stating that this is my sole object. A historian may be allowed the privilege of a naturalist; I have regarded my subject as the metamorphosis of an insect.

The Ancient Régime (1876) 1931:viii.

3 Facts only seem to exist, but in reality there are only abstract, universals. The more I study the things of the mind the more mathematical I find them. In them as in mathematics it is a question of quantities; they must be treated with precision. I have never had more satisfaction than in proving this in the realms of art, politics and history.

Life and Letters of H. Taine 1908:239.

4 *Après la collection des faits, la recherche des causes* [After the collection of facts, the search for causes].

Quoted in Benedetto Croce, *History* (1915) 1921:65.

Frank W. Taussig 1859–1940
U.S. economist

1 Gradations, hierarchies, shining leaders, cumulative aspirations — all these appear spontaneously whenever men get together, whether for play, for mutual help, for voluntary association, or for the great compulsory association of the state. Every Englishman is said to love a lord; every American is said to love a title.

Inventors and Money-Makers (1915) 1930:126.

R. H. Tawney 1880–1962
British historian

1 If men are fascinated. . . by the brilliant prizes of plutocracy, they must bear the burden of its limitations. Poverty, economic oppression, and industrial strife are not superficial and transitory incidents of the present industrial order. They are an expression of its essential nature as fundamental as its mechanical perfection and imposing material prizes.

The Conditions of Economic Liberty (1918) 1964:109.

2 The faith upon which our economic civilization reposes, the faith that riches are not a means but an end, implies that all economic activity is equally estimable, whether it is subordinated to a social purpose or not. Hence it divorces gain from service, and justifies rewards for which no function is performed, or which are out of all proportion to it. Wealth in modern societies is distributed according to opportunity; and while opportunity depends partly upon talent and energy, it depends still more upon birth, social position, access to education and inherited wealth; in a word, upon property. For talent and energy can create opportunity. But property need only wait for it. It is the sleeping partner who draws the dividends which the firm produces, the residuary legatee who always claims his share in the estate.

The Acquisitive Society (1920) 1948:33–34.

3 As the history of the Poor Law in the nineteenth century was to prove, there is no touchstone, except the treatment of childhood, which reveals the true character of a social philosophy more clearly than the spirit in which it regards the misfortunes of those of its members who fall by the way.

Religion and the Rise of Capitalism (1926) 1954:222.

4 It is not till it is discovered that high individual incomes will not purchase the mass of mankind immunity from cholera, typhus, and ignorance, still less secure them the positive advantages of educational opportunity and economic security, that slowly and reluctantly, amid prophecies of moral degeneration and economic disaster, society begins to make collective provision for needs which no ordinary individual, even if he works overtime all his life, can provide himself.

Equality (1931) 1952:134–135.

5 The State is an important instrument; hence the struggle to control it. But it is an instrument, and nothing more. Fools will use it, when they can, for foolish ends, and criminals for criminal ends. Sensible and decent men will use it for ends which are sensible and decent. We, in England, have repeatedly re-made the State, and are re-making it now, and shall re-make it again. Why, in heaven's name, should we be afraid of it?

Social Democracy in Britain (1949) 1964:164.

Sol Tax 1907–
U.S. anthropologist

1 The title of this book is intended to be catchy, but it should also convey in two words what the book describes: a society which is "capitalist" on a microscopic scale. There are no machines, no factories, no co-ops or corporations. Every man is his own firm and works ruggedly for himself. Money there is, in small denominations; trade there is, with what men carry on their backs; free entrepreneurs, the impersonal market place, competition — these are in the rural economy. But commerce is without credit, as production is without machines. It turns out that the difference between a poor people and a rich one is the difference between the hand and the machine, between money and credit, between the merchant and the firm; and that all these are differences between the "modern" economy and the primitive "underdeveloped" ones.

Penny Capitalism: A Guatemalan Indian Economy (1953) 1963:ix.

Frederick W. Taylor 1856–1915
U.S. industrial engineer

1 Scientific management is not any efficiency device, not a device of any kind for securing efficiency; nor is it any bunch or group of efficiency devices. It is not a new system of figuring costs; it is not a new scheme of paying men; it is not a piecework system; it is not a bonus system; it is not a premium system; it is no scheme for paying men; it is not holding a stop watch on a man and writing things down about him; it is not time study; it is not motion study nor an analysis of the movements of men; it is not the printing and ruling and unloading of a ton or two of blanks on a set of men and saying, "Here's your system; go use it." It is not divided foremanship or functional foremanship; it is not any of the devices which the average man calls to mind when scientific management is spoken of. . .

In its essence, scientific management involves a complete mental revolution on the part of the workingman engaged in any particular establishment or industry — a complete mental revolution on the part of these men as to their duties toward their work, toward their fellow men, and toward their employers. And it involves the equally complete mental revolution on the part of those on the management's side—the foreman, the superintendent, the owner of the business, the board of directors—a complete mental revolution on their part as to their duties toward their fellow workers in the management, toward their workmen, and toward all of their daily problems. And without this complete mental revolution on both sides scientific management does not exist.

Testimony before the Special House Committee (1911–1912) 1947:26–27.

Terence ?185–?159 B.C.
North African-born Roman playwright

1 [*Chremes*]: I am a man, and nothing human is foreign to me.

The Self-Tormentor:xviii.

Wagner Thielens, Jr.
See PAUL F. LAZARSFELD AND WAGNER THIELENS, JR.

Dorothy Swaine Thomas
See W. I. THOMAS AND DOROTHY SWAINE THOMAS.

W. I. Thomas 1863–1947
U.S. sociologist

1 The world of modern intellectual life is in reality a white man's world. Few women and perhaps no blacks have ever entered this world in the fullest sense. To enter it in the fullest sense would be to be in it at every moment from the time of birth to the time of death, and to absorb it unconsciously and consciously, as the child absorbs language. When something like this happens, we shall be in a position to judge of the mental efficiency of woman and the lower races. At present we seem justified in inferring that the differences in mental expressions are no greater than they should be in view of the existing differences in opportunity. . . Certain it is that no civilization can remain the highest if another civilization adds to the intelligence of its men the intelligence of its women.

The Mind of Woman and the Lower Races 1907:469.

2 The human wishes have a great variety of concrete forms but are capable of the following general classification:
1. The desire for new experience.
2. The desire for security.
3. The desire for response.
4. The desire for recognition.

The Four Wishes (1917) 1951:121.

3 Preliminary to any self-determined act of behavior there is always a stage of examination and deliberation which we may call the definition of the situation. And actually

not only concrete acts are dependent on the definition of the situation, but gradually a whole life-policy and the personality of the individual himself follow from a series of such definitions.

The Unadjusted Girl (1923) 1969:42.

4 We do not. . . lead our lives, make our decisions, and reach our goals in everyday life either statistically or scientifically. We live by inference. I am, let us say, your guest. You do not know, you cannot determine scientifically, that I will not steal your money or your spoons. But inferentially I will not, and inferentially you have me as a guest.

The Relation of Research to the Social Process (1931) 1951:93.

5 An adjustive effort of any kind is preceded by a decision to act or not act along a given line, and the decision is itself preceded by a *definition of the situation,* that is to say, an *interpretation,* or *point of view,* and eventually a policy and a behavior pattern. In this way quick judgments and decisions are made at every point in everyday life. Thus when approached by a man or beast in a lonely spot we first define the situation, make a judgment, as to whether the object is dangerous or harmless, and then decide ("make up our mind") what we are going to do about it.

Primitive Behavior 1937:8.

W. I. Thomas 1863–1947
and
Dorothy Swaine Thomas 1899–1977
U.S. sociologists

1 In any interpretative study, by selecting out only those factors which are at the moment capable of quantitative expression, there is necessary overweighting of those factors as against factors not readily expressed quantitatively.

The Child in America 1928:567.

2 The warden of Dannemora prison recently refused to honor the order of the court to send an inmate outside the prison walls for some specific purpose. He excused himself on the ground that the man was too dangerous. He had killed several persons who had the unfortunate habit of talking to themselves on the street. From the movement of their lips he imagined that they were calling him vile names, and he behaved as if this were true. If men define situations as real, they are real in their consequences.

The Child in America 1928:572. → Known since 1938 as "The Thomas Theorem." Although it appears in a book written jointly by W. I. Thomas and Dorothy Swaine Thomas, it is ascribed to him alone since Dorothy Thomas insisted — e.g., in a letter to one of the editors — that she had written only the statistical portions of the book and that "the concept of 'defining the situation' was strictly W. I.'s."

W. I. Thomas 1863–1947
U.S. sociologist
and
Florian Znaniecki 1882–1958
Polish-born U.S. sociologist

1 [Social disorganization is] a decrease of the influence of existing social rules of behavior upon individual members of the group.

The Polish Peasant in Europe and America (1918–1920) 1958:Vol. 2, 1128.

2 Personal life-records, as complete as possible, constitute the *perfect* type of sociological material, and. . . [if] social science has to use other materials at all it is only because of the practical difficulty of obtaining at the moment a sufficient number of records.

The Polish Peasant in Europe and America (1918–1920) 1958:Vol. 2, 1832.

Thomas Aquinas
See THOMAS AQUINAS.

E. P. Thompson 1924–
British historian

1 I am seeking to rescue the poor stockinger, the Luddite cropper, the "obsolete" hand-loom weaver, the "utopian" artisan, and even the deluded follower of Joanna Southcott, from the enormous condescension of posterity.

The Making of the English Working Class 1963:12.

William Thompson 1775–1833
Irish-born British political economist

1 *Without labour there is no wealth.* Labor is its distinguishing attribute. The agency of nature constitutes nothing an object of wealth: its energies are exerted altogether equally and in common, in the production of all the means of enjoyment or desire, whether objects of wealth or not objects of wealth. Labour is the *sole* parent of wealth. . .

Land, air, heat, light, the electric fluid, men, horses, water, *as such,* are equally unentitled to the appellation of wealth. They may be objects of desire, of happiness; but, till touched by the transforming hand of labor, they are not wealth.

An Inquiry into the Principles of the Distribution of Wealth (1824) 1963:6–7.

2 That the advancement of knowledge and benevolence, leading to the perception of man's true interest, will *ultimately* lead, in spite of the opposing tendency of the system of individual competition, to the equalization of knowledge, rights, wealth, and happiness, between the two great branches of the human race, men and women, may perhaps be presumed.

An Inquiry into the Principles of the Distribution of Wealth (1824) 1963:373.

William Thomson

See Lord Kelvin.

Henry David Thoreau 1817–1862

U.S. writer

1 I heartily accept the motto, "That government is best which governs least"; and I should like to see it acted up to more rapidly and systematically. Carried out, it finally amounts to this, which also I believe, — "That government is best which governs not at all"; and when men are prepared for it, that will be the kind of government which they will have.

Civil Disobedience (1849) 1950:1. → See O'Sullivan:1.

2 The objections which have been brought against a standing army, and they are many and weighty, and deserve to prevail, may also at last be brought against a standing government.

Civil Disobedience (1849) 1950:1.

3 To my astonishment I was informed on leaving college that I had studied navigation! — why, if I had taken one turn down the harbour I should have known more about it. Even the *poor* student studies and is taught only *political* economy, while that economy of living which is synonymous with philosophy is not even sincerely professed in our colleges. The consequence is, that while he is reading Adam Smith, Ricardo, and Say, he runs his father in debt irretrievably.

Walden (1854) 1927:44.

Edward L. Thorndike 1874–1949

U.S. psychologist

1 Nature is quite as truly "red in tooth and claw," quite as truly an unchanging machine, quite as truly a master against whom our revolt is beginning to succeed, quite as truly a mere collection of things to be turned to the service of our conscious ends. It is above all, on any reasonable ground, a thing to *study, to know about, to see thro*, and one can readily show that the emotionally indifferent attitude of the scientific observer is ethically a far higher attitude than the loving interest of the poet.

Sentimentality in Science-Teaching 1899:61–62.

2 Our reasons for believing in the existence of other people's minds are our experiences of their physical actions.

The Human Nature Club (1900) 1914:202.

3 Darwin showed psychologists that the mind not only is, but has grown, that it has a history as well as a character, that this history is one of hundreds of thousands of years, and that the mind's present can be fully understood only in the light of its total past. . . Our intellects and characters are no more subjects for magic, crude or refined, than the ebb and flow of the tides or the sequence of day and night.

Darwin's Contribution to Psychology 1909:70, 78.

4 The Law of Effect is that, other things being equal, *the greater the satisfyingness of the state of affairs which accompanies or follows a given response to a certain situation, the more likely that response is to be made to that situation in the future.* Conversely, the greater the discomfort or annoyingness of the state of affairs which comes with or after a response to a situation, the more likely that response is *not* to be made to that situation in the future.

Education (1912) 1973:96.

5 The Law of Effect is the fundamental law of learning and teaching. By it a crab learns to respond to the situation, *two paths*, by taking the one, choice of which has in the past brought food. By it a dog will learn to respond to the situation, *a white box and a black box*, by neglecting the latter if opening it in the past has been promptly followed by an electric shock. By it animals are taught their tricks; by it babies learn to smile at the sight of the bottle or the kind attendant, and to manipulate spoon and fork; by it the player at billiards or golf improves his game; by it the man of science preserves those ideas that satisfy him by their promise, and discards futile fancies. It is the great weapon of all who wish — in industry, trade, government, religion or education — to change men's responses, either by reinforcing old and adding new ones, or by getting rid of those that are undesirable.

Education (1912) 1973:97.

6 Whatever exists, exists in some amount. To measure it is simply to know its varying amounts.

Measurement (1913) 1962:148.

7 It is no more necessary, and is much less accurate, to describe man loosely as possessed of an "instinct of self-preservation" than it is to describe oxygen as possessed of an "instinct of rust production."

The Original Nature of Man (1913) 1919:14.

8 Practice without zeal — with equal comfort at success and failure — does *not* make perfect, and the nervous system grows *away* from the modes in which it is *exercised with resulting discomfort.* When the law of effect is omitted — when habit-formation is reduced to the supposed effect of mere repetition — two results are almost certain. By the resulting theory, little in human behavior can be explained by the law of habit; and by the resulting practice, unproductive or extremely wasteful forms of drill are encouraged.

The Psychology of Learning 1913:22.

Thucydides 5th century B.C.

Greek historian

1 The absence of romance in my history will, I fear, detract somewhat from its interest; but if it be judged useful by those inquirers who desire an exact knowledge of the past as an aid to the interpretation of the future, which in the course of human things must resemble if it does not reflect it, I shall be content. In fine, I have written my

work, not as an essay which is to win the applause of the moment, but as a possession for all time.

The Peloponnesian War:Book 1, chap. 1, 14–15.

2 Revolution. . . ran its course from city to city, and the places which it arrived at last, from having heard what had been done before carried to a still greater excess the refinement of their inventions, as manifested in the cunning of their enterprises and the atrocity of their reprisals. Words had to change their ordinary meaning and to take that which was now given them. Reckless audacity came to be considered the courage of a loyal ally; prudent hesitation, specious cowardice; moderation was held to be a cloak for unmanliness; ability to see all sides of a question inaptness to act on any. Frantic violence became the attribute of manliness; cautious plotting, a justifiable means of self-defence. The advocate of extreme measures was always trustworthy; his opponent a man to be suspected.

The Peloponnesian War:Book 3, chap. 10, 189.

Johann Heinrich von Thünen 1783–1850
German economist

1 Hypothesis: Imagine a very large town, at the centre of a fertile plain which is crossed by no navigable river or canal. Throughout the plain the soil is capable of cultivation and of the same fertility. Far from the town, the plain turns into an uncultivated wilderness which cuts off all communication between this State and the outside world.

There are no other towns on the plain. The central town must therefore supply the rural areas with all manufactured products, and in return it will obtain all its provisions from the surrounding countryside.

The mines that provide the State with salt and metals are near the central town which, as it is the only one, we shall in future call simply "the Town."

Von Thünen's Isolated State (1826) 1966:7. → Thünen used the model of an "isolated state" in order to test his economic theories.

2 A [natural wage] = $\sqrt{ap}$.

Tombstone inscription 1850. Quoted in Peter Hall, Introduction to *Von Thünen's Isolated State* (1826) 1966:xviii. → This formula summarizes Thünen's theory of the relation of wages to the rate of interest and the rent of land; it was carved on his tombstone at his request.

Charles Tilly 1929–
U.S. sociologist and historian

1 Sociologists have cut themselves off from a rich inheritance by forgetting the obvious: that all history is past social behavior, that all archives are brimming with news on how men used to act, and how they are acting still.

The Vendée 1964:342.

Charles Tilly 1929–
U.S. sociologist and historian
and
C. Harold Brown 1933–
U.S. sociologist

1 The ghost of Robert Ezra Park will not be silent. Turn to the study of urban spatial arrangements; there is his idea that the city's landscape records its pattern of social mobility. Turn to the writings on ethnic relations; there is his metaphor of social distance. Turn to the analysis of migration; there is the theory of the marginal man.

On Uprooting, Kinship, and the Auspices of Migration 1967:139. → See PARK:1 and 4.

Edward B. Titchener 1867–1927
British-born U.S. psychologist

1 An experiment is an observation that can be repeated, isolated and varied. The more frequently you can *repeat* an observation, the more likely are you to see clearly what is there and to describe accurately what you have seen. The more strictly you can *isolate* an observation, the easier does your task of observation become, and the less danger is there of your being led astray by irrelevant circumstances, or of placing emphasis on the wrong point. The more widely you can *vary* an observation, the more clearly will the uniformity of experience stand out, and the better is your chance of discovering laws.

A Text-Book of Psychology (1896) 1926:20.

2 "Mind" is understood to mean simply the sum total of mental processes experienced by the individual during his lifetime. Ideas, feelings, impulses, etc., are mental processes; the whole number of ideas, feelings, impulses, etc., experienced by me during my life constitutes my "mind."

An Outline of Psychology (1897) 1906:11.

3 The primary aim of the experimental psychologist has been to analyze the structure of the mind; to ravel out the elemental processes from the tangle of consciousness, or (if we may change the metaphor) to isolate the constituents in the given conscious formation. His task is a vivisection, but a vivisection which shall yield structural, not functional results. He tries to discover, first of all, what is there and in what quantity, not what it is there for.

The Postulates of a Structural Psychology 1898:450.

4 The instinctive tendency of the scientific man is toward the existential substrate that appears when use and purpose — cosmic significance, artistic value, social utility, personal reference — have been removed. He responds positively to the bare "what" of things; he responds negatively to any further demand for interest or appreciation.

Systematic Psychology 1929:32.

5 The great difference between science and technology is a difference of initial attitude. The scientific man follows his method whithersoever it may take him. He seeks ac-

quaintance with his subject-matter, and he does not at all care about what he shall find, what shall be the content of his knowledge when acquaintance-with is transformed into knowledge-about. The technologist moves in another universe; he seeks the attainment of some determinate end, which is his sole and obsessing care; and he therefore takes no heed of anything that he cannot put to use as means toward that end.

Systematic Psychology 1929:66.

Richard M. Titmuss 1907–1973
British sociologist

1 The ways in which society organizes and structures its social institutions — and particularly its health and welfare systems — can encourage or discourage the altruistic in man; such systems can foster integration or alienation; they can allow the "theme of the gift" (to recall Mauss's words) — of generosity towards strangers — to spread among and between social groups and generations.

The Gift Relationship 1971:225. → See MAUSS:3.

2 From our study of the private market in blood in the United States we have concluded that the commercialization of blood and donor relationships represses the expression of altruism, erodes the sense of community, lowers scientific standards, limits both personal and professional freedoms, sanctions the making of profits in hospitals and clinical laboratories, legalizes hostility between doctor and patient, subjects critical areas of medicine to the laws of the marketplace, places immense social costs on those least able to bear them — the poor, the sick and the inept — increases the danger of unethical behaviour in various sectors of medical science and practice, and results in situations in which proportionately more and more blood is supplied by the poor, the unskilled, the unemployed, Negroes and other low-income groups and categories of exploited human populations of high blood yielders. Redistribution in terms of blood and blood products from the poor to the rich appears to be one of the dominant effects of the American blood banking systems.

The Gift Relationship (1971) 1972:245–246.

James Tobin 1918–
U.S. economist

1 Revolutions and revelations in economics are rare. They have generally occurred at intervals of thirty to sixty years and have taken decades to influence public opinion and policy. The Keynesian revolution, initiated by a forbidding theoretical book in 1935, made its way only gradually through academe to lay intellectuals, media pundits, business and labour leaders, bureaucrats and politicians. When, after considerable resistance and revision, J. M. Keynes's ideas became explicit rationales for American macroeconomics strategy in 1961–5, the press hailed them as the "New" Economics.

Supply-side Economics (1981) 1987:126.

Alexis de Tocqueville 1805–1859
French political theorist and statesman

1 Nothing is easier than becoming rich in America; naturally, the human spirit, which needs a dominant passion, in the end turns all its thoughts toward gain. As a result, at first sight this people seems to be a company of merchants joined together for trade, and as one digs deeper into the national character of the Americans, one sees that they have sought the value of everything in this world only in the answer to this single question: how much money will it bring in?

Letter to Ernest de Chabrol, 9 June 1831. 1985:39.

2 It is not without having carefully reflected that I decided to write the book I am just now publishing. I do not hide from myself what is annoying in my position: it is bound to attract active sympathy from no one. Some will find that at bottom I do not like democracy and that I am severe toward it; others will think that I favor its development imprudently. It would be most fortunate for me if the book were not read, and that is a piece of good fortune that may perhaps come to pass. I know all that, but this is my response: nearly ten years ago I was already thinking about part of the things I have just now set forth. I was in America only to become clear on this point. The penitentiary system was a pretext: I took it as a passport that would let me enter thoroughly into the United States.

Letter to Louis de Kergorlay, January 1835. 1985:95. → The first part of *Democracy in America* appeared in 1835. See BEAUMONT:1.

3 If there is a country in the world where the doctrine of the sovereignty of the people can be fairly appreciated, where it can be studied in its application to the affairs of society, and where its dangers and its advantages may be judged, that country is assuredly America.

Democracy in America (1835–1840) 1945:Vol. 1, 57.

4 There is no medium between servitude and license; in order to enjoy the inestimable benefits that the liberty of the press ensures, it is necessary to submit to the inevitable evils that it creates.

Democracy in America (1835–1840) 1945:Vol. 1, 192.

5 It cannot be denied that the unrestrained liberty of association for political purposes is the privilege which a people is longest in learning how to exercise. If it does not throw the nation into anarchy, it perpetually augments the chances of that calamity. On one point, however, this perilous liberty offers a security against dangers of another kind; in countries where associations are free, secret societies are unknown. In America there are factions, but no conspiracies.

Democracy in America (1835–1840) 1945:Vol. 1, 202–203.

6 American functionaries are far more independent within the sphere that is prescribed to them than the French civil officers. Sometimes, even, they are allowed by the

popular authority to exceed those bounds; and as they are protected by the opinion and backed by the power of the majority, they dare do things that even a European, accustomed as he is to arbitrary power, is astonished at. By this means habits are formed in the heart of a free country which may some day prove fatal to its liberties.

Democracy in America (1835–1840) 1945:Vol. 1, 272–273.

7 In America the majority raises formidable barriers around the liberty of opinion; within these barriers an author may write what he pleases, but woe to him if he goes beyond them.

Democracy in America (1835–1840) 1945:Vol. 1, 274.

8 Scarcely any political question arises in the United States that is not resolved, sooner or later, into a judicial question.

Democracy in America (1835–1840) 1945:Vol. 1, 290.

9 If it be of the highest importance to man, as an individual, that his religion should be true, it is not so to society. Society has no future life to hope for or to fear; and provided the citizens profess a religion, the peculiar tenets of that religion are of little importance to its interests.

Democracy in America (1835–1840) 1945:Vol. 1, 314.

10 Despotism may govern without faith, but liberty cannot. Religion is much more necessary in the republic which they set forth in glowing colors than in the monarchy which they attack; it is more needed in democratic republics than in any others. How is it possible that society should escape destruction if the moral tie is not strengthened in proportion as the political tie is relaxed? And what can be done with a people who are their own masters if they are not submissive to the Deity?

Democracy in America (1835–1840) 1945:Vol. 1, 318.

11 The philosophers of the eighteenth century explained in a very simple manner the gradual decay of religious faith. Religious zeal, said they, must necessarily fail the more generally liberty is established and knowledge diffused. Unfortunately, the facts by no means accord with their theory.

Democracy in America (1835–1840) 1945:Vol. 1, 319.

12 The Americans never use the word *peasant,* because they have no idea of the class which that term denotes; the ignorance of more remote ages, the simplicity of rural life, and the rusticity of the villager have not been preserved among them; and they are alike unacquainted with the virtues, the vices, the coarse habits, and the simple graces of an early stage of civilization.

Democracy in America (1835–1840) 1945:Vol. 1, 328.

13 I am obliged to confess that I do not regard the abolition of slavery as a means of warding off the struggle of the two races in the Southern states. The Negroes may long remain slaves without complaining; but if they are once raised to the level of freemen, they will soon revolt at being deprived of almost all their civil rights; and as they cannot become the equals of the whites, they will speedily show themselves as enemies.

Democracy in America (1835–1840) 1945:Vol. 1, 394.

14 The whole life of an American is passed like a game of chance, a revolutionary crisis, or a battle.

Democracy in America (1835–1840) 1945:Vol. 1, 443.

15 Democratic nations care but little for what has been, but they are haunted by visions of what will be; in this direction their unbounded imagination grows and dilates beyond all measure. . . Democracy, which shuts the past against the poet, opens the future before him.

Democracy in America (1835–1840) 1945:Vol. 2, 78.

16 Historians who write in aristocratic ages are inclined to refer all occurrences to the particular will and character of certain individuals; and they are apt to attribute the most important revolutions to slight accidents. They trace out the smallest causes with sagacity, and frequently leave the greatest unperceived.

Historians who live in democratic ages exhibit precisely opposite characteristics. Most of them attribute hardly any influence to the individual over the destiny of the race, or to citizens over the fate of a people; but, on the other hand, they assign great general causes to all petty incidents.

Democracy in America (1835–1840) 1945:Vol. 2, 90.

17 Democracy leads men not to draw near to their fellow creatures; but democratic revolutions lead them to shun each other and perpetuate in a state of equality the animosities that the state of inequality created.

The great advantage of the Americans is that they have arrived at a state of democracy without having to endure a democratic revolution, and that they are born equal instead of becoming so.

Democracy in America (1835–1840) 1945:Vol. 2, 101.

18 Not only does democracy make every man forget his ancestors, but it hides his descendants and separates his contemporaries from him; it throws him back forever upon himself alone and threatens in the end to confine him entirely within the solitude of his own heart.

Democracy in America (1835–1840) 1945:Vol. 2, 106.

19 The Americans make associations to give entertainments, to found seminaries, to build inns, to construct churches, to diffuse books, to send missionaries to the antipods; in this manner they found hospitals, prisons, and schools. If it is proposed to inculcate some truth or to foster some feeling by the encouragement of a great example, they form a society. Wherever at the head of some new undertaking you see the government in France, or a man of rank in England, in the United States you will be sure to find an association.

Democracy in America (1835–1840) 1945:Vol.2, 114.

20 Among the laws that rule human societies there is one which seems to be more precise and clear than all others.

If men are to remain civilized or to become so, the art of associating together must grow and improve in the same ratio in which the equality of conditions is increased.

Democracy in America (1835–1840) 1945:Vol. 2, 118.

21 The Americans entertain with respect to different callings. In America no one is degraded because he works, for everyone about him works also; nor is anyone humiliated by the notion of receiving pay, for the President of the United States also works for pay. He is paid for commanding, other men for obeying orders. In the United States professions are more or less laborious, more or less profitable; but they are never either high or low: every honest calling is honorable.

Democracy in America (1835–1840) 1945:Vol. 2, 162.

22 Although the women of the United States are confined within the narrow circle of domestic life, and their situation is in some respects one of extreme dependence, I have nowhere seen woman occupying a loftier position; and if I were asked, now that I am drawing to the close of this work, in which I have spoken of so many important things done by the Americans, to what the singular prosperity and growing strength of that people ought mainly to be attributed, I should reply: To the superiority of their women.

Democracy in America (1835–1840) 1945:Vol. 2, 225.

23 I have already observed that in democracies no such thing as a regular code of good breeding can be laid down. . . This has some inconveniences and some advantages. In aristocracies the rules of propriety impose the same demeanor on everyone; they make all the members of the same class appear alike in spite of their private inclinations; they adorn and they conceal the natural man. Among a democratic people manners are neither so tutored nor so uniform, but they are frequently more sincere. They form, as it were, a light and loosely woven veil through which the real feelings and private opinions of each individual are easily discernible. The form and the substance of human actions, therefore, often stand there in closer relation; and if the great picture of human life is less embellished, it is more true. Thus it may be said, in one sense, that the effect of democracy is not exactly to give men any particular manners, but to prevent them from having manners at all.

Democracy in America (1835–1840) 1945:Vol. 2, 230.

24 In no country in the world is the love of property more active and more anxious than in the United States; nowhere does the majority display less inclination for those principles which threaten to alter, in whatever manner, the laws of property.

Democracy in America (1835–1840) 1945:Vol. 2, 270.

25 If ever America undergoes great revolutions, they will be brought about by the presence of the black race on the soil of the United States; that is to say, they will owe their origin, not to the equality, but to the inequality of condition.

Democracy in America (1835–1840) 1945:Vol. 2, 270.

26 There are two things that a democratic people will always find very difficult, to begin a war and to end it.

Democracy in America (1835–1840) 1945:Vol. 2, 283.

27 All those who seek to destroy the liberties of a democratic nation ought to know that war is the surest and the shortest means to accomplish it. This is the first axiom of the science.

Democracy in America (1835–1840) 1945:Vol. 2, 284.

28 People did not fall from the excess of evil into revolution, but from the excess of progress into revolution. Having come to the middle of the staircase, they threw themselves out the window in order to arrive at the bottom sooner. Thus, moreover, does the world almost always go. It is almost never when a state of things is the most detestable that it is smashed, but when, beginning to improve, it permits men to breathe, to reflect, to communicate their thoughts with each other, and to gauge by what they already have the extent of their rights and their grievances. The weight, although less heavy, seems then all the more unbearable.

Letter to Pierre Freslon, 23 September 1853. 1985:296.

29 It is not always when things are going from bad to worse that revolutions break out. On the contrary, it oftener happens that when a people which has put up with an oppressive rule over a long period without protest suddenly finds the government relaxing its pressure, it takes up arms against it. Thus the social order overthrown by a revolution is almost always better than the one immediately preceding it, and experience teaches us that, generally speaking, the most perilous moment for a bad government is one when it seeks to mend its ways.

The Old Régime and the French Revolution (1856) 1945:176–177. → An early statement of "the revolution of rising expectations."

Alvin Toffler 1928–

U.S. writer

1 The term "future shock" [was coined] to describe the shattering stress and disorientation that we induce in individuals by subjecting them to too much change in too short a time. . . Future shock is no longer a distantly potential danger, but a real sickness from which increasingly large numbers already suffer. This psycho-biological condition can be described in medical and psychiatric terms. It is the disease of change.

Future Shock 1970:4.

Edward C. Tolman 1886–1959

U.S. psychologist

1 The psychology of animal learning — not to mention that of child learning — has been and still is primarily a mat-

ter of agreeing or disagreeing with Thorndike, or trying in minor ways to improve upon him. Gestalt psychologists, conditioned-reflex psychologists, sign-gestalt psychologists — all of us here in America seem to have taken Thorndike, overtly or covertly, as our starting point.

The Determiners of Behavior at a Choice Point 1938:11.

2 What, by way of summary, can we now say as to the contributions of us rodent psychologists to human behavior? What is it that we rat runners still have to contribute to the understanding of the deeds and the misdeeds, the absurdities and the tragedies of our friend, and our enemy — *homo sapiens*? The answer is that, whereas man's successes, persistences, and socially unacceptable divagations — that is, his intelligences, his motivations, and his instabilities — are all ultimately shaped and materialized by specific cultures, it is still true that most of the formal underlying laws of intelligence, motivation, and instability can still be studied in rats as well as, and more easily than, in men.

A Stimulus-Expectancy Need-Cathexis Psychology 1945:166.

3 I have always wanted my psychology to be as wide as the study of a life career and as narrow as the study of a rat's entrance into a specific blind. But, actually, I have for the most part studied only average numbers of entrances into specific blinds, or jumps to a particular type of door, and have hoped that the principles found there would have something to do with a really interesting piece of behavior — say, the choice and pursuit of a life career.

Principles of Purposive Behavior 1959:97.

4 Our language is full of spatial terms: e.g., "this when *approached* is seen to be that," "this is the *opposite* of that," "this is a more *direct* solution than that," "this is a more clumsy, more *roundabout*, *longer*, way to do it than that," "this *leads* to that." The spatial concepts of distance and direction seem to me of the very warp and woof of all our thinking about performances whether these performances involve actual space or mere mechanics or mere logic.

Principles of Purposive Behavior 1959:146.

Leo Tolstoy 1828–1910
Russian novelist and social critic

1 Man lives consciously for himself, but is an unconscious instrument in the attainment of the historic, universal, aims of humanity.

War and Peace (1865–1869) 1970:Book 9, chap. 1, 670.

2 In historic events, the so-called great men are labels giving names to events, and like labels they have but the smallest connection with the event itself.

Every act of theirs, which appears to them an act of their own will, is in an historical sense involuntary and is related to the whole course of history and predestined from eternity.

War and Peace (1865–1869) 1970:Book 9, chap. 1, 671.

3 In quiet and untroubled times it seems to every administrator that it is only by his efforts that the whole population under his rule is kept going, and in this consciousness of being indispensable every administrator finds the chief reward of his labor and efforts. While the sea of history remains calm the ruler-administrator in his frail bark, holding on with a boat hook to the ship of the people and himself moving, naturally imagines that his efforts move the ship he is holding on to. But as soon as a storm arises and the sea begins to heave and the ship to move, such a delusion is no longer possible. The ship moves independently with its own enormous motion, the boat hook no longer reaches the moving vessel, and suddenly the administrator, instead of appearing a ruler and a source of power, becomes an insignificant, useless, feeble man.

War and Peace (1865–1869) 1970:Book 11, chap. 12, 988.

4 Happy families are all alike; every unhappy family is unhappy in its own way.

Anna Karenina (1875–1877) 1939:Vol. 1, part 1, chap. 1, 3.

Ferdinand Tönnies 1855–1936
German sociologist

1 The group which is formed through this positive type of relationship is called an association (*Verbindung*) when conceived of as a thing or being which acts as a unit inwardly and outwardly. The relationship itself, and also the resulting association, is conceived of either as real and organic life — this is the essential characteristic of the Gemeinschaft (community); or as imaginary and mechanical structure — this is the concept of Gesellschaft (society).

Community & Society (1887) 1957:33.

2 All intimate, private, and exclusive living together, so we discover, is understood as life in Gemeinschaft (community). Gesellschaft (society) is public life — it is the world itself. In Gemeinschaft with one's family, one lives from birth on, bound to it in weal and woe. One goes into Gesellschaft as one goes into a strange country.

Community & Society (1887) 1957:33–34.

3 All praise of rural life has pointed out that the Gemeinschaft among people is stronger there and more alive; it is the lasting and genuine form of living together. In contrast to Gemeinschaft, Gesellschaft is transitory and superficial. Accordingly, Gemeinschaft should be understood as a living organism, Gesellschaft as a mechanical aggregate and artifact.

Community & Society (1887) 1957:35.

4 Public opinion, which brings the morality of Gesellschaft into rules and formulas and can rise above the state, has

nevertheless decided tendencies to urge the state to use its irresistible power to force everyone to do what is useful and to leave undone what is damaging. Extension of the penal code and the police power seems the right means to curb the evil impulses of the masses. Public opinion passes easily from the demand for freedom (for the upper classes) to that of despotism (against the lower classes).

Community & Society (1887) 1957:230.

5 Public opinion is the common way of thought, the corporate spirit of any group or association, in so far as these opinions are built upon thought and knowledge rather than on unproven imaginings, beliefs or authority.

Kritik der öffentlichen Meinung 1922:77–78.

Arnold Toynbee 1852–1883
British economist

1 The essence of the Industrial Revolution is the substitution of competition for the mediaeval regulations which had previously controlled the production and distribution of wealth.

The Industrial Revolution (1884) 1956:58. → First published as *Lectures on the Industrial Revolution of the Eighteenth Century* from Toynbee's lecture notes after his sudden death in the midst of a series of debates with Henry George. The book introduced the phrase "industrial revolution" to the English-speaking world. According to S. G. Checkland, the term itself originated in France. In 1837, Jérôme-Adolphe Blanqui wrote that "la révolution industrielle se met en possession de l'Angleterre." See S. G. Checkland, Industrial Revolution (1987:811).

2 The effects of the Industrial Revolution prove that free competition may produce wealth without producing well-being. We all know the horrors that ensued in England before it was restrained by legislation and combination.

The Industrial Revolution (1884) 1956:66.

Arnold J. Toynbee 1889–1975
British historian

1 The "intelligible fields of historical study". . . are societies which have a greater extension, in both Space and Time, than national states or city-states, or any other political communities. . . Societies, not states, are "the social atoms" with which students of history have to deal.

A Study of History 1934:Vol. 1, 44–45.

2 The so-called racial explanation of differences in human performance and achievement is either an ineptitude or a fraud.

A Study of History 1934:Vol. 1, 245.

3 Civilizations. . . are wholes whose parts all cohere with one another and all affect one another reciprocally.

A Study of History 1934:Vol. 3, 380.

4 An essential difference between civilizations and primitive societies *as we know them* (the *caveat* will be found to be important) is the direction taken by mimesis or imitation. . . In primitive societies, as we know them, mimesis is directed towards the older generation and towards dead ancestors who stand, unseen but not unfelt, at the back of the living elders, reinforcing their prestige. On the other hand, in societies in process of civilization, mimesis is directed towards creative personalities who command a following because they are pioneers. In such societies, "the cake of custom," as Walter Bagehot called it in his *Physics and Politics*, is broken.

A Study of History [Somervell abridgement of vols. 1–6] 1947:49. → See BAGEHOT:7.

5 The nature of the breakdowns of civilizations can be summed up in three points: a failure of creative power in the minority, an answering withdrawal of mimesis on the part of the majority and a consequent loss of social unity in the society as a whole.

A Study of History [Somervell abridgement of vols. 1–6] 1947:246.

6 Though sixteen civilizations may have perished already to our knowledge, and nine others may be now at the point of death, we — the twenty-sixth — are not compelled to submit the riddle of our fate to the blind arbitrament of statistics. The divine spark of creative power is still alive in us, and, if we have the grace to kindle it into flame, then the stars in their courses cannot defeat our efforts to attain the goal of human endeavour.

A Study of History [Somervell abridgement of vols. 1–6] 1947:254.

7 Of the twenty or so civilizations known to modern Western historians, all except our own appear to be dead or moribund, and when we diagnose each case, *in extremis* or *post mortem*, we invariably find that the cause of death has been either War or Class or some combination of the two. To date, these two plagues have been deadly enough, in partnership, to kill off nineteen out of twenty representatives of this recently evolved species of human society; but, up to now, the deadliness of these scourges has had a saving limit.

Civilization on Trial 1948:23.

8 Civilizations, I believe, come to birth and proceed to grow by successfully responding to successive challenges. They break down and go to pieces if and when a challenge confronts them which they fail to meet.

Civilization on Trial 1948:56.

Heinrich von Treitschke 1834–1896
German historian

1 The greatness of war is just what at first sight seems to be its horror — that for the sake of their country men will overcome the natural feelings of humanity, that they will slaughter their fellow-men who have done them no injury, nay, whom they perhaps respect as chivalrous foes. Man will not only sacrifice his life, but the natural and justified instincts of his soul; his very self he must offer up for the sake of patriotism; here we have the sublimity

of war. When we pursue this thought further we see how war, with all its brutality and sternness, weaves a bond of love between man and man, linking them together to face death, and causing all class distinctions to disappear. He who knows history knows also that to banish war from the world would be to mutilate human nature.

Politics (1897–1898) 1963:244–245.

George Macaulay Trevelyan 1876–1962
British historian

1 Social history might be defined negatively as the history of the people with the politics left out.

English Social History (1942) 1946:vii.

2 Our modern system of popular Education was indeed indispensable and has conferred great benefits on the country, but it has been a disappointment in some important respects. . . It has produced a vast population able to read but unable to distinguish what is worth reading.

English Social History (1942) 1946:582.

H. R. Trevor-Roper 1914–
British historian

1 History is not merely what happened: it is what happened in the context of what might have happened. Therefore it must incorporate, as a necessary element, the alternatives, the might-have-beens.

History and Imagination 1980:15.

2 It is only if we place ourselves before the alternatives of the past, as of the present, only if we live for a moment, as the men of the time lived, in its still fluid context and among its still unresolved problems, if we see those problems coming upon us, as well as look back on them after they have gone away, that we can draw useful lessons from history. That is what was meant by the famous phrase of Ranke — of the young Ranke, still uncorrupted by the philosophical determinism of Berlin: the phrase which has been so often quoted, and almost as often misapplied, *"wie es eigentlich gewesen."*

History and Imagination 1980:16. → See RANKE:1.

Diana Trilling 1905–
U.S. literary and cultural critic

1 There is all the difference in the world between a society which *permits* such of its women as have other than female capacities to pursue extra-domestic lives, and a society [like our own] that virtually *compels* its women to seek extra-domestic occupations in order to feel valued.

Men, Women, and Sex (1950) 1964:62.

2 The irony of bringing Freud into immediate conjunction with the subject of women's liberation lies in his having had such an invidious view of the female sex. I am afraid that the man who sought to liberate the human psyche from the hindrances put upon it in infancy was interested not at all in liberating women from the special restraints imposed upon them in our society. Nowhere in his writings does Freud express sympathy for the problems which pertain to women alone. On the contrary, his misogyny is now taken for granted even by his most admiring students.

Female Biology in a Male Culture (1970) 1977:190.

3 We are all of us, men and women both, the creatures of culture: we do and feel what our societies ask us to, and the demands put upon us are not always consistent or precisely correlated with biology.

Female Biology in a Male Culture (1970) 1977:195.

Lionel Trilling 1900–1975
U.S. literary and cultural critic

1 Freud may be right or he may be wrong in the place he gives to biology in human fate, but I think we must stop to consider whether this emphasis on biology, correct or incorrect, is not so far from being a reactionary idea that it is actually a liberating idea. It proposes to us that culture is not all-powerful. It suggests that there is a residue of human quality beyond the reach of cultural control, and that this residue of human quality, elemental as it may be, serves to bring culture itself under criticism and keeps it from being absolute.

Freud (1955) 1965:98.

2 We nowadays say "role" without taking thought of its original histrionic meaning: "in my professional role," "in my masculine, or feminine role." But the old histrionic meaning is present whether or not we let ourselves be aware of it, and it brings with it the idea that somewhere under all the roles there is Me, that poor old ultimate actuality, who, when all the roles have been played, would like to murmer "Off, off, you lendings!" and settle down with his own original actual self.

Sincerity and Authenticity 1972:910.

3 Society is a concept that is readily hypostatized — the things that are said about it suggest that it has a life of its own and its own laws. . . Society is a kind of entity different from a kingdom or realm; and even "commonwealth," as Hobbes used that word, seems archaic to denote what he has in mind.

Sincerity and Authenticity 1972:19.

4 For Karl Marx, . . . the city was to be praised for at least one thing, the escape it offers from what he called "the idiocy of village life." He no doubt had in mind the primitive meaning of the word "idiot," which is not a mentally deficient person, nor yet an uncouth and ignorant person, but a private person, one "who does not hold public office": a person who is not a participant in society as Marx understood it. For Marx the working out of the historical process, and therefore the essential life of man, could take place only in cities, where the classes confront each other, where men in the mass demonstrate the nature and destiny of mankind.

Sincerity and Authenticity 1972:20. → See MARX AND ENGELS:7.

5 Seen in its totality, seen historically, the life of mind consists as much in its failed efforts as in its successes, in its false starts, its mere approximations, its very errors. It is carried on, we may say, even in the vicissitudes it makes for itself, including its mistrust or denial of its own ideal nature. All these are manifestations of the energies of mind, and William James, a philosopher in whose peculiar largeness of spirit we may perceive an affinity with Jefferson's, was at pains to remind us that they, in all their ill-conditioned disorder, are actually a function of mind's ideal achievement. Mind does not move toward its ideal purposes over a royal straight road but finds its way through the thicket of its own confusions and contradictions.

Mind in the Modern World (1973) 1981:127.

Ernst Troeltsch 1865–1923
German sociologist and historian

1 The Church is that type of organization which is overwhelmingly conservative, which to a certain extent accepts the secular order, and dominates the masses; in principle, therefore, it is universal, i.e. it desires to cover the whole life of humanity. The sects, on the other hand, are comparatively small groups; they aspire after personal inward perfection, and they aim at a direct personal fellowship between the members of each group.

The Social Teaching of the Christian Churches (1912) 1981:Vol. 1, 331.

Frances Trollope 1780–1863
British social, economic, and political critic

1 Should the women ever discover what their power might be, and compare it with what it is, much improvement might be hoped for. While, at Philadelphia, among the handsomest, the wealthiest, and the most distinguished of the land, their comparative influence in society, with that possessed in Europe by females holding the same station, occurred forcibly to my mind.

Domestic Manners of the Americans (1832) 1949:280.

Leon Trotsky 1879–1940
[Lev Davidovitch Bronstein]
Russian revolutionary leader

1 Since the greatest enigma is the fact that a backward country was the *first* to place the proletariat in power, it behooves us to seek the solution of that enigma in the *peculiarities* of that backward country — that is, in its differences from other countries.

The History of the Russian Revolution (1932) 1957:Vol. 1, xx.

2 The law of combined development of backward countries — in the sense of a peculiar mixture of backward elements with the most modern factors — here rises before us in its most finished form, and offers a key to the fundamental riddle of the Russian revolution. If the agrarian problem, as a heritage from the barbarism of the old Russian history, had been solved by the bourgeoisie, if it could have been solved by them, the Russian proletariat could not possibly have come to power in 1917. In order to realise the Soviet state, there was required a drawing together and mutual penetration of two factors belonging to completely different historic species: a peasant war — that is, a movement characteristic of the dawn of bourgeois development — and a proletarian insurrection, the movement signalising its decline. That is the essence of 1917.

The History of the Russian Revolution (1932) 1957: Vol. 1, 50–51.

3 A party for whom everybody votes except that minority who know what they are voting for, is no more a party, than the tongue in which babies of all countries babble is a national language.

The History of the Russian Revolution (1932) 1957: Vol. 1, 223.

4 The basis of bureaucratic rule is the poverty of society in objects of consumption, with the resulting struggle of each against all. When there is enough goods in a store, the purchasers can come whenever they want to. When there is little goods, the purchasers are compelled to stand in line. When the lines are very long, it is necessary to appoint a policeman to keep order. Such is the starting point of the power of the Soviet bureaucracy. It "knows" who is to get something and who has to wait.

The Revolution Betrayed (1937) 1945:112.

5 The increasingly insistent deification of Stalin is, with all its elements of caricature, a necessary element of the regime. . . In Stalin each [Soviet bureaucrat] easily finds himself. But Stalin also finds in each one a small part of his own spirit. Stalin is the personification of the bureaucracy. That is the substance of his political personality.

The Revolution Betrayed (1937) 1945:277.

6 The perspective of permanent revolution may be summarized in the following way: the complete victory of the democratic revolution in Russia is conceivable only in the form of the dictatorship of the proletariat, leaning on the peasantry. The dictatorship of the proletariat, which would inevitably place on the order of the day not only democratic but socialistic tasks as well, would at the same time give a powerful impetus to the international socialist revolution. Only the victory of the proletariat in the West could protect Russia from bourgeois restoration and assure it the possibility of rounding out the establishment of socialism.

Stalin 1941:433.

David B. Truman 1913–
U.S. political scientist

1 It is. . . multiple memberships in potential groups based on widely held and accepted interests that serve as a bal-

ance wheel in a going political system like that of the United States.

The Governmental Process (1951) 1971:514.

Anne Robert Jacques Turgot 1727–1781
French economist

1 Colonies are like fruits which cling to the tree only until they have reached their maturity: once they had become self-sufficient they did what Carthage was to do later, and what America will one day do.

A Philosophical Review (1750) 1973:47.

2 Universal history embraces the consideration of the successive progress of humanity, and the detailed causes which have contributed to it: the earliest beginnings of man, the formation and mixture of nations; the origins and revolutions of government; the development of language; of morality, custom, arts and sciences; the revolutions which have brought about the succession of empires, nations, and religions.

Plan de deux discours sur l'histoire universelle (1750) 1844:627.

3 The primitive dispositions are equally active among barbarians and civilized peoples. They are probably the same in every place and time. Genius is spread throughout humankind somewhat like gold in a mine. The more ore you mine, the more metal you extract. The more men you have, the more great ones or ones fitting to become great. The chances of education and circumstances develop them or let them be buried in obscurity.

Plan de deux discours sur l'histoire universelle (1750) 1844:645.

4 The ambitious ones themselves in forming the great nations have contributed to the views of Providence, to the progress of enlightenment, and consequently to the increase of the happiness of the human species, a thing which did not at all interest them. Their passions, their very rages, have led them without their knowing where they were going.

Plan du premier discours sur la formation des gouvernements et le mélange des nations (1751?) 1913:283.

5 The study of language, if well done, would perhaps be the best of logics. In analyzing, in comparing the words of which they are fashioned, in tracing from the beginning the different meanings which they acquired, in following the thread of ideas, we will see through which stages, through which metamorphoses men passed. . . This kind of experimental metaphysics would be at one and the same time the history of the human mind and the history of the progress of its thoughts, always fitted to the needs which gave birth to them. Languages are at once their expression and their measure.

Réflexions sur les langues (1751?) 1913:347.

6 Before we have learned that things are in a given situation they have already been altered several times. Thus we always become aware of events when it is too late, and politics has to foresee the present, so to speak.

Plan d'un ouvrage sur la géographie politique (date uncertain) 1913:321.

Frederick Jackson Turner 1861–1932
U.S. historian

1 Each age tries to form its own conception of the past. *Each age writes the history of the past anew with reference to the conditions uppermost in its own time.*

The Significance of History (1891) 1961:17.

2 Up to our own day American history has been in a large degree the history of the colonization of the Great West. The existence of an area of free land, its continuous recession, and the advance of American settlement westward, explain American development.

The Significance of the Frontier in American History (1893) 1962:1. → The so-called "Frontier Thesis" that dominated much of American historical thought from the turn of the century until the 1930s. Based upon Census reports, Turner used 1880 as the date for the closing of the frontier. See PORTER:1.

3 What the Mediterranean Sea was to the Greeks, breaking the bond of custom, offering new experiences, calling out new institutions and activities, that, and more, the ever retreating frontier has been to the United States directly, and to the nations of Europe more remotely. And now, four centuries from the discovery of America, at the end of a hundred years of life under the Constitution, the frontier has gone, and with its going has closed the first period of American history.

The Significance of the Frontier in American History (1893) 1962:38.

Victor W. Turner 1920–1983
Scottish-born U.S. anthropologist

1 Myths are not merely a guide to culture, although they are this as well; they point to the generative power underlying human life, a power which from time to time oversteps cultural limits.

Myth and Symbol 1968:581.

2 The attributes of liminality or of liminal *personae* ("threshold people") are necessarily ambiguous, since this condition and these persons elude or slip through the network of classifications that normally locate states and positions in cultural space. Liminal entities are neither here nor there; they are betwixt and between the positions assigned and arrayed by law, custom, convention, and ceremonial.

The Ritual Process 1969:95.

Victor W. Turner 1920–1983
Scottish-born U.S. anthropologist
and
Edith Turner 1921–
U.S. anthropologist

1 *Inferiority.* A value-bearing category that refers to the powers of the weak, countervailing against structural power, fostering continuity, creating the sentiment of the wholeness of the total community, positing the model of an undifferentiated whole whose units are total human beings. The powers of the weak are often assigned in hierarchic and stratified societies to females, the poor, autochthons, and outcastes.

Image and Pilgrimage in Christian Culture 1978:251.

Edward Burnett Tylor 1832–1917
British anthropologist

1 Culture or Civilization, taken in its wide ethnographic sense, is that complex whole which includes knowledge, belief, art, morals, law, custom, and any other capabilities and habits acquired by man as a member of society.

The Origins of Culture (1871) 1958:1. → Originally published as chapters one to ten of *Primitive Culture.*

2 The fact is that a stone arrow-head, a carved club, an idol, a grave-mound where slaves and property have been buried for the use of the dead, an account of a sorcerer's rites in making rain, a table of numerals, the conjugation of a verb, are things which each express the state of a people as to one particular point of culture, as truly as the tabulated numbers of deaths by poison, and of chests of tea imported, express in a different way other partial results of the general life of a whole community.

The Origins of Culture (1871) 1958:12.

3 Rudimentary as the science of culture still is, the symptoms are becoming very strong that even what seem its most spontaneous and motiveless phenomena will, nevertheless, be shown to come within the range of distinct cause and effect as certainly as the facts of mechanics.

The Origins of Culture (1871) 1958:18.

4 It is quite wonderful, even if we hardly go below the surface of the subject, to see how large a share stupidity and unpractical conservatism and dogged superstition have had in preserving for us traces of the history of our race, which practical utilitarianism would have remorselessly swept away.

The Origins of Culture (1871) 1958:156.

5 It is no more reasonable to suppose the laws of mind differently constituted in Australia and in England, in the time of the cave-dwellers and in the time of the builders of sheet-iron houses, than to suppose that the laws of chemical combination were of one sort in the time of coal-measures, and are of another now. The thing that has been will be; and we are to study savages and old nations to learn the laws that under new circumstances are working for good or ill in our own development.

The Origins of Culture (1871) 1958:158–159.

6 The sense of an absolute psychical distinction between man and beast, so prevalent in the civilized world, is hardly to be found among the lower races. Men to whom the cries of beasts and birds seem like human language, and their actions guided as it were by human thought, logically enough allow the existence of souls to beasts, birds, and reptiles, as to men.

Religion in Primitive Culture (1871) 1958:53. → Originally published as chapters eleven to nineteen of *Primitive Culture.*

7 It is a harsher, and at times even painful, office of ethnography to expose the remains of crude old cultures which have passed into harmful superstition, and to mark these out for destruction. Yet this work, if less genial, is not less urgently needful for the good of mankind. Thus, active at once in aiding progress and in removing hindrance, the science of culture is essentially a reformer's science.

Religion in Primitive Culture (1871) 1958:539.

V

Thorstein Veblen 1857–1929

U.S. economist and sociologist

1 It is the characteristic of man to do something, not simply to suffer pleasures and pains through the impact of suitable forces. He is not simply a bundle of desires that are to be saturated by being placed in the path of the forces of the environment, but rather a coherent structure of propensities and habits which seeks realisation and expression in an unfolding activity.

Why Is Economics Not an Evolutionary Science? (1898) 1948:233.

2 In order to gain and to hold the esteem of men it is not sufficient merely to possess wealth or power. The wealth or power must be put in evidence, for esteem is awarded only on evidence. And not only does the evidence of wealth serve to impress one's importance on others and to keep their sense of his importance alive and alert, but it is scarcely less use in building up and preserving one's self-complacency.

The Theory of the Leisure Class (1899) 1973:42.

3 Conspicuous consumption of valuable goods is a means of reputability to the gentleman of leisure.

The Theory of the Leisure Class (1899) 1973:64.

4 From the foregoing survey of the growth of conspicuous leisure and consumption, it appears that the utility of both alike for the purposes of reputability lies in the element of waste that is common to both. In the one case it is a waste of time and effort, in the other it is a waste of goods.

The Theory of the Leisure Class (1899) 1973:71.

5 The instinct of workmanship is present in all men, and asserts itself even under very adverse circumstances. So that however wasteful a given expenditure may be in reality, it must at least have some colorable excuse in the way of an ostensible purpose.

The Theory of the Leisure Class (1899) 1973:75.

6 With the exception of the instinct of self-preservation, the propensity for emulation is probably the strongest and most alert and persistent of the economic motives proper.

The Theory of the Leisure Class (1899) 1973:85.

7 "Classic" always carries [the] connotation of wasteful and archaic, whether it is used to denote the dead languages or the obsolete or obsolescent forms of thought and diction in the living language, or to denote items of scholarly activity or apparatus to which it is applied with less aptness.

The Theory of the Leisure Class (1899) 1973:256.

8 A breach of the proprieties in spelling is extremely annoying and will discredit any writer in the eyes of all persons who are possessed of a developed sense of the true and beautiful. English orthography satisfies all the requirements of the canons of reputability under the law of conspicuous waste. It is archaic, cumbrous, and ineffective; its acquisition consumes much time and effort; failure to acquire it is easy of detection. Therefore it is the first and readiest test of reputability in learning, and conformity to its ritual is indispensable to a blameless scholastic life.

The Theory of the Leisure Class (1899) 1973:257.

9 The data with which any scientific inquiry has to do are trivialities in some other bearing than that one in which they are of account.

The Place of Science in Modern Civilisation (1906) 1961:42.

10 In making use of the expression, "instinct of workmanship" or "sense of workmanship," it is not here intended to assume or to argue that the proclivity so designated is in the psychological respect a simple or irreducible element; still less, of course, is there any intention to allege that it is to be traced back in the physiological respect to some one isolable tropismatic sensibility or some single enzymotic or visceral stimulus. All that is matter for the attention of those whom it may concern. The expression

may as well be taken to signify a concurrence of several instinctive aptitudes, each of which might or might not prove simple or irreducible when subjected to psychological or physiological analysis. For the present inquiry it is enough to note that in human behaviour this disposition is effective in such consistent, ubiquitous and resilient fashion that students of human culture will have to count with it as one of the integral hereditary traits of mankind.

The Instinct of Workmanship (1914) 1964:27–28.

11 The instinct of workmanship brought the life of mankind from the brute to the human plane, and in all the later growth of culture it has never ceased to pervade the works of man.

The Instinct of Workmanship (1914) 1964:37.

12 If the "efficiency engineers" are to be credited, it is probably within the mark to say that the net aggregate gains from industry fall short of what they might be by some fifty per cent, owing to the trained inability of the businessmen in control to appreciate and give effect to the visible technological requirements of the industries from which they draw their gains.

The Instinct of Workmanship (1914) 1964:193.

13 Invention is the mother of necessity.

The Instinct of Workmanship (1914) 1964:316. → See PLATO:6.

14 It is not intended, seriously and as a practical measure, to propose the abolition of the president's office, or of the governing board; nor is it intended to intimate that the captain of erudition can be dispensed with in fact. He is too dear to the commercialized popular imagination, and he fits too convincingly into the businessmen's preconceived scheme of things, to permit any such sanguine hope of surcease from skilled malpractice and malversation. All that is here intended to be said is nothing more than the *obiter dictum* that, as seen from the point of view of the higher learning, the academic executive and all his works are anathema, and should be discontinued by the simple expedient of wiping him off the slate; and that the governing board, in so far as it presumes to exercise any other than vacantly perfunctory duties, has the same value and should with advantage be lost in the same shuffle.

The Higher Learning in America (1918) 1965:286.

Giovanni Battista Vico 1668–1744
Italian jurist, philologist, and philosopher

1 The useful historians are not those who give general descriptions of facts and explain them by reference to general conditions, but those who go into the greatest detail and reveal the particular cause of each event.

De antiquissima italorum sapientia ex linguae originibus eruenda (1710) 1914:135.

2 Common sense is judgment without reflection, shared by an entire class, an entire nation, or the entire human race.

The New Science (1725) 1984:Book 1, par. 142, 63.

3 Uniform ideas originating among entire peoples unknown to each other must have a common ground of truth.

The New Science (1725) 1984:Book 1, par. 144, 63.

4 Men first feel necessity, then look for utility, next attend to comfort, still later amuse themselves with pleasure, thence grow dissolute in luxury, and finally go mad and waste their substance.

The nature of peoples is first crude, then severe, then benign, then delicate, finally dissolute.

The New Science (1725) 1984:Book 1, par. 241–242, 78–79.

5 But in the night of thick darkness enveloping the earliest antiquity, so remote from ourselves, there shines the eternal and never failing light of a truth beyond all question: that the world of civil society has certainly been made by men, and that its principles are therefore to be found within the modifications of our own human mind. Whoever reflects on this cannot but marvel that the philosophers should have bent all their energies to the study of the world of nature, which, since God made it, He alone knows; and that they should have neglected the study of the world of nations, or civil world, which, since men had made it, men could come to know.

The New Science (1725) 1984:Book 1, par. 331, 96.

6 We observe that all nations, barbarous as well as civilized, though separately founded because remote from each other in time and space, keep these three human customs: all have some religion, all contract solemn marriages, all bury their dead.

The New Science (1725) 1984:Book 1, par. 333, 97.

7 Our Science comes to be at once a history of the ideas, the customs, and the deeds of mankind. From these three we shall derive the principles of the history of human nature, which we shall show to be the principles of universal history, which principles it seems hitherto to have lacked.

The New Science (1725) 1984:Book 2, par. 368, 112.

8 It is true that men themselves made this world of nations (and we took this as the first incontestable principle of our Science. . .), but this world without doubt has issued from a mind often diverse, at times quite contrary, and always superior to the particular ends that men had proposed to themselves; which narrow ends, made means to serve wider ends, it has always employed to preserve the human race upon this earth. Men mean to gratify their bestial lust and abandon their offspring, and they inaugurate the chastity of marriage from which the families arise. The fathers mean to exercise without restraint their paternal power over their clients, and they subject them to the civil powers from which the cities arise. The

reigning orders of nobles mean to abuse their lordly freedom over the plebeians, and they are obliged to submit to the laws which establish popular liberty. The free peoples mean to shake off the yoke of their laws, and they become subject to monarchs. The monarchs mean to strengthen their own positions by debasing their subjects with all the vices of dissoluteness, and they dispose them to endure slavery at the hands of stronger nations. The nations mean to dissolve themselves, and their remnants flee for safety to the wilderness, whence, like the phoenix, they rise again. That which did all this was mind, for men did it with intelligence; it was not fate, for they did it by choice; not chance, for the results of their always so acting are perpetually the same.

The New Science (1725) 1984:Conclusion, par. 1108:425.

Paul Vidal de la Blache 1845–1918
French geographer

1 A region is a reservoir of energy whose origin lies in nature but whose development depends upon man. It is man, who, by molding the land to his own purposes, brings out its individuality. He establishes a connection between its separate features. He substitutes for the incoherent effect of local circumstances a systematic concourse of forces. It is thus that a region defines and differentiates itself and becomes as it were a medal struck off in the effigy of a people.

Tableau de la géographie de la France 1903:8.

Voltaire 1694–1778
[François Marie Arouet]
French historian and critic

1 If there were only one religion in England, there would be danger of tyranny; if there were two, they would cut each other's throats; but there are thirty, and they live happily together in peace.

On the Presbyterians (1732) 1961:26.

2 *Il faut écrire l'histoire en philosophe* [History must be written as a philosopher would write it].

Letter to Thieriot, 31 October 1738. → Unpublished translation by Yole G. Sills.

3 *Ce corps qui s'appelait et qui s'appelle encore le saint empire romain n'était en aucune manière ni saint, ni romain, ni empire* [This body, which called itself and still calls itself the Holy Roman Empire, was neither Holy, nor Roman, nor an Empire].

Essai sur les moeurs et les esprit des nations 1756:Chap. 70. → Unpublished translation by Yole G. Sills.

4 There is no complete language, no language which can express all our ideas and all our sensations; their shades are too numerous, too imperceptible. Nobody can make known the precise degree of sensation he experiences. One is obliged, for example, to designate by the general names of "love" and "hate" a thousand loves and a thousand hates all different from each other; it is the same with our pleasures and our pains. Thus all languages are, like us, imperfect.

Philosophical Dictionary (1764) 1923:178.

5 One distinguishes between the tyranny of one man and that of many. . . Under which tyranny would you like to live? Under neither; but if I had to choose, I should detest the tyranny of one man less than that of many. A despot always has his good moments; an assembly of despots never.

Philosophical Dictionary (1764) 1923:308.

6 The art of writing history well is very rare. It requires a grave, pure, varied, agreeable style. There are laws for writing history as there are for all other arts of the spirit; many precepts, and few great artists.

Histoire 1778–1782:555–572.

7 Ideas have changed the world.

Introduction à l'Abrégé de l'histoire universelle 1785–1789:51.

Ludwig von Mises 1881–1973
Austrian-born U.S. economist

1 The fallacies implied in the Keynesian full-employment doctrine are, in a new attire, essentially the same errors which Smith and Say long since demolished.

The Theory of Money and Credit (1912) 1971:424.

2 It is true that economics is a theoretical science and as such abstains from any judgment of value. It is not its task to tell people what ends they should aim at. It is a science of the means to be applied for the attainment of ends chosen, not, to be sure, a science of the choosing of ends. Ultimate decisions, the valuations and the choosing of ends, are beyond the scope of any science. Science never tells a man how he should act; it merely shows how a man must act if he wants to attain definite ends.

Human Action (1949) 1966:10.

3 The market economy is the social system of the division of labor under private ownership of the means of production. Everybody acts on his own behalf; but everybody's actions aim at the satisfaction of other people's needs as well as at the satisfaction of his own. Everybody in acting serves his fellow citizens. Everybody, on the other hand, is served by his fellow citizens. Everybody is both a means and an end in himself, an ultimate end for himself and a means to other people in their endeavors to attain their own ends.

Human Action (1949) 1966:257.

4 The market is not a place, a thing, or a collective entity. The market is a process, actuated by the interplay of the actions of the various individuals cooperating under the division of labor.

Human Action (1949) 1966:257.

5 Every step a government takes beyond the fulfillment of its essential functions of protecting the smooth operation of the market economy against aggression, whether on the part of domestic or foreign disturbers, is a step forward on a road that directly leads into the totalitarian system where there is no freedom at all.

Human Action (1949) 1966:282.

6 The market economy as such does not respect political frontiers. Its field is the world.

Human Action (1949) 1966:323.

7 The concept of a "just" or "fair" price is devoid of any scientific meaning; it is a disguise for wishes, a striving for a state of affairs different from reality. Market prices are entirely determined by the value judgments of men as they really act.

Human Action (1949) 1966:332. → See AQUINAS:5.

8 If one takes pleasure in calling the gold standard a "barbarous relic," one cannot object to the application of the same term to every historically determined institution. Then the fact that the British speak English — and not Danish, German, or French — is a barbarous relic too, and every Briton who opposes the substitution of Esperanto for English is no less dogmatic and orthodox than those who do not wax rapturous about the plans for a managed currency.

Human Action (1949) 1966:471.

9 Laissez faire does not mean: Let soulless mechanical forces operate. It means: Let each individual choose how he wants to cooperate in the social division of labor; let the consumers determine what the entrepreneurs should produce. Planning means: Let the government alone choose and enforce its rulings by the apparatus of coercion and compulsion.

Human Action (1949) 1966:731.

10 Everybody thinks of economics whether he is aware of it or not. In joining a political party and in casting his ballot, the citizen implicitly takes a stand upon essential economic theories.

Human Action (1949) 1966:878.

11 The fundamental thesis of historicism is the proposition that, apart from the natural sciences, mathematics, and logic, there is no knowledge but that provided by history. There is no regularity in the concatenation and sequence of phenomena and events in the sphere of human action. Consequently the attempts to develop a science of economics and to discover economic laws are vain.

Theory and History 1957:199.

John von Neumann 1903–1957
Hungarian-born U.S. mathematician and computer scientist
and
Oskar Morgenstern 1902–1977
German-born U.S. economist

1 The great progress in every science came when, in the study of problems which were modest as compared with ultimate aims, methods were developed which could be extended further and further. The free fall is a very trivial physical phenomenon, but it was the study of this exceedingly simple fact and its comparison with the astronomical material, which brought forth mechanics.

Theory of Games and Economic Behavior (1944) 1953:6–7.

2 We think that the procedure of the mathematical theory of games of strategy gains definitely in plausibility by the correspondence which exists between its concepts and those of social organizations. On the other hand, almost every statement which we — or for that matter anyone else — ever made concerning social organizations, runs afoul of some existing opinion. And, by the very nature of things, most opinions thus far could hardly have been proved or disproved within the field of social theory. It is therefore a great help that all our assertions can be borne out by specific examples from the theory of games of strategy.

Theory of Games and Economic Behavior (1944) 1953:43.

3 An important viewpoint in classifying games is this: Is the sum of all payments received by all players (at the end of the game) always zero; or is this not the case? If it is zero, then one can say that the players pay only to each other, and that no production or destruction of goods is involved. All games which are actually played for entertainment are of this type. But the economically significant schemes are most essentially not such. There the sum of all payments, the total social product, will in general not be zero, and not even constant. I.e., it will depend on the behavior of the players — the participants in the social economy. . . We shall call games of the first-mentioned type *zero-sum* games, and those of the latter type *non-zero-sum* games.

Theory of Games and Economic Behavior (1944) 1953:46–47.

L. S. Vygotsky 1896–1934
Russian psychologist

1 We need to concentrate not on the *product* of development but on the very *process* by which higher forms are established. To do so the researcher is often forced to alter the automatic, mechanized, fossilized character of the higher form of behavior and the turn it back to its source through the experiment. This is the aim of dynamic analysis.

Mind in Society (1960) 1978:64.

2 If the fundamental and most general activity of the cerebral hemispheres of animals and humans is signalization, then the basic and most general activity of humans, the activity that above all distinguishes humans from animals from the psychological point of view, is *signification*. . . Signification is the creation and use of signs, that is, artificial signals.

Razvitie vysshykh psikhicheskikh funktstil [The Development of Higher Mental Functions] 1960:111–112.

3 The very mechanism underlying higher mental functions is a copy from social interaction; all higher mental functions are internalized social relationships.

The Genesis of Higher Mental Functions (1979) 1981:164.

4 Formerly, psychologists tried to derive social behavior from individual behavior. They investigated individual responses observed in the laboratory and then studied them in the collective. They studied how the individual's responses change in the collective setting. Posing the problem in such a way is, of course, quite legitimate; but genetically speaking, it deals with the second level in behavioral development. The first problem is to show how the individual response emerges from the forms of collective life.

The Genesis of Higher Mental Functions (1979) 1981:164–165.

Francis A. Walker 1840–1897
U.S. economist and statistician

1 It is the future, not the past, to which employers look, and which determines the amount of labor they will purchase and the amount they can afford to pay.

Address on the Wages Question 1874:5.

2 Value is the power which an article confers upon its possessor, irrespective of legal authority or personal sentiments, of commanding, in exchange for itself, the labor, or the products of the labor, of others. . . Value is power in exchange.

Political Economy (1883) 1888:5.

3 It has not been by accident, or whim, or from any notion respecting the comparative dignity of the several claimants to the product of industry, that rent, interest, and profits have been discussed before wages. . . Wages *equal* the product of industry *minus* the three parts already determined in their nature and amount.

Political Economy (1883) 1888:248.

Alfred Russel Wallace 1823–1913
British naturalist

1 It suddenly flashed upon me that this self-acting process would necessarily *improve the race*, because in every generation the inferior would inevitably be killed off and the superior would remain — that is, the *fittest would survive*. . . The more I thought over it the more I became convinced that I had at length found the long-sought-for law of nature that solved the problem of the origin of species.

My Life (1905) 1974:362. → See DARWIN:4 and SPENCER:8.

Anthony F. C. Wallace 1923–
U.S. anthropologist

1 It can be argued that all organized religions are relics of old revitalization movements, surviving in routinized form in stabilized cultures, and that religious phenomena per se originated (if it is permissible still in this day and age to talk about the "origins" of major elements of culture) in the revitalization process — i.e., in visions of a new way of life by individuals under extreme stress.

Revitalization Movements 1956:268.

2 A world view is not merely a philosophical by-product of each culture, like a shadow, but the very skeleton of concrete cognitive assumptions on which the flesh of customary behavior is hung. World view, accordingly, may be expressed, more or less systematically in cosmology, philosophy, ethics, religious ritual, scientific belief, and so on, but it is implicit in almost every act. In Parsonian terms, it constitutes the set of cognitive orientations of the members of a society.

Culture and Personality 1961:101.

Graham Wallas 1858–1932
British political scientist

1 Economists have invented the term The Great Industry for the special aspect of this change [in scale] which is dealt with by their science, and sociologists may conveniently call the whole result The Great Society.

The Great Society (1914) 1932:3.

2 The little girl had the making of a poet in her who, being told to be sure of her meaning before she spoke, said, "How can I know what I think till I see what I say?"

The Art of Thought 1926:106.

Willard W. Waller
See EDWARD R. HAWKINS AND WILLARD W. WALLER.

Léon Walras 1834–1910
French economist

1 *Pure economics* is, in essence, the theory of the determination of prices under a hypothetical regime of perfectly free competition. The sum total of all things, material or immaterial, on which a price can be set because they are

scarce (i.e. both *useful* and *limited in quantity*), constitutes *social wealth*. Hence pure economics is also the theory of *social wealth*.

Elements of Pure Economics (1874) 1977:40.

2 By *social wealth* I mean all things, material or immaterial (it does not matter which in this context), that are *scarce*, that is to say, on the one hand, *useful* to us and, on the other hand, only available to us in *limited quantity*.

Elements of Pure Economics (1874) 1977:65.

3 The question of whether a drug is wanted by a doctor to cure a patient, or by a murderer to kill his family is a very serious matter, but from our point of view, it is totally irrelevant. So far as we are concerned, the drug is useful in both cases, and may even be more so in the latter case than in the former.

Elements of Pure Economics (1874) 1977:65.

4 Unquestionably competition is also the primary force in setting the value of the doctor's and the lawyer's consultations, of the musician's and the singer's recitals, etc. In fact, the whole world may be looked upon as a vast general market made up of diverse special markets where social wealth is bought and sold. Our task then is to discover the laws to which these purchases and sales tend to conform automatically. To this end, we shall suppose that the market is perfectly competitive, just as in pure mechanics we suppose, to start with, that machines are perfectly frictionless.

Elements of Pure Economics (1874) 1977:84.

5 Demand ought to be considered as the principal fact and offer as the accessory fact where two commodities are exchanged for each other in kind. No one ever makes an offer simply for the sake of offering. The only reason one offers anything is that one cannot demand anything without making an offer. Offer is only a consequence of demand.

Elements of Pure Economics (1874) 1977:89.

Lester F. Ward 1841–1913
U.S. sociologist

1 It is the misfortune of all truly great minds to be wedded to errors as well as to truths.

Dynamic Sociology (1883) 1926:Vol. 1, 83.

W. Lloyd Warner 1898–1970
U.S. anthropologist

1 Approximately half the population of Yankee City is either foreign-born or native-born of at least one foreign parent. . . These groups, with the exception of the first, we have called "ethnics."

The Social Life of a Modern Community (1941) 1966:211. → Written with Paul S. Lunt.

John B. Watson 1878–1958
U.S. psychologist

1 Psychology, as the behaviorist views it, is a purely objective, experimental branch of natural science which needs introspection as little as do the sciences of chemistry and physics. It is granted that the behavior of animals can be investigated without appeal to consciousness. Heretofore the viewpoint has been that such data have value only in so far as they can be interpreted by analogy in terms of consciousness. The position is taken here that the behavior of man and the behavior of animals must be considered in the same plane.

Psychology as the Behaviorist Views It 1913:176.

2 The rule, or measuring rod, which the behaviorist puts in front of him always is: Can I describe this bit of behavior I see in terms of "stimulus and response"? By stimulus we mean any object in the general environment or any change in the tissues themselves due to the physiological condition of the animal, such as the change we get when we keep an animal from sex activity, when we keep it from feeding, when we keep it from building a nest. By response we mean anything the animal does — such as turning toward or away from a light, jumping at a sound, and more highly organized activities such as building a skyscraper, drawing plans, having babies, writing books, and the like.

Behaviorism (1924) 1930:6.

3 "Give me a dozen healthy infants, well-formed, and my own specified world to bring them up in and I'll guarantee to take any one at random and train him to become any type of specialist I might select — doctor, lawyer, artist, merchant chief, and yes, even beggarman and thief, regardless of his talents, penchants, tendencies, abilities, vocations, and race of his ancestors." I am going beyond the facts and I admit it, but so have the advocates of the contrary and they have been doing it for many thousands of years.

Behaviorism (1924) 1930:104.

4 The universe will change if you bring up your children, not in the freedom of the libertine, but in behavioristic freedom — a freedom which we cannot even picture in words, so little do we know of it. Will not these children in turn, with their better ways of living and thinking, replace us as society and in turn bring up their children in a still more scientific way, until the world finally becomes a place fit for human habitation?

Behaviorism (1924) 1930:303–304.

5 There are. . . for us no instincts — we no longer need the term in psychology. Everything we have been in the habit of calling an "instinct" today is a result largely of training — belonging to man's *learned behavior*.

What the Nursery Has to Say about Instincts 1926:1.

6 At three years of age the child's whole emotional life plan has been laid down, his emotional disposition set. At that age the parents have already determined for him whether he is to grow into a happy person, wholesome and good-natured, whether he is to be a whining, complaining neurotic, an anger-driven, vindictive, over-bearing slave driver, or one whose every move in life is definitely controlled by fear.

Are You Giving Your Child a Chance? 1927:74.

7 From the time of [Wilhelm] Wundt on, consciousness becomes the keynote of psychology. It is the keynote to-day. It has never been seen, touched, smelled, tasted, or moved. It is plain assumption just as unprovable as the old concept of the soul. And to the Behaviorist the two terms are essentially identical, so far as their metaphysical implications are concerned.

Behaviorism — The Modern Note in Psychology 1929:14.

8 The Behaviorist cannot find consciousness in the test-tube of his science. He finds no evidence anywhere for a stream of consciousness, not even for one so convincing as that described by William James. He does, however, find convincing proof of an ever-widening stream of behavior.

Behaviorism — The Modern Note in Psychology 1929:26. → See JAMES:11.

9 I would rather see the behavior of one white rat observed carefully from the moment of birth until death than to see a large volume of accurate statistical data on how 2,000 rats learned to open a puzzle box.

Introduction to G. V. Hamilton and Kenneth Macgowan, *What Is Wrong with Marriage* 1929:xx.

Sidney Webb 1859–1947
[1st Baron Passfield]
British economist and socialist

1 It would not be of much use to have all babies born from good stocks, if generation after generation they were made to grow up into bad men and women. A world of well-born, but physically and morally perverted adults is not attractive!

Eugenics and the Poor Law 1910:236.

2 Once we face the necessity of putting our principles first into Bills, to be fought through committee clause by clause; and then into the appropriate administrative machinery for carrying them into execution from one end of the Kingdom to the other — and this is what the Labour Party has done with its Socialism — the inevitability of gradualness cannot fail to be appreciated.

The Labour Party on the Threshold 1923:11.

Alfred Weber 1868–1958
German sociologist and economist

1 A sociologist — or the discipline as such — asks questions about human fate in a historical setting, and for that reason should never lose the awareness that in essence he looks at life, which is forever changing and in flux. . . Modern academic sociology. . . has lost sight of this basic fact, and has therefore become estranged from life. [The sociologist] has trapped himself into setting up categories and systems, which are useful as tools but satisfy no one. [He] is discovering all kinds of social phenomena, types of relationships, without seeing the clear evidence of their existential significance. He has given up the effort to comprehend and analyze the totality of the stream of life [*Lebenstrom*] and can no longer answer vital questions [*Lebensfragen*].

Ideen zur Staats-und Kultursoziologie 1927:5. → Unpublished translation by Beate S. Riesterer.

2 One must keep in mind that society and existence are two different things. The subject matter of sociology is not just society, but *existence*, enveloping the human being.

Einführung in die Soziologie 1955:209.

Max Weber 1864–1920
German sociologist and economist

1 The type of social science in which we are interested is an *empirical science* of concrete *reality* (*Wirklichkeitswissenschaft*). Our aim is the understanding of the characteristic uniqueness of the reality in which we move. We wish to understand on the one hand the relationships and the cultural significance of individual events in their contemporary manifestations and on the other the causes of their being historically *so* and not *otherwise*.

"Objectivity" in Social Science and Social Policy (1904) 1949:72.

2 The impulse to acquisition, pursuit of gain, of money, of the greatest possible amount of money, has in itself nothing to do with capitalism. This impulse exists and has existed among waiters, physicians, coachmen, artists, prostitutes, dishonest officials, soldiers, nobles, crusaders, gamblers, and beggars. One may say that it has been common to all sorts and conditions of men at all times and in all countries of the earth, wherever the objective possibility of it is or has been given.

The Protestant Ethic and the Spirit of Capitalism (1904–1905) 1930:17.

3 Christian asceticism, at first fleeing from the world into solitude, had already ruled the world which it had renounced from the monastery and through the Church. But it had, on the whole, left the naturally spontaneous character of daily life in the world untouched. Now it strode into the market-place of life, slammed the door of the monastery behind it, and undertook to penetrate just that daily routine of life with its methodicalness, to fashion it into a life in the world, but neither of nor for this world.

The Protestant Ethic and the Spirit of Capitalism (1904–1905) 1930:154.

4 The Puritan wanted to work in a calling; we are forced to do so. For when asceticism was carried out of monastic cells into everyday life, and began to dominate worldly morality, it did its part in building the tremendous cosmos of the modern economic order. This order is now bound to the technical and economic conditions of machine production which to-day determine the lives of all the individuals who are born into this mechanism, not only those directly concerned with economic acquisition, with irresistible force. Perhaps it will so determine them until the last ton of fossilized coal is burnt. In [Richard]

Baxter's view the care for external goods should only lie on the shoulders of the "saint like a light cloak, which can be thrown aside at any moment." But fate decreed that the cloak should become an iron cage [*ein stahlhartes Gehäuse*].

The Protestant Ethic and the Spirit of Capitalism (1904–1905) 1930:181. → For a discussion of the translation of this phrase as "iron cage," see Edward A. Tiryakian, The Sociological Import of a Metaphor: Tracking the Source of Max Weber's "Iron Cage" (1981).

5 No one knows who will live in this cage in the future, or whether at the end of this tremendous development entirely new prophets will arise, or there will be a great rebirth of old ideas and ideals, or, if neither, mechanized petrification, embellished with a sort of convulsive self-importance. For of the last stage of this cultural development, it might well be truly said: "Specialists without spirit, sensualists without heart; this nullity imagines that it has attained a level of civilization never before achieved."

The Protestant Ethic and the Spirit of Capitalism (1904–1905) 1930:182.

6 To this day there has never existed a bureaucracy which could compare with that of Egypt. This is known to everyone who knows the social history of ancient times; and it is equally apparent that to-day we are proceeding towards an evolution which resembles that system in every detail. . . But horrible as the thought is that the world may one day be peopled with professors — we would retire on to a desert island if such a thing were to happen — it is still more horrible to think that the world could one day be filled with nothing but those little cogs, little men clinging to little jobs and striving towards bigger ones. . . This passion for bureaucracy. . . is enough to drive one to despair.

Bureaucratization (1909) 1955:127.

7 *Man muss, wie oft gesagt worden ist, "nicht Caesar sein, um Caesar zu verstehen." Sonst wäre alle Geschichtsschreibung sinnlos* [As is often said, "one need not be Caesar to understand Caesar." Otherwise, all historical writing would be meaningless].

Über einige Kategorien der verstehenden Soziologie 1913:254. → Noting Georg Simmel's earlier use of this aphorism, Weber drew upon it here and elsewhere. It has since been adopted by others, including Alfred Schutz. See SIMMEL:11 and SCHUTZ:1.

8 In spite of all "social welfare policies," the whole course of the state's inner political functions, of justice and administration, is repeatedly and unavoidably regulated by the objective pragmatism of "reasons of state." The state's absolute end is to safeguard (or to change) the external and internal distribution of power; ultimately, this end must seem meaningless to any universalist religion of salvation. This fact has held and still holds, even more so, for foreign policy. It is absolutely essential for every political association to appeal to the naked violence of coercive means in the face of outsiders as well as in the face of internal enemies. It is only this very appeal to violence that constitutes a political association in our terminology. The state is an association that claims the monopoly of the *legitimate use of violence*, and cannot be defined in any other manner.

Religious Rejections of the World and Their Directions (1915) 1946:334.

9 Not ideas, but material and ideal interests, directly govern men's conduct. Yet very frequently the "world images" that have been created by "ideas" have, like switchmen, determined the tracks along which action has been pushed by the dynamic of interest. "From what" and "for what" one wished to be redeemed and, let us not forget, "could be" redeemed, depended on one's image of the world.

The Social Psychology of the World Religions (1915) 1946:280.

10 Like everyone else, the professor has other facilities for the diffusion of his ideals. When these facilities are lacking, he can easily create them in an appropriate form, as experience has shown in the case of every honest attempt. But the professor should not demand the right as a professor to carry the marshal's baton of the statesman or reformer in his knapsack.

The Meaning of "Ethical Neutrality" in Sociology and Economics (1917) 1949:5.

11 What we must vigorously oppose is the view that one may be "scientifically" contented with the conventional self-evidentness of very widely accepted value-judgments. The specific function of science, it seems to me, is just the opposite: namely, to ask questions about these things which convention makes self-evident.

The Meaning of "Ethical Neutrality" in Sociology and Economics (1917) 1949:13.

12 The possibility of questioning the meaning of the world presupposes the capacity to be astonished about the course of events.

Ancient Judaism (1917–1919) 1952:207.

13 I am slowly working away on the [new] edition of "The Protestant Ethic" and other articles, and I shall see things through. I think I shall manage in the winter too, after a good rest and the fading of all the depression that is weighing me down.

Letter to Karl Rothenbücher, 1919 1988:665.

14 The early Christians knew full well the world is governed by demons and that he who lets himself in for politics, that is, for power and force as means, contracts with diabolical powers and for his action it is *not* true that good can follow only from good and evil only from evil, but that often the opposite is true. Anyone who fails to see this is, indeed, a political infant.

Politics as a Vocation (1919) 1946:123. → See GOETHE:1.

15 Politics is a strong and slow boring of hard boards. It takes both passion and perspective. Certainly all historical experience confirms the truth — that man would not have attained the possible unless time and again he had

reached out for the impossible. But to do that a man must be a leader, and not only a leader but a hero as well, in a very sober sense of the word. And even those who are neither leaders nor heroes must arm themselves with that steadfastness of heart which can brave even the crumbling of all hopes. This is necessary right now, or else men will not be able to attain even that which is possible today. Only he has the calling for politics who is sure that he shall not crumble when the world from his point of view is too stupid or too base for what he wants to offer. Only he who in the face of all this can say "In spite of all!" has the calling for politics.

Politics as a Vocation (1919) 1946:128.

16 One's own work must inevitably remain highly imperfect. Only by strict specialization can the scientific worker become fully conscious, for once and perhaps never again in his lifetime, that he has achieved something that will endure. A really definitive and good accomplishment is today always a specialized accomplishment. And whoever lacks the capacity to put on blinders, so to speak, and to come up to the idea that the fate of his soul depends upon whether or not he makes the correct conjecture at this passage of this manuscript may as well stay away from science. He will never have what one may call the "personal experience" of science. Without this strange intoxication, ridiculed by every outsider; without this passion, this "thousands of years must pass before you enter into life and thousands more wait in silence" — according to whether or not you succeed in making this conjecture; without this, you have *no* calling for science and you should do something else. For nothing is worthy of man as man unless he can pursue it with passionate devotion.

Science as a Vocation (1919) 1946:135.

17 No sociologist. . . should think himself too good, even in his old age, to make tens of thousands of quite trivial computations in his head and perhaps for months at a time. One cannot with impunity try to transfer this task entirely to mechanical assistants if one wishes to figure something, even though the final result is often small indeed.

Science as a Vocation (1919) 1946:135.

18 In science, each of us knows that what he has accomplished will be antiquated in ten, twenty, fifty years. That is the fate to which science is subjected; it is the very *meaning* of scientific work, to which it is devoted in a quite specific sense, as compared with other spheres of culture for which in general the same holds. Every scientific "fulfilment" raises new "questions"; it *asks* to be "surpassed" and outdated. Whoever wishes to serve science has to resign himself to this fact. Scientific works certainly can last as "gratifications" because of their artistic quality, or they may remain important as a means of training. Yet they will be surpassed scientifically — let that be repeated — for it is our common fate and, more, our common goal. We cannot work without hoping that others will advance further than we have. In principle, this progress goes on *ad infinitum*.

Science as a Vocation (1919) 1946:138.

19 The fate of our times is characterized by rationalization and intellectualization and, above all, by the "disenchantment of the world." Precisely the ultimate and most sublime values have retreated from public life either into the transcendental realm of mystic life or into the brotherliness of direct and personal human relations. It is not accidental that our greatest art is intimate and not monumental.

Science as a Vocation (1919) 1946:155.

20 "Power" (*Macht*) is the probability that one actor within a social relationship will be in a position to carry out his own will despite resistance, regardless of the basis on which this probability rests.

"Domination" (*Herrschaft*) is the probability that a command with a given specific content will be obeyed by a given group of persons. "Discipline" is the probability that by virtue of habituation a command will receive prompt and automatic obedience in stereotyped forms, on the part of a given group of persons.

Economy and Society (1922) 1968:Vol. 1, 53.

21 There are three pure types of legitimate domination. The validity of their claims to legitimacy may be based on:

1. Rational grounds — resting on a belief in the legality of enacted rules and the right of those elevated to authority under such rules to issue commands (legal authority).

2. Traditional grounds — resting on an established belief in the sanctity of immemorial traditions and the legitimacy of those exercising authority under them (traditional authority); or finally,

3. Charismatic grounds — resting on devotion to the exceptional sanctity, heroism or exemplary character of an individual person, and of the normative patterns or order revealed or ordained by him (charismatic authority).

Economy and Society (1922) 1968:Vol. 1, 215.

22 The whole administrative staff [of a bureaucracy] consists, in the purest type, of individual officials. . . who are appointed and function according to the following criteria:

(1) They are personally free and subject to authority only with respect to their impersonal official obligations.

(2) They are organized in a clearly defined hierarchy of offices.

(3) Each office has a clearly defined sphere of competence in the legal sense.

(4) The office is filled by a free contractual relationship. . .

(5) Candidates are selected on the basis of technical qualifications. . . They are *appointed*, not elected. . .

(6) They are remunerated by fixed salaries in money. . .

(7) The office is treated as the sole, or at least the primary, occupation of the incumbent.

(8) It constitutes a career. . .

(9)The official works entirely separated from ownership of the means of administration and without appropriation of his position.

(10) He is subject to strict and systematic discipline and control in the conduct of the office.

Economy and Society (1922) 1968:Vol. 1, 220–221.

23 Bureaucratic administration is, other things being equal, always the most rational type from a technical point of view, [and] the needs of mass administration make it today completely indispensable. The choice is only that between bureaucracy and dilletantism in the field of administration.

Economy and Society (1922) 1968:Vol. 1, 223.

24 Bureaucratic domination has the following social consequences:

(1) The tendency to "levelling" in the interest of the broadest possible basis of recruitment in terms of technical competence.

(2) The tendency to plutocracy growing out of the interest in the greatest possible length of technical training. Today this often lasts up to the age of thirty.

(3) The dominance of a spirit of formalistic impersonality: "*Sine ira et studio,*" without hatred or passion, and hence without affection or enthusiasm. The dominant norms are concepts of straightforward duty without regard to personal considerations. Everyone is subject to formal equality of treatment; that is, everyone in the same empirical situation. This is the spirit in which the ideal official conducts his office.

Economy and Society (1922) 1968:Vol. 1, 225.

25 The term "charisma" will be applied to a certain quality of an individual personality by virtue of which he is considered extraordinary and treated as endowed with supernatural, superhuman, or at least specifically exceptional powers or qualities. These are such as are not accessible to the ordinary person, but are regarded as of divine origin or as exemplary, and on the basis of them the individual concerned is treated as a "leader."

Economy and Society (1922) 1968:Vol. 1, 241.

26 If proof and success elude the leader for long, if he appears deserted by his god or his magical or heroic powers, above all, if his leadership fails to benefit his followers, it is likely that his charismatic authority will disappear. This is the genuine meaning of the divine right of kings *(Gottesgnadentum).*

Economy and Society (1922) 1968:Vol. 1, 242.

27 In its pure form charismatic authority has a character specifically foreign to everyday routine structures. The social relationships directly involved are strictly personal, based on the validity and practice of charismatic personal qualities. If this is not to remain a purely transitory phenomenon, but to take on the character of a permanent relationship, a "community" of disciples or followers or a party organization or any sort of political or hierocratic organization, it is necessary for the character of charismatic authority to become radically changed. Indeed, in its pure form charismatic authority may be said to exist only *in natu nascendi*. It cannot remain stable, but becomes either traditionalized or rationalized, or a combination of both.

Economy and Society (1922) 1968:Vol. 1, 246.

28 We may speak of a "class" when (1) a number of people have in common a specific causal component of their life chances, insofar as (2) this component is represented exclusively by economic interests in the possession of goods and opportunities for income, and (3) is represented under the conditions of the commodity or labor markets. This is [a] "class situation."

Economy and Society (1922) 1968:Vol. 2, 927.

29 The contributions of the city in the whole field of culture are extensive. The city created the party and the demagogue. . . The city and it alone has brought forth the phenomena of the history of art. Hellenic and Gothic art, in contrast with Mycaenean and Roman, are city art. So also the city produced science in the modern sense. . . Furthermore, the city is the basis of specific religious institutions. Not only was Judaism, in contrast with the religion of Israel, a thoroughly urban construction — a peasant could not conform with the ritual of the law — but early Christianity is also a city phenomenon; the larger the city the greater was the percentage of Christians, and the case of Puritanism and Pietism was also the same. . . Finally, the city alone produced theological thought, and on the other hand again, it alone harbored thought untrammeled by priestcraft. The phenomenon of Plato, with his question of how to make men useful citizens as the dominant problem of his thought, is unthinkable outside the environment of a city.

General Economic History (1923) 1981:316–317.

C. V. Wedgwood 1910–
British historian

1 It is impossible now, indeed it was always impossible, to disentangle sincere and self-interested motives among Protestants on the one side or Catholics on the other. At all times some men will be moved by deep spiritual motives incomprehensible to the materialist, unpredictable and inexplicable in terms of politics and economics. It adds something to knowledge to know the economic thrust behind the Reformation, but it diminishes knowledge to see that and nothing else. Some men made a good thing out of the new religion: others died for it in agony. Some men saw their interests bound up with the old Church, others perished rather than deny it.

William the Silent (1944) 1967:26.

Alvin Weinberg 1915–
U.S. physicist

1 We nuclear people have made a Faustian bargain with society. On the one hand, we offer. . . an inexhaustible source of energy. . . But the price that we demand of society for this magical energy source is both a vigilance

and a longevity of our social institutions that we are quite unaccustomed to.

Social Institutions and Nuclear Energy 1972:33.

H. G. Wells 1866–1946
British novelist and historian

1 The Baileys, it seemed to me, loved a world as flat and metallic as Sidney Cooper's cows. If they had the universe in hand I know they would take down all the trees and put up stamped tin green shades and sunlight accumulators. Altiora thought trees hopelessly irregular and sea cliffs a great mistake.

The New Machiavelli 1910:201. → From Wells's fictional depiction of Sidney and Beatrice Webb, written after his falling out with them and his resignation from the Fabian Society.

Rebecca West 1892–1983
[Cicily Isabel Fairfield]
Irish-born British journalist

1 One of [the James brothers] grew up to write fiction as though it were philosophy and the other to write philosophy as though it were fiction.

Henry James 1916:11.

Leslie A. White 1900–1975
U.S. anthropologist

1 The technology is the independent variable, the social system the dependent variable. Social systems are therefore determined by systems of technology; as the latter change, so do the former.

The Science of Culture 1949:365.

2 A cultural system that can launch earth satellites can dispense with gods entirely.

Unpublished paper, 1957. Quoted in Robert L. Carneiro, Leslie A. White 1981:222. → Spoken at a meeting of the American Anthropological Association a few months after the Soviet launching of the first Sputnik, this remark was quoted in the *New York Times*, the *Detroit News*, and other papers, and reportedly nearly led to White's dismissal from the University of Michigan.

Lynn T. White, Jr. 1907–1987
U.S. historian

1 The greatest spiritual revolutionary in Western history, Saint Francis, proposed what he thought was an alternative Christian view of nature and man's relation to it: he tried to substitute the idea of the equality of all creatures, including man, for the idea of man's limitless rule of creation. He failed. Both our present science and our present technology are so tinctured with orthodox Christian arrogance toward nature that no solution for our ecologic crisis can be expected from them alone. Since the roots of our trouble are so largely religious, the remedy must also be essentially religious, whether we call it that or not. We must rethink and refeel our nature and destiny. The profoundly religious, but heretical, sense of the primitive Franciscans for the spiritual autonomy of all parts of nature may point a direction. I propose Francis as a patron saint for ecologists.

The Historical Roots of Our Ecologic Crisis 1967:1207.

2 Some of the most perceptive systems analysts are pondering today how to incorporate into their procedures for decision the so-called fragile or nonquantifiable values to supplement and rectify their traditional quantifications. Unhappy clashes with aroused groups of ecologists have proved that when a dam is being proposed, kingfishers may have as much political clout as kilowatts. How do you apply cost-benefit analysis to kingfishers? Systems analysts are caught in Descartes's dualism between the measurable *res extensa* and the incommensurable *res cogitans*, but they lack his pineal gland to connect what he thought were two sorts of reality. In the long run the entire Cartesian assumption must be abandoned for recognition that quantity is only one of the qualities and that all decisions, including the quantitative, are inherently qualitative. That such a statement to some ears has an ominously Aristotelian ring does not automatically refute it.

Technology Assessment from the Stance of a Medieval Historian 1974:3.

Alfred North Whitehead 1861–1947
British mathematician and philosopher

1 It is a profoundly erroneous truism, repeated by all copybooks and by eminent people when they are making speeches, that we should cultivate the habit of thinking of what we are doing. The precise opposite is the case. Civilization advances by extending the number of important operations which we can perform without thinking about them. Operations of thought are like cavalry charges in a battle — they are strictly limited in number, they require fresh horses, and must only be made at decisive moments.

An Introduction to Mathematics 1911:61.

2 To come very near to a true theory, and to grasp its precise application, are two very different things, as the history of science teaches us. Everything of importance has been said before by somebody who did not discover it.

The Organisation of Thought 1917:127. → See SCHOPENHAUER:2.

3 This new tinge to modern minds is a vehement and passionate interest in the relation of general principles to irreducible and stubborn facts. All the world over and at all times there have been practical men, absorbed in "irreducible and stubborn facts": all the world over and at all times there have been men of philosophic temperament who have been absorbed in the weaving of general principles. It is this union of passionate interest in the

detailed facts with equal devotion to abstract generalisation which forms the novelty in our present society.

Science and the Modern World (1925) 1948:10. → Whitehead notes that William James had written to his brother Henry, as he was finishing his *Principles of Psychology,* that "I have to forge every sentence in the teeth of irreducible and stubborn facts."

4 Spatialisation is the expression of more concrete facts under the guise of very abstract logical constructions. There is an error; but it is merely the accidental error of mistaking the abstract for the concrete. It is an example of what I will call the "Fallacy of Misplaced Concreteness."

Science and the Modern World (1925) 1948:52.

5 The safest general characterization of the European philosophical tradition is that it consists of a series of footnotes to Plato.

Process and Reality (1929) 1979:39.

6 The ideas of Freud were popularized by people who only imperfectly understood them, who were incapable of the great effort required to grasp them in their relationship to larger truths, and who therefore assigned to them a prominence out of all proportion to their true importance.

Dialogue 28, 3 June 1943. 1954:211.

Walt Whitman 1819–1892
U.S. poet

1 Who are you indeed who would talk or sing to America?
Have you studied out the land, its idioms and men?
Have you learn'd the physiology, phrenology, politics, geography, pride, freedom, friendship of the land? its substratums and objects?
Have you consider'd the organic compact of the first day, of the first year of Independence, sign'd by the Commissioners, ratified by the States, and read by Washington at the head of the army?
Have you possess'd yourself of the Federal Constitution?
Do you see who have left all feudal processes and poems behind them, and assumed the poems and processes of Democracy?

By Blue Ontario's Shore (1856) 1926:291.

William Dwight Whitney 1827–1894
U.S. linguist

1 A language is, in very truth, a grand system, of a highly complicated and symmetrical structure; it is fitly comparable with an organized body; but this is not because any human mind has planned such a structure and skilfully worked it out. Each single part is conscious and intentional; the whole is instinctive and natural. The unity and symmetry of the system is the unconscious product of the efforts of the human mind, grappling with the facts of the world without and the world within itself, and recording each separate result in speech.

Language (1867) 1891:50.

2 Everything in language goes by analogy; what a language is in the habit of doing, it can do, but nothing else; and habits are of very slow growth; a lost habit cannot be revived; a new one cannot be formed except gradually, and almost or quite unconsciously.

The Life and Growth of Language (1875) 1979:150.

Benjamin L. Whorf 1897–1941
U.S. linguist

1 The WHY of understanding may remain for a long time mysterious but the HOW or logic of understanding — its background of laws or regularities — is discoverable. It is the grammatical background of our mother tongue, which includes not only our way of constructing propositions but the way we dissect nature and break up the flux of experience into objects and entities to construct propositions about. This fact is important for science, because it means that science CAN have a rational or logical basis even though it be a relativistic one and not Mr. Everyman's natural logic.

Languages and Logic (1941) 1956:239.

2 We cut up and organize the spread and flow of events as we do, largely because, through our mother tongue, we are parties to an agreement to do so, not because nature itself is segmented in exactly that way for all to see. Languages differ not only in how they build their sentences but also in how they break down nature to secure the elements to put in those sentences.

Languages and Logic (1941) 1956:240.

3 People act about situations in ways which are like the ways they talk about them.

The Relation of Habitual Thought and Behavior to Language (1941) 1956:148.

4 "Common sense," as its name shows, and "practicality" as its name does not show, are largely matters of talking so that one is readily understood.

The Relation of Habitual Thought and Behavior to Language (1941) 1956:152.

5 Thinking is most mysterious, and by far the greatest light upon it that we have is thrown by the study of language. This study shows that the forms of a person's thoughts are controlled by inexorable laws of pattern of which he is unconscious. These patterns are the unperceived intricate systematizations of his own language — shown readily enough by a candid comparison and contrast with other languages, especially those of a different linguistic family.

Language, Mind, and Reality (1942) 1956:252.

6 **What needs to be clearly seen by anthropologists, who to a large extent may have gotten the idea that linguistics is merely a highly specialized and tediously technical pigeonhole in a far corner of the anthropological workshop, is that linguistics is essentially the quest of MEANING. It may seem to the outsider to be inordinately absorbed in recording hair-splitting distinctions of sound, performing**

phonetic gymnastics, and writing complex grammars which only grammarians read. But the simple fact is that its real concern is to light up the thick darkness of the language, and thereby of much of the thought, the culture, and the outlook upon life of a given community, with the light of this "golden something," as I have heard it called, this transmuting principle of meaning.

A Linguistic Consideration of Thinking in Primitive Communities 1956:73. → Written in 1937 and found among Whorf's papers after his death.

William F. Whyte 1914–
U.S. sociologist

The middle-class person looks upon the slum district as a formidable mass of confusion, a social chaos. The insider finds in Cornerville a highly organized and integrated social system.

Street Corner Society (1943) 1955:xvi.

The code of the corner boy [in a Boston slum] requires him to help his friends when he can and to refrain from doing anything to harm them. When life in the group runs smoothly, the obligations binding members to one another are not explicitly recognized. Once Doc asked me to do something for him, and I said that he had done so much for me that I welcomed the chance to reciprocate. He objected: "I don't want it that way. I want you to do this for me because you're my friend. That's all."

Street Corner Society (1943) 1955:256–257.

The economic man will be laid to rest only when we are able to build a new model socioeconomic man. That requires a new theoretical statement regarding the motivation of man in the industrial production process.

Money and Motivation (1955) 1977:7. → Written with Melville Dalton, Donald Roy, Leonard Sayles, Orvis Collins, Frank Miller, George Strauss, Friedrich Fuerstenberg, and Alex Bavelas.

William H. Whyte, Jr. 1917–
U.S. writer

This book is about the organization man. If the term is vague, it is because I can think of no other way to describe the people I am talking about. They are not the workers, nor are they the white-collar people in the usual, clerk sense of the word. These people only work for The Organization. The ones I am talking about *belong* to it as well. They are the ones of our middle class who have left home, spiritually as well as physically, to take the vows of organization life, and it is they who are the mind and soul of our great self-perpetuating institutions.

The Organization Man 1956:3.

Knut Wicksell 1851–1926
Swedish economist

The definition of political economy as a practical science is the theory of the manner of satisfying human needs which gives the greatest possible satisfaction to society as a whole, having regard for future generations as well as the present. . . As soon as we begin seriously to regard economic phenomena *as a whole* and to seek for the conditions of the welfare of the whole, consideration for the interests of the proletariat must emerge; and from thence to the proclamation of *equal* rights for all is only a short step.

The very concept of political economy, therefore, or the existence of a science with such a name, implies, strictly speaking, a thoroughly revolutionary programme. It is not surprising that the concept is vague, for that often happens with a revolutionary programme.

Lectures on Political Economy (1901–1906) 1967:Vol. 1, 3–4.

2 In the hands of the Socialists (especially [Johann Karl] Rodbertus, and Marx still more so) the theory of value became a terrible weapon against the existing order. It almost rendered all other criticism of society superfluous.

Lectures on Political Economy (1901–1906) 1967:Vol. 1, 28.

3 Every rise or fall in the price of a particular commodity presupposes a disturbance of the equilibrium between the supply of and the demand for that commodity, whether the disturbance has actually taken place or is merely prospective. What is true *in this respect* of each commodity separately must doubtless be true of all commodities collectively. A general rise in prices is therefore only conceivable on the supposition that the general demand has for some reason become, or is expected to become, greater than the supply. . . Any theory of money worthy of the name must be able to show how and why the monetary or pecuniary demand for goods exceeds or falls short of the supply of goods in given conditions.

Lectures on Political Economy (1901–1906) 1967:Vol. 2, 159–160.

Philip Henry Wicksteed 1844–1927
British economist

1 In stating the law of diminishing returns, it is assumed that the factor of land is constant, and if, when a number of factors co-operate to produce a result, you double some of them without doubling others, of course you cannot expect to double the result. If you double the pastry without doubling the apples, you do not double the pie. If you double the diners without doubling the dinner, or double the dinner without doubling the diners, you do not double the dining experience. In like manner if you double the land without doubling the operations on it, or double the operations without doubling the land, you cannot expect to double the crop.

The Commonsense of Political Economy (1910) 1938:Vol. 2, 528.

Norbert Wiener 1894–1964
U.S. mathematician

1 We have decided to call the entire field of control and communication theory, whether in the machine or in the animal, by the name *Cybernetics*, which we form from the Greek χνβερνήτηξ or *steersman*. In choosing this

term, we wish to recognize that the first significant paper on feedback mechanisms is an article on governors, which was published by Clerk Maxwell in 1868, and that *governor* is derived from a Latin corruption of *χνβερνήτηξ*. We also wish to refer to the fact that the steering engines of a ship are indeed one of the earliest and best-developed forms of feedback mechanisms.

Cybernetics (1948) 1961:11–12.

2 Society can only be understood through a study of the messages and communication facilities which belong to it.

The Human Use of Human Beings (1950) 1954:16.

3 The future offers very little hope for those who expect that our new mechanical slaves will offer us a world in which we may rest from thinking. Help us they may, but at the cost of supreme demands upon our honesty and our intelligence. The world of the future will be an ever more demanding struggle against the limitations of our intelligence, not a comfortable hammock in which we can lie down to be waited upon by our robot slaves.

God and Golem, Inc. (1964) 1966:69.

Friedrich von Wieser 1851–1926
Austrian economist and sociologist

1 Whenever the business man speaks of incurring costs, he has in mind the quantity of productive means required to achieve a certain end; but the associated idea of a sacrifice which his efforts demand is also aroused. In what does this sacrifice consist?. . . The sacrifice consists in the exclusion or limitation of possibilities by which other products might have been turned out, had the material not been devoted to one particular product.

Social Economics (1914) 1927:99. → Wieser's "sacrifices" are now generally called "opportunity costs": the cost of opportunities foregone. See BUCHANAN:3.

William of Ockham
See WILLIAM OF OCKHAM.

Robin M. Williams, Jr. 1914–
U.S. sociologist

1 Focalization of hostility upon a given group is probably inhibited by a multiplicity of vulnerable minorities in the society; a society riven by many minor cleavages is in less danger of open mass conflict than a society with only one or a few cleavages.

The Reduction of Intergroup Tensions 1947:59. → See ROSS:1.

2 [A source of cohesion in American society is] *the unity coming directly from diversity.* There is no real paradox here. One outcome of diversity in this society is a multiple overlapping of groups and social categories that blurs considerably the sharp edges of potential cleavage — for example, the "cross-pressures" that operate upon individuals whose different membership and reference groups pull them toward different political alignments, or the internal heterogeneity of the major political parties. Without these relatively fluid, crisscrossing allegiances it seems highly probable that conflict would be increased, assuming that class differentiation did not diminish. American society is simply riddled with cleavages. The remarkable phenomenon is the extent to which the various differences "cancel out" — are noncumulative in their incidence. There is thus much realistic sociological meaning in *e pluribus unum.*

American Society 1951:531.

Edward O. Wilson 1929–
U.S. biologist

1 How can altruism, which by definition reduces personal fitness, possibly evolve by natural selection? The answer is kinship: if the genes causing the altruism are shared by two organisms because of common descent, and if the altruistic act by one organism increases the joint contribution of these genes to the next generation, the propensity to altruism will spread through the gene pool. This occurs even though the altruist makes less of a solitary contribution to the gene pool as the price of its altruistic act.

Sociobiology 1975:3–4.

2 When a person (or animal) increases the fitness of another at the expense of his own fitness, he can be said to have performed an act of *altruism.* Self-sacrifice for the benefit of offspring is altruism in the conventional but not in the strict genetic sense, because individual fitness is measured by the number of surviving offspring. But self- sacrifice on behalf of second cousins is true altruism at both levels; and when directed at total strangers such abnegating behavior is so surprising (that is, "noble") as to demand some kind of theoretical explanation. In contrast, a person who raises his own fitness by lowering that of others is engaged in *selfishness.* While we cannot publicly approve the selfish act we do understand it thoroughly and may even sympathize. Finally, a person who gains nothing or even reduces his own fitness in order to diminish that of another has committed an act of *spite.* The action may be sane, and the perpetrator may seem gratified, but we find it difficult to imagine his rational motivation. We refer to the commitment of a spiteful act as "all too human" — and then wonder what we meant.

Sociobiology 1975:117.

3 True spite is a commonplace in human societies, undoubtedly because human beings are keenly aware of their own blood lines and have the intelligence to plot intrigue. Human beings are unique in the degree of their capacity to lie to other members of their own species.

Sociobiology 1975:119.

4 Can the cultural evolution of higher ethical values gain a direction and momentum of its own and completely replace genetic evolution? I think not. The genes hold culture on a leash. The leash is very long, but inevitably values will be constrained in accordance with their effects on the human gene pool.

On Human Nature 1978:167.

William Julius Wilson 1935–
U.S. sociologist

1 The recent mobility patterns of blacks lend strong support to the view that economic class is clearly more important than race in predetermining job placement and occupational mobility. In the economic realm. . . the black experience has moved historically from economic racial oppression experienced by virtually all blacks to economic subordination for the black underclass.

The Declining Significance of Race 1978:152.

2 The hidden agenda for liberal policymakers is to improve the life chances of truly disadvantaged groups such as the ghetto underclass by emphasizing programs to which the more advanced groups of all races and class backgrounds can positively relate.

The Truly Disadvantaged 1987:155.

Woodrow Wilson 1856–1924
U.S. political scientist and statesman

1 I do not like the term political science. Human relationships, whether in the family or in the state, in the counting house or in the factory, are not in any proper sense the subject-matter of science. They are stuff of insight and sympathy and spiritual comprehension. I prefer the term Politics, therefore, to include both the statesmanship of thinking and the statesmanship of action.

The Law and the Facts 1911:10–11. → From a presidential address to the American Political Science Association.

2 Yesterday, and ever since history began, men were related to one another as individuals. To be sure there were the family, the Church, and the State, institutions which associated men in certain wide circles of relationship. But in the ordinary concerns of life, in the ordinary work, in the daily round, men dealt freely and directly with one another. To-day, the everyday relationships of men are largely with great impersonal concerns, with organizations, not with other individual men.

Now this is nothing short of a new social age, a new era of human relationships, a new stagesetting for the drama of life.

The New Freedom 1913:6–7.

3 You deal in the raw material of opinion and, if my convictions have any validity, opinion ultimately governs the world.

Remarks to the Associated Press, 20 April 1915. 1980:37.

4 Open covenants of peace, openly arrived at, after which there shall be no private international understandings of any kind but diplomacy shall proceed always frankly and in the public view.

An Address to a Joint Session of Congress, 8 January 1918. 1984:536. → This is the first of Wilson's "Fourteen Points."

Louis Wirth 1897–1952
U.S. sociologist

1 In a community composed of a larger number of individuals than can know one another intimately and can be assembled in one spot, it becomes necessary to communicate through indirect media and to articulate individual interests by a process of delegation. Typically in the city, interests are made effective through representation. The individual counts for little, but the voice of the representative is heard with a deference roughly proportional to the numbers for whom he speaks.

Urbanism as a Way of Life (1938) 1964:72–73.

Karl A. Wittfogel 1896–1988
German-born U.S. historian

1 *Total terror — total submission — total loneliness.* . . What happens to man's desire for autonomy under the conditions of total power? One variant of total power, hydraulic despotism, tolerates no relevant political forces besides itself. In this respect it succeeds on the institutional level because it blocks the development of such forces; and it succeeds on the psychological level, because it discourages man's desire for independent political action. In the last analysis, hydraulic government is government by intimidation.

Oriental Despotism 1957:137.

Ludwig Wittgenstein 1889–1951
Austrian-born British philosopher

1 The world is all that is the case [*Die Welt ist alles, was der Fall ist*].

Tractatus Logico-Philosophicus (1921) 1972:1, 6–7.

2 What we cannot speak about we must pass over in silence [*Wovon man nicht sprechen kann, darüber muss man schweigen*].

Tractatus Logico-Philosophicus (1921) 1972:7, 150–151. → Karl Popper, in *Conjectures and Refutations* [(1963) 1968:7], reported that Franz Urbach had once replied to this statement: "But it is only here that speaking becomes worthwhile." See GELLNER:1.

3 For a *large* class of cases — though not for all — in which we employ the word "meaning" it can be defined thus: the meaning of a word is its use in the language [*Man kann für eine* grosse *Klasse von Fällen der Benützung des Wortes* "Bedeutung" — *wenn auch nicht für alle Fälle seiner Benützung — dieses Wort so erklären: Die Bedeutung eines Wortes ist sein Gebrauch in der Sprache*].

Philosophical Investigations (1953) 1967:20, 20e.

4 Like everything metaphysical the harmony between thought and reality is to be found in the grammar of the language [*Wie alles Metaphysische ist die Harmonie zwischen Gedanken und Wirklichkeit in der Grammatik der Sprache aufzufinden*].

Zettel 1967:12–12e.

C. Vann Woodward 1908–
U.S. historian

1 One of the strangest things about the career of Jim Crow [i.e., the legally-sanctioned pattern of racial segregation in the United States] was that the system was born in the North and reached an advanced age before moving South in force.

The Strange Career of Jim Crow (1955) 1974:17.

2 Southerners have repeated the American rhetoric of self admiration and sung the perfection of American institutions ever since the Declaration of Independence. But for half that time they lived intimately with a great social evil and the other half with its aftermath. . . The South's preoccupation was with guilt, not with innocence, with the reality of evil, not with the dream of perfection. Its experience. . . was on the whole a thoroughly un-American one.

The Burden of Southern History 1960:20–21.

Robert S. Woodworth 1869–1962
U.S. psychologist

1 Behaviorism meant to many young men and women of the time a new orientation and a new hope when the old guides had become hopelessly discredited in their eyes. It was a religion to take the place of religion.

Contemporary Schools of Psychology (1931) 1948:94.

Dennis H. Wrong 1923–
Canadian-born U.S. sociologist

1 Sociological theory originates in the asking of general questions about man and society. The answers lose their meaning if they are elaborated without reference to the questions, as has been the case in much contemporary theory. An example is the Hobbesian question of how men become tractable to social controls. The two-fold answer of contemporary theory is that man "internalizes" social norms and seeks a favorable self-image by conforming to the "expectations" of others. Such a model of man denies the very possibility of his being anything but a thoroughly socialised being and thus denies the reality of the Hobbesian question. The Freudian view of man, on the other hand, which sociologists have misrepresented, sees man as a social though never a fully socialised creature. Sociologists need to develop a more complex, dialectical conception of human nature instead of relying on an implicit conception that is tailor-made for special sociological problems.

The Oversocialized Conception of Man in Modern Sociology 1961:183.

Wilhelm Wundt 1832–1920
German psychologist

1 The new statistics has provided extremely rich materials which have as yet scarcely been used by psychologists. Beyond opening up new realms for investigation, statistics offers the boundless advantage of replacing guesswork with unshakeable certainties. It enables one to draw conclusions with mathematical precision rather than relying upon imprecise deductions. . . One can say without exaggeration that more psychology can be learned through the use of statistical methods than from all the philosophers with the exception of Aristotle.

Beiträge zur Theorie der Sinneswahrnehmung 1862:xxiv–xxv. → Unpublished translation by Edward J. Doherty.

2 Ideas, like all other mental experiences, are not *objects*, but *processes, occurrences*.

Lectures on Human and Animal Psychology (1864–1865) 1894:236.

3 The endeavour to observe oneself must inevitably introduce changes into the course of mental events, — changes which could not have occurred without it, and whose usual consequence is that the very process which was to have been observed disappears from consciousness.

Principles of Physiological Psychology (1873) 1904:Vol. 1, 5.

4 The psychologist who wants to concentrate on his own consciousness will notice only one thing: that this wish remains unfulfilled. There is nothing unusual about a person attentively observing some external object. But the idea of a person observing himself is irresistibly comical. His situation is exactly like that of Münchhausen who wanted to pull himself out of a swamp with his own pigtail. The object of observation is the observer himself.

Die Aufgaben der experimentellen Psychologie 1882:8–9. → Unpublished translation by Adrian Brock.

5 Since language consists always in a *communication* of ideas, the original word-creation cannot have been the work of any *individual* inventor; it must have proceeded from a community of individuals, endowed with similar mental capacities and living under the same external conditions. So is it with custom, which, like language, is a mode of *common* conduct arising from community of ideas.

Ethics (1886) 1922:Vol. 1, 161.

Y

Michael Young 1915–
British sociologist

The fundamental change of the last century. . . is that intelligence has been redistributed between the classes, and the nature of the classes changed. The talented have been given the opportunity to rise to the level which accords with their capacities, and the lower classes consequently reserved for those who are also lower in ability.

The Rise of the Meritocracy (1958) 1961:14. → *The Rise of the Meritocracy* is an anti-utopian history of the future, set in the year 2034, depicting a society in which the current emphasis upon equality of opportunity has led to an anti-egalitarian society.

2 Today we frankly recognize that democracy can be no more than aspiration, and have rule not so much by the people as by the cleverest people; not an aristocracy of birth, not a plutocracy of wealth, but a true meritocracy of talent.

The Rise of the Meritocracy (1958) 1961:21.

Z

Israel Zangwill 1864–1926
British playwright and novelist

1 [*Vera*]: The Crucible? I don't understand!
[*David*]: Not understand! . . . Not understand that America is God's Crucible, the great Melting-Pot where all the races of Europe are melting and reforming!

The Melting-Pot (1909) 1932:33. → With this play, Zangwill introduced the term "melting pot" into the language. See GLAZER AND MOYNIHAN:1.

David Zeaman 1921–
U.S. psychologist

1 One of the differences between the natural and the social sciences is that in the natural sciences, each succeeding generation stands on the shoulders of those that have gone before, while in the social sciences, each generation steps in the faces of its predecessors.

Skinner's Theory of Teaching Machines 1959:167. → See BERNARD OF CHARTRES:1, NEWTON:1, and HOLTON:1.

Florian Znaniecki 1882–1958
Polish-born U.S. sociologist

1 By conceiving society as a synthesis of psychological individuals we preclude the possibility of a rational solution of all particular problems which can be solved only with the help of common social schemes acting in and through individuals and yet existing independently of each of them. By conceiving the individual as synthesis of social schemes, we preclude the possibility of the solution of all those problems in which the continuity of personal life or the uniformity of experiences in all conscious individuals independent of the social groups to which they belong are the necessary presuppositions.

Cultural Reality 1919:285–286.

2 Every cultural system is found by the investigator to exist for certain conscious and active historical subjects. . . For the scientist this cultural system is really and objectively as it was (or is) given to those historical subjects themselves when they were (or are) experiencing it and actively dealing with it. In a word, the data of the cultural student are always "somebody's," never "nobody's" data. This essential character of cultural data we call the *humanistic coefficient*.

The Method of Sociology (1934) 1968:36–37.

3 In contrast with the natural scientist, who seeks to discover an order among empirical data entirely independent of conscious human agents, the student of culture seeks to discover any order among empirical data which depends upon conscious human agents, is produced, and is maintained by them. To perform this task he takes every empirical datum which he investigates with what we have called its humanistic coefficient, i.e., as it appears to those human individuals who experience it and use it.

Cultural Sciences (1952) 1963:132.

[*See also* W. I. THOMAS AND FLORIAN ZNANIECKI.]

Bibliography

[Dates in parentheses are dates of first publication]

ABRAHAM, KARL (1909) 1955 Dreams and Myths: A Study in Folk-Psychology. In *Clinical Papers and Essays on Psycho-Analysis*. London: Hogarth.

ABRAHAM, KARL (1920) 1955 The Cultural Significance of Psycho-Analysis. In volume 2 of *Selected Papers of Karl Abraham*. New York: Basic Books.

ACTON, J. E. E. D. (1878) 1985 The History of Freedom in Antiquity. In volume 1 of *Selected Writings of Lord Acton*. Indianapolis, Ind.: Liberty Fund.

ACTON, J. E. E. D. (1887) 1955 Letter to Mandell Creighton, 5 April 1887. In *Essays on Freedom and Power*. New York: Meridian.

ACTON, J. E. E. D. 1902 Introductory Note. In volume 1 of *Cambridge Modern History*. Cambridge Univ. Press.

ACTON, J. E. E. D. (1906) 1952 *Lectures on Modern History*. London: Macmillan.

ADAMS, HENRY (1907) 1946 *The Education of Henry Adams: An Autobiography*. Boston: Houghton Mifflin.

ADAMS, JAMES TRUSLOW (1928) 1932 *Jeffersonian Principles and Hamiltonian Principles*. Boston: Little, Brown.

ADAMS, JOHN (1774) 1969 Novanglus: Or, a History of the Dispute with America. In volume 4 of *The Works of John Adams*. Freeport, N.Y.: Books for Libraries Press.

[ADAMS, JOHN] (1780) 1826 *The Constitution of the State of Massachusetts*. Boston: Richardson and Lord.

ADLER, ALFRED 1914 Individual Psychology, Its Assumptions and Its Results. In *The Practice and Theory of Individual Psychology*. San Diego, Calif.: Harcourt.

ADLER, ALFRED (1927) 1946 *Understanding Human Nature*. New York: Greenberg.

ADLER, ALFRED 1930 Individual Psychology. In Carl Murchison (editor), *Psychologies of 1930*. Worcester, Mass.: Clark Univ. Press.

ADLER, ALFRED 1930 *Problems of Neurosis*. New York: Cosmopolitan Book.

ADORNO, T. W. (1951) 1978 *Minimi moralia: Reflections from Damaged Life*. London: NLB.

ADORNO, T. W. 1978 The Sociology of Knowledge and Its Consciousness. In Andrew Arato and Eike Gebhardt (editors), *The Essential Frankfurt School Reader*. New York: Urizen.

ALLPORT, FLOYD H. (1924) 1967 *Social Psychology*. New York: Johnson.

ALLPORT, GORDON W. 1937 *Personality: A Psychological Interpretation*. New York: Holt.

ALLPORT, GORDON W. 1946 Geneticism versus Ego-Structure in Theories of Personality. *British Journal of Educational Psychology* 16:57–68.

ALLPORT, GORDON W. 1954 The Historical Background of Modern Social Psychology. In volume 1 of Gardner Lindzey (editor), *Handbook of Social Psychology*. Reading, Mass.: Addison-Wesley.

ALLPORT, GORDON W. 1955 *Becoming: Basic Considerations for a Psychology of Personality*. New Haven, Conn.: Yale Univ. Press.

ALTHUSSER, LOUIS 1964–1965 Freud et Lacan. *La nouvelle critique* no. 161–162. Quoted in Sherry Turkle, *Psychoanalytic Politics: Freud's French Revolution* 1978:91. New York: Basic Books.

AQUINAS, THOMAS Commentary, *I Ethics*. Quoted in Thomas Gilby, *St. Thomas Aquinas: Philosophical Texts* 1951:4. Oxford Univ. Press.

AQUINAS, THOMAS 1979 *On Kingship: To the King of Cyprus*. Westport, Conn.: Hyperion.

AQUINAS, THOMAS 1966 *Summa theologiae*. Volume 28, 1a2ae 90–97. New York: McGraw-Hill.

AQUINAS, THOMAS 1972 *Summa theologiae*. Volume 35, 2a2ae 34–46. New York: McGraw-Hill.

AQUINAS, THOMAS 1975 *Summa theologiae*. Volume 38, 2a2ae 63–79. New York: McGraw- Hill.

ARCHILOCHOS 1977 Fragment 201. In *Archilochos*. London: Secker & Warburg.

ARENDT, HANNAH (1951) 1979 *The Origins of Totalitarianism*. San Diego, Calif.: Harcourt.

ARENDT, HANNAH 1958 *The Human Condition*. Univ. of Chicago Press.

ARENDT, HANNAH (1963) 1964 *Eichmann in Jerusalem: A Report on the Banality of Evil*. New York: Viking.

ARISTOTLE 1980 *The Metaphysics*. In volume 17 of *Aristotle in Twenty-Three Volumes*. Cambridge, Mass.: Harvard Univ. Press.

ARISTOTLE 1982 *The Nicomachean Ethics*. In volume 19 of *Aristotle in Twenty-Three Volumes*. Cambridge, Mass.: Harvard Univ. Press.

ARISTOTLE 1973 *The Poetics*. In volume 23 of *Aristotle in Twenty-Three Volumes*. Cambridge, Mass.: Harvard Univ. Press.

ARISTOTLE 1943 *Politics*. New York: Modern Library.

ARON, RAYMOND (1955) 1985 *The Opium of the Intellectuals*. Lanham, Md.: University Press of America.

ARON, RAYMOND (1965) 1968 *Main Currents in Sociological Thought*. New York: Doubleday.

ARON, RAYMOND (1971) 1978 On the Historical Condition of the Sociologist. In *Politics and History*. New York: Free Press.

ARROW, KENNETH J. (1952) 1983 The Principle of Rationality in Collective Decisions. In volume 1 of *Collected Papers of Kenneth J. Arrow*. Cambridge, Mass.: Harvard Univ. Press.

ARROW, KENNETH J. (1971) 1984 Exposition of the Theory of Choice under Uncertainty. In volume 3 of *Collected Papers of Kenneth J. Arrow*. Cambridge, Mass.: Harvard Univ. Press.

ARROW, KENNETH J. 1974 *The Limits of Organization*. New York: Norton.

ARROW, KENNETH J. (1974) 1984 On the Agenda of Organizations. In volume 4 of *Collected Papers of Kenneth J. Arrow*. Cambridge, Mass.: Harvard Univ. Press.

ARROW, KENNETH J.; AND HAHN, F. H. 1971 *General Competitive Analysis*. San Francisco: Holden-Day.

ASCH, SOLOMON E. 1952 *Social Psychology*. Englewood Cliffs, N.J.: Prentice-Hall.

AUBREY, JOHN 1950 *Aubrey's Brief Lives*. London: Secker & Warburg.

AUDEN, W. H. 1933 *The Dance of Death*. London: Faber & Faber.

AUDEN, W. H. (1939) 1976 Heavy Date. In *W. H. Auden: Collected Poems.* New York: Random House.

AUDEN, W. H. (1939) 1976 In Memory of Sigmund Freud. In *W. H. Auden: Collected Poems.* New York: Random House.

AUDEN, W. H. (1946) 1976 Under Which Lyre: A Reactionary Tract for the Times. In *W. H. Auden: Collected Poems.* New York: Random House.

AUGUSTINE (413–427) 1950 *The City of God.* New York: Modern Library.

AUSTEN, JANE (1818) 1985 *Northanger Abbey.* New York: Bantam Books.

BABBAGE, CHARLES 1832 *The Economy of Machinery and Manufacturers.* Philadelphia, Pa.: Carey & Lea.

BABBAGE, CHARLES 1842? Letter to Alfred Tennyson. c. 1842. Quoted in Henry D. Turner, Charles Babbage: Father of the Computer. *The New Scientist* 1958:4, no. 107, 1428.

BACON, FRANCIS (1597) 1892 De haeresibus. In *Meditationes sacrae.* Volume 7 of *The Works of Francis Bacon.* London: Longmans.

BACON, FRANCIS (1605) 1963 *The Advancement of Learning.* Oxford Univ. Press.

BACON, FRANCIS (1620) 1960 *The New Organon.* In *The New Organon and Related Writings.* Indianapolis, Ind.: Bobbs-Merrill.

BACON, FRANCIS (1625) 1936 Of Seditions and Troubles. In *The Essays of Francis Bacon.* Boston: Houghton Mifflin.

BACON, FRANCIS (1627) 1965 *New Atlantis.* In *Francis Bacon: A Selection of His Works.* Indianapolis, Ind.: Bobbs-Merrill.

BAGEHOT, WALTER (1852) 1968 Letters on the French *Coup d'État* of 1851, Letter III 20 January 1852. In volume 4 of *The Collected Works of Walter Bagehot.* London: The Economist.

BAGEHOT, WALTER (1855) 1965 The First Edinburgh Reviewers. In volume 1 of *The Collected Works of Walter Bagehot.* London: The Economist.

BAGEHOT, WALTER (1856) 1968 The Character of Sir Robert Peel. In volume 3 of *The Collected Works of Walter Bagehot.* London: The Economist.

BAGEHOT, WALTER (1867) 1974 *The English Constitution.* In volume 5 of *The Collected Works of Walter Bagehot.* London: The Economist.

BAGEHOT, WALTER (1872) 1974 *Physics and Politics.* In volume 7 of *The Collected Works of Walter Bagehot.* London: The Economist.

BAGEHOT, WALTER (1880) 1978 *Economic Studies.* In volume 11 of *The Collected Works of Walter Bagehot.* London: The Economist.

BAILYN, BERNARD 1967 *The Ideological Origins of the American Revolution.* Cambridge, Mass.: Harvard Univ. Press.

BAILYN, BERNARD 1974 *The Ordeal of Thomas Hutchinson.* Cambridge, Mass.: Harvard Univ. Press.

BAILYN, BERNARD (1986) 1988 *The Peopling of British North America: An Introduction.* New York: Random House.

BARBER, BERNARD (1952) 1962 *Science and the Social Order.* New York: Collier Books.

BARBER, BERNARD 1983 *The Logic and Limits of Trust.* New Brunswick, N.J.: Rutgers Univ. Press.

BARNARD, CHESTER I. (1938) 1968 *The Functions of the Executive.* Cambridge, Mass.: Harvard Univ. Press.

BARTLETT, F. C. (1932) 1967 *Remembering: A Study in Experimental and Social Psychology.* Cambridge Univ. Press.

BARTLETT, F.C. (1940) 1973 *Political Propaganda.* New York: Octagon Books.

BARTLETT, F. C. 1958 *Thinking: An Experimental and Social Study.* London: Allen & Unwin.

BARUCH, BERNARD 1960 *Baruch: The Public Years.* New York: Holt.

BARZUN, JACQUES 1937 *Race: A Study in Modern Superstition*. San Diego, Calif.: Harcourt.

BARZUN, JACQUES (1946) 1962 Bagehot, or the Human Comedy. In *The Energies of Art*. New York: Random House.

BARZUN, JACQUES 1974 *Clio and the Doctors: Psycho-History, Quanto-History & History*. Univ. of Chicago Press.

BASTIAT, FRÉDÉRIC (1846) 1877 Government. In *Essays on Political Economy*. New York: Putnam.

BASTIAT, FRÉDÉRIC (1850) 1964 *Economic Harmonies*. Princeton, N.J.: Van Nostrand.

BATESON, GREGORY (1935) 1972 Culture Contact and Schismogenesis. In *Steps to an Ecology of Mind: Collected Essays in Anthropology, Psychiatry, Evolution, and Epistemology*. San Francisco: Chandler.

BATESON, GREGORY (1936) 1958 *Naven: A Survey of the Problems Suggested by a Composite Picture of the Culture of a New Guinea Tribe Drawn from Three Points of View*. Stanford Univ. Press.

BATESON, GREGORY (1956) 1972 Toward a Theory of Schizophrenia. In *Steps to an Ecology of Mind: Collected Essays in Anthropology, Psychiatry, Evolution, and Epistemology*. San Francisco: Chandler.

BATESON, GREGORY 1972 Effects of Conscious Purpose on Human Adaptation. In *Steps to an Ecology of Mind: Collected Essays in Anthropology, Psychiatry, Evolution, and Epistemology*. San Francisco: Chandler.

BEARD, CHARLES A. (1913) 1935 *An Economic Interpretation of the Constitution of the United States*. New York: Macmillan.

BEARD, CHARLES A. (1922) 1924 *The Economic Basis of Politics*. New York: Knopf.

BEARD, CHARLES A. (1932) 1955 Introduction to J.B. Bury, *The Idea of Progress*. New York: Dover.

BEARD, CHARLES A. 1935 That Noble Dream. *American Historical Review* 41:74–87.

BEARD, CHARLES A.; AND BEARD, MARY R. 1939 *America in Midpassage*. New York: Macmillan.

BEAUMONT, GUSTAVE AUGUSTE DE 1831 Letter to his Father, 25 April 1831. Quoted in André Jardin, *Tocqueville: A Biography* (1984) 1988:94. New York: Farrar, Straus.

BEAUVOIR, SIMONE DE (1949) 1968 *The Second Sex*. New York: Modern Library.

BECCARIA (1764) 1963 *On Crimes and Punishments*. Indianapolis, Ind.: Bobbs-Merrill.

BECKER, CARL L. 1932 Everyman His Own Historian. *American Historical Review* 37, no. 2:221–236.

BECKER, CARL L. (1936) 1949 *Progress and Power*. New York: Knopf.

BECKER, GARY S. 1976 Marriage, Fertility, and the Family. In *The Economic Approach to Human Behavior*. Univ. of Chicago Press.

BECKER, GARY S. 1981 *A Treatise on the Family*. Cambridge, Mass.:Harvard Univ. Press.

BECKER, GARY S. 1988 Family Economics and Macro Behavior. *American Economic Review* 78:1–13.

BELL, DANIEL (1960) 1965 The End of Ideology in the West: An Epilogue. In *The End of Ideology: On the Exhaustion of Political Ideas in the Fifties*. New York: Free Press.

BELL, DANIEL (1973) 1976 *The Coming of Post-Industrial Society: A Venture in Social Forecasting*. New York: Basic Books.

BENDA, JULIEN (1928) 1969 *The Treason of the Intellectuals*. New York: Norton.

BENEDICT, RUTH (1934) 1959 Anthropology and the Abnormal. In *An Anthropologist at Work: Writings of Ruth Benedict*. Boston: Houghton Mifflin.

Benedict, Ruth (1934) 1959 *Patterns of Culture*. Boston: Houghton Mifflin.

Benedict, Ruth 1943 Obituary: Franz Boas. *Science* 97:60–62.

Benedict, Ruth 1946 *The Chrysanthemum and the Sword: Patterns of Japanese Culture*. Boston: Houghton Mifflin.

Benjamin, Walter (1937) 1978 Eduard Fuchs: Collector and Historian. In Andrew Arato and Eike Gebhardt (editors), *The Essential Frankfurt School Reader*. New York: Urizen.

Bentham, Jeremy (1776) 1948 *A Fragment on Government*. In *A Fragment on Government* and *An Introduction to the Principles of Morals and Legislation*. Oxford (United Kingdom): Basil Blackwell.

Bentham, Jeremy (1789) 1948 *An Introduction to the Principles of Morals and Legislation*. New York: Hafner.

Bentham, Jeremy (1793–1795) 1952 *Manual of Political Economy*. In volume 1 of *Jeremy Bentham's Economic Writings*. New York: Burt Franklin.

Bentham, Jeremy (1801) 1954 *The True Alarm*. In volume 3 of *Jeremy Bentham's Economic Writings*. New York: Burt Franklin.

Bentham, Jeremy (1802) 1931 *The Theory of Legislation*. San Diego, Calif.: Harcourt.

Bentham, Jeremy (1816) 1987 *Anarchical Fallacies: Being an Examination of the Declaration of Rights Issued During the French Revolution*. In Jeremy Waldron (editor), *Nonsense Upon Stilts: Bentham, Burke and Marx on the Rights of Man*. London: Methuen.

Bentham, Jeremy (1822) 1954 The Psychology of Economic Man. In volume 3 of *Jeremy Bentham's Economic Writings*. New York: Burt Franklin.

Bentham, Jeremy (1825) 1843 *The Rationale of Reward*. In volume 2 of *The Works of Jeremy Bentham*. Edinburgh: Tait and Tait.

Bentham, Jeremy 1932 *The Theory of Fictions*. In C. K. Ogden, *Bentham's Theory of Fictions*. London: Kegan Paul.

Bentley, Arthur F. 1895 The Units of Investigation in the Social Sciences. *Publications of the American Academy of Political and Social Science* 149:87–113.

Bentley, Arthur F. 1908 *The Process of Government: A Study of Social Pressures* Univ. of Chicago Press.

Berelson, Bernard et al. 1954 *Voting: A Study of Opinion Formation in a Presidential Campaign*. Univ. of Chicago Press.

Berelson, Bernard 1963 Introduction to the Behavioral Sciences. In *The Behavioral Sciences Today*. New York: Basic Books.

Berger, Peter L. (1967) 1969 *The Sacred Canopy: Elements of a Sociological Theory of Religion*. New York: Doubleday.

Berger, Peter L.; and Kellner, Hansfried 1981 *Sociology Reinterpreted: An Essay on Method and Vocation*. New York: Doubleday.

Berger, Peter L.; and Luckmann, Thomas 1966 *The Social Construction of Reality: A Treatise in the Sociology of Knowledge*. New York: Doubleday.

Bergson, Henri 1946 *The Creative Mind: An Introduction to Metaphysics*. New York: Philosophical Library.

Berle, Adolf A.; and Means, Gardiner C. (1932) 1968 *The Modern Corporation and Private Property*. San Diego, Calif.: Harcourt.

Berlin, Isaiah (1939) 1973 *Karl Marx: His Life and Environment*. Oxford Univ. Press.

Berlin, Isaiah (1950) 1969 Political Ideas in the Twentieth Century. In *Four Essays on Liberty*. Oxford Univ. Press.

Berlin, Isaiah 1954 *Historical Inevitability*. Oxford Univ. Press.

Berlin, Isaiah (1958) 1969 Two Concepts of Liberty. In *Four Essays on Liberty*. Oxford Univ. Press.

Berlin, Isaiah (1958) 1981 Chaim Weizmann. In *Personal Impressions*. New York: Viking.

BERLIN, ISAIAH 1969 Introduction. *Four Essays on Liberty*. Oxford Univ. Press.

BERNARD, CLAUDE (1865) 1957 *An Introduction to the Study of Experimental Medicine*. New York: Dover.

BERNOULLI, DANIEL (1738) 1954 Exposition of a New Theory on the Measurement of Risk. *Econometrica* 22, no. 1:23–36

BERNOULLI, JAKOB 1713 *Ars conjectandi*. Quoted in Bertrand de Jouvenel, *The Art of Conjecture*. 1967:21. New York: Basic Books.

BERNSTEIN, BASIL (1965) 1974 A Socio-linguistic Approach to Social Learning. In volume 1 of *Class, Codes, and Control*. London: Routledge.

BERNSTEIN, BASIL (1971) 1974 A Socio-linguistic Approach to Socialization. In volume 1 of *Class, Codes, and Control*. London: Routledge.

BERNSTEIN, EDUARD 1898 Die Zusammenbruchstheorie und die Kolonialpolitik. *Die Neue Zeit* 16. Quoted in David McLellan, *Marxism After Marx* 1979:31. Boston: Houghton Mifflin.

BERNSTEIN, EDUARD (1899) 1961 *Evolutionary Socialism: A Criticism and Affirmation*. New York: Schocken Books.

BERNSTEIN, EDUARD (1899) 1961 Preface to English Edition. *Evolutionary Socialism: A Criticism and Affirmation*. New York: Schocken Books.

BERTALANFFY, LUDWIG VON 1968 *General System Theory: Foundations, Development, Applications*. New York: Braziller.

BESTE, HENRY DIGBY 1829 Late Duke of Gloucester and Gibbon. In *Personal and Literary Memorials*. London: Henry Colburn. Published anonymously.

BETTELHEIM, BRUNO (1943) 1979 Individual and Mass Behavior in Extreme Situations. In *Surviving and Other Essays*. New York: Knopf.

BEVERIDGE, W.I.B. (1950) 1961 *The Art of Scientific Investigation*. New York: Random House.

BEVERIDGE, WILLIAM HENRY 1938 Epigraph. Lancelot Hogben (editor), *Political Arithmetic: A Symposium of Population Studies*. New York: Macmillan.

BEVERIDGE, WILLIAM HENRY (1944) 1945 *Full Employment in a Free Society*. New York: Norton.

BICKEL, ALEXANDER M. 1962 *The Least Dangerous Branch: The Supreme Court at the Bar of Politics*. Indianapolis, Ind.: Bobbs-Merrill

BINET, ALFRED 1888 *Études de psychologie expérimentale: Le fétichisme dans l'amour*. Paris: Octave Doin. Quoted in Jacqueline L. Cunningham, French Historical Views on the Acceptability of Evidence Regarding Child Abuse. *Psychological Reports* 1988:Vol. 63, 348.

BINET, ALFRED 1900 *La suggestibilité*. Paris: Schleicher Frères.

BINET, ALFRED 1905 Méthodes nouvelles pour le diagnostic du niveau intellectuel des anormaux. *L'année psychologique* 11:191–244. Quoted in Theta H. Wolf, *Alfred Binet* 1973:178. Univ. of Chicago Press.

BINET, ALFRED (1905) 1907 *The Mind and the Brain*. London: Kegan Paul.

BINET, ALFRED 1909 *Les idées modernes sur les enfants*. Paris: Flammarion. Quoted in Theta H. Wolf, *Alfred Binet* 1973:205.

BINET, ALFRED; AND SIMON, THÉODORE 1906 Méthodes nouvelles pour diagnostiquer l'idiotie, l'imbécillité et la débilité mentale. In *Atti del V Congresso internazionale di psicologia*. Rome: Forziani. Quoted in Theta H. Wolf, *Alfred Binet* 1973:141. Univ. of Chicago Press.

BINET, ALFRED; AND SIMON, THÉODORE 1910 Hystérie: Historique. *L'année psychologique* 16:67–70.

BISMARCK, OTTO VON (1867) 1924 Gespräch mit dem Journalisten Friedrich Meyer von Waldeck am 11 August 1867 in Berlin. In *Gespräche*. Volume 7 of *Bismarck: Die gesammelten Werke*. Berlin: Otto Stollberg & Co.

BLACKSTONE, WILLIAM (1765–1769) 1858 *Commentaries on the Laws of England*. New York: Harper.

BLAU, PETER M. 1968 Interaction: Social Exchange. In volume 7 of *International Encyclopedia of the Social Sciences*. New York: Macmillan and Free Press.

BLAU, PETER M. 1974 Parameters of Social Structure. *American Sociological Review* 39:615–635.

BLAU, PETER M. 1977 *Inequality and Heterogeneity: A Primitive Theory of Social Structure*. New York: Free Press.

BLOCH, MARC 1931 Feudalism: European. In *Encyclopaedia of the Social Sciences*. New York: Macmillan.

BLOCH, MARC (1949) 1953 *The Historian's Craft*. New York: Random House.

BLOOMFIELD, LEONARD 1927 Literate and Illiterate Speech. *American Speech* 2:432–439.

BLOOMFIELD, LEONARD 1927 On Recent Work in General Linguistics. *Modern Philology* 25, no. 2:211–230.

BLOOMFIELD, LEONARD 1930 Linguistics as a Science. *Studies in Philology* 27:553–557.

BLOOMFIELD, LEONARD 1933 *Language*. New York: Holt.

BLUMER, HERBERT 1969 *Symbolic Interactionism: Perspective and Method*. Englewood Cliffs, N.J.: Prentice-Hall.

BOAS, FRANZ (1887) 1982 The Principles of Ethnological Classification. In *A Franz Boas Reader*. Univ. of Chicago Press.

BOAS, FRANZ (1889) 1982 The Aims of Ethnology. In *Race, Language and Culture*. Univ. of Chicago Press.

BOAS, FRANZ (1911) 1966 *Introduction to Handbook of American Indian Languages*. Lincoln: Univ. of Nebraska Press.

BOAS, FRANZ (1911) 1963 *The Mind of Primitive Man*. New York: Collier Books.

BOAS, FRANZ (1930) 1940 Some Problems of Methodology in the Social Sciences. In *Race, Language and Culture*. New York: Macmillan.

BODIN, JEAN (1576) 1962 *The Six Bookes of a Commonweale*. Cambridge, Mass.: Harvard Univ. Press.

BÖHM-BAWERK, EUGEN VON (1888) 1923 *The Positive Theory of Capital*. New York: G. E. Stechert.

BÖHM-BAWERK, EUGEN VON (1896) 1984 *Karl Marx and the Close of His System*. Philadelphia, Pa.: Orion.

BÖHM-BAWERK, EUGEN VON (1896) 1962 Unresolved Contradiction in the Marxian Economic System. In volume 1 of *Shorter Classics of Eugen von Böhm-Bawerk*. South Holland, Ill.: Libertarian Press.

BOLINGBROKE, LORD (1730) 1841 *Remarks on the History of England*. In volume 1 of *The Works of Lord Bolingbroke*. Philadelphia, Pa.: Carey and Hart.

BOLINGBROKE, LORD (1734) 1777 *A Dissertation upon Parties*. In volume 2 of *The Works of the Late Right Honorable Henry St. John, Lord Viscount Bolingbroke*. London.

BOOTH, CHARLES (1889) 1904 *Life and Labour of the People in London*. First Series: Poverty. London: Macmillan.

BOOTH, CHARLES 1903 *Life and Labour of the People in London*. Final Volume. London: Macmillan.

BORGESE, GIUSEPPE ANTONIO 1934 The Intellectual Origins of Fascism. *Social Research* 1:458–485.

BORING, EDWIN G. 1919 Mathematical vs. Scientific Significance. *Psychological Bulletin* 16:335–338.

BORING, EDWIN G. 1920 The Logic of the Normal Law of Error in Mental Measurement. *American Journal of Psychology* 31:1–33.

BORING, EDWIN G. 1929 The Psychology of Controversy. *Psychological Review* 36, no. 2:97–121.

BORING, EDWIN G. 1957 When Is Human Behavior Predetermined? *Scientific Monthly* 84, no. 4:189–196.

Boswell, James (1791) 1980 *Life of Johnson.* Oxford Univ. Press.

Boudon, Raymond (1975) 1980 The Three Basic Paradigms of Macrosociology: Functionalism, Neo-Marxism and Interaction Analysis. In *The Crisis of Sociology.* New York: Columbia Univ. Press.

Boudon, Raymond (1977) 1982 *The Unintended Consequences of Social Action.* London: Macmillan.

Boulding, Kenneth E. 1953 *The Organizational Revolution: A Study in the Ethics of Economic Organization.* New York: Harper.

Boulding, Kenneth E. 1956 Some Contributions of Economics to the General Theory of Value. *Philosophy of Science* 23, no. 1:1–14.

Boulding, Kenneth E. 1962 Social Justice in Social Dynamics. In Richard R. Brandt (editor), *Social Justice.* Englewood Cliffs, N.J.: Prentice-Hall.

Boulding, Kenneth E. (1973) 1981 The Welfare Economics of Grants. In *A Preface to Grants Economics: The Economy of Love and Fear.* New York: Praeger.

Boulding, Kenneth E. 1978 Reflections on Law and Justice. *Cornell Review* Spring:11–18.

Bourdieu, Pierre (1973) 1977 Cultural Reproduction and Social Reproduction. In Jerome Karabel and A.H. Halsey (editors), *Power and Ideology in Education.* Oxford Univ. Press.

Bourdieu, Pierre (1979) 1984 *Distinction: A Social Critique of the Judgement of Taste.* Cambridge, Mass.: Harvard Univ. Press.

Bourdieu, Pierre (1984) 1988 *Homo academicus.* Cambridge (United Kingdom): Polity Press.

Bourdieu, Pierre; and Passeron, Jean-Claude (1970) 1977 *Reproduction in Education, Society and Culture.* Newbury Park, Calif: Sage.

Box, George E. P. 1966 Use and Abuse of Regression. *Technometrics* 8:625–629.

Braudel, Fernand (1949) 1973 *The Mediterranean and the Mediterranean World in the Age of Philip II.* New York: Harper.

Braudel, Fernand (1958) 1972 History and the Social Sciences. In Peter Burke (editor), *Economy and Society in Early Modern Europe: Essays from* Annales. New York: Harper.

Braudel, Fernand (1979) 1984 *The Perspective of the World.* New York: Harper.

Brentano, Franz (1874) 1973 *Psychology from an Empirical Standpoint.* New York: Humanities.

Breuer, Josef; and Freud, Sigmund (1893–1895) 1955 *Studies on Hysteria.* Volume 2 of *The Complete Psychological Works of Sigmund Freud.* London: Hogarth.

Brewster, David (1855) 1965 *Memoirs of the Life, Writings, and Discoveries of Sir Isaac Newton.* New York: Johnson.

Brinton, C. Crane (1933) 1962 *English Political Thought in the 19th Century.* New York: Harper.

Bronfenbrenner, Urie 1977 Toward an Experimental Ecology of Human Development. *American Psychologist* 32:513–531.

Brontë, Charlotte (1849) 1965 *Shirley.* London: Dent.

Brown, Roger; and McNeill, David 1966 The "Tip of the Tongue" Phenomenon. *Journal of Verbal Learning and Verbal Behavior* 5:325–337.

Bruner, Jerome S. et al. 1956 *A Study of Thinking.* New York: Wiley.

Bruner, Jerome S. 1960 *The Process of Education.* Cambridge, Mass.: Harvard Univ. Press.

Bruner, Jerome S. 1962 Art as a Mode of Knowing. In *On Knowing: Essays for the Left Hand.* Cambridge, Mass.: Harvard Univ. Press.

Bruner, Jerome S. (1970) 1971 *The Relevance of Education*. New York: Norton.

Bryce, James (1888) 1910 *The American Commonwealth*. New York: Macmillan.

Bryce, James 1921 *Modern Democracies*. New York: Macmillan.

Buber, Martin (1957) 1965 Elements of the Interhuman. In *The Knowledge of Man: Selected Essays*. New York: Harper.

Buchanan, James M. 1978 *The Consequences of Mr Keynes: An Analysis of the Misuse of Economic Theory for Political Profiteering, with Proposals for Constitutional Disciplines*. London: Institute of Economic Affairs.

Buchanan, James M. (1979) 1984 Politics without Romance: A Sketch of Positive Public Choice Theory and Its Normative Implications. In *The Theory of Public Choice-II*. Ann Arbor: Univ. of Michigan Press.

Buchanan, James M. 1987 Opportunity Cost. In volume 3 of *The New Palgrave: A Dictionary of Economics*. London: Macmillan.

Buckle, Henry Thomas (1857–1861) 1913 *History of Civilization in England*. New York: Hearst's International Library.

Buffon, Comte de 1777 *Essai d'arithmétique morale*. In volume 4 of the *Supplément* to *Histoire naturelle, générale et particulière*. Paris: L'imprimerie Royale.

Bunche, Ralph J. (1936) 1968 *A World View of Race*. Port Washington, N.Y.: Kennikat Press.

Burckhardt, Jacob (1860) 1958 *The Civilization of the Renaissance in Italy*. New York: Harper.

Burckhardt, Jacob (1905) 1979 *Reflections on History*. Indianapolis, Ind.: Liberty Fund.

Burke, Edmund (1770) 1865 *Thoughts on the Cause of the Present Discontents*. In volume 1 of *The Works of the Right Honorable Edmund Burke*. Boston: Little, Brown.

Burke, Edmund (1774) 1904 Speech on American Taxation, 19 April 1774. In volume 2 of *The Works of the Right Honorable Edmund Burke*. Boston: Little, Brown.

Burke, Edmund (1774) 1904 Speech to the Electors of Bristol, 3 November 1774. In volume 2 of *The Works of the Right Honorable Edmund Burke*. Boston: Little, Brown.

Burke, Edmund (1775) 1904 Speech on Moving His Resolutions for Conciliation with the Colonies, 22 March 1775. In volume 2 of *The Works of the Right Honorable Edmund Burke*. Boston: Little, Brown.

Burke, Edmund (1780) 1904 Speech at the Guildhall in Bristol. In volume 2 of *The Works of the Right Honorable Edmund Burke*. Boston: Little, Brown.

Burke, Edmund (1790) 1865 *Reflections on the Revolution in France, and on the Proceedings in Certain Societies in London Relative to that Event*. In volume 3 of *The Works of the Right Honorable Edmund Burke*. Boston: Little, Brown.

Burke, Edmund (1796) 1904 Letter to a Noble Lord. In volume 5 of *The Works of the Right Honorable Edmund Burke*. Boston: Little, Brown.

Burke, Edmund (1796–1797) 1904 Three Letters to a Member of Parliament on the Proposals for Peace with the Regicide Directory of France. In volume 5 of *The Works of the Right Honorable Edmund Burke*. Boston: Little, Brown.

Burke, Kenneth 1935 *Permanence and Change: An Anatomy of Purpose*. New York: New Republic Books.

Burns, Arthur F. 1953 Business Cycle Research and the Needs of Our Time. In *Thirty-Third Annual Report*. Cambridge, Mass.: National Bureau of Economic Research.

Burt, Cyril 1921 *Mental and Scholastic Tests*. London County Council.

Bury, J. B. (1909) 1958 *The Ancient Greek Historians*. New York: Dover.

Bury, J. B. (1920) 1955 *The Idea of Progress: An Inquiry into Its Origin and Growth.* New York: Dover.

Butler, Joseph (1736) 1892 *The Analogy of Religion, Natural and Revealed, to the Constitution and Course of Nature.* New Haven, Conn.: A. H. Maltby.

Butterfield, Herbert (1931) 1965 *The Whig Interpretation of History.* New York: Norton.

Butterfield, Herbert 1944 *The Englishman and His History.* Cambridge Univ. Press.

Butterfield, Herbert 1949 *The Origins of Modern Science: 1300–1800.* London: G. Bell and Sons.

Cairnes, John Elliott (1857) 1875 *The Character and Logical Method of Political Economy.* London: Macmillan.

Cairnes, John Elliott 1874 *Some Leading Principles of Political Society Newly Expounded.* New York: Harper.

Campbell, Donald T. 1969 Reforms as Experiments. *American Psychologist* 24:409–429.

Campbell, Joseph 1949 *The Hero with a Thousand Faces.* New York: Random House.

Campbell, Lewis; and Garnett, William (1882) 1969 *The Life of James Clerk Maxwell.* New York: Johnson.

Cannan, Edwin (1914) 1928 *Wealth: A Brief Explanation of the Causes of Economic Welfare.* London: P. S. King.

Cantillon, Richard (1775) 1931 *Essai sur la nature du commerce en général.* London: Macmillan.

Čapek, Karel (1923) 1961 *R.U.R. (Rossum's Universal Robots).* Oxford Univ. Press.

Cardozo, Benjamin 1921 A Ministry of Justice. *Harvard Law Review* 35, no. 2:113–153.

Cardozo, Benjamin (1921) 1949 *The Nature of the Judicial Process.* New Haven, Conn.: Yale Univ. Press.

Cardozo, Benjamin 1928 *The Paradoxes of Legal Science.* New York: Columbia Univ. Press.

Carlyle, Thomas (1839) 1904 *Chartism.* In volume 29 of *The Works of Thomas Carlyle in Thirty Volumes.* New York: Scribner.

Carlyle, Thomas (1841) 1903 *On Heroes, Hero-Worship, and the Heroic in History.* In volume 5 of *The Works of Thomas Carlyle in Thirty Volumes.* New York: Scribner.

Carlyle, Thomas (1843) 1903 *Past and Present.* In volume 10 of *The Works of Thomas Carlyle in Thirty Volumes.* New York: Scribner.

Carlyle, Thomas (1849) 1904 The Nigger Question. In volume 29 of *The Works of Thomas Carlyle in Thirty Volumes.* New York: Scribner.

Carnegie, Andrew 1889 Wealth. *North American Review* 148:653–664.

Carneiro, Robert L. 1981 Leslie A. White. In Sydel Silverman (editor), *Totem and Teachers: Perspectives on the History of Anthropology.* New York: Columbia Univ. Press.

Carr, E. H. 1961 *What Is History?* New York: Knopf.

Carroll, John B. 1951 The Interdisciplinary Summer Seminar on Linguistics and Psychology. *Items* 5:40–42.

Carroll, Lewis (1872) 1960 *Through the Looking Glass and What Alice Found There.* In *The Annotated Alice.* New York: New American Library.

Carus, Carl Gustav 1846 *Psyche: Zur Entwicklungsgeschichte der Seele.* Pforzheim (Germany): Flammer und Hoffmann.

Cassirer, Ernst (1944) 1975 *An Essay on Man: An Introduction to a Philosophy of Human Culture.* New Haven, Conn.: Yale Univ. Press.

CATTELL, JAMES MCKEEN 1904 The Conceptions and Methods of Psychology. *Popular Science Monthly* December.

CATTELL, RAYMOND B. 1950 *An Introduction to Personality Study*. London and New York: Hutchinson's University Library.

CHERRY, COLIN 1957 *On Human Communication: A Review, a Survey, and a Criticism*. Cambridge, Mass.: Technology Press of M.I.T.

CHESTERTON, G. K. (1911) 1983 The Invisible Man. In *The Father Brown Omnibus*. New York: Dodd, Mead.

CHOMSKY, NOAM (1957) 1964 *Syntactic Structures*. The Hague: Mouton.

CHOMSKY, NOAM (1959) 1964 A review of B. F. Skinner, *Verbal Behavior*. In Jerry A. Fodor and Jerrold J. Katz (editors), *The Structure of Language: Readings in the Philosophy of Language*. Englewood Cliffs, N.J.: Prentice-Hall.

CHOMSKY, NOAM 1965 *Aspects of the Theory of Syntax*. Cambridge, Mass.: M.I.T. Press.

CHOMSKY, NOAM (1977) 1979 *Language and Responsibility: Based on Conversations with Mitsou Ronat*. New York: Random House.

CHURCHILL, WINSTON (1941) 1974 The War Situation, 30 September 1941. In volume 6 of *Winston S. Churchill: His Complete Speeches; 1897–1963*. New York: Bowker.

CHURCHILL, WINSTON (1943) 1974 A Sense of Crowd and Urgency. In volume 7 of *Winston S. Churchill: His Complete Speeches 1897–1963*. New York: Bowker.

CHURCHILL, WINSTON (1946) 1974 The Sinews of Peace. In volume 7 of *Winston S. Churchill: His Complete Speeches; 1897–1963*. New York: Bowker.

CHURCHILL, WINSTON (1947) 1974 Parliament Bill, 11 November 1947. In volume 7 of *Winston S. Churchill: His Complete Speeches; 1897–1963*. New York: Bowker.

CICERO, MARCUS TULLIUS 1928 *De legibus*. In volume 16 of *Cicero in Twenty-Eight Volumes*. Cambridge, Mass.: Harvard Univ. Press.

CICERO, MARCUS TULLIUS 1933 *De natura deorum*. In volume 19 of *Cicero in Twenty-Eight Volumes*. Cambridge, Mass.: Harvard Univ. Press.

CICERO, MARCUS TULLIUS 1942 *De oratore*. Cambridge, Mass.: Harvard Univ. Press.

CICERO, MARCUS TULLIUS 1931 On Behalf of Milo [Pro Milone]. In volume 14 of *Cicero in Twenty-Eight Volumes*. Cambridge, Mass.: Harvard Univ. Press.

CLARK, JOHN BATES 1896 The Theory of Economic Progress. American Economic Association, *Economic Studies* 1, no. 1:5–22.

CLARK, JOHN BATES 1898 Introduction to Karl Rodbertus, *Overproduction and Crises*. London: Swan Sonnenschein & Co.

CLARK, JOHN BATES (1899) 1965 *The Distribution of Wealth: A Theory of Wages, Interest and Profit*. Fairfield, N.J.: Augustus M. Kelley.

CLARK, JOHN BATES (1907) 1968 *Essentials of Economic Theory as Applied to Modern Problems of Industry and Public Policy*. Fairfield, N.J.: Augustus M. Kelley.

CLARK, JOHN MAURICE 1922 The Empire of Machines. *Yale Review* 12, no. 1:132–143.

CLARK, KENNETH B. (1965) 1989 *Dark Ghetto: Dilemmas of Social Power*. Middletown, Conn.: Wesleyan Univ. Press.

CLAUSEWITZ, KARL VON (1832–1834) 1962 *On War*. London: Routledge.

COCHRAN, WILLIAM G. ET AL. 1954 Principles of Sampling. *Journal of the American Statistical Association* 49:13–35.

COHEN, I. BERNARD 1952 *General Education in Science*. Cambridge, Mass.: Harvard Univ. Press.

COHEN, I. BERNARD 1980 *The Newtonian Revolution*. Cambridge Univ. Press.

COHEN, MORRIS R. 1936 The Statistical View of Nature. *Journal of the American Statistical Association* 31:327–347.

COKE, SIR EDWARD (1628) 1832 *The First Part of the Institutes of the Laws of England: Or, a Commentary upon Littleton.* London: Clarke.

COKE, SIR EDWARD (1644) 1809 *The Third Part of the Institutes of the Laws of England: Concerning High Treason, and Other Pleas of the Crown.* London: Clarke.

COLE, G. D. H. 1956 *The Second International: 1889–1914.* London: Macmillan.

COLE, MARGARET (1945) 1946 *Beatrice Webb.* San Diego, Calif.: Harcourt.

COLEMAN, JAMES S. 1961 *The Adolescent Society: The Social Life of the Teenager and Its Impact on Education.* New York: Free Press.

COLEMAN, JAMES S. 1986 Introduction. *Individual Interests and Collective Action: Selected Essays.* Cambridge Univ. Press.

COLEMAN, JAMES S. 1990 *Foundations of Social Theory.* Cambridge, Mass.: Harvard Univ. Press.

COLEMAN, JAMES S. ET AL. 1966 *Equality of Educational Opportunity.* Washington, D.C.: Government Printing Office.

COLLINGWOOD, R. G. (1946) 1956 *The Idea of History.* Oxford Univ. Press.

COMTE, AUGUSTE (1822) 1911 Plan for the Scientific Operations Necessary for Reorganizing Society. In *Early Essays on Social Philosophy.* London: Routledge.

COMTE, AUGUSTE (1830–1842) 1839 *Cours de philosophie positive.* Paris: Bachelier, Impremeuv-Libraire.

COMTE, AUGUSTE (1830–1842) 1983 *The Positive Philosophy.* In *Auguste Comte and Positivism: The Essential Writings.* Univ. of Chicago Press.

CONDILLAC, ÉTIENNE BONNOT DE (1746) 1971 *An Essay on the Origin of Human Knowledge: Being a Supplement to Mr. Locke's* Essay on the Human Understanding. Gainesville, Fla.: Scholars' Facsimiles & Reprints.

CONDILLAC, ÉTIENNE BONNOT DE 1746 *Essai.* Quoted in Roy Harris and Talbot J. Taylor, *Landmarks in Linguistic Thought: The Western Tradition from Socrates to Saussure* 1989:120. London: Routledge.

CONDILLAC, ÉTIENNE BONNOT DE 1780 *Grammaire.* Quoted in Roy Harris and Talbot J. Taylor, *Landmarks in Linguistic Thought: The Western Tradition from Socrates to Saussure* 1989:120–121. London: Routledge.

CONDORCET (1795) 1955 *Sketch for a Historical Picture of the Progress of the Human Mind.* London: Weidenfeld and Nicolson.

COOLEY, CHARLES H. (1902) 1964 *Human Nature and the Social Order.* New York: Schocken Books.

COOLEY, CHARLES H. (1909) 1962 *Social Organization: A Study of the Larger Mind.* New York: Schocken Books.

COOLEY, CHARLES H. (1918) 1966 *Social Process.* Carbondale: Southern Illinois Univ. Press.

COON, CARLETON S. (1948) 1958 *A Reader in General Anthropology.* New York: Holt.

COSER, LEWIS A. 1956 *The Functions of Social Conflict.* New York: Free Press.

COSER, LEWIS A. 1974 *Greedy Institutions: Patterns of Undivided Commitment.* New York: Free Press.

COURNOT, ANTOINE AUGUSTIN (1838) 1971 *Researches into the Mathematical Principles of the Theory of Wealth.* Fairfield, N.J.: Augustus M. Kelley.

COURNOT, ANTOINE AUGUSTIN (1872) 1934 *Considérations sur la marche des idées et des événements dans les temps modernes.* Paris: Boivin. Quoted in Julián Marías, Generations: The Concept, in volume 6 of *International Encyclopedia of the Social Sciences* 1968:88. New York: Free Press and Macmillan.

Cousin, Victor (1828) 1832 *Introduction to the History of Philosophy*. Boston: Hilliard.

Cremin, Lawrence A. 1990 *Popular Education and Its Discontents*. New York: Harper.

Crévecoeur, J. Hector St. John de (1782) 1981 *Letters from an American Farmer*. New York: Penguin.

Croce, Benedetto (1915) 1921 *History: Its Theory and Practice*. San Diego, Calif.: Harcourt.

Croce, Benedetto 1919 La storia ridotta sotto il concetto generale dell'arte. In *Primi saggi*. Quoted in H. Stuart Hughes, *Consciousness and Society: The Reorientation of European Social Thought; 1890–1930* (1958) 1977:205–206. New York: Random House.

Croce, Benedetto (1938) 1970 *History as the Story of Liberty*. Chicago: Henry Regnery.

Dahl, Robert A. (1955) 1956 Hierarchy, Democracy, and Bargaining in Politics and Economics. In Heinz Eulau et al. (editors), *Political Behavior: A Reader in Theory and Research*. New York: Free Press.

Dahl, Robert A. (1956) 1963 *A Preface to Democratic Theory*. Univ. of Chicago Press.

Dahl, Robert A. 1957 The Concept of Power. *Behavioral Science* 2, no. 3:201–215.

Dahl, Robert A. (1961) 1967 *Who Governs? Democracy and Power in an American City*. New Haven, Conn.: Yale Univ. Press.

Dahrendorf, Ralf (1958) 1973 Sociology and Human Nature. In *Homo sociologicus*. London: Routledge.

Dahrendorf, Ralf 1961 Democracy without Liberty: An Essay on the Politics of Other-Directed Man. In Seymour Martin Lipset and Leo Lowenthal (editors), *Culture and Social Character*. New York: Free Press.

Dahrendorf, Ralf 1988 *The Modern Social Conflict: An Essay on the Politics of Liberty*. New York: Weidenfeld & Nicolson.

Darnton, Robert 1982 *The Literary Underground of the Old Regime*. Cambridge, Mass.: Harvard Univ. Press.

Darnton, Robert 1984 *The Great Cat Massacre and Other Episodes in French Cultural History*. New York: Basic Books.

Darnton, Robert 1985 The Social Life of Rousseau: Anthropology and the Loss of Innocence. *Harper's Magazine* July.

Darwin, Charles (1838) 1987 *Notebooks*, 16 August 1838. In *Charles Darwin's Notebooks, 1836–1844*. Ithaca, N.Y.: Cornell Univ. Press.

Darwin, Charles (1844) 1987 Letter to Joseph Dalton Hooker, 11 January 1844. In volume 3 of *The Correspondence of Charles Darwin: 1844–1846*. Cambridge Univ. Press.

Darwin, Charles (1857) 1896 Letter to A. R. Wallace, 22 December 1857. In *The Life and Letters of Charles Darwin*. New York: Appleton.

Darwin, Charles (1859) 1964 *On the Origin of Species*. Cambridge, Mass.: Harvard Univ. Press.

Darwin, Charles (1871) 1981 *The Descent of Man, and Selection in Relation to Sex*. Princeton Univ. Press.

Darwin, Francis (1876) 1958 *The Autobiography of Charles Darwin* and *Selected Letters*. New York: Dover.

Davenant, Charles 1698 *Discourses on the Publick Revenues, and on the Trade of England*. London: James Knapton.

Davies, James C. (1962) 1969 Toward a Theory of Revolution. In Barry McLaughlin (editor), *Studies in Social Movements: A Social Psychological Perspective*. New York: Free Press.

Davis, Kingsley 1945 The World Demographic Transition. American Academy of Political and Social Science, *Annals* 237:1–11.

DAVIS, KINGSLEY 1967 Population Policy: Will Current Programs Succeed? *Science* 158:730–740.

DAVIS, KINGSLEY; AND MOORE, WILBERT E. 1945 Some Principles of Stratification. *American Sociological Review.* 10:242–249.

DAVIS, NATALIE ZEMON (1973) 1975 The Rites of Violence. In *Society and Culture in Early Modern France.* Stanford Univ. Press.

DAVIS, NATALIE ZEMON 1975 Women on Top. In *Society and Culture in Early Modern France.* Stanford Univ. Press.

DEBOW, J.D.B. 1854 Introduction. *Statistical View of the United States.* Washington, D.C.: A. O. P. Nicholson.

DE MORGAN, AUGUSTUS 1845 Theory of Probabilities. In volume 2 of *Encyclopaedia metropolitana.* London: B. Fellowes.

DE MORGAN, AUGUSTUS (1872) 1915 *A Budget of Paradoxes.* Chicago: Open Court.

DESCARTES, RENÉ (1637) 1958 *Discourse on Method.* In *Descartes: Philosophical Writings.* New York: Modern Library.

DEVEREUX, GEORGE 1955 *A Study of Abortion in Primitive Societies.* New York: Julian Press.

DEWEY, JOHN 1900 Psychology and Social Practice. *Psychological Review* 7:105–124.

DEWEY, JOHN (1910) 1933 *How We Think: A Restatement of the Relation of Reflective Thinking to the Educative Process.* Boston: D. C. Heath.

DEWEY, JOHN (1915) 1979 *Schools of To-Morrow.* In volume 8 of *John Dewey: The Middle Works; 1899–1924.* Carbondale: Southern Illinois Univ. Press.

DEWEY, JOHN (1916) 1980 An Added Note as to the "Practical." In volume 10 of *John Dewey: The Middle Works, 1899–1924.* Carbondale: Southern Illinois Univ. Press.

DEWEY, JOHN 1922 *Human Nature and Conduct: An Introduction to Social Psychology.* New York: Holt.

DEWEY, JOHN (1922) 1983 Pragmatic America. In volume 13 of *John Dewey: The Middle Works, 1899–1924.* Carbondale: Southern Illinois Univ. Press.

DEWEY, JOHN 1927 *The Public and Its Problems.* New York: Holt.

DEWEY, JOHN (1929) 1984 *The Quest for Certainty.* In volume 4 of *John Dewey: The Later Works, 1925–1953.* Carbondale: Southern Illinois Univ. Press.

DEWEY, JOHN (1935) 1987 *Liberalism and Social Action.* In volume 11 of *John Dewey: The Later Works, 1925–1953.* Carbondale: Southern Illinois Univ. Press.

DEWEY, JOHN (1938) 1986 *Logic: The Theory of Inquiry.* In volume 12 of *John Dewey: The Later Works, 1925–1953.* Carbondale: Southern Illinois Univ. Press.

DEWEY, JOHN (1941) 1988 My Philosophy of Law. In volume 14 of *John Dewey: The Later Works, 1925–1953.* Carbondale: Southern Illinois Univ. Press.

DIACONIS, PERSI; AND MOSTELLER, FREDERICK 1989 Methods for Studying Coincidences. *Journal of the American Statistical Association* 84:853–861.

DIDEROT, DENIS 1765 Société. In volume 15 of *Encyclopédie, ou dictionnaire raisonné des sciences, des arts et des metiers.* Paris: Briasson. Quoted in Ralf Dahrendorf, On the Origin of Social Inequality. In Peter Laslett and W. G. Runciman (editors), *Philosophy, Politics and Society* 1964:89. Oxford (United Kingdom): Basil Blackwell.

DILTHEY, WILHELM (1883) 1989 *Selected Works.* Volume 1. *Introduction to the Human Sciences.* Princeton Univ. Press.

DILTHEY, WILHELM (1905–1910) 1927 *Gesammelte Schriften.* Quoted in Trygve R. Tholfsen, *Historical Thinking: An Introduction* 1967:248. New York: Harper.

DISRAELI, BENJAMIN(1833) 1982 *Letters: 1815–1834.* Univ. of Toronto Press.

DISRAELI, BENJAMIN (1845) 1980 *Sybil: Or the Two Nations*. Harmondsworth (United Kingdom): Penguin.

DISRAELI, BENJAMIN (1859) 1867 Reform Bill, 28 February 1859. In *Parliamentary Reform: A Series of Speeches on that Subject Delivered in the House of Commons by the Right Hon. B. Disraeli*. London: Longmans.

DOBB, MAURICE H. (1937) 1975 *Political Economy and Capitalism: Some Essays in Economic Tradition*. Westport, Conn.: Greenwood.

DOBB, MAURICE H. (1973) 1979 *Theories of Value and Distribution since Adam Smith: Ideology and Economic Theory*. Cambridge Univ. Press.

DOBZHANSKY, THEODOSIUS 1955 *Evolution, Genetics, and Man*. New York: Wiley.

DOBZHANSKY, THEODOSIUS (1962) 1967 *Mankind Evolving: The Evolution of the Human Species*. New Haven, Conn.: Yale Univ. Press.

The Doctrine of Saint-Simon: An Exposition; First Year, 1828–1829. (1830) 1958 Boston: Beacon.

DOLLARD, JOHN ET AL. 1939 *Frustration and Aggression*. New Haven, Conn.: Yale Univ. Press.

DOSTOYEVSKI, FYODOR MIKHAYLOVICH (1864) 1981 *Notes from Underground*. New York: Bantam Books.

DOUGLAS, MARY 1966 *Purity and Danger: An Analysis of the Concepts of Pollution and Taboo*. New York: Praeger

DOUGLAS, MARY 1971 Deciphering a Meal. In Clifford Geertz (editor), *Myth, Symbol, and Culture*. New York: Norton.

DOUGLAS, MARY 1980 *Evans-Pritchard*. Brighton, Sussex: Harvester Press.

DOYLE, ARTHUR CONAN (1891) 1986 A Scandal in Bohemia. In volume 1 of *The Annotated Sherlock Holmes*. New York: Clarkson N. Potter.

DOYLE, ARTHUR CONAN (1894) 1953 Silver Blaze. In *The Complete Sherlock Holmes*. New York: Doubleday.

DOYLE, ARTHUR CONAN (1914) 1953 *The Valley of Fear*. In *The Complete Sherlock Holmes*. New York: Doubleday.

DRYDEN, JOHN (1672) 1978 *The Conquest of Granada by the Spaniards*. In volume 11 of *The Works of John Dryden*. Berkeley and Los Angeles: Univ. of California Press.

DUBOIS, W. E. B. 1899 *The Philadelphia Negro: A Social Study*. Philadelphia, Pa.: Univ. of Pennsylvania.

DUBOIS, W. E. B. (1903) 1953 *The Souls of Black Folk*. New York: Blue Heron Press.

DUBOIS, W. E. B. 1909 *John Brown*. Philadelphia, Pa.: George W. Jacobs.

DUBOIS, W. E. B. (1920) 1969 *Darkwater: Voices from Within the Veil*. New York: Schocken Books.

DUBOIS, W. E. B. (1935) 1956 *Black Reconstruction: An Essay Toward a History of the Part Which Black Folk Played in the Attempt to Reconstruct Democracy in America, 1860–1880*. New York: S. A. Russell.

DUNCAN, OTIS DUDLEY 1968 Ability and Achievement. *Eugenics Quarterly* 15, no.1:1–11.

DUNCAN, OTIS DUDLEY (1970) 1971 Observations on Population. *The New Physician* 20:243–245 April.

DUNCAN, OTIS DUDLEY 1975 *Introduction to Structural Equation Models*. New York: Academic Press.

DUNCAN, OTIS DUDLEY 1984 *Notes on Social Measurement: Historical and Critical*. Russell Sage Foundation.

DURKHEIM, ÉMILE (1892) 1960 Montesquieu's Contribution to the Rise of Social Science. In *Montesquieu and Rousseau: Forerunners of Sociology*. Ann Arbor: Univ. of Michigan Press.

DURKHEIM, ÉMILE (1893) 1964 *The Division of Labor in Society*. New York: Free Press.

DURKHEIM, ÉMILE (1895) 1958 *The Rules of Sociological Method*. New York: Free Press.

DURKHEIM, ÉMILE (1897) 1966 *Suicide: A Study in Sociology*. New York: Free Press.

DURKHEIM, ÉMILE (1902–1906) 1973 *Moral Education: A Study in the Theory and Application of the Sociology of Education*. New York: Free Press.

DURKHEIM, ÉMILE (1912) 1965 *The Elementary Forms of the Religious Life*. New York: Free Press.

DURKHEIM, ÉMILE 1928 *Le socialisme: Sa définition, ses débuts, la doctrine saint-simonienne*. Quoted in H. Stuart Hughes, *Consciousness and Society: The Reorientation of European Social Thought; 1890–1930* (1958) 1977:77. New York: Random House.

DURKHEIM, ÉMILE (1950) 1957 *Professional Ethics and Civic Morals*. London: Routledge.

EASTERLIN, RICHARD A. 1987 Easterlin Hypothesis. In volume 2 of *The New Palgrave: A Dictionary of Economics*. London: Macmillan.

EBBINGHAUS, HERMANN 1873 *Über die hartmannsche Philosophie des Unbewussten*. Quoted in David Shakow, Hermann Ebbinghaus 1968:326. In volume 4 of *International Encyclopedia of the Social Sciences*. New York: Macmillan and Free Press.

EBBINGHAUS, HERMANN (1885) 1913 Epigraph. On title page of *Memory: A Contribution to Experimental Psychology*. New York: Teachers College, Columbia Univ.

EBBINGHAUS, HERMANN (1885) 1913 *Memory: A Contribution to Experimental Psychology*. New York: Teachers College, Columbia Univ.

EBBINGHAUS, HERMANN 1908 *Psychology: An Elementary Text-Book*. Boston: D. C. Heath.

ECKERMANN, J. P. (1836–1848) 1964 *Conversations with Goethe*. New York: Frederick Ungar.

EDGEWORTH, FRANCIS YSIDRO 1881 *Mathematical Psychics: An Essay on the Application of Mathematics to the Moral Sciences*. London: Kegan Paul.

EDGEWORTH, FRANCIS YSIDRO Observations and Statistics: An Essay on the Theory of Errors of Observation and the First Principles of Statistics. *Transactions of the Cambridge Philosophical Society* 14:138–169.

EDGEWORTH, FRANCIS YSIDRO 1887 *Metretike: Or the Method of Measuring Probability and Utility*. London: Temple.

EDGEWORTH, FRANCIS YSIDRO (1894) 1925 The Pure Theory of International Values. In volume 2 of *Papers Relating to Political Economy*. London: Macmillan.

EINSTEIN, ALBERT 1919 Einstein on His Theory. *The Times* (London) 28 November.

EISELE, CAROLYN 1987 Peirce's Pragmaticism. In volume 2 of Herbert Stachowiak (editor), *Pragmatik: Handbuch pragmatschen Denkens*. Hamburg: Felix Meiner Verlag.

EISENSTADT, S.N. (1956) 1971 *From Generation to Generation: Age Groups and Social Structure*. New York: Free Press.

EISENSTADT, S.N. (1964) 1973 Political Modernization: Some Comparative Notes. In *Tradition, Change, and Modernity*. New York: Wiley.

EISENSTEIN, ELIZABETH L. 1979 *The Printing Press as an Agent of Change: Communications and Cultural Transformations in Early-modern Europe*. Cambridge Univ. Press.

ELIADE, MIRCEA (1949) 1971 *The Myth of the Eternal Return: Or, Cosmos and History*. Princeton Univ. Press.

ELIADE, MIRCEA (1949) 1958 *Patterns in Comparative Religion*. New York: Sheed & Ward.

ELIAS, NORBERT 1969 *Über den Prozess der Zivilisation*. Quoted in Reinhard Bendix, Foreword. Norbert Elias, *What Is Sociology?* 1978:12. New York: Columbia Univ. Press.

ELIAS, NORBERT (1970) 1978 *What Is Sociology?* New York: Columbia Univ. Press.

ELLIS, HAVELOCK (1897) 1936 *Studies in the Psychology of Sex*. New York: Random House.

ELLUL, JACQUES (1977) 1980 *The Technological System*. New York: Continuum.

ELSTER, JON 1978 *Logic and Society: Contradictions and Possible Worlds*. New York: Wiley.

ELSTER, JON (1979) 1984 *Ulysses and the Sirens: Studies in Rationality and Irrationality*. Cambridge Univ. Press.

ELSTER, JON 1983 *Sour Grapes: Studies in the Subversion of Rationality*. Cambridge Univ. Press.

EMERSON, RALPH WALDO (1841) 1940 Self-Reliance. In *The Complete Essays and Other Writings of Ralph Waldo Emerson*. New York: Modern Library.

EMERSON, RALPH WALDO (1841) 1950 History. In *The Selected Writings of Ralph Waldo Emerson*. New York: Modern Library.

EMERSON, RALPH WALDO (1860) 1979 Fate. In *The Conduct of Life*. New York: AMS Press.

ENGEL, ERNST (1857) 1895 Die Productions-und Consumtionsverhältnisse des Königreichs Sachsen. L'institut International de Statistique, *Bulletin* 9:1–54.

ENGELS, FRIEDRICH (1859) 1980 Review of Karl Marx's *A Contribution to the Critique of Political Economy*. In volume 16 of *Karl Marx and Frederick Engels: Collected Works*. New York: International Publishers.

ENGELS, FRIEDRICH (1878) 1987 *Anti-Dühring*. In volume 25 of *Karl Marx and Frederick Engels: Collected Works*. London: Lawrence and Wishart.

ENGELS, FRIEDRICH (1882) 1967 Letter to Eduard Bernstein, 2–3 November 1882. In volume 35 of *Karl Marx and Friedrich Engels: Werke*. Berlin: Dietz Verlag.

ENGELS, FRIEDRICH (1883) 1956- Letter to Eduard Bernstein, 10 February 1883. In volume 35 of Karl Marx and Friedrich Engels, *Werke*. Berlin: Dietz. Quoted in Gérard Bekerman, *Marx and Engels: A Conceptual Concordance (1981) 1986:165*. Oxford (United Kingdom): Basil Blackwell.

ENGELS, FRIEDRICH (1883) 1950 Speech at the Graveside of Karl Marx. In volume 2 of *Karl Marx and Frederick Engels: Selected Works*. London: Lawrence and Wishart.

ENGELS, FRIEDRICH (1884) 1950 *The Origin of the Family, Private Property and the State*. In volume 2 of *Karl Marx and Frederick Engels: Selected Works*. London: Lawrence and Wishart.

ENGELS, FRIEDRICH (1888) 1950 *Ludwig Feuerbach and the End of Classical German Philosophy*. In volume 2 of *Karl Marx and Frederick Engels: Selected Works*. London: Lawrence and Wishart.

ENGELS, FRIEDRICH (1890) 1956 Letter to Joseph Bloch, 21–22 September 1890. In *Karl Marx and Frederick Engels: Selected Correspondence*. London: Lawrence and Wishart.

ENGELS, FRIEDRICH (1893) 1956 Letter to Franz Mehring, 14 July 1893. In *Karl Marx and Frederick Engels: Selected Correspondence*. London: Lawrence and Wishart.

ERIKSON, ERIK H. (1950) 1963 *Childhood and Society*. New York: Norton.

ERIKSON, ERIK H. (1950) 1968 Life Cycle. In volume 9 of *International Encyclopedia of the Social Sciences*. New York: Macmillan and Free Press.

Erikson, Erik H. 1957 The First Psychoanalyst. In Benjamin Nelson (editor), *Freud and the 20th Century*. New York: Meridian.

Erikson, Erik H. (1958) 1962 *Young Man Luther: A Study in Psychoanalysis and History*. New York: Norton.

Erikson, Erik H. 1968 *Identity: Youth and Crisis*. New York: Norton.

Erikson, Erik H. (1970) 1975 "Identity Crisis" in Autobiographic Perspective. In *Life History and the Historical Moment*. New York: Norton.

Erikson, Erik H. 1974 *Dimensions of a New Identity*. New York: Norton.

Erikson, Kai T. 1976 *Everything in Its Path: Destruction of Community in the Buffalo Creek Flood*. New York: Simon & Schuster.

Euripides 1959 *Orestes*. In volume 4 of David Grene and Richmond Lattimore (editors), *The Complete Greek Tragedies*. Univ. of Chicago Press.

Evans-Pritchard, E. E. 1936 Science and Sentiment: An Exposition and Criticism of the Writings of Pareto. Egyptian University, *Bulletin of the Faculty of Arts* Part 2:163–192. Quoted in Mary Douglas, *Edward Evans-Pritchard* 1980:28. New York: Viking.

Evans-Pritchard, E. E. (1948) 1964 Social Anthropology. In *Social Anthropology and Other Essays*. New York: Free Press.

Evans-Pritchard, E. E. (1950) 1964 Social Anthropology: Past and Present. In *Social Anthropology and Other Essays*. New York: Free Press.

Evans-Pritchard, E. E. (1961) 1964 Anthropology and History. In *Social Anthropology and Other Essays*. New York: Free Press.

Evans-Pritchard, E. E. 1963 *The Comparative Method in Social Anthropology*. London: Athlone Press.

Fanon, Frantz (1961) 1966 *The Wretched of the Earth*. New York: Grove Press.

Febvre, Lucien (1922) 1966 *A Geographical Introduction to History*. New York: Barnes & Noble.

Febvre, Lucien (1930) 1973 Civilisation: Evolution of a Word and a Group of Ideas. In *A New Kind of History: From the Writings of Febvre*. New York: Harper.

Femia, Joseph V. 1979 The Gramsci Phenomenon: Some Reflections. *Political Studies* 27:472–483.

Festinger, Leon 1957 *A Theory of Cognitive Dissonance*. New York: Harper.

Festinger, Leon 1961 The Psychological Effects of Insufficient Rewards. *American Psychologist* 16, no. 1:1–11.

Feuerbach, Ludwig Andreas (1841) 1957 *The Essence of Christianity*. New York: Harper.

Feuerbach, Ludwig Andreas 1846 *Sämtliche Werke*. Quoted in Sidney Hook, *From Hegel to Marx: Studies in the Intellectual Development of Karl Marx* (1950) 1962:223. Ann Arbor: Univ. of Michigan Press.

Feyerabend, Paul (1975) 1988 *Against Method*. London: Verso.

Firth, J. R. (1935) 1957 The Technique of Semantics. In *Papers in Linguistics: 1934–1951*. Oxford Univ. Press.

Firth, Raymond (1938) 1958 *Human Types: An Introduction to Social Anthropology*. New York: New American Library.

Firth, Raymond (1957) 1964 Introduction: Malinowski as Scientist and as Man. In Raymond Firth (editor), *Man and Culture: An Evaluation of the Work of Bronislaw Malinowski*. New York: Harper.

Fisher, Irving (1911) 1922 *The Purchasing Power of Money: Its Determination and Relation to Credit, Interest and Crises*. New York: Macmillan.

Fisher, Irving (1930) 1954 *The Theory of Interest*. New York: Kelley & Millman.

Fisher, R. A. (1926) 1972 The Arrangement of Field Experiments. In volume 2 of *Collected Papers of R. A. Fisher*. Univ. of Adelaide (Australia).

FISHER, R. A. (1935) 1971 *The Design of Experiments.* New York: Hafner.

FLEAY, FREDERICK GARD 1874 On Metrical Tests as Applied to Dramatic Poetry. New Shakespeare Society, *Transactions* 1:1–16.

FLECK, LUDWIK (1935) 1979 *Genesis and Development of a Scientific Fact.* Univ. of Chicago Press.

FOGEL, ROBERT WILLIAM 1989 *Without Consent or Contract: The Rise and Fall of American Slavery.* New York: Norton.

FOGEL, ROBERT WILLIAM; AND ELTON, GEOFFREY RUDOLPH 1983 *Which Road to the Past? Two Views of History.* New Haven, Conn.: Yale Univ. Press.

FOGEL, ROBERT WILLIAM; AND ENGERMAN, STANLEY L. 1974 *Time on the Cross: The Economics of American Negro Slavery.* Boston: Little, Brown.

FOLLETT, MARY PARKER (1918) 1920 *The New State: Group Organization, the Solution of Popular Government.* New York: Longmans.

FORTES, MEYER (1949) 1963 Time and Social Structure: An Ashanti Case Study. In *Social Structure.* New York: Russell & Russell.

FOUCAULT, MICHEL (1966) 1973 *The Order of Things.* New York: Random House.

FOUCAULT, MICHEL (1969) 1976 *The Archeology of Knowledge.* New York: Harper.

FOUCAULT, MICHEL (1971) 1977 Nietzsche, Genealogy, History. In *Language, Counter-Memory, Practice: Selected Essays and Interviews.* Ithaca, N.Y.: Cornell Univ. Press.

FOUCAULT, MICHEL (1976) 1978 *The History of Sexuality.* New York: Random House.

FOUCAULT, MICHEL (1976) 1980 Two Lectures. In *Power/Knowledge: Selected Interviews and Other Writings 1972–1977.* New York: Random House.

FOUCAULT, MICHEL (1977) 1980 Truth and Power. In *Power/Knowledge: Selected Interviews and Other Writings 1972–1977.* New York: Random House.

FOUCAULT, MICHEL (1982) 1983 The Subject and Power. In *Michel Foucault: Beyond Structuralism and Hermeneutics.* Univ. of Chicago Press.

FRANCE, ANATOLE (1894) 1917? *The Red Lily.* New York: Modern Library.

FRANKLIN, BENJAMIN (1739) 1987 *Poor Richard's Almanack.* In *Benjamin Franklin: Writings.* New York: Viking.

FRANKLIN, BENJAMIN (1789) 1907 Letter to Jean Baptiste Le Roy. In volume 10 of *The Writings of Benjamin Franklin.* New York: Macmillan.

FRAZER, JAMES GEORGE (1890) 1922 *The Golden Bough: A Study in Magic and Religion.* Abridged edition. London: Macmillan.

FRAZER, JAMES GEORGE (1894) 1927 William Robertson Smith. In *The Gorgon's Head and Other Literary Pieces.* London: Macmillan.

FRAZIER, E. FRANKLIN 1949 The Negro Family. In Ruth Nanda Anshen (editor), *The Family: Its Function and Destiny.* New York: Harper.

FREEMAN, EDWARD AUGUSTUS 1886 *The Methods of Historical Study.* London: Macmillan.

FRENKEL-BRUNSWIK, ELSE 1949 Dynamic and Cognitive Personality Organization as Seen through the Interviews. In T. W. Adorno et al. (editors), *The Authoritarian Personality.* New York: Harper.

FREUD, SIGMUND (1885) 1961 Letter to Martha Bernays, 24 November 1885. In *Letters of Sigmund Freud: 1873–1939.* London: Hogarth.

FREUD, SIGMUND (1886) 1960 Letter to Martha Bernays, 2 February 1886. In *Letters of Sigmund Freud: 1873–1939.* New York: Basic Books.

FREUD, SIGMUND (1896) 1962 The Aetiology of Hysteria. Volume 3 of *The Standard Edition of the Complete Psychological Works of Sigmund Freud.* London: Hogarth.

FREUD, SIGMUND (1898) 1954 Letter to Wilhelm Fliess, 10 March 1898. In *The Origins of Psycho-Analysis: Letters to Wilhelm Fliess, Drafts and Notes; 1887–1902.* New York: Basic Books.

FREUD, SIGMUND (1898) 1962 Sexuality in the Aetiology of the Neuroses. Volume 3 of *The Standard Edition of the Complete Psychological Works of Sigmund Freud*. London: Hogarth.

FREUD, SIGMUND (1899) 1954 Letter to Wilhelm Fliess, 19 February 1899. In *The Origins of Psycho-Analysis: Letters to Wilhelm Fliess, Drafts and Notes*. New York: Basic Books.

FREUD, SIGMUND (1900) 1958 *The Interpretation of Dreams*. Volumes 4–5 of *The Standard Edition of the Complete Psychological Works of Sigmund Freud*. London: Hogarth.

FREUD, SIGMUND (1905) 1953 Fragment of an Analysis of a Case of Hysteria. Volume 7 of *The Standard Edition of the Complete Psychological Works of Sigmund Freud*. London: Hogarth.

FREUD, SIGMUND (1905) 1953 *Three Essays on the Theory of Sexuality*. Volume 7 of *The Standard Edition of the Complete Psychological Works of Sigmund Freud*. London: Hogarth.

FREUD, SIGMUND 1906 Letter to Carl Gustav Jung, 6 December 1906. Quoted in Peter Gay, *Freud: A Life for Our Time* 1988:301. New York: Norton.

FREUD, SIGMUND (1912) 1957 On the Universal Tendency to Debasement in the Sphere of Love. Volume 11 of *The Standard Edition of the Complete Psychological Works of Sigmund Freud*. London: Hogarth.

FREUD, SIGMUND (1912) 1958 Recommendations to Physicians Practising Psycho-Analysis. Volume 12 of *The Standard Edition of the Complete Psychological Works of Sigmund Freud*. London: Hogarth.

FREUD, SIGMUND (1913) 1958 On Beginning the Treatment. Volume 12 of *The Standard Edition of the Complete Psychological Works of Sigmund Freud*. London: Hogarth.

FREUD, SIGMUND (1913) 1958 *Totem and Taboo*. Volume 13 of *The Standard Edition of the Complete Psychological Works of Sigmund Freud*. London: Hogarth.

FREUD, SIGMUND (1915) 1958 Observations on Transference-Love. Volume 12 of *The Standard Edition of the Complete Psychological Works of Sigmund Freud*. London: Hogarth.

FREUD, SIGMUND (1915) 1957 Thoughts for the Times on War and Death. Volume 14 of *The Standard Edition of the Complete Psychological Works of Sigmund Freud*. London: Hogarth.

FREUD, SIGMUND (1916–1917) 1961 *Introductory Lectures on Psycho-Analysis*. Volume 15 of *The Standard Edition of the Complete Psychological Works of Sigmund Freud*. London: Hogarth.

FREUD, SIGMUND (1917) 1955 A Difficulty in the Path of Psycho-Analysis. Volume 17 of *The Standard Edition of the Complete Psychological Works of Sigmund Freud*. London: Hogarth.

FREUD, SIGMUND (1921) 1955 *Group Psychology and the Analysis of the Ego*. Volume 18 of *The Standard Edition of the Complete Psychological Works of Sigmund Freud*. London: Hogarth.

FREUD, SIGMUND (1925) 1959 *An Autobiographical Study*. Volume 20 of *The Standard Edition of the Complete Psychological Works of Sigmund Freud*. London: Hogarth.

FREUD, SIGMUND (1926) 1959 *The Question of Lay Analysis: Conversations with an Impartial Person*. Volume 20 of *The Standard Edition of the Complete Psychological Works of Sigmund Freud*. London: Hogarth.

FREUD, SIGMUND (1928) 1961 *Dostoevsky and Parricide*. Volume 21 of *The Standard Edition of the Complete Psychological Works of Sigmund Freud*. London: Hogarth.

FREUD, SIGMUND (1930) 1961 *Civilization and Its Discontents*. Volume 21 of *The Standard Edition of the Complete Psychological Works of Sigmund Freud*. London: Hogarth.

FREUD, SIGMUND (1933) 1964 *New Introductory Lectures on Psycho-Analysis*. Volume 22 of *The Standard Edition of the Complete Psychological Works of Sigmund Freud*. London: Hogarth.

FREUD, SIGMUND (1935) 1961 Letter to Mrs. . . . 9 April 1935. In *Letters of Sigmund Freud: 1873–1939*. London: Hogarth.

FREUD, SIGMUND (1937) 1964 Analysis Terminable and Interminable. Volume 23 of *The Standard Edition of the Complete Psychological Works of Sigmund Freud*. London: Hogarth.

FREUD, SIGMUND (1940) 1964 *An Outline of Psycho-Analysis*. Volume 23 of *The Standard Edition of the Complete Psychological Works of Sigmund Freud*. London: Hogarth.

FREYRE, GILBERTO (1933) 1963 *The Masters and the Slaves: A Study in the Development of Brazilian Civilization*. New York: Knopf.

FRIEDAN, BETTY (1963) 1983 *The Feminine Mystique*. New York: Norton.

FRIEDMAN, MILTON (1951) 1953 Comments on Monetary Policy. In *Essays in Positive Economics*. Univ. of Chicago Press.

FRIEDMAN, MILTON 1962 *Capitalism and Freedom*. Univ. of Chicago Press.

FRIEDMAN, MILTON (1963) 1968 Inflation: Causes and Consequences. In *Dollars and Deficits*. Englewood Cliffs, N.J.: Prentice-Hall.

FRIEDMAN, MILTON 1966 Letter to the Editor, *Time* 4 February.

FRIEDMAN, MILTON (1968) 1987 The Case for the Negative Income Tax. In *The Essence of Friedman*. Stanford, Calif.: Hoover Institution Press.

FRIEDMAN, MILTON 1970 Defense of Usury. *Newsweek* 6 April.

FRIEDMAN, MILTON (1976) 1987 Inflation and Unemployment. In *The Essence of Friedman*. Stanford, Calif.: Hoover Institution Press.

FRIEDRICH, CARL J.; AND BRZEZINSKI, ZBIGNIEW K. (1956) 1961 *Totalitarian Dictatorship and Autocracy*. New York: Praeger.

FRISCH, RAGNAR 1933 Editorial. *Econometrica* 1:1–4.

FROMM, ERICH (1932) 1978 The Method and Function of an Analytic Social Psychology: Notes on Psychoanalysis and Historical Materialism. In Andrew Arato and Eike Gebhardt (editors), *The Essential Frankfurt School Reader*. New York: Urizen.

FROMM, ERICH 1941 *Escape from Freedom*. New York: Holt.

FROMM, ERICH 1944 Individual and Social Origins of Neurosis. *American Sociological Review* 9:380–384.

FROST, ROBERT (1914) 1939 The Black Cottage. In *Collected Poems of Robert Frost*. New York: Halcyon House.

FURET, FRANÇOIS (1982) 1984 *In the Workshop of History*. Univ. of Chicago Press.

FUSTEL DE COULANGES, NUMA DENIS (1864) 1979 *The Ancient City: A Study on the Religion, Laws, and Institutions of Greece and Rome*. Gloucester, Mass.: Smith.

FUSTEL DE COULANGES, NUMA DENIS 1893 *Questions historiques*. Paris: Hachette. Quoted in Trygve R. Tholfsen, *Historical Thinking: An Introduction* 1967:197. New York: Harper.

GABELENTZ, HANS GEORG VON DER (1891) 1901 *Die Sprachwissenschaft: Ihre Aufgaben, Methoden und bisherigen Ergebnisse*. Revised edition. Leipzig: T. O. Weigel.

GALBRAITH, JOHN KENNETH (1952) 1980 *American Capitalism: The Concept of Countervailing Power*. Armonk, N.Y.: M. E. Sharpe.

GALBRAITH, JOHN KENNETH 1958 *The Affluent Society*. Boston: Houghton Mifflin.

GALBRAITH, JOHN KENNETH 1975 *Money: Whence It Came, Where It Went*. Boston: Houghton Mifflin.

GALBRAITH, JOHN KENNETH 1977 *The Age of Uncertainty*. Boston: Houghton Mifflin.

GALIANI, FERDINANDO 1770 *Dialogues sur le commerce des blés*. Quoted in Henry William Spiegel, *The Development of Economic Thought: Great Economists in Perspective* 1952:65. New York: Wiley.

GALTON, FRANCIS 1863 *Meteorographica: Methods of Mapping the Weather*. London: Macmillan.

GALTON, FRANCIS 1877 Typical Laws of Heredity. *Nature* 15:492–495, 512–514, 532–533.

GALTON, FRANCIS 1885 Section H: Anthropology; Opening Address. *Nature* 32:507–510.

GALTON, FRANCIS 1888 Co-relations and Their Measurement, Chiefly from Anthropometric Data. Royal Society of London, *Proceedings* 45:135–145.

GALTON, FRANCIS 1889 *Natural Inheritance*. London: Macmillan.

GANDHI, MOHANDAS K. (1951) 1961 *Non-Violent Resistance (Satyagraha)*. New York: Schocken. Quoted in Christian Bay, Civil Disobedience. In volume 2 of *International Encyclopedia of the Social Sciences* 1968:478. New York: Macmillan and Free Press.

GANTT, W. HORSLEY 1941 Introduction to volume 2 of Ivan Petrovich Pavlov, *Lectures on Conditioned Reflexes* (1923). New York: International Publishers.

GARFINKEL, HAROLD 1967 *Studies in Ethnomethodology*. Englewood Cliffs, N.J.: Prentice-Hall.

GAY, PETER 1974 Macaulay: Intellectual Voluptuary. In *Style in History*. New York: Basic Books.

GAY, PETER 1988 *Freud: A Life for Our Time*. New York: Norton.

GAY, PETER; AND CAVANAUGH, GERALD J. 1975 Lewis B. Namier. In volume 4 of *Historians at Work*. New York: Harper.

GEERTZ, CLIFFORD 1962 The Growth of Culture and the Evolution of Mind. In Jordan M. Scher (editor), *Theories of the Mind*. New York: Free Press.

GEERTZ, CLIFFORD 1964 Ideology as a Cultural System. In David E. Apter (editor), *Ideology and Discontent*. New York: Free Press.

GEERTZ, CLIFFORD (1966) 1973 The Impact of the Concept of Culture on the Concept of Man. In *The Interpretation of Cultures*. New York: Basic Books.

GEERTZ, CLIFFORD (1966) 1973 Religion as a Cultural System. In *The Interpretation of Cultures*. New York: Basic Books.

GEERTZ, CLIFFORD 1973 Thick Description: Toward an Interpretive Theory of Culture. In *The Interpretation of Cultures*. New York: Basic Books.

GEERTZ, CLIFFORD 1988 *Works and Lives: The Anthropologist as Author*. Stanford Univ. Press.

GELDERMAN, CAROL 1981 *Henry Ford: The Wayward Capitalist*. New York: The Dial Press.

GELLNER, ERNEST (1959) 1979 *Words and Things: An Examination of, and an Attack on, Linguistic Philosophy*. London: Routledge.

GELLNER, ERNEST (1964) 1965 *Thought and Change*. Univ. of Chicago Press.

GELLNER, ERNEST 1969 *Saints of the Atlas*. Univ. of Chicago Press.

GENNEP, ARNOLD VAN (1908) 1966 *The Rites of Passage*. Univ. of Chicago Press.

GEORGE, HENRY (1879) 1942 *Progress and Poverty*. New York: Walter J. Black.

GIBBON, EDWARD (1776–1788) 1974 *The History of the Decline and Fall of the Roman Empire*. New York: AMS Press.

GIBBON, EDWARD (1796) 1961 *The Autobiography of Edward Gibbon*. New York: Meridian.

GIDDENS, ANTHONY 1984 *The Constitution of Society: Outline of the Theory of Structuration*. Berkeley and Los Angeles: Univ. of California Press.

GIDDENS, ANTHONY 1987 *Social Theory and Modern Sociology*. Cambridge (United Kingdom): Polity Press.

GIDDINGS, FRANKLIN H. (1896) 1970 *The Principles of Sociology*. New York: Johnson.

GIDDINGS, FRANKLIN H. (1922) 1926 *Studies in the Theory of Human Society*. New York: Macmillan.

GLANVILL, JOSEPH (1661) 1970 *The Vanity of Dogmatizing*. Brighton, Sussex: Harvester Press.

GLAZER, NATHAN; AND MOYNIHAN, DANIEL PATRICK 1963 *Beyond the Melting Pot: The Negroes, Puerto Ricans, Jews, Italians, and Irish of New York City*. Cambridge, Mass.: M.I.T. Press.

GODWIN, WILLIAM (1793) 1926 *An Enquiry Concerning Political Justice and Its Influence on General Virtue and Happiness*. New York: Knopf.

GOETHE, JOHANN WOLFGANG VON (1808) 1970 *Goethe's Faust*. Univ. of Toronto Press.

GOFFMAN, ERVING 1952 On Cooling the Mark Out: Some Aspects of Adaptation to Failure. *Psychiatry* 15:451–463

GOFFMAN, ERVING (1956) 1973 *The Presentation of Self in Everyday Life*. Woodstock, N.Y.: Overlook Press.

GOFFMAN, ERVING (1963) 1968 *Stigma: Notes on the Management of Spoiled Identity*. Harmondsworth (United Kingdom): Penguin.

GOFFMAN, ERVING 1971 *Relations in Public: Microstudies of the Public Order*. New York: Basic Books.

GOFFMAN, ERVING 1974 *Frame Analysis: An Essay on the Organization of Experience*. New York: Harper.

GOFFMAN, ERVING 1983 The Interaction Order. *American Sociological Review* 48:1–17.

GOOCH, G. P. (1913) 1959 *History and Historians in the Nineteenth Century*. Boston: Beacon.

GOODE, WILLIAM J. 1963 *World Revolution and Family Patterns*. New York: Free Press.

GOSSET, WILLIAM SEALY (1929) 1938 Letter to E. S. Pearson, 18 May 1929. In E. S. Pearson, "Student" as Statistician. *Biometrika* 30: 244.

GOSSET, WILLIAM SEALY (1938) 1943 Comparison between Balanced and Random Arrangements of Field Plots. In *"Student's" Collected Papers*. London: University College, Biometrika Office.

GOULD, STEPHEN JAY 1981 *The Mismeasure of Man*. New York: Norton.

GOULD, STEPHEN JAY 1985 *The Flamingo's Smile: Reflections in Natural History*. New York: Norton.

GOULD, STEPHEN JAY 1989 *Wonderful Life: The Burgess Shale and the Nature of History*. New York: Norton.

GOULDNER, ALVIN W. 1970 *The Coming Crisis of Western Sociology*. New York: Basic Books.

GRAHAM, LOREN R. 1987 *Science, Philosophy, and Human Behavior in the Soviet Union*. New York: Columbia Univ. Press.

GRAMSCI, ANTONIO (1920) 1977 The Factory Council. In *Selections from Political Writings: 1910–1920*. London: Lawrence and Wishart.

GRAMSCI, ANTONIO (1933–1934) 1971 *Selections from the Prison Notebooks of Antonio Gramsci*. New York: International Publishers.

GRANOVETTER, MARK 1982 The Strength of Weak Ties: A Network Theory Revisited. In Peter V. Marsden and Nan Lin (editors), *Social Structure and Network Analysis*. Newbury Park, Calif.: Sage.

GRAUNT, JOHN (1662) 1899 *Observations upon the Bills of Mortality*. In *The Economic Writings of Sir William Petty*. Cambridge Univ. Press.

GREEN, T. H. (1881) 1888 Lecture on Liberal Legislation and Freedom of Contract. In *Works of Thomas Hill Green*. New York: Longmans.

GRUBER, HOWARD E. 1982 Piaget's Mission. *Social Research* 49, no. 1:239–264.

Grunberg, Emile; and Modigliani, Franco 1954 The Predictability of Social Events. *Journal of Political Economy* 62, no. 6:465–478.

Habermas, Jürgen (1963) 1973 *Theory and Practice*. Boston: Beacon.

Habermas, Jürgen (1968) 1971 *Knowledge and Human Interests*. Boston: Beacon.

Habermas, Jürgen (1969) 1971 *Toward a Rational Society: Student Protest, Science, and Politics*. London: Heinemann.

Habermas, Jürgen (1981) 1983 Modernity: An Incomplete Project. In *The Anti-Aesthetic: Essays on Postmodern Culture*. Port Townsend, Wash.: Bay Press.

Hacker, Andrew 1957 Liberal Democracy and Social Control. *American Political Science Review* 51:1009–1026.

Hacking, Ian 1965 *Logic of Statistical Inference*. Cambridge Univ. Press.

Hahn, F. H. 1970 Some Adjustment Problems. *Econometrica* 38:1–17.

Hahn, F. H. 1973 The Winter of Our Discontent. *Economica* 40:322–330.

Hahn, F. H. 1982 Reflections on the Invisible Hand. *Lloyds Bank Review* 144:1–21.

Halévy, Élie (1901–1904) 1955 *The Growth of Philosophic Radicalism*. Boston: Beacon.

Halévy, Élie (1930) 1966 The World Crisis of 1914–1918: An Interpretation. In *The End of Tyrannies: Essays on Socialism and War*. New York Univ. Press.

Hall, G. Stanley 1878 The Muscular Perception of Space. *Mind* October.

Hall, G. Stanley (1904) 1911 *Adolescence: Its Psychology and Its Relations to Physiology, Anthropology, Sociology, Sex, Crime, Religion and Education*. New York: Appleton.

Hamilton, Alexander (1787) 1961 No. 22. *The Federalist Papers*. New York: New American Library.

Hamilton, Alexander (1788) 1961 No. 31. *The Federalist Papers*. New York: New American Library.

Hamilton, Alexander (1788) 1961 No. 68. *The Federalist Papers*. New York: New American Library.

Hand, Learned (1932) 1953 Democracy: Its Presumptions and Realities. In *The Spirit of Liberty: Papers and Addresses of Learned Hand*. New York: Knopf.

Hand, Learned (1952) 1959 A Plea for the Open Mind and Free Discussion. In *The Spirit of Liberty: Papers and Addresses of Learned Hand*. New York: Random House.

Hardin, Garrett 1968 The Tragedy of the Commons. *Science* 162:1243–1248.

Harrington, Michael 1962 *The Other America: Poverty in the United States*. New York: Macmillan.

Harris, C. Alexander (1896) 1906 Gresham's Law. In volume 2 of R. H. Inglis Palgrave, *Dictionary of Political Economy*. London: Macmillan.

Harrod, R. F. 1951 *The Life of John Maynard Keynes*. San Diego, Calif.: Harcourt.

Hartley, David (1749) 1966 *Observations on Man: His Frame, His Duty, and His Expectations*. Gainesville, Fla.: Scholars' Facsimiles & Reprints.

Hartmann, Heinz (1950) 1964 Comments on the Psychoanalytic Theory of the Ego. In *Essays on Ego Psychology: Selected Problems in Psychoanalytic Theory*. New York: International Universities Press.

Harvey, William (1628) 1923 *The Circulation of the Blood*. London: Dent.

Hawkins, Edward R., and Waller, Willard W. 1936 Critical Notes on the Cost of Crime. *Journal of the American Institute of Criminal Law and Criminology* 26:679–694.

Hayek, Friedrich A. von 1942 Scientism and the Study of Society. *Economica* 9:267–291.

Hayek, Friedrich A. von (1944) 1972 *The Road to Serfdom*. Univ. of Chicago Press.

Hayek, Friedrich A. von (1945) 1948 The Use of Knowledge in Society. In *Individualism and Economic Order*. Univ. of Chicago Press.

Hayek, Friedrich A. von (1952) 1964 *The Counter-Revolution of Science: Studies in the Abuse of Reason*. New York: Free Press.

Hayek, Friedrich A. von 1967 *Studies in Philosophy, Politics and Economics*. Univ. of Chicago Press.

Hayek, Friedrich A. von (1976) 1978 *Law, Legislation and Liberty: A New Statement of the Liberal Principles of Justice and Political Economy*. Univ. of Chicago Press.

Hegel, Georg Wilhelm Friedrich (1821) 1952 *Philosophy of Right*. Oxford Univ. Press.

Hegel, Georg Wilhelm Friedrich (1837) 1956 *The Philosophy of History*. New York: Dover.

Hegel, Georg Wilhelm Friedrich 1840 Die Logik. In *Enzyklopädie*, Erster Theil. Berlin. Quoted in Karl Marx, *Capital* (1867) 1967: 179. New York: International Publishers.

Heilbroner, Robert L. (1953) 1980 *The Worldly Philosophers*. New York: Simon & Schuster.

Heilbroner, Robert L. 1960 *The Future as History*. New York: Harper.

Heilbroner, Robert L. 1968 Putting Marx to Work. *New York Review of Books* 5 December 1968.

Heilbroner, Robert L. 1987 Capitalistic and Acapitalistic Production. In volume 1 of *The New Palgrave: A Dictionary of Economics*. London: Macmillan.

Heilbroner, Robert L. 1989 Reflections: The Triumph of Capitalism. *The New Yorker* 23 January.

Hempel, Carl G. 1942 The Function of General Laws in History. *Journal of Philosophy* 39, no. 2:35–48.

Henderson, L. J. 1941 *The Study of Man*. Philadelphia, Pa.: Univ. of Pennsylvania Press.

Heraclitus 1979 *Heracleitus on the Universe*. Cambridge, Mass.: Harvard Univ. Press.

Herder, Johann Gottfried von (1774) 1892 *Uebers Erkennen und Empfinden in der menschlichen Seele*. In volume 8 of *Sämtliche Werke*. Berlin: Weidmannsche.

Herder, Johann Gottfried von (1784–1791) 1968 *Reflections on the Philosophy of the History of Mankind*. Univ. of Chicago Press.

Herder, Johann Gottfried von (1785) 1887 *Ideen zur Philosophie der Geschichte der Menschheit*. In volume 13 of *Sämtliche Werke*. Berlin: Weidmannsche. Pages 257–258, quoted in F. M. Barnard, Introduction. *J. G. Herder on Social and Political Culture* 1969:41. Cambridge Univ. Press. Page 341, quoted in Isaiah Berlin, *Vico and Herder: Two Studies in the History of Ideas* 1976:158. New York: Viking.

Herder, Johann Gottfried von 1877–1913 *Sämtliche Werke*. Quoted in Isaiah Berlin, *Vico and Herder: Two Studies in the History of Ideas* 1976:158, 204. New York: Viking.

Herodotus 1987 *The History*. Univ. of Chicago Press.

Herold, J. Christopher (editor) 1955 *The Mind of Napoleon*. New York: Columbia Univ. Press.

Herschel, John F. W. (1850) 1857 Quetelet on Probabilities. In *Essays from the Edinburgh and Quarterly Reviews*. London: Longmans.

Herskovits, Melville Jean 1961 The Study of African Oral Art. *Journal of American Folklore* 74:451–456.

Hexter, J. H. (1961) 1963 *Reappraisals in History: New Views on History and Society in Early Modern Europe*. New York: Harper.

HEXTER, J. H. 1968 Historiography: The Rhetoric of History. In volume 6 of *International Encyclopedia of the Social Sciences*. New York: Macmillan and Free Press.

HICKS, JOHN R. (1932) 1968 *The Theory of Wages*. New York: St. Martins.

HICKS, JOHN R. 1936 *Economic Theory and the Social Sciences*. Quoted in Robert K. Merton, The Bearing of Sociological Theory on Empirical Research (1948) 1968:143. In *Social Theory and Social Structure*. New York: Free Press.

HICKS, JOHN R. (1942) 1943 *The Social Framework: An Introduction to Economics*. Oxford Univ. Press.

HICKS, JOHN R. 1977 *Economic Perspectives: Further Essays on Money and Growth*. Oxford Univ. Press.

HIMMELFARB, GERTRUDE 1959 *Darwin and the Darwinian Revolution*. New York: Doubleday.

HIMMELFARB, GERTRUDE (1984) 1987 "History with the Politics Left Out." In *The New History and the Old*. Cambridge, Mass.: Harvard Univ. Press.

HIRSCHMAN, ALBERT O. 1967 *Development Projects Observed*. Washington, D.C.: The Brookings Institution.

HIRSCHMAN, ALBERT O. 1970 *Exit, Voice, and Loyalty: Responses to Decline in Firms, Organizations, and States*. Cambridge, Mass.: Harvard Univ. Press.

HIRSCHMAN, ALBERT O. (1978) 1981 Exit, Voice, and the State. In *Essays in Trespassing: Economics to Politics and Beyond*. Cambridge Univ. Press.

HIRSCHMAN, ALBERT O. (1980) 1981 Morality and the Social Sciences: A Durable Tension. In *Essays in Trespassing: Economics to Politics and Beyond*. Cambridge Univ. Press.

HIRSCHMAN, ALBERT O. (1984) 1986 Against Parsimony: Three Easy Ways of Complicating Some Categories of Economic Discourse. In *Rival Views of Market Society and Other Recent Essays*. New York: Viking.

HIRSCHMAN, ALBERT O. 1989 Reactionary Rhetoric. *The Atlantic Monthly* May.

HOBBES, THOMAS (1651) 1946 *Leviathan: Or the Matter, Forme and Power of a Commonwealth, Ecclesiasticall and Civil*. Oxford (United Kingdom): Basil Blackwell.

HOBSON, JOHN A. (1902) 1965 *Imperialism: A Study*. Ann Arbor: Univ. of Michigan Press.

HOCART, A. M. (1936) 1970 *Kings and Councillors: An Essay in the Comparative Anatomy of Human Society*. Univ. of Chicago Press.

HODGSKIN, THOMAS (1825) 1963 *Labour Defended against the Claims of Capital*. Fairfield, N.J.: Augustus M. Kelley.

HODGSKIN, THOMAS 1827 *Popular Political Economy*. London: Charles Tate.

HOFSTADTER, RICHARD (1944) 1955 *Social Darwinism in American Thought*. Boston: Beacon.

HOFSTADTER, RICHARD 1948 *The American Political Tradition and the Men Who Made It*. New York: Vintage.

HOFSTADTER, RICHARD (1954) 1965 The Pseudo-conservative Revolt — 1954. In *The Paranoid Style in American Politics and Other Essays*. New York: Knopf.

HOFSTADTER, RICHARD (1955) 1956 *The Age of Reform: From Bryan to F. D. R.* New York: Knopf

HOFSTADTER, RICHARD (1968) 1970 *The Progressive Historians: Turner, Beard, Parrington*. New York: Vintage.

HOGBEN, LANCELOT 1937 Preface on Prejudices. In Cedric Dover, *Half-Caste*. London: Secker & Warburg.

HOGBEN, LANCELOT 1938 Prolegomena to Political Arithmetic. In Lancelot Hogben (editor), *Political Arithmetic: A Symposium of Population Studies*. New York: Macmillan.

HOLMES, OLIVER WENDELL (1881) 1967 *The Common Law*. Cambridge, Mass.: Harvard Univ. Press.

HOLMES, OLIVER WENDELL (1895) 1913 Speech at Harvard Law School, 25 June 1895. In *Speeches*. Boston: Little, Brown.

HOLMES, OLIVER WENDELL (1897) 1943 The Path of the Law. In *The Mind and Faith of Justice Holmes: His Speeches, Essays, Letters and Judicial Opinions*. New York: Modern Library.

HOLMES, OLIVER WENDELL (1934) 1962 The Profession of the Law. In *The Occasional Speeches of Justice Oliver Wendell Holmes*. Cambridge, Mass.: Harvard Univ. Press.

HOLTON, GERALD 1961 On the Recent Past of Physics. *American Journal of Physics* 29, no. 12:805–810.

HOLTON, GERALD (1981) 1986 Thematic Presuppositions and the Direction of Scientific Advance. In *The Advancement of Science, and Its Burdens*. Cambridge Univ. Press.

HOLTON, GERALD (1982) 1986 Science, Technology, and the Fourth Discontinuity. In *The Advancement of Science, and Its Burdens*. Cambridge Univ. Press.

HOMANS, GEORGE C. 1961 *Human Behavior: Its Elementary Forms*. San Diego, Calif.: Harcourt.

HOMANS, GEORGE C. 1964 Bringing Men Back In. *American Sociological Review* 29:809–818.

HOMANS, GEORGE C. 1967 *The Nature of Social Science*. San Diego, Calif.: Harcourt.

HOOTON, EARNEST A. (1934) 1937 The Biology of Primitive Human Societies. In *Apes, Men, and Morons*. New York: Putnam.

HOOTON, EARNEST A. (1936) 1937 Plain Statements about Race. In *Apes, Men, and Morons*. New York: Putnam.

HORNEY, KAREN 1937 *The Neurotic Personality of Our Time*. New York: Norton.

HORNEY, KAREN (1939) 1966 *New Ways in Psychoanalysis*. New York: Norton.

HORNEY, KAREN 1945 *Our Inner Conflicts: A Constructive Theory of Neurosis*. New York: Norton.

HOUSEHOLDER, FRED W. 1952 Review of *Methods in Structural Linguistics* by Zellig S. Harris. *International Journal of American Linguistics* 18:260–268.

HUGHES, EVERETT C. (1948) 1971 The Study of Ethnic Relations. In *The Sociological Eye: Selected Papers*. Chicago: Aldine.

HUGHES, H. STUART 1964 *History as Art and as Science: Twin Vistas on the Past*. New York: Harper.

HUIZINGA, JOHAN (1919) 1952 *The Waning of the Middle Ages*. London: Edward Arnold.

HUIZINGA, JOHAN (1938) 1955 *Homo ludens: A Study of the Play-element in Culture*. Boston: Beacon.

HULL, CLARK L. (1927) 1962 Diary Entry, March 1927. In Psychology of the Scientist: IV. Passages from the "Idea Books" of Clark L. Hull. *Perceptual and Motor Skills* 15:807–882.

HULL, CLARK L. (1930) 1962 Diary Entry, 26 June 1930. In Psychology of the Scientist: IV. Passages from the "Idea Books" of Clark L. Hull. *Perceptual and Motor Skills* 15:807–882.

HULL, CLARK L. 1943 *Principles of Behavior: An Introduction to Behavior Theory*. New York: Appleton.

HUMBOLDT, FRIEDRICH WILHELM VON (1836) 1988 *On Language: The Diversity of Human Language-structure and Its Influence on the Mental Development of Mankind*. Cambridge Univ. Press.

HUME, DAVID (1739–1740) 1975 *A Treatise of Human Nature*. Oxford Univ. Press.

HUME, DAVID (1740) 1955 *An Abstract of a Treatise of Human Nature.* In *An Inquiry Concerning Human Understanding* with a Supplement: *An Abstract of a Treatise of Human Understanding.* Indianapolis, Ind.: Bobbs-Merrill.

HUME, DAVID (1741) 1985 Of the First Principles of Government. In *Essays: Moral, Political, and Literary.* Indianapolis, Ind.: Liberty Fund.

HUME, DAVID (1741) 1985 Of the Independency of Parliament. In *Essays: Moral, Political, and Literary.* Indianapolis, Ind.: Liberty Fund.

HUME, DAVID (1742) 1985 The Skeptic. In *Essays: Moral, Political, and Literary.* Indianapolis, Ind.: Liberty Fund.

HUME, DAVID (1742) 1985 The Stoic. In *Essays: Moral, Political, and Literary.* Indianapolis, Ind.: Liberty Fund.

HUME, DAVID (1748) 1955 *An Inquiry Concerning Human Understanding.* Indianapolis, Ind.: Bobbs-Merrill.

HUME, DAVID (1748) 1985 Of National Characters. In *Essays: Moral, Political, and Literary.* Indianapolis, Ind.: Liberty Fund.

HUME, DAVID (1752) 1955 Of Money. In *David Hume: Writings on Economics.* Edinburgh: Nelson.

HUME, DAVID (1754) 1985 Of Commerce. In *Essays: Moral, Political, and Literary.* Indianapolis, Ind.: Liberty Fund.

HUME, DAVID (1758) 1985 Of the Jealousy of Trade. In *Essays: Moral, Political, and Literary.* Indianapolis, Ind.: Liberty Fund.

HUME, DAVID (1779) 1948 *Dialogues Concerning Natural Religion.* New York: Hafner.

HUNTINGTON, ELLSWORTH 1916 Weather and Civilizations. *Bulletin of the Geographical Society of Philadelphia* 14:1–21.

HUNTINGTON, SAMUEL P. 1968 *Political Order in Changing Societies.* New Haven, Conn.: Yale Univ. Press.

HUTCHESON, FRANCIS (1725) 1726 *An Inquiry Concerning Moral Good and Evil.* In *An Inquiry into the Original of Our Ideas of Beauty and Virtue; In Two Treatises.* London: J. Darby et al.

HUXLEY, JULIAN; AND HADDON, ALFRED CORT 1935 *We Europeans: A Survey of "Racial" Problems.* London: Jonathan Cape.

HUXLEY, T. H. (1854) 1971 On the Educational Value of the Natural History Sciences. In *T. H. Huxley on Education.* Cambridge Univ. Press.

HUXLEY, T. H. (1863) 1959 *Man's Place in Nature.* Ann Arbor: Univ. of Michigan Press.

HUXLEY, T. H. (1870) 1896 Biogenesis and Abiogenesis. In *Discourses: Biological and Geological Essays.* New York: Appleton.

HUXLEY, T. H. 1871 On the Physical Basis of Life. In *Lay Sermons, Addresses, and Reviews.* London: Macmillan.

HUXLEY, T. H. (1880) 1896 The Coming of Age of "The Origin of Species." In *Darwiniana: Essays.* New York: Appleton.

HYMAN, HERBERT H. 1968 Reference Groups. In volume 13 of *International Encyclopedia of the Social Sciences.* New York: Macmillan and Free Press.

HYMES, DELL (1967) 1974 Why Linguistics Needs the Sociologist. In *Foundations in Sociolinguistics: An Ethnographic Approach.* Philadelphia, Pa.: Univ. of Pennsylvania Press.

HYMES, DELL (1971) 1972 On Communicative Competence. In J. B. Pride and Janet Holmes (editors), *Sociolinguistics.* Harmondsworth (United Kingdom): Penguin.

IBN KHALDÛN (1377) 1950 *An Arab Philosophy of History: Selections from the Prolegomena of Ibn Khaldun.* London: Murray.

IBN KHALDÛN (1377) 1958 *The Muqaddimah.* New York: Bollingen Foundation.

JACOBI, JOLAN 1943 *The Psychology of Jung.* New Haven, Conn.: Yale Univ. Press.

JAKOBSON, ROMAN (1929) 1971 Retrospect. In volume 2 of *Roman Jakobson: Selected Writings*. The Hague: Mouton.

JAKOBSON, ROMAN 1960 Closing Statement: Linguistics and Poetics. In Thomas A. Sebeok (editor), *Style in Language*. Cambridge, Mass.: Technology Press of M.I.T.

JAKOBSON, ROMAN (1961) 1987 Poetry of Grammar and Grammar of Poetry. In *Language in Literature*. Cambridge, Mass.: Harvard Univ. Press.

JAMES, WILLIAM (1868) 1920 Letter to Thomas W. Ward. In volume 1 of *The Letters of William James*. Boston: Atlantic Monthly Press.

JAMES, WILLIAM (1878) 1920 Letter to Mrs. James. In volume 1 of *The Letters of William James*. Boston: Atlantic Monthly Press.

JAMES, WILLIAM 1880–1897 Lecture Notes. Quoted in Ralph Barton Perry, *The Thought and Character of William James* 1936:Vol. 1, 482. Boston: Little, Brown.

JAMES, WILLIAM (1880) 1910 Great Men and Their Environment. In *The Will to Believe and Other Essays in Popular Philosophy*. New York: Longmans.

JAMES, WILLIAM (1882) 1910 The Sentiment of Rationality. In *The Will to Believe and Other Essays in Popular Philosophy*. New York: Longmans.

JAMES, WILLIAM (1887) 1920 Letter to Carl Stumpf, 6 February 1887. In volume 1 of *The Letters of William James*. Boston: Atlantic Monthly Press.

JAMES, WILLIAM (1890) 1950 *The Principles of Psychology*. New York: Dover.

JAMES, WILLIAM (1892) 1928 *Psychology: Briefer Course*. New York: Holt.

JAMES, WILLIAM (1896) 1910 The Will to Believe. In *The Will to Believe and Other Essays in Popular Philosophy*. New York: Longmans.

JAMES, WILLIAM (1899) 1923 *Talks to Teachers on Psychology and to Students on Some of Life's Ideals*. New York: Holt.

JAMES, WILLIAM (1907) 1946 *Pragmatism: A New Name for Some Old Ways of Thinking*. New York: Longmans.

JAMES, WILLIAM (1910) 1911 The Moral Equivalent of War. In *Memories and Studies*. New York: Longmans.

JANEWAY, ELIZABETH 1980 *Powers of the Weak*. New York: Knopf.

JANOWITZ, MORRIS 1964 *The Military in the Political Development of New Nations: An Essay in Comparative Analysis*. Univ. of Chicago Press.

JEFFERSON, THOMAS (1785) 1830 Letter to General Chastellux. In volume 1 of *Memoir, Correspondence, and Miscellanies, from the Papers of Thomas Jefferson*.

JEFFERSON, THOMAS (1785) 1984 *Notes on the State of Virginia*. In *Thomas Jefferson: Writings*. New York: Library of America.

JEFFERSON, THOMAS (1787) 1984 Letter to Edward Carrington, 16 January 1787. In *Thomas Jefferson: Writings*. New York: Library of America.

JEFFERSON, THOMAS (1787) 1984 Letter to James Madison, 30 January 1787. In *Thomas Jefferson: Writings*. New York: Library of America.

JEFFERSON, THOMAS (1787) 1984 Letter to William S. Smith, 13 November 1787. In *Thomas Jefferson: Writings*. New York: Library of America.

JEFFERSON, THOMAS (1789) 1984 Letter to James Madison, 6 September 1789. In *Thomas Jefferson: Writings*. New York: Library of America.

JEFFERSON, THOMAS (1801) 1984 First Inaugural Address, 4 March 1801. In *Thomas Jefferson: Writings*. New York: Library of America.

JEFFERSON, THOMAS (1802) 1967 Letter to the Danbury [Connecticut] Baptist Association, 1 January 1802. In volume 1 of *The Jefferson Cyclopedia*. New York: Russell & Russell.

JEFFERSON, THOMAS (1813) 1984 Letter to John Adams, 28 October 1813. In *Thomas Jefferson: Writings*. New York: Library of America.

JEFFERSON, THOMAS (1820) 1905 Letter to William Charles Jarvis, September 28, 1820. In volume 12 of *The Works of Thomas Jefferson*. New York: Putnam.

JEFFERSON, THOMAS (1823) 1984 Letter to James Monroe, 24 October 1823. In *Thomas Jefferson: Writings.* New York: Library of America.

JEFFERSON, THOMAS (1825) 1984 Letter to Henry Lee, 8 May 1825. In *Thomas Jefferson: Writings.* New York: Library of America.

JEFFERSON, THOMAS (1826) 1984 Letter to Roger C. Weightman, 24 June 1826. In *Thomas Jefferson: Writings.* New York: Library of America.

JEFFERSON, THOMAS (1826) 1984 Epitaph. In *Thomas Jefferson: Writings.* New York: Library of America.

JESPERSEN, OTTO (1922) 1964 *Language: Its Nature, Development, and Origin.* New York: Norton.

JEVONS, WILLIAM STANLEY (1860) 1886 Letter to Herbert Jevons, 1 June 1860. *Letters and Journal of W. Stanley Jevons.* London: Macmillan.

JEVONS, WILLIAM STANLEY (1865) 1866 *The Coal Question: An Inquiry Concerning the Progress of the Nation, and the Probable Exhaustion of Our Coal-Mines.* London: Macmillan.

JEVONS, WILLIAM STANLEY (1871) 1957 *The Theory of Political Economy.* New York: Kelley & Millman.

JOHN OF SALISBURY (1169) 1955 *The Metalogicon of John of Salisbury.* Berkeley and Los Angeles: Univ. of California Press.

JOHN OF SALISBURY (1476?) 1979 *Policraticus: The Statesman's Book.* New York: Frederick Ungar.

JOLL, JAMES (1964) 1966 *The Anarchists.* New York: Grosset & Dunlap.

JONES, ERNEST 1953–1957 *The Life and Work of Sigmund Freud.* New York: Basic Books.

JOOS, MARTIN (1957) 1958 Preface. *Readings in Linguistics: The Development of Descriptive Linguistics in America since 1925.* New York: American Council of Learned Societies.

JUNG, CARL GUSTAV (1916) 1953 *The Structure of the Unconscious.* In volume 7 of *The Collected Works of C. G. Jung.* London: Routledge.

JUNG, CARL GUSTAV (1921) 1971 *Psychological Types.* In volume 6 of *The Collected Works of C. G. Jung.* London: Routledge.

JUNG, CARL GUSTAV (1928) 1953 The Relations between the Ego and the Unconscious. In volume 7 of *The Collected Works of C. G. Jung.* London: Routledge.

JUNG, CARL GUSTAV (1930) 1956 Dream Analysis in Its Practical Application. In *Modern Man in Search of a Soul.* San Diego, Calif.: Harcourt.

JUNG, CARL GUSTAV (1931) 1956 The Aims of Psychotherapy. In *Modern Man in Search of a Soul.* San Diego, Calif.: Harcourt.

JUNG, CARL GUSTAV (1931) 1956 Archaic Man. In *Modern Man in Search of a Soul.* San Diego, Calif.: Harcourt.

JUNG, CARL GUSTAV (1931) 1956 The Basic Postulates of Analytical Psychology. In *Modern Man in Search of a Soul.* San Diego, Calif.: Harcourt.

JUNG, CARL GUSTAV (1931) 1956 A Psychological Theory of Types. In *Modern Man in Search of a Soul.* San Diego, Calif.: Harcourt.

JUNG, CARL GUSTAV (1933) 1964 *The Meaning of Psychology for Modern Man.* In volume 10 of *The Collected Works of C. G. Jung.* London: Routledge.

JUNG, CARL GUSTAV (1961) 1963 *Memories, Dreams, Reflections.* New York: Random House.

KANT, IMMANUEL (1784) 1963 Idea for a Universal History from a Cosmopolitan Point of View. In *On History.* Indianapolis, Ind.: Bobbs-Merrill.

KANT, IMMANUEL (1785) 1909 *Critique of Practical Reason.* In *Critique of Practical Reason and Other Works on the Theory of Ethics.* New York: Longmans.

KANT, IMMANUEL (1785) 1959 *Foundations of the Metaphysics of Morals.* Indianapolis, Ind.: Bobbs-Merrill.

KANT, IMMANUEL (1798) 1964 *Anthropologie in pragmatischer Hinsicht.* In volume 6 of *Werke.* Darmstadt (Germany). Quoted in Lucio Colletti, *From Rousseau to Lenin: Studies in Ideology and Society* (1969) 1972:206–207. New York: Monthly Review Press.

KARDINER, ABRAM 1945 *The Psychological Frontiers of Society.* New York: Columbia Univ. Press.

KARDINER, ABRAM; AND PREBLE, EDWARD 1961 *They Studied Man.* Cleveland, Ohio: World Publishing.

KARR, ALPHONSE (1849) 1853 *Les Guêpes.* Paris: Victor Lecou.

KATZ, DANIEL; AND ALLPORT, FLOYD H. 1952 *Students' Attitudes: A Report of the Syracuse University Reaction Study.* Syracuse, N.Y.: Craftsman Press.

KATZ, ELIHU, AND LAZARSFELD, PAUL F. 1955 *Personal Influence.* New York: Free Press.

KAUDER, EMIL 1968 Böhm-Bawerk, Eugen von. In volume 2 of *International Encyclopedia of the Social Sciences.* New York: Macmillan and Free Press.

KAUTSKY, KARL (1892) 1971 *The Class Struggle (Erfurt Program).* New York: Norton.

KAUTSKY, KARL (1899) 1979 *Bernstein und das sozialdemokratische Programm.* Bonn: J. H. W. Dietz Nachf.

KAUTSKY, KARL 1929 Natur und Gesellschaft. *Die Gesellschaft* 6, no. 2:481–505.

KELSEN, HANS 1945 *General Theory of Law and State.* Cambridge, Mass.: Harvard Univ. Press.

KELVIN, LORD (1883) 1891 Electrical Units of Measurement. In volume 1 of *Popular Lectures and Addresses.* London: Macmillan.

[KENNAN, GEORGE F.] 1947 The Sources of Soviet Conduct. *Foreign Affairs* 25, July:566–582.

KENNAN, GEORGE F. 1954 The Two Planes of International Reality. In *Realities of American Foreign Policy.* Princeton Univ. Press.

KENNAN, GEORGE F. 1961 *Russia and the West under Lenin and Stalin.* Boston: Little, Brown.

KENNAN, GEORGE F. 1977 *The Cloud of Danger: Current Realities of American Foreign Policy.* Boston: Little, Brown.

KENNEDY, ROBERT F. (1968) 1987 Campaign speech. Quoted in E. J. Dionne, Biden Was Accused of Plagiarism in Law School. *The New York Times* 17 September.

KERNER, OTTO 1968 Introduction. In *Report of the National Advisory Commission on Civil Disorders.* Washington, D.C.: The Commission.

KEYFITZ, NATHAN 1987 The Social and Political Context of Population Forecasting. In William Alonso and Paul Starr (editors), *The Politics of Numbers.* New York: Russell Sage Foundation.

KEYNES, JOHN MAYNARD (1919) 1971 *The Economic Consequences of the Peace.* In volume 2 of *The Collected Writings of John Maynard Keynes.* London: Macmillan.

KEYNES, JOHN MAYNARD (1923) 1971 *A Tract on Monetary Reform.* In volume 4 of *The Collected Writings of John Maynard Keynes.* London: Macmillan.

KEYNES, JOHN MAYNARD (1924) 1951 Alfred Marshall: 1842–1924. In *Essays in Biography.* London: Rupert Hart-Davis.

KEYNES, JOHN MAYNARD (1925) 1972 Am I a Liberal? In volume 9 of *The Collected Writings of John Maynard Keynes.* London: Macmillan.

KEYNES, JOHN MAYNARD 1926 *The End of Laissez-Faire.* In *Laissez-Faire and Communism.* New York: New Republic Books.

KEYNES, JOHN MAYNARD (1930) 1972 Economic Possibilities for Our Grandchildren. In volume 9 of *The Collected Writings of John Maynard Keynes.* London: Macmillan.

KEYNES, JOHN MAYNARD (1930) 1971 *A Treatise on Money*. In volume 6 of *The Collected Writings of John Maynard Keynes*. London: Macmillan.

KEYNES, JOHN MAYNARD (1932) 1972 The Consequences to the Banks of the Collapse of Money Values. In volume 9 of *The Collected Writings of John Maynard Keynes*. London: Macmillan.

KEYNES, JOHN MAYNARD (1935) 1982 Letter to George Bernard Shaw, New Year's Day, 1935. In volume 28 of *The Collected Writings of John Maynard Keynes*. London: Macmillan.

KEYNES, JOHN MAYNARD (1936) 1973 *The General Theory of Employment, Interest and Money*. Volume 7 of *The Collected Writings of John Maynard Keynes*. London: Macmillan.

KEYNES, JOHN MAYNARD 1951 William Stanley Jevons. In *Essays in Biography*. New York: Horizon.

KEYNES, JOHN NEVILLE (1891) 1955 *The Scope and Method of Political Economy*. New York: Kelley & Millman.

KIERKEGAARD, SØREN (1841) 1971 *The Concept of Irony with Constant Reference to Socrates*. Bloomington: Indiana Univ. Press.

KING, MARTIN LUTHER, JR. (1959) 1986 The Social Organization of Nonviolence. In *A Testament of Hope: The Essential Writings of Martin Luther King, Jr.* New York: Harper.

KING, MARTIN LUTHER, JR. (1961) 1986 The Time for Freedom Has Come. In *A Testament of Hope: The Essential Writings of Martin Luther King, Jr.* New York: Harper.

KING, MARTIN LUTHER, JR. (1962) 1986 The Case against "Tokenism." In *A Testament of Hope: The Essential Writings of Martin Luther King, Jr.* New York: Harper.

KING, MARTIN LUTHER, JR. (1963) 1986 I Have a Dream. In *A Testament of Hope: The Essential Writings of Martin Luther King, Jr.* New York: Harper.

KING, MARTIN LUTHER, JR. (1963) 1986 The Strength to Love. In *A Testament of Hope: The Essential Writings of Martin Luther King, Jr.* New York: Harper.

KLEIN, MELANIE (1930) 1948 The Importance of Symbol-formation in the Development of the Ego. In *Contributions to Psycho-Analysis: 1921–1945*. London: Hogarth.

KLUCKHOHN, CLYDE 1944 *Navaho Witchcraft*. Cambridge, Mass.: Peabody Museum.

KLUCKHOHN, CLYDE; AND MURRAY, HENRY A. (1944) 1967 Personality Formation. In *Personality in Nature, Society, and Culture*. New York: Knopf.

KNIGHT, FRANK H. (1921) 1971 *Risk, Uncertainty and Profit*. Univ. of Chicago Press.

KNIGHT, FRANK H. (1922) 1935 Ethics and the Economic Interpretation. In *The Ethics of Competition and Other Essays*. New York: Harper.

KNIGHT, FRANK H. (1923) 1935 The Ethics of Competition. In *The Ethics of Competition and Other Essays*. London: Allen & Unwin.

KNIGHT, FRANK H. 1932 The Newer Economics and the Control of Economic Activity. *Journal of Political Economy* 40:433–476.

KNIGHT, FRANK H. (1939) 1947 Ethics and Economic Reform. In *Freedom and Reform: Essays in Economics and Social Philosophy*. New York: Harper.

KNIGHT, FRANK H. (1940) 1956 "What is Truth" in Economics? In *On the History and Method of Economics: Selected Essays*. Univ. of Chicago Press.

KNIGHT, FRANK H. (1951) 1956 The Role of Principles in Economics and Politics. In *On the History and Method of Economics: Selected Essays*. Univ. of Chicago Press.

KNIGHT, FRANK H. 1960 *Intelligence and Democratic Action*. Cambridge, Mass.: Harvard Univ. Press.

KOESTLER, ARTHUR (1940) 1941 *Darkness at Noon*. New York: Macmillan.

KOFFKA, KURT 1931 Gestalt. In volume 6 of *Encyclopaedia of the Social Sciences*. New York: Macmillan.

KOFFKA, KURT 1935 *Principles of Gestalt Psychology*. San Diego, Calif.: Harcourt.

KÖHLER, WOLFGANG (1917) 1925 *The Mentality of Apes*. London: Kegan Paul.

KÖHLER, WOLFGANG 1929 *Gestalt Psychology*. New York: Liveright.

KÖHLER, WOLFGANG 1938 *The Place of Value in a World of Facts*. New York: Liveright.

KÖHLER, WOLFGANG 1940 *Dynamics in Psychology*. New York: Liveright.

KOLAKOWSKI, LESZEK 1961 *Der Mensch ohne Alternative*. Quoted in Albert O. Hirschman, *Development Projects Observed* 1967:32. Washington, D.C.: The Brookings Institution.

KOLAKOWSKI, LESZEK (1966) 1972 *Positivist Philosophy: From Hume to the Vienna Circle*. London: Penguin.

KOMAROVSKY, MIRRA 1953 *Women in the Modern World: Their Education and Their Dilemmas*. Boston: Little, Brown.

KOMAROVSKY, MIRRA 1965 *Women in College: Shaping New Feminine Identities*. New York: Basic Books.

KONDRATIEFF, N. D. (1925) 1935 The Long Waves in Economic Life. *The Review of Economic Statistics* 17, no. 6:105–115.

KOYRÉ, ALEXANDRE 1943 Galileo and Plato. *Journal of the History of Ideas* 4:400–427.

KOYRÉ, ALEXANDRE (1950) 1965 The Significance of the Newtonian Synthesis. In *Newtonian Studies*. Cambridge, Mass.: Harvard Univ. Press.

KOYRÉ, ALEXANDRE (1957) 1958 *From the Closed World to the Infinite Universe*. New York: Harper.

KRACAUER, SIEGFRIED 1969 *History: The Last Things before the Last*. Oxford Univ. Press.

KROEBER, ALFRED L. (1917) 1952 The Superorganic. In *The Nature of Culture*. Univ. of Chicago Press.

KROEBER, ALFRED L. (1923) 1948 *Anthropology: Race, Language, Culture, Psychology, Prehistory*. New York: Harcourt.

KROEBER, ALFRED L. (1928) 1931 Sub-human Culture Beginnings. In A. L. Kroeber and T. T. Waterman, *Source Book in Anthropology*. San Diego, Calif.: Harcourt.

KROEBER, ALFRED L. 1944 *Configurations of Culture Growth*. Berkeley and Los Angeles: Univ. of California Press.

KROEBER, ALFRED L. 1953 Introduction. *Anthropology Today: An Encyclopedic Inventory*. Univ. of Chicago Press.

KROEBER, ALFRED L. 1957 *Style and Civilizations*. Ithaca, N.Y.:Cornell Univ. Press.

KROEBER, ALFRED L.; AND KLUCKHOHN, CLYDE 1952 *Culture: A Critical Review of Concepts and Definitions*. Cambridge, Mass.: Peabody Museum.

KROPOTKIN, P'ETR (1902) 1972 *Mutual Aid: A Factor of Evolution*. New York Univ. Press.

KRUSKAL, WILLIAM H. 1988 The n Cultures. Bureau of the Census, Fourth Annual Research Conference, *Proceedings*. Washington, D.C.: Bureau of the Census.

KRUSKAL, WILLIAM H.; AND MOSTELLER, FREDERICK 1979 Representative Sampling, II: Scientific Literature, Excluding Statistics. *International Statistical Review* 47:111–127.

KUHN, THOMAS S. (1962) 1970 *The Structure of Scientific Revolutions.* Univ. of Chicago Press.

KUHN, THOMAS S. 1977 *The Essential Tension: Selected Studies in Scientific Tradition and Change.* Univ. of Chicago Press.

LACAN, JACQUES (1966) 1977 *Écrits: A Selection.* New York: Norton.

LAMPRECHT, KARL 1906 Historical Development and Present Character of the Science of History. In volume 2 of Howard J. Rogers (editor), *Congress of Arts and Science: Universal Exposition; St. Louis, 1904.* Boston: Houghton Mifflin.

LANGE, OSKAR 1934–1935 Marxian Economics and Modern Economic Theory. *Review of Economic Studies* 2:189–201.

LANGE, OSKAR (1936–1937) 1938 On the Economic Theory of Socialism. In Oskar Lange and F. M. Taylor, *On the Economic Theory of Socialism.* Minneapolis: Univ. of Minnesota Press.

LANGE, OSKAR (1959) 1963 *Political Economy.* New York: Macmillan.

LANGER, SUSANNE K. (1956) 1962 The Growing Center of Knowledge. In *Philosophical Sketches.* Baltimore, Md.: Johns Hopkins Univ. Press.

LAPLACE, PIERRE SIMON DE (1814) 1951 *A Philosophical Essay on Probabilities.* New York: Dover.

LAPLACE, PIERRE SIMON DE (1814) 1986 *Essai philosophique sur les probabilités.* Paris: Christian Bourgois.

LA ROCHEFOUCAULD, FRANÇOIS DE (1665) 1959 Maxim No. 436. In *The Maxims of La Rochefoucauld.* New York: Random House.

LASHLEY, KARL S. 1951 The Problem of Serial Order in Behavior. In *Cerebral Mechanisms in Behavior: The Hixon Symposium.* New York: Wiley.

LASKI, HAROLD J. (1918) 1968 The Problem of Administrative Areas. In *The Foundations of Sovereignty and Other Essays.* Freeport, N.Y.: Books for Libraries Press.

LASKI, HAROLD J. 1919 *Authority in the Modern State.* New Haven, Conn.: Yale Univ. Press.

LASKI, HAROLD J. 1919 Introduction to Leon Duguit, *Law in the Modern State* (1913). New York: B. W. Huebsch.

LASKI, HAROLD J. (1925) 1938 *A Grammar of Politics.* London: Allen & Unwin.

LASKI, HAROLD J. 1933 Liberty. In volume 9 of *Encyclopaedia of the Social Sciences.* New York: Macmillan.

LASLETT, PETER (1965) 1973 *The World We Have Lost.* New York: Scribner.

LASLETT, PETER 1983 *The World We Have Lost Further Explored.* London: Methuen.

LASSALLE, FERDINAND 1859 *Franz von Sickingen: Eine historische Tragödie.* Berlin: Franz Duncker.

LASSALLE, FERDINAND (1862) 1879 *Open Letter to the National Labor Association of Germany.* Cincinnati, Ohio: National Executive Committee of the Socialistic Labor Party.

LASSWELL, HAROLD D. (1930) 1960 *Psychopathology and Politics.* New York: Viking.

LASSWELL, HAROLD D. (1935) 1950 *World Politics and Personal Insecurity.* New York: Free Press.

LASSWELL, HAROLD D. (1936) 1951 *Politics: Who Gets What, When, How.* In *The Political Writings of Harold D. Lasswell.* New York: Free Press.

LASSWELL, HAROLD D. (1948) 1964 The Structure and Function of Communication in Society. In Lyman Bryson (editor), *The Communication of Ideas: A Series of Addresses.* New York: Cooper Square Publishers.

LASSWELL, HAROLD D. 1949 The Language of Power. In Harold D. Lasswell and Nathan Leites (editors), *Language of Politics: Studies in Quantitative Semantics.* New York: Stewart.

LASSWELL, HAROLD D. 1963 *The Future of Political Science.* New York: Atherton.

LASSWELL, HAROLD D.; AND KAPLAN, ABRAHAM 1950 *Power and Society*. New Haven, Conn.: Yale Univ. Press.

LAW, JOHN (1705) 1720 *Money and Trade Consider'd: With a Proposal for Supplying the Nation with Money*. London: W. Lewis.

LAZARSFELD, PAUL F. ET AL. (1944) 1948 *The People's Choice: How the Voter Makes Up His Mind in a Presidential Campaign*. New York: Columbia Univ. Press.

LAZARSFELD, PAUL F. (1959) 1982 Problems in Methodology. In *The Varied Sociology of Paul F. Lazarsfeld*. New York: Columbia Univ. Press.

LAZARSFELD, PAUL F. (1961) 1972 The Mass Media and the Intellectual Community. In *Qualitative Analysis: Historical and Critical Essays*. Boston: Allyn and Bacon.

LAZARSFELD, PAUL F. (1962) 1972 Philosophy of Science and Empirical Social Research. In *Qualitative Analysis: Historical and Critical Essays*. Boston: Allyn and Bacon.

LAZARSFELD, PAUL F. (1964) 1972 The Obligations of the 1950 Pollster to the 1984 Historian. In *Qualitative Analysis: Historical and Critical Essays*. Boston: Allyn and Bacon.

LAZARSFELD, PAUL F. (1968) 1982 An Episode in the History of Social Research: A Memoir. In *The Varied Sociology of Paul F. Lazarsfeld*. New York: Columbia Univ. Press.

LAZARSFELD, PAUL F. 1976 Interview with Paul Lazarsfeld. *Kölner Zeitschrift für Soziologie und Sozialpsychologie* 4:794–802. Quoted in Michael Pollak, Paul F. Lazarsfeld: A Sociointellectual Biography. *Knowledge: Creation, Diffusion, Utilization* 1980:Vol. 2, no. 2, 164.

LAZARSFELD, PAUL F.; AND ROSENBERG, MORRIS 1955 General Introduction. *The Language of Social Research: A Reader in the Methodology of Social Research*. New York: Free Press.

LAZARSFELD, PAUL F.; AND THIELENS, WAGNER, JR. 1958 *The Academic Mind: Social Scientists in a Time of Crisis*. New York: Free Press.

LEACH, EDMUND R. (1957) 1970 The Epistemological Background to Malinowski's Empiricism. In *Man and Culture: An Evaluation of the Work of Bronislaw Malinowski*. London: Routledge.

LEACH, EDMUND R. (1961) 1968 *Pul Eliya: A Village in Ceylon*. Cambridge Univ. Press.

LEACH, EDMUND R. 1961 Time and False Noses. In *Rethinking Anthropology*. London: Athlone Press.

LEACH, EDMUND R. 1965 Culture and Social Cohesion: An Anthropologist's View. In *Science and Culture: A Study of Cohesive and Disjunctive Forces*. Boston: Houghton Mifflin.

LEACH, EDMUND R. 1982 *Social Anthropology*. Oxford Univ. Press.

LE BON, GUSTAVE (1895) 1979 *The Crowd*. In *Gustave Le Bon: The Man and His Works*. Indianapolis, Ind.: Liberty Fund.

LENIN, V. I. (1902) 1961 *What Is to Be Done?* In volume 5 of *V. I. Lenin: Collected Works*. Moscow: Progress Publishers.

LENIN, V. I. (1916) 1964 *Imperialism, the Highest Stage of Capitalism: A Popular Outline*. In volume 22 of *V. I. Lenin: Collected Works*. Moscow: Progress Publishers.

LENIN, V. I. (1918) 1937 Report Delivered to the Seventh Congress of the Russian Communist Party (Bolsheviks), 7 March 1918. In volume 7 of *V. I. Lenin: Selected Works*. New York: International Publishers.

LENIN, V. I. (1920) 1966 Report on the Work of the Council of People's Commissars, 22 December 1920. In volume 31 of *V. I. Lenin: Collected Works*. Moscow: Progress Publishers.

LEONTIEF, WASSILY (1954) 1985 Gibbs and Mathematical Economics. In *Essays in Economics: Theories, Theorizing, Facts, and Policies*. New Brunswick, N.J.: Transaction Books.

LEONTIEF, WASSILY 1971 Theoretical Assumptions and Nonobserved Facts. *American Economic Review* 61:1–7.

LEONTIEF, WASSILY 1977 Natural Resources, Environmental Disruption, and Growth Prospects of the Developed and Less Developed Countries. The American Academy of Arts and Sciences, *Bulletin* 30, no. 8:20–30.

LE PLAY, FRÉDÉRIC (1855) 1877–1879 *Les ouvriers européens*. Quoted in Catherine Bodard Silver, *Frédéric Le Play on Family, Work, and Social Change* 1982:68. Univ. of Chicago Press.

LERNER, MAX 1950 Introduction to Niccolò Machiavelli, *The Prince*. New York: Modern Library.

LEVI, PRIMO (1985) 1989 The Moon and Us. In *Other People's Trades*. New York: Summit Books.

LEVINE, DONALD N. 1985 *The Flight from Ambiguity*. Univ. of Chicago Press.

LÉVI-STRAUSS, CLAUDE 1945 French Sociology. In Georges Gurvitch and Wilbert E. Moore (editors), *Twentieth Century Sociology*. New York: Philosophical Library.

LÉVI-STRAUSS, CLAUDE 1953 Discussion. In Sol Tax et al. (editors), *An Appraisal of* Anthropology Today. Univ. of Chicago Press.

LÉVI-STRAUSS, CLAUDE (1955) 1974 *Tristes tropiques*. New York: Atheneum.

LÉVI-STRAUSS, CLAUDE (1958) 1967 *Structural Anthropology*. New York: Doubleday.

LÉVI-STRAUSS, CLAUDE (1959) 1969 Culture and Language. In G. Charbonnier, *Conversations with Claude Lévi-Strauss*. London: Jonathan Cape.

LÉVI-STRAUSS, CLAUDE (1964) 1983 *The Raw and the Cooked*. Univ. of Chicago Press.

LÉVI-STRAUSS, CLAUDE 1966 Anthropology: Its Achievements and Future. *Current Anthropology* 7:124–127.

LÉVY-BRUHL, LUCIEN (1927) 1966 *The "Soul" of the Primitive*. New York: Praeger.

LÉVY-BRUHL, LUCIEN (1949) 1975 *The Notebooks on Primitive Mentality*. Oxford (United Kingdom): Basil Blackwell.

LEWIN, KURT (1936) 1948 Some Social-psychological Differences between the United States and Germany. In *Resolving Social Conflicts: Selected Papers on Group Dynamics*. New York: Harper.

LEWIN, KURT (1939) 1976 Field Theory and Experiment in Social Psychology. In *Field Theory in Social Science*. Univ. of Chicago Press.

LEWIN, KURT (1946) 1976 Behavior and Development as a Function of the Total Situation. In *Field Theory in Social Science: Selected Theoretical Papers*. Univ. of Chicago Press.

LEWIN, KURT 1947 Group Decision and Social Change. In T. M. Newcomb and E. L. Hartley (editors), *Readings in Social Psychology*. New York: Holt.

LEWIS, OSCAR 1958 The Culture of the Vecindad in Mexico City. *Actas de XXXIII Congreso Internacional de Americanistas*:387–402. Quoted in Douglas Butterworth, Obituary: Oscar Lewis. *American Anthropologist* 1972:Vol. 74, 750.

LEWIS, OSCAR 1961 *The Children of Sanchez: Autobiography of a Mexican Family*. New York: Random House.

LINCOLN, ABRAHAM (1858?) 1989 Speech on Slavery and Democracy. In *Abraham Lincoln: Speeches and Writings; 1832–1858*. New York: Library of America.

LINCOLN, ABRAHAM (1861) 1989 First Inaugural Address, 4 March 1861. In *Abraham Lincoln: Speeches and Writings; 1859–1865*. New York: Library of America.

LINCOLN, ABRAHAM (1862) 1989 Annual Message to Congress, 1 December 1862. In *Abraham Lincoln: Speeches and Writings; 1859–1865*. New York: Library of America.

LINDBLOM, CHARLES E. 1979 Still Muddling, Not Yet Through. *Public Administration Review* November/December:517–526.

LINDZEY, GARDNER 1967 Some Remarks Concerning Incest, the Incest Taboo, and Psychoanalytic Theory. *American Psychologist* 22, no. 12:1051–1059.

LINTON, RALPH (1936) 1964 *The Study of Man: An Introduction*. New York: Appleton.

LINTON, RALPH (1937) 1971 One Hundred Per Cent American. Quoted in Adelin Linton and Charles Wagley, *Ralph Linton* 1971:35–36. New York: Columbia Univ. Press.

LINTON, RALPH 1945 *The Cultural Background of Personality*. New York: Appleton.

LIPPMANN, WALTER 1913 *A Preface to Politics*. New York: Kennerley.

LIPPMANN, WALTER 1920 *Liberty and the News*. San Diego, Calif.: Harcourt.

LIPPMANN, WALTER (1922) 1965 *Public Opinion*. New York: Free Press.

LIPPMANN, WALTER 1943 *U.S. Foreign Policy: Shield of the Republic*. Boston: Little, Brown.

LIPSET, SEYMOUR MARTIN ET AL. 1956 *Union Democracy: The Internal Politics of the International Typographical Union*. New York: Free Press.

LIPSET, SEYMOUR MARTIN (1960) 1981 The Sociology of Politics. In *Political Man: The Social Bases of Politics*. Baltimore, Md.: Johns Hopkins Univ. Press.

LIPSET, SEYMOUR MARTIN (1963) 1979 *The First New Nation: The United States in Historical and Comparative Perspective*. New York: Norton.

LIST, FRIEDRICH (1841) 1966 *The National System of Political Economy*. Fairfield, N.J.: Augustus M. Kelley.

LLEWELLYN, KARL N. 1934 The Constitution as an Institution. *Columbia Law Review* 34, no. 1:1–40.

LLOYD, WILLIAM FORSTER (1837) 1968 Two Lectures on the Checks to Population. In *Lectures on Population, Value, Poor-Laws and Rent*. New York: Augustus M. Kelley.

LOCKE, JOHN (1689) 1963 *A Letter Concerning Toleration*. The Hague: Martinus Nijhoff.

LOCKE, JOHN (1690) 1959 *An Essay Concerning Human Understanding*. New York: Dover.

LOCKE, JOHN (1690) 1965 *Two Treatises of Government*. New York: New American Library.

LOEB, JACQUES 1912 The Significance of Tropisms for Psychology. In *The Mechanistic Conception of Life*. Univ. of Chicago Press.

LOVEJOY, ARTHUR O. (1936) 1960 *The Great Chain of Being: A Study of the History of an Idea*. New York: Harper.

LOWENTHAL, LEO (1944) 1984 The Triumph of Mass Idols. In *Literature and Mass Culture*. New Brunswick, N.J.: Transaction Books.

LOWENTHAL, LEO (1948) 1984 On Sociology of Literature. In *Literature and Mass Culture*. New Brunswick, N.J.: Transaction Books.

LOWENTHAL, LEO (1950) 1984 Historical Perspectives of Popular Culture. In *Literature and Mass Culture*. New Brunswick, N.J.: Transaction Books.

LOWENTHAL, LEO 1986 Social Meanings in Literature. In *Literature and the Image of Man*. New Brunswick, N.J.: Transaction Books.

LOWIE, ROBERT H. (1920) 1961 *Primitive Society*. New York: Harper.

LOWIE, ROBERT H. (1927) 1962 *The Origin of the State*. New York: Russell & Russell.

LOWIE, ROBERT H. (1934) 1940 *An Introduction to Cultural Anthropology*. New York: Farrar & Rinehart.

LUCIAN 1905 The Way to Write History. In volume 2 of *The Works of Lucian of Samosata*. Oxford Univ. Press.

LUHMANN, NIKLAS (1975) 1982 World-Time and System History. In *The Differentiation of Society.* New York: Columbia Univ. Press.

LUHMANN, NIKLAS (1976) 1982 The Future Cannot Begin. In *The Differentiation of Society.* New York: Columbia Univ. Press.

LUHMANN, NIKLAS (1977) 1982 The Differentiation of Society. In *The Differentiation of Society.* New York: Columbia Univ. Press.

LUHMANN, NIKLAS (1986) 1989 *Ecological Communication.* Univ. of Chicago Press.

LUHMANN, NIKLAS 1986 Preface to the English edition of *Love as Passion: The Codification of Intimacy* (1982). Cambridge (United Kingdom): Polity Press.

LUKÁCS, GYÖRGY (1923) 1971 *History and Class Consciousness: Studies in Marxist Dialectics.* Cambridge, Mass.: M.I.T. Press.

LUXEMBURG, ROSA (1899) 1971 Social Reform or Revolution. In *Selected Political Writings of Rosa Luxemburg.* New York: Monthly Review Press.

LUXEMBURG, ROSA (1904) 1961 *Leninism or Marxism?* In *The Russian Revolution* and *Leninism or Marxism?* Ann Arbor: Univ. of Michigan Press.

LUXEMBURG, ROSA (1906) 1971 *The Mass Strike.* New York: Harper.

LUXEMBURG, ROSA (1913) 1968 *The Accumulation of Capital.* New York: Modern Reader.

LYND, ROBERT S. (1939) 1946 *Knowledge for What? The Place of Social Science in American Culture.* Princeton Univ. Press.

LYND, ROBERT S.; AND LYND, HELEN MERRELL 1929 *Middletown: A Study in American Culture.* San Diego, Calif.: Harcourt.

LYND, ROBERT S.; AND LYND, HELEN MERRELL (1937) 1965 *Middletown in Transition: A Study in Cultural Conflicts.* San Diego, Calif.: Harcourt.

LYOTARD, JEAN FRANÇOIS (1982) 1984 What Is Postmodernism? In *The Postmodern Condition: A Report on Knowledge.* Minneapolis: Univ. of Minnesota Press.

MACAULAY, THOMAS BABINGTON (1824) 1843 On Mitford's History of Greece. In volume 3 of *Critical and Miscellaneous Essays.* Philadelphia, Pa.: Carey and Hart.

MACAULAY, THOMAS BABINGTON (1825) 1843 Milton. In volume 1 of *Critical and Miscellaneous Essays.* Philadelphia, Pa.: Carey and Hart.

MACAULAY, THOMAS BABINGTON (1827) 1843 Machiavelli. In volume 3 of *Critical and Miscellaneous Essays.* Philadelphia, Pa.: Carey and Hart.

MACAULAY, THOMAS BABINGTON (1828) 1843 History. In volume 1 of *Critical and Miscellaneous Essays.* Philadelphia, Pa.: Carey and Hart.

MACAULAY, THOMAS BABINGTON (1828) 1880 Review of *The Poetical Works of John Dryden.* In volume 1 of *Miscellaneous Works of Lord Macaulay.* New York: Harper.

MACAULAY, THOMAS BABINGTON (1829) 1844 Mill's *Essay on Government.* In volume 5 of *Critical and Miscellaneous Essays.* Philadelphia, Pa.: Carey and Hart.

MACAULAY, THOMAS BABINGTON (1830) 1843 Southey's Colloquies on Society. In volume 1 of *Critical and Miscellaneous Essays.* Philadelphia, Pa.: Carey and Hart.

MACAULAY, THOMAS BABINGTON (1831) 1898 Speech Delivered in the House of Commons, 2 March 1831. In volume 1 of *The Works of Lord Macaulay: Speeches, Poems, & Miscellaneous Writings.* London: Longmans.

MACAULAY, THOMAS BABINGTON (1840) 1843 Ranke's *History of the Popes.* In volume 1 of *Critical and Miscellaneous Essays.* Philadelphia, Pa.: Carey and Hart.

MACAULAY, THOMAS BABINGTON (1848) 1901 *The History of England: From the Accession of James the Second.* Boston: Houghton Mifflin.

MCDOUGALL, WILLIAM (1908) 1928 *An Introduction to Social Psychology.* London: Methuen.

McDougall, William 1912 *Psychology: The Study of Behaviour*. New York: Holt.

McGahey, Richard 1982 Poverty's Voguish Stigma. *The New York Times* 12 March.

Machiavelli, Niccolò (1513) 1961 Letter to Francesco Vettori, 10 December 1513. In *The Letters of Machiavelli: A Selection of His Letters*. New York: Capricorn Books.

Machiavelli, Niccolò (1532) 1974 *The Discourses*. Harmondsworth (United Kingdom): Penguin.

Machiavelli, Niccolò (1532) 1977 *The Prince*. New York: Norton.

MacIver, Robert M. (1917) 1924 *Community: A Sociological Study*. London: Macmillan.

MacIver, Robert M. (1921) 1931 *The Elements of Social Science*. London: Methuen.

MacIver, Robert M. (1947) 1965 *The Web of Government*. New York: Free Press.

MacIver, Robert M. 1950 *The Ramparts We Guard*. New York: Macmillan.

Mackinder, Halford (1919) 1942 *Democratic Ideals and Reality: A Study in the Politics of Reconstruction*. New York: Holt.

Macleod, Henry Dunning 1858 *The Elements of Political Economy*. London: Longmans.

McLuhan, Marshall 1964 *Understanding Media: The Extensions of Man*. New York: McGraw-Hill.

McLuhan, Marshall; and Fiore, Quentin 1967 *The Medium Is the Massage: An Inventory of Effects*. New York: Bantam Books.

McNeill, William H. 1986 Mythistory, or Truth, Myth, History, and Historians. *American Historical Review* 91:1–10.

Madison, James (1787) 1961 No. 10. *The Federalist Papers*. New York: New American Library.

Madison, James (1788) 1961 No. 47. *The Federalist Papers*. New York: New American Library.

Madison, James (1788) 1961 No. 49. *The Federalist Papers*. New York: New American Library.

Madison, James (1788) 1961 No. 51. *The Federalist Papers*. New York: New American Library.

Madison, James (1792) 1906 Parties. In volume 6 of *The Writings of James Madison*. New York: Putnam.

Madison, James (1798) 1906 Letter to Thomas Jefferson, 2 April 1798. In volume 6 of *The Writings of James Madison*. New York: Putnam.

Mahan, Alfred Thayer (1890) 1918 *The Influence of Sea Power upon History: 1660–1783*. Boston: Little, Brown.

Maine, Henry Sumner (1861) 1917 *Ancient Law*. London: Dent.

Maine, Henry Sumner (1871) 1880 *Village Communities in the East and West*. New York: Holt.

Maine, Henry Sumner 1875 *Lectures on the Early History of Institutions*. New York: Holt.

Maine, Henry Sumner (1885) 1918 Prospects of Popular Government. In *Popular Government: Four Essays*. London: Murray.

Maitland, Frederic William (1911) 1968 The Body Politic. In *Frederic William Maitland: Selected Essays*. Freeport, N.Y.: Books for Libraries Press.

Maitland, James 1804 *An Inquiry into the Nature and Origin of Public Wealth*. Edinburgh: Constable.

Malinowski, Bronislaw (1916) 1954 Baloma: The Spirits of the Dead in the Trobriand Islands. In *Magic, Science and Religion and Other Essays*. New York: Doubleday.

Malinowski, Bronislaw (1922) 1961 *Argonauts of the Western Pacific: An Account of Native Enterprise and Adventure in the Archipelagoes of Melanesian New Guinea.* New York: Dutton.

Malinowski, Bronislaw (1923) 1953 The Problem of Meaning in Primitive Languages. In C. K. Ogden and I. A. Richards, *The Meaning of Meaning: A Study of the Influence of Language upon Thought and of the Science of Symbolism.* San Diego, Calif.: Harcourt.

Malinowski, Bronislaw (1925) 1954 Magic, Science and Religion. In *Magic, Science and Religion and Other Essays.* New York: Doubleday.

Malinowski, Bronislaw 1926 Anthropology. In volume 29 of Encyclopaedia Britannica. Chicago: Encyclopaedia Britannica.

Malinowski, Bronislaw (1926) 1951 *Crime and Custom in Savage Society.* London: Routledge.

Malinowski, Bronislaw (1926) 1971 *Myth in Primitive Psychology.* Westport, Conn.: Greenwood.

Malinowski, Bronislaw (1929) 1932 *The Sexual Life of Savages in North-Western Melanesia.* London: Routledge. Quoted in Ashley Montagu (editor), *Frontiers of Anthropology* 1974:476. New York: Putnam.

Malinowski, Bronislaw 1931 Culture. In volume 4 of *Encyclopaedia of the Social Sciences.* New York: Macmillan.

Malinowski, Bronislaw 1939 The Group and the Individual in Functional Analysis. *American Journal of Sociology* 44:938–964.

Malthus, Thomas Robert (1798) 1970 *An Essay on the Principle of Population.* In *An Essay on the Principle of Population* and *A Summary View of the Principle of Population.* New York: Penguin.

Malthus, Thomas Robert 1814 *Observations on the Effects of the Corn Laws and of a Rise or Fall in the Price of Corn on the Agriculture and General Wealth of the Country.* London: J. Johnson.

Malthus, Thomas Robert (1830) 1970 *A Summary View of the Principle of Population.* In *An Essay on the Principle of Population* and *A Summary View of the Principle of Population.* New York: Penguin.

Mandeville, Bernard (1705) 1924 The Grumbling Hive: Or, Knaves Turn'd Honest. In volume 1 of *The Fable of the Bees: Or, Private Vices, Publick Benefits.* Oxford Univ. Press.

Mandeville, Bernard (1714–1729) 1924 *The Fable of the Bees: Or, Private Vices, Publick Benefits.* 2 vols. Oxford Univ. Press.

Mandeville, Bernard (1723) 1924 A Vindication of the Book. In *The Fable of the Bees: Or, Private Vices, Publick Benefits.* Oxford Univ. Press.

Mandler, George; and Kessen, William 1959 *The Language of Psychology.* New York: Wiley.

Mannes, Marya 1963 The Problems of Creative Women. In Seymour M. Farber and Roger H. L. Wilson (editors), *The Potential of Woman.* New York: McGraw-Hill.

Mannheim, Karl (1927) 1952 The Problem of Generations. In *Essays on the Sociology of Knowledge.* Oxford Univ. Press.

Mannheim, Karl (1929–1931) 1946 *Ideology and Utopia: An Introduction to the Sociology of Knowledge.* San Diego, Calif.: Harcourt.

Mannheim, Karl 1952 Competition as a Cultural Phenomenon. In *Essays on the Sociology of Knowledge.* London: Routledge.

Manuel, Frank E. (1962) 1965 *The Prophets of Paris.* New York: Harper.

Manuel, Frank E.; and Manuel, Fritzie P. 1979 *Utopian Thought in the Western World.* Cambridge, Mass.: Harvard Univ. Press.

Mao Zedong 1967 *Quotations from Chairman Mao Tse-Tung.* New York: Bantam Books.

Marcuse, Herbert (1955) 1966 *Eros and Civilization: A Philosophical Inquiry into Freud.* Boston: Beacon Press.

MARCUSE, HERBERT (1964) 1966 *One-Dimensional Man: Studies in the Ideology of Advanced Industrial Society*. Boston: Beacon.

MARCUSE, HERBERT 1969 *An Essay on Liberation*. Boston: Beacon.

MARETT, ROBERT RANULPH 1912 *Anthropology*. New York: Holt.

MARSHALL, ALFRED (1885) 1956 The Present Position of Economics. In *Memorials of Alfred Marshall*. New York: Kelley & Millman.

MARSHALL, ALFRED (1890) 1961 *Principles of Economics*. New York: Macmillan.

MARSHALL, ALFRED (1906) 1956 Letter to A. L. Bowley, 27 February 1906. In *Memorials of Alfred Marshall*. New York: Kelley & Millman.

MARSHALL, ALFRED 1907 The Social Possibilities of Economic Chivalry. *Economic Journal* 17, no. 65:7–29.

MARSHALL, ALFRED (1923) 1960 *Money, Credit & Commerce*. Fairfield, N.J.: Augustus M. Kelley.

MARSHALL, ALFRED 1956 Undated Fragment. In *Memorials of Alfred Marshall*. New York: Kelley & Millman.

MARSHALL, T. H. (1946) 1964 Sociology at the Crossroads. In *Class, Citizenship, and Social Development*. New York: Doubleday.

MARSHALL, T. H. (1950) 1964 Citizenship and Social Class. In *Class, Citizenship, and Social Development*. New York: Doubleday.

MARSILIUS OF PADUA (1324) 1980 *Defensor pacis*. Univ. of Toronto Press.

MARTINEAU, HARRIET 1837 *Society in America*. New York: Saunders and Otley.

MARTINEAU, HARRIET 1838 *How to Observe: Morals and Manners*. Philadelphia, Pa.: Lea & Blanchard.

MARX, KARL (1844) 1975 *Contribution to the Critique of Hegel's Philosophy of Law*. In volume 3 of *Karl Marx and Frederick Engels: Collected Works*. New York: International Publishers.

MARX, KARL (1844) 1975 *Economic and Philosophic Manuscripts of 1844*. In volume 3 of *Karl Marx and Frederick Engels: Collected Works*. New York: International Publishers.

MARX, KARL (1845) 1976 Theses on Feuerbach. In volume 5 of *Karl Marx and Frederick Engels: Collected Works*. New York: International Publishers.

MARX, KARL (1852) 1963 *The Eighteenth Brumaire of Louis Bonaparte*. New York: International Publishers.

MARX, KARL (1852) 1983 Letter to Joseph Weydemeyer, 5 March 1852. In volume 39 of *Karl Marx and Frederick Engels: Collected Works*. London: Lawrence and Wishart.

MARX, KARL (1857–1858) 1971 *The Grundrisse*. New York: Harper.

MARX, KARL (1859) 1970 *A Contribution to the Critique of Political Economy*. New York: International Publishers.

MARX, KARL (1862) 1985 Letter to Friedrich Engels, 18 June 1862. In volume 41 of *Karl Marx and Frederick Engels: Collected Works*. London: Lawrence and Wishart.

MARX, KARL (1867) 1967 *Capital: A Critique of Political Economy*. New York: International Publishers.

MARX, KARL (1875) 1938 *Critique of the Gotha Programme*. New York: International Publishers.

MARX, KARL; AND ENGELS, FRIEDRICH (1845) 1975 *The Holy Family: Or Critique of Critical Criticism*. In volume 4 of *Karl Marx and Frederick Engels: Collected Works*. New York: International Publishers.

MARX, KARL; AND ENGELS, FRIEDRICH (1845–1846) 1976 *The German Ideology*. In volume 5 of *Karl Marx and Frederick Engels: Collected Works*. New York: International Publishers.

MARX, KARL; AND ENGELS, FRIEDRICH (1848) 1964 *The Communist Manifesto*. New York: Modern Reader.

MASLOW, ABRAHAM H. 1954 *Motivation and Personality.* New York: Harper.

MAUSS, MARCEL 1902 L'enseignment de l'histoire des religions des peuples non-civilises à l'École des Hautes Études. *Revue de l'histoire des religions* 45:36–55. Quoted in Seth Leacock, The Ethnological Theory of Marcel Mauss. *American Anthropologist* 1954:Vol. 56, 60.

MAUSS, MARCEL 1923 On Language and Primitive Forms of Classification [Discussion]. *Journal de psychologie: Normale et pathologique* 20:944–947. Quoted in Dell Hymes, *Language in Culture and Society: A Reader in Linguistics and Anthropology* 1964:125. New York: Harper.

MAUSS, MARCEL (1925) 1967 *The Gift: Forms and Functions of Exchange in Archaic Societies.* New York: Norton.

MAY, ROLLO 1953 *Man's Search for Himself.* New York: Norton.

MAYO, ELTON (1933) 1946 *The Human Problems of an Industrial Civilization.* Cambridge, Mass.: Harvard Univ. Press.

MAYO, ELTON 1945 *The Social Problems of an Industrial Civilization.* Boston: Graduate School of Business Administration, Harvard Univ.

MAYR, ERNST 1959 Darwin and the Evolutionary Theory in Biology. In Betty J. Meggers (editor), *Evolution and Anthropology: A Centennial Appraisal.* Washington, D.C.: The Anthropological Society of Washington.

MAYR, ERNST 1964 Introduction to Charles Darwin, *On the Origin of Species.* Cambridge, Mass.: Harvard Univ. Press.

MAYR, ERNST 1982 *The Growth of Biological Thought: Diversity, Evolution, and Inheritance.* Cambridge, Mass.: Harvard Univ. Press.

MEAD, GEORGE HERBERT 1918 The Psychology of Punitive Justice. *American Journal of Sociology* 23, no. 5:577–602.

MEAD, GEORGE HERBERT (1921–1925) 1964 The Genesis of the Self and Social Control. In *Selected Writings.* Indianapolis, Ind.: Bobbs-Merrill.

MEAD, GEORGE HERBERT (1927) 1982 1927 Class Lectures in Social Psychology. In *The Individual and the Self: Unpublished Work of George Herbert Mead.* Univ. of Chicago Press.

MEAD, GEORGE HERBERT 1932 *The Philosophy of the Present.* Chicago: Open Court.

MEAD, GEORGE HERBERT (1934) 1962 *Mind, Self, and Society: From the Standpoint of a Social Behaviorist.* Univ. of Chicago Press.

MEAD, GEORGE HERBERT 1936 *Movements of Thought in the Nineteenth Century.* Univ. of Chicago Press.

MEAD, MARGARET (1928) 1939 *Coming of Age in Samoa.* In *From the South Seas: Studies of Adolescence and Sex in Primitive Societies.* New York: Morrow.

MEAD, MARGARET (1930) 1939 *Growing Up in New Guinea.* In *From the South Seas: Studies of Adolescence and Sex in Primitive Societies.* New York: Morrow.

MEAD, MARGARET (1935) 1939 *Sex and Temperament.* In *From the South Seas: Studies of Adolescence and Sex in Primitive Societies.* New York: Morrow.

MEAD, MARGARET 1940 Warfare Is Only an Invention — Not a Biological Necessity. *Asia* 40:403–405.

MEAD, MARGARET (1942) 1949 *And Keep Your Powder Dry: An Anthropologist Looks at America.* New York: Morrow.

MEAD, MARGARET 1949 *Male and Female: A Study of the Sexes in a Changing World.* New York: Morrow. A 1964 New American Library edition includes the 1954 introduction.

MEAD, MARGARET 1953 National Character. In Alfred L. Kroeber (editor), *Anthropology Today: An Encyclopedic Inventory.* Univ. of Chicago Press.

MEHRING, FRANZ (1918) 1935 *Karl Marx: The Story of His Life.* New York: Covici, Friede.

MEHTA, VED 1971 *John Is Easy to Please: Encounters with the Written and Spoken Word.* New York: Farrar, Straus.

MEILLET, ANTOINE 1925 *La méthode comparative en linguistique historique.* Oslo: H. Aschehoug.

MEILLET, ANTOINE 1936 *Linguistique historique et linguistique générale.* Paris: Librairie C. Klincksieck.

MEINECKE, FRIEDRICH 1915 *Die deutsche Erhebung von 1914.* Stuttgart: J. G. Gotta'sche.

MEINECKE, FRIEDRICH 1924 *Die Idee der Staatsräson in der neueren Geschichte.* Munich: R. Oldenbourg.

MENGER, CARL (1871) 1950 *Principles of Economics.* New York: Free Press.

MENGER, CARL (1883) 1963 *Problems of Economics and Sociology.* Urbana, Ill.: Univ. of Illinois Press.

MERRIAM, CHARLES E. 1926 Progress in Political Research. *American Political Science Review* 20, no. 1, 1–13.

MERRIAM, CHARLES E. (1934) 1964 *Political Power.* New York: Collier Books.

MERRIAM, CHARLES E. 1945 *Systematic Politics.* Univ. of Chicago Press.

MERTON, ROBERT K. (1942) 1973 The Normative Structure of Science. In *The Sociology of Science: Theoretical and Empirical Investigations.* Univ. of Chicago Press.

MERTON, ROBERT K. (1948) 1968 The Self-Fulfilling Prophecy. In *Social Theory and Social Structure.* New York: Free Press.

MERTON, ROBERT K. (1949) 1968 Manifest and Latent Functions. In *Social Theory and Social Structure.* New York: Free Press.

MERTON, ROBERT K. (1965) 1985 *On the Shoulders of Giants: A Shandean Postscript.* San Diego, Calif.: Harcourt.

MERTON, ROBERT K. (1968) 1973 The Matthew Effect in Science. In *The Sociology of Science: Theoretical and Empirical Investigations.* Univ. of Chicago Press.

MERTON, ROBERT K. ET AL. 1984 The Kelvin Dictum and Social Science: An Excursion into the History of an Idea. *Journal of the History of the Behavioral Sciences* 20:319–331.

MERZ, JOHN THEODORE 1903 *A History of European Thought in the Nineteenth Century.* Edinburgh: William Blackwood.

MICHELS, ROBERT (1911) 1949 *Political Parties: A Sociological Study of the Oligarchical Tendencies of Modern Democracy.* New York: Free Press.

MICHELS, ROBERT (1927) 1949 The Sociological Character of Political Parties. In *First Lectures in Political Sociology.* New York: Harper.

MICHELS, ROBERT 1930 Authority. In volume 2 of *Encyclopaedia of the Social Sciences.* New York: Macmillan.

MILL, JAMES (1820) 1955 *An Essay on Government.* New York: Liberal Arts Press.

MILL, JAMES (1829) 1967 *Analysis of the Phenomena of the Human Mind.* Fairfield, N.J.: Augustus M. Kelley.

MILL, JOHN STUART (1835) 1969 Sedgwick's Discourse. In volume 10 of *Collected Works of John Stuart Mill.* Univ. of Toronto Press.

MILL, JOHN STUART (1844) 1967 Of the Influence of Consumption on Production. In volume 4 of *Collected Works of John Stuart Mill.* Univ. of Toronto Press.

MILL, JOHN STUART (1848) 1965 *Principles of Political Economy, with Some of Their Applications to Social Philosophy.* In volume 3 of *Collected Works of John Stuart Mill.* Univ. of Toronto Press.

MILL, JOHN STUART (1859) 1977 *On Liberty.* In volume 18 of *Collected Works of John Stuart Mill.* Univ. of Toronto Press.

MILL, JOHN STUART (1861) 1977 *Considerations on Representative Government.* In volume 19 of *Collected Works of John Stuart Mill.* Univ. of Toronto Press.

MILL, JOHN STUART (1861) 1969 *Utilitarianism.* In volume 10 of *Collected Works of John Stuart Mill.* Univ. of Toronto Press.

MILL, JOHN STUART (1869) 1984 *The Subjection of Women.* In volume 21 of *Collected Works of John Stuart Mill.* Univ. of Toronto Press.

MILLER, GEORGE A. (1956) 1967 The Magical Number Seven, Plus or Minus Two: Some Limits on Our Capacity for Processing Information. In *The Psychology of Communication.* New York: Basic Books.

MILLER, GEORGE A. 1978 Review of *Language, Thought, and Reality: Selected Writings of Benjamin Lee Whorf. Human Nature* 1, no. 6:92–96

MILLER, NEAL E.; AND DOLLARD, JOHN (1941) 1953 *Social Learning and Imitation.* New Haven, Conn.: Yale Univ. Press.

MILLS, C. WRIGHT (1956) 1959 *The Power Elite.* Oxford Univ. Press.

MILLS, C. WRIGHT 1959 *The Sociological Imagination.* Oxford Univ. Press.

MILLS, C. WRIGHT (1959) 1963 Culture and Politics. In *Power, Politics and People: The Collected Essays of C. Wright Mills.* Oxford Univ. Press.

MILLS, C. WRIGHT (1962) 1963 *The Marxists.* New York: Doubleday.

MITCHELL, WESLEY C. (1913) 1941 *Business Cycles and Their Causes.* Berkeley and Los Angeles: Univ. of California Press.

MITCHELL, WESLEY C. (1916) 1937 The Role of Money in Economic Theory. In *The Backward Art of Spending Money and Other Essays.* New York: McGraw-Hill.

MITCHELL, WESLEY C. (1928) 1952 Letter to John Maurice Clark, 9 August 1928. In Arthur F. Burns (editor), *Wesley Clair Mitchell: The Economic Scientist.* Cambridge, Mass.: National Bureau of Economic Research.

MITCHELL, WESLEY C. 1929 Obituary: Thorstein Veblen: 1857–1929. *The Economic Journal* 39:646–650.

MODIGLIANI, FRANCO 1944 Liquidity Preference and the Theory of Interest and Money. *Econometrica* 12:45–88.

MODIGLIANI, FRANCO 1975 The Life Cycle Hypothesis of Saving Twenty Years Later. In M. Parkin (editor), *Contemporary Issues in Economics.* Manchester Univ. Press.

MODIGLIANI, FRANCO (1985) 1986 Life Cycle, Individual Thrift, and the Wealth of Nations. *American Economic Review* 76, no. 3:297–313.

MONTAGU, ASHLEY (1942) 1964 *Man's Most Dangerous Myth: The Fallacy of Race.* New York: World.

MONTESQUIEU (1748) 1949 *The Spirit of the Laws.* New York: Hafner.

MOODY, ERNEST A. 1974 William of Ockham. In volume 10 of *Dictionary of Scientific Biography.* New York: Scribner.

MORENO, JACOB L. 1934 *Who Shall Survive? A New Approach to the Problem of Human Interrelations.* Washington, D.C.: Nervous and Mental Disease Publishing Co.

MORGAN, C. LLOYD 1894 *An Introduction to Comparative Psychology.* London: Walter Scott.

MORGAN, LEWIS HENRY (1851) 1972 *League of the Iroquois.* Secaucus, N.J.: Citadel Press.

MORGAN, LEWIS HENRY 1870 *Systems of Consanguinity and Affinity of the Human Family.* Washington, D.C.: The Smithsonian Institution.

MORGAN, LEWIS HENRY (1877) 1964 *Ancient Society.* Cambridge, Mass.: Harvard Univ. Press.

MORGENSTERN, OSKAR (1950) 1963 *On the Accuracy of Economic Observations.* Princeton Univ. Press.

MORISON, SAMUEL ELIOT 1965 *The Oxford History of the American People.* Oxford Univ. Press.

MOSCA, GAETANO (1896) 1939 *The Ruling Class.* New York: McGraw-Hill.

MOSTELLER, FREDERICK ET AL. 1983 *Beginning Statistics with Data Analysis.* Reading, Mass.: Addison-Wesley.

MOSTELLER, FREDERICK; AND BUSH, ROBERT R. 1954 Selected Quantitative Techniques. In Gardner Lindzey (editor), *Handbook of Social Psychology.* Reading, Mass.: Addison-Wesley.

MOSTELLER, FREDERICK; AND WALLACE, DAVID L. 1964 *Inference and Disputed Authorship: The Federalist.* Reading, Mass.: Addison-Wesley.

MÜLLER, FRIEDRICH MAX (1866) 1875 *Lectures on the Science of Language.* New York: Scribner.

MUMFORD, LEWIS 1938 *The Culture of Cities.* San Diego, Calif.: Harcourt.

MUMFORD, LEWIS 1944 *The Condition of Man.* San Diego, Calif.: Harcourt.

MUMFORD, LEWIS 1951 *The Conduct of Life.* San Diego, Calif.: Harcourt.

MUMFORD, LEWIS 1961 *The City in History: Its Origins, Its Transformations, and Its Prospects.* San Diego, Calif.: Harcourt.

MÜNSTERBERG, HUGO 1904 *The Americans.* New York: McClure, Phillips.

MURDOCK, GEORGE P. (1949) 1960 *Social Structure.* New York: Macmillan.

MURDOCK, GEORGE P. 1972 Anthropology's Mythology. Royal Anthropological Institute of Great Britain and Ireland, *Proceedings* 1971:17–24.

MURPHY, GARDNER 1947 *Personality: A Biosocial Approach to Origins and Structure.* New York: Harper.

MURRAY, GILBERT 1925 *Five Stages of Greek Religion.* Oxford Univ. Press.

MURRAY, HENRY A. ET AL. 1938 *Explorations in Personality: A Clinical and Experimental Study of Fifty Men of College Age.* Oxford Univ. Press.

MURRAY, HENRY A. 1959 Preparations for the Scaffold of a Comprehensive System. In volume 3 of Sigmund Koch (editor), *Psychology: A Study of a Science.* New York: McGraw-Hill.

MURRAY, HENRY A. 1968 Components of an Evolving Personological System. In volume 12 of *International Encyclopedia of the Social Sciences.* New York: Macmillan and Free Press.

MURRAY, HENRY A.; AND KLUCKHOHN, CLYDE (1948) 1967 Outline of a Conception of Personality. In Henry A. Murray and Clyde Kluckhohn (editors), *Personality: In Nature, Society, and Culture.* New York: Knopf.

MYRDAL, GUNNAR 1944 *An American Dilemma: The Negro Problem and Modern Democracy.* New York: Harper.

MYRDAL, GUNNAR 1953 The Relation between Social Theory and Social Policy. *British Journal of Sociology* 4:210–242.

MYRDAL, GUNNAR (1962) 1963 *Challenge to Affluence.* London: Victor Gollancz.

MYRDAL, GUNNAR 1969 *Objectivity in Social Research.* New York: Random House.

NAGEL, ERNEST 1961 *The Structure of Science: Problems in the Logic of Scientific Explanation.* San Diego, Calif.: Harcourt.

NAMIER L. B. (1941) 1942 Symmetry and Repetition. In *Conflicts: Studies in Contemporary History.* London: Macmillan.

NAMIER, L. B. (1946) 1964 *1848: The Revolution of the Intellectuals.* New York: Doubleday.

NAMIER, L. B. 1952 History. In *Avenues of History.* London: Hamish Hamilton.

NEUMANN, FRANZ (1953) 1957 The Concept of Political Freedom. In *The Democratic and Authoritarian State.* New York: Free Press.

NEUMANN, SIGMUND 1942 *Permanent Revolution: The Total State in a World at War.* New York: Harper.

NEURATH, OTTO (1921) 1973 Anti-Spengler. In *Empiricism and Sociology.* Dordrecht (Holland): D. Reidel.

NEVINS, ALLAN (1938) 1962 *The Gateway to History.* New York: Doubleday.

NEVINS, ALLAN (1947) 1975 *Ordeal of the Union.* New York: Scribner.

NEWELL, ALLEN 1983 Intellectual Issues in the History of Artificial Intelligence. In Fritz Machlup and Una Mansfield (editors), *The Study of Information: Interdisciplinary Messages*. New York: Wiley.

NEWMAN, JAMES R. 1956 Commentary on Sir Francis Galton. In volume 2 of James R. Newman (editor), *The World of Mathematics*. New York: Simon & Schuster.

NEWTON, ISAAC (1675/6) 1959 Letter to Robert Hooke, 5 February 1675/6. In volume 1 of *The Correspondence of Isaac Newton: 1661–1665*. Cambridge Univ. Press.

NEYMAN, JERZY 1938 *Lectures and Conferences on Mathematical Statistics*. Washington, D.C.: Graduate School of the United States Department of Agriculture.

NIEBUHR, REINHOLD 1944 *The Children of Light and the Children of Darkness: A Vindication of Democracy and a Critique of Its Traditional Defence*. New York: Scribner.

NIETZSCHE, FRIEDRICH WILHELM (1878) 1964 *Human All-Too-Human: A Book for Free Spirits*. New York: Russell & Russell.

NIETZSCHE, FRIEDRICH WILHELM (1882) 1974 *The Gay Science*. New York: Random House.

NIETZSCHE, FRIEDRICH WILHELM (1887) 1968 *On the Genealogy of Morals*. In *Basic Writings of Nietzsche*. New York: Modern Library.

NIETZSCHE, FRIEDRICH WILHELM (1889) 1911 *The Twilight of the Idols*. In volume 16 of *The Complete Works of Friedrich Nietzsche*. London: Allen & Unwin.

NIGHTINGALE, FLORENCE (1891) 1924 Letter to Francis Galton, 7 February 1891. In volume 2 of Karl Pearson, *The Life, Letters and Labours of Francis Galton*. Cambridge Univ. Press.

NISBET, ROBERT A. 1966 *The Sociological Tradition*. New York: Basic Books.

NISBET, ROBERT A. 1973 *The Social Philosophers: Community and Conflict in Western Thought*. New York: Thomas I. Crowell.

NISBET, ROBERT A. 1982 Historical Necessity. In *Prejudices: A Philosophical Dictionary*. Cambridge, Mass.: Harvard Univ. Press.

NISBET, ROBERT A. 1986 *The Making of Modern Society*. Brighton (United Kingdom): Harvester.

NOELLE-NEUMANN, ELISABETH (1980) 1984 *The Spiral of Silence: Public Opinion — Our Social Skin*. Univ. of Chicago Press.

NOONAN, JOHN T., JR. 1976 *Persons and Masks of the Law: Cardozo, Holmes, Jefferson, and Wythe as Makers of the Masks*. New York: Farrar, Straus.

NORTH, DUDLEY (1691) 1822 *Discourses upon Trade*. Edinburgh: Ballantyne.

OAKESHOTT, MICHAEL 1933 *Experience and Its Modes*. Cambridge Univ. Press.

OAKESHOTT, MICHAEL 1946 Introduction to Thomas Hobbes, *Leviathan* (1651). Oxford (United Kingdom): Basil Blackwell.

OGBURN, WILLIAM FIELDING 1922 Bias, Psychoanalysis, and the Subjective in Relation to the Social Sciences. *Publications of the American Sociological Society* 17:62–74.

OGBURN, WILLIAM FIELDING 1922 *Social Change, With Respect to Culture and Original Nature*. New York: B. W. Huebsch.

[OGBURN, WILLIAM FIELDING] 1933 *Recent Social Trends in the United States: Report of the President's Research Committee on Social Trends*. New York: McGraw-Hill.

OGDEN, C. K. AND RICHARDS, I. A. 1923 *The Meaning of Meaning: A Study of the Influence of Language upon Thought and of the Science of Symbolism*. San Diego, Calif.: Harcourt.

OLSON, MANCUR 1965 *The Logic of Collective Action: Public Goods and the Theory of Groups*. Cambridge, Mass.: Harvard Univ. Press.

Olson, Mancur 1987 Collective Action. In volume 1 of *The New Palgrave: A Dictionary of Economics*. London: Macmillan.

Oppenheimer, J. Robert 1947 *Physics in the Contemporary World*. The Arthur Dehon Little Memorial Lecture at the Massachusetts Institute of Technology, Cambridge, Massachusetts, 25 November 1947. Privately printed.

Oresme, Nicole (c. 1373) 1956 A Treatise on the Origin, Nature, Law and Alterations of Money [*De moneta*]. In *The De Moneta of Nicholas Oresme*. London: Thomas Nelson.

Ortega y Gasset, José (1921) 1937 *Invertebrate Spain*. New York: Norton.

Ortega y Gasset, José (1923) 1961 *The Modern Theme*. New York: Harper.

Ortega y Gasset, José (1930) 1957 *The Revolt of the Masses*. New York: Norton.

Orwell, George (1945) 1987 *Animal Farm*. In volume 8 of *The Complete Works of George Orwell*. London: Secker & Warburg.

Orwell, George 1949 *Nineteen Eighty-Four*. San Diego, Calif.: Harcourt.

O'Sullivan, John Louis (1838) 1967 Introduction. In *The United States Magazine, and Democratic Review*. New York: AMS Press.

Paine, Thomas (1776) 1942 *Common Sense*. In *Basic Writings of Thomas Paine*. New York: Willey.

Paine, Thomas (1791–1792) 1958 *The Rights of Man*. London: Dent.

Pais, Abraham (1982) 1983 *"Subtle Is the Lord. . .": The Science and Life of Albert Einstein*. Oxford Univ. Press.

Palmer, R. R. 1959 *The Age of the Democratic Revolution: The Challenge*. Princeton Univ. Press.

Palmer, R. R. 1964 *The Age of the Democratic Revolution: The Struggle*. Princeton Univ. Press.

Pareto, Vilfredo (1892) 1984 Letter to Maffeo Pantaleoni, 5 January 1892. In volume 1 of *Lettere a Maffeo Pantaleoni: 1890–1923*. Geneva: Libraire Droz.

Pareto, Vilfredo 1896–1897 *Cours d'économie politique*. Lausanne: F. Rouge. Quoted in John S. Chipman, Compensation Principle 1987:525. In volume 1 of *The New Palgrave: A Dictionary of Economics*. London: Macmillan.

Pareto, Vilfredo (1896–1897) 1964 *Cours d'économie politique*. Geneva: Libraire Droz.

Pareto, Vilfredo (1896) 1966 *Cours d'économie politique*. In *Sociological Writings*. New York: Praeger.

Pareto, Vilfredo (1902–1903) 1966 *Les systèmes socialistes*. In *Sociological Writings*. New York: Praeger.

Pareto, Vilfredo (1906) 1966 *Le manuel d'économie politique*. In *Sociological Writings*. New York: Praeger.

Pareto, Vilfredo (1906) 1971 *Manual of Political Economy*. Fairfield, N.J.: Augustus M. Kelley.

Pareto, Vilfredo (1916) 1935 *The Mind and Society*. San Diego, Calif.: Harcourt.

Pareto, Vilfedo (1921) 1946 *Trasformazioni della democrazia*. Rome: Guanda.

Park, Robert E. (1925) 1952 The Urban Community as a Spatial Pattern and a Moral Order. In *Human Communities: The City and Human Ecology*. New York: Free Press.

Park, Robert E. 1926 Behind Our Masks. *Survey* (New York) 56, no. 3:135–139.

Park, Robert E. (1926) 1927 Human Nature and Collective Behavior. *American Journal of Sociology* 32:733–741.

Park, Robert E. 1928 Human Migration and the Marginal Man. *American Journal of Sociology* 33:881–893.

Park, Robert E. 1929 The City as a Social Laboratory. In T. V. Smith and Leonard D. White (editors), *Chicago: An Experiment in Social Science Research.* Univ. of Chicago Press.

Park, Robert E. (1939) 1974 The Nature of Race Relations. In *Race and Culture.* Volume 1 of *The Collected Papers of Robert Ezra Park.* New York: Arno Press.

Park, Robert E.; and Burgess, Ernest W. (1921) 1924 *Introduction to the Science of Sociology.* Univ. of Chicago Press.

Park, Robert E; and Burgess, Ernest W. 1925 *The City.* Univ. of Chicago Press.

Parkinson, C. Northcote 1957 *Parkinson's Law and Other Studies in Administration.* Boston: Houghton Mifflin.

Parsons, Elsie Clews 1913 *The Old-Fashioned Woman: Primitive Fancies about the Sex.* New York: Putnam.

Parsons, Elsie Clews 1916 *Social Rule: A Study of the Will to Power.* New York: Putnam.

Parsons, Talcott (1937) 1968 *The Structure of Social Action: A Study in Social Theory with Special Reference to a Group of Recent European Writers.* New York: Free Press.

Parsons, Talcott (1940) 1964 An Analytical Approach to the Theory of Social Stratification. In *Essays in Sociological Theory.* New York: Free Press.

Parsons, Talcott 1947 Introduction to Max Weber, *The Theory of Social and Economic Organization.* Oxford Univ. Press.

Parsons, Talcott 1951 *The Social System.* New York: Free Press.

Pascal, Blaise (1670) 1958 *Pensées.* New York: Dutton.

Pasteur, Louis (1854) 1939 Discours. In volume 7 of *Oeuvres de Pasteur.* Paris: Masson.

Patinkin, Don 1976 *Keynes' Monetary Thought: A Study of Its Development.* Durham, N.C.: Duke Univ. Press.

Patinkin, Don 1982 *Anticipations of the General Theory? and Other Essays on Keynes.* Univ. of Chicago Press.

Pavlov, Ivan Petrovich (1906) 1967 Scientific Study of the So-Called Psychical Processes in the Higher Animals. In volume 1 of *Lectures on Conditioned Reflexes: Twenty-Five Years of Objective Study of the Higher Nervous Activity (Behavior) of Animals.* New York: International Publishers.

Pavlov, Ivan Petrovich (1909) 1928 Natural Science and the Brain. In volume 1 of *Lectures on Conditioned Reflexes: Twenty-Five Years of Objective Study of the Higher Nervous Activity (Behaviour) of Animals.* New York: International Publishers.

Pavlov, Ivan Petrovich (1910–1911) 1967 Some Fundamental Laws of the Work of the Cerebral Hemispheres. In volume 1 of *Lectures on Conditioned Reflexes: Twenty-Five Years of Objective Study of the Higher Nervous Activity (Behavior) of Animals.* New York: International Publishers.

Pavlov, Ivan Petrovich (1911–1912) 1928 Some Principles of the Activity of the Central Nervous System as Shown from the Study of Conditioned Reflexes. In volume 1 of *Lectures on Conditioned Reflexes: Twenty-Five Years of Objective Study of the Higher Nervous Activity (Behavior) of Animals.* New York: International Publishers.

Pavlov, Ivan Petrovich (1913) 1928 The Objective Study of the Highest Nervous Activity of Animals. In volume 1 of *Lectures on Conditioned Reflexes: Twenty-Five Years of Objective Study of the Higher Nervous Activity (Behaviour) of Animals.* New York: International Publishers.

Pavlov, Ivan Petrovich (1932) 1941 Physiology of the Higher Nervous Activity. In volume 2 of *Lectures on Conditioned Reflexes: Conditioned Reflexes and Psychiatry.* New York: International Publishers.

Pavlov, Ivan Petrovich (1935) 1957 The Conditioned Reflex. In *Experimental Psychology and Other Essays.* New York: Philosophical Library.

PEARSON, KARL 1892 *The Grammar of Science*. London: Walter Scott.

PEARSON, KARL (1894) 1897 The Scientific Aspect of Monte Carlo Roulette. In *The Chances of Death and Other Studies in Evolution*. London: Edward Arnold.

PEARSON, KARL 1905 Discussion of a paper on eugenics by Francis Galton. In Francis Galton et al., *Sociological Papers*. London: Macmillan.

PEARSON, KARL 1924 *The Life, Letters, and Labours of Francis Galton*. Cambridge Univ. Press.

PEIRCE, CHARLES SANDERS (1867) 1966 Review of John Venn's *The Logic of Chance*. In volume 8 of *Collected Papers of Charles Sanders Peirce*. Cambridge, Mass.: Harvard Univ. Press.

PEIRCE, CHARLES SANDERS (1877) 1960 The Fixation of Belief. In volume 5 of *Collected Papers of Charles Sanders Peirce*. Cambridge, Mass.: Harvard Univ. Press.

PEIRCE, CHARLES SANDERS (1878) 1923 The Doctrine of Chances. In *Chance, Love and Logic: Philosophical Essays*. London: Kegan Paul.

PEIRCE, CHARLES SANDERS (1905) 1965 What Pragmatism Is. In *Collected Papers of Charles Sanders Peirce*. Volume 5, Pragmatism and Pragmaticism. Cambridge, Mass.: Harvard Univ. Press.

PERELMAN, S. J. 1946 *Keep It Crisp*. New York: Random House.

PETERSEN, WILLIAM (1958) 1964 A General Typology of Migration. In *The Politics of Population*. New York: Doubleday.

PETTY, WILLIAM (1662) 1963 A Treatise of Taxes and Contributions. In volume 1 of *The Economic Writings of Sir William Petty*. Fairfield, N.J.: Augustus M. Kelley.

PETTY, WILLIAM (1683) 1963 Another Essay in Political Arithmetick Concerning the Growth of the City of London, 1682. In volume 2 of *The Economic Writings of Sir William Petty*. Fairfield, N.J.: Augustus M. Kelley.

PETTY, WILLIAM (1690) 1963 *Political Arithmetick*. In volume 1 of *The Economic Writings of Sir William Petty*. Fairfield, N.J.: Augustus M. Kelley.

PETTY, WILLIAM (1691) 1963 *Verbum sapienti*. In volume 1 of *The Economic Writings of Sir William Petty*. Fairfield, N.J.: Augustus M. Kelley.

PIAGET, JEAN (1923) 1969 *The Language and Thought of the Child*. New York: Meridian.

PIAGET, JEAN 1927 La première année de l'enfant. *British Journal of Psychology* 18:97–120.

PIAGET, JEAN (1932) 1965 *The Moral Judgment of the Child*. New York: Free Press.

PIAGET, JEAN (1936) 1952 *The Origins of Intelligence in Children*. New York: International Universities Press.

PIAGET, JEAN (1937) 1954 *The Construction of Reality in the Child*. New York: Basic Books.

PIAGET, JEAN (1947) 1950 *The Psychology of Intelligence*. London: Routledge.

PIAGET, JEAN 1966 Response to Brian Sutton-Smith. *Psychological Review* 73, no. 1:111–112.

PIAGET, JEAN (1968) 1977 Structuralism: Introduction and Location of Problems. In *The Essential Piaget*. New York: Basic Books.

PIAGET, JEAN (1970) 1983 Piaget's Theory. In volume 1 of Paul H. Mussen (editor), *Handbook of Child Psychology*. New York: Wiley.

PIAGET, JEAN; AND SZEMINSKA, ALINA (1941) 1952 *The Child's Conception of Number*. London: Routledge.

PIGOU, ARTHUR CECIL (1920) 1978 *The Economics of Welfare*. New York: AMS Press.

PIGOU, ARTHUR CECIL 1936 Mr. J. M. Keynes' *General Theory of Employment, Interest and Money*. *Economica* 3:115–132.

PLANCK, MAX (1948) 1949 *Scientific Autobiography and Other Papers*. New York: Philosophical Library.

PLATO 1961 *Cratylus*. In *The Collected Dialogues of Plato*. New York: Bollingen Foundation.

PLATO 1961 *Phaedo*. In *The Collected Dialogues of Plato*. New York: Random House.

PLATO 1961 *Phaedrus*. In *The Collected Dialogues of Plato*. New York: Random House.

PLATO 1961 *Protagoras*. In *The Collected Dialogues of Plato*. New York: Random House.

PLATO 1982 *Republic*. New York: Modern Library.

PLATO 1961 *Socrates' Defense (Apology)*. In *The Collected Dialogues of Plato*. New York: Random House.

PLATO 1961 *Theaetetus*. In *The Collected Dialogues of Plato*. New York: Random House.

PLAYFAIR, WILLIAM 1798 *Lineal Arithmetic: Applied to Shew the Progress of the Commerce and Revenue of England during the Present Century*. London: Privately printed.

PLAYFAIR, WILLIAM 1801 *The Statistical Breviary: Shewing on a Principle Entirely New, the Resources of Every State and Kingdom in Europe*. London: T. Bensley.

PLUMB, J. H. 1970 *The Death of the Past*. Boston: Houghton Mifflin.

PLUMB, J. H. 1973 Is History Sick? *Encounter* 40, no. 4:63–66.

PLUTARCH 1946 *The Lives of the Noble Grecians and Romans*. New York: Modern Library.

POINCARÉ, JULES HENRI (1896) 1912 *Calcul des probabilités*. Paris: Gauthier-Villars.

POINCARÉ, JULES HENRI (1908) 1952 *Science and Method*. New York: Dover.

POINCARÉ, JULES HENRI (1911) 1913 *The Value of Science*. In *The Foundations of Science*. New York: Science Press.

POLANYI, KARL (1944) 1975 *The Great Transformation*. New York: Octagon Books.

POLANYI, MICHAEL (1958) 1964 *Personal Knowledge: Towards a Post-Critical Philosophy*. New York: Harper.

POLLOCK, FREDERICK; AND MAITLAND, FREDERIC WILLIAM (1895) 1968 *The History of English Law before the Time of Edward I*. Cambridge Univ. Press.

POLYBIUS 1926 *Fragment of Book 16*. In *The Histories*. Cambridge, Mass.: Harvard Univ. Press.

POPE, ALEXANDER (1733) 1950 *An Essay on Man*. London: Methuen.

POPPER, KARL (1945) 1950 *The Open Society and Its Enemies*. Princeton Univ. Press.

POPPER, KARL (1948) 1968 Prediction and Prophecy in the Social Sciences. In *Conjectures and Refutations: The Growth of Scientific Knowledge*. New York: Harper.

POPPER, KARL 1957 *The Poverty of Historicism*. Boston: Beacon.

POPPER, KARL (1963) 1968 *Conjectures and Refutations: The Growth of Scientific Knowledge*. New York: Harper.

POPPER, KARL 1968 Plato. In volume 11 of *International Encyclopedia of the Social Sciences*. New York: Macmillan and Free Press.

POPPER, KARL (1968) 1972 Epistemology without a Knowing Subject. In *Objective Knowledge: An Evolutionary Approach*. Oxford Univ. Press.

POPPER, KARL (1971) 1972 Conjectural Knowledge: My Solution of the Problem of Induction. In *Objective Knowledge: An Evolutionary Approach*. Oxford Univ. Press.

PORTER, ROBERT P. 1895 Progress of the Nation: 1790 to 1890. In part 1 of *Report on Population of the United States at the Eleventh Census*: 1890. Washington, D.C.: Government Printing Office.

POUND, ROSCOE 1906 The Causes of Popular Dissatisfaction with the Administration of Justice. In *Report of the Twenty-Ninth Annual Meeting of the American Bar Association*. Philadelphia, Pa.: Dando.

POUND, ROSCOE (1922) 1959 *An Introduction to the Philosophy of Law*. New Haven, Conn.: Yale Univ. Press.

POUND, ROSCOE 1944 The Humanities in an Absolutist World. In Norman Foerster (editor), *The Humanities after the War*. Princeton Univ. Press.

PRICE, DEREK J. DE SOLLA (1963) 1986 *Little Science, Big Science. . . And Beyond*. New York: Columbia Univ. Press.

PROUDHON, PIERRE JOSEPH (1840) 1966 *What Is Property? An Enquiry into the Principle of Right and of Government*. New York: Howard Fertig.

PROUDHON, PIERRE JOSEPH 1843–1846 *Carnets*. Paris: Rivière. Quoted in James Joll, *The Anarchists* 1966:68. New York: Grosset & Dunlap.

PROUDHON, PIERRE JOSEPH 1848 Statement in the Constituent Assembly of 1848. Quoted in E. H. Carr, *Michael Bakunin* 1961:136–137. New York: Random House.

PROUDHON, PIERRE JOSEPH (1851) 1923 *General Idea of the Revolution in the Nineteenth Century*. London: Freedom Press.

PROUDHON, PIERRE JOSEPH (1851) 1929 *L'idée générale de la révolution au 19e siècle*. Quoted in James Joll, *The Anarchists* 1966:78–79. New York: Grosset & Dunlap.

PROUDHON, PIERRE JOSEPH 1865 *De la capacité politique des classes ouvrières*. Quoted in James Joll, *The Anarchists* 1966:80. New York: Grosset & Dunlap.

PUTNAM, HILARY 1981 Philosophers and Human Understanding. In A. F. Heath (editor), *Scientific Understanding*. Oxford Univ. Press.

QUESNAY, FRANÇOIS (1758) 1888 Maximes générales du gouvernement économique d'un royaume agricole et notes sur ces maximes. In Auguste Oncken (editor), *Oeuvres économiques et philosophiques de F. Quesnay*. Paris: Jules Peelman.

QUESNAY, FRANÇOIS (1763) 1963 Extract from *Rural Philosophy*. In Ronald L. Meek (editor), *The Economics of Physiocracy: Essays and Translations*. Cambridge, Mass.: Harvard Univ. Press.

QUESNAY, FRANÇOIS (1766) 1888 Réponse au mémoire de M. H. In Auguste Oncken (editor), *Oeuvres économiques et philosophiques de F. Quesnay*. Paris: Jules Peelman.

QUETELET, ADOLPHE (1835) 1842 *A Treatise on Man and the Development of His Faculties*. Edinburgh: William and Robert Chambers.

QUETELET, ADOPHE 1848 *Du système social et des lois qui le régissent*. Paris: Guillaumin.

RADCLIFFE-BROWN, A. R. (1922) 1948 *The Andaman Islanders*. New York: Free Press.

RADCLIFFE-BROWN, A. R. 1934 Social Sanction. In volume 13 of *Encyclopaedia of the Social Sciences*. New York: Macmillan.

RADCLIFFE-BROWN, A. R. (1935) 1965 On the Concept of Function in Social Science. In *Structure and Function in Primitive Society*. New York: Free Press.

RADCLIFFE-BROWN, A. R. (1940) 1970 Preface to Meyer Fortes and E. E. Evans-Pritchard, *African Political Systems*. Oxford Univ. Press.

RADCLIFFE-BROWN, A. R. (1948) 1957 *A Natural Science of Society*. New York: Free Press.

RADCLIFFE-BROWN, A. R. 1949 Functionalism: A Protest. *American Anthropologist* 51:320–323.

Radin, Paul (1956) 1972 *The Trickster: A Study in American Indian Mythology.* New York: Schocken Books.

Rae, John (1834) 1905 *The Sociological Theory of Capital.* New York: Macmillan.

Ramsey, Frank Plumpton (1931) 1965 *The Foundations of Mathematics.* London: Routledge. Selections quoted in John Maynard Keynes, Frank Ramsey. In *Essays in Biography.* Volume 10 of *The Collected Writings of John Maynard Keynes* 1972:341, 345. London: Macmillan.

Rank, Otto 1912 *Das Inzestmotiv in Dichtung und Sage.* Vienna: Deuticke. Quoted in Erwin R. Wallace, IV, *Freud and Anthropology* 1983:44. New York: International Universities Press.

Rank, Otto 1929 Beyond Psychoanalysis. *Psycholanalytic Review* 16, no. 1:1–11.

Rank, Otto (1941) 1958 *Beyond Psychology.* New York: Dover.

Ranke, Leopold von (1824) 1885 *Geschichten der romanischen und germanischen Völker von 1494 bis 1514.* Leipzig: Duncker & Humblot.

Rapoport, Anatol 1974 Prisoner's Dilemma — Recollections and Observations. In volume 2 of *Game Theory as a Theory of Conflict Resolution.* Dordrecht (Holland): D. Reidel.

Rawls, John 1971 *A Theory of Justice.* Cambridge, Mass.: Harvard Univ. Press.

Redfield, Robert 1947 The Folk Society. *American Journal of Sociology* 52, no. 4:293–308.

Redfield, Robert (1949) 1962 Social Science among the Humanities. In volume 1 of *Human Nature and the Study of Society: The Papers of Robert Redfield.* Univ. of Chicago Press.

Redfield, Robert 1952 The Primitive World View. In *Proceedings.* Vol. 96. Philadelphia, Pa.: The American Philosophical Society.

Redfield, Robert 1953 *The Primitive World and Its Transformations.* Ithaca, N.Y.: Cornell Univ. Press.

Redfield, Robert 1955 *The Little Community: Viewpoints for the Study of a Human Whole.* Univ. of Chicago Press.

Redfield, Robert (1958) 1962 Civilizations as Cultural Structures? In volume 1 of *Human Nature and the Study of Society: The Papers of Robert Redfield.* Univ. of Chicago Press.

Redfield, Robert (1960) 1962 How Human Society Operates. In volume 1 of *Human Nature and the Study of Society: The Papers of Robert Redfield.* Univ. of Chicago Press.

Reuter, Peter 1983 *Disorganized Crime: The Economics of the Visible Hand.* Cambridge, Mass.: M.I.T. Press.

Ricardo, David (1815) 1951 An Essay on the Influence of a Low Price of Corn on the Profits of Stock. In volume 4 of *The Works and Correspondence of David Ricardo.* Cambridge Univ. Press.

Ricardo, David (1817) 1963 *The Principles of Political Economy and Taxation.* Homewood, Ill.: Richard D. Irwin.

Rice, Stuart A. 1930 The Historico-Statistical Approach to Social Studies. In *Statistics in Social Studies.* Philadelphia, Pa.: Univ. of Pennsylvania Press.

Richardson, Lewis Fry 1960 *Arms and Insecurity.* Pittsburgh, Pa.: Boxwood Press.

Rieff, Philip (1959) 1979 *Freud: The Mind of the Moralist.* Univ. of Chicago Press.

Riesman, David 1950 *The Lonely Crowd: A Study of the Changing American Character.* New Haven, Conn.: Yale Univ. Press.

Riley, Matilda White (1980) 1982 Aging and Social Change. In volume 2 of Matilda White Riley et al. (editors), *Aging from Birth to Death.* Boulder, Co.: Westview Press.

RIVERS, W. H. R. 1914 *The History of Melanesian Society*. Cambridge Univ. Press.

RIVERS, W. H. R. 1922 The Psychological Factor. In *Essays on the Depopulation of Melanesia*. Cambridge Univ. Press.

RIVERS, W. H. R. 1922 *History and Ethnology*. London: Society for Promoting Christian Knowledge.

RIVLIN, ALICE M. 1987 Taming the Economic Policy Monster. *The New York Times* 18 January.

ROBBINS, LIONEL (1932) 1984 *An Essay on the Nature and Significance of Economic Science*. New York Univ. Press.

ROBINSON, JAMES HARVEY; AND BEARD, CHARLES A. 1908 *The Development of Modern Europe: An Introduction to the Study of Current History*. Boston: Ginn.

ROBINSON, JOAN 1936 Review of R. F. Harrod, *The Trade Cycle*. *Economic Journal* 46:691–693.

ROBINSON, JOAN (1955) 1980 Marx, Marshall and Keynes. In volume 2 of *Collected Economic Papers*. Cambridge, Mass.: M.I.T. Press.

ROBINSON, JOAN (1962) 1963 The Keynesian Revolution. In *Economic Philosophy*. Chicago: Aldine.

ROBINSON, JOAN (1962) 1963 Metaphysics, Morals and Science. In *Economic Philosophy*. Chicago: Aldine.

ROBINSON, JOAN (1962) 1963 What Are the Rules of the Game? In *Economic Philosophy*. Chicago: Aldine.

ROBINSON, JOAN (1968) 1980 Economics versus Political Economy. In volume 4 of *Collected Economic Papers*. Cambridge, Mass.: M.I.T. Press.

ROBINSON, JOAN (1979) 1980 Thinking about Thinking. In *Further Contributions to Modern Economics*. Oxford (United Kingdom): Basil Blackwell.

ROETHLISBERGER, F. J. 1941 *Management and Morale*. Cambridge, Mass.: Harvard Univ. Press.

ROGERS, CARL R. (1951) 1965 *Client-Centered Therapy: Its Current Practice, Implications, and Theory*. Boston: Houghton Mifflin.

ROGERS, CARL R. 1961 *On Becoming a Person: A Therapist's View of Psychotherapy*. Boston: Houghton Mifflin.

RÓHEIM, GÉZA 1934 *The Riddle of the Sphinx*. London: Leonard and Virginia Woolf.

ROOSEVELT, FRANKLIN DELANO (1937) 1946 Second Inaugural Address, 20 January 1937. In *Nothing to Fear: The Selected Addresses of Franklin Delano Roosevelt; 1932–1945*. Freeport, N.Y.: Books for Libraries Press.

ROOSEVELT, FRANKLIN DELANO (1940) 1946 Address at the Jackson Day Dinner. In *Nothing to Fear: The Selected Addresses of Franklin Delano Roosevelt; 1932–1945*. Freeport, N.Y.: Books for Libraries Press.

ROOSEVELT, FRANKLIN DELANO (1941) 1946 Speech, 6 January 1946. In *Nothing to Fear: The Selected Addresses of Franklin Delano Roosevelt; 1932–1945*. Freeport, N.Y.: Books for Libraries Press.

RORTY, RICHARD (1981) 1982 Method, Social Science, and Social Hope. In *Consequences of Pragmatism*. Minneapolis: Univ. of Minnesota Press.

ROSCHER, WILHELM (1854) 1878 *Principles of Political Economy*. New York: Holt.

ROSS, EDWARD A. 1920 *The Principles of Sociology*. New York: Century.

ROSZAK, THEODORE (1963) 1969 *The Making of a Counter Culture: Reflections on the Technocratic Society and Its Youthful Opposition*. New York: Doubleday.

ROUSSEAU, JEAN JACQUES (1750) 1964 *Discourse on the Sciences and Arts*. In *The First and Second Discourses*. New York: St. Martins.

ROUSSEAU, JEAN JACQUES (1755) 1963 *Discourses on the Origin and Foundations of Inequality among Men*. In *The First and Second Discourses*. New York: St. Martins.

ROUSSEAU, JEAN JACQUES (1755) 1973 *A Discourse on Political Economy*. In *The Social Contract* and *Discourses*. London: Dent.

ROUSSEAU, JEAN JACQUES (1758) 1982 *Politics and the Arts: Letter to M. d'Alembert on the Theatre*. Ithaca, N.Y.: Cornell Univ. Press.

ROUSSEAU, JEAN JACQUES (1762) 1979 *Émile: Or on Education*. New York: Basic Books.

ROUSSEAU, JEAN JACQUES (1762) 1973 *Social Contract*. In *The Social Contract* and *Discourses*. London: Dent.

ROUSSEAU, JEAN JACQUES (1781) 1877 Essai sur l'origine des langues. In volume 1 of *Oeuvres complètes*. Paris: Hachette. Quoted in Robert Derathé, Jean Jacques Rousseau. In volume 13 of *International Encyclopedia of the Social Sciences* 1968:570. New York: Macmillan and Free Press.

RUSSELL, BERTRAND 1921 *The Analysis of Mind*. London: Allen & Unwin.

RUSSELL, BERTRAND 1929 *Our Knowledge of the External World*. New York: Norton.

SAHLINS, MARSHALL 1976 *Culture and Practical Reason*. Univ. of Chicago Press.

SAINT-SIMON (1819) 1964 *The Organizer*. In *Social Organization, the Science of Man and Other Writings*. New York: Harper.

SAMUELSON, PAUL A. 1946 Lord Keynes and the General Theory. *Econometrica* 14:187–200.

SAMUELSON, PAUL A. (1947) 1961 *Foundations of Economic Analysis*. Cambridge, Mass.: Harvard Univ. Press.

SAMUELSON, PAUL A. (1963) 1966 A Brief Survey of Post-Keynesian Developments. In volume 2 of *The Collected Scientific Papers of Paul A. Samuelson*. Cambridge, Mass.: M.I.T. Press.

SAMUELSON, PAUL A. (1965) 1972 Proof That Properly Anticipated Prices Fluctuate Randomly. In volume 3 of *The Collected Scientific Papers of Paul A. Samuelson*. Cambridge, Mass.: M.I.T. Press.

SAMUELSON, PAUL A. (1968) 1983 Monetarism Pure and Neat, No. In E. Cary Brown and Robert M. Solow (editors), *Paul Samuelson and Modern Economic Theory*. New York: McGraw-Hill.

SAMUELSON, PAUL A. (1970) 1972 Economics in a Golden Age: A Personal Memoir. In Gerald Holton (editor), *The Twentieth-Century Sciences: Studies in the Biography of Ideas*. New York: Norton.

SAMUELSON, PAUL A.; AND NORDHAUS, WILLIAM D. (1948) 1985 *Economics*. New York: McGraw-Hill.

SANTAYANA, GEORGE (1905–1906) 1953 *The Life of Reason: Or the Phases of Human Progress*. New York: Scribner.

SAPIR, EDWARD (1921) 1949 *Language: An Introduction to the Study of Speech*. San Diego, Calif.: Harcourt.

SAPIR, EDWARD (1924) 1949 The Grammarian and His Language. In *Selected Writings of Edward Sapir in Language, Culture, and Personality*. Berkeley and Los Angeles: Univ. of California Press.

SAPIR, EDWARD (1925) 1959 Letter to Ruth Benedict, 14 June 1925. In *An Anthropologist at Work: Writings of Ruth Benedict*. Boston: Houghton Mifflin.

SAPIR, EDWARD (1929) 1949 The Status of Linguistics as a Science. In *Selected Writings of Edward Sapir in Language, Culture, and Personality*. Berkeley and Los Angeles: Univ. of California Press.

SAPIR, EDWARD 1931 Communication. In volume 4 of *Encyclopaedia of the Social Sciences*. New York: Macmillan.

SAPIR, EDWARD 1931 Fashion. In volume 6 of *Encyclopaedia of the Social Sciences*. New York: Macmillan.

SAPIR, EDWARD (1932) 1949 Cultural Anthropology and Psychiatry. In *Selected Writings of Edward Sapir in Language, Culture, and Personality*. Berkeley and Los Angeles: Univ. of California Press.

SAPIR, EDWARD 1933 Language. In volume 9 of *Encyclopaedia of the Social Sciences*. New York: Macmillan.

SARTON, GEORGE (1930) 1988 The History of Science and the History of Civilization. In *The History of Science and the New Humanism*. New Brunswick, N.J.: Transaction Books.

SARTON, GEORGE (1935) 1962 Quetelet (1796–1874). In *Sarton on the History of Science*. Cambridge, Mass.: Harvard Univ. Press.

SAUSSURE, FERDINAND DE (1916) 1966 *Course in General Linguistics*. New York: McGraw-Hill.

SAUVY, ALFRED (1966) 1969 *General Theory of Population*. New York: Basic Books.

SAY, JEAN BAPTISTE (1803) 1841 *A Treatise on Political Economy: Or the Production, Distribution, and Consumption of Wealth*. Philadelphia, Pa.: Grigg and Elliot.

SCHATTSCHNEIDER, E. E. 1942 *Party Government*. New York: Holt.

SCHELLING, THOMAS C. 1960 *The Strategy of Conflict*. Cambridge, Mass.: Harvard Univ. Press.

SCHELLING, THOMAS C. (1967) 1984 What Is Game Theory? In *Choice and Consequence*. Cambridge, Mass.: Harvard Univ. Press.

SCHILLER, FRIEDRICH VON (1795) 1916 *Essays Aesthetical and Philosophical*. Quoted in Ernst Cassirer, *An Essay on Man: An Introduction to a Philosophy of Human Culture* (1944) 1962:165. New Haven, Conn.: Yale Univ. Press.

SCHLESINGER, ARTHUR M., JR. (1949) 1962 *The Vital Center: The Politics of Freedom*. Boston: Houghton Mifflin.

SCHLESINGER, ARTHUR M., JR. (1966) 1967 The Inscrutability of History. In *The Bitter Heritage: Vietnam and American Democracy; 1941–1966*. Boston: Houghton Mifflin.

SCHLESINGER, ARTHUR M., JR. 1986 Foreword. *The Cycles of American History*. Boston: Houghton Mifflin.

SCHOPENHAUER, ARTHUR (1844) 1928 On History. In *The Works of Schopenhauer*. Abridged edition. New York: Frederick Ungar.

SCHOPENHAUER, ARTHUR (1851) 1974 *Parerga and Paralipomena*. Oxford Univ. Press.

SCHOPENHAUER, ARTHUR (1851) 1988 *Parerga und Paralipomena*. Zurich: Haffmans Verlag.

SCHUMACHER, E. F. 1973 *Small Is Beautiful: A Study of Economics as if People Mattered*. London: Blond & Briggs.

SCHUMPETER, JOSEPH A. (1912) 1934 *The Theory of Economic Development: An Inquiry into Profits, Capital, Credit, Interest, and the Business Cycle*. Cambridge, Mass.: Harvard Univ. Press.

SCHUMPETER, JOSEPH A. (1918) 1954 The Crisis of the Tax State. In Alan T. Peacock et al. (editors), *International Economic Papers No. 4: Translations Prepared for the International Economic Association*. London: Macmillan.

SCHUMPETER, JOSEPH A. (1927) 1955 *Social Classes in an Ethnically Homogeneous Environment*. In *Imperialism* and *Social Classes*. New York: Meridian.

SCHUMPETER, JOSEPH A. (1935) 1951 The Analysis of Economic Change. In *Essays of J. A. Schumpeter*. Reading, Mass.: Addison-Wesley.

SCHUMPETER, JOSEPH A. (1937) 1951 Preface to the Japanese edition of *Theorie der wirtschaftlichen Entwicklung*. In *Essays of J. A. Schumpeter*. Reading, Mass.: Addison-Wesley.

SCHUMPETER, JOSEPH A. (1939) 1982 *Business Cycles*. Philadelphia, Pa.: Porcupine Press.

SCHUMPETER, JOSEPH A. (1942) 1975 *Capitalism, Socialism, and Democracy.* New York: Harper.

SCHUMPETER, JOSEPH A. (1949) 1951 Vilfredo Pareto: 1848–1923. In *Ten Great Economists: From Marx to Keynes.* Oxford Univ. Press.

SCHUMPETER, JOSEPH A. 1954 *History of Economic Analysis.* Oxford Univ. Press.

SCHUTZ, ALFRED (1942–1967) 1970 Interactional Relationships. In *Alfred Schutz on Phenomenology and Social Relations.* Univ. of Chicago Press.

SCHUTZ, ALFRED (1944) 1962 Some Leading Concepts of Phenomenology. In volume 1 of *Collected Papers.* The Hague: Martinus Nijhoff.

SELIGMAN, EDWIN R. A. (1902) 1903 *The Economic Interpretation of History.* New York: Columbia Univ. Press.

SELZNICK, PHILIP 1949 *TVA and the Grass Roots: A Study in the Sociology of Formal Organization.* Berkeley and Los Angeles: Univ. of California Press.

SELZNICK, PHILIP 1952 *The Organizational Weapon.* New York: McGraw-Hill.

SENIOR, NASSAU WILLIAM (1830) 1831 The Causes and Remedies of the Present Disturbances. In *Three Lectures on the Rate of Wages.* London: Murray.

SENIOR, NASSAU WILLIAM (1836) 1965 *An Outline of the Science of Political Economy.* Fairfield, N.J.: Augustus M. Kelley.

SHAKESPEARE, WILLIAM 1940 *As You Like It.* In *The Complete Works of William Shakespeare.* New York: Garden City.

SHAKESPEARE, WILLIAM 1940 *Hamlet.* In *The Complete Works of William Shakespeare.* New York: Garden City.

SHAKESPEARE, WILLIAM 1940 *The Second Part of King Henry IV.* In *The Complete Works of William Shakespeare.* New York: Garden City.

SHAKESPEARE, WILLIAM 1940 *The Tempest.* In *The Complete Works of William Shakespeare.* New York: Garden City.

SHAKESPEARE, WILLIAM 1940 *The Tragedy of Macbeth.* In *The Complete Works of William Shakespeare.* New York: Garden City.

SHAW, GEORGE BERNARD (1906) 1985 *The Doctor's Dilemma.* In *Three Plays: Major Barbara, Caesar and Cleopatra, The Doctor's Dilemma.* New York: New American Library.

SHAW, GEORGE BERNARD (1912) 1930 *Pygmalion.* New York: Dodd, Mead.

SHERRINGTON, CHARLES (1906) 1961 *The Integrative Action of the Nervous System.* New Haven, Conn.: Yale Univ. Press.

SHILS, EDWARD (1957) 1975 Primordial, Personal, Sacred, and Civil Ties. In *Center and Periphery: Essays in Macrosociology.* Univ. of Chicago Press.

SHILS, EDWARD 1961 The Calling of Sociology. In volume 2 of Talcott Parsons et al. (editors), *Theories of Society: Foundations of Modern Sociological Theory.* New York: Free Press.

SHILS, EDWARD (1961) 1975 Center and Periphery. In *Center and Periphery: Essays in Macrosociology.* Univ. of Chicago Press.

SHKLAR, JUDITH N. 1969 *Men and Citizens: A Study of Rousseau's Social Theory.* Cambridge Univ. Press.

SICHEL, WERNER (editor) 1989 *The State of Economic Science: Views of Six Nobel Laureates.* Kalamazoo, Mich.: W. E. Upjohn Institute for Employment Research.

SILVERSTEIN, MICHAEL 1979 Language Structure and Linguistic Ideology. In Paul R. Clyne et al. (editors), *The Elements: A Parasession on Linguistic Units and Levels.* Chicago Linguistic Society, University of Chicago.

SIMEY T. S.; AND SIMEY, M. B. 1960 *Charles Booth: Social Scientist.* Oxford Univ. Press.

SIMMEL, GEORG 1890 *Über soziale Differenzierung.* Quoted in David Frisby, *Georg Simmel* 1984:84. London: Tavistock.

SIMMEL, GEORG (1900) 1978 *The Philosophy of Money.* London: Routledge.

SIMMEL, GEORG (1902) 1950 The Isolated Individual and the Dyad. In *The Sociology of Georg Simmel.* New York: Free Press.

SIMMEL, GEORG (1903) 1971 The Metropolis and Mental Life. In *Georg Simmel: On Individuality and Social Forms.* Edited by Donald N. Levine. Univ. of Chicago Press.

SIMMEL, GEORG 1905 *Die Probleme der Geschichtsphilosophie: Eine erkenntnistheoretische Studie.* Second, completely revised edition. Leipzig: Duncker & Humblot. The first edition was published in 1892.

SIMMEL, GEORG (1908) 1950 Friendship and Love. In *The Sociology of Georg Simmel.* New York: Free Press.

SIMMEL, GEORG (1908) 1955 *Conflict.* In *Conflict* and *The Web of Group Affiliations.* New York: Free Press.

SIMMEL, GEORG (1908) *Soziologie.* Quoted in R. M. MacIver, *Community: A Sociological Study.* (1917) 1924:129. London: Macmillan.

SIMMEL, GEORG (1908) 1950 The Stranger. In *The Sociology of Georg Simmel.* New York: Free Press.

SIMMEL, GEORG (1908) 1950 Superordination and Subordination. In *The Sociology of Georg Simmel.* New York: Free Press.

SIMMEL, GEORG (1917) 1950 Faithfulness and Gratitude. In *The Sociology of Georg Simmel.* New York: Free Press.

SIMMEL, GEORG (1918) 1971 The Transcendent Character of Life. *Georg Simmel: On Individuality and Social Forms.* Edited by Donald N. Levine. Univ. of Chicago Press.

SIMON, HERBERT A. (1945) 1961 *Administrative Behavior: A Study of Decision-making Processes in Administrative Organization.* New York: Macmillan.

SIMON, HERBERT A. (1945) 1961 Introduction to the 1957 edition. *Administrative Behavior: A Study of Decision-making Processes in Administrative Organization.* New York: Macmillan.

SIMON, HERBERT A. 1957 Rationality and Administrative Decision Making. In *Models of Man: Social and Rational.* New York: Wiley.

SIMON, HERBERT A. 1969 *The Sciences of the Artificial.* Cambridge, Mass.: M.I.T. Press.

SIMON, HERBERT A. 1983 *Reason in Human Affairs.* Stanford Univ. Press.

SIMON, HERBERT A. 1985 What We Know about the Creative Process. In Robert Lawrence Kuhn (editor), *Frontiers in Creative and Innovative Management.* Cambridge, Mass.: Ballinger.

SIMONDE DE SISMONDI, J. C. L. 1837 *Études sur l'économie politique.* Paris: Treuttel et Würtz. Quoted in Jacques Barzun, *Darwin, Marx, Wagner: Critique of a Heritage* 1958:149, 150. New York: Doubleday.

SIMONS, HENRY C. 1934 *A Positive Program for Laissez Faire.* Univ. of Chicago Press.

SKINNER, B. F. 1938 *The Behavior of Organisms: An Experimental Analysis.* New York: Appleton.

SKINNER, B. F. 1945 The Operational Analysis of Psychological Terms. *Psychological Review* 52:270–277.

SKINNER, B. F. (1948) 1976 *Walden Two.* New York: Macmillan.

SKINNER, B. F. 1953 *Science and Human Behavior.* New York: Macmillan.

SKINNER, B. F. 1963 Behaviorism at Fifty. *Science* 140:951–958.

SMELSER, NEIL J. 1959 *Social Change in the Industrial Revolution: An Application of Theory to the British Cotton Industry.* Univ. of Chicago Press.

SMELSER, NEIL J. 1980 Issues in the Study of Work and Love in Adulthood. In Neil J. Smelser and Erik H. Erikson (editors), *Themes of Work and Love in Adulthood.* Cambridge, Mass.: Harvard Univ. Press.

SMELSER, NEIL J. 1988 Introduction. *Handbook of Sociology.* Newbury Park, Calif.: Sage.

SMITH, ADAM (1759) 1982 *The Theory of Moral Sentiments.* Indianapolis, Ind.: Liberty Fund.

SMITH, ADAM (1764) 1977 Letter to David Hume, 5 July 1764. In *The Correspondence of Adam Smith*. Oxford Univ. Press.

SMITH, ADAM (1776) 1937 *An Inquiry into the Nature and Causes of the Wealth of Nations*. New York: Modern Library.

SMITH, WILLIAM ROBERTSON (1889) 1901 *Lectures on the Religion of the Semites*. London: Adam and Charles Black.

SNOW, C. P. (1959) 1964 *The Two Cultures and a Second Look*. Cambridge Univ. Press.

SOLOW, ROBERT M. 1963 *Capital Theory and the Rate of Return*. Amsterdam: North-Holland.

SOLOW, ROBERT M. 1970 *Growth Theory: An Exposition*. Oxford Univ. Press.

SOLOW, ROBERT M. 1972 Notes on "Doomsday Models." National Academy of Sciences, *Proceedings* 69:3832–3833.

SOLOW, ROBERT M. 1988 Growth Theory and After. *American Economic Review* 78:307–317.

SOMBART, WERNER 1930 Capitalism. In volume 3 of *Encyclopaedia of the Social Sciences*. New York: Macmillan.

SOREL, GEORGES (1899) 1987 The Ethics of Socialism. In *From Georges Sorel: Essays in Socialism and Philosophy*. New Brunswick, N.J.: Transaction Books.

SOREL, GEORGES (1908) 1961 *Reflections on Violence*. New York: Collier Books.

SOROKIN, PITIRIM A. (1927) 1959 *Social Mobility*. In *Social and Cultural Mobility*. New York: Free Press.

SOROKIN, PITIRIM A. 1937–1941 *Social and Cultural Dynamics*. New York: American Book.

SOROKIN, PITIRIM A. 1947 *Society, Culture, and Personality: Their Structure and Dynamics; A System of General Sociology*. New York: Harper.

SOROKIN, PITIRIM A. 1956 Preface. *Fads and Foibles in Modern Sociology and Related Sciences*. Chicago: Henry Regnery.

SPENCER, HERBERT (1850) 1954 *Social Statics: The Conditions Essential to Human Happiness Specified, and the First of Them Developed*. New York: Schalkenbach Foundation.

SPENCER, HERBERT (1852) 1966 The Development Hypothesis. In volume 1 of *Essays: Scientific, Political & Speculative*. Osnabrück (Germany): Otto Zeller.

SPENCER, HERBERT (1857) 1966 Progress: Its Law and Cause. In volume 1 of *Essays: Scientific, Political & Speculative*. Osnabrück (Germany): Otto Zeller.

SPENCER, HERBERT 1860 *Education: Intellectual, Moral, and Physical*. New York: Appleton.

SPENCER, HERBERT (1862) 1888 *First Principles*. New York: Appleton.

SPENCER, HERBERT (1864–1867) 1966 *The Principles of Biology*. In volume 2 of *The Works of Herbert Spencer*. Osnabrück (Germany): Otto Zeller.

SPENCER, HERBERT (1872) 1966 Mr. Martineau on Evolution. In volume 1 of *Essays: Scientific, Political, & Speculative*. Osnabrück (Germany): Otto Zeller.

SPENCER, HERBERT (1876) 1906 *The Principles of Sociology*. New York: Appleton.

SPENCER, HERBERT 1904 *An Autobiography*. New York: Appleton.

SPENGLER, OSWALD (1918) 1926 *The Decline of the West: Form and Actuality*. New York: Knopf.

SPENGLER, OSWALD (1922) 1928 *The Decline of the West: Perspectives of World-History*. New York: Knopf.

SPINOZA, BARUCH (1677) 1955 *The Ethics*. In volume 2 of *The Chief Works of Benedict de Spinoza*. New York: Dover.

SPINOZA, BARUCH (1677) 1955 *A Political Treatise*. In volume 1 of *The Chief Works of Benedict de Spinoza*. New York: Dover.

SRAFFA, PIERO 1932 Dr. Hayek on Money and Capital. *Economic Journal* 42:42–53.

Stamp, Josiah 1929 *Some Economic Factors in Modern Life.* London: P. S. King.

Stein, Herbert 1989 *The Triumph of the Adaptive Society.* Memphis, Tenn.: P. K. Seidman Foundation.

Stern, Fritz 1956 *The Varieties of History: From Voltaire to the Present.* New York: Meridian.

Stern, Fritz 1972 Introduction to Germany Revisited. In *The Failure of Illiberalism: Essays on the Political Culture of Modern Germany.* New York: Knopf.

Stern, Fritz 1987 Einstein's Germany. In *Dreams and Delusions: The Drama of German History.* New York: Knopf.

Sterne, Laurence (1760) 1819 *The Life and Opinions of Tristram Shandy.* In volume 2 of *The Works of Laurence Sterne.* London: Cadell and Davies.

Steuart Denham, James 1767 *An Inquiry into the Principles of Political Oeconomy: Being an Essay on the Science of Domestic Policy in Free Nations.* London: A. Millar and T. Cadell.

Steward, Julian H. (1955) 1979 *Theory of Culture Change: The Methodology of Multilinear Evolution.* Urbana: Univ. of Illinois Press.

Stigler, George J. 1946 *The Theory of Price.* New York: Macmillan.

Stigler, George J. (1951) 1986 The Division of Labor Is Limited by the Extent of the Market. In *The Essence of Stigler.* Stanford, Calif.: Hoover Institution Press.

Stigler, George J. 1954 The Early History of Empirical Studies of Consumer Behavior. *Journal of Political Economy* 62:95–113.

Stigler, George J. (1961) 1986 The Economics of Information. In *The Essence of Stigler.* Stanford, Calif.: Hoover Institution Press.

Stigler, George J. (1962) 1986 What Can Regulators Regulate? The Case of Electricity. In *The Essence of Stigler.* Stanford, Calif.: Hoover Institution Press.

Stigler, George J. 1963 The Government of the Economy. In George J. Stigler and Paul A. Samuelson, *A Dialogue on the Proper Economic Role of the State.* Selected Papers No. 7. University of Chicago Graduate School of Business.

Stigler, George J. (1965) 1986 The Economist and the State. In *The Essence of Stigler.* Stanford, Calif.: Hoover Institution Press.

Stigler, George J. (1971) 1975 Smith's Travels on the Ship of State. In Andrew S. Skinner and Thomas Wilson (editors), *Essays on Adam Smith.* Oxford Univ. Press.

Stigler, George J. (1981) 1986 The Economist as Preacher. In *The Essence of Stigler.* Stanford, Calif.: Hoover Institution Press.

Stigler, George J. (1982) 1986 The Process and Progress of Economics. In *The Essence of Stigler.* Stanford, Calif.: Hoover Institution Press.

Stigler, Stephen M. 1987 Testing Hypotheses or Fitting Models? Another Look at Mass Extinctions. In Matthew H. Nitecki and Antoni Hoffman (editors), *Neutral Models in Biology.* Oxford Univ. Press.

Stinchcombe, Arthur L. 1968 *Constructing Social Theories.* San Diego, Calif.: Harcourt.

Stinchcombe, Arthur L. 1975 [A] Theory of Social Structure. In Lewis A. Coser (editor), *The Idea of Social Structure.* San Diego, Calif.: Harcourt.

Stinchcombe, Arthur L. 1978 *Theoretical Methods in Social History.* New York: Academic Press.

Stone, Lawrence 1972 *The Causes of the English Revolution: 1529–1642.* New York: Harper.

Stone, Lawrence 1987 *The Past and the Present Revisited.* London: Routledge.

Stonequist, Everett V. 1937 *The Marginal Man: A Study in Personality and Culture Conflict.* New York: Scribner.

STOUFFER, SAMUEL A. (1955) 1962 The Younger Generation Has More Schooling — What Does this Fact Portend? In *Social Research to Test Ideas: Selected Writings of Samuel A. Stouffer*. New York: Free Press.

STRACHEY, LYTTON 1918 *Eminent Victorians: Cardinal Manning, Florence Nightingale, Dr. Arnold, General Gordon*. New York: Putnam.

STRAUSS, LEO 1953 *Natural Right and History*. Univ. of Chicago Press.

STRAUSS, LEO (1955) 1973 *What Is Political Philosophy?* Westport, Conn.: Greenwood.

STUBBS, WILLIAM (1874) 1880 *The Constitutional History of England in Its Origin and Development*. Oxford Univ. Press.

SULLIVAN, HARRY STACK (1940) 1953 The Human Organism and Its Necessary Environment. In *Conceptions of Modern Psychiatry: The First William Alanson White Memorial Lectures*. New York: Norton.

SULLIVAN, HARRY STACK (1940) 1953 Therapeutic Conceptions. In *Conceptions of Modern Psychiatry: The First William Alanson White Memorial Lectures*. New York: Norton.

SUMNER, WILLIAM GRAHAM (1883) 1969 *The Forgotten Man and Other Essays*. Freeport, N.Y.: Books for Libraries Press.

SUMNER, WILLIAM GRAHAM (1906) 1940 *Folkways: A Study of the Sociological Importance of Usages, Manners, Customs, Mores, and Morals*. Boston: Ginn.

SUMNER, WILLIAM GRAHAM (1911) 1970 Sociology. In *War and Other Essays*. Freeport, N.Y.: Books for Libraries Press.

SUMNER, WILLIAM GRAHAM; AND KELLER, ALBERT GALLOWAY 1927 *The Science of Society*. New Haven, Conn.: Yale Univ. Press.

SUTHERLAND, EDWIN H. (1949) 1983 *White Collar Crime: The Uncut Version*. New Haven, Conn.: Yale Univ. Press.

TAINE, HIPPOLYTE ADOLPHE (1864) 1900 *History of English Literature*. New York: Colonial Press.

TAINE, HIPPOLYTE ADOLPHE (1876) 1931 *The Ancient Régime*. New York: Peter Smith.

TAINE, HIPPOLYTE ADOLPHE 1908 *Life and Letters of H. Taine*. London: Constable.

TAUSSIG, FRANK W. (1915) 1930 *Inventors and Money-Makers: Lectures on some Relations Between Economics and Psychology Delivered at Brown University in Connection with the Celebration of the 150th Anniversary of the Foundation of the University*. New York: Macmillan.

TAWNEY, R. H. (1918) 1964 The Conditions of Economic Liberty. In *The Radical Tradition: Twelve Essays on Politics, Education and Literature*. New York: Random House.

TAWNEY, R. H. (1920) 1948 *The Acquisitive Society*. San Diego, Calif.: Harcourt.

TAWNEY, R. H. (1926) 1954 *Religion and the Rise of Capitalism: A Historical Study*. New York: New American Library.

TAWNEY, R. H. (1931) 1952 *Equality*. London: Allen & Unwin.

TAWNEY, R. H. (1949) 1964 Social Democracy in Britain. In *The Radical Tradition: Twelve Essays on Politics, Education and Literature*. New York: Random House.

TAX, SOL (1953) 1963 *Penny Capitalism: A Guatemalan Indian Economy*. Univ. of Chicago Press.

TAYLOR, FREDERICK W. (1911–1912) 1947 Testimony before the Special House Committee. In *Scientific Management*. New York: Harper.

TEITELBAUM, MICHAEL S. 1979 As Societies Age. In *1979: Britannica Book of the Year*. Chicago: Encyclopaedia Britannica.

TERENCE 1988 The Self-Tormentor. In *The Complete Comedies of Terence*. New Brunswick, N.J.: Rutgers Univ. Press.

THOLFSEN, TRYGVE R. 1967 *Historical Thinking: An Introduction*. New York: Harper.

THOMAS, W. I. 1907 The Mind of Woman and the Lower Races. *American Journal of Sociology* 12, no. 4:435–469.

THOMAS, W. I. (1917) 1951 The Four Wishes. In *Social Behavior and Personality*. New York: Social Science Research Council.

THOMAS, W. I. (1923) 1969 *The Unadjusted Girl: With Cases and Standpoint for Behavior Analysis*. Montclair, N.J.: Patterson Smith.

THOMAS, W. I. (1931) 1951 The Relation of Research to the Social Process. In *Social Behavior and Personality: Contributions of W. I. Thomas to Theory and Social Research*. New York: Social Science Research Council.

THOMAS, W. I. 1937 *Primitive Behavior: An Introduction to the Social Sciences*. New York: McGraw-Hill.

THOMAS, W. I.; AND THOMAS, DOROTHY SWAINE 1928 *The Child in America: Behavior Problems and Programs*. New York: Knopf.

THOMAS, W. I.; AND ZNANIECKI, FLORIAN (1918–1920) 1958 *The Polish Peasant in Europe and America*. New York: Dover.

THOMPSON, E. P. 1963 *The Making of the English Working Class*. London: Victor Gollancz.

THOMPSON, JAMES WESTFALL (1942) 1967 *A History of Historical Writing*. Gloucester, Mass.: Smith.

THOMPSON, WILLIAM (1824) 1963 *An Inquiry into the Principles of the Distribution of Wealth Most Conducive to Human Happiness*. Fairfield, N.J.: Augustus M. Kelley.

THOREAU, HENRY DAVID (1849) 1950 *Civil Disobedience*. Saugatuck, Conn.: The 5X8 Press.

THOREAU, HENRY DAVID (1854) 1927 *Walden: Or Life in the Woods*. London: Chapman & Hall.

THORNDIKE, EDWARD L. 1899 Sentimentality in Science-Teaching. *Educational Review* 17, January:57–64.

THORNDIKE, EDWARD L. (1900) 1914 *The Human Nature Club: An Introduction to the Study of Mental Life*. New York: Longmans.

THORNDIKE, EDWARD L. 1909 Darwin's Contribution to Psychology. *University of California Chronicle* 12:65–80.

THORNDIKE, EDWARD L. (1912) 1973 *Education: A First Book*. New York: Arno Press.

THORNDIKE, EDWARD L. (1913) 1962 Measurement. In *Psychology and the Science of Education: Selected Writings of Edward L. Thorndike*. New York: Teachers College, Columbia Univ.

THORNDIKE, EDWARD L. (1913) 1919 *The Original Nature of Man*. New York: Teachers College, Columbia Univ.

THORNDIKE, EDWARD L. 1913 *The Psychology of Learning*. New York: Teachers College, Columbia Univ.

THUCYDIDES 1951 *The Peloponnesian War*. In *The Complete Writings of Thucydides: The Peloponnesian War*. New York: Modern Library.

THÜNEN, JOHANN HEINRICH VON (1826) 1966 *Von Thünen's Isolated State*. Oxford (United Kingdom): Pergamon.

TILLY, CHARLES 1964 *The Vendée*. Cambridge, Mass.: Harvard Univ. Press.

TILLY, CHARLES; AND BROWN, C. HAROLD 1967 On Uprooting, Kinship, and the Auspices of Migration. *International Journal of Comparative Sociology* 8, no. 2:139–164.

TIRYAKIAN, EDWARD A. 1981 The Sociological Import of a Metaphor: Tracking the Source of Max Weber's "Iron Cage." *Sociological Inquiry* 51, no. 1:27–33.

TITCHENER, EDWARD B. (1896) 1926 *A Text-Book of Psychology*. New York: Macmillan.

TITCHENER, EDWARD B. (1897) 1906 *An Outline of Psychology.* New York: Macmillan.

TITCHENER, EDWARD B. 1898 The Postulates of a Structural Psychology. *Philosophical Review* 7, no. 5:449–465.

TITCHENER, EDWARD B. 1929 *Systematic Psychology: Prolegomena.* New York: Macmillan.

TITMUSS, RICHARD (1971) 1972 *The Gift Relationship: From Human Blood to Social Policy.* New York: Random House.

TOBIN, JAMES (1981) 1987 Supply-side Economics: What Is It? Will It Work? In *Policies for Prosperity: Essays in a Keynesian Mode.* Cambridge, Mass.: M.I.T. Press.

TOCQUEVILLE, ALEXIS DE (1831) 1985 Letter to Ernest de Chabrol, 9 June 1831. In *Alexis de Tocqueville: Selected Letters on Politics and Society.* Berkeley and Los Angeles: Univ. of California Press.

TOCQUEVILLE, ALEXIS DE (1835) 1985 Letter to Louis de Kergorlay, January 1835. In *Alexis de Tocqueville: Selected Letters on Politics and Society.* Berkeley and Los Angeles: Univ. of California Press.

TOCQUEVILLE, ALEXIS DE (1835–1840) 1945 *Democracy in America.* New York: Vintage.

TOCQUEVILLE, ALEXIS DE (1853) 1985 Letter to Pierre Freslon, 23 September 1853. In *Alexis de Tocqueville: Selected Letters on Politics and Society.* Berkeley and Los Angeles: Univ. of California Press.

TOCQUEVILLE, ALEXIS DE (1856) 1945 *The Old Régime and the French Revolution.* New York: Doubleday.

TOFFLER, ALVIN 1970 *Future Shock.* New York: Random House.

TOLMAN, EDWARD C. 1938 The Determiners of Behavior at a Choice Point. *Psychological Review* 45:1–41.

TOLMAN, EDWARD C. 1945 A Stimulus-Expectancy Need-Cathexis Psychology. *Science* 101:160–166.

TOLMAN, EDWARD C. 1959 Principles of Purposive Behavior. In Sigmund Koch (editor), *Psychology: A Study of a Science.* New York: McGraw-Hill.

TOLSTOY, LEO (1865–1869) 1970 *War and Peace.* New York: Simon & Schuster.

TOLSTOY, LEO (1875–1877) 1939 *Anna Karenina.* New York: Random House.

TÖNNIES, FERDINAND (1887) 1957 *Community & Society (Gemeinschaft und Gesellschaft).* East Lansing: Michigan State Univ. Press.

TÖNNIES, FERDINAND 1922 *Kritik der öffentlichen Meinung.* Berlin: Springer. Quoted in Gillian Lindt Gollin and Albert E. Gollin, Tönnies on Public Opinion. In Werner J. Cahnman (editor), *Ferdinand Tönnies: A New Evaluation* 1973:193. Leiden: E. J. Brill.

TOYNBEE, ARNOLD (1884) 1956 *The Industrial Revolution.* Boston: Beacon.

TOYNBEE, ARNOLD J. 1934 *A Study of History.* Oxford Univ. Press.

TOYNBEE, ARNOLD J. 1947 *A Study of History.* Somervell abridgement. Oxford Univ. Press.

TOYNBEE, ARNOLD J. 1948 *Civilization on Trial.* Oxford Univ. Press.

TREITSCHKE, HEINRICH VON (1897–1898) 1963 *Politics.* San Diego, Calif.: Harcourt.

TREVELYAN, GEORGE MACAULAY (1942) 1946 *English Social History: A Survey of Six Centuries; Chaucer to Queen Victoria.* London: Longmans.

TREVOR-ROPER, H. R. 1958 Introduction to Jacob Burckhardt, *Judgments on History and Historians* (1957). Boston: Beacon.

TREVOR-ROPER, H. R. 1980 *History and Imagination.* Oxford Univ. Press.

TRILLING, DIANA (1950) 1964 Men, Women, and Sex. In *Claremont Essays.* San Diego, Calif.: Harcourt.

TRILLING, DIANA (1970) 1977 Female Biology in a Male Culture. In *We Must March My Darlings.* San Diego, Calif.: Harcourt.

TRILLING, LIONEL (1940) 1950 Freud and Literature. In *The Liberal Imagination: Essays on Literature and Society.* New York: Viking.

TRILLING, LIONEL (1955) 1965 Freud: Within and Beyond Culture. In *Beyond Culture: Essays on Literature and Learning.* San Diego, Calif.: Harcourt.

TRILLING, LIONEL 1972 *Sincerity and Authenticity.* Cambridge, Mass.: Harvard Univ. Press.

TRILLING, LIONEL (1973) 1981 Mind in the Modern World. In *The Last Decade: Essays and Reviews, 1965–75.* San Diego, Calif.: Harcourt.

TROELTSCH, ERNST (1912) 1981 *The Social Teaching of the Christian Churches.* Univ. of Chicago Press.

TROLLOPE, FRANCES (1832) 1949 *Domestic Manners of the Americans.* New York: Knopf.

TROTSKY, LEON (1932) 1957 *The History of the Russian Revolution.* Ann Arbor: Univ. of Michigan Press.

TROTSKY, LEON (1937) 1945 *The Revolution Betrayed: What Is the Soviet Union and Where Is It Going?* New York: Pioneer Publishers.

TROTSKY, LEON 1941 *Stalin: An Appraisal of the Man and His Influence.* New York: Grosset & Dunlap.

TRUMAN, DAVID B. (1951) 1971 *The Governmental Process: Political Interests and Public Opinion.* New York: Knopf.

TURGOT, ANNE ROBERT JACQUES (1750) 1973 A Philosophical Review of the Successive Advances of the Human Mind. In *Turgot on Progress, Sociology, and Economics.* Cambridge Univ. Press.

TURGOT, ANNE ROBERT JACQUES (1750) 1844 *Plan de deux discours sur l'histoire universelle.* Paris: Guillaumin. Quoted in Marvin Harris, *The Rise of Anthropological Theory* (1968) 1970:14. New York: Crowell.

TURGOT, ANNE ROBERT JACQUES (1751?) 1913 Plan du premier discours sur la formation des gouvernements et le mélange des nations. In volume 1 of *Oeuvres de Turgot et documents le concernant.* Paris: Libraire Alcan. Quoted in Frank E. Manuel, *The Prophets of Paris: Turgot, Condorcet, Saint-Simon, Fourier, and Comte* 1965:47. New York: Harper.

TURGOT, ANNE ROBERT JACQUES (1751?) 1913 *Réflexions sur les langues.* In volume 1 of *Oeuvres de Turgot et documents le concernant.* Paris: Libraire Feliz Alcan. Quoted in Frank E. Manuel, *The Prophets of Paris: Turgot, Condorcet, Saint-Simon, Fourier, and Comte* 1965:30. New York: Harper.

TURGOT, ANNE ROBERT JACQUES (date uncertain) 1913 Plan d'un ouvrage sur la géographie politique. In *Pensées diverses sur la morale.* Volume 1 of *Oeuvres de Turgot et documents le concernant.* Paris: Libraire Feliz Alcan. Quoted in Frank E. Manuel, *The Prophets of Paris: Turgot, Condorcet, Saint-Simon, Fourier, and Comte* 1965:22. New York: Harper.

TURNER, FREDERICK JACKSON (1891) 1961 The Significance of History. In *Frontier and Section: Selected Essays of Frederick Jackson Turner.* Englewood Cliffs, N.J.: Prentice-Hall.

TURNER, FREDERICK JACKSON (1893) 1962 The Significance of the Frontier in American History. In *The Frontier in American History.* New York: Holt.

TURNER, VICTOR W. 1968 Myth and Symbol. In volume 10 of *International Encyclopedia of the Social Sciences.* New York: Macmillan and Free Press.

TURNER, VICTOR W. 1969 *The Ritual Process: Structure and Anti-Structure.* Chicago: Aldine.

TURNER, VICTOR W.; AND TURNER, EDITH 1978 *Image and Pilgrimage in Christian Culture: Anthropological Perspectives.* New York: Columbia Univ. Press.

TWAIN, MARK 1924 *Mark Twain's Autobiography.* New York: Harper.

TYLOR, EDWARD BURNETT (1871) 1958 *The Origins of Culture.* New York: Harper.

TYLOR, EDWARD BURNETT (1871)1958 *Religion in Primitive Culture.* New York: Harper.

VEBLEN, THORSTEIN (1898) 1948 Why Is Economics Not an Evolutionary Science? In *The Portable Veblen*. New York: Viking.

VEBLEN, THORSTEIN (1899) 1973 *The Theory of the Leisure Class*. Boston: Houghton Mifflin.

VEBLEN, THORSTEIN (1906) 1961 The Place of Science in Modern Civilisation. In *The Place of Science in Modern Civilisation and Other Essays*. New York: Russell & Russell.

VEBLEN, THORSTEIN (1914) 1964 *The Instinct of Workmanship and the State of the Industrial Arts*. Fairfield, N.J.: Augustus M. Kelley.

VEBLEN, THORSTEIN (1918) 1965 *The Higher Learning in America: A Memorandum on the Conduct of Universities by Business Men*. Fairfield, N.J.: Augustus M. Kelley.

VICO, GIOVANNI BATTISTA (1710) 1914 *De antiquissima italorum sapientia ex linguae originibus eruenda*. In volume 1 of *Opere*. Bari (Italy): Laterza. Quoted in Isaiah Berlin, *Vico and Herder* 1976:1. New York: Viking.

VICO, GIOVANNI BATTISTA (1725) 1984 *The New Science of Giambattista Vico*. Ithaca, N.Y.: Cornell Univ. Press.

VIDAL DE LA BLACHE, PAUL 1903 Tableau de la géographie de la France. Volume 1, part 1 of Ernest Lavisse, *Histoire de France depuis les origines jusqu'à la Révolution*. Paris: Hachette. Quoted in Rupert B. Vance, Region. Volume 1 of *International Encyclopedia of the Social Sciences* 1968:379. New York: Macmillan and Free Press.

VOLTAIRE (1732) 1961 On the Presbyterians. In *Philosophical Letters*. Indianapolis, Ind.: Bobbs-Merrill.

VOLTAIRE 1738 Letter to Thieriot, 31 October 1738. Quoted in J. B. Black, *The Art of History* (1926) 1965:1. New York: Russell & Russell.

VOLTAIRE 1756 *Essai sur les moeurs et les esprit des nations*. Quoted in Jeanne Matignon et al. (editors), *Noveau dictionnaire de citations françaises* 1970:500. Paris: Hachette-Tchou.

VOLTAIRE (1764) 1923 *Voltaire's Philosophical Dictionary*. London: Allen & Unwin.

VOLTAIRE 1778–1782 Histoire. In volume 17 of Denis Diderot (editor), *Encyclopédie, ou Dictionnaire raisonné des sciences, des arts et des métiers*. Lausanne and Bern. Quoted in James Westfall Thompson, *A History of Historical Writing*. (1942) 1967:Vol. 2, 67. Gloucester, Mass.: Peter Smith.

VOLTAIRE 1785–1789 Introduction à l'Abrégé de l'histoire universelle. In volume 24 of *Oeuvres*. Quoted in J. B. Black, *The Art of History* 1965:84. New York: Russell & Russell.

VON MISES, LUDWIG (1912) 1971 *The Theory of Money and Credit*. Irvington, N.Y.: Foundation for Economic Education.

VON MISES, LUDWIG (1949) 1966 *Human Action: A Treatise on Economics* Chicago: Henry Regnery.

VON MISES, LUDWIG 1957 *Theory and History: An Interpretation of Social and Economic Evolution*. New Haven, Conn.: Yale Univ. Press.

VON NEUMANN, JOHN; AND MORGENSTERN, OSKAR (1944) 1953 *Theory of Games and Economic Behavior*. Princeton Univ. Press.

VYGOTSKY, L. S. (1960) 1978 *Mind in Society: The Development of Higher Psychological Processes*. Cambridge, Mass.: Harvard Univ. Press.

VYGOTSKY, L. S. 1960 *Razvitie vysshykh psikhicheskikh funktstil* [The Development of Higher Mental Functions]. Moscow: Izdatel'stvo Akademii Pedagogicheskikh Nauk. Quoted in James V. Wertsch, *Vygotsky and the Social Formation of the Mind* 1985:90. Cambridge, Mass.: Harvard Univ. Press.

VYGOTSKY, L. S. (1979) 1981 The Genesis of Higher Mental Functions. In James V. Wertsch (editor), *The Concept of Activity in Soviet Psychology*. Armonk, N.Y.: M. E. Sharpe.

WALKER, FRANCIS A. 1874 Address on the Wages Question. *The New York Times* 9 July.

Walker, Francis A. (1883) 1888 *Political Economy*. New York: Holt.

Wallace, Alfred Russel (1905) 1974 *My Life: A Record of Events and Opinions*. New York: AMS Press.

Wallace, Anthony F. C. 1956 Revitalization Movements. *American Anthropologist* 58:264–281.

Wallace, Anthony F. C. 1961 *Culture and Personality*. New York: Random House.

Wallas, Graham (1914) 1932 *The Great Society: A Psychological Analysis*. London: Macmillan.

Wallas, Graham 1926 *The Art of Thought*. London: Jonathan Cape.

Walras, Léon (1874) 1977 *Elements of Pure Economics: Or the Theory of Social Wealth*. Fairfield, N.J.: Augustus M. Kelley.

Ward, Lester F. (1883) 1926 *Dynamic Sociology: Or Applied Social Science, as Based upon Statistical Sociology and the Less Complex Sciences*. New York: Appleton.

Warner, W. Lloyd; and Lunt, Paul S. (1941) 1966 *The Social Life of a Modern Community*. New Haven, Conn.: Yale Univ. Press.

Watson, John B. 1913 Psychology as the Behaviorist Views It. *Psychological Review* 20, no. 2:158–197.

Watson, John B. (1924) 1930 *Behaviorism*. Univ. of Chicago Press.

Watson, John B. 1926 What the Nursery Has to Say about Instincts. In Madison Bentley et al., *Psychologies of 1925: Powell Lectures in Psychological Theory*. Worcester, Mass.: Clark Univ. Press.

Watson, John B. 1927 Are You Giving Your Child a Chance? The Behaviorist Speaks. *McCall's Magazine* October.

Watson, John B. 1929 Behaviorism — The Modern Note in Psychology. In *The Battle of Behaviorism: An Exposition and an Exposure*. New York: Norton.

Watson, John B. 1929 Introduction to G. V. Hamilton and Kenneth Macgowan, *What Is Wrong with Marriage*. New York: A & C Boni.

Webb, Sidney 1910 Eugenics and the Poor Law. *Eugenics Review* 2, no. 3:233–241.

Webb, Sidney 1923 *The Labour Party on the Threshold*. London: The Fabian Society.

Weber, Alfred 1927 *Ideen zur Staats- und Kultursoziologie*. Karlsruhe (Germany): G. Braun.

Weber, Alfred 1953 *Der dritte oder vierte Mensch: Von Sinn des geschichtlichen Daseins*. Munich: Piper.

Weber, Alfred 1955 *Einführung in die Soziologie*. Munich: Piper.

Weber, Max (1904) 1949 "Objectivity" in Social Science and Social Policy. In *Max Weber on the Methodology of the Social Sciences*. New York: Free Press.

Weber, Max (1904–1905) 1930 *The Protestant Ethic and the Spirit of Capitalism*. New York: Scribner.

Weber, Max (1909) 1979 Bureaucratization. In J. P. Mayer, *Max Weber and German Politics*. New York: Arno Press.

Weber, Max 1913 Über einige Kategorien der verstehenden Soziologie. *Logos: Internationale Zeitschrift für Philosophie der Kultur* 4:253–294.

Weber, Max (1915) 1946 Religious Rejections of the World and Their Directions. In *From Max Weber: Essays in Sociology*. Edited by H. H. Gerth and C. Wright Mills. Oxford Univ. Press.

Weber, Max (1915) 1946 The Social Psychology of the World Religions. In *From Max Weber: Essays in Sociology*. Edited by H. H. Gerth and C. Wright Mills. Oxford Univ. Press.

Weber, Max (1917) 1949 The Meaning of "Ethical Neutrality" in Sociology and Economics. In *Max Weber on the Methodology of the Social Sciences*. New York: Free Press.

WEBER, MAX (1917–1919) 1952 *Ancient Judaism*. New York: Free Press.

WEBER, MAX (1919) 1946 Politics as a Vocation. In *From Max Weber: Essays in Sociology*. Edited by H. H. Gerth and C. Wright Mills. Oxford Univ. Press.

WEBER, MAX (1919) 1946 Science as a Vocation. In *From Max Weber: Essays in Sociology*. Edited by H. H. Gerth and C. Wright Mills. Oxford Univ. Press.

WEBER, MAX (1919) 1988 Letter to Karl Rothenbücher. In Marianne Weber, *Max Weber: A Biography*. New Brunswick, N.J.: Transaction Books.

WEBER, MAX (1922) 1968 *Economy and Society: An Outline of Interpretive Sociology*. New York: Bedminster.

WEBER, MAX (1923) 1981 *General Economic History*. New Brunswick, N.J.: Transaction Books.

WEDGEWOOD, C. V. (1944) 1967 *William the Silent*. London: Jonathan Cape.

WEINBERG, ALVIN 1972 Social Institutions and Nuclear Energy. *Science* 177:27–34.

WELLS, H. G. 1910 *The New Machiavelli*. New York: Duffield.

WEST, REBECCA 1916 *Henry James*. London: Nisbet.

WHITE, LESLIE A. 1949 *The Science of Culture: A Study of Man and Civilization*. New York: Farrar, Straus.

WHITE, LYNN T., JR. 1967 The Historical Roots of Our Ecologic Crisis. *Science* 155:1203–1207.

WHITE, LYNN T., JR. 1974 Technology Assessment from the Stance of a Medieval Historian. *American Historical Review* 79:1–13.

WHITEHEAD, ALFRED NORTH 1911 *An Introduction to Mathematics*. New York: Holt.

WHITEHEAD, ALFRED NORTH 1917 The Organisation of Thought. In *The Organisation of Thought: Educational and Scientific*. London: Williams and Norgate.

WHITEHEAD, ALFRED NORTH (1925) 1948 *Science and the Modern World: Lowell Lectures, 1925*. New York: New American Library.

WHITEHEAD, ALFRED NORTH (1929) 1979 *Process and Reality: An Essay in Cosmology*. New York: Free Press.

WHITEHEAD, ALFRED NORTH (1943) 1954 Dialogue 28, 3 June 1943. In *Dialogues of Alfred North Whitehead*. Boston: Atlantic Monthly Press.

WHITMAN, WALT (1856) 1926 By Blue Ontario's Shore. In *Leaves of Grass*. New York: Doubleday.

WHITNEY, WILLIAM DWIGHT (1867) 1891 *Language and the Study of Language*. New York: Scribner.

WHITNEY, WILLIAM DWIGHT (1875) 1979 *The Life and Growth of Language: An Outline of Linguistic Science*. New York: Dover.

WHORF, BENJAMIN L. (1941) 1956 Languages and Logic. In *Language, Thought, and Reality: Selected Writings of Benjamin Lee Whorf*. Cambridge, Mass.: Technology Press of M.I.T.

WHORF, BENJAMIN L. (1941) 1956 The Relation of Habitual Thought and Behavior to Language. In *Language, Thought, and Reality: Selected Writings of Benjamin Lee Whorf*. Cambridge, Mass.: Technology Press of M.I.T.

WHORF, BENJAMIN L. (1942) 1956 Language, Mind, and Reality. In *Language, Thought, and Reality: Selected Writings of Benjamin Lee Whorf*. Cambridge, Mass.: Technology Press of M.I.T.

WHORF, BENJAMIN L. 1956 A Linguistic Consideration of Thinking in Primitive Communities. In *Language, Thought, and Reality: Selected Writings of Benjamin Lee Whorf*. Cambridge, Mass.: Technology Press of M.I.T.

WHYTE, LANCELOT LAW 1960 *The Unconscious before Freud*. New York: Basic Books.

WHYTE, WILLIAM F. (1943) 1955 *Street Corner Society: The Social Structure of an Italian Slum*. Univ. of Chicago Press.

WHYTE, WILLIAM F. ET AL. (1955) 1977 *Money and Motivation: An Analysis of Incentives in Industry*. Westport, Conn.: Greenwood.

WHYTE, WILLIAM H., JR. 1956 *The Organization Man*. Simon & Schuster.

WICKSELL, KNUT (1901–1906) 1967 *Lectures on Political Economy*. New York: Augustus M. Kelley.

WICKSTEED, PHILIP HENRY (1910) 1938 *The Commonsense of Political Economy*. London: Routledge.

WIENER, NORBERT (1948) 1961 *Cybernetics: Or Control and Communication in the Animal and the Machine*. Cambridge, Mass.: M.I.T. Press.

WIENER, NORBERT (1950) 1954 *The Human Use of Human Beings: Cybernetics and Society*. New York: Doubleday.

WIENER, NORBERT (1964) 1966 *God and Golem, Inc.: A Comment on Certain Points Where Cybernetics Impinges on Religion*. Cambridge, Mass.: M.I.T. Press.

WIESER, FRIEDRICH VON (1914) 1927 *Social Economics*. New York: Adelphi.

WILLIAMS, ROBIN M., JR. 1947 *The Reduction of Intergroup Tensions: A Survey of Research on Problems of Ethnic, Racial, and Religious Group Relations*. New York: Social Science Research Council.

WILLIAMS, ROBIN M., JR. 1951 *American Society: A Sociological Interpretation*. New York: Knopf.

WILSON, EDWARD O. 1975 *Sociobiology: The New Synthesis*. Cambridge, Mass.: Harvard Univ. Press.

WILSON, EDWARD O. 1978 *On Human Nature*. Cambridge, Mass.: Harvard Univ. Press.

WILSON, WILLIAM JULIUS 1978 *The Declining Significance of Race: Blacks and Changing American Institutions*. Univ. of Chicago Press.

WILSON, WILLIAM JULIUS 1987 *The Truly Disadvantaged: The Inner City, the Underclass, and Public Policy*. Univ. of Chicago Press.

WILSON, WOODROW 1911 The Law and the Facts. *American Political Science Review* 5, no. 1:1–11.

WILSON, WOODROW 1913 *The New Freedom*. New York: Doubleday.

WILSON, WOODROW (1915) 1980 Remarks to the Associated Press, 20 April 1915. In volume 33 of *The Papers of Woodrow Wilson*. Princeton Univ. Press.

WILSON, WOODROW (1918)1984 An Address to a Joint Session of Congress, 8 January 1918. In volume 45 of *The Papers of Woodrow Wilson*. Princeton Univ. Press.

WIRTH, LOUIS (1938) 1964 Urbanism as a Way of Life. In *Louis Wirth on Cities and Social Life: Selected Papers*. Univ. of Chicago Press.

WITTFOGEL, KARL A. 1957 *Oriental Despotism: A Comparative Study of Total Power*. New Haven, Conn.: Yale Univ. Press.

WITTGENSTEIN, LUDWIG (1921) 1981 *Tractatus Logico-Philosophicus*. London: Routledge.

WITTGENSTEIN, LUDWIG (1953) 1967 *Philosophical Investigations*. New York: Macmillan.

WITTGENSTEIN, LUDWIG 1967 *Zettel*. Berkeley and Los Angeles: Univ. of California Press.

WOODWARD, C. VANN (1955) 1974 *The Strange Career of Jim Crow*. Oxford Univ. Press.

WOODWARD, C. VANN 1960 *The Burden of Southern History*. Baton Rouge: Louisiana State Univ. Press.

WOODWORTH, ROBERT S. (1931) 1948 *Contemporary Schools of Psychology*. New York: Ronald Press.

WRONG, DENNIS H. 1961 The Oversocialized Conception of Man in Modern Sociology. *American Sociological Review* 26:183–193.

WUNDT, WILHELM 1862 *Beiträge zur Theorie der Sinneswahrnehmung*. Leipzig: Winter.

WUNDT, WILHELM (1864–1865) 1894 *Lectures on Human and Animal Psychology*. London: Swan Sonnenschein & Co.

WUNDT, WILHELM (1873) 1904 *Principles of Physiological Psychology*. London: Swan Sonnenschein & Co.

WUNDT, WILHELM 1882 Die Aufgaben der experimentellen Psychologie. *Unsere Zeit* 3.

WUNDT, WILHELM (1886) 1922 *Ethics: An Investigation of the Facts and Laws of the Moral Life*. London: Allen & Unwin.

WYMAN, JEFFRIES; AND GILL, STANLEY J. 1987 Conversations with Jeffries Wyman. *Annual Review of Biophysics and Biophysical Chemistry* 16:1–23.

YINGER, J. MILTON 1960 Contraculture and Subculture. *American Sociological Review* 25:625–635.

YOUNG, MICHAEL (1958) 1961 *The Rise of the Meritocracy: 1870–2033*. London: Penguin.

ZANGWILL, ISRAEL (1909) 1932 *The Melting-Pot: Drama in Four Acts*. New York: Macmillan.

ZEAMAN, DAVID 1959 Skinner's Theory of Teaching Machines. In Eugene Galenter (editor), *Automatic Teaching: The State of the Art*. New York: Wiley.

ZNANIECKI, FLORIAN 1919 *Cultural Reality*. Univ. of Chicago Press.

ZNANIECKI, FLORIAN (1934) 1968 *The Method of Sociology*. New York: Octagon.

ZNANIECKI, FLORIAN (1952) 1963 *Cultural Sciences: Their Origin and Development*. Urbana: Univ. of Illinois Press.

Index

Each subentry in the index is followed by the author's name and the number of the indexed quotation. Main entries in **boldface** signify the author of one or more of the quotations in the text.

society is nexus of a., Bentley: 1
unintended repercussions of intentional human a., Popper: 4
activity:
conservation is necessary for all rational a., Piaget and Szeminska: 1
use of words in all forms of human a. an indispensable correlate of bodily behavior, Malinowski: 16
Acton, J.E.E.D.:
[Turner] most reminiscent of Lord A., Hofstadter: 5
acts:
men begin with a., not thoughts, Sumner: 3
O Mr. Marx, you know economic reasons for our a., Auden: 1
Adams, Henry
Adams, James Truslow
Adams, John
Adler, Alfred
administered:
whate'er is best a. is best, Pope: 2
administration:
choice only between bureaucracy and dilettantism in field of a., Weber, Max: 23
fatal defect of current principles of a. that they occur in pairs, Simon: 1
true test of good government is aptitude to produce good a., Hamilton: 3
administrative staff:
whole a.s. consists of officials who are appointed and function according to criteria, Weber, Max: 22
administrative theory:
central concern of a.t. is boundary between rational and non-rational aspects of human social behavior, Simon: 3
adolescence:
genius is intensified and prolonged a., Hall: 3
genius lives in perpetual a., Cattell, Raymond B.: 1
adolescent's energy:
structure secondary education so that it captures a.e., Coleman: 1
Adorno, T. W.
advanced:
terms such as a. and backward when comparing a society may generate conflicts of pride and meaning, Smelser: 1
advantage:
who has seen men acting solely for sake of a.?, Dostoevsky: 1
advantages:
no longer speak of goods but of a., Arrow: 1
advertising:
a. treated with hostility economists normally reserve for monopolists, Stigler, George J.: 2
aesthetic:
to [Freud], a. work is way of mastering, or disguising failure to master, world, Gay: 2
affections:
numberless are ways in which a. infect understanding, Bacon: 6
age(s):
a. of chivalry is gone, Burke, Edmund: 10
a. of intellectual organization of political hatreds, Benda: 1
[a.] serves as a category for allocating roles, Eisenstadt: 1
at three years of a. emotional life plan laid down, Watson: 6
each a. tries to form its own conception of the past, Turner, Frederick Jackson: 1
every a. creates its own Rousseau, Darnton: 3
every a. must be free to act for itself, Paine: 2
great man actualizes his a., Hegel: 3
his acts being seven a., Shakespeare: 1
[historian's] view is conditioned by mentality of his own a., Bury: 1
true spirit of an a. revealed in its mode of expressing commonplace things, Huizinga: 3
Agesilaus
aggregation of action:
a.o.a. model should play important role in sociology, Boudon: 1
aggression:
a. always consequence of frustration, Dollard: 1
children cannot find their ways to acts of sexual a. unless they have been seduced previously, Freud: 3
hostility toward lawbreaker has advantage of uniting community in emotional solidarity of a., Mead, George Herbert: 1
aging:
[a. society is comprised] of old people ruminating over old ideas, Sauvy: 2
dynamic interplay between people growing older and society undergoing change, Riley: 1
agnostic:
as judges we are neither Catholic nor a., Frankfurter: 2
agriculture:
a. multiplies wealth [from land], Quesnay: 1
aid: [*see* mutual aid]
aim:
a. much higher than real target to accomplish real end, Machiavelli: 8
show us not the a. without the way, Lassalle: 1
ale-houses:
not multitude of a.-h. that [causes] drunkenness; but that disposition arising from other causes gives employment to multitude of a.h., Smith, Adam: 20
Alexander the Great:
kingdoms are great robberies, Augustine: 1
alienated:
a. consciousness is undialectical consciousness, Berger: 1
alienation:
a. is the process whereby the dialectical relationship between individual and his world is lost to consciousness, Berger: 1
free choice among variety of goods and services does not signify freedom if they sustain a., Marcuse: 2
theory of a. demonstrated that man does not realize himself in his labor, Marcuse: 1
alliances:
entangling a. with none, Jefferson: 10, 14
Allport, Floyd H.
Allport, Gordon W.
Althusser, Louis
altruism:
a. evolves by natural selection [through] kinship, Wilson, Edward O.: 1, 2
commercialization of blood and donor relationships represses expression of a., Titmuss: 2
when [individual] increases fitness of another at expense of own fitness, has performed act of a., Wilson, Edward O.: 2
altruistic:
a. suicide [when] basis of existence appears situated beyond life itself, Durkheim: 14
in a. gift-giving, act of giving evaluated positively above pleasure [of] recipient, Elster: 3
structuring of social institutions can encourage or discourage the a. in man, Titmuss: 1
ambiguities:
benefits to be gained from a. of scientific discourse, Levine: 1
ambiguity:
intolerance of a. part of ego-ideal of Nazi ideology exponents in professional psychology, Frenkel-Brunswik: 1
ambiguous:
attributes of liminality (threshold people) are ambiguous, Turner, Victor W.: 2
America:
A. country where doctrine of sovereignty of the people can be fairly appreciated, Tocqueville: 3
A. discovered accidentally [and] named after man who discovered no part of New World, Morison: 1
A. has contributed to concept of ghetto restriction on basis of skin color, Clark, Kenneth B.: 1
A. is great Melting-Pot, Zangwill: 1
GNP can tell everything about A. except why we are proud, Kennedy: 1
if ever A. undergoes great revolutions, will be brought about by presence of the black race, Tocqueville: 25
in A. majority raises barriers around liberty of opinion, Tocqueville: 7
in A. no one is degraded because he works, Tocqueville: 21
in A. there are factions, but no conspiracies, Tocqueville: 5
Negroes' status in A. so precarious they have to get allies in white camp, Myrdal: 5
never entangle in broils of Europe [nor] suffer Europe to intermeddle with A., Jefferson: 14

nothing easier than becoming rich in A., Tocqueville: 1
once colonies become self-sufficient they do what A. will one day do, Turgot: 1
other A., the A. of poverty, Harrington: 1
scarcely any political quesion arises that is not resolved into judicial, Tocqueville: 8
who are you who would talk or sing to A.?, Whitman: 1
[*see also* United States]
American:
A. creed, valuations preserved on the general plane, Myrdal: 2
A. Dilemma, the ever-raging conflict between high precepts and specific planes of individual and group living, Myrdal: 2
A. functionaries independent within prescribed sphere, Tocqueville: 6
A. Negro problem is problem in the heart of the A., Myrdal: 2
anticipate fundamental changes in A. race relations [and] development toward A. ideal, Myrdal: 1
every A. is said to love a title, Taussig: 1
experience [of South] thoroughly un-A., Woodward: 2
hardly surprising that first historian to emphasize accelerating velocity of history [Henry Adams] should have been an A., Schlesinger: 4
irony of A. race relations is that rejected Negro must find strength to free privileged white, Clark, Kenneth B.: 2
life of A. passed like game of chance, Tocqueville: 14
present-day A. social science dedicated to proposition that all men endowed by evolutionary process, but with no natural right, Strauss: 1
real losers [in A. Revolution] were A. loyalists, Bailyn: 2
thank Hebrew deity in Indo-European language that he is 100 percent A., Linton: 5
three characteristics of A. education — popularization, multitudinousness, politicalization, Cremin: 1
to decry wars, to refuse to go, as A. as apple pie, Lipset: 3
[Tocqueville and I] have ambitious plans. . . [for] book that gives accurate notion of the A. people, Beaumont: 1
unity coming directly from diversity [in A. society], Williams: 2
what, then, is the A., this new man?, Crèvecoeur: 1
American flag:
protect with equal vigor right to destroy [A.f.] and right to wave it, Rothstein: 1
American history:
A.h. has been history of colonization of Great West, Turner, Frederick Jackson: 2
frontier has gone [closing] first period of A.h., Turner, Frederick Jackson: 3
American Revolution:
Burke: 4
real losers [in A.R.] were American loyalists, Bailyn: 2
Americanization:
concepts of identity and identity crisis grounded in experience of A., Erikson, Erik H: 8
Americans:
A. are born equal instead of becoming so, Tocqueville: 17
A. are nation because they once obeyed a king, Maine: 8
A. never use word peasant because have no idea what class term denotes, Tocqueville: 12
old A. are "WASPs," Hacker: 1
to superiority of their women that singular prosperity [of A.] be attributed, Tocqueville: 22
to think as A. were doing before Independence, was to reconceive fundamentals of government, Bailyn: 1
America's:
Treatment of Negro is A. greatest and most conspicuous scandal, Myrdal: 6
analysis:
dream a. stands or falls with unconscious, Jung: 6
moral obtuseness is necessary condition for scientific a., Strauss: 3
successful economic a. certain to be group product, Solow: 6
thematic a. is identification of particular map of themata which can characterize a scientist, Holton: 2
[*see also* psychoanalysis]
analytical economics:
further development of a.e. along lines of comparative dynamics must rest with future, Samuelson: 3
anarchism:
a. no more merits serious discussion than a fairy-tale, Pareto: 3
Proudhon: 5
anatomy:
a. is destiny, Freud: 20
am I saying that a. is destiny? Yes, Erikson, Erik H.: 6
to learn and to teach a. from dissections, Harvey: 1
ancestors:
democracy makes every man forget his a., Tocqueville: 18
people will not look forward to posterity, who never look backward to their a., Burke, Edmund: 7
ancient:
a. religion part of social order which embraces gods and men alike, Smith, William Robertson: 4
from most a. subject shall produce the newest science, Ebbinghaus: 2
I enter a. courts of a. men and give myself over to them, Machiavelli: 1
in study of a. religions begin with ritual and traditional usage, Smith, William Robertson: 1
ancients:
to understand the a., must study them without comparison with us, Fustel de Coulanges: 3
angels:
if men were a., no government would be necessary, Madison: 7
animal:
in Darwin, a. kingdom figures as civil society, Marx: 13
man is human a. transformed by social experience into a human being, Sullivan: 1
man more of political a. [because] man is only a. endowed with gift of speech, Aristotle: 8
Morgan's canon on parsimony in a. research, Morgan, C. Lloyd: 1
mutual aid as much law of a. life as mutual struggle, Kropotkin: 2
psychology of a. learning matter of agreeing or disagreeing with Thorndike, Tolman: 1
what is a. becomes human and human a., Marx: 3
animals:
all a. equal but some more than others, Orwell: 1
behavior of man and behavior of a. must be considered in same plane, Watson: 1
man is best of a., Aristotle: 9
anomic suicide:
a.s. results from activity's lacking regulation, Durkheim: 13, 14
anomie (anomy):
a. state of mind of one pulled up from his moral roots, MacIver: 6
Durkheim able to offer explanation of why diversity of ethical opinion associated with a., Parsons, Talcott: 6
state of de-regulation or a. is heightened by passions, Durkheim: 13
antagonism:
by a. I mean the unsocial sociability of men, Kant: 1
democratic republic does not abolish a. between classes, Engels: 6
anthropologist:
a. must relinquish his comfortable position on the verandah, Malinowski: 15
social a. seeks to reveal underlying structural order, Evans-Pritchard: 2
anthropologists:
a. learn to think of one whole, Mead, Margaret: 8
historical a. dispute with evolutionists on social forms, Murdock: 2
anthropology:
a. [attracted] me because of structural affinity between civilizations it studies and my way of thinking, Lévi-Strauss: 3
a. found its Galileo in Rivers, its Newton in Mauss, Lévi-Strauss: 9
a. outcome of historical process which has made larger part of mankind subservient to other, Lévi-Strauss: 15
a. will have choice between being history and being nothing, Maitland, Frederic William: 1

awe of mother-in-law familiar fact of a., Frazer: 3
Boas [changed] a. to discipline in which he delimited possibilities from impossibilities, Benedict: 6
cultural a. is valuable because it is constantly rediscovering the normal, Sapir: 12
Evans-Pritchard described as Stendhal of a., Douglas: 4
generation of his [Malinowski] followers believes that social a. began in Trobriand islands in 1914, Leach: 1
in a. generalization supports comparison, Lévi-Strauss: 6
object of study [of a.] is the individual, Boas: 1
quantitative approach in cultural a. lies in thesis that human culture proceeded from simpler to complex, Coon: 1
Rivers is the Rider Haggard of a.; I shall be the Conrad: Malinowski: 21
Rousseau invented a. by doing it to himself, Darnton: 3
social a. interprets rather than explains, Evans-Pritchard: 3
theology is A., Feuerbach: 1
title of Functional School of A. has been bestowed by myself, on myself, Malinowski: 19

anti-functionalist:
I may be called an a.-f., Radcliffe-Brown: 8

anxiety:
a. is biological concept, Rank: 2
act of birth first experience of a. and source of affect of a., Freud: 11

anxious:
freedom has made [modern man] isolated and, thereby a., Fromm: 2

anything goes:
principle that can be defended under *all* circumstances is principle: a.g., Feyerabend: 1

Apocalypse:
who could pay attention to humdrum legislation when date of A. just announced by a computer?, Solow: 5

applicability:
disdain of pure scientist for questions of a., Mandler and Kessen: 1

Aquinas, Thomas

archaeology:
evidence of a. and history supports the simple-to-more-complex theory of cultural development, Coon: 1

archaic:
classic always carries connotation of wasteful and a., Veblen: 7
human psyche shows countless a. traits, Jung: 9, 10

Archilochos

Arendt, Hannah

aristocracies:
history is graveyard of a., Pareto: 14

aristocracy:
Democracy and A. second political form in history, Hegel: 6
intrusion of humanitarian feelings invariably presages decadence of a., Pareto: 7
virtue and talents grounds of natural a., Jefferson: 12

aristocrat:
nouns democrat and a. were unknown before 1780s, Palmer: 1

Aristotle:
more psychology can be learned through statistical methods than from all philosophers with exception of A., Wundt: 1
Sullivan: 1

arithmetic:
by Political a. mean Art of Reasoning by Figures, upon things relating to Government, Davenant: 1
I have taken course (as Specimen of the Political A. I have longed aimed at) to express myself in terms of number, weight, or measure, Petty: 4
if constitution be a problem in a., Burke, Edmund: 9

armaments:
world-wide reduction [in] a. [to achieve] freedom from fear, Roosevelt: 3

army:
objections brought against standing a., may also be brought against standing government, Thoreau: 2

Aron, Raymond

Arrow, Kenneth J.

art:
a. imitating nature, Hobbes: 1
if history is not science it must be a., Croce: 1
language is most massive, inclusive a. we know, Sapir: 3
State as a work of a., Burckhardt: 1
with language, city remains man's greatest work of a., Mumford: 1

artificial intelligence:
a.i. saw computers [encoding] everything into symbols, even numbers, Newell: 1

artificial signals:
signification is creation and use of a.s., Vygotsky: 2

artist:
a. [appears] unmasked as human who requires no interpreter, Rank: 3
a. firing arrows at moon, Pigou: 4
a. represents atavistic stage, Rank: 1
a. tends to justify or defy society rather than [chronicle] it, Lowenthal: 4

arts:
a. spread garlands of flowers over iron chains, Rousseau: 1
impact of a. on politics and of politics on [a.], Lasswell: 9

Aryan:
A. is man with white skin, thick skin, and foreskin, Schapera: 1

asceticism:
a. carried into everyday life, Weber, Max: 3
Christian a. strode into the marketplace of life, Weber, Max: 3
empirical social science has become kind of applied a., Lowenthal: 3

Asch, Solomon E.

associating:
art of a. together must grow in same ratio in which equality of conditions increased, Tocqueville: 20

association:
in United States will be sure to find an a., Tocqueville: 19
single a., never reinforced, results in life-long dynamic system, Allport, Gordon W.: 3

associations:
essence of language lies in employment of fixed a., Russell: 1

assumptions:
what can be accounted for by fewer a. is explained in vain by more, Ockham: 1

atomic weapons:
physicists felt responsibility for the realization of a.w., Oppenheimer: 1

atoms:
a. of pleasure are not easy to distinguish, Edgeworth: 4
reciprocities between a. of society, Simmel: 15
societies are "social a.," Toynbee, Arnold J.: 1

attachments:
celibacy and promiscuity fulfill identical functions — prevention of particularistic a., Coser: 2

attitude:
a. of generalized other is a. of whole community, Mead, George Herbert: 12
child who plays in game must be ready to take a. of [others] involved, Mead, George Herbert: 11
emotionally indifferent a. [toward nature] of scientific observer ethically higher than loving interest of poet, Thorndike: 1
great difference between science and technology is difference of initial a., Titchener: 5

attitudes:
if human being is experimented upon, his a. toward experiment becomes important factor, Roethlisberger: 1
in shaping a. men orient themselves to reference groups, Hyman: 1
pluralistic ignorance made possible exaggerated impression of universality of a., Katz and Allport: 1
self-consciousness is awakening of a. we are arousing in others, Mead, George Herbert: 14
social control depends upon individuals able to assume a. of others, Mead, George Herbert: 3

Aubrey, John

Auden, W. H.

Augustine

Austen, Jane

author:
difference slight, to the influence of a., whether read by five hundred, or by five hundred thousand; if he can select the five hundred, Adams, Henry: 1

authoritative:
person will accept communication as a. only when four conditions simultaneously obtain, Barnard: 1

identical forms of b. toward one another, Simmel: 2
economics studies human b. as relationship between ends and scarce means, Robbins: 1
every b. fulfils vital function, Malinowski: 12
everything we have been calling an instinct is learned b., Watson: 5
facts about b. are not treated in their own right, Skinner: 1
human b. reveals uniformities which constitute natural laws, Pareto: 2, 8
hypothesis that man is not free essential to application of scientific method to study of human b., Skinner: 8
it is in form of the generalized other that social process influences the b. of individuals, Mead, George Herbert: 12, 13
linguistic codes transmit the culture and so constrain b., Bernstein, Basil: 1
man behaves because of consequences which followed similar past b., Skinner: 4
mankind will possess control over human b. when the human mind will contemplate itself from within, Pavlov: 1
man's b. in a social group [enables him] to become an object to himself, Mead, George Herbert: 9
most b. is multimotivated, Maslow: 2
non-logical conduct plays minor part in b. of primitive or civilized man, Evans-Pritchard: 1
only possible "science" of conduct is that which treats b. of the economic man, Knight: 3
operant conditioning shapes b. as sculptor shapes clay, Skinner: 5
pattern of b. shaped by [coincidental] forces ends tenuously related to those forces, Geertz: 2
phenomena of b. desirable in concepts of mathematical and physical sciences, Lashley: 1
pluralistic b. is subject-matter of sociology, Giddings: 2
[psychology] is the positive science of b., McDougall: 1
rather see b. of one white rat observed from birth until death than statistical data on how 2,000 rats learned to open puzzle box, Watson: 9
science of b. concerned with talking about talking and knowing about knowing, Skinner: 3
simple reflexes ever combined into unitary harmonies termed b., Sherrington: 1
social b. displays many features at same time [and so it is] intolerable we can say only one thing at time, Homans: 1
social disorganization is decrease of influence of social rules of b. upon individual members, Thomas and Znaniecki: 1
sociologists cut themselves off from rich inheritance by forgetting that all history is past social b., Tilly: 1
striving to achieve an end is mark of b., McDougall: 3
theories that explain social phenomena are about b. of men, Homans: 2
this adaptation [by Nazis' prisoners] produced interesting types of b., Bettelheim: 1
when we think we can explain [human b.], general principles turn out to be psychological, Homans: 2
world view is the very skeleton of concrete cognitive assumptions on which flesh of cognitive b. is hung, Wallace, Anthony F.C.: 2

behavioral:
no contradiction between intuitive model of thinking and b. model, Simon: 6

behavioral sciences:
b.s. are here to stay, Berelson: 3
difficult to conceive how b.s. could be simultaneously trivial and threatening, Smelser: 3

behaviorism:
b. was a religion to take place of religion, Woodworth: 1

behaviorist:
b. cannot find consciousness in the test-tube of his science, Watson: 8
b. [questions]: Can I describe this behavior in terms of stimulus and response?, Watson: 2
b. views psychology as purely objective, experimental branch of natural science, Watson: 1
to b. consciousness is as unprovable as old concept of the soul, Watson: 7

behavioristic:
universe will change if you bring up your children in b. freedom, Watson: 4

behaviors:
single kind of deprivation strengthens many kinds of b., Skinner: 6

belief:
b. in [Progress of humanity] is act of faith, Bury: 2
questions about human society clustered around power, b., wealth, Gellner: 4
why abandon a b. because it ceases to be true, Frost: 1

belief systems:
collective irrationality arises only from incompatibility of b.s., Elster: 1

beliefs:
its b. are his b., Benedict: 2

Bell, Daniel

Benda, Julien

Benedict, Ruth:
B. and others show how common culture shapes separate lives, Auden: 2

benefit:
by utility is meant property in any object to produce b., Bentham: 3
whatever is for the [public] b. is for his b., Mill, John Stuart: 17

benefits:
difference principle [is] agreement to regard distribution of natural talents as common assets and share b., Rawls: 4
private Vices by dextrous Management of skilful Politician, may be turn'd into publick B., Mandeville: 5

benevolence:
b. [will] atrophy when not adequately practiced and [be] scarce when relied on to excess, Hirschman: 5
entire Motive to good Action not always B. alone, Hutcheson: 1
not from b. of butcher that we expect our dinner, but from [his] regard to own interest, Smith, Adam: 7

Benjamin, Walter

Bentham, Jeremy:
B. divorced himself from history, Maine: 7
B. first to disclose manifold "linguistic fictions," Jakobson: 3
B. on distance between conviction and practice, Friedman: 8

Bentley, Arthur F.

Berelson, Bernard

Berger, Peter L.

Berger, Peter L., and Luckmann, Thomas

Berger, Peter L., and Kellner, Hansfried

Bergson, Henri:
grateful to B. for defence of the irrational, Jung: 1

Berle, Adolph A., and Means, Gardiner C.

Berlin, Isaiah:
fox-hedgehog metaphor for types of thinkers, Archilochos: 1

Bernard, Claude

Bernard of Chartres:
Newton: 1

Bernoulli, Daniel:
response to method of estimating limits of moral probabilities, Buffon: 1

Bernoulli, Jakob

Bernstein, Basil

Bernstein, Eduard

Bertalanffy, Ludwig von

best:
b. government that which governs least, O'Sullivan: 1
whate'er is b. administer'd is b., Pope: 2

Beste, Henry Digby

Bettelheim, Bruno

Beveridge, William Henry

Beveridge, W. I. B.

bias:
steps be taken to identify value b. when occurs, Nagel: 1

bible:
newspaper is b. of democracy, Lippmann, Walter: 1

Bickel, Alexander M.

Big Brother:
no love, except love of B.B., Orwell: 3

Bills of Mortality:
now having engaged my thoughts upon the *B.o.M.*, Graunt: 1

history teaches that c. that bears lance forces its rule upon c. that handles spade, Mosca: 2
interest of the landlord always opposed to interest of every other c., Ricardo: 1
politicians are symbols of fact that every c. must take every other c. into account, Ortega y Gasset: 1
ruling ideas of each age have been ideas of ruling c., Marx and Engels: 9
[social] c. defined as much by its consumption as by its position in relations of production, Bourdieu: 3
that which constitutes a c. is always some community of Interest, Mill, James: 3
to that c. give name *élite*, Pareto: 12
to understand middle c. we have only to see what is around us, Mills: 2
"underclass" of unemployed, and gradually, unemployable persons, Myrdal: 9
white collar crimes defined as crime committed by upper c. [related to] occupation, Sutherland: 1

class situation:
c.s. when number of people have in common specific causal component of life chances, Weber, Max: 28

class struggle:
c.s. leads to dictatorship of proletariat, Marx: 9
correct ideas come from c.s., Mao Zedong: 1

class struggles:
history of all existing society is history of c.s., Marx and Engels: 5

class system:
in twentieth century, citizenship and capitalist c.s. have been at war, Marshall, T. H.: 2

class war:
c.w. will find me on side of educated *bourgeoisie*, Keynes: 7

classes:
Bourdieu: 1
democratic republic does not abolish antagonism between the c., Engels: 6
dictatorship of proletariat transition to abolition of c. Marx: 9
do not claim to have discovered existence of c. or struggle between them, Marx: 9
economics concerned with relations between persons and c., Engels: 1
effect of compulsory schooling [on] dominated c., Bourdieu and Passeron: 1
in both lower and upper c. irrational expenditure is current practice, Mauss: 6
intelligence been redistributed between the c. and nature of c. changed as talented rise, Young: 1
IQ is primary leaven preventing c. from hardening into castes, Duncan: 1
only in cities, where c. confront each other, Trilling, Lionel: 4

classic:
c. always carries connotation of wasteful and archaic, Veblen: 7

classical:
linguistics has power of c. spirit, Sapir: 5

classifier:
taste classifies the c., Bourdieu: 2

classifying:
man is c. animal, Jespersen: 1

classless society:
dictatorship of proletariat transition to c.s., Marx: 9

Clausewitz, Karl von

clear:
c. and imminent danger, Holmes: 11, 12

cleavage:
division into working and business class that constitutes outstanding c. in Middletown, Lynd and Lynd: 1
focus on sources of c. in study of conditions encouraging democracy, Lipset: 2

cleavages:
society riven by many minor c. less in danger of open mass conflict than a society with few c., Williams: 1

clerks:
designate "c." all whose activity is not the pursuit of practical aims, Benda: 2
political realism of the "c." bound up with essence of modern world, Benda: 3

climate:
stimulating c. essential condition for civilization, Huntington, Ellsworth: 1

climate(s) of opinion:
best ideas in social sciences participate in fostering the c.o.o., Giddens: 1
[Freud] is whole c.o.o., Auden: 3
larger Souls that have travell'd divers C.o.O. are more cautious in their resolves, Glanvill: 1

cliometrics:
c. is quantitative history [in which] data are dug out in vast detail and given computer assimilation, Nisbet: 3
new "c." history — born of marriage between historical problems and advanced statistical analysis, Fogel and Elton: 1

cloak:
light c. becomes iron cage, Weber, Max: 4

club:
category of paradoxes given by Groucho Marx's saying "would not dream of belonging to c. willing to have me," Elster: 4

coastal sailing:
[*see* sailing]

Cochran, William G.

codes:
linguistic c. transmit the culture and so constrain behaviour, Bernstein, Basil: 1

coefficient:
essential character of cultural data we call humanistic c., Znaniecki: 2, 3

coercion:
category of facts external to individual and endowed with power of c., Durkheim: 5
planning means: Let government choose and enforce its rulings by c., von Mises: 9

coexistence:
human race unable to do without peaceful c., Kant: 5

cognitive assumptions:
world view is the very skeleton of concrete c.a. on which flesh of customary behavior is hung, Wallace, Anthony F. C.: 2

cognitive dissonance:
[c.] dissonance will motivate person to reduce it and actively avoid situations likely to increase it, Festinger: 1

Cohen, I. Bernard

Cohen, Morris R.

cohort size hypothesis:
Easterlin: 1

coincidence:
behavior shaped by certain set of forces by mysterious c. [serves] ends but tenuously related to those forces, Geertz: 2
if a c. occurs to one person in a million each day, then we expect 250 occurrences a day, Diaconis and Mosteller: 1

Coke, Edward

cold war:
Soviets waging new kind of war, the c. w., Baruch: 1

Cole, G. D. H.:
belonging to the A's of the world, Cole, Margaret: 1

Cole, Margaret

Coleman, James S.

collective:
c. forces which made for strife [World War I], Halévy: 2
c. irrationality arises only from incompatibility of belief systems, Elster: 1
c. mind is formed in organized crowd, Le Bon: 1
cannot be completely consistent meaning to c. rationality, Arrow: 3
contradictions generate c. action [to overcome] the contradictions, Elster: 2
first problem [of psychologists] is to show how individual response emerges from c. life, Vygotsky: 4
illusion is most tenacious weed in c. consciousness, Gramsci: 4
individual within the [thought] c. is never conscious of the prevailing thought style, Fleck: 2
no society which does not feel need of upholding c. sentiments and ideas, Durkheim: 21
only memory organization possesses is c. memory of its participants, Simon: 2

conspiracy:
c. theory of society, Popper: 3
difference between locating conspiracies in history and saying that history is a c., Hofstadter: 4
people of same trade seldom meet together but conversation ends in c. against the public, Smith, Adam: 17
Constantine:
conversion of C. broke violence of fall of Roman Empire, Gibbon: 5
constitution:
c. not intended to embody a particular economic theory, Holmes: 6
I voted against c. because it is a c., Proudhon: 4
if c. be a problem in arithmetic, Burke, Edmund: 9
Constitution (English):
that the king can do no wrong is fundamental principle of the C., Blackstone: 3
Constitution (U.S.):
American C. has changed, is changing, Bryce: 1
[C.] is experiment, as all life is experiment, Holmes: 13
C. supposes that the Ex. is branch most interested in war and accordingly vested question of war in the Legisl., Madison: 9
Fourteenth Amendment [to the U.S. Constitution] does not enact Mr. Herbert Spencer's Social Statics, Holmes: 6
if possible to have economic biography of all connected with [Constitution's] framing and adoption, materials for scientific analysis and classification would be available, Beard: 1
people made C., and people can unmake it, Marshall, John: 2
we [judges] owe equal attachment to C., Frankfurter: 2
when C. was framed no respectable person a democrat, Beard and Beard: 1
constitutional monarchy:
under c.m. sovereign has three rights, Bagehot: 5
consumer economy:
c.e. [has] created second nature which ties [man] to commodity form, Marcuse: 3
free choice among variety of goods and services does not signify freedom if they sustain alienation, Marcuse: 2
consumer goods:
society which sets as highest goal production of private c.g. will entrust public decisions to men who regard any other goal as incredible, Galbraith: 5
consumption:
articles of which the c. is not conspicuous, are incapable of gratifying, Rae: 1
c. is sole end of production, Smith, Adam: 23
c. of other people can enter in utility function, Elster: 3
conspicuous c. is means of reputability, Veblen: 2-4
Engel's law, Engel: 1
increase c. as income increases, but not by as much, Keynes: 19
[magazine] heros are idols of production and c., Lowenthal: 1
no act of saving subtracts in least from c., Say: 1
[social] class defined as much by its c. as by its position in relations of production, Bourdieu: 3
containment:
firm and vigilant c. of Russian expansive tendencies, Kennan: 1
contract:
c. replaces reciprocity in rights and duties which have origin in the Family, Maine: 2
each puts his person and power in common under general will [in social c.], Rousseau: 14
fundamental problem of which social c. provides solution, Rousseau: 13
movement from Status to C., Maine: 3
society is a c., Burke, Edmund: 12
contracts:
[government's] business to provide against c. that become instrument of disguised oppression, Green: 1
terms in which c. are made matter, Arrow and Hahn: 1
contradictions:
c. generate collective action [to overcome] c., Elster: 2
counterfinality is species of real c., Elster: 1
no final solution of eternal c., Beard: 2
contrast conception:
Negro becomes "c.c.," Myrdal: 4
control:
decided to call field of c. and communication theory Cybernetics, Wiener: 1
even feminism has not succeeded in giving women any c. over men, Parsons, Elsie Clews: 2
men of greater ability are subject to c. of incapable, Saint-Simon: 1
must first enable government to c. governed; and oblige it to c. itself, Madison: 7
control groups (social experiments):
Bacon: 5; Cicero: 2
controlling:
c. and controlled — story of man in society, Barnard: 4
controls:
language c. us, Pollock and Maitland: 2
who c. the past. . . c. the future: who c. the present c. the past, Orwell: 2
controversy:
scientific truth must come about by c., Boring: 3
conventional wisdom:
The ultimate triumph of the c.w., Galbraith: 4
conversation:
most of give-and-take of c. is stereotyped, Firth, J.R.: 1
[*see also* phatic communion; phatic function]
Cooley, Charles H.
Coon, Carlton
co-operate:
supreme merit of exchange mechanism is that it enables vast number to c. in use of means to achieve ends, Knight: 11
cooperation:
by primary groups I mean those characterized by c., Cooley: 6
conflict and c. are phases of one process, Cooley: 8
to understand conception of justice must make conception of social c. explicit, Rawls: 2
writing about c. means writing at same time about rejection, Douglas: 5
cooperative:
public opinion is c. product, Cooley: 7
coöptation:
c. is absorbing new elements into leadership of organization [to avert] threats to its stability, Selznick: 1
coping:
compulsive drives are specifically neurotic and represent ways of c., Horney: 5
corn:
c. is not high because rent is paid, but rent is paid because c. is high, Ricardo: 4
Cornerville:
insider finds in C. a highly organized social system, Whyte, William F.: 1
corporate:
c. actors created when persons combine portion of their resources to create distinct acting entity, Coleman: 3
corporations:
[c.] have become social institutions, Berle and Means: 1
control of great c. should develop into neutral technocracy, Berle and Means: 2
must be outright dismantling of our gigantic c., Simons: 1
through size, c. become an institution, Brandeis: 8
correlation coefficient:
two variable organs co-related when variation of one is accompanied by variation of other in same direction, Galton: 4
corruption:
between business and politics as reasonable to assert that c. goes one way as the other, Knight: 6
corrupts:
absolute power c. absolutely, Acton: 3
weakness in face of power c. equally, Knight: 12
Coser, Lewis A.
cosmopolitans:
only c. and provincials, Spengler: 2

cost:
c. is price [the purchaser] pays, added to c. of verifying degree of goodness for which he contracts, Babbage: 1
c. of liberty less than price of repression, even though that c. be blood, DuBois: 5
opportunity c. the anticipated value of "that which might be" if choices were made differently, Buchanan: 3
value is governed by c. of production, Marshall, Alfred: 7
cosymptom:
psychotherapy is a c. treatment, Campbell, Donald T.: 1
count:
people cannot c., at least not very high, Mosteller and Wallace: 1
whenever you can, c., Galton: 6
counterculture:
arising among the young a c., Roszak: 1
counterfinality:
c. is species of real contradictions, Elster: 1
countervailing power:
counterpart of competition I shall call c.p., Galbraith: 1, 2
counting:
good of c. [is] it brings every thing to a certainty, Johnson: 3
not from c. as from measuring that advantage of mathematical treatment comes, Peirce: 4
though c. heads not ideal way to govern, better than breaking them, Hand: 1
country:
any alternative should be adopted which will save life of one's c., Machiavelli: 6
c. more developed industrially shows, to less developed, the image of its future, Marx: 14
exercise of faculties bounded within ways of own c., Locke: 5
give me map of any c., and I [can] tell you quality of man and part its inhabitants will act in history, Cousin: 1
greatest enigma is that backward c. was first to place proletariat in power, Trotsky: 1
habits formed in heart of free c. may some day prove fatal to its liberties, Tocqueville: 6
if we [historians] make deliberate misstatements in interest of our c., what difference is there between us and those who gain their living by their pens, Polybius: 1
when safety of c. wholly depends on decision, no attention should be paid to justice or injustice, Machiavelli: 6
Cournot, Antoine Augustin
courts:
laws are a dead letter without c., Hamilton: 1
legislature and c. move in proud and silent isolation [from each other], Cardozo: 1
courtship:
all c. systems are market exchange systems, Goode: 1
Cousin, Victor
covenants:
open c. of peace, openly arrived at, Wilson, Woodrow: 4
creative:
before problem of c. writer, analysis must lay down its arms, Freud: 34
c. power still alive in us, Toynbee, Arnold J.: 6
failure of c. power in minority [leading to] breakdowns of civilizations, Toynbee, Arnold J.: 5
in societies in process of civilization, mimesis is directed towards c. persons [and] "cake of custom" is broken, Toynbee, Arnold J.: 4
creativity:
not necessary to surround c. with mystery and obfuscation, Simon: 7
credit:
an excessive increase of currency, causes it to lose c., Marshall, A.: 12
misallocation of c. for scientific work described as Matthew effect, Merton: 4
nothing is more fantastical and nice than C., Davenant: 3
Cremin, Lawrence A.
Crèvecoeur, J. Hector St. John de
crime:
action is c. because it shocks common conscience, Durkheim: 3
great injustice to persecute homosexuality as c., Freud: 39
society prepares c., and the guilty are only the instruments by which it is executed, Quetelet: 4
white collar c. defined as crime committed by upper class [related to] occupation, Sutherland: 1
crimes:
punishment must be proportionate to the c., Beccaria: 2
to declare that Government may commit c. to secure conviction could bring terrible retribution, Brandeis: 6
criminal:
[for] originality of idealist [to] find expression, necessary that originality of c. also be possible, Durkheim: 8
criminals:
less evil that some c. escape than government play an ignoble part, Holmes: 17
Croce, Benedetto
cross-disciplinary research:
Snow: 3
cross-pressures:
c.-p. [on] individuals whose different reference groups pull them toward different political alignments, Williams: 2
crowds:
characteristics of reasoning of c., Le Bon: 2
collective mind formed, subject to law of mental unity of c., Le Bon: 1
even in extreme cases of violence, c. do not act in mindless way, Davis, Natalie Zemon: 2
Cui bono?:
Cicero: 4
cultural:
c. facts [remain] after every consideration of individuals involved [have been] exhausted, Kroeber: 4
c. system that can launch earth satellites can dispense with gods entirely, White, Leslie A.: 2
c. crusader cannot win in mass society, Lazarsfeld: 3
can c. evolution of higher ethical values completely replace genetic evolution?, Wilson, Edward O.: 4
essential character of c. data [we call] humanistist coefficient, Znaniecki: 2, 3
every human society has made [a] selection of its c. institutions, Benedict: 4
genuine knowledge about [relation of] physical characteristics of human communities to their c. capabilities can be written on back of postage stamp, Hogben: 2
great import of c. conditions on neuroses [supersede] biological conditions considered by Freud to be their root, Horney: 1, 2
human potentialities are helpless without a c. milieu, Mead, Margaret: 3
language is most perfect of all c. systems, Lévi-Strauss: 12
no c. forms survive unless they constitute responses which are adjustive or adaptive, Kluckhohn: 1, 2
structure and tradition different aspects of single c. complex, Park and Burgess: 3
without c. forms there would be no men, Geertz: 1
cultural anthropology:
c.a. is valuable because it is constantly rediscovering the normal, Sapir: 12
Coon: 1
cultural capital:
c.c. added to c.c. and distribution of c.c. between social classes be thereby reproduced, Bourdieu: 1
cultural lag:
Ogburn: 2
culture:
all parts of c. are inter-dependent, Putnam: 1
arising among the young a counter c., Roszak: 1
both men and women creatures of c., and demands not always consistent with biology, Trilling, Diana: 3
c. and social structure are epiphenomena, Murdock: 3
c. [can] be shown to come within range of cause and effect, Tylor: 3
c. consists of patterns, Kroeber and Kluckhohn: 1

information occupies slum dwelling in town of e., Stigler, George J.: 2
Keynes' dictum that e. should be like dentistry, Hahn: 2
Keynesian e. has destroyed constraint on politicians' appetites to spend without the necessity to tax, Buchanan: 1
man of the future is the master of e., Holmes: 4
Marx did not have much to say about e. of socialism, Robinson, Joan: 7
must assume that people in models do not know what is going to happen and know that they do not know, Hicks: 4
new doctrine [Keynes] was that private virtues were public vices, Robinson, Joan: 4
politics gives birth to permanent organisations in so far as it identifies itself with e., Gramsci: 2
Principle of Survival of the Fittest could be regarded as one vast generalisation of Ricardian e., Keynes: 8
problem of E. [is] the mode of employing labour which will maximise utility of the produce, Jevons: 12
pure e. is also theory of social wealth, Walras: 1
pure e. is theory of determination of prices under perfectly free competition, Walras: 1
purpose of studying e. to learn how to avoid being deceived by economists, Robinson, Joan: 2
revolutions and revelations in e. are rare, Tobin: 1
superiority of Marxian e. is only partial, Lange: 1
supply-side e. [means] e. supplied to meet demand of politicians to rationalize [their intent], Stein: 2
with Malthus and Ricardo e. became the dismal science, Galbraith: 7
[*see also* political economy]

economies:
worth looking at figures to see if steady state gives summary of advanced industrial e., Solow: 2

economist:
[e.] always wants to hand over the problem in the end to some sociologist, Hicks: 2
Boulding: 2
know of no e. of any standing who has favored legal limit on rate of interest, Friedman: 8
Marshall was first great e., Keynes: 6
no English gentleman was ever sorry for the death of a political e., Bagehot: 2
no modern e. would think as he does if Marx never existed, Aron: 2
nothing so quickly marks an [e.] as incompetently trained as remark on legitimacy of desire for more food and frivolity of desire for more elaborate automobile, Galbraith: 3
practical men, slaves of some defunct e., Keynes: 24
role of the e. [is] to prescribe what should be done in light of what can be done, politics aside, Friedman: 1
Wealth, not Happiness, subject treated by the Political E., Senior: 2
what e. calls equilibrium of behavior, psychologists call frustration, Boulding: 4
without theory of value e. can have no theory of international trade, Stigler, George J.: 8

economists:
advertising treated with hostility e. normally reserve for monopolists, Stigler, George J.: 2
all the great e. have envisaged an eventual end to the capitalist period of history, Heilbroner: 4
both doctors and e. need humility, but neither should abandon their patients to quacks, Rivlin: 1
competent e. are rarest of birds, Keynes: 4
e. are only beginning to attribute a dominant role to the family, Becker, Gary S.: 1
e. familiar with perverse effects, Boudon: 2
e. have invented term The Great Industry, Wallas: 1
[great e.] can be called the worldly philosophers, Heilbroner: 1
if e. could get themselves thought of as competent [as] dentists, that would be splendid!, Keynes: 11
mania on part of mathematical e. to find reason [to] support protection, Pareto: 1
political e. have been reproached with too small a use of facts, and too large an employment of theory, Babbage: 2
purpose of studying economics is to learn how to avoid being deceived by e., Robinson, Joan: 2

economy:
best way of understanding economics of capitalism may be to think about socialist e., Solow: 1
capitalism [is] that form of private property e. in which innovations [are] carried out by borrowed money, Schumpeter: 8
capitalism must everywhere fight battle of annihilation against every historical form of natural e., Luxemburg: 5
direct factual study and quantitative descriptions offer only promising approach to understanding modern e., Leontief: 1
economics once more became Political E., Robinson, Joan: 4
even *poor* student is taught only *political* e., while e. of living is not professed in our colleges, Thoreau: 3
every step a government takes beyond protecting smooth operation of market e. is step [toward] totalitarian system, von Mises: 5
existence of a political e. implies revolutionary programme, Wicksell: 1
families have large effects on the e., and evolution of the e. greatly changes structure and decisions of families, Becker, Gary S.: 4
few sectors of e. whose efficiency would be greater if [population were] larger, Duncan: 2
have attempted to treat E. as a Calculus of Pleasure and Pain, Jevons: 3
[of political e.] I cannot read other books on subject without indignation, Jevons: 1
long [cyclical] waves arise out of causes inherent in capitalistic e., Kondratieff: 1
market e. does not respect political frontiers, von Mises: 6
market e. is system of division of labor under private ownership of means of production, von Mises: 3
not surprising that international trade should mean something else in Political E., Edgeworth: 9
of highest presumption in kings and ministers to watch over e. of private people, Smith, Adam: 18
only through principle of competition political e. has any pretension to character of a science, Mill, John Stuart: 6
political e. came to him [Ricardo], Bagehot: 8
Political E. has much analogous to mathematical sciences, Roscher: 1
political e. is study of mankind in ordinary business of life, Marshall, Alfred: 3
principle of identity of interests can always be applied in political e., Halévy: 1
world-e. only concerns fragment of the world, Braudel: 8

economy of means:
principle of e.o.m. variant of principle of economic rationality, Lange: 3

Edgeworth, Francis Ysidro

education:
e. introduced into an organization by its youngest and newest members, Arrow: 5
easier for society to change e. than for e. to change society, Lewin: 1
in e. [we] make our nervous system our ally, James: 8
modern system of E. produced population able to read but unable to distinguish what is worth reading, Trevelyan: 2
my favorite "principle" in e. [is] "it's knowin' so derned much that ain't so," Knight: 9
social science lays groundwork for ever more effective e., Myrdal: 10
structure secondary e. to capture [adolescent's] energy, Coleman: 1
three characteristics of American e. — popularization, multitudinousness, politicalization, Cremin: 1

through e., each generation transmits to the following [generations], a groundwork of ideas, Cournot: 5
effect:
all reasonings concerning matter of fact are founded on relation of cause and e., Hume: 7
culture [can] be shown to come within range of cause and e., Tylor: 3
every cause produces more than one e., Spencer: 4
law of e. is fundamental law of learning and teaching, Thorndike: 5
law of e. is great weapon to change men's responses, Thorndike: 5
law of e. relates initial emotional response to subsequent emotional responses, Thorndike: 4
[Law of E. that] man behaves because of consequences which followed similar behavior in past, Skinner: 4
[Law of E] shapes behavior as sculptor shapes clay, Skinner: 5
principle of greatest e. variant of principle of economic rationality, Lange: 3
effecting of all things possible:
End of our Foundation is the knowledge of Causes and the e.o.a.t.p., Bacon: 11
e.o.a.t.p. [is] primary imperative of technology, Holton: 3
effective scope:
e.s. characterizes what [man] perceives, has contact with, and reaches for, Lazarsfeld and Thielens: 1
effects:
linguistic facts are e. rather than causes, Mauss: 2
perverse e. [cause] of social imbalances and change, Boudon: 2
efficiency:
Industrial Revolution accompanied by demographic transition represents gain in human e., Davis, Kingsley: 2
principle of greatest e., Lange: 3
ego:
the e. has tendency to oppose the drives, but one of main functions is to help them toward gratification, Hartmann: 1
the e. needs to bind itself to others and work with them, Asch: 2
the e. not master in its own house, Freud: 29
where id was, there e. shall be, Freud: 38
ego-centrism:
e.-c. closely connected with child's incapacity for true causal explanation, Piaget: 2
egoistic:
dreams are completely e., Freud: 10
e. suicide results from no longer finding basis for existence in life, Durkheim: 14
egoists:
strongest e. as children can become most helpful citizens, Freud: 27
Egypt:
never existed a bureaucracy which could compare with that of E., Weber, Max: 6
Eichmann, Adolf:
grotesque silliness of [E.'s] last words taught us banality of evil, Arendt: 3
Einstein, Albert
Eisenstadt, S.N.
Eisenstein, Elizabeth L.
elasticity:
e. of demand [related to] rise and fall in price, Marshall, Alfred: 5
elderly:
e. people in our culture are frequently oriented towards the past, Lynd: 1
elders:
greater schooling of younger generation [should make it] more tolerant [as it ages] than its e., Stouffer: 1
electrification:
communism is Soviet power plus e. of whole country, Lenin: 6
Eliade, Mircea
Elias, Norbert
elite:
organizations [are] weapons when used by power-seeking e., Selznick: 2
those who get the most are the e., Lasswell: 6
to class of people who have highest indices in their branch of activity give name *e.*, Pareto: 12
elites:
circulation of *e.*, Pareto: 13
Ellis, Havelock
Ellul, Jacques
Elster, Jon
emancipation:
first premise for e. of women is [their reintroduction] into public industry, Engels: 6
Emerson, Ralph Waldo
emotion:
e. can be controlled or destroyed by another e. with more power, Spinoza: 4
feeling of bodily changes [that] follow perception of exciting fact is the e., James: 18
emotional:
at three years of age e. life plan has been laid down, Watson: 6
e. attitude of man has greater sway over custom than reason, Malinowski: 6
law of effect relates initial e. response to subsequent emotional responses, Thorndike: 4
empathy:
drama is artistic expression of e., Adler: 2
empires:
the life-span of e. cannot be plotted by events, Braudel: 1
empirical:
e. science of concrete reality, Weber, Max: 1
e. social science has become kind of applied asceticism, Lowenthal: 3
explication of differential aspects of e. social research needs attention, Lazarsfeld: 4
from a nonempirical base of axioms you never get e. results, Samuelson: 5
student of culture seeks to discover any order among e. data that depends upon conscious human agents, Znaniecki: 3
study of language no different from e. investigation of other phenomena, Chomsky: 3
empiricism:
test between science and e. is "Can you say, not only of what kind, but how much?," Fleay: 1
employers:
it is the future, not the past, to which e. look, Walker: 1
employment:
different e. for the sexes may be traced in all communities, in every age and history, Hodgskin: 2
[drunkenness] arising from other causes gives e. to multitude of ale-houses, Smith, Adam: 20
fallacies implied in Keynesian full-e. doctrine are same errors which Smith and Say demolished, von Mises: 1
full e. means that unemployment is reduced to short intervals of standing by, Beveridge, William Henry: 2
emptiness:
chief problem of people is e., May: 1
empty:
senses let in particular ideas, and furnish e. cabinet, Locke: 4
emulation:
propensity for e. is strongest of economic motives, Veblen: 6
end:
aim higher than real target to accomplish real e., Machiavelli: 8
chief e. of Men uniting into Commonwealths is Preservation of their Property, Locke: 19
everybody is both a means and e. in himself, von Mises: 3
faith that riches not means but e. implies all economic activity is equally estimable, Tawney: 2
folly to fasten upon single e. and blot from perception all undesired consequences, Dewey: 5
man exists as e. in himself and not merely as a means, Kant: 4
principle that e. justifies means is only rule of political ethics, Koestler: 1
striving to achieve an e. is mark of behaviour, McDougall: 3
ends:
curious adapting of means to e., throughout all nature, Hume: 23
e. and means are so entangled, Lassalle: 1
e. are not compromised when referred to the means necessary to realize them, Dewey: 1
economics is entirely neutral between e., Robbins: 2

economics studies human behaviour as relationship between e. and scarce means, Robbins: 1
exchange mechanism enables vast number to co-operate in use of means to achieve e., Knight: 11
men adapt means to approach efficiency, Parsons, Talcott: 3
relations of means to achievement of e. verifiable by empirical methods, Parsons, Talcott: 3
science merely shows how man must act to attain definite e., von Mises: 2
world issued from mind superior to particular e. that men proposed, Vico: 8

enemies:
I always feel intimate with my e., Follett: 2

enemy:
every stranger an e. is [universal] ethnographic feature, Malinowski: 6
social group clear who it holds to be its e., Simmel: 1

energy:
dynamo most expressive symbol of e., Adams, Henry: 3
region is reservoir of e. whose origin lines in nature but whose development depends upon man, Vidal de la Blache: 1

Engel, Ernst

Engel's law of consumption:
Engel: 1

Engels, Friedrich

engine:
[economic doctrine] an e. for discovery of concrete truth, Marshall, Alfred: 1

engineers:
victorious revolution requires e., Lazarsfeld: 6

England:
in E. repeatedly re-made State, re-making it now, and shall re-make it again, Tawney: 5
Ricardo conquered E. as completely as the Holy Inquisition conquered Spain, Keynes: 17
thirty [religions] in E. [and so] they live happily in peace, Voltaire: 1

English:
E. orthography satisfies all requirements under law of conspicuous waste, Veblen: 8
[E.] sovereign has three rights, Bagehot: 5
in our [E.] law, the king is said never to die, Blackstone: 2
no E. gentleman was ever sorry for the death of a political economist, Bagehot: 2
secrecy essential to utility of E. royalty, Bagehot: 4
that the king can do no wrong is fundamental principle of the E. Constitution, Blackstone: 3

Englishman:
every E. is said to love a lord, Taussig: 1

entangling alliances:
e.a. with none, Jefferson: 10, 14

entertainment:
all games played for e. are zero-sum games, von Neumann and Morgenstern: 3

enthusiasm:
Catholic Church neither submits to e. nor proscribes it, but uses it, Macaulay: 10

entrepreneur:
successful e. led by invisible hand to bring modern conveniences to poorest homes, Hayek: 8

environment:
behavior (B) is function (F) of person (P) and of his e. (E), Lewin: 3
complexity of [man's] behavior largely a reflection of the complexity of [his] e., Simon: 5
e. is product of culture, Leach: 5
eliminating [dirt] is positive effort to organise the e., Douglas: 1
for any system the e. is more complex than system itself, Luhmann: 5
general systems theory and cybernetics made it possible to relate structures and processes of systems to the e., Luhmann: 3
man discovered new method of adapting to his e. [symbolic system], Cassirer: 1
personality is dynamic organization that determines unique adjustments to e., Allport, Gordon W.: 1
potential knowledge contained in man's e., Bruner: 4

environmental:
social system consists of individual actors interacting in situation which has e. aspect, Parsons, Talcott: 12

environments:
e. have children, Pigou: 3

ephemera:
events are the e. of history, Braudel: 6

epitaphs:
here was buried Thomas Jefferson, Jefferson: 17
philosophers only interpreted world; point is to change it, Marx: 5
Thünen: 1

equal:
all animals e. but some more e. than others, Orwell: 1
all men created e., Jefferson: 1
Americans are born e. instead of becoming so, Tocqueville: 17
inferiors revolt that they may be e., Aristotle: 14
no greater inequality than e. treatment of unequals, Frankfurter: 3
social group in which all members are e. does not exist, Sorokin: 1

equal rights:
when regard economic phenomena as whole, [ultimate step] is proclamation of e.r. for all, Wicksell: 1

equality:
art of associating together must grow in same ratio in which e. of conditions increased, Tocqueville: 20
[democracy] dispensing e. to equals and unequals alike, Plato: 11
development of social problems theory oriented to values of freedom and e. rather than order, Gouldner: 1
e. disappeared from moment one man needed help of another, Rousseau: 4
e. is luxury of rich societies, Boulding: 3
e. of educational opportunity must imply a strong effect of schools independent of child's social environment, Coleman: 2
e. that meant a wider diffusion of liberty, Palmer: 2
feeling of e. will crop out where nature designed none, Münsterberg: 1
greatest good reduces to liberty and e., Rousseau: 17
human e. is contingent fact of history, Gould: 2
Indians of North America on a level with whites, Jefferson: 3
joins ideal of liberty to e. in name of social justice, Laski: 7
Left is dominated by three ideas: liberty, organisation, and e., Aron: 1
Liberty, E., Severity, Proudhon: 3
majestic e. of the laws, France: 1
race, translated realistically for American Negro, means there must never be e. between white and black, Bunche: 1
radical transformations that realization of sex e. would require, Komarovsky: 2
society makes [men] lose it [e.], and they recover it only by protection of laws, Montesquieu: 4

equals:
e. [revolt] that they may be superior, Aristotle: 14

equilibrium:
nothing must disturb the e. lest whole mechanism [of society] overturn, Galiani: 1
rise or fall in price of commodity presupposes disturbance of e. between supply and demand, Wicksell: 3
what economist calls e. of behavior, psychologists call frustration, Boulding: 4
women became social problem because technological and social changes have disturbed old e. without replacing it, Komarovsky: 1

Erikson, Erik H.

Erikson, Kai T.

Eros:
one of two basic instincts, Freud: 42

erotic:
distinction between e. life of antiquity and our own [is that] ancients [emphasized] instinct, whereas we emphasize its object, Freud: 17

erres:
[Hobbes] e. so ingeniosely one rather erre with him than hitt the marke, Aubrey: 2

evolutionists:
[e.] dispute with historical anthropologists on social forms, Murdock: 2
exaggeration:
cause of error is e., Ibn Khaldûn: 1
exaggerations:
in psycho-analysis nothing is true except the e., Adorno: 1
examination:
life without e. is not worth living, Plato: 13
view that e. results are lottery popular among those placed in the third class, Carr: 2
example:
custom and e. have more persuasive power than any certitude obtained by inquiry, Descartes: 2
turning e. into precedent and precedent into institution, MacIver: 4
excess:
e. of liberty seems only to pass into e. of slavery, Plato: 12
people did not fall from e. of evil but from e. of progress into revolution, Tocqueville: 28
excesses:
e. resulting from extreme familiarity with things holy are characteristic of periods of unshaken faith, Huizinga: 2
exchange:
concept of social interaction as an e. process follows assumption that men seek rewards, Blau: 1
division of labor is consequence of propensity to e. one thing for another, Smith, Adam: 6
e. is one of functions that creates a society, Simmel: 4
e. *is* political economy, Bastiat: 3
e. not a fundamental law of the distribution of produce, Mill, John Stuart: 7
impossible to have correct idea of Economics without perfect comprehension of the Theory of E., Jevons: 6, 7, 8
money makes possible secrecy, invisibility and silence of e., Simmel: 7
no chemist has discovered e.-value in pearl or diamond, Marx: 17
nothing more useful than water; but scarce any thing can be had in e. for it, Smith, Adam: 8
supreme merit of the e. mechanism is that it enables vast number to co-operate in use of means to achieve ends, Knight: 11
value in e., Smith, Adam: 8
exchangeable value:
utility not measure of e.v., although essential to it, Ricardo: 2
excitation:
nervous activity consists in e. and inhibition, Pavlov: 3
executive:
Constitution supposes that the E. is branch most interested in war, Madison: 9
informal e. organizations make possible development of personal influences, Barnard: 3
legislative department shall never exercise the e. and judicial powers, Adams, John: 2
necessary that judicial be separated and independent from e. power, Smith, Adam: 24
[unless] legislative, e., and judiciary powers are separate there can be no liberty, Montesquieu: 5
existence:
question concerning the e. or non-e. of God is nothing but question concerning the e. or non-e. of man, Feuerbach: 2
social e. determines [men's] consciousness, Marx: 12
subject matter of sociology is e., Weber, Alfred: 2
existing order:
all doctrines which deny value of e.o. may produce either puritans or libertines, Joll: 1
expectation(s):
e. are themselves predictions, Grunberg and Modigliani: 1
revolution of rising e., Davies: 1; Tocqueville: 28
expenditure:
in both lower and upper classes irrational e. is current practice, Mauss: 6
experience:
all our knowledge is founded on E., Locke: 7
almost every major systematic error which has deluded for thousands of years relied on practical e., Polanyi, Michael: 2
case before us must be considered in light of our whole e., Holmes: 14
dealing with e. from standpoint of society, Mead, George Herbert: 5
desire for new e., Thomas: 2
enlarge specific e. to become accessible as e. to men of another country or epoch, Lévi-Strauss: 5
experimental observations are only e. carefully planned in advance, Fisher, R.A.: 5
history of human race is one in source, one in e., and one in progress, Morgan, Lewis Henry: 5
if past be no rule for the future, all e. becomes useless, Hume: 14
life of law not logic [but] e., Holmes: 1
self arises in process of social e., Mead, George Herbert: 8
experiences:
by borrowing from our daily e. we derive elements which help us restore the past, Bloch: 2
for our lived e., [sociology] substitutes indicators, Aron: 4
individual e. himself indirectly, Mead, George Herbert: 10
no such thing as isolated repetition of isolated experiences, Horney: 4
people with similar e. behave in similar ways, Homans: 4
portrayal of *how* [man] reacts to common human e. that matters, Lowenthal: 4
experiment:
e. is observation that can be repeated, isolated and varied, Titchener: 1
I passionately desire to live to see completion of this historical social e., Pavlov: 8
if human being is experimented upon, his attitudes toward e. become important, Roethlisberger: 1
it [Constitution] is an e., as all life is an e., Holmes: 13
no isolated e. can suffice, Fisher, R. A.: 6
no one believes hypothesis except originator but everyone believes e. except experimenter, Beveridge, W. I. B.: 1
observation by e. as means of exploration, Comte: 7
one well-constructed e. often suffices for the establishment of a law, Durkheim: 9
experimental:
behaviorist views psychology as e. branch of natural science, Watson: 1
e. observations are only experience carefully planned in advance, Fisher, R. A.: 5
experimental psychologist:
e.p. tries to discover what is there, not what it is there for, Titchener: 3
experimenter:
our government [Soviet Union] also an e., Pavlov: 8
experiments:
isolated scientists daily run risk [of] repeating e. made by others, Saint-Simonians: 1
experts:
become e. in the practical by so many separate acts, James: 9
explanation:
desire for e. that generates science, Nagel: 1
every e. matter of less or greater probability, Murray, Henry A.: 4
every psychological e. [leans] on biology or on logic, Piaget: 8
exploitation:
communism is e. of strong by weak, Proudhon: 2
e. is factual description of a socio-economic relationship, Dobb: 2
for e., veiled by illusions, [bourgeoisie] substituted direct brutal e., Marx and Engels: 7
property is e. of weak by strong, Proudhon: 2
exploration:
means of e. are three [types of observation], Comte: 7
explorations:
Quetelet said "Let the e. be carried out," Nightingale: 1
expropriators:
e. are expropriated, Marx: 21
externalities:
also ignored are the free-rider problems created as e., Coleman: 7

presence of e. [is] market failure, Samuelson and Nordhaus: 1
extinct:
single words, like whole languages, gradually become e., Darwin: 8
extraordinary:
charisma [is] quality by virtue of which [individual] is considered e., Weber, Max: 25
extraverted:
if man lives in way directly correlated with objective conditions, he is e., Jung: 3
extreme:
advocate of e. measures was always trustworthy; his opponent suspected, Thucydides: 2
e. instances are rare, Plato: 2
extremes:
everything good, he [Montagu] said, trims between e., Macaulay: 13
eye-witnesses:
shall build modern history on e.-w. and original documents, Ranke: 3

Fabian Society:
Wells: 1
face-to-face:
by primary group I mean f.-t.-f. associations and cooperation, Cooley: 6
f.-t.-f. interaction never been treated as subject in own right, Goffman: 4
f-.t.-f. interactions must meet key requirements of real situations, Goffman: 2
[in] f-.t.-f. gatherings can fit shape and form to matters that aren't otherwise palpable to senses, Goffman: 7
fact:
all reasonings concerning matter of f. are founded on relation of cause and effect, Hume: 7
all scientist creates in a f. is language in which he enunciates it, Poincaré: 2
every linguistic f. reveals a f. of civilization, Meillet: 2
f. not phenomenon, but proposition *about* phenomena, Parsons, Talcott: 4
Freud's respect for the singular f., Jones: 1
great tragedy of Science — slaying of beautiful hypothesis by ugly f., Huxley, T. H.: 3
if we infer a soul quality from the social f. and use the quality to explain the f., we put ourselves on a level with animists in the most savage tribes, Bentley: 2
the past is f. that cannot be destroyed, Chateaubriand: 1
scientific f. experimentally established, Fisher, R. A.: 1
social f. exerts external constraint on individual, Durkheim: 6
this is how a [scientific] fact arises, Fleck: 4
when [Freud] got hold of significant f. he would know it was example of something universal, Jones: 1
faction:
by a f. I understand a number of citizens, adverse to rights of other citizens or aggregate interests of the community, Madison: 1
liberty is to f. what air is to fire, Madison: 2
to secure public good and private rights against danger of f. is object [of] our inquiries, Madison: 4
factions:
in America there are f., but no conspiracies, Tocqueville: 5
most common source of f. has been unequal distribution of property, Madison: 3
factory:
no matter how degraded the f. hand, he is not real estate, DuBois: 7
revolutionary process takes place in the f., Gramsci: 1
facts:
after the collection of f., the search for causes, Taine: 4
aim of thick-description ethnology to draw large conclusions from small, densely textured f., Geertz: 8
certain authors on social subjects claim f. "speak for themselves," Parsons, Talcott: 2
conclusive f. are inseparable from inconclusive except by a head that already understands, Carlyle: 1
consider social f. as things, Durkheim: 7
errors which arise from absence of f. more durable than those which result from unsound reasoning respecting true data, Babbage: 2
explanation of f. the establishment of a connection between single phenomena and general f., Comte: 5
f. about behavior are not treated in their own right, Skinner: 1
f. are the mere dross of history, Macaulay: 4
f. only seem to exist, Taine: 3
f. speak only when the historian calls on them, Carr: 1
false f. are highly injurious to the progress of science, Darwin: 9
good observer quick to take a hint from the f., Mayo: 2
history gives particular f. while poetry general truths, Aristotle: 6
imaginations people have of another are the solid f. of a society, Cooley: 1
mental f. cannot be studied apart from [their] physical environment, James: 19
most important f. that sociologists have to deal with are opinions, Park and Burgess: 1
most reckless of all theorists is he who professes to let f. and figures speak for themselves, Marshall, Alfred: 2
only laws and generalizations are scientific f., Malinowski: 1
practical politics consists in ignoring f., Adams, Henry: 2
relation of general principles to irreducible and stubborn f. which forms novelty in present society, Whitehead: 3
science disciplines speculation with f., Simon: 8
spatialisation expression of concrete f. under guise of abstract logical construction, Whitehead: 4
that f. will "speak for themselves" is illusion, Becker, Carl L.: 1
those who reject Theory of Evolution as not supported by f., forget their own theory is supported by no f. at all, Spencer: 2
when theories and f. in conflict, theories must yield, Simon: 8
failure:
few positions in life that do not throw together persons there by virtue of f. and [others] by virtue of success, Goffman: 1
failure of nerve:
Murray, Gilbert: 1
fair:
concept of f. price is devoid of any scientific meaning, von Mises: 7
true civilization will demand f. play, Huizinga: 6
faith:
belief in [progress of humanity] is act of f., Bury: 2
despotism may govern without f., but liberty cannot, Tocqueville: 10
excesses resulting from extreme familiarity with things holy are characteristic of periods of unshaken f., Huizinga: 2
ritual is bridge between f. and action, Firth, Raymond: 2
faithfulness:
without f., society could not exist, Simmel: 19
fallacies:
f. implied in Keynesian full-employment doctrine are same errors which Smith and Say demolished, von Mises: 1
fallacy:
F. of Misplaced Concreteness, Whitehead: 4
false:
f. views [in science] do little harm, as every one takes salutary pleasure in proving their falseness, Darwin: 9
from f. assumptions and irreproducible experiments an important discovery has resulted, Fleck: 3
ideology is process accomplished consciously, but with a f. consciousness, Engels: 9
political judgment which describes connections of institutions with other institutions can be true or f., Dilthey: 1
stifling [f. opinion] would be an evil still, Mill, John Stuart: 14
falsehood:
we should in vain attempt to demonstrate as f. [that sun will or will not rise tomorrow], Hume: 13

successful staging of false f. involves use of real techniques, Goffman: 2
you might prove anything by f., Carlyle: 1
file:
politics are a smooth f., Montesquieu: 7
final solution:
belief that there is a f.s. responsible for slaughter of individuals on altars of great historical ideas, Berlin: 8
moment philosophy supposes it can find a f.s., it becomes apologetics or propaganda, Dewey: 10
recognition that there is no f.s. of eternal contradictions is beginning of wisdom — and statesmanship, Beard: 2
finality:
f. is not the language of politics, Disraeli: 3
finance capital:
imperialism is capitalism at stage at which dominance of f.c. is established, Lenin: 4
Fiore, Quentin
Firth, J. R.
Firth, Raymond
fiscal:
spirit of a people written in its f. history, Schumpeter: 2
Fisher, Irving
Fisher, R. A.
fitness:
people may be fitted by being fit in an unfit f., Burke, Kenneth: 1
person who gains nothing or reduces own f. to diminish another has committed act of spite, Wilson, Edward O.: 2
person who raises own f. by lowering others is engaged in selfishness, Wilson, Edward O.: 2
when [individual] increases f. of another at expense of own f., has performed act of altruism, Wilson, Edward O.: 2
fittest:
[competition] best for the race because insures survival of f., Carnegie: 1
expression used by Spencer of survival of the f. is more accurate, Darwin: 4
f. may also be the gentlest, Dobzhansky: 2
f. would survive [and improve the race], Wallace, Alfred Russel: 1
only the f. [forms of action] survive, Pollack and Maitland: 3
Spencer suggested substituting for natural selection the term "survival of the f." which is easily consider tautological, Mayr: 1
survival of f. is what Darwin called natural selection, Spencer: 7
survival of f., not better or stronger, Spencer: 8
flag:
protect with equal vigor right to destroy [f.] and right to wave it, Rothstein: 1
Flag Protection Act of 1989:
Rothstein: 1
Fleay, Frederick Gard
Fleck, Ludwik
flower girl:
difference between lady and f.g. is how she's treated, Shaw: 2
focus:
f. upon A involves neglect of B, Burke, Kenneth: 3
Fogel, Robert William
Fogel, Robert William, and Elton, Geoffrey Rudolph
Fogel, Robert William, and Engerman, Stanley
folk society:
[f.] s. is small, isolated, nonliterate, and homogeneous, Redfield: 1
[in] f.s. technical order is subordinated within the moral order, Redfield: 4
folkways:
in f., whatever is, is right, Sumner: 7
Follett, Mary Parker
food:
f. categories encode social events, Douglas; 3
f. is necessary to existence of man, Malthus: 1
poorer a family, greater proportion of its total expenditure devoted to f., Engel: 1
fool:
better to be Socrates dissatisfied than f. satisfied, Mill, John Stuart: 21
force:
every active f. produces more than one change, Spencer: 4
f. is foundation of all social organisation, Pareto: 9
meeting physical f. with soul f., King: 4
notion that f. is creator of government is one of part-truths that beget total errors, MacIver: 3
violence not to be confused with f., Pareto: 7
forces:
pattern of behavior shaped by certain set of f. by mysterious coincidence [serves] ends but tenuously related to those f., Geertz: 2
Ford, Henry
foreign:
if either f.-born or native-born of at least one f. parent we have called ethnics, Warner: 1
foreign relations:
conduct of f.r. ought not be purpose in itself for political society, Kennan: 2
foreplay:
no accident that Freud called reward from [aesthetic work] f., Gay: 2
foreskin:
Aryan is man with white skin, thick skin, and f., Schapera: 1
forgetting:
[failure of recall] as "tip of the tongue (TOT)" phenomenon, Brown and McNeill: 1
in use of intellect, f. as important as recollecting, James: 16
forgotten man:
F.M. always pays, is not seldom a woman, Sumner: 2
Fortes, Meyer
fortune:
F. exerts all her power where there is no strength prepared to oppose her, Machiavelli: 17
F. governs half of our actions, Machiavelli: 17
F. is a woman, and man who wants to hold her down must beat and bully her, Machiavelli: 18
Foucault, Michel
fountains of knowledge:
he that makes ill use of language [impedes] f.o.k., Locke: 10
four freedoms:
seek world founded upon f.f., Roosevelt: 3
Fourteen Points:
Wilson, Woodrow: 4
Fourteenth Amendment [to the U. S. Constitution]:
the F.A. does not enact Mr. Herbert Spencer's Social Statics, Holmes: 6
Fourth Estate:
in Reporters' Gallery sat F.E., Carlyle: 6
fox:
f. knows many tricks, hedgehog only one, Archilochos: 1
have to be a f. to be wary of traps, Machiavelli: 16
France, Anatole
Francis [St.]:
I propose F. as patron saint for ecologists, White, Lynn T., Jr.: 1
Frankenstein monster:
such is the F.m. States have created by their corporation laws, Brandeis: 8
Frankfurter, Felix
Franklin, Benjamin:
F.'s famous reply "What good is a new-born child?," Mandler and Kessen: 1
Frazer, James George
Frazier, E. Franklin
free:
could calculate a man's conduct for the future [and nevertheless] maintain that the man is f., Kant: 2
East knew that One is f.; Greek and Roman world that some are f.; German World that All are f., Hegel: 6
f. and unfree — story of man in society, Barnard: 4
hypothesis that man is not f. essential to application of scientific method to study of human behavior, Skinner: 8
I am as f. as Nature first made man, Dryden: 1
man is born f.; everywhere he is in chains, Rousseau: 11
free choice:
f.c. among variety of goods and services does not signify freedom if they sustain alienation, Marcuse: 2
free commerce:
under system of perfectly f.c.,

pursuit of individual advantage is connected with the universal good of the whole, Ricardo: 7
free competition:
f.c. of entrepreneurs, Pareto: 6
pure economics is theory of determination of prices under perfectly f.c., Walras: 1
free country:
habits formed in a f.c. may prove fatal to its liberties, Tocqueville: 6
free enterprise:
f.e. system rightly compared to gigantic computing machine, Leontief: 2
free rider:
also ignored are the f.-r. problems created as externalities, Coleman: 7
free speech:
f.s. basis of U. S. Constitutional guarantees, Brandeis 1, 3, 4
[f.s.] is matrix of every other freedom, Cardozo: 4
f.s. would not protect man falsely shouting fire, Holmes: 11
only [creating] present danger warrants setting limit to [f.s.], Holmes: 11, 12, 13
right of f.s. same in peace and in war, Brandeis: 1
free thought:
[f.t.] is matrix of every other freedom, Cardozo: 4
not f.t. for those who agree with us but for the thought we hate, Holmes: 18
that régime forbids f.t. is necessary basis for greatest good, Bagehot: 7
freedom:
capital a necessary condition for political f., Friedman: 2
development of social problems theory oriented to values of f. and equality rather than order, Gouldner: 1
f. has made [modern man] isolated and, thereby, anxious and powerless, Fromm: 2
f. in a commons brings ruin to all, Hardin: 1
f. [of thought and speech] is matrix of every other f., Cardozo: 4
for flag to endure as symbol of f., protect with equal vigor right to destroy and right to wave it, Rothstein: 1
History of the World nothing but development of Idea of F., Hegel: 7
in giving f. to the slave, we assure f. [for] the free, Lincoln: 3
let us not seek to satisfy our thirst for f. by drinking from the cup of bitterness, King: 3
social science can give us f., Barber: 2
system of private property is most important guaranty of f. [even] for those who do not own property, Hayek: 3
truth of political theory is political f., Neumann, Franz: 1
universe will change if you bring up your children in behavioristic f., Watson: 4
freedoms:
seek world founded upon four f., Roosevelt: 3
Freeman, Edward Augustus
French Resistance:
Bloch: 4
French Revolution:
thesis of perverse effect first put forward in wake of F.R., Hirschman: 6
Frenkel-Brunswik, Else
Freud, Sigmund:
exhilarating yet terrifying to read F. as moralist, Rieff: 1
F. created new professional identity, Erikson, Erik H.: 7
F. said never abandon sexual theory, Jung: 14
F. showed that human subject is decentered, Althusser: 1
[F.'s] emphasis on biology actually liberating idea, Trilling, Lionel: 1
[F.'s] great strength was respect he had for singular fact, Jones: 1
[F.'s] misogyny taken for granted even by most admiring students, Trilling, Diana: 2
ideas of F. assigned prominence out of all proportion to their true importance, Whitehead: 6
if F. had brought to man's knowledge nothing more than that there is such thing as the true, there would be no Freudian discovery, Lacan: 2
Napoleon I: 1
no accident that F. called reward from [aesthetic work] forepleasure, Gay: 2
[our interest in work and love] rooted in phrase reportedly uttered by F., Smelser: 2
strict adherence to all of F.'s theoretical interpretations is danger of stagnation, Horney: 1, 2
to us he [F.] is whole climate of opinion, Auden: 3
Totem and Taboo was sweet revenge on the crown prince [Jung], Gay: 3
what was F.'s Galapagos?, Erikson: Erik H.: 4
with this work F. [opens] royal road to unconscious, Lacan: 3
Freyre, Gilberto
Friedan, Betty
Friedman, Milton:
F.'s voice is like voice of ten, Samuelson: 7
Friedrich, Carl J., and Zbigniew K. Brzezinski
friend:
social group clear who it holds to be its f., Simmel: 1
friends:
code of corner boy requires him to help f. and refrain from [harming] them, Whyte, William F.: 2
differentiated friendships require that f. do not look into sphere which would make them feel limits of their mutual understanding, Simmel: 14
Perfect Christian and the Economic Man have one thing in common: neither would have any f., Knight: 14
friendship:
in modern society differentiated f. [emerges], Simmel: 14
to refuse to give and refuse to accept is refusal of f., Mauss: 5
Frisch, Ragnar:
word Econometrics is [F.'s], Schumpeter: 15
Fromm, Erich
frontier:
f. can have [no] place in census reports, Porter: 1
f. has gone [thus closing] first period of American history, Turner, Frederick Jackson: 3
Frontier Thesis:
Porter: 1; Turner, Frederick Jackson: 2
frontiers:
continuous creation of new f., Bailyn: 3
market economy does not respect political f., von Mises: 6
Frost, Robert
frustration:
aggression is always a consequence of f., Dollard: 1
what economist calls equilibrium of behavior, psychologists call f., Boulding: 4
full employment:
f.e. means that unemployment is reduced to short intervals of standing by, Beveridge, William Henry: 2
fallacies implied in Keynesian f.-e. doctrine are same errors which Smith and Say demolished, von Mises: 1
function(s):
behavior (*B*) is f. (*F*) of person (*P*) and of his environment (E), Lewin: 3
celibacy and promiscuity fulfill identical sociological f., Coser: 2
every custom, material object, idea and belief fulfils vital f., Malinowski: 12
final cause is the f.; form is the definition, Aristotle: 2
use word f. because social phenomena do not exist for the useful results they produce, Durkheim: 10
[*see also* latent; manifest]
functional:
social system has f. unity, Radcliffe-Brown: 4
society shifts in direction of f. differentiation if everybody can buy anything and pursue any occupation, Luhmann: 4
title of F. School of Anthropology has been bestowed by myself, on myself, Malinowski: 19
functional autonomy:
Allport, Gordon W.: 4
functionalism:
alienation of young sociologists from F., Gouldner: 1

question concerning existence of G. is nothing but question concerning existence of man, Feuerbach: 2
where fear of G. is wanting, [either] kingdom ruined, or kept going by fear of a prince, Machiavelli: 5
gods:
ancient religion part of social order which embraces g. and men alike, Smith, William Robertson: 4
cultural system that can launch earth satellites can dispense with g. entirely, White, Leslie A.: 2
man born into fixed relation to certain g., Smith, William Robertson: 3
we are the only people who think themselves risen from savages; everyone else believes they descend from g., Sahlins: 1
God's truth:
"G.t." position in metaphysics of linguistics, Householder: 1
Godwin, William
Goethe, Johann Wolfgang von:
Napoleon : 1
Goffman, Erving
gold:
not by gold or by silver but by labour wealth of the world purchased, Smith, Adam: 10
gold standard:
if [call] g.s. "barbarous relic," cannot object to application of same term to every historically determined institution, von Mises: 8
golden age:
to revive a G.A., must be as free, for Acorns, as for Honesty, Mandeville: 2
golden eggs:
capital lays g.e., Marx: 18
golden sands of life:
we cannot count the g.s.o.l., Edgeworth: 3
good:
bad money drives out g. money, Gresham: 1; Macleod: 1
everything is g. as it leaves Author of things; everything degenerates in hands of man, Rousseau: 9
g. government is one in which vices of mankind conspire for the common g., Aron: 3
g. laws, lead to the making of better ones, Rousseau: 19
g. or evil, only in reference to pleasure or pain, Locke: 8
general will always for common g., Rousseau: 6
greatest g. reduces to liberty and equality, Rousseau: 17
in place of absolute g. and evil, we speak of ranking, Arrow: 1
knowledge is power to do g. and evil alike, but cannot throw away the power, Barber: 2
men do g. despite themselves, Condorcet: 3
never known much g. done by those who affected to trade for public g., Smith, Adam: 21
not true that g. can follow only from g., Weber, Max: 14
part of the force that always tries to do evil and always does g., Goethe: 1
prince must learn how not to be g., Machiavelli: 14
pursuit of individual advantage connected with universal g. of whole, Ricardo: 7
social g. is an abstraction from individual values of members of society, Arrow: 3
state exists for sake of a g. life, and not for sake of a life only, Aristotle: 12
things only G. and Evil in reference to something else, Mandeville: 4
we deem thing to be g., because we strive for it, Spinoza: 3
good sense:
g.s. is most equitably distributed; for everyone thinks himself amply provided with it, Descartes: 1
Goode, William J.
goodness:
cost is the price [the purchaser] pays, added to the cost of verifying the degree of g. for which he contracts, Babbage: 1
goods:
no longer speak of g. but of advantages, Arrow: 1
value is importance that g. acquire for individuals, Menger: 1
Gosset, William Sealy
Gould, Stephen Jay
Gouldner, Alvin W.
govern:
against natural order for the many to g. and few to be governed, Rousseau: 18
despotism may g. without faith, but liberty cannot, Tocqueville: 10
though counting heads not ideal way to g., better than breaking them, Hand: 1
to g. well a family, and a kingdom, different sorts of business, Hobbes: 5
governed:
by what was world ever g., but by opinion of person or persons?, Macaulay: 8
deriving powers from consent of the g., Jefferson: 1
easiness with which many are g. by few, Hume: 8
figures tell us whether [world] is being governed well or badly, Goethe: 2
great error of present age is believing men can be g. by reasoning, Pareto: 9
must first enable government to control the g.; and oblige it to control itself, Madison: 7
necessary that there exist means by which group may be g., Aquinas: 2
public spirit is as superfluous in the g., as it ought to be all-powerful in the statesman, Steuart Denham: 1
to be g. is to be watched over, betrayed, dishonoured, Proudhon: 5
governing:
g. beyond the grave is most insolent of all tyrannies, Paine: 2
were a people to become disinterested, would be no possibility of g. them, Steuart Denham: 1
government:
all g. is founded on compromise and barter, Burke, Edmund: 4
best g. that which governs least, O'Sullivan: 1
by consenting to make one Body Politick under One G., every Man puts himself under Obligation to submit to majority, Locke: 17
by Political Arithmetick mean Art of Reasoning by Figures, upon things relating to G., Davenant: 1
chief end of Mens under G. is Preservation of their Property, Locke: 19
civil disobedience is phenomenon of private as well as public g., Merriam: 3
commonweale is a lawfull g. of many families with a puissant soveraigntie, Bodin: 1
democracy, a charming form of g., Plato: 11
democracy is worst form of G. except all those forms that have been tried from time to time, Churchill: 4
error alone that needs support of g., Jefferson: 5
every g. is in some respects a problem for every other g., Kennan: 3
every step a g. takes beyond protecting smooth operation of market economy is step [toward] totalitarian system, von Mises: 5
for Forms of G. let fools contest, Pope: 2
g. best which governs not at all, Thoreau: 1
g. can have no more than two legitimate purposes, Godwin: 1
g. could print good edition of Shakespeare's works, but could not get them written, Marshall, Alfred: 11
g. in best state is but necessary evil, Paine: 1
g. is adjustment of interest groups in particular group or system, Bentley: 3
g. is badge of lost innocence, Paine: 1
g. is based upon patterns of action in types of situations, Merriam: 1
g. is great fiction, Bastiat: 1
G. keen on amassing statistics, but every figure comes from village watchman who puts down what he damn pleases, Stamp: 1
g. of laws, not of men, Adams, John: 1, 2
g. [with] power and will to remedy capitalist system would have will and power to abolish it, Robinson, Joan: 1
good g. is one in which vices of mankind conspire for the common good, Aron: 3

happened:
historian's one task is to tell thing as it h., Lucian: 1
history is what h. in context of what might have h., Trevor-Roper: 1
this work wants only to show what actually h., Ranke: 1
happiness:
diversity of ethical opinion associated with *anomie* rather than increase of h., Parsons, Talcott: 6
for moral calculus compare h. of one person with h. of another and different average h., Edgeworth: 2
great end of all human industry, is h., Hume: 12
greatest h. of greatest number the measure of right and wrong, Bentham: 1
never have laws been dictated from point of view: greatest h. shared by the greatest number, Beccaria: 1
pursuit of H., Jefferson: 1
Wealth, not H., subject treated by the Political Economist, Senior: 2
happy:
choose rather to be h. citizens than subtle disputants, Burke, Edmund: 4
h. families are all alike, Tolstoy: 4
hard data:
h.d. those which resist solvent influence of critical reflection, Russell: 2
[*see also* data]
Hardin, Garrett
harm:
any h. you do to a man should be done in such way that you need not fear his revenge, Machiavelli: 7
only purpose for which power can be rightfully exercised over member of community is to prevent h. to others, Mill, John Stuart: 12
harmony:
h. between thought and reality to be found in grammar of the language, Wittgenstein: 4
[Man] is a multitudinous h., Herder: 2
Harrington, Michael
Hartley, David
Hartmann, Heinz
Harvey, William:
Machiavelli, like H. [with the circulation of the blood], recognized existence of power politics and subjected it to scientific study, Lerner: 1
hate:
h. menaces stable government, Brandeis: 3
history neither written nor made without love or h., Mommsen: 1
misery generates h., Brontë: 1
hatred:
h. can unleash upheavals, but it produces nothing, Sorel: 1
hatreds:
age of intellectual organization of political h., Benda: 1
Hawkins, Edward R., and Waller, Willard W.
Hawthorne effect:
if human being is experimented upon, his attitude toward experiment becomes important, Roethlisberger: 1
Hayek, Friedrich A. von
healer:
myth and action form pair associated with duality of patient and h., Lévi-Strauss: 10
hearing:
[h.], cannot be measured independently, Cherry: 2
heart:
religion is h. of a h.-less world, Marx: 1
specialists without spirit, sensualists without h., Weber, Max: 5
to compare worths of what exists and what does not, must consult our h., James: 22
heartland:
who rules East Europe commands the H., Mackinder: 1
hearts:
Socialism is in our h., Sorel: 2
heavenly:
h. city makes use of peace until this mortal condition which necessitates it shall pass away, Augustine: 2
hedgehog:
h. knows only one trick: a good one, Archilochos: 1
Hegel, Georg Wilhelm Friedrich:
can be truly said that Marx stood H. on his head, Elster: 4
H. remarks that all facts and personages in history occur twice, Marx: 6
H. showed we are free only to degree that we know laws of nature, Plekhanov: 1
only one [pupil] understood me [H.], and he misunderstood, Mehring: 1
reminiscent of H.'s *Phenomenology*, Marx: 13
with [H.] it [dialectic] is standing on its head, Marx: 15
hegemony:
h. protected by armour of coercion, Gramsci: 3
some speak of h., others simply of power, Dahrendorf: 3
Heilbroner, Robert L.
help:
code of corner boy requires him to h. friends and refrain from [harming] them, Whyte, William F.: 2
from moment one man needed h. of another, equality disappeared, Rousseau: 4
Hempel, Carl J.
Henderson, L. J.
Henry IV, Emperor:
to believe Pope Gregory VII about H., Bloch: 3
Heraclitus
Herder, Johann Gottfried von
hereditary:
crown becomes h. in the wearer of it, Blackstone: 2
h. drill, Bagehot: 7
h. faculty for culture that is most distinctive feature of man, Kroeber: 7
idea of h. legislators as absurd as h. mathematician, Paine: 3
heredity:
h. as explanation diverts from social and intellectual factors that make up personality, Barzun: 1
h. invents nothing, has no imagination, Binet: 1
h. [produces] given series of characters with increasing economy and speed [law of tachygenesis], Hall: 2
heresies:
covert h. have given Christian creed buoyancy, Mumford: 3
fate of new truths to begin as h. and end as superstitions, Huxley, T. H.: 5
hermeneutical:
current movement to make social sciences h. makes reasonable Deweyan point, Rorty: 1
hero:
h. [appears] unmasked as human who requires no interpreter, Rank: 3
Herodotus
heroes:
Carlyle: 5
h. [in popular magazines] are idols of production and consumption, Lowenthal: 1
men of science to be the h. of the future, Robinson and Beard: 1
heroic:
I would as soon be descended from that h. little monkey as from a savage who delights to torture his enemies, Darwin: 10
Herschel, John F. W.
Herskovits, Melville Jean
heterogeneous:
progress is transformation of homogeneous into h., Spencer: 3, 6
Hexter, J. H.
Hicks, John R.
hiding hand:
H.H. beneficially hides difficulties from us, Hirschman: 1
hierarchy:
basic human needs organized into h. of relative prepotency, Maslow: 1
[h.] pole of medieval mind, Huizinga: 14
hierophany:
man trying by means of h. to give being to his most ordinary act, Eliade: 2
higgling:
proportion between two different quantities of labour adjusted by h. and bargaining of the market, Smith, Adam: 11
Himmelfarb, Gertrude
Hirschman, Albert O.
historian:
after great h. has done his work, others should not be able to practise in terms of preceding era, Namier: 4

all h. can do is to enlarge specific experience to dimensions of more general, Lévi-Strauss: 5
cause of the event [for h.] is the inside of the event itself, Collingwood: 1, 2, 3
facts speak only when the h. calls on them, Carr: 1
goal [of h.] to have complete knowledge for reasons and origin of every event, Ibn Khaldûn: 5
great abilities are not requisite for H., Johnson: 1
h. looks through [events] to discern thought within them, Collingwood: 1, 2
h. may be allowed privilege of a naturalist, Taine: 2
h. must keep eye on universal aspect, Ranke: 2
h. of science [is] guardian of man's most precious heritage, Sarton: 3
h. tells what happened and [poet] what might happen, Aristotle: 6
hardly surprising that first h. to emphasize accelerating velocity of history [Henry Adams] should have been an American, Schlesinger: 4
ignorance is first requisite of h., Strachey: 1
no modern h. would think as he does if Marx never existed, Aron: 2
not only political history that social h. denies [but] reason itself, Himmelfarb: 2
to arrive at interpretation, h. synthesizes material to illustrate dominant idea, Nevins: 2
true history begins when h. has discerned the living, active man, Taine: 1

historian's:
h. one task is to tell the thing as it happened, Lucian: 1
h. powers are limited, Beard: 5
h. sole rule is to think of the yet unborn who shall seek his converse, Lucian: 1
[h.] view is conditioned by mentality of his own age, Bury: 1
history is h. experience, Oakeshott: 1
history of thought is reenactment of past thought in h. own mind, Collingwood: 3
one h. truth becomes another's myth, McNeill: 1

historians:
by borrowing from our daily experiences [h.] derive elements which help us restore the past, Bloch: 2
h. have stepped upon territory of our science [economics] like foreign conquerors, Menger: 3
[h.] imagine the past and remember the future, Namier: 1
h. must be alert for the casual reference that will open up a whole unsuspected realm of understanding, Hughes, H. Stuart: 1
h. relate what they would have believed, Franklin: 1
h. who live in democratic ages assign great general causes to all petty incidents, Tocqueville: 16
h. who refuse to grow up, Foucault: 2
if we [h.] make deliberate misstatements in interest of our country, what difference is there between us and those who live by their pens, Polybius: 1
invocation to h. to suppress moral or psychological evaluation one of most destructive fallacies, Berlin: 3
movement to narrative by new h. marks end of attempt to produce coherent explanation of change in past, Stone: 2
peculiarity of historical vocabulary enabled h. to conceal their ignorance, Hexter: 1
quotation is necessity for h., Hexter: 2
to suppose that facts "speak for themselves" is illusion of those h. who found special magic in word "scientific," Becker, Carl L.: 1
useful h. reveal particular cause of each event, Vico: 1

historical:
all historical knowledge is with view to ourselves, here and now, Laslett: 2
arbitrary character of sign alone makes comparative method in h. linguistics possible, Meillet: 1
belief in final solution responsible for slaughter of individuals on altars of great h. ideas, Berlin: 8
critical h. process helped weaken the past, Plumb: 1
extensive occurrence of diffusion lays axe to the theory of h. laws, Lowie: 1
for Marx, working out of h. process could take place only in cities, Trilling, Lionel: 4
h. knowledge of great intrinsic interest because it is about people with whom we can identify, Laslett: 2
h. sense — intuitive understanding of how things do not happen, Namier: 3
inscrutability [of] h. process, Schlesinger: 3
only a very vulgar h. materialism denies power of ideas, Berlin: 7
peculiarity of h. vocabulary — enabled historians to conceal their ignorance, Hexter: 1
something in nature of h. events which twists course of history, Butterfield: 3
sources of error in h. writings, Ibn Khaldûn: 1, 2, 3
strict conception of cause, introduced into h. experience, brings darkness, Oakeshott: 4
thought collective provides carrier for h. development of any field of thought, Fleck: 1
wealth of h. facts dash all attempts at theoretical treatment, Luhmann: 6

historical anthropologists:
[h.a.] dispute with evolutionists on social forms, Murdock: 2

historical materialism:
Plekhanov: 1

historical relativism:
Beard: 5

historical school of ethnology:
[h.s.o.e. believes] that many customs have long and tortuous history, Rivers: 2

historically:
idea of regarding religions h. hardly suggested before the nineteenth century, Frazer: 7

historicism:
[consequence] of thesis of h. [is that] attempts to develop a science of economics are vain, von Mises: 11

histories:
to converse with men, as L. Histories, Aubrey: 1

historiography:
Foucault: 2
h. considered domain of the common people, Ibn Khaldûn: 5
quotation is indispensable to h., Hexter: 2

history:
according to materialist conception of h., the ultimately determining element is production and reproduction of real life, Engels: 8
all facts and personages in h. appear first as tragedy, second as farce, Marx: 6
American h. has been h. of colonization of Great West, Turner, Frederick Jackson: 2
anthropology will have choice between being h. and being nothing, Maitland, Frederic William: 1
art of writing h. well is very rare, Voltaire: 6
can understand structure of a society without knowing its h., Evans-Pritchard: 4
cannot escape h., Lincoln: 3
[current forms of h. are] psychohistory and cliometrics, Nisbet: 3
Darwin showed that mind has h. as well as character, Thorndike: 3
democratic currents of h. resemble successive waves, Michels: 5
discussion whether h. is art or science seems futile, Namier: 4
endeavor to relate h. of the people as well as h. of the government, Macaulay: 11
events are the ephemera of h., Braudel: 6
events of h. are never mere phenomena, Collingwood: 1, 2, 3
facts are the mere dross of h., Macaulay: 4
first book of h., Herodotus: 1
first political form we observe in h. is Despotism, second Democracy and Aristocracy, third Monarchy, Hegel: 6
first task of ethnologist to unravel h. [of customs], Rivers: 2

how man reacts to common h. experiences that matters, Lowenthal: 4
how transitory all h. structures are, Herder: 3
hypothesis that man is not free essential to scientific study of h. behavior, Skinner: 8
I am a man and nothing h. is foreign to me, Terence: 1
I have laboured carefully to understand h. actions, Spinoza: 6
Industrial Revolution accompanied by demographic transition represents gain in h. efficiency, Davis, Kingsley: 2
mankind will possess control over h. behavior when h. mind will contemplate itself from within, Pavlov: 1
mystical mentality more observable among primitive people, but is present in every h. mind, Lévy-Bruhl: 2
principles of civil society found within h. mind, Vico: 5
racial explanation of differences in h. performance is ineptitude or fraud, Toynbee, Arnold J. (historian): 2
refer to spiteful act as "all too h," — and wonder what we meant, Wilson, Edward O.: 2
social organization necessary to h. species, Ibn Khaldûn: 7, 8
task of social theory to explain unintended consequences of h. action, Hayek: 7
to call someone a great man is to claim he has taken a large step in satisfying central h. interests, Berlin: 6
use of words in all forms of h. activity an indispensable correlate of bodily behavior, Malinowski: 16
we are not trapped in individual solipsistic hells but engage in h. dialogue, Putnam: 1
what influence occupation has on h. vision of the h. fate, Auden: 2
what is h. becomes animal, and animal h., Marx: 3
world is something h., Langer: 1

human behavior:
economics studies h.b. as relationship between ends and scarce means, Robbins: 1
general principles [to] explain h.b. turn out to be psychological, Homans: 3
theories that explain social phenomena are about [h.b.], Homans: 2

human being:
better to be a h.b. dissatisfied than a pig satisfied, Mill, John Stuart: 21
for social psychologist, man is human animal transformed into h.b., Sullivan: 1
if h.b. is experimented upon, his attitudes toward experiment become important factor, Roethlisberger: 1

human beings:
behold! h.b. living in underground den [where] they can see only shadows, Plato: 9
h.b. do not pursue their daily lives as automata, Rivers: 1
h.b. are concept-bearing agents, Giddens: 3
[h.b.] are item of history, not embodiment of general principles, Gould: 3
h.b. do not wish to be modest, Sapir: 11
h.b. unique in degree of capacity to lie, Wilson, Edward O.: 3
historians [should] view h.b. as creatures with purposes and motives, Berlin: 3
social reality has specific meaning for h.b., Schutz: 3
social sciences deal with relations between h.b. [in which] they interact on basis of mutually attributed meanings, Barber: 1
true spite commonplace because h.b. have intelligence to plot intrigue, Wilson, Edward O.: 3
what is it that we h.b. want, Lynd: 2
[*see also* individual; man; men; woman; women]

human capital:
h.c. created by changing persons to give them skills [to] act in new ways, Coleman: 5

human life:
myths point to generative power underlying h.l., Turner, Victor W.: 1

human nature:
all sciences have a relation to h.n., Hume: 1, 2
city [best place] to study h.n., Park: 5
city is product of nature, particularly of h.n., Park and Burgess 2, 3
every culture clings to belief that own feelings are the normal expression of h.n., Horney: 2
in most social science, h.n. is part of the method, Redfield: 2
only solid foundation [for study of h.n.] based on experience and observation, Hume: 2
principles of history of h.n. principles of universal history, Vico: 7
sociologists need to develop more complex, dialectical conception of h.n., Wrong: 1
to banish war would mutilate h.n., Treitschke: 1

human potentialities:
h.p. are helpless without a cultural milieu, Mead, Margaret: 3
to achieve richer culture, must recognize gamut of h.p., Mead, Margaret: 2

human race:
h.r. unable to do without peaceful coexistence, Kant: 5
history of h.r. is one in source, one in experience, and one in progress, Morgan, Lewis Henry: 5
little ground for claiming that mother of young children is more responsible than husband or brothers for welfare of h.r., Mead, Margaret: 13

human relations:
h.r. not subject matter of science, Wilson, Woodrow: 1

human society:
every h.s. from the point of view of another ignores fundamentals and exploits irrelevancies, Benedict: 4
questions about h.s. clustered around power, belief, wealth, Gellner: 4

humanistic coefficient:
essential character of cultural data [called] h.e., Znaniecki: 2, 3

humanists:
ominous conflict of outlook between h. and scientists, Sarton: 1; Snow: 1-3

humanitarian:
h. feelings invariably presage decadence of aristocracy, Pareto: 7

humanities:
linguistics opening small door between h. and the social sciences, Lévi-Strauss: 8

humanity:
belief in [progress of h.] is act of faith, Bury: 2
great technological breakthroughs have not shaken h. at its foundations, Levi: 1
man is unconscious instrument in attainment of universal aims of h., Tolstoy: 1
must use one's own h. as means to understanding, Redfield: 2
universal history embraces detailed causes of successive progress of h., Turgot: 2

Humboldt, Wilhelm von

Hume, David

humility:
both doctors and economists need h., but neither should abandon their patients to quacks, Rivlin: 1

hunger:
took as starting-point saying of Schiller that h. and love [move] world, Freud: 35

Huntington, Ellsworth

Huntington, Samuel P.

Hutcheson, Francis

Huxley, Julian, and Haddon, Alfred Cort

Huxley, T. H.

hybrid:
disposes of theory that h. peoples are inferior, Linton: 1
every civilized group has been h., Linton: 1

hydraulic:
h. government is government by intimidation, Wittfogel: 1

Hyman, Herbert H.:
James: 14
reference group, Cooley: 4

Hymes, Dell

hypotheses:
beware of testing too many h., Stigler, Stephen M.: 1
economics limps along with one foot in untested h., Robinson, Joan: 5
statistics affords only secure ground

on which h. can be brought to test, Herschel: 1
hypothesis:
body of positive knowledge grows by failure of tentative h. to predict phenomena the h. professes to explain, Friedman: 9
great tragedy of Science — slaying of beautiful h. by ugly fact, Huxley, T. H.: 3
h. grows stronger by every thing you see, hear, read, or understand, Sterne: 1
I have no need for this h., Laplace: 6
no one believes h. except originator, Beveridge, W. I. B.: 1
whenever attempt to test a h. we try to avoid errors in judging it, Neyman: 1
hysterics:
h. suffer mainly from reminiscences, Breuer and Freud: 1

Ibn Khaldûn
id:
where i. was, there ego shall be, Freud: 38
idea:
every i. fulfils vital function, Malinowski: 12
[i.] as act of intelligence, Binet: 4
i. is process which can cause chemical changes in body, Loeb: 1
truth of i. not stagnant, James: 28
ideal:
i. interests directly govern men's conduct, Weber, Max: 9
i. type of perfect government must be representative, Mill, John Stuart: 18
man who neglects the real to study the i. will learn how to accomplish his ruin, Machiavelli: 14
men hoist banner of the i. and then march in direction that concrete conditions reward, Dewey: 8
your i. made up of traits suggested by past men's words and actions, James: 1
idealist:
[for] originality of i. [to] find expression, necessary that originality of criminal also be possible, Durkheim: 8
ideas:
[aging society is comprised] of old people ruminating over old i., Sauvy: 2
belief there is a final solution responsible for the slaughter of individuals on altars of great historical i., Berlin: 8
correct i. come from social practice, Mao Zedong: 1
custom is mode of common conduct arising from community of i., Wundt: 5
difficulty lies not in new i., but in escaping from old ones, Keynes: 15
history of i. is history of misunderstandings, Kracauer: 1
hostility with which human societies receive all new i., Pearson: 1
how plastic limited number of observations become in hands of men with plastic i., Galton: 1
i. are not objects, but processes, Wundt: 2
i. govern the world or throw it into chaos, Comte: 7
i. have changed world, Voltaire: 7
i., not vested interests, which are dangerous for good or evil, Keynes: 24
i. of time, space, class, cause, personality constructed out of social elements, Durkheim: 17
i. seem to flow *from* [mass media] to opinion leaders and *from them* to population, Katz and Lazarsfeld: 1
intellectual revolutions often only synthesize and popularize long current i., Himmelfarb: 1
intimate relation exists between men's i. and social state, Fustel de Coulanges: 1
inviolable liberty to make words stand for what i. he pleases, Locke: 9
linguistic system is series of phonetic differences of sound combined with series of differences of i., Saussure: 6
look into past for criterion of i. which turn out to be ideological or utopian, Mannheim: 10
not only does ideology transform i., it transforms people, Bell: 2
ruling i. of each age have been i. of its ruling class, Marx and Engels: 9
senses let in particular i., and furnish empty cabinet, Locke: 4
social forces remain blind and undirected unless they clothe themselves in i., Berlin: 7
soon as a man connects i. with signs of own choosing, his memory is formed, Condillac: 2
through education, each generation transmits groundwork of i. to following, Cournot: 5
true i. are those we can verify, James: 27, 28
uniform i. originating among peoples unknown to each other must have common ground of truth, Vico: 3
within same language, all words used to express related i. limit each other reciprocally, Saussure: 5
without Locke we should have possessed a just theory of origin of human i., Macaulay: 6
woman with i. is social embarrassment, Mannes: 1
world largely ruled by i., Beard: 3
ideation:
i. [is aspect of] consciousness, Mead, George Herbert: 5
identification:
i. with one's office attractive [because] it offers easy compensation for personal deficiencies, Jung: 5
in act of devouring [primal father] accomplished their i. with him, Freud: 24
identities:
mathematics issues in i., Ramsey: 1
identity:
every time child speaks or listens, social structure reinforced in him and his social i. shaped, Bernstein, Basil: 2
study of i. as strategic in our time as study of sexuality was in Freud's time, Erikson, Erik H.: 2
identity crisis:
concept of i.c. grounded in experience of emigration and Americanization, Erikson, Erik H.: 8
identity of interests:
principle of i.o.i. can always be applied in political economy, Halévy: 1
ideological:
criterion of what is i. and what is utopian, Mannheim: 10
i. leaders subject to excessive fears which they can master only by reshaping thoughts of contemporaries, Erikson, Erik H.: 5
i. man, Berelson: 2
ideology:
analysis of i. belongs properly in discussion of the intelligentsia, Bell: 1
concept i. reflects the one discovery which emerged from political conflict, Mannheim: 4
every political i. has its root in volition, Kelsen: 1
i. is process accomplished with a false consciousness, Engels: 9
implicit in i. that collective unconscious obscures real condition of society and thereby stabilizes it, Mannheim: 4
not only does i. transform ideas, it transforms people, Bell: 2
sociology of knowledge, related, but distinguishable from theory of i., Mannheim: 11
total conception of i. develops simple theory of i. into sociology of knowledge, Mannheim: 6
idiocy:
i. of rural life, Marx and Engels: 8
idiot:
characteristic and diffferential signs of the i., Binet and Simon: 1
idols:
four classes of I. which beset men's minds, Bacon: 4
i. of production and consumption, Lowenthal: 1
ignorance:
i. is first requisite of historian, Strachey: 1
i. of the law excuseth not, Coke: 1
pluralistic i. made possible exaggerated impression of universality of attitudes, Katz and Allport: 1
term pluralistic i. could be applied to polarization, Noelle-Neumann: 2
though no such thing as chance, i. of real cause has same influence on the understanding, Hume: 16

understand nothing of what takes place in the group, Durkheim: 12
life-policy and personality of i. follow from definition of situation, Thomas: 3, 5
not say of culture patterns that they act upon an i., Radcliffe-Brown: 7
object of study is the i., Boas: 1
out of social interweaving something emerges that has [not] been planned by the i., Elias: 1
personality is organization within the i. that determines unique adjustment to environment, Allport, Gordon W.: 1
preference ordering for i., represents his entire social ethic, Arrow: 1
psychologists have not treated i. as unit in social system, Parsons, Talcott: 10
pursuit of i. advantage is connected with universal good of whole, Ricardo: 7
society provides remedy for inconveniences when every i. labours a-part, Hume: 6
strength of opinion in each i. [depends] on number he supposes to have entertained same opinion, Madison: 6
the i. does not fully realize his own nature, except that he is involved in society, Durkheim: 16
society infinitely surpasses i. in time and space, Durkheim: 11
Trickster represents undifferentiated past and present within every i., Radin: 1
weak ties are vital for an i.'s integration into modern society, Granovetter: 1

individuals:
capacity of i. to comprehend and to respond to each other's experiences [is] decisive psychological fact about society, Asch: 1
cultural facts [remain] after every consideration of i. involved exhausted, Kroeber: 4
culture and social structures are derivative products of social interaction of pluralities of i., Murdock: 3
easier to change i. in group than to change any one separately, Lewin: 4
greater number of i. observed, the more do individual peculiarities become effaced, Quetelet: 2
once i. come into one another's presence, promissory, evidential character of social life becomes pronounced, Goffman: 7
original word-creation must have proceeded from community of i., Wundt: 5
rational, self-interested i. will not act voluntarily to achieve group interests, Olson: 1
science cannot describe i., but only types, Durkheim: 1
sciences speak always of species; history of i., Schopenhauer: 1
social control depends upon i. able to assume attitudes of others, Mead, George Herbert: 3
social process in form of generalized other influences behavior of i., Mead, George Herbert: 12, 13
social systems more malleable than i., Elster: 6
society expresses sum of relationships in which i. find themselves, Marx: 11
society not mere sum of i., Durkheim: 12
various kinds of collectivism differ from liberalism in refusing to recognize spheres in which ends of the i. are supreme, Hayek: 2
[*see also* human beings; man; men; woman; women]

induction:
method of i. for use in noble science of politics, Macaulay: 7

inductive:
i. inference is only process by which new knowledge comes into the world, Fisher, R. A.: 4

industrial:
concept "post-i." is counterposed to that of "pre-i." and "i.," Bell: 3
i. civilization will exist when utopian experiment of self-regulating market will be no more than memory, Polanyi, Karl: 1
new theoretical statement [on] motivation in i. production required, Whyte, William F.: 3
poverty, economic oppression and i. strife not transitory incidents of i. order, Tawney: 1

Industrial Revolution:
effects of I.R. prove free competition may produce wealth without producing well-being, Toynbee, Arnold (economist): 2
essence of I.R. is substitution of competition for mediaeval distribution of wealth, Toynbee, Arnold (economist): 1
I.R. has been accompanied by a demographic transition representing gain in human efficiency, Davis, Kingsley: 2

industry:
economists have invented term The Great I., Wallas: 1
i. is ecology of science, Gellner: 2
need is father of i., Quesnay: 3
net aggregate gains from i. fall short owing to trained inability of businessmen, Veblen: 12
wages equal the product of i. minus rent, interest, and profits, Walker: 3

inequalities:
without sharp i. we would not have had great cultural achievements of past civilizations, Boulding: 3

inequality:
citizenship itself becoming architect of social i., Marshall, T. H.: 4
i. of economic advantages tend toward progressive increase of i., Knight: 5
no greater i. than equal treatment of unequals, Frankfurter: 3
no more i. between stations in life than among characters in a comedy, Diderot: 1
social i. is device by which societies insure that the most important positions are filled by the most qualified persons, Davis and Moore: 1

inertia:
[analysis of] migration includes not only concept of forces but also that of i., Petersen: 1

inevitability:
i. of gradualness cannot fail to be appreciated, Webb: 2

inexplicable:
we tolerate unexplained but not the i., Goffman: 6

infantile:
artist a survival from i. stage, Rank: 1
culture is consequence of i. experience, Róheim: 1
dreaming is piece of i. mental life that has been superseded, Freud: 12
entirety of i. experiences combines to form character structure, Horney: 4

infants:
give me dozen healthy i., and I'll guarantee to take any one at random and train him to become any type of specialist I select, Watson: 3

inference:
every i. matter of less or greater probability, Murray, Henry A.: 4
inductive i. is only process by which new knowledge comes into the world, Fisher, R. A.: 4
scientist cannot excuse himself from duty of getting his head clear on principles of scientific i., Fisher, R. A.: 3
we live by i., Thomas: 4

inferior:
disposes of theory that hybrid peoples are i., Linton: 1
in every generation the i. would be killed off, Wallace, Alfred Russel: 1

inferiority:
i. [is] value-bearing category that refers to powers of weak, Turner, Victor W.: 1

inferiority complex:
pessimists are individuals who have acquired an i.c., Adler: 4

inflation:
i. always and everywhere a monetary phenomenon, Friedman: 5
[no grounds for believing] that government will resist i. with as much tenacity as depression, Burns: 1

influence:
difference is slight, to the i. of an author, whether he is read by five hundred or five thousand; if he can select the five hundred, Adams, Henry: 1
i. is complex, bilateral relation, Koyré: 3
nobody wishes that his i. should completely determine other individual, Simmel: 18

influential:
i. are those who get the most of what there is to get, Lasswell: 6
study of politics is study of i., Lasswell: 5
influentials:
who or what influences the i.?, Katz and Lazarsfeld: 1
informal organization:
Barnard: 3
Moreno: 1
Roethlisberger: 1
Selznick: 1
information:
fundamental reason why Soviet rulers unable to achieve goals is lack of reliable i., Elster: 5
i. occupies slum dwelling in town of economics, Stigler, George J.: 2
must look at price system as a mechanism for communicating i., Hayek: 5
necessary to aim at facility in communicating i., Playfair: 1
one has i. only to extent one has tended to communicate, Sullivan: 4
ingratitude:
accusation of i. serves as social sanction to discourage men from forgetting obligations, Blau: 1
inheritance:
i. of economic advantages tend toward progressive increase of inequality, Knight: 5
inherited:
ideology of the conjugal family asserts worth of individual against i. elements, Goode: 2
man's unconscious contains all patterns of life and behavior i. from his ancestors, Jung: 10
inhibition:
nervous activity consists in excitation and i., Pavlov: 3
injustice:
great i. to persecute homosexuality as crime, Freud: 39
inclination to i. makes democracy necessary, Niebuhr: 1
to die slowly our life long, imprisoned in an Infinite I., Carlyle: 7
inner conflicts:
society is sewn together by its i.c., Ross: 1
inner-directed people:
society of transitional population growth develops i.-d.p., Riesman: 1
innocence:
difficult to recapture preconceptual i., Bruner: 1
innocent:
better that ten guilty persons escape than that one i. suffer, Blackstone: 4
innovate:
to i. is not to reform, Burke, Edmund: 13
innovations:
i. are changes in production functions, Schumpeter: 4
i. carried out by borrowed money, Schumpeter: 8
most radical i. in any culture amount to no more than a minor revision, Benedict: 5
inquiry:
custom and example have more persuasive power than any certitude obtained by i., Descartes: 2
inscrutability:
salient fact about historical process is its i., Schlesinger: 3
insects:
i. too can conduct complex communities without use of reason, Lowell: 1
insinuate:
[in philosophy] that which one would i., thereof one must speak, Gellner: 1
instability:
underlying laws of i. can be studied in rats as well and more easily than in man, Tolman: 2
instances:
extreme i. are rare, while intermediate ones are plentiful, Plato: 2
instinct:
equations [on causes of war] are description of what would occur if i. were allowed to act uncontrolled, Richardson: 1
everything we have been calling an i. is learned behavior, Watson: 5
i. of workmanship is present in all men, Veblen: 5, 11
[not] necessary to describe man as possessed of i. of self-preservation, Thorndike: 7
instinctive:
i. logic still directs the mind, Bernard: 1
take away i. dispositions and the organism would become incapable of activity, McDougall: 2
instincts:
great decisions of human life have more to do with i., Jung: 8
only two basic i., Eros and the destructive instinct, Freud: 42
institution:
i. is lengthened shadow of one man, Emerson: 2
political judgment which condemns an i. [can only be] correct or incorrect [in appraising] institution's goal, Dilthey: 1
political judgment which describes connections of i. with other institutions can be true or false, Dilthey: 1
turning example into precedent and precedent into i., MacIver: 4
institutions:
all our i. are determined and maintained by privileged males, Adler: 3
History of I. cannot be mastered — without an effort, Stubbs: 1
how can i. which serve common welfare come into being without a common will?, Menger: 2
how oppressive the best i. become in course of a few generations, Herder: 3
human beings do not pursue their daily lives as automata conforming to i. into which they have been born, Rivers: 1
i. must be reformed or abolished if unjust, Rawls: 1
i. require to be adapted not to good men, but to bad, Mill, John Stuart: 25
i. which arise as result of conscious actions are often unwanted byproducts of such actions, Popper: 2
need for status is met by public recognition of just i., Rawls: 5
organization man [is] mind and soul of our great self-perpetuating i., Whyte, William H., Jr.: 1
press no substitute for i., Lippmann, Walter: 4
science has produced i. that bind people more than "superstitions" they replaced, Berger and Kellner: 2
so long as [man] keeps human shape he is enchained by our i., Rousseau: 10, 11
to be celebrated requires access to major i., Mills: 1
instructing:
to history assigned office of judging past, i. present for benefit of future generations, Ranke: 1
insufficient data:
temptation to form premature theories upon insufficient data, Doyle: 3
integration:
i. of large societies depends on weak social ties of individuals, Blau: 3
weak ties vital for an individual's i. into modern society, Granovetter: 1
integument:
[capitalist] i. is burst asunder, Marx: 21
intellect:
in use of i., forgetting as important as recollecting, James: 16
judgment of i. is only half-truth, Jung: 4
intellectual:
capitalism that set him [i.] loose and presented him with printing press, Schumpeter: 12
civil society figures as an "i. animal kingdom" in Hegel's *Phenomenology*, Marx: 13
conception of i. operations is to transform reality and assimilate it to schemes of transformation, Piaget: 10
difficult sociological problem raised by existence of the i., Mannheim: 8
Marxism remains the most powerful among i. forces permanently transforming ways in which men think and act, Berlin: 1
our i. ancestors are freely chosen, Koyré: 3
what the priest is to religion, the i. is to ideology, Bell: 1
world of modern i. life is white man's world, Thomas: 1

psychology which has no place for concepts of m. and value cannot be complete, Koffka: 2
[social science] refuses to enter sphere of m., Lowenthal: 3
there are things we can measure, yet our minds do not grasp their m., MacIver: 2
things we cannot measure, yet m. clear, MacIver: 2

meanings:
social sciences deal with relations between human beings [in which] they interact on basis of mutually attributed m., Barber: 1
symbolic interactionism rests on m., Blumer: 1

means:
curious adapting of m. to ends, throughout all nature, Hume: 23
economics studies human behaviour as relationship between ends and scarce m., Robbins: 1
ends and m. are so entangled, Lassalle: 1
ends are not compromised when referred to the m. necessary to realize them, Dewey: 1
everybody is both a m. and end in himself, von Mises: 3
faith that riches not m. but end implies all economic activity is equally estimable, Tawney: 2
man exists as end in himself and not merely as a m., Kant: 4
never has object [money] that owes its value exclusively to its quality as a m. so thoroughly developed into a psychological absolute value, Simmel: 6
principle of minimum outlay of m. variant of principle of economic rationality, Lange: 3
principle that end justifies the m. is only rule of political ethics, Koestler: 1
relations of m. to achievement of ends verifiable by empirical methods, Parsons, Talcott: 3
supreme merit of exchange mechanism is that it enables vast number to co-operate in use of m. to achieve ends, Knight: 11

means of production:
market economy is system of division of labor under private ownership of m.o.p., von Mises: 3

measurable:
range of the m. not the range of knowable, MacIver: 2

measure:
if cannot weigh, m., and number results, must not hope to convince others, Fleay: 1
in [economics], Kelvin dictum means, "if you cannot m., m. anyhow!," Knight: 8
instrument to m. amount of organization shown by social groups is called sociometric test, Moreno: 1
m. and express in numbers, Kelvin: 1
things we can m., yet our minds do not grasp their meaning, MacIver: 2
things we cannot m., yet meaning clear, MacIver: 2
to m. is simply to know varying amounts, Thorndike: 6

measurement:
our salvation would lie in art of m., Plato: 4
science will grow in the social studies in direct ratio to use of m., Ogburn: 1
sociology of m. is needed, Duncan: 4

measurements:
different m. of same man are observations; m. of different men are statistics, Edgeworth: 7

measures:
scientific revolution of exact m., Koyré: 2

measuring:
not from counting as from m. that advantage of mathematical treatment comes, Peirce: 4

"Mécanique Sociale":
"M.S." may one day take her place along with "Mécanique Celeste," Edgeworth: 5

mechanical:
future offers little hope for those who expect our new m. slaves will offer rest from thinking, Wiener: 3
no star [has] exerted greater influence in human affairs than these m. discoveries [printing, gunpowder, magnet], Bacon: 9
without a speeding up of social invention or slowing down of m. invention, grave maladjustments certain to result, Ogburn: 3

mechanistic psychology:
greatest problem confronting m.p. is to discover [how] habits control and evoke other habit units, Hull: 1, 2

media:
[*see* magazine; mass media; newspapers]

medieval:
fifteenth century still m. at heart, Huizinga: 4
[*see* Middle Ages]

medium:
m. is the message, McLuhan: 1

meek:
proposition that m. inherit the earth is iron law of evolution, Boulding: 1

Mehring, Franz

Meillet, Antoine

Meinecke, Friedrich

melting pot:
America is great M.-P., Zangwill: 1
Crèvecoeur: 1
point about the m.p. is that it did not happen, Glazer and Moynihan: 1

memberships:
multiple m. in groups serve as balance wheel in going political system, Truman: 1

memory:
as soon as a man connects ideas with signs of own choosing, his memory is formed, Condillac: 2
m. is evidence [of] flexible and creative relation to time, May: 2
only m. organization possesses is collective m. of its participants, Simon: 2

men:
all m. are created equal, Jefferson: 1
ancient religion but part of social order which embraces gods and m. alike, Smith, William Robertson: 4
custom is what m. do, average m., Leach: 2
demands put upon us [m. and women both] not always consistent or correlated with biology, Trilling, Diana: 3
did M. content themselves with bare Necessaries, we should have poor World, North: 1
even feminism has not succeeded in giving women any control over m., Parsons, Elsie Clews: 2
every man like all other m., some other man, no other man, Kluckhohn and Murray: 1
feminism only changed distribution of women, removing vast numbers from class supported by m. to class working for them, Parsons, Elsie Clews: 2
government of laws, and not of m., Adams, John: 1, 2
if m. define situations as real, they are real in their consequences, Thomas and Thomas: 2
instinct of workmanship present in all m., Veblen: 5, 10, 11
m. are jealous one of another, Simmel: 15
m. are perverse, Rousseau: 2
m. are what their mothers made them, Emerson: 3
m. begin with acts, not thoughts, Sumner: 3
[m.] created different [but lose] individual autonomy in seeking to become like each other, Riesman: 4
m. do good despite themselves, Condorcet: 3
m. do not give their own understandings fair play, Hamilton: 2
m. live by positive goals, seldom predictable, at times incompatible, Berlin: 2
m. make their own history, but not as they please, Marx: 7
m. not required as preliminary to marriage to prove they are fit to be trusted with absolute power, Mill, John Stuart: 25
more worthy of our knowledge to study actions of m. than actions of beast, Spinoza: 5
most unreasonable things become most reasonable, because of unruliness of m., Pascal: 1
must be taken for granted that all m. are wicked, Machiavelli: 3
no culture has said there is no difference between m. and women, Mead, Margaret: 7

m. is total of mental processes experienced by individual during lifetime, Titchener: 2
m. takes form in city, Mumford: 1
mankind will possess control over human behavior when human m. will contemplate itself from within, Pavlov: 1
more I study things of the m. the more mathematical I find them, Taine: 3
mystical mentality more observable among primitive people, but is present in every human m., Lévy-Bruhl: 2
no more reasonable to suppose the laws of m. differ from time and place than do laws of chemical combination, Tylor: 5
phenomena of m. desirable in concepts of mathematical and physical sciences, Lashley: 1
principles of civil society found within human m., Vico: 5
whole m. working together, James: 23

minds:
four classes of Idols which beset men's m., Bacon: 4
how myths operate in men's m. without their being aware, Lévi-Strauss: 13
majestic forces pervading civilization will be evident when cease to look upon discovery as inherent faculty of individual m., Kroeber: 2
misfortune of all truly great m. to be wedded to errors as well as to truths, Ward: 1
reasons for believing in existence of other people's m. are our experiences of their actions, Thorndike: 2

minimum outlay of means:
principle of m.o.o.m. variant of principle of economic rationality, Lange: 3

minorities:
characteristics of democracy greatly extend diversity of m. whose preferences will influence decisions, Dahl: 2
focalization of hostility upon given group inhibited by multiplicity of vulnerable m. in society, Williams: 1

minority:
m. of directors and majority of directed, Michels: 1
party for whom everybody votes except that m. who know what they are voting for, Trotsky: 3

miserable:
to live m. [and] know not why makes a man wretched, Carlyle: 7

misery:
m. generates hate, Brontë: 1

misfortune(s):
by attending to people's response to m. he [Evans-Pritchard] justified the claims of [anthropology], Douglas: 4
touchstone which reveals true character of a social philosophy [is] spirit in which it regards m. of its members, Tawney: 3

misogyny:
[Freud's] m. taken for granted even by most admiring students, Trilling, Diana: 2

misplaced concreteness:
Fallacy of M.C., Whitehead: 4

missionaries:
most British m. not whit concerned to "sanctify the spirit of Imperialism," Hobson: 3

mistakes:
[Hobbes] erres so ingeniosely that one had rather erre with him than hitt the marke with Clavius, Aubrey: 2
some men's m. more seminal than other men's valid insights, Miller, George A.: 3

misunderstanding:
in social so-called sciences, absurd m. can continue for hundred years, Robinson, Joan: 8

misunderstandings:
history of ideas, history of m., Kracauer: 1

misunderstood:
only one understood me [Hegel], and he m., Mehring: 1

Mitchell, Wesley C.

mob:
m. psychology destroys web of nation's social structure, Neumann, Sigmund: 1

mobility:
economic class is more important than race in predetermining occupational m., Wilson, William Julius: 1

model:
building larger scale econometric m. may be what God made graduate students for, Solow: 4
m. is a pattern to be abandoned easily at the demand of progress, Boring: 4
object [in social sciences] is to construct a m., Lévi-Strauss: 4

models:
Doomsday M. divert attention from remedial public policy, Solow: 5
m. are the only reality, Lévi-Strauss: 2
one must assume that people in m. do not know what is going to happen, Hicks: 4

modern:
postmodern that which, in the m., puts forward the unpresentable in presentation itself, Lyotard: 1

modern history:
time coming when we shall build m.h. on eye-witnesses and original documents, Ranke: 3

modern society:
m.s. is held together by infinity of personal attachments and civil sense, Shils: 1

modern world:
political realism of the "clerks" bound up with essence of m. w., Benda: 3

modernization:
Eisenstadt: 2

modest:
human beings do not wish to be m., Sapir: 11

Modigliani, Franco

Mommsen, Theodor

monarchy:
division of power, which constitute a limited m., Bolingbroke: 1
M. is third political form we observe in history, Hegel: 6
under constitutional m. sovereign has three rights, Bagehot: 5
what no m. has been able to accomplish, Proudhon: 6

monetary:
inflation is always and everywhere a m. phenomenon, Friedman: 5

monetary theory:
if serious m.t. written, fact that contracts are made in terms of money will be of importance, Arrow and Hahn: 1
m.t. is little more than elaboration of the truth that "it all comes out in the wash," Keynes: 12

money:
Americans have sought value of everything in answer to how much m. will it bring in, Tocqueville: 1
bad m. drives out good m., Gresham: 1
by doubling quantity of m. in a State the prices are not always doubled, Cantillon: 1
good and bad m. cannot circulate together, Macleod: 1
importance of m. [as] link between past and present, Arrow and Hahn: 1
innovations carried out by borrowed m., Schumpeter: 8
m. is but the Fat of the Body-politick, Petty: 5
m. is like muck, not good except it be spread, Bacon: 10
m. is link between present and future, Keynes: 23
m. is machine for doing quickly what would be done without it, Mill, John Stuart: 9
m. is root of economic science, Mitchell: 2
m. is standard [by which] all kinds of relations between men are fixed, Sraffa: 1
m. [is the] oil used to enable machine to run smoothly, Marshall, Alfred: 12
m. is the oil which renders motion of wheels [of commerce] more smooth, Hume: 20
m. makes possible secrecy, invisibility and silence of exchange, Simmel: 7
m. may be compared to language, Simmel: 8
never has object [m.] that owes its value exclusively to its quality as a means so thoroughly developed into a psychological absolute value, Simmel: 6

one well-made o. will be enough in many cases, Durkheim: 9
political economy proceeds by way of o., Bastiat: 2
politics ought [to be elevated] to rank of a science of o., Comte: 1
without speculation there is no original o., Darwin: 3
observations:
all that is necessary to reduce nature to laws is sufficient o. and [complex] mathematics, Condorcet: 2
different measurements of the same man are o., Edgeworth: 7
experimental o. are only experience carefully planned in advance, Fisher, R. A.: 5
fundamental difference in [economics] between data and o., Morgenstern: 1
how plastic limited number of o. become in hands of men with preconceived ideas, Galton: 1
o. and statistics agree in being quantities grouped about a Mean, Edgeworth: 7
observe:
to o. oneself, one must introduce changes whose consequence is that very process to be observed disappears from consciousness, Wundt: 3
you see, but you do not o., Doyle: 1
observed:
social structure as whole can only be o. in its functioning, Radcliffe-Brown: 3
theory capable of explaining anything that might be o. is hardly a theory, Solow: 2
observer:
good o. quick to take hint from facts, Mayo: 2
traveller who should report manners exclusive of morals does not merit name of o., Martineau: 3
observing:
idea of person o. himself is comical, Wundt: 4
occult:
Freud fearful of occultism, Jung: 14
positivists object only to accounting for invisible causes of observed phenomenon in terms of o., Kolakowski: 3
spell is part of magic which is o., Malinowski: 10
when philosopher cannot account for anything, ascribes it to o. quality, Bagehot: 6
occupation:
society shifts [toward] functional differentiation if everybody can buy anything and pursue any o., Luhmann: 4
what influence o. has on human vision of the human fate, Auden: 2
white collar crimes defined as crime committed by upper class [related to] o., Sutherland: 1
occupational:
economic class is more important than race in predetermining o. mobility, Wilson, William Julius: 1
occupations:
difference between society which *permits* women to pursue extra-domestic o. and society that *compels* [them] in order to feel valued, Trilling, Diana: 1
occurrences:
ideas are not objects, but o., Wundt: 2
Ockham, William of
Ockham's Razor:
what can be accounted for by fewer assumptions is explained in vain by more, Ockham: 1
Oedipus situation:
in love with one parent and hating other, Freud: 8
Samoa culture demonstrates [that] the O.s. is not created by young child's biological impulses, Mead, Margaret: 11
offer:
o. is only a consequence of demand, Walras: 5
office:
identification with one's o. attractive [because] offers easy compensation for personal deficiencies, Jung: 5
no worse heresy than that the o. sanctifies holder of it, Acton: 4
Ogburn, William Fielding
Ogden, C. K., and Richards, I. A.
old:
o. people ruminating over o. ideas [in aging society], Sauvy: 2
old history:
if we abandon the o.h., we will lose conception of man as a rational, political animal, Himmelfarb: 3
older:
dynamic interplay between people growing o. and society undergoing change, Riley: 1
oligarchy:
iron law of o., Michels: 1, 3, 6
real difference between democracy and o. is poverty and wealth, Aristotle: 11
ruin of o. is ruin of democracy, Plato: 12
where some possess much and others nothing, there may arise a pure o., Aristotle: 13
Olson, Mancur
omnipotence:
o. through technology, Holton: 3
o.-cum-impotence of despotism classically captured by Tocqueville, Elster: 5
omniscience:
o. through science, Holton: 3
100 percent American:
thank Hebrew deity in Indo-European language that he is 100.p.A., Linton: 5
ontological:
[hermeneutical movement] goes too far [in] announcing that o. difference dictates methodological difference, Rorty: 1
open:
o. convenants of peace, openly arrived at, Wilson, Woodrow: 4
operant conditioning:
o.c. shapes behavior as sculptor shapes clay, Skinner: 5
[o.c. means] man behaves because of consequences which followed similar behavior in past, Skinner: 4
operationism:
o. defined, Skinner: 2
ophelimity:
free competition of entrepreneurs yields same values for production coefficients as by determining them [to achieve] maximum o. for each individual in society, Pareto: 6
opinion:
all social mechanism rests upon o., Comte: 7
anticipating what average o. expects average o. to be, Keynes: 22
basis of our governments is o. of the people, Jefferson: 6
best ideas in social sciences participate in fostering climate of o., Giddens: 1
by what was world ever governed, but by o.?, Macaulay: 8
empire of o. [acts] upon morals of a people, Rousseau: 8
[Freud] is whole climate of o., Auden: 3
governors have nothing to support them but o., Hume: 8
in America majority raises barriers around liberty of o., Tocqueville: 7
inaccurate estimate of group o. is universally accepted, Katz and Allport: 1
larger Souls that have travell'd the divers Climates of O. are more cautious in their resolves, Glanvill: 1
o. is one of the greatest social forces, Mill, John Stuart: 16
o. that they were the best troops really made them such, Hume: 19
o. ultimately governs the world, Wilson, Woodrow: 3
once an o. is adopted, human understanding draws all things else to support and agree with it, Bacon: 5
protection against tyranny of the prevailing o., Mill, John Stuart: 11
sociable man knows how to live only in o. of others, Rousseau: 5
stifling [even false] o. an evil, Mill, John Stuart: 14
strength of o. in each individual [depends] on number which he supposes to have entertained same o., Madison: 6
to us [Freud] is whole climate of o., Auden: 3
variety of o. necessary for objective knowledge, Feyerabend: 2
what is asserted by a man is o.; by a woman is opinionated, Mannes: 1
worship of O. is established religion of United States, Martineau: 1

poorer:
p. a family, greater proportion of its total expenditure devoted to food, Engel: 1
poorest:
arrival in political life of most numerous and p. class, Proudhon: 7
entrepreneur led by invisible hand of market to bring modern conveniences to p. homes, Hayek: 8
Pope, Alexander
Popper, Karl R.
popular conscience:
aroused p.c. sears conscience of people's representatives, Frankfurter: 4
popularity:
fatal penalty [of suburbs] — penalty of p., Mumford: 4
popularization:
p. characteristic of American education, Cremin: 1
population:
governments perceived they were dealing with a "p.," Foucault: 4
growth of the earth's p. like powder fuse that burns slowly until it explodes, Davis, Kingsley: 1
hardly any social problem whose solution would be easier if our p. were larger, Duncan: 2
moral restraint is only mode of keeping p. on level with means of subsistence, Malthus: 5
p., when unchecked, increases in geometrical ratio, Malthus: 2
preventive and positive checks to natural increase of p., Malthus: 3
use of family planning for implementing p. policy poses unacknowledged limits on intended reduction in fertility, Davis, Kingsley: 3
zero p. growth as ultimate goal, Davis, Kingsley: 3
populationist:
p. stresses uniqueness of everything, Mayr: 1
porcupines:
Schopenhauer's simile of freezing p., Freud: 30
Porter, Robert P.
positions:
few p. in life that do not throw together some persons by virtue of failure and [others] by virtue of success, Goffman: 1
positive philosophy:
expression [p.p.] spoiled by writers who have not understood true meaning, Comte: 2
positive reinforcement:
Skinner: 3
positivism:
p. does not prejudge how men arrive at knowledge, Kolakowski: 2
p. stands or falls with principle of scientism, Habermas: 2
positivists:
p. object to accounting for invisible causes of observed phenomenon in terms of occult, Kolakowski: 3
possess:
laws are of use to those who p. and harmful to those who have nothing, Rousseau: 15
possessions:
not p. but the desires of mankind which require to be equalized, Aristotle: 10
possessor:
value is the power which an article confers upon its p., Walker: 2
possibilities:
[in] history selections are made from horizon of p., Luhmann: 1
man, as master of p., is the judge of their use, Febvre: 1
possible:
politics is the art of the p., Bismarck: 1
post-industrial:
concept "p.-i." is counterposed to that of "pre-industrial" and "industrial," Bell: 3
post-Keynesians:
we are all p.-K. now, Samuelson: 7
posterity:
I am seeking to rescue poor stockinger from enormous condescension of p., Thompson, E. P.: 1
people will not look forward to p., who never look backward to their ancestors, Burke, Edmund: 7
postmodern:
p. that which, in the modern, puts forward the unpresentable in presentation itself, Lyotard: 1
potatoes:
French nation is formed much as p. in a sack form a sack of p., Marx: 8
potentialities:
[human] p. are passive without cultural milieu in which to grow, Mead, Margaret: 3
to achieve richer culture, must recognize gamut of human p., Mead, Margaret: 4
Pound, Roscoe
poverty:
culture of p., Lewis: 1
culture of p. gets to young early, Bruner: 5
hard to find single direct [positive] assault on p. which has not failed or entailed other [greater] evils, Sumner: 10
other America of p., Harrington: 1
p. [is] not transitory incident of present industrial order, Tawney: 1
p. is way of life, passed down from generation to generation, Lewis: 2
rabble created only when there is joined to p. an inner indignation against the rich, Hegel: 1
real difference between democracy and oligarchy is p. and wealth, Aristotle: 11
study of causes of p. is study of causes of degradation, Marshall, Alfred: 4
third freedom is freedom from want, Roosevelt: 3
underclass is latest in long line of labels that stigmatize poor people for their p., McGahey: 1
power:
A has p. over B to extent that he can get B to do something he would not otherwise do, Dahl: 3
absolute p. corrupts absolutely, Acton: 3
accumulation of all p. in same hands definition of tyranny, Madison: 5
adjustments that women have made over centuries as subordinate partners illuminate range of p. situations, Janeway: 1
arbitrary p. can never be delegated, Steuart Denham: 2
both p.-seeking attitude and servility are inherently to be condemned, Knight: 12
division of p., which constitutes a limited monarchy, Bolingbroke: 1
emotion can be controlled or destroyed by another emotion with more p., Spinoza: 4
great Question is not whether there be P. in World, but who should have it, Locke: 14
greatest enigma is that backward country was first to place proletariat in p., Trotsky: 1
knowledge is p., Bacon: 1
knowledge is p. to do good and evil alike, but cannot throw away the p., Barber: 2
language of politics is language of p., Lasswell: 8
Man can never be oblig'd to submit to any P., unless satisfied who is Person who has Right to Exercise that P., Locke: 13
men not required as preliminary to marriage to prove fit to be trusted with absolute p., Mill, John Stuart: 25
more p. in socially organized masses on the march, King: 1
necessary that judicial be independent from executive p., Smith, Adam: 24
only purpose for which p. can be rightfully exercised over member of community is to prevent harm to others, Mill, John Stuart: 12
p. and economic value are paradigm of social reality, Polanyi, Karl: 2
p. comes from below, Foucault: 4, 5
p. derives efficacy from comparative amount, Mill, James: 2
p. is legitimate to degree that p.-holder can call upon sufficient other centers of p. as reserves, Stinchcombe: 1
p. is probability that one actor within social relationship [can] carry out his own will despite resistance, Weber, Max: 20
p. of civil government hath nothing to do with world to come, Locke: 1
p. of Habit and Custom, Hartley: 1
p. of reason is blind reason of those who currently hold p., Adorno: 2
p. to tax involves p. to destroy, Marshall, John: 1

direct factual study and q. descriptions offer only promising approach to understanding modern economy, Leontief: 1
essence of q. approach in cultural anthropology, Coon: 1
factors capable of q. expression are overweighted against factors not readily expressed quantitatively, Thomas and Thomas: 1
quantity:
goods have a Value from the greater or lesser Q. of them in proportion to the Demand, Law: 1
quantity theory [of money]:
Fisher, Irving: 1
many see Keynes' trilogy as Saga of Man's Struggle for Freedom from the Q.T., Patinkin: 1
Quesnay, François
question:
great Q. not whether there be Power in the World, but who should have it, Locke: 14
pragmatism asks its usual q., James: 27
"What does a woman want?" is great q. that has never been answered, Freud: 43
you never get a q. answered literally, even when answered truly, Chesterton: 1
questionnaire(s):
Nature will best respond to a logical and carefully thought out q., Fisher, R. A.: 2
thou shalt not answer q., Auden: 4
questions:
specific function of science is to ask q. about things convention makes self-evident, Weber, Max: 11
Quetelet, Adolphe:
[Q.'s] abuse of term social physics, Comte: 2
Buffon: 1
Q. has better claim than Comte to title [founder of sociology], Sarton: 2
Q. said "Let the explorations be carried out," Nightingale: 1
quotation:
q. is a necessity for historians, indispensable to historiography, Hexter: 2

rabble:
a r. created only when there is joined to poverty an inner indignation against the rich, Hegel: 1
race:
close connection between r. and personality never been established, Boas: 4
[competition] best for the r. because insures survival of the fittest, Carnegie: 1
dark world is going to submit to its present treatment just as long as it must and not one moment longer, DuBois: 6
economic class more important than r. in predetermining occupational mobility, Wilson, William Julius: 1
how large a share stupidity had in preserving traces of history of our r., Tylor: 4
[in America] individuals of all nations are melted into new r., Crèvecoeur: 1
popular and scientific views of r. no longer coincide, Huxley and Haddon: 1
primitive people are not r.-conscious to extent of civilized populations, Hooton: 1
r. consciousness enforces social distances, Park: 6
r. is the witchcraft of our time, Montagu: 1
r. refers to difference of origin, Herder: 4
r., translated realistically for American Negro, means there must never be equality between white and black, Bunche: 1
r.-thinking diverts from social and intellectual factors that make up personality, Barzun: 1
self-acting process [survival of fittest] would improve the r., Wallace, Alfred Russel: 1
softmindedness is one of the basic causes of r. prejudice, King: 6
when philosopher cannot account for anything, ascribes it to occult quality in some r., Bagehot: 6
race relations:
anticipate fundamental changes in American r.r., Myrdal: 1
[Park's] metaphor of social distance, Tilly and Brown: 1
poetic irony of American r.r. is that rejected Negro must somehow find strength to free privileged white, Clark, Kenneth B.: 2
r.r. are [relations] between individuals conscious of differences, Park: 6
races:
America is great Melting-Pot where all r. of Europe are reforming!, Zangwill: 1
sense of absolute psychical distinction between man and beast hardly found among lower r., Tylor: 6
racial:
civilization has grown and spread with serene indifference to r. lines, Linton: 2
futile to try to explain fleeting phenomena of culture by a r. constant, Lowie: 4
so-called r. explanation of differences in human performance is ineptitude or fraud, Toynbee, Arnold J. (historian): 2
racial oppression:
black experience moved from economic r.o. to economic subordination for black underclass, Wilson, William Julius: 1
racial segregation:
Jim Crow [r.s.] born and reached advanced age in North before moving South in force, Woodward: 1
racial suicide:
measures [once] used chiefly to prevent illegitimacy have become instrument of r.s., Rivers: 2
racism:
American blacks held on cross not just by chains of slavery but also by spikes of r., Fogel and Engerman: 1
Radcliffe-Brown, A. R.
radical:
to be r. is to grasp root of matter, Marx: 2
Radin, Paul
Rae, John
Ramsey, Frank Plumpton
randomization:
r. most democratic means of allocating scarce resources, Campbell, Donald T.: 2
Rank, Otto
rank:
system of artificial r. gives stamp to base metal in Europe which cannot be given in republican country, Bryce: 2
Ranke, Leopold von:
famous phrase of R., Trevor-Roper: 2
ranking:
in place of absolute good and evil, we speak of r., Arrow: 1
Rapoport, Anatol
rare:
truly r. events are bound to be plentiful in a population of 250 million, Diaconis and Mosteller: 1
rash:
better to be r. than timid, Machiavelli: 18
rat(s):
underlying laws of intelligence, motivation, and instability can be studied in r. as well and more easily than in man, Tolman: 2
would rather see behavior of one white r. observed from moment of birth until death than statistical data on how 2,000 r. learned to open puzzle box, Watson: 9
ratio of exchange:
market theoretically perfect only when all traders have perfect knowledge of r.o.e., Jevons: 7
rational:
conservation is necessary for all r. activity, Piaget and Szeminska: 1
human action is r. [with qualifications], Parsons, Talcott: 3
if we abandon old history, we will lose conception of man as a r. animal, Himmelfarb: 3
processes amenable to r. analysis, Mannheim: 12
r. grounds [for one] type of legitimate domination, Weber, Max: 21
routine [is] necessary condition of r. action, Garfinkel: 2
science can have r. or logical basis even though it be relativistic, Whorf: 1
social justice is principle of r. prudence applied to welfare of group, Rawls: 3

routine:
  r. [is] necessary condition of rational action, Garfinkel: 2
royal road:
  Freud [opens] r.r. to unconscious, Lacan: 3
  interpretation of dreams is r.r. to unconscious, Freud: 14
  mind does not move toward its ideal purposes over r.r., Trilling, Lionel: 5
royalty:
  secrecy essential to utility of English r., Bagehot: 4
ruin:
  freedom in a commons brings r. to all, Hardin: 1
  r. is destination toward which all men rush, Hardin: 1
  r. of oligarchy is r. of democracy, Plato: 12
rule:
  r. by true meritocracy of talent, Young: 2
  r. of the Robots, Čapek: 1
  violation of a r. has different consequence according to type, Habermas: 5
  well-ordered State where they who r. are truly rich in virtue and wisdom, Plato: 10
rules:
  civilization will always be played according to certain r., Huizinga: 5
  if r. decide cases, one judge as good as another, Llewellyn: 1
  making and maintaining commonwealths consisteth in r. which hitherto man [had not the] leisure or curiosity to find out, Hobbes: 14
  public opinion brings morality of Gesellschaft into r., Tönnies: 4
  social disorganization is decrease of influence of social r. of behavior upon individual members, Thomas and Znaniecki: 1
ruling:
  r. groups can become so intensively interest-bound they no longer see facts which would undermine their domination, Mannheim: 4
  r. ideas of each age been ideas of r. class, Marx and Engels: 9
Runciman, W. C.:
  as shown by R. crucial intutition upon which *Social Contract* rests later called "Prisoner's Dilemma," Boudon: 1
rural life:
  all praise of r.l. has pointed out that Gemeinschaft among people is stronger there, Tönnies: 3
  rescued from idiocy of r.l., Marx and Engels: 8
Russell, Bertrand:
  belonging to the A's of the world, Cole, Margaret: 1
Russia:
  only victory of proletariat in West could protect R. from bourgeois restoration, Trotsky: 6
Russian:
  firm and vigilant containment of R. expansive tendencies, Kennan: 1
  he [Jakobson] speaks R. fluently in six languages, Jakobson: 4
  [*see also* Soviet; Soviet Union]
Russian revolution:
  law of combined development of backward countries offers key to riddle of R.r., Trotsky: 2
Ryle, Gilbert:
  ethnology as "thick description," Geertz: 7

sack of potatoes:
  French nation is formed much as potatoes in a sack form a s.o.p., Marx: 8
sacred:
  a religion is a unified system relative to s. things, Durkheim: 19
  s. things are those which the interdictions protect, Durkheim: 18
sacrifice:
  s. [is] limitation of other products which might have been turned out, had material not been devoted to one particular product, Wieser: 1
Sahlins, Marshall
said:
  difference between what is not s. because no occasion to say it, and what is not s. because [can't] find way to say it, Hymes: 1
sailing:
  coastal s. commands no magic, Malinowski: 18
  Morison: 1
  Neurath: 1
  Putnam: 1
  with s., so with politics: make your cloth too taut, and your ship will dip and keel, Euripedes: 1
Saint-Simon
Saint-Simonians
salvation:
  s. of men's souls cannot belong to magistrate, Locke: 1
Samoa:
  S. culture demonstrates [that] Oedipus situation is not created by young child's biological impulses, Mead, Margaret: 11
sample:
  any member of group, provided that his position is specified, is perfect s. of group-wide pattern, Mead, Margaret: 12
  with large enough s., any outrageous thing is likely to happen, Diaconis and Mosteller: 1
Samuelson, Paul A.
Samuelson, Paul A., and Nordhaus, William D.
sanctification:
  in totalitarian societies history is s., Plumb: 1
sanction:
  application of any s. is direct affirmation of social sentiments by community, Radcliffe-Brown: 2
Santayana, George
Sapir, Edward:
  S. served as Leibniz of America Linguistics, Joos: 1
Sarton, George
satellites:
  cultural system that can launch earth s. can dispense with gods entirely, White, Leslie A.: 2
satisfaction:
  each act looks no further than immediate s., Sumner: 4
  value is importance that goods acquire for individuals for s. of their needs, Menger: 1
satisfice:
  behavior of human beings who *satisfice* because they have not the wits to *maximize*, Simon: 3
Satyagraha:
  S. largely appears as Civil Disobedience, Gandhi: 1
Saussure, Ferdinand de
Sauvy, Alfred
savage:
  awe and dread with which untutored s. contemplates his mother-in-law, Frazer: 3
  in dreams we all resemble the s., Nietzsche: 1
  more liberty under despotism than under apparent freedom of s. life, Frazer: 1
  noble s., Dryden: 1
  our resemblances to the s. still more numerous than our differences, Frazer: 4
  plan of Supreme Intelligence to develop a barbarian out of a s., and civilized man out of this barbarian, Morgan, Lewis Henry: 7
  s. lives within himself, Rousseau: 5
savages:
  only people who think themselves risen from s., Sahlins: 1
  s. have no knowledge of total outline of their social structure, Malinowski: 5
save:
  few would s. without reward, Marshall, Alfred: 6
saving:
  because of relation between s. and productive capital thrift regarded as socially beneficial act, Modigliani: 3
  no act of s. subtracts in least from consumption, Say: 1
  s. = investment, Keynes: 18
say:
  "How can I know what I think till I see what I s.?," Wallas: 2
  social behavior displays many features at same time [so] intolerable we can s. only one thing at a time, Homans: 1
  we hear what we s. to others as well as what others s. to us, Mead, George Herbert: 4
Say, Jean Baptiste:
  errors and contradictions of [S.] easily corrected by theory of productive powers, List: 1
  fallacies implied in Keynesian full-employment doctrine are same errors which S. demolished, von Mises: 1

science fiction:
 not his [Marx's] business to write s.f., Robinson, Joan: 7
science of politics:
 that noble s.o.p., Macaulay: 7
science's:
 s. systematic denial of personality, James: 1
sciences:
 all s. have a relation to human nature, Hume: 1, 2
 difference between systems in social s. and natural s. seen in their evolution, Henderson: 1
 exact s. are no others than the mathematical ones, Peirce: 3
 general laws have analogous functions in history and in natural s., Hempel: 1
 in natural s. each succeeding generation stands on shoulders of those that have gone before, Zeaman: 1
 in s., we sit side-by-side with the giants on whose shoulders we stand, Holton: 1
 in social s. each generation steps in faces of its predecessors, Zeaman: 1
 men become attached to particular s. because fancy selves inventors thereof, or because most habituated to them, Bacon: 7
 practical s. build up; theoretical s. resolve into components, Aquinas: 1
 s. all speak of that which always is, Schopenhauer: 1
 s. spread garlands of flowers over iron chains with which men are burdened, Rousseau: 1
scientific:
 benefits to be gained from ambiguities of s. discourse, Levine: 1
 data [of] any s. inquiry are trivialities in some other bearing, Veblen: 9
 every s. fulfilment raises new questions, Weber, Max: 18
 linguistics shows by its data and methods possibility of truly s. study of society, Sapir: 8
 mathematical measures of difference may need to be discounted in arriving at a s. conclusion, Boring: 1
 misallocation of credit for s. work described as Matthew effect, Merton: 4
 moral obtuseness is necessary condition for s. analysis, Strauss: 3
 not one s. description of concrete social situation is cited [in holistic method], Popper: 5
 popular and s. views of race no longer coincide, Huxley and Haddon: 1
 s. development depends on process of non-incremental or revolutionary change, Kuhn: 4
 s. discourse demands a s. reading, Bourdieu: 4
 special magic in the word "s.," Becker, Carl L.: 1
 thematic analysis is identification of particular map of themata which can characterize a scientist or part of s. community, Holton: 2
scientific doomsday:
 s.d. is less than a century distant, Price: 2
scientific experiment:
 correct ideas come from s.e., Mao Zedong: 1
scientific fact(s):
 experimentally established only if experiment rarely fails to give 5 per cent level of significance, Fisher, R. A.: 1
 only laws and generalizations are s.f., Malinowski: 1
scientific historian:
 s.h. taken to be one who set forth the facts without injecting extraneous meaning into them, Becker, Carl L.: 1
scientific history:
 new "s." h. — born of marriage between historical problems and advanced statistical analysis, Fogel and Elton: 1
scientific man:
 instinctive tendency of s.m. is toward existential substrate, Titchener: 4
scientific management:
 without complete mental revolution on both sides [labor and management] s.m. does not exist, Taylor: 1
scientific method:
 discovered s.m. by which unconscious can be studied, Freud: 33
 hypothesis that man is not free essential to application of s.m. to study of human behavior, Skinner: 8
 s.m. devised for elucidating under controlled conditions, Polanyi, Michael: 2
scientific observer:
 emotionally indifferent attitude [toward nature] of s.o. ethically far higher than loving interest of poet, Thorndike: 1
scientific opinion:
 confessions obtained under duress not admissible in court of s.o., Stigler, Stephen M.: 1
scientific revolution:
 few expressions more commonly used than "s.r.," Cohen, I. Bernard: 2
 question of when this s.r. occurred arouses as much scholarly disagreement as question of what it was, Cohen, I. Bernard: 2
 s.r. of exact measures, Koyré: 2
 [the s.r.] outshines everything since the rise of Christianity, Butterfield: 4
scientific truth:
 new s.t. [triumphs] because its opponents die, and new generation grows up familiar with it, Planck: 1
 s.t. must come about by controversy, Boring: 3
scientism:
 positivism stands or falls with principle of s., Habermas: 2
scientist:
 all s. creates in a fact is language in which he enunciates it, Poincaré: 2
 disdain of pure s. for questions of applicability, Mandler and Kessen: 1
 thematic analysis is identification of particular map of themata which can characterize a s., Holton: 2
scientists:
 between literary intellectuals and s. a gulf of mutual incomprehension, Snow: 1-3
 80 to 90 percent of all s. that ever lived are alive now, Price: 1
 isolated s. run risk [of] repeating experiments already made by others, Saint-Simonians: 1
 led by a new paradigm, s. see new and different things when looking in places they have looked before, Kuhn: 2
 ominous conflict of difference of outlook between humanists and s., Sarton: 1
 [s.] to be the heroes of the future, Robinson and Beard: 1
 social, biological and physical s. all have same problems, main difference being decimal place in which they appear, Cochran: 1
 [some groups of s.] constitute an invisible college, Price: 3
 we [s.] cannot work without hoping others will advance further, Weber, Max: 18
scissors:
 dispute whether upper or under blade cuts, Marshall, Alfred: 7
 theory and data are two blades of s., Simon: 8
scope:
 effective s. characterizes what [man] perceives, has contact with, and reaches for, Lazarsfeld and Thielens: 1
scouts:
 thoughts are to the desires as s. to range abroad, Hobbes: 6
scribble:
 "always s., s., s.!, Eh! Mr. Gibbon?," Beste: 1
scribbler:
 madmen in authority are distilling their frenzy from some academic s., Keynes: 24
sea power:
 history of S.P. narrative of contests between nations, Mahan: 1
seamless web:
 such is unity of history that to tell piece of it tears a s.w., Pollack and Maitland: 1
seashore:
 like boy playing on s. whilst great ocean of truth lay all undiscovered, Newton: 2
 Quetelet said "only few pebbles picked up on vast s. to be explored," Nightingale: 1
secrecy:
 s. essential to utility of English royalty, Bagehot: 4
secret:
 no mortal can keep s., Freud: 16
sects:
 s. aspire after personal inward perfection, Troeltsch: 1

Shakespeare, William:
a government could print good edition of S.'s works, but could not get them written, Marshall, Alfred: 11
"bloody and invisible hand," Smith, Adam: 1
"one touch of nature makes the whole world kin," Marett: 1
shape:
we s. our buildings, afterwards buildings s. us, Churchill: 2
Shaw, George Bernard:
Keynes: 14
Shays's Rebellion:
God forbid we should ever be 20 years without such a rebellion, Jefferson: 8
Shils, Edward
ship:
steering engines of s. one of earliest forms of feedback mechanisms, Wiener: 1
shipwreck:
[no] names inscribed of those who perished, Laplace: 4
nowhere any pictures of those drowned at sea, Cicero: 2
where are they painted that were drowned?, Bacon: 5
Shklar, Judith N.
shock:
future s. is disease of change, Toffler: 1
shopkeepers:
nation of s., Smith, Adam: 22
short-term:
s.-t. most capricious and deceptive form of time, Braudel: 7
[*see also* long run; long term]
shoulders of giants:
dwarfs perched on the s. of g., Bernard of Chartres: 1
if I have seen further it is by standing on ye s. of G., Newton: 1
in natural sciences each succeeding generation stands on s. of those before, Zeaman: 1
sit side-by-side with the giants on whose s. we stand, Holton: 1
shreds and patches:
that thing of s.a.p. called civilization, Lowie: 2
sick society:
acquisitiveness of a s.s., Mayo: 1
sign:
arbitrary character of s. alone makes possible comparative method in historical linguistics, Meillet: 1
signals:
signification is creation and use of artificial s., Vygotsky: 2
significance:
main purpose of s. test is to inhibit natural enthusiasm of investigator, Mosteller and Bush: 1
scientific fact experimentally established only if experiment rarely fails to give 5 per cent level of s., Fisher, R. A.: 1
s. of man is that he is insignificant and aware of it, Becker, Carl: 3
significant others:
self is approved by s.o., Sullivan: 3
signification:
s. is creation and use of artificial signals, Vygotsky: 2
signs:
as soon as a man connects ideas with s. of own choosing, his memory is formed, Condillac: 2
I have distinguished three sorts of s.: accidental, natural, and instituted, Condillac: 1
semiology would show what constitutes s., Saussure: 1
silence:
spiral of s., Noelle-Neumann: 1
what we cannot speak about we must pass over in s., Wittgenstein: 2
silencing:
mankind no more justified in s. one person, than justified in s. mankind, Mill, John Stuart: 13
silk stockings:
capitalist achievement [to bring] s.s. within reach of factory girls, Schumpeter: 10
Silverstein, Michael
Simmel, Georg
Simon, Herbert A.
Simonde de Sismondi, J. C. L.
Simons, Henry C.
simple reflexes:
s.r. ever combined into unitary harmonies termed behaviour, Sherrington: 1
singing:
emotionally true s. is rarer than technically correct s., Ebbinghaus: 3
man is s. creature though the notes are coupled with thought, Humboldt: 3
situation:
life-policy and personality of individual [follow] from definition of s., Thomas: 3, 5
situations:
face-to-face interactions must meet key requirements of real s., Goffman: 2
if men define s. as real, they are real in their consequences, Thomas and Thomas: 2
people act about s. in ways like the ways they talk about them, Whorf: 3
people define s., but do not define them as they please, Stinchcombe: 2
skepticism:
organized s. an institutional imperative of modern science, Merton: 1
skilled labor:
difference between wages of s.l. and common labor founded upon principle [of capital investment], Smith, Adam: 16
skills:
just as we learn new s., we learn new motives, Allport, Gordon W.: 4
s. put us in a position to solve problems, Habermas: 5
skin:
America has contributed to concept of ghetto restriction on basis of s. color, Clark, Kenneth B.: 1
Aryan is man with white s., thick s., and foreskin, Schapera: 1
Skinner, B. F.
slave:
as I would not be a s., so I would not be a master, Lincoln: 1
in giving freedom to the s., we assure freedom for the free, Lincoln: 3
reason is, and ought only to be s. of passions, Hume: 3
slavery:
civil man is born, lives, and dies in s., Rousseau: 10
excess of liberty seems only to pass into excess of s., Plato: 12
if men wait for liberty till they become wise in s., they may wait for ever, Macaulay: 2
political forces were the overriding factors in the destruction of s., Fogel: 1
tragedy of [slave's] position was absolute subjection to owner, Du-Bois: 7
when we abolish the s. of half of humanity, the human couple will find its true form, Beauvoir: 2
slaves:
practical men usually the s. of some defunct economist, Keynes: 24
sleeping princess:
economics was a s.p., Samuelson: 8
Keynes woke the s.p., Robinson, Joan: 4
slogans:
economics limps along with other [foot] in untestable s., Robinson, Joan: 5
slum:
in s. there is vast conspiracy against forces of law and order, Harrington: 2
middle-class person looks upon s. as social chaos, Whyte, William F.: 1
small:
man is s., and therefore, s. is beautiful, Schumacher: 1
Smelser, Neil J.
Smith, Adam:
economic doctrine of S. is doctrine of Mandeville set in rational and scientific form, Halévy 1
errors and contradictions of [S.] easily corrected by theory of productive powers, List: 1
fallacies implied in Keynesian full-employment doctrine are same errors which S. demolished, von Mises: 1
individual hunter or fisher, who forms starting point with S., an insipid illusion, Marx: 10
now recognize scope and limitations of his [S.'] market doctrine, Samuelson and Nordhaus: 1
S. describes accumulation process reaching plateau and decline, Heilbroner: 4
S. reasons 100 times better than modern [mathematical] economists, Pareto: 1
venerable master [S.] offered clear advice that conduct of economic affairs best left to private citizens, Stigler, George J.: 5

man's behavior in s.g. enables him to become an object to himself, Mead, George Herbert: 9
s.g. clear who its friend and who its enemy, Simmel: 1
social groups:
a man [the] intersection point of circles representing s.g., Cooley: 2
instrument to measure amount of organization shown by s.g. called sociometric test, Moreno: 1
most diverse s.g. may show identical forms of behavior toward one another, Simmel: 2
[*see also* group(s); reference groups]
social historian:
not only political history that s.h. denies [but] reason itself, Himmelfarb: 2
social history:
s.h. defined negatively as history with politics left out, Trevelyan: 1
social inequality:
citizenship itself becoming architect of s.i., Marshall, T. H.: 4
s.i. device by which societies insure that most important positions filled by most qualified persons, Davis and Moore: 1
social institutions:
[corporations] have become s.i., Berle and Means: 1
ways s.i. [structured] can encourage or discourage altruistic in man, Titmuss: 1
social interaction:
conception of s.i. as an exchange process follows from assumption that men seek rewards, Blau: 1
meanings arise out of s.i. with fellows, Blumer: 1
social interweaving:
out of s.i. something emerges that has [not] been planned by individual, Elias: 1
social justice:
s.j. is principle of rational prudence applied to welfare of group, Rawls: 3
[state] joins ideal of liberty to equality in name of s.j., Laski: 7
social life:
communication renders true s.l. practicable, Cherry: 1
derive from s.l. more convenience than injury, Spinoza: 5
once individuals come into one another's presence promissory evidential character of s.l. becomes pronounced, Goffman: 6, 7
seek explanation of s.l. in nature of society itself, Durkheim: 11
social mobility:
[Park's idea was] that city's landscape records its pattern of s.m., Tilly and Brown: 1
social movement:
s.m. can rouse people when it can do three things, Bell: 2
social order:
a revolutionary party is never able to foresee forms of new s.o. it strove to usher in, Kautsky: 1
ancient religion is part of s.o. which embraces gods and men alike, Smith, William Robertson: 4
in studying political organization have to deal with s.o., Radcliffe-Brown: 6
trust [defined] as expectation of persistence of moral s.o., Barber: 3
social organism:
s.o. grows [and] becomes more complex, Spencer: 10
social organization:
s.o. necessary to the human species, Ibn Khaldûn 7, 8
theoretical questions about s.o. seldom focused on how to organize action without generating undesirable externalities, Coleman: 7
totem meal beginning of s.o., Freud: 24
social organizations:
theory of games of strategy gains plausibility by correspondence between its concepts and those of s.o., von Neumann and Morgenstern: 2
social phenomena:
theories that explain s.p. are about behavior of men, Homans: 2
use word function because s.p. do not exist for useful results they produce, Durkheim: 10
social phenomenon:
law is s.p., Dewey: 11
social philosophy:
touchstone of true character of a s.p. [is] spirit in which it regards misfortunes of its members, Tawney: 3
social physics:
my term s.p. abused by [Quetelet] who adopted it as title of book of elementary statistics, Comte: 2
new term [sociology] exactly equivalent to s.p., Comte: 3
social policy:
s.p. has been primary, Myrdal: 8
social positions:
man figures in sociological analysis to extent he complies with expectations associated with his s.p., Dahrendorf: 1
social practice:
correct ideas come from s.p., Mao Zedong: 1
social problem:
hardly any s.p. whose solution would be easier if our population were larger, Duncan: 2
social problems:
by conceiving of society as synthesis of individuals and individual as synthesis of social schemes we preclude solutions of particular [s.p.], Znaniecki: 1
development of s.p. theory oriented to values of freedom and equality rather than order, Gouldner: 1
social projection:
[s.p. is] self-reaction to others, Allport, Floyd H.: 1
social psychologist:
for s.p., man is human animal transformed into human being, Sullivan: 1
social psychology:
task of s.p. to show how man's energies become productive forces, Fromm: 3
social reality:
no two languages sufficiently similar [to represent] same s.r., Sapir: 7
power and economic value are paradigm of s.r., Polanyi, Karl: 2
social relationship:
power is probability that actor within s.r. [can] carry out own will despite resistance, Weber, Max: 20
social relationships:
all higher mental functions are internalized s.r., Vygotsky: 3
social research:
explication of differential aspects of empirical s.r. needs attention, Lazarsfeld: 4
social science:
empirical s.s. has become kind of applied asceticism, Lowenthal: 3
history is verification of s.s., Mill, John Stuart: 1
human nature part of the method in most s.s., Redfield: 2
in s.s. today have greater trust in improvability of man and society than since the Enlightenment, Myrdal: 7
new kind of s.s. is search for knowledge for the reconstruction of society, Coleman: 6
present-day American s.s. dedicated to proposition that all men endowed by evolutionary process, but with no natural right, Strauss: 1
s.s. can give us freedom, Barber: 2
s.s. lays groundwork for ever more effective education, Myrdal: 10
s.s. not confined to practical politics, Lynd: 2
s.s. of concrete reality, Weber, Max: 1
s.s. virtually abhors the event, Braudel: 7
saying often quoted from Lord Kelvin applied to s.s. is misleading and pernicious, Knight: 8
thou shalt not commit a s.s., Auden: 4
whoever studies s.s. implicitly admits existence of uniformities, Pareto: 2, 8
social sciences:
best ideas in the s.s. participate in fostering the climate of opinion, Giddens: 1
current movement to make s.s. hermeneutical makes reasonable point, Rorty: 1
difference between systems in s.s. and natural sciences is seen in their evolution, Henderson: 1
difficult to conceive how s.s. could be simultaneously trivial and threatening, Smelser: 3
essential characteristic of s.s. is that they deal with relations between human beings who interact on basis of mutually attributed meanings, Barber: 1

fundamental terms which s.s. trying to adopt from physics have originated in social field, Cohen, Morris R.: 1
in s. [so-called] s. absurd misunderstanding can continue for hundred years, Robinson, Joan: 8
in s.s. each generation steps in faces of its predecessors, Zeaman: 1
in the very young s.s. Marx's work able to attain great influence because most powerful support is in hearts of its disciples, Böhm-Bawerk: 4
linguistics opening small door between humanities and the s.s., Lévi-Strauss: 8
main task of s.s. to trace unintended repercussions of intentional human actions, Popper: 4
methodological individualism [is] closely connected with subjectivism of the s.s., Hayek: 1
object [in s.s.] to construct model, Lévi-Strauss: 4
serious error in wishing to generalize everything connected with the s.s., Simonde de Sismondi: 1
s.s. have received impetus more from urge to improve society than from curiosity about its working, Myrdal: 8
[s.s.] need to be approached with acquired wisdom, Pound: 3
[*see also* behavioral sciences]

social scientist(s):
more serious as s.s., more completely we develop indifference to any goal, Strauss: 3
s.s. act as interpreters for those with whom we are not sure how to talk, Rorty: 2
to be adequate s.s. must come to grips with ideas of marxism, Mills: 6

social situation:
not one scientific description of concrete s.s. is cited [in holistic method], Popper: 5

social stability:
one of strongest factors in s.s. is hostility with which human societies receive all new ideas, Pearson: 1

social state:
intimate relation which exists between men's ideas and s.s., Fustel de Coulanges: 1
s.s. is advantageous to men only when all have something and none too much, Rousseau: 15

social stratification:
[*see* class; social class; stratification]

social structure:
culture and s.s. are epiphenomena, Murdock: 3
every time child speaks or listens, s.s. reinforced in him, Bernstein, Basil: 2
mob psychology destroys web of nation's s.s., Neumann, Sigmund: 1
savages have no knowledge of the total outline of their s.s., Malinowski: 5
s.s. as whole can only be observed in its functioning, Radcliffe-Brown: 3
to speak of s.s. is to speak of differentiation among people, Blau: 2
weak social ties of individuals integrate various groups into a coherent s.s., Blau: 3
[with] structural point of view, study [customs and beliefs] in their relations to s.s., Radcliffe-Brown: 5

social studies:
science will grow in the s.s. in direct ratio to use of measurement, Ogburn: 1

social system:
conflicts serve to sew the s.s. together by cancelling each other out, Coser: 1
generalized s.s. is conceptual scheme, Parsons, Talcott: 9
psychologists have not treated individual as unit in functioning s.s., Parsons, Talcott: 10
s.s. consists of individual actors interacting in situation which has environmental aspect, Parsons, Talcott: 12
s.s. has functional unity, Radcliffe-Brown: 4

social systems:
power relations between persons as actors and corporate actors in s.s., Coleman: 3
s.s. are determined by systems of technology, White, Leslie A.: 1
s.s. more malleable than individuals, Elster: 6

social theorists:
custom was the lens without which [s.t.] could not see, Benedict: 3

social theory:
social policy has been primary, s.t. has been secondary, in impetus of social science, Myrdal: 8
task of s.t. to explain unintended consequences of human action, Hayek: 7

social thought:
formation of schools of s.t., Parsons, Talcott: 11

social wealth:
by s.w. I mean all things that are scarce, Walras: 2
prospects of socialism depend on increase of s.w., Bernstein, Eduard: 3
pure economics is also theory of s.w., Walras: 1
whole world [is] vast [perfectly competitive] market where s.w. is bought and sold, Walras: 4

socialism:
can be more s. in a good factory law than in nationalisation of factories, Bernstein, Eduard: 1
contest between capitalism and s. is over: capitalism has won: Heilbroner: 5
defeated revolution [s.] calls for psychology, Lazarsfeld: 6
final goal of s. is nothing to me, the movement is everything, Bernstein, Eduard: 1
general strike the myth in which S. is comprised, Sorel: 5
how can a doctrine [Marxian S.] so illogical have exercised so powerful an influence, Keynes: 9
Marx did not have much to say about economics of s., Robinson, Joan: 7
method, not results, decisive in Marxian s., Kautsky: 2
only victory of proletariat in West could assure [Russia] possibility of establishing s., Trotsky: 6
prospects of s. depend on increase of social wealth, Bernstein, Eduard: 3
real issue [in s.] is compatibility of capitalistic system with economic progress, Lange: 2
s. is a cry of pain, Durkheim: 22
[S.] not outside us; it is in our hearts, Sorel: 2
s. proceeds by way of imagination, Bastiat: 2
socialists might conquer, but s. would perish, Michels: 2
to violence that S. owes high ethical values by which it brings salvation to modern world, Sorel: 6

socialist:
best way of understanding economics of capitalism may be to think about s. economy, Solow: 1
both s. State which kept good books and intelligent *laissez-faire* democracy would soon discard Imperialism, Hobson: 1
term and concept of capitalism traced primarily to writings of s. theoreticians, Sombart: 1

socialists:
in hands of S., theory of value became terrible weapon against existing order, Wicksell: 2
s. might conquer, but socialism would perish, Michels: 2
S. no longer want to leap into the unknown, Sorel: 1

socially constructed reality:
human reality is s.c.r., Berger and Luckmann: 1

societal:
nature is a s. category, Lukács: 2

societies:
hostility with which human s. receive all new ideas, Pearson: 1
integration of large s. depends on weak social ties of individuals, Blau: 3
s. are "social atoms" with which students of history have to deal, Toynbee, Arnold J.: 1
s. in good working order do not foster ideas hostile to their fundamental working arrangements, Hofstadter: 2
social anthropology studies s. as moral systems, Evans-Pritchard: 3
two s., one black, one white — separate and unequal, Kerner: 1

society:
acquisitiveness of a sick s., Mayo: 1; Tawney 2
actions of a s. compared to those of individual possess unswerving accuracy and expediency, Simmel: 1

s. nothing but series of generations exerting pressure upon one which follows it, Piaget: 4
s. practices social tyranny more formidable than many kinds of political oppression, Mill, John Stuart: 11
s. prepares crime, and the guilty are only the instruments by which it is executed, Quetelet: 4
s. provides remedy for inconveniences when every individual labours a-part, Hume: 6
s. riven by many minor cleavages less in danger of open mass conflict than s. with few cleavages, Williams: 1
s. shifts in direction of functional differentiation if everybody can buy anything and pursue any occupation, Luhmann: 4
s. without power relations can only be an abstraction, Foucault: 9
seek the explanation of social life in nature of s. itself, Durkheim: 11
self and s. are twin-born, Cooley: 5
story of man in s., Barnard: 4
subject matter of sociology is not just s., but existence, Weber, Alfred: 2
suicide is product of general condition of society, Buckle: 1
terms such as advanced and backward when comparing a s. may generate conflicts of pride and meaning, Smelser: 1
The Great Society, a [new] term for use by sociologists, Wallas: 1
thesis of perverse effect asserts attempt to push s. in certain direction will result in its moving in opposite direction, Hirschman: 6
those united onto one Body, and have common Law and Judicature, are in Civil S., Locke: 16
to him only who has studied principles of morals will manners be index to internal movements of s., Martineau: 4
to love the little platoon we belong to in s. is first link towards love of country and mankind, Burke, Edmund: 8
top of modern s. often inaccessible, bottom often hidden, Mills: 2
true founder of s. [was] first person [who] fenced off plot [and said] *this is mine*, Rousseau: 3
we nuclear people have made Faustian bargain with s., Weinberg: 1
what is new in s. traceable to a new technology, Kautsky: 3
where there is s. there is power, Dahrendorf: 3
without faithfulness, s. could not exist, Simmel: 19
without trust s. would disintegrate, Simmel: 5

socioeconomic:
economic man will be laid to rest when we build new model s. man, Whyte, William F.: 3
exploitation is factual description of a s.-e. relationship, Dobb: 2

sociogenesis:
social interweaving secret of s., Elias: 1

sociolinguistics:
s. can draw little from sociology, Chomsky: 4
[*see also* linguistics; psycholinguistics]

sociological:
difficult s. problem raised by existence of the intellectual, Mannheim: 8
man figures in s. analysis to extent he complies with expectations associated with his social positions, Dahrendorf: 1
personal life-records constitute *perfect* type of s. material, Thomas and Znaniecki: 2
realistic s. meaning in *e pluribus unum*, Williams: 2
s. purpose to explain differences rather than similarities, Evans-Pritchard: 5

sociological imagination:
s. i. enables us to grasp history and biography and [their] relations, Mills: 4
s.i. is capacity to shift from one perspective to another, Mills: 5

Sociological Society:
a S.S. until we have found great sociologist is a herd without its leader, Pearson: 4

sociological theory:
prevailing direction of [s.t.] that appreciates [man's] cognitive, moral and appreciative humanity, Shils: 2
s.t. nowhere near complex enough and not elaborated in sufficiently abstract terms to tackle wealth of historical data, Luhmann: 6

sociologist:
analysis of mass literature offers a field and a challenge to s., Lowenthal: 2
distinctive contributions of s. found in study of unintended consequences, Merton: 3
[economist] wants to hand over problem to some s., Hicks: 2
no s. [should] think himself too good to make trivial computations in his head, Weber, Max: 17

sociologists:
most important facts that s. have to deal with are opinions, Park and Burgess: 1
s. cut themselves off from rich inheritance by forgetting that all history is past social behavior, Tilly: 1
s. may call result The Great Society, Wallas: 1
s. need to develop more complex, dialectical conception of human nature, Wrong: 1

sociology:
aggregation of action model should play important role in s., Boudon: 1
coming crisis of Western S. manifested by drift of Functionalist and Parsonian models toward Marxism, Gouldner: 1
Comte was right in pointing to action of one generation upon another as most important phenomenon of s., Piaget: 4
even one well-made observation will be enough in many cases, Durkheim: 9
general formulation of ideology develops into s. of knowledge, Mannheim: 6
great injustice when Comte called founder of s., for Quetelet has better claim to title, Sarton: 2
I profess to teach s. from the conduct of mankind, Beveridge, William Henry: 1
in s. study of concrete furthers more explanations than study of abstract, Mauss: 7
many a vain and specious formula has been set forward in name of s., MacIver: 1
modern academic s. has become estranged from life, Weber, Alfred: 1
no-man's or everyman's land developed that might be called economic s., Schumpeter: 13
pluralistic behavior is the subject-matter of s., Giddings: 2
pure s. abstracts mere elements of sociation, Simmel: 2
s. creates distance between the world in which one lives and in which one thinks, Aron: 4
s. gives constant awareness of force of consequences, including unintended consequences, Berger and Kellner: 1
[s.] I risk introducing this new term, Comte: 3
s. is science with greatest number of methods and least results, Poincaré: 1
s. must be in continuous conversation with both history and philosophy, Berger and Luckmann: 2
s. of knowledge implies that s. takes its place in company of sciences that deal with man *as* man, Berger and Luckmann: 2
s. of knowledge is related to, but distinguishable from theory of ideology, Mannheim: 11, 12
s. of knowledge understands human reality as socially constructed reality, Berger and Luckmann: 1
s. of measurement is needed, Duncan: 4
s. should be thought of as science of action, Parsons, Talcott: 8
sociolinguistics can draw little from s., Chomsky: 4
statistics have significance for s. because social relations inevitably correlated with spatial relations, Park: 1
subject matter of s. is not just society, but existence, Weber, Alfred: 2

sociometric test:
instrument to measure amount of organization shown by social groups is called s.t., Moreno: 1

Socrates:
better to be S. dissatisfied than fool satisfied, Mill, John Stuart: 21
in S. that irony has its inception, Kierkegaard: 1
soft data:
s.d. those which become to our minds doubtful, Russell: 2
[*see also* data; hard data]
soil:
rent is portion of produce of earth paid to landlord for use of s., Ricardo: 3
solidarity:
true function of division of labor is to create feeling of s., Durkheim: 2
writing about s. means writing at same time about mistrust, Douglas: 5
solitary:
life of man, s., poor, nasty, brutish, and short, Hobbes: 11
what change in an individual's s. performance occurs when other people are present?, Allport, Gordon W.: 5
solitude:
chimpanzee kept in s. not a real chimpanzee, Köhler: 1
Solon:
S. replied laws he gave Athenians "best they were able to bear," Montesquieu: 9
Solow, Robert M.
solutions:
by conceiving of society as synthesis of individuals and individual as synthesis of social schemes we preclude s. of particular [social] problems, Znaniecki: 1
Sombart, Werner
sophistry:
commit to flames [books of] s. and illusion, Hume: 17
Sophocles:
legend of King Oedipus and S. drama which bears his name, Freud: 8
Sorel, Georges
Sorokin, Pitirim A.
soul:
dream is a little hidden door in the innermost recesses of the s., Jung: 13
if we infer a s. quality from the social fact and use the quality to explain the fact, we put ourselves on a level with animists in the most savage tribes, Bentley: 2
measuring one's s. by the tape of a world that looks on in amused contempt and pity, DuBois: 2
meeting physical force with s. force, King: 4
movements of each s. may continually be realising the Divine love of the universe, Edgeworth: 5
psychology studies the properties and laws of the s., Brentano: 1
to Behaviorist consciousness is as unprovable as old concept of the s., Watson: 7
souls:
existence of s. to beasts, as to men, Tylor: 6
religion did not exist for saving of s. but for preservation of society, Smith, William Robertson: 2
salvation of men's s. cannot belong to magistrate, Locke: 1
sound(s):
linguistic system is series of phonetic differences of s. combined with series of differences of ideas, Saussure: 6
meaning of a word an active effect of the s. uttered within context of situation, Malinowski: 16
three sorts of s.: accidental, natural, and instituted, Condillac: 1
South:
experience [of S.] thoroughly un-American one, Woodward: 2
Jim Crow system was born and reached advanced age in North before moving S. in force, Woodward: 1
South's:
S. preoccupation was with guilt, Woodward: 2
sovereign:
common law the articulate voice of some s. that can be identified, Holmes: 9
s. has three rights, Bagehot: 5
sovereignty:
America country where doctrine of s. of the people can be fairly appreciated, Tocqueville: 3
s. is the most absolute power over the citizens in a commonweale, Bodin: 1, 2
Soviet:
communism is S. power plus electrification of whole country, Lenin: 6
fundamental reason why S. rulers unable to achieve goals is lack of reliable information, Elster: 5
[S.] government also an experimenter, Pavlov: 8
starting point of power of S. bureaucracy [is] it knows who is to get something and who has to wait, Trotsky: 4
Soviet Union:
great changes will occur [in S.U.] once lid taken off, Elster: 6
in S.U. reliable information does not exist, Elster: 5
main element of United States policy toward S.U. must be containment, Kennan: 1
only victory of proletariat in West could protect Russia from bourgeois restoration, Trotsky: 6
we in the USSR are striving to discover how [child] can become what he not yet is, Leont'ev: 1
Soviets:
S. waging new kind of war, the cold war, Baruch: 1
[*see also* Russia; Russian]
span of absolute judgment:
s.o.a.j. in neighborhood of seven, Miller: George A.: 1
spatial:
s. concepts of distance and direction [are] very warp and woof of all thinking about performances, Tolman: 4
s. relations are determining conditions of relationships among men and symbols as well, Simmel: 16
statistics significant for sociology because social relations correlate with s. relations, Park: 1
spatialisation:
s. is expression of concrete facts under guise of abstract logical construction, Whitehead: 4
speak:
certain authors on social subjects claim "facts s. for themselves," Parsons, Talcott: 2
most reckless of all theorists is he who professes to let facts s. for themselves, Marshall, Alfred: 2
not I who s., but History, Fustel de Coulanges: 5
that facts "will speak for themselves" is an illusion, Becker, Carl L.: 1
that which one would not insinuate, thereof one must s., Gellner: 1
the facts s. only when the historian calls on them, Carr: 1
what we cannot s. about we must pass over in silence, Wittgenstein: 2
speaker-listener:
linguistic theory concerned with an ideal s.-l., Chomsky: 3
speaking:
all s., good or bad, is careless, Bloomfield: 1
language is speech less s., Saussure: 2
process of s. is distributing phenomena into different classes, Jespersen: 1
speaks:
every time child s. or listens, social structure reinforced in him and his social identity shaped, Bernstein, Basil: 2
leading Polish linguist once said that Jakobson s. Russian fluently in six languages, Jakobson: 4
science s. in terms of phonemes, Bloomfield: 3
specialists:
s. without spirit, sensualists without heart, Weber, Max: 5
species:
favourable variations would tend to be preserved and unfavourable ones destroyed [resulting in] a new s., Darwin: 12
higher the s., more rapid is transit through lower stages, Hall: 2
I had found the long-sought-for law that solved the problem of the origin of s., Wallace, Alfred Russel: 1
s. are not immutable, Darwin: 2
sciences speak always of s.; history of individuals, Schopenhauer: 1
spectre:
s. haunting Europe, the s. of Communism, Marx and Engels: 4

state of the world:
to formalize theory of choice under uncertainty, introduce concept of s.o.t.w., Arrow: 2
states:
moral behavior [codes] for individuals [are] not suitable for s., Hirschman: 4
[no] theories valid for present constitutional and parliamentary s., Pareto: 15
statesman:
professor should not demand right as professor to carry baton of s., Weber, Max: 10
public spirit is as superfluous in the governed, as it ought to be all-powerful in the s., Steuart Denham: 1
s. must defend present life by keeping aggressions of men in balance, Barzun: 2
statesmanship:
term politics [should] include s. of thinking and s. of action, Wilson, Woodrow: 1
statesmen:
regulation of various and interfering interests constitutes principal task of modern s., Beard: 2
stationary state:
picture of s.s. as goal of competitive industry [completes] impression of dismalness made by the political economy of the early period, Clark, John Bates: 1
statistical:
new "scientific" or "cliometric" history — born of marriage between historical problems and advanced s. analysis, Fogel and Elton: 1
s. ability, divorced from scientific observations, leads nowhere, Boring: 1
s. accounts are to be referred to as a grammar [for young men], Playfair: 2
statistical method:
s.m. will produce an average result from which we estimate the Mean Man, Maxwell: 1
statistical methods:
more psychology can be learned through s.m. than from all philosophers with exception of Aristotle, Wundt: 1
statistician:
s. cannot excuse himself from duty of getting his head clear on principles of scientific inference, Fisher, R. A.: 3
s. keeps his finger on pulse of Humanity, Sarton: 3
statisticians:
difficult to understand why s. limit inquiries to Averages, Galton: 5
thou shalt not sit with s., Auden: 4
statistics:
Government keen on amassing s., but every figure comes from village watchman who puts down what he damn pleases, Stamp: 1
I find s. full of beauty and interest, Galton: 5
"judicious man" looks at S. to save himself from ignorance, Carlyle: 2
lies, damned lies and s., Disraeli: 4
man of the future is the man of s., Holmes: 4
measurements of different men are s., Edgeworth: 7
no study less alluring than s., Playfair: 4
observations and s. agree [as] quantities grouped about a Mean, Edgeworth: 7
science of s. arisen from uncertainty in life, Merz: 1
s. affords only secure ground on which theories and hypotheses can be brought to test, Herschel: 1
[s.] are only tools [to cut] through formidable thicket of difficulties that bars path of those who pursue Science of man, Galton: 5
s. constitute ledger of a nation, DeBow: 1
s. have significance for sociology because social relations inevitably correlated with spatial relations, Park: 1
S. ought to be honourable science; a wise head requisite for carrying it on, Carlyle: 1
study of s. was her [Florence Nightingale] religious duty, Pearson: 5
status:
movement from S. to Contract, Maine: 3
need for s. is met by public recognition of just institutions, Rawls: 5
role represents dynamic aspect of s., Linton: 4
s. a matter of social distance, Park: 1
S. derived from powers and privileges anciently residing in the Family, Maine: 3
s. simply collection of rights and duties, Linton: 3, 4
status politics:
s.p. [is] clash of projective rationalizations arising from personal motives, Hofstadter: 3
steady state:
anticipate the arrival of a s.s., Heilbroner: 4
s.s. not bad place for theory of growth to start, but dangerous place for it to end, Solow: 3
worth looking at figures to see if s.s. gives summary of advanced industrial economies, Solow: 2
steam:
all s. in world could not build Chartres, Adams, Henry: 4
statistics is a science not to be carried on by s., Carlyle: 1
steering engines:
s.e. of ship one of earliest forms of feedback mechanisms, Wiener: 1
Stein, Herbert
stepping stones:
wide generalizations and interpretation of concrete phenomena need s.s. in middle distance, Marshall, T. H.: 1
stereotyped:
most of give-and-take of conversation is s., Firth, J. R.: 1
stereotypes:
subtlest, most pervasive influences those which create s., Lippmann, Walter: 3
Stern, Fritz
Sterne, Laurence
Steuart Denham, James
Steward, Julian H.
Stigler, George J.
Stigler, Stephen M.
stigma:
three types of s. [are] abominations of body, blemishes of individual character, tribal, Goffman: 3
stigmatize:
underclass is latest in long line of labels that s. poor people for their poverty, McGahey: 1
stimulus and response:
behaviorist [questions]: Can I describe this behavior in terms of s.a.r.?, Watson: 2
Stinchcombe, Arthur L.
stock exchange:
[s.e.] highest vocation for capitalist whose property merges directly with theft, Engels: 3
Stone, Lawrence
Stonequist, Everett V.
Stouffer, Samuel A.
Strachey, Lytton
stranger:
every s. an enemy is [universal] ethnographic feature, Malinowski: 6
[s.] is the freer man, Simmel: 17
sociological form of s. synthesis of wandering and attachment, Simmel: 16
strategy:
theory of games of s. gains plausibility by correspondence between its concepts and those of social organizations, von Neumann and Morgenstern: 2
stratification:
s. approaches its limits if subsystems define their clientele in universalistic terms, Luhmann: 4
stratified:
any social group is always a s. body, Sorokin: 1
[*see also* class; classes; social class; social classes]
Strauss, Leo
stream of consciousness:
[Behaviorist] finds no evidence for a s.o.c., Watson: 8
let us call it the s.o.c., James: 11
strength:
Fortune exerts all her power where there is no s. prepared to oppose her, Machiavelli: 17
strength of weak ties:
integration of large societies depends on the weak social ties of individuals, Blau: 3
weak ties are vital for an individual's integration into modern society, Granovetter: 1
strike:
general s. the myth in which Socialism is comprised, Sorel: 5
mass s. does not produce revolution, but revolution produces the mass s., Luxemburg: 4

Toffler, Alvin
toil:
turn work into hated t., Marx: 20
tolerant:
greater schooling which younger generation has received [should make it] more t. [as it ages] than its elders, Stouffer: 1
liberalism is too t. of what should be intolerable, Stern: 1
Tolman, Edward C.
Tolstoy, Leo
torture:
more you t. data, more likely they are to confess, Stigler, Stephen N.: 1
total:
t. terror — t. submission — t. loneliness [under] conditions of t. power, Wittfogel: 1
totalitarian:
every step government takes beyond protecting smooth operation of market economy is step [toward] t. system, von Mises: 5
in t. societies history is sanctification, Plumb: 1
traits of a t. dictatorship, Friedrich and Brzezinski: 1
totalitarianism:
t. has discovered means of dominating human beings from within, Arendt: 1
totality:
point of view of t. in historical explanation constitutes decisive difference between Marxism and bourgeois thought, Lukács: 2
primacy of the category of t. is bearer of principle of revolution in science, Lukács: 2
Totem and Taboo:
T.a.T papers were weapons in Freud's competition with Jung, Gay: 3
totem meal:
ancient t.m. revived in form of communion, Freud: 25
t.m. beginning of social organization, Freud: 24
tough-minded:
t.-m. intellectual temperament, James: 24
t-m. person always examines facts before reaching conclusions, King: 6
Toynbee, Arnold
Toynbee, Arnold J.
trade:
main spur to T. is exorbitant Appetites of Man, North: 1
never much good done by those who affected to t. for public good, Smith, Adam: 21
people of same t. seldom meet together but conversation ends in conspiracy against public, Smith, Adam: 17
restraint of t. must be treated as major crime, Simons: 1
t. is social act, Mill, John Stuart: 15
without theory of value economist can have no theoryu of international t., Stigler, George J.: 8
trade union:
average t.u. contains only one formal organization, Lipset: 1
every professional union becomes divided into minority of directors and majority of directed, Michels: 1
tradition:
every t. grows more venerable, the farther off lies its origin, Nietzsche: 2
no mechanical substitute for a living t., Mumford: 2
real structure of t. is intricate system of relationships between levels of t., Redfield: 6
structure and t. different aspects of single cultural complex, Park and Burgess: 3
super-ego becomes vehicle of t., Freud: 37
t. of dead generations weighs on brain of the living, Marx: 7
tradition-directed people:
society of high growth potential develops t.-d.p., Riesman: 1
traditional:
t. grounds [for] a type of legitimate domination, Weber, Max: 21
traditions:
t. which arise as conscious actions are the often unwanted by-products of such actions, Popper: 2
tragedy:
great T. of Science: slaying of beautiful hypothesis by ugly fact, Huxley, T. H.: 3
t. of the age that men know so little of men, DuBois: 4
t. of the commons, Hardin: 1; Lloyd: 1
trained inability:
net aggregate gains from industry fall short owing to t.i. of businessmen, Veblen: 12
training:
adopting measures in keeping with past t. may lead to adopting wrong measures, Burke, Kenneth: 1
traitors:
rather risk that some t. escape than spread spirit of suspicion, Hand: 2
traits:
contribution that psychodynamics makes is to demonstrate that t. are related, Kardiner: 1
Trajan:
t. was strong, not violent, Pareto: 7
transaction:
uncertainty casts shadow on every business t. into which time enters, Fisher, Irving: 5
transference:
[t.] provides impulsion for translating unconscious, Freud: 19
transform:
not only does ideology t. ideas, it t. people, Bell: 2
to know or to understand is to t. reality and to assimilate it, Piaget: 9
transformations:
revolutionary advances in science consist of series of t., Cohen, I. Bernard: 3
treatment:
psychotherapy is a cosymptom t., Campbell, Donald T.: 1
tree of liberty:
t.o.l. must be refreshed from time to time with blood of patriots & tyrants, Jefferson: 8
Treitschke, Heinrich von
Trevelyan, George Macaulay
Trevor-Roper, H. R.
tricks:
fox knows many t., hedgehog only one: a good one, Archilochos: 1
Trickster:
every generation occupies itself with interpreting T. anew, Radin: 1
Trilling, Diana
Trilling, Lionel
Trimmers:
Montagu was chief of politicians called T., Macaulay: 13
trivial:
data of a scientific inquiry t. in other bearings, Veblen: 9
difficult to conceive how behavioral and social sciences could be simultaneously t. and threatening, Smelser: 3
Trobriand islands:
generation of [Malinowski's] followers believes social anthropology began in T.i. in 1914, Leach: 1
Troeltsch, Ernst
Trollope, Frances
Trotsky, Leon
true:
if Freud had only brought to man's knowledge the truth that there is such thing as the t., there would be no Freudian discovery, Lacan: 2
political judgment which describes connections of institutions with other institutions can be t. or false, Dilthey: 1
t. ideas are those we can verify, James: 27, 28
t. [in psychology] not new, new not t., Ebbinghaus: 1
thing not recognized as t., does not function as t. in the community, Mead, George Herbert: 15
things we apprehend very clearly and distinctly are t., Descartes: 3
why abandon a belief because it ceases to be t., Frost: 1
Truman, David B.
trust:
t. [defined] as expectation of persistence of moral social order, Barber: 3
without t., society would disintegrate, Simmel: 5
truth:
all possible t. is practical, Hall: 1
any science contains not only t. but half-t., sham-t., and error, Sorokin: 5
by singular coincidence error was t., Morgan, Lewis Henry: 4
cannot find objective t. of history, Beard: 5
each society has its régime of t., Foucault: 7, 8

economic doctrine an engine for discovery of concrete t., Marshall, Alfred: 1
great ocean of t. lay all undiscovered before me, Newton: 2
he alone is author of a t. who has recognized it from its grounds and thought it out to its consequents, Schopenhauer: 2
history's first law that author tell t. and whole t., Cicero: 3
if a man will start upon it [history], he must sacrifice to no God but T., Lucian: 1
judgment of intellect is only half-t., Jung: 4
meaning of t., James: 27
new scientific t. [triumphs] because its opponents die, and new generation grows up familiar with it, Planck: 1
one historian's t. becomes another's myth, McNeill, William H.: 1
ongoing t. of certain descriptive propositions is maintained by altering other propositions, Bateson: 4
ray from the infinite source of t., Huxley, T. H.: 2
science is none other than the t., Pareto: 4
study of errors serves as stimulating introduction to study of t., Lippmann, Walter: 5
t. can stand by itself, Jefferson: 5
t. made true by events, James: 28
t. of idea not stagnant, James: 28
t. of the universal struggle for life, Darwin: 5
t. valuable only in community where it has universal acceptance, Mead, George Herbert: 15
t. would be nothing but shadows of images, Plato: 9
takes great man to find t. in public opinion, Hegel: 3
to search for some great t. one has first to refute some great error, Fustel de Coulanges: 4
uniform ideas originating among peoples unknown to each other must have common ground of t., Vico: 3
with language, dimension of t. appears, Lacan: 4

truths:
change we think we see is due to t. being in and out of favour, Frost: 2
fate of new t. is to begin as heresies and end as superstitions, Huxley, T. H.: 5
part-t. that beget total errors, MacIver: 4
poetry tends to give general t., Aristotle: 6
we hold these t. to be self-evident, Jefferson: 1

Tucker, A. W.:
Prisoner's Dilemma, Rapoport: 1

Turgot, Anne Robert Jacques

Turner, Frederick Jackson:
Porter: 1
[T.] most reminiscent of Lord Acton, whose high repute might have been considerably diminished if he had taken trouble to do them [unwritten books], Hofstadter: 5

Turner, Victor W.

Turner, Victor W., and Turner, Edith

turning points:
t.p., moments of decision between progress and regression, Erikson, Erik H.: 1

twentieth century:
behavioral sciences are one of the major intellectual and cultural inventions of the t.c., Berelson: 3
in t.c., citizenship and capitalist class system have been at war, Marshall, T. H.: 2
problem of the t.c. is problem of the color-line, DuBois: 3

two:
number t. is dangerous [and] why dialectic is dangerous process, Snow: 3
t. are not always better than one, Keynes: 21

two cultures:
gap between humanists and scientists, Sarton: 1
literary intellectuals and scientists who had almost ceased to communicate, Snow: 1–3

two nations:
t.n.: THE RICH AND THE POOR, Disraeli: 2

two-party system:
shape of House of Commons building linked to t.p.s., Churchill: 2

two societies:
t.s., separate and unequal, Kerner: 1

Tylor, Edward Burnett

typologist:
for t. the type is real and variation an illusion, Mayr: 1

tyrannical:
in all t. governments the right of both making and of enforcing laws is vested in one man or body of men, Blackstone: 1

tyrannies:
governing beyond the grave is most insolent of all t., Paine: 2

tyranny:
accumulation of all powers in same hands the definition of t., Madison: 5
bad laws are the worst sort of t., Burke, Edmund: 5
if only one religion in England, would be danger of t., Voltaire: 1
protection against t. of prevailing opinion, Mill, John Stuart: 11
rebel [produces] t., Berger and Kellner: 1
t. may grow out of either extreme [some citizens possessing much and others nothing], Aristotle: 13
t. of next-door neighbor, Bagehot: 3
t. quickly succeeds t., Sorel: 1
where-ever Law ends T. begins, Locke: 20

tyrant:
between a t. and prince: difference [is] that latter obeys law and rules by its dictates, John of Salisbury: 1

unanticipated/unintended consequences:
distinctive contributions of sociologist found in study of u.c., Merton: 3
events in history that are unanticipated results of innumerable decisions of innumerable men, Mills: 3
folly to fasten upon single end and blot from perception all undesired c., Dewey: 5
hard to exaggerate importance of u.c. of intentional conduct, Giddens: 2
in history an additional result is produced by human actions beyond that which they aim at. . . called the cunning of reason, Hegel: 5
in history it is u.c. that really matter, Stone: 1
knowing and not knowing about c. of our actions [we] are like chess player, Simmel: 20
main task of social sciences is to trace u. repercussions of intentional human actions, Popper: 4
out of individual interests and intentions emerge [c.] neither planned nor intended, Elias: 1
pattern of behavior shaped by forces turns out to serve ends but tenously related to those forces, Geertz: 2
part of the force that always tries to do evil and always does good, Goethe: 1
perverse effects are one of the fundamental causes of social imbalances and change, Boudon: 2
Pride and Vanity have built more Hospitals than all the Virtues together, Mandeville: 3
sociology gives one a constant awareness of force of c., including u.c., Berger and Kellner: 1
task of social theory to explain u.c. of human action, Hayek: 7
these results are consequences which were never conscious, and never foreseen or intended, Sumner: 4
thesis of perverse effect asserts attempt to push society in certain direction will result in its moving in opposite direction, Elster: 1
u.c. arise when each individual in group acts upon an assumption that, when generalized, yields contradiction, Elster: 1

uncertain:
if an intelligence knew all forces that animate nature, nothing would be u., Laplace: 2

uncertainty:
theory of choice under u., Arrow: 2
u. casts shadow on every business transaction into which time enters, Fisher, Irving: 5
u. still main characteristic of our life, Merz: 1

essence of Industrial Revolution is substitution of competition for mediaeval distribution of w., Toynbee, Arnold (economist): 1
if laboring classes produce ample amount of w. and get only a part of it, many will become revolutionists, Clark, John Bates: 3
Instruments which produce W. may be indefinitely increased by using their Products as means of further Production, Senior: 4
Labour is Father of W., as Lands are Mother, Petty: 2
labour is not only source of w., Marx: 16
land is only source of w., Quesnay: 1
laws and conditions of production of w. partake of physical truths, Mill, John Stuart: 3
most worldly of all man's activities — his drive for w., Heilbroner: 1
nothing but impossibility of general combination protects the public w. against rapacity of private avarice, Maitland, James: 1
Political Economy expounds the laws of phenomena of w., Cairnes: 1
prospects of socialism depend on increase of social w., Bernstein, Eduard: 3
pure economics is also theory of social w., Walras: 1
questions about human society clustered around power, belief, w., Gellner: 4
real difference between democracy and oligarchy is poverty and w., Aristotle: 11
theory of w. can be only slowly developed as commercial relations progress, Cournot: 3
to gain esteem of men, w. or power must be put in evidence, Veblen: 2
w. derives efficacy from comparative amount, Mill, James: 2
w. distributed according to opportunity, Tawney: 2
w. is made up of promises, Pound: 2
w. is w. because it is scarce, Robbins: 3
W., not Happiness, subject treated by the Political Economist, Senior: 2
whole world [is] vast [perfectly competitive] market where social w. is bought and sold, Walras: 4
without labour there is no w., Thompson, William: 1
without profit no accumulation of w., Schumpeter: 1

Wealth of Nations:
I have begun to write a book to pass away the time, Smith, Adam: 3
W.o.N. does not contain single *analytic* idea new in 1776, Schumpeter: 14
W.o.N. is stupendous palace erected upon granite of self-interest, Stigler, George J.: 6

wealthy:
to be w. requires access to major institutions, Mills: 1

Webb, Beatrice:
described herself as belonging to the B's of the world, Cole, Margaret: 1
Wells: 1

Webb, Sidney:
described as belonging to the B's of the world, Cole, Margaret: 1
W. had a "civil service" mind, Cole, G. D. H.: 1
Wells: 1

Weber, Alfred

Weber, Max:
Montesquieu: 7
Parsons, Talcott: 10
Schutz: 1
Simmel: 11
W. [compared with Veblen] was on totally different level of scientific and cultural sophistication, Parsons, Talcott: 11
W. theory of bureaucracy has impeded theory of formal organizations, Coleman: 7

Wedgwood, C. V.

weigh:
if cannot w., measure, and number results, must not hope to convince others, Fleay: 1

Weinberg, Alvin

Weismann, August:
[Spencer's] famous controversy with W., Mayr: 2

welfare state:
w.s. not built for desperate, but for those already capable of helping themselves, Harrington: 3

well-being:
effects of Industrial Revolution prove free competition may produce wealth without producing w.-b., Toynbee, Arnold (economist): 2

well-born:
world of w.-b., but physically and morally perverted adults is not attractive!, Webb: 1

Wells, H. G.

West, Rebecca

West:
American history has been history of colonization of Great W., Turner, Frederick Jackson: 2

Western civilization:
"Decline of the West" comprises nothing less than problem of Civilization, Spengler: 1
thought either Platonic or anti-Platonic, Popper: 7
to unravel the underlying causes of one of the greatest dramas [Reformation] of W.c., Bloch: 3

Wheeler, William Morton:
to W. who has shown that [insects] too can conduct complex communities without use of reason, Lowell: 1

Whig:
"the w. interpretation of history" is to produce a story which ratifies the present, Butterfield: 1

White, Leslie A.

White, Lynn T., Jr.

white:
Aryan is man with w. skin, thick skin, and foreskin, Schapera: 1
dark ghetto's invisible walls have been erected by w. society, Clark, Kenneth B.: 1
poetic irony of American race relations is that rejected Negro must somehow find strength to free privileged w., Clark, Kenneth B.: 2

white collar crimes:
w.c.c. defined as crime committed by the upper class [related to] occupation, Sutherland: 1

Whitehead, Alfred North

white man's:
in sphere of w.m. mind, Negro is inferior, Myrdal: 4
w.m. rank order of discriminations, Myrdal: 3
world of modern intellectual life is w.m. world, Thomas, W.I.: 1

Whitman, Walt

Whitney, William Dwight

whole:
anthropologists learn to think of one w., Mead, Margaret: 8
dynamic w. has properties different from properties of parts or sum of parts, Lewin: 2
gestalt psychology found it necessary to mention segregation wherever dealing with definite w., Köhler: 3, 4

wholeness:
idea of w. in notion of structure, Piaget: 10

wholes:
child discovers true quantification only when capable of constructing w. that are preserved, Piaget and Szeminska: 2
gestalt category signifies attempt to find coherent functional w., Koffka: 1-3

Whorf, Benjamin:
theme of indeterminacy, Silverstein: 1

why:
W. of understanding may remain mysterious but HOW is discoverable, Whorf: 1

Whyte, William F.

Whyte, William H., Jr.

wicked:
in constituting and legislating for a commonwealth it must be taken for granted that all men are w., Machiavelli: 3

Wicksell, Knut

Wicksteed, Philip Henry

Wiener, Norbert

Wieser, Friedrich von

will:
absolute authority concerns itself no less with [man's] w. than with his actions, Rousseau: 7
difference between the w. of all and the general w., Rousseau: 16
general w. always for common good, Rousseau: 6
[in social contract] each puts his person and power in common under direction of general w., Rousseau: 14
power is probability that one actor within social relationship [can] carry out own w. despite resistance, Weber, Max: 20

w. of those who operate machine of government gets registered, Laski: 3
will (legal document):
to Romans belongs credit of inventing the W., Maine: 4
William of Ockham
Williams, Robin M., Jr.
will-to-dominate:
even the abstract w.-t.-d. is case of interaction, Simmel: 18
will-to-power:
volume on "w.-t.p." as exciting as biography of Napoleon, Murray, Henry A.: 3
Wilson, Edward O.
Wilson, William Julius
Wilson, Woodrow
win:
real motive of rich and powerful business men is to w. at biggest game yet invented, Knight: 1
situation in which can't w. called double bind, Bateson: 3
world to w., Marx and Engels: 10
wiretapping:
unconstitutional search or seizure, Brandeis: 5, 6
Wirth, Louis
wisdom:
men filled with the conceit of w. will be burden to their fellows, Plato: 3
[social sciences] need to be approached with acquired w., Pound: 3
well-ordered State where they who rule are truly rich in virtue and w., Plato: 10
wise:
words are w. men's counters, Hobbes: 4
wish:
not give patient translation of w., Freud: 23
w. was father to that thought, Shakespeare: 3
who wants to w. according to graphs?, Dostoevsky: 2
wish fulfillment:
reality — w.-f. contrasting pair [from which] mental life springs, Freud: 6
w.-f. theory gives only the psychological explanation, Freud: 4
wishes:
classification of human w., Thomas: 2
dreams fulfill w. along short path of regression, Freud: 12
wit:
w. [is] reverting to freedom enjoyed in early childhood, Abraham: 2
witchcraft:
race is the w. of our time, Montagu: 1
withers:
state w. away, Engels: 2
Wittfogel, Karl A.
Wittgenstein, Ludwig
woman:
all burdens fall on Forgotten Man [who] is not seldom a w., Sumner: 2
balance, by artificial advantages, unavoidable evils nature has given w., Thompson, William: 2
charge of unwomanliness has been whip against would-be w. rebel, Parsons, Elsie Clews: 3
Fortune is a w., and man who wants to hold her down must beat and bully her, Machiavelli: 18
modern family is based on domestic enslavement of w., Engels: 5, 6
new w. means the w. new not only to men, but to herself, Parsons, Elsie Clews: 3
one is not born, but becomes a w., Beauvoir: 1
w. with ideas is social embarrassment, Mannes: 1
"what does a w. want?," Freud: 43
women:
adjustments that w. have made over centuries as subordinate partners illuminate range of power situations, Janeway: 1
degradation of working classes varies uniformly with amount of rough work done by w., Marshall, Alfred: 8
demands put upon men and w. both not always consistent with biology, Trilling, Diana: 3
difference between society which *permits* w. to pursue extra-domestic occupations and society that *compels* [them] in order to feel valued, Trilling, Diana: 1
even feminism not succeeded in giving w. control over men, Parsons, Elsie Clews: 2
first premise for the emancipation of w. is [their] reintroduction into public industry, Engels: 6
inner voice driving w. to become complete, Friedan: 2
know of no culture that has said there is no difference between men and w., Mead, Margaret: 7
legal subordination of one sex to other — is wrong, Mill, John Stuart: 22
men taking out-door work and leaving to w. most of the domestic occupations, Hodgskin: 2
nature of w. is artificial — result of forced repression, Mill, John Stuart: 24
no civilization can remain highest if another civilization adds to intelligence of its men the intelligence of its w., Thomas: 1
nowhere in his writings does Freud express sympathy for problems which pertain to w. alone, Trilling, Diana: 2
problem that has no name stirring minds of American w. today, Friedan: 1
sex-role revolution [allows] men and w. to "make love, not war," Friedan: 3
sexual life of adult w. is "dark continent" for psychology, Freud: 32
should w. ever discover what their power might be, much improvement might be hoped for, Trollope: 1
subjection of w. to men being universal, any departure appears unnatural, Mill, John Stuart: 23
to superiority of their w. that Americans' singular prosperity must be attributed, Tocqueville: 22
w. became social problem because technological and social changes have disturbed an old equilibrium without replacing it, Komarovsky: 1
w. try hard to live down to what is expected of them, Parsons, Elsie Clews: 1
when the slavery of half of humanity is abolished, the human couple will find its true form, Beauvoir: 2
who knows what w. can be when free to become themselves?, Friedan: 2
women's liberation:
irony of bringing Freud into conjunction with w.l. lies in his invidious view of the female sex, Trilling, Diana: 2
Woodward, C. Vann
Woodworth, Robert S.
word:
gap of one w. does not feel like gap of another, James: 12
meaning of a w. is an active effect of the sound uttered within context of situation, Malinowski: 16
meaning of a w. is its use in the language, Wittgenstein: 3
never waste of time to study the history of a w., Febvre: 2
original w.-creation cannot have been work of any individual, Wundt: 5
"tip of the tongue" phenomenon: one cannot quite recall familiar w. but can recall words of similar form and meaning, Brown and McNeill: 1; James: 12
w. may vary in color and content according to circumstances, Holmes: 10, 14
words:
inviolable liberty to make w. stand for what ideas he pleases, Locke: 9
these simple w. have enabled historians to conceal their ignorance, Hexter: 1
w. are instruments, Ogden and Richards: 1
w. are wise men's counters, Hobbes: 4
w. in Phatic Communion fulfil a social function, Malinowski: 7
w., like whole languages, gradually become extinct, Darwin: 8
within same language, all w. used to express related ideas limit each other reciprocally, Saussure: 5
work:
[capitalism] destroys charm of w. and [turns it] into hated toil, Marx: 20
cryptic phrase, reportedly uttered by Freud, to love and to w., Smelser: 4
degradation of working classes varies uniformly with amount of rough